# Every PROPHECY of the BIBLE

# Every PROPHECY of the BIBLE

# JOHN F. WALVOORD

Formerly titled
The Prophecy Knowledge Handbook

*Chariot Victor Publishing*
A Division of Cook Communications

Chariot Victor Publishing
A division of Cook Communications, Colorado Springs, Colorado 80918
Cook Communications, Paris, Ontario
Kingsway Communications, Eastbourne, England

Unless otherwise indicated, all Scripture quotations are from the *Holy Bible, New International Version,* © 1973, 1978, 1984, International Bible Society. Used by permission of Zondervan Bible Publishers. Other quotations are from the *New American Standard Bible* (NASB), © the Lockman Foundation 1960, 1962, 1963, 1968, 1971, 1972, 1973, 1975, 1977. Used by permission; the *American Standard Version* (ASV); and the *King James Version* (KJV).

Cover Design: Bill Gray
Cover Photos: Image Bank

**Library of Congress Cataloging-in-Publication Data**

Walvoord. John F.
    Every prophecy of the Bible/by John Walvoord.
        p.    cm.
    ISBN 1-56476-758-2
    1. Bible--Prophecies.    I. Title.
    BS647.2.W274      1999
    220.1'5--dc21                              98-43533
                                               CIP

    3 4 5 6 7 8 9 10 Printing / Year 02  01 00

# CONTENTS

# PREFACE

For many years I had been urged to compile a list of all significant prophecies of Scripture and provide an exposition of them. This book, in an attempt to meet this need, explains one thousand passages of the Bible and, for the first time in current literature, all the prophecies of the Bible are explained in one volume. The significance is especially striking with the arrival of the twenty-first century which has continued to sharpen interest in prophetic interpretation.

The leading problem in the interpretation of prophecy is whether the Scripture should be interpreted in its natural or literal sense. This is discussed in the Introduction. It is also important to understand that in the interpretation of prophecy, every prophecy is related to other prophecies like the piece of a tapestry to the whole. Accordingly, a system had to be used that would unfold prophecy in an orderly way and relate prophecies to each other. To achieve this, the general method of study of prophetic Scripture was approached from the biblical point of view, beginning in Genesis and ending in Revelation. In the Gospels the chronological approach was modified to deal with major prophecies in the Synoptic Gospels and to consider separately prophecy in the Gospel of John. Biblical quotations are from the *Holy Bible, New International Version.*

Most significant is the fact that half of these prophecies—five hundred of them—have already been literally fulfilled, establishing beyond any intellectual question that the Bible was intended to be interpreted literally in prophetic passages. Unmistakably, the evidence is overwhelming that God means exactly what He says as prophecy after prophecy has already been literally fulfilled. When history has run its course, every prophecy will be fulfilled.

Though it is impossible in one volume to deal at length with each interpretation, the goal of this volume is to provide an explanatory exposition of each significant prophecy of Scripture with some mention of alternative views. The reader will in this way be provided with a workable and intelligent interpretation of prophecy that fits into the larger scheme of prophecy as fulfilled or to be fulfilled and will be given an introductory understanding of the prophecy as a basis for further study.

The competent work of Karen Grassmick as stenographer did much to enhance the book. The cooperation of the administration of Dallas Seminary in allowing me free time is gratefully acknowledged.

John F. Walvoord
Summer 1998

# INTRODUCTION

## THE IMPORTANCE OF PROPHECY

In the history of the church the eschatological or prophetic portions of Scripture have suffered more from inadequate interpretation than any other major theological subject. The reason for this is that the church turned aside from a normal and grammatical literal interpretation of prophecy to one that is nonliteral and subject to the caprice of the interpreter. This false approach to interpreting prophecy is contradicted beyond question by the fact that so many hundreds of prophecies have already been literally fulfilled.

In the first two centuries of the Christian era the church was predominantly premillennial, interpreting Scripture to teach that Christ would fulfill the prophecy of His second coming to bring a thousand-year reign on earth before the eternal state will begin. This was considered normal in Orthodox theology. The early interpretation of prophecy was not always cogent and sometimes fanciful but, for the most part, prophecy was treated in the same way as other Scripture.

In the last ten years of the second century and in the third century the heretical school of theology at Alexandria, Egypt advanced the erroneous principle that the Bible should be interpreted in a nonliteral or allegorical sense. In applying this to the Scriptures, they subverted all the major doctrines of the faith, including prophecy. The early church rose up and emphatically denied the Alexandrian system and to a large extent restored the interpretation of Scripture to its literal, grammatical, historical sense. The problem was that in prophecy there were predictions that had not yet been fulfilled. This made it more difficult to prove that literal fulfillment was true of prophecy. The result was somewhat catastrophic for prophecy, and the church floundered in the area of interpretation of the future.

Augustine (354–430) rescued the church from uncertainty as far as nonprophetic Scripture is concerned but continued to treat prophecy in a nonliteral way with the purpose of eliminating a millennial kingdom on earth. Strangely, Augustine held to a literal Second Coming, a literal heaven, and a literal hell, but not to a literal millennium. This arbitrary distinction has never been explained.

Because amillennialism, which denies a literal millennial kingdom on earth following the Second Coming, is essentially negative and hinders intelligent literal interpretation of prophecy, there was little progress in this area. However the church continued to believe in heaven and hell and purgatory but neglected or explained away long passages having to deal with Israel in prophecy and the kingdom on earth as frequently revealed in the Old Testament. Even in the Protestant Reformation prophecy was not rescued from this hindrance in its interpretation.

Though remnants of the church still advanced the premillennial view, it was not until the nineteenth and twentieth centuries that a movement to restore the literal truth of prophecy began to take hold. The twentieth century has been especially significant in the progress of prophetic interpretation and is one in which many details of prophecy have been debated and clarified in a way that had never been possible before. Though amillennialism continues to be the majority view of the church, among those who hold a high view of Scripture the premillennial interpretation has been given detailed exposition, serving to provide an intelligent view of the present and the future from the standpoint of biblical prophecy.

The importance of prophecy should be evident, even superficially, in examining the Christian faith, for about one-fourth of the Bible was prophecy when it was written. It is evident that God intended to draw aside the veil of the future and to give some indication of what His plans and purposes were for the human race and for the universe as a whole. The fact that Scriptures supporting the premillennial interpretation have been neglected and misinterpreted is now to some extent being corrected in the twentieth century.

In the nature of Christian faith a solid hope for the future is essential. Christianity without a future would not be basic Christianity. In contrast to the eschatology of heathen religions, which often paint the future in a forbidding way, Christianity's hope is bright and clear and offers a Christian the basic fact that the life to come is better than our present life. As Paul stated it in 2 Corinthians 5:8, "We are confident, I say, and would prefer to be away from the body and at home with the Lord." In the Christian faith the future is painted as one of bliss and happiness in the presence of the Lord without the ills that are common to this life.

The revelation of prophecy in Scripture serves as an important evidence that the Scriptures are accurate in their interpretation of the future. Because approximately half of the prophecies of the Bible have already been fulfilled in a literal way, it gives a proper intellectual basis for assuming that prophecy yet to be fulfilled will likewise have a literal fulfillment. At the same time it justifies the conclusion that the Bible is inspired of the Holy Spirit and that prophecy which goes far beyond any scheme of man is instead a revelation by God of that which is certain to come to pass. The fact that prophecy has been literally fulfilled serves as a guide to interpret the prophecies which are yet ahead.

Scriptural prophecy, properly interpreted, also provides a guideline for establishing the value of human conduct and the things that pertain to this life. For a Christian, the ultimate question is whether God considers what He is doing of value or not, and it is in contrast to the world's system of values which is largely materialistic.

Prophecy is also a support for the scriptural revelation of the righteousness of God and a support for the assertion that the Christian faith has an integral relationship to morality. Obviously, the present life does not demonstrate fully the righteousness of God as many wicked situations are not actively judged. Scripture that is prophetic dealing with this indicates that every act will be brought into divine judgment according to the infinite standard of the holy God, and accordingly, prophecy provides a basis for morality based on the character of God Himself.

Prophecy also provides a guide to the meaning of history. Though philosophers will continue to debate a philosophy of history, actually the Bible indicates that history is the unfolding of God's plan and purpose of revealing Himself and manifesting His love and grace and righteousness in a way which would be impossible without human history. In the Christian faith history has its climax in God's plan for the future in which the earth in its present situation will be destroyed and a new earth will be created. A proper interpretation of prophecy serves to support and enhance all other areas of theology, and without a proper interpretation of prophecy all other areas to some extent become incomplete revelation.

In attempting to communicate the meaning of Scripture relative to the prophetic past and future, prophecy serves to bring light and understanding to many aspects of our present life as well as our future hope. In an effort to understand and interpret prophecy correctly as a justifiable theological exercise, it is necessary to establish a proper base of interpretation.

# THE INTERPRETATION OF PROPHECY
## *General Assumptions in Biblical Interpretation*

As in all sciences, theology is based on assumptions. Mankind finds itself living in an ordered world with observable natural laws and evidence of design. The nature of the ordered world in which we live reveals an evident interrelationship of purposes requiring the existence of a God who is infinite in power, rational, and having the basic elements of personality, intellect, sensibility, and will. The observable facts of nature as well as revelation through Scripture must be consistent with such a God. These facts, organized into a rational system, are the substance of theology, making it a science embracing the revealed facts about God, Creation, and history. To the observable facts in nature, Scripture reveals the additional truth that the God of history is gracious, holy, loving, patient, faithful, and good, and has infinite attributes of knowledge, power, and rational purpose.

What is true of theology as a whole is especially true of biblical interpretation. In approaching the interpretation of the Bible, at least four assumptions are essential.

1. In order to have a coherent and consistent interpretation of the Bible, it is necessary to assume that there are ample proofs that the Bible was inspired by the Holy Spirit and that the human authors were guided in the writing of Scripture and in the selection of the very words that they used. Accordingly, the Bible is an inerrant revelation containing all the truth that God intended to be included and excluding all facts that were not to be included. As the inspired Word of God, it should be expected that, properly interpreted, the Bible does not contradict itself.

2. The Bible was intended to communicate truth about God and the universe, to record historical facts, to reveal ethical principles, to provide wisdom for human judgments, to reveal moral and material values, and to provide prediction of future events.

3. The Bible progressively reveals the truth of God in such a way that changes in the moral rule of life are recognized, such as the contrast between the Mosaic Law and the present age of grace. Later revelation may replace earlier revelation as a standard of faith without contradicting it.

4. Though the Bible is an unusual book, in many respects it is a normative piece of literature, using words to convey truth, and yet providing a great variety of literary forms, such as history, poetry, and prophecy, and sometimes using normal figures of speech.

Though a supernatural book, the Bible nevertheless speaks in normative ways which can be illustrated in literature outside the Bible.

### General Rules of Biblical Interpretation

Though the interpretation of the Bible is an exceedingly complex problem, if certain general rules are followed, they will keep the interpreter from misunderstanding Scripture.

1. In approaching Scripture, first of all there must be study of the words that are used, their general usages, variety of meaning, historical context, theological context, and any determination of the probable meaning of the word used in a particular context.

2. Words in Scripture are used in a grammatical context which should be observed, including such matters as whether the word is used in a statement of fact, a command, a desired goal, or an application to a particular situation.

3. In any interpretation it is most important to decide to whom the Scripture is addressed, as this involves the application of the statement.

4. Scripture should never be interpreted in isolation from its context. Careful thought should be given to the immediate context, the general context, and the context of the whole of Scripture. This will serve to relate the revelation contained to other divine revelation.

5. The literary character of the Scripture interpreted should be taken into consideration as the Bible is written in a variety of scriptural styles—such as history, poetry, worship, prediction—and uses a variety of figures of speech. These factors determine the interpretation of a particular text.

6. If the Scripture is inspired by the Holy Spirit and without error, it is important to compare any particular text to all other Scripture that might be relative. For instance, the Book of Revelation may often be interpreted through a study of the Book of Daniel. One Scripture will serve to cast light on other Scripture.

7. Though the Bible is largely written in factual style to be interpreted as a normal, factual presentation, the Bible, like all other literature, uses figures of speech, and they should be recognized for their intended meaning. All forms of biblical literature ultimately yield a factual truth.

8. In interpreting the Bible, one must seek the guidance of the indwelling Holy Spirit who casts light on the Scriptures and guides its interpretation.

## *Guidelines for Interpretation of Prophecy*

The interpretation of prophecy has its own peculiar problems of interpretation when prophecy reveals some future event or is couched in figurative or apocalyptic form. In some instances it is difficult to determine the precise meaning of the text because there is no corroborative comparison with history. In general, however, prophecy is factual. Because so many prophecies have already been literally fulfilled, the nature of this fulfillment provides guidelines for the interpretation of prophecy which is yet unfulfilled. In addition to the general rules of interpreting the Bible, certain additional guidelines assist the interpretation of prophecy.

1. As is true in the interpretation of all Scripture, it is most important to determine the meaning of significant words in the interpretation of prophecy. Often these words have a historical background that will help in understanding the reference.

2. One of the important decisions necessary in the interpretation of prophecy is the determination of whether the prophecy concerns the present or the future, that is, whether it refers to a situation now past or present or is prophetic of future events. A biblical prophet, especially in the Old Testament, often delivered contemporary messages that dealt with current problems which were not necessarily futuristic in their revelation. This problem is compounded by the fact that many times prophecy was given in the past tense, where the writer of Scripture took a position of looking back on the prophecy as if it were already fulfilled. Normally, however, it is possible to determine quickly whether the prophecy deals with the past, present, or the future.

3. Many prophecies of Scripture were fulfilled shortly after their revelation. At least half of the prophecies of the Bible have already been fulfilled literally. Such fulfillment confirms the fact that unfulfilled prophecy will also be literally fulfilled as one could anticipate from fulfillment of prophecy already achieved. Fulfilled prophecy is an important guide in interpreting prophecy unfulfilled and generally confirms the concept of literal interpretation of a prophecy.

4. Prophecies may be conditional or unconditional. This becomes an important part in the conclusion that may be reached from the revelation of the prophecy. If a prophecy is conditional, it is possible it will never be fulfilled. If it is unconditional, then it is certain to be fulfilled, regardless of human response. This is an area of confusion in the interpretation of prophecy, as some have assumed that

prophecy is conditional when there is no supporting data that indicates this.

5. Prophecies sometimes have more than one fulfillment. This is referred to as the law of double reference. It is not unusual in Scripture for a prophecy to be partially fulfilled early and then later have a complete fulfillment. Accordingly, what seems to be a partial fulfillment of a prophecy should not be assumed to be the final answer as the future may record a more complete fulfillment.

6. One of the most important questions in the interpretation of prophecy is whether a prophecy is literal or figurative. As discussed earlier, early in the history of the church, especially in the third century, a school of prophetic interpretation arose in Alexandria which attempted to interpret all the Bible in an allegorical or a nonliteral sense. The influence of this school was one of the major reasons why premillennialism in the early church faded and a form of amillennialism became dominant.

Though the Alexandrian school of theology is labeled by all theologians as heretical, the effect of nonliteral interpretation on prophecy was rendered acceptable by the theological writings of Augustine who applied allegorical interpretation only to prophecy and not to other forms of Scripture revelation. This influence continued through the Protestant Reformation to the present day.

Among conservative interpreters of the Bible, the issue of literal versus figurative or allegorical interpretation is a major issue because on it hangs the question as to whether the Bible teaches a future millennial kingdom following the Second Advent, or whether it does not. Because the church is divided on this issue, full attention should be given to the interpretation of prophecy as this unfolds in the Bible to see what the Scriptures themselves indicate concerning literal versus nonliteral interpretation.

Confusion also reigns in terminology which sometimes contrasts the literal to the spiritual or the literal to the typical. The nonliteral interpretation of the Bible is not necessarily more spiritual than the literal. The consideration of types in this connection is another confusing aspect. Types, however, depend on the historical fact which is then used as an illustration of a later truth, but is not prophetic in the ordinary sense. Though it may be demonstrated that most prophecy should be interpreted literally, this does not rule out figurative revelation, allegories, apocalyptic Scriptures, or other forms of nonliteral prophecy. Though it is difficult to deal with these things in the abstract, when studying a particular Scripture, it is not too difficult to determine to what extent it is literal.

7. Apocalyptic literature is in a place all by itself because all agree that this is not, strictly speaking, literal in its revelation. Outstanding examples, of course, are the Books of Daniel, Ezekiel, and Revelation. The fact that such revelation is not literal, however, does not deny it reveals specific facts. Here, skill in interpretation is most necessary, and careful comparison of Scripture with Scripture is essential in determining the actual meaning. This will be illustrated as prophecies of Scripture are interpreted.

As in reading all other types of literature, it may be presumed in studying prophecy that a statement predicting a future event is factual and literal unless there are good reasons for taking it in another sense. Here, the good judgment of the interpreter and avoidance of prejudice and preconceived concepts are most important to let the passage speak for itself.

### Major Theological Interpretations of Prophecy

*Amillennial interpretations.* Within orthodox interpretation of the Bible the most prominent theological interpretation of prophecy since the fourth century of the Christian era has been amillennial or nonmillennial. Beginning with Augustine, the amillennial interpretation held that there would be no literal future thousand-year reign of Christ on earth, but that the Millennium referred to the present age or possibly the last thousand years of the present age. Because this did not provide a literal interpretation of millennial passages, it has been designated as amillennial since the nineteenth century.

The amillennial interpretation within the limits of orthodox theology has had various explanations of fulfillment of the millennial prophecies. The most popular, the Augustinian interpretation, relates the Millennium in the present age as a spiritual kingdom ruling in the hearts of Christians or embodied in the progress of the Gospel in the church.

Amillenarians of the nineteenth and twentieth centuries have offered varied interpretations, some holding that the Millennium is fulfilled in the time between the death and resurrection of a Christian. Some in the twentieth century hold that the Millennium will be fulfilled in the new heaven and the new earth described in Revelation 21–22. Some amillenarians have also suggested that the millennial passages are conditional and will not be fulfilled due to the departure of Israel from the faith. Still others suggest that the kingdom on earth was fulfilled in the reign of Solomon who controlled the land promised to Abraham (Gen. 15:18).

Within twentieth-century amillennialism the neoorthodox interpretation of Scripture may also be considered. This view considers the kingdom being fulfilled now in the experience of individual Christians. Generally speaking, neoorthodox scholars hold that God directly communicates to Christians supernaturally, but the Bible is not considered in itself an infallible record of revelation.

All liberal theologians also are amillennial in the sense that they do not believe any future millennium will ever take place.

*Postmillennial Interpretation.* Beginning with Daniel Whitby in the eighteenth century an interpretation of prophecy became popular which held specifically that the Millennium would be the last 1,000 years of the present age. Adherents of this view believed the Gospel would triumph to such an extent in the world that the whole world would be Christianized, bringing in a golden age which would correspond to the millennial kingdom. Like amillennialism, it places the second coming of Christ at the end of the Millennium. Postmillennialism in its original form was a biblical interpretation and attempted a more literal interpretation of the Millennium than was followed by the later postmillenarians of the twentieth century.

In the twentieth century, however, postmillennialism, influenced by evolution, has become less biblical and adopted the concept of spiritual progress over a long period of time as in a general way bringing in a golden age. These postmillenarians, however, are not considered orthodox. As a theological movement postmillennialism largely died in the first part of the twentieth century, but small groups have attempted to revive it in current theological discussion.

*Premillennial Interpretation.* From the first century Bible scholars have held that the second coming of Christ will be premillennial, that is, the Second Coming will be followed by a thousand years of Christ's literal reign on earth. This was a predominant view of the early church as witnessed by the early church fathers. By the third century, however, the Alexandria school of theology, bringing in sweeping allegorical interpretation of Scripture, succeeded in displacing the premillennial view.

In the last few centuries, however, premillennialism has been revived by biblical scholars and now is held by many who are orthodox in other respects. Unlike amillennialism and postmillennialism, the premillennial interpretation has no liberal adherents as it builds on the concept that the Bible is the Word of God and that prophecies are to be interpreted in their normal literal sense.

The premillennial view has much to commend it as it has the same principles of interpretation regarding prophecy as is normal in other areas of theological interpretation. The premillennial view is generally adopted in the interpretation of prophecy in this work. The fact that so many prophecies have already been literally fulfilled lends support for the expectation that prophecies yet to be fulfilled will have the same literal fulfillment.

# 1

# PROPHECY IN
# THE PENTATEUCH

# THE BEGINNINGS OF PROPHETIC REVELATION
## *First Prophecy of Judgment*

*Genesis 2:16-17.* When the divine work of Creation had been completed and Adam had been created, God gave him the first command which is in the form of a conditional prophecy. According to verses 16-17, "The LORD God commanded the man, 'You are free to eat from any tree in the garden; but you must not eat from the tree of the knowledge of good and evil, for when you eat of it you will surely die.' "

*Genesis 3:1-3.* After Eve was created, Satan approached her in the form of a serpent (cf. Rev. 20:2). The serpent said to the woman, "Did God really say, 'You must not eat from any tree in the garden'?" (Gen. 3:1) The question implies the restriction necessarily deprived her of something that is rightfully hers. In reply, Eve said, "We may eat fruit from the trees in the garden, but God did say, 'You must not eat fruit from the tree that is in the middle of the garden, and you must not touch it, or you will die' " (v. 2).

In her reply Eve added the restriction that she was not to touch the fruit and omitted the word "surely." The devil immediately attacked the statement of the certainty of death by denying that Eve would surely die. He found fault with the restriction by affirming that when the fruit was eaten they would be like God and would know good and evil. What he did not say was that they would know the good without being able to do it and know the evil without being able to avoid it.

Genesis recorded, "When the woman saw that the fruit of the tree was good for food and pleasing to the eye, and also desirable for gaining wisdom, she took some and ate it. She also gave some to her husband, who was with her, and he ate it" (v. 6).

The temptation which was faced followed the pattern described in 1 John 2:16, "For everything in the world—the cravings of sinful man, the lust of his eyes and the boasting of what he has and does—comes not from the Father but from the world." The temptation which Eve faced was her belief that the fruit was good and appealed to actual desires of man described in 1 John as "the cravings of sinful man." That it was "pleasing to the eye" corresponds to "the lust of his eyes." That it was "desirable for gaining wisdom" appealed to pride which relates to "the boasting of what he has and does."

In approaching Christ in His temptation Satan tempted Christ along these same lines: appeal to the desires of the natural man, appeal to hunger, and appeal to pride in tempting Christ to cast Himself down from the temple as the Son of God. In the revelation of the glory of the kingdoms of the world, Satan appealed to the desire of the eyes for beauty (Matt. 4:1-11; Mark 1:12-13; Luke 4:1-13). The same avenues of temptation are illustrated in Saul who was tempted by pride (1 Sam. 13:1-14), David who was tempted by the desires of the human nature (2 Sam. 11:2-27), and the desire for beautiful things as illustrated in Solomon (1 Kings 10:14-29; 2 Chron. 9:13-28).

### The Judgment and Promise of Salvation

*Genesis 3:14-24.* This first prophecy was fulfilled by the spiritual death of Adam and Eve and their ultimate physical death (vv. 7-24; 5:5). In fulfilling the prophecy of death, God added other prophecies including the curse on the serpent (3:14-15). God prophesied that Eve would give birth to children in pain and that her husband would rule over her. To Adam, God predicted that the ground would be cursed and he would have difficulty raising the food necessary for his continued existence.

In the midst of these promises enlarging on the judgment that had come on mankind because of the entrance of sin, a plan for redemption was also revealed.

In pronouncing the curse on the devil and the serpent, it was prophesied that there would always be enmity between the serpent and the descendants of the woman (v. 15). Referring to one of the woman's Descendants (Christ), God said, "He will crush your head." In regard to the judgment on Satan, made sure by the Cross of Christ, the prophecy was further enlarged, "you will strike His heel" (v. 15). This referred to the fact that Christ would die, but, unlike the effect on Satan, His death would be conquered by resurrection. This was fulfilled in Christ's death and resurrection (Rom. 3:24-25).

### Importance of the First Two Major Prophecies of Scripture

In subsequent prophecies both the judgment on sin and the promise of salvation can be traced throughout Scripture. The importance of these prophecies can be seen in the context of the early chapters of Genesis.

The divine plan for man was stated in detail in Genesis 1:26-27, "Then God said, 'Let Us make man in Our image, in Our likeness, and let them rule over the fish of the sea and the birds of the air, over the livestock, over all the earth, and over all the creatures that move along the ground.' So God created man in His own image, in the image of God He created him; male and female He created them.

"God blessed them and said to them, 'Be fruitful and increase in number; fill the earth and subdue it. Rule over the fish of the sea and the birds of the air and over every living creature that moves on the ground' " (v. 28). The fulfillment of this was hindered by the fact that sin had entered the human race. The ultimate fulfillment, of course, will be by Christ as "the last Adam" (1 Cor. 15:45) who will rule the earth in the millennial kingdom (Ps. 72:8-11).

The fulfillment of these first prophecies of Scripture provide the first insight into the normal rule of interpreting prophecy, that is, to interpret prophecy literally. When Adam and Eve sinned they literally died spiritually and later physically. The prophecies of cursing on the serpent and Satan, the prophecies of Eve's suffering pain in childbirth and being subject to her husband, and the prophecies to Adam of raising food with great toil have all been subject to literal fulfillment (vv. 14-19).

## PROPHECY CONCERNING CAIN AND ABEL
### The Birth of Cain and Abel

*Genesis 4:1-15.* In keeping with the prophecy that Eve would bear children, Cain and Abel were born (vv. 1-2). When they were grown, "Abel kept flocks, and Cain worked the soil" (v. 2). Cain brought an offering to the Lord of the fruits of the soil (v. 3), but "Abel brought fat portions from some of the firstborn of his flock" (v. 4).

God rejected the offering of Cain and accepted the offering of Abel (v. 5). Though Scripture does not indicate the reason for this, Scripture emphasizes that a bloody sacrifice is necessary for the forgiveness of sins (Heb. 9:22). It may also be that Cain did not bring his offering in the proper spirit. God may have given instruction concerning offerings which Cain had ignored.

### The Curse on Cain

Because of God's rejection of his offering, Cain attacked Abel and murdered him (Gen. 4:8). As a result, God prophesied a curse on him, stating, "When you work the ground, it will no longer yield its crops for you. You will be a restless wanderer on the earth" (v. 12). This prophecy was fulfilled when Cain left his home in Eden and established a civilization to the east (v. 16).

# PROPHECY RELATED TO THE DAYS OF NOAH
## The Prediction of the Flood

*Genesis 6:1-22.* Because of the wickedness of the human race, God declared His purpose to destroy the human race, "I will wipe mankind, whom I have created, from the face of the earth—men and animals, and creatures that move along the ground, and birds of the air—for I am grieved that I have made them" (v. 7).

Of all the people on earth, apparently Noah and his family were the only ones who found favor with God (vv. 8-10). God revealed His purpose to destroy the human race to Noah, "I am going to put an end to all people, for the earth is filled with violence because of them. I am surely going to destroy both them and the earth" (v. 13). After describing the major dimensions of the ark which Noah was instructed to build, God added, "I am going to bring floodwaters on the earth to destroy all life under the heavens, every creature that has the breath of life in it. Everything on earth will perish" (v. 17).

In obedience to God, Noah directed the animals into the ark (vv. 19-20). Noah was to provide food for them in the ark (v. 21) and was to bring his wife, his sons, and their wives also into the ark (v. 18).

*Genesis 7:1-24.* God further revealed that in seven days after the ark was finished the Flood would come (vv. 1-4). Scriptures recorded the fulfillment of the coming Flood by which every living person on the face of the earth was destroyed except for Noah and his family (vv. 21-23).

## God's Covenant with Noah

*Genesis 8:1–9:17.* After the flood subsided and Noah and his family were able to leave the ark, according to 8:20, "Then Noah built an altar to the LORD and, taking some of all the clean animals and clean birds, he sacrificed burnt offerings on it." The Lord was pleased with Noah's offering and prophesied, "Never again will I curse the ground because of man, even though every inclination of his heart is evil from childhood. And never again will I destroy all living creatures, as I have done. As long as the earth endures, seedtime and harvest, cold and heat, summer and winter, day and night will never cease" (vv. 21-22).

Additional details concerning the covenant with Noah were given in 9:1-17. As part of God's prophetic program for Noah and his family, mankind for the first time was given permission to eat

23

meat, but not the blood. For the first time capital punishment was established as an essential ingredient in the concept of government. According to verse 6, "Whoever sheds the blood of man, by man shall his blood be shed; for in the image of God has God made man." In addition to emphasizing provisions of the covenant, God established the rainbow as the sign of the covenant (v. 13). God said, "Never again will the waters become a flood to destroy all life. Whenever the rainbow appears in the clouds, I will see it and remember the everlasting covenant between God and all living creatures of every kind on the earth" (vv. 15-16).

### Noah's Prophecy

*Genesis 9:18-29.* Because Ham, Noah's son, the father of Canaan, treated Noah with disrespect (vv. 20-24), Noah delivered a prophecy concerning his descendants, "When Noah awoke from his wine and found out what his youngest son had done to him, he said, 'Cursed be Canaan! The lowest of slaves will he be to his brothers.' He also said, 'Blessed be the LORD, the God of Shem! May Canaan be the slave of Shem. May God extend the territory of Japheth; may Japheth live in the tents of Shem, and may Canaan be his slave' " (vv. 24-27). This was fulfilled in history (10:1-32).

### The Failure of Man under the Covenant with Noah

*Genesis 11:1-9.* Symbolic of their rejection of God, those who were living in the Babylonian area said to each other, " 'Come, let's make bricks and bake them thoroughly.' They used brick instead of stone, and tar for mortar. Then they said, 'Come, let us build ourselves a city, with a tower that reaches to the heavens, so that we may make a name for ourselves and not be scattered over the face of the whole earth' " (vv. 3-4).

God judged this effort and confused their language so that they could not understand each other (v. 7). The stage was now set for God's tremendous revelation given to Abram.

## THE PROPHETIC COVENANT WITH ABRAHAM

### Background of the Covenant

*Genesis 11:10-31.* The historical background of Abraham is given in Genesis 11. He and his family were descendants of the line of Shem. According to verses 31-32 Terah took his son Abram and his grandson Lot and their wives and started out for the land of Canaan. However, when they came to Haran they settled down until Terah died. The fuller explanation is given in Scripture which follows, giving the precise provisions of the covenant which was revealed to Abraham.

### Provisions of the Covenant

*Genesis 12:1-3.* God had revealed to Abram the basic provisions of His covenant with him while Abram was still in Ur of the Chaldeans: "The LORD had said to Abram, 'Leave your country, your people and your father's household and go to the land I will show you. I will make you into a great nation and I will bless you; I will make your name great, and you will be a blessing. I will bless those who bless you, and whoever curses you I will curse; and all peoples on earth will be blessed through you'" (vv. 1-3).

The covenant with Abram was a major step in divine revelation indicating that God was selecting Abram and his posterity to fulfill His purpose of revealing Himself to the world and bringing salvation for mankind. Though only eleven chapters were used to trace the whole history of the world prior to Abram, including Creation and all the major events which followed, the rest of the Book of Genesis was devoted to Abram and his immediate descendants, indicating the importance of this covenant.

The covenant required Abram to leave his country and his people and go to the land which God would show him. The expression, "You will be a blessing" (v. 2), could be translated "be a blessing." Abram was essential to God's program of bringing blessing and revelation to the world and ultimately salvation through Jesus Christ. In keeping with Abram's obedience, God made the promises: (1) "I will make you into a great nation." (2) "I will bless you." (3) "I will make your name great" (vv. 2-3).

The promise of a great nation was fulfilled in the nation Israel which has had a large place in the history of the world. Their number would be like the stars of the heavens, innumerable (15:5) and like the sand of the sea (32:12). As Abram had no children at that time, the promise seemed too extensive to be true.

The promise of personal blessing on Abram (12:2) is evident in God's special dealing with him in calling him, choosing him for his important role, and in caring for him throughout his life. It followed that Abram would be famous (v. 2), as his name is prominent in the Old Testament as well as the New Testament and highly regarded in Judaism, Christianity, and the Muslim faith. These promises have been literally fulfilled (Heb. 11:8-19).

Through Abram and the nation which would descend from him

came the blessing promised to "all peoples on earth" (Gen. 12:3). God's promises included blessing on those who blessed Abram and his descendants, curses on those who would curse Abram and his descendants, and the promise of blessing to all peoples of the earth. While most of these promises had direct effect on Israel, the promised blessing on all peoples would include the Gentiles mentioned in Galatians 3:6-9. These basic provisions of God's covenant with Abram were subsequently enlarged in the Book of Genesis and throughout Scripture. Later prophecies emphasized the fact that Israel would continue as a nation throughout human history.

### The Prophecy of Possession of the Land

*Genesis 12:7.* Though not included in the basic provisions of the covenant with Abram, the narrative of the Book of Genesis immediately picked up the central feature of the promise of the land. This was part of the original revelation that God gave to Abram when he was still in Ur (v. 1). Now it became an important proof of God's continuing purpose for Abram and his people.

According to verse 7, "The LORD appeared to Abram and said, 'To your offspring I will give this land.' " From this point on throughout the Old Testament the land became one of the central features of God's prophetic program for Israel. As simple and direct as this prophecy is, interpreters of prophecy have made this a decisive point of departure, some interpreting the land as not a literal reference to the Holy Land but rather a promise of heaven. Those who interpret this prophecy in a nonliteral sense point to Hebrews 11:9-10, "By faith he made his home in the promised land like a stranger in a foreign country; he lived in tents, as did Isaac and Jacob, who were heirs with him of the same promise. For he was looking forward to the city with foundations, whose architect and builder is God."

All serious interpreters of Scripture agree that Abram had an eternal hope of dwelling forever in the New Jerusalem (Rev. 21–22). This eternal hope, however, does not satisfy the Old Testament description of a literal land in human history. The point is that Abram had a future temporal hope—the land—as well as the eternal hope—the New Jerusalem. It is not too much to say that the interpretation of Genesis 12:7 determines in large measure the prophetic interpretation of the rest of the Bible.

As in all interpretive problems the important rule of hermeneutics is that usage should determine the meaning of a term. Accordingly, the many references to the Promised Land throughout the Old Testament should provide guidance as to its interpretation here. The concept of the land being heaven, though a popular concept, does not satisfy the scriptural prophecy.

The land was the place of blessing as Abram soon discovered when he went down to Egypt to avoid the famine and left the land. Though this move increased his wealth, it also created a problem for him in that Hagar, the handmaid who would be the mother of Ishmael, was taken from Egypt to the Promised Land on this visit.

*Genesis 13:1-18.* In the original command to Abram in Ur of the Chaldeans, he was told to leave his kindred. Instead, his father and his nephew Lot traveled with him. His arrival in the Promised Land was delayed until the death of his father. In Genesis 13 the herds of Lot and Abram became so large they could not occupy the same area. Because of this Abram offered Lot the choice of the land. At the time Abram and Lot were in the land, archeology supports the concept that the Jordan Valley was "well watered, like the garden of the LORD" (v. 10). Lot chose the valley of the Jordan. Unfortunately, it was also the place where Sodom and Gomorrah were located which ultimately led to his downfall.

After Lot had separated himself from Abram, a further prophetic revelation is given to Abram, "The LORD said to Abram after Lot had parted from him, 'Lift up your eyes from where you are and look north and south, east and west. All the land that you see I will give to you and your offspring forever. I will make your offspring like the dust of the earth, so that if anyone could count the dust, then your offspring could be counted. Go, walk through the length and breadth of the land, for I am giving it to you' " (vv. 14-17). From this passage it is clear that Abram understood the promise of Genesis 12:7 as referring to the literal land which God had promised him. This was confirmed by God's instruction for him to look in all directions because what he saw was what his offspring would inherit.

*Genesis 15:1-6.* The promise of the land was complicated by the fact that Abram had no children. How could the promise be fulfilled if he had no heirs? In this situation Abram suggested to God that he consider Eliezer of Damascus as his child and his children would therefore be Abram's children and could inherit the promise. The reply of the Lord was direct, "Then the word of the LORD came to him: 'This man will not be your heir, but a son coming from your own body will be your heir' " (v. 4). The prophesied son of Abram was just as literal as the promise of the land.

In verse 6 the simple statement was made, "Abram believed the LORD, and He credited it to him as righteousness." Abram's faith was in the character of God and the revelation of God and illustrates the true nature of faith which in all dispensations is the basis for righteousness with God.

*Genesis 15:9-21.* In verses 9-17 prediction of the land was further supported by a solemn ceremony in which blood was shed, certifying that this covenant with Abram would have literal fulfillment.

Further, the boundaries of the land were indicated in verses 18-21, "On that day the LORD made a covenant with Abram and said, 'To your descendants I give this land, from the river of Egypt to the great river, the Euphrates — the land of the Kenites, Kenizzites, Kadmonites, Hittites, Perizzites, Rephaites, Amorites, Canaanites, Girgashites and Jebusites.' " It is difficult to understand how capable expositors of the Word of God can make this description of the land symbolic of heaven.

*Genesis 16:7-16.* The problem of who would inherit the land was complicated when Abram had a son, Ishmael, by Hagar, the handmaiden he had brought from Egypt. Hagar, attempting to flee Sarai, was instructed to return. Her child was to be named Ishmael. She was told her son would live in hostility in relation to his brothers (v. 12). After Ishmael was born, Scriptures were silent about the next thirteen years.

*Genesis 17:1-8.* When Abram was ninety-nine years old and Sarai was ninety, having a child in old age now became humanly impossible. In this situation God spoke to Abram, changing his name to Abraham, meaning "father of many," and emphasizing the certain fulfillment of the promises, "I will make you very fruitful; I will make nations of you, and kings will come from you. I will establish My covenant as an everlasting covenant between Me and you and your descendants after you for the generations to come, to be your God and the God of your descendants after you. The whole land of Canaan, where you are now an alien, I will give as an everlasting possession to you and your descendants after you; and I will be their God" (vv. 6-8).

*Genesis 17:9-21.* The rite of circumcision was instituted as representing a sign of the covenant of Abram. At the same time God changed the name of Sarai, Abram's wife, to Sarah, meaning "princess." Though Abraham found it difficult to believe that a son could be born to Sarah and him in their old age, God reiterated the promise. He also heeded Abraham's request that Ishmael be blessed (v. 20). But God made it clear, "But My covenant I will establish with Isaac, whom Sarah will bear to you by this time next year" (v. 21).

### Isaac and Jacob

*Genesis 21:1-21.* The rule that prophecy is normally interpreted literally is illustrated once again in the birth of Isaac. Impossible as it seemed, Abraham and Sarah were the parents of Isaac. Hagar and Ishmael were sent away with Abraham's blessing, but without the promises which Isaac would inherit (vv. 9-20). The promises to Ishmael were also fulfilled (1 Chron. 1:28-29).

*Genesis 22:15-18.* Because Abraham had obeyed God, he was promised again innumerable blessings, victory over enemies, and that all nations would be blessed because of him. This is fulfilled in history and prophecy.

*Genesis 24:1–26:6.* Isaac was promised that the blessing on Abraham would pass to him and he would fulfill in part the promise of a great nation and blessing on the whole world. The place of blessing was in the land that God had promised to Abraham. In that land God provided a bride for Isaac (24:1-66). Isaac and Rebekah were childless for nineteen years, and it seemed that Isaac would have the same problem that Abraham had of having a suitable heir. Twenty years after marriage when Isaac was sixty years old, Jacob and Esau were born (25:20, 26).

The promise of the land was also repeated in Genesis 26. Isaac, like his father, sought to go to Egypt because of the famine in the land. In confirmation of earlier prophecies, verses 2-6 repeated the promise of the land, "The LORD appeared to Isaac and said, 'Do not go down to Egypt; live in the land where I tell you to live. Stay in this land for a while, and I will be with you and will bless you. For to you and your descendants will I give all these lands and will confirm the oath I swore to your father Abraham. I will make your descendants as numerous as the stars in the sky and will give them all these lands, and through your offspring all nations on earth will be blessed, because Abraham obeyed Me and kept My requirements, My commands, My decrees and My laws.' So Isaac stayed in Gerar."

*Genesis 27:1-40.* Though Jacob was not the firstborn, he connived with his mother Rebekah to deceive Isaac, who now was old and blind, into bestowing the blessing that normally would be on the firstborn. The Scriptures record that Isaac blessed Jacob with a prophetic benediction, "Ah, the smell of my son is like the smell of a field that the LORD has blessed. May God give you of heaven's dew and of earth's richness—an abundance of grain and new wine. May nations serve you and peoples bow down to you. Be lord over your brothers, and may the sons of your mother bow down to you. May those who curse you be cursed and those who bless you be blessed" (vv. 27-29). When Esau came in later Isaac also blessed him and prophesied his future (vv. 39-40). It was the will of God, however, that Jacob and not Esau should be the one who inherited the Abrahamic promises. These promises were fulfilled in history and prophecy.

*Genesis 27:41–28:22.* The promise of the land, however, continued to be the magnet around which the history of Abraham, Isaac, and Jacob would unfold. Because of Esau's hatred of Jacob, his mother Rebekah arranged to send him back to her people. On the way the Lord reiterated the promise of the land, "I am the LORD, the God of your father Abraham and the God of Isaac. I will give you and your descendants the land on which you are lying. Your descendants will be like the dust of the earth, and you will spread out to the west and to the east, to the north and to the south. All peoples on earth will be blessed through you and your offspring. I am with you and will watch over you wherever you go, and I will bring you back to this land. I will not leave you until I have done what I have promised you" (28:13-15).

This prophecy is of utmost importance because it makes clear that the promise of the land, as well as other promises specifically given to the promised seed of Abraham, were given to Isaac, not Ishmael, and to Jacob, not Esau. While some of the promises of blessing extended to all of Abraham's descendants, the promise of the land was limited to Jacob and his heirs.

*Genesis 36:1–37:36; 39:1–48:22.* The latter chapters of Genesis described the history of Jacob. It was summarized in Genesis 37:1, "Jacob lived in the land where his father had stayed, the land of Canaan." As the story of Jacob and his children unfolded, Joseph was sold as a slave into Egypt (vv. 1-36) and in the end rescued his people and brought them down to Egypt to escape the famine (41:1-43; 45:9–46:7). In Joseph's prophetic dream (37:5-7) it was predicted that his brethren would bow down to him (vv. 8-11). This was later fulfilled in Egypt (42:6). A number of prophetic utterances were recorded in the closing chapters of Genesis. These prophecies included the prediction that Pharaoh's butler would be restored (40:12-13; 21) and his baker would be hanged (vv. 18-19, 22). Both prophecies were fulfilled (vv. 21-22). Later this paved the way to interpret Pharaoh's dream (41:1-42) which predicted seven years of plenty to be followed by seven years of famine (vv. 25-36). This was later fulfilled (vv. 47-57). Joseph was elevated to a position next to Pharaoh and put in charge of grain storage (vv. 37-42). This made it possible for Jacob to see Joseph again, the prophecy predicted (46:4) and fulfilled (v. 29). Toward the close of his life Jacob pronounced his blessing on Joseph and his sons (48:15-20).

*Genesis 49:1-28.* Jacob had gathered his sons about his bed to give them his final prophetic blessing.

Reuben, the firstborn, was commended with the description, "My might, the first sign of my strength, excelling in honor, excelling in power" (v. 3). Further praise of Reuben, however, was cut short by the fact that he had defiled his father's bed. As Jacob expressed it, "Turbulent as the waters, you will no longer excel, for you went up onto your father's bed, onto my couch and defiled it" (v. 4). The reference here is to Reuben's adultery with Jacob's concubine Bilhah (35:22). Though Reuben as firstborn would normally receive the double inheritance and be given the place of leadership (1 Chron. 5:1-2), there is no evidence that he received his inheritance, and he did not provide leadership for Israel (cf. Jud. 5:15-16).

Simeon and Levi are grouped in Jacob's prophecy (Gen. 49:5-7). They were characterized as being violent with the sword and having "killed men in their anger" (v. 6). They were both guilty of anger, ferocity, and cruelty, and Jacob predicted that they would be scattered in the land (v. 7).

Judah is a subject of major recognition prophetically (vv. 8-12). Jacob predicted that Judah would triumph over his enemies and be strong like a lion (vv. 8-9). The most significant prophecy was given that the scepter, referring to the future Messiah, would come from the tribe of Judah. Jacob predicted, "The scepter will not depart from Judah, nor the ruler's staff from between his feet, until He comes to whom it belongs and the obedience of the nations is His" (v. 10). This was fulfilled in Christ (Rev. 2:27; 12:5; 19:15). This clearly refers to Christ coming from the family of David which is a part of the tribe of Judah. He is described poetically, "He will tether His donkey to a vine, His colt to the choicest branch; He will wash His garments in wine, His robes in the blood of grapes. His eyes will be darker than wine, His teeth whiter than milk" (Gen. 49:11-12). The poetic language indicates the abundance which will characterize the millennial kingdom when there will be an abundance of vines so that they can tether a donkey to them. Wine will be so plentiful that it can be regarded as wash water. The whiteness of the teeth would come from drinking milk. This is a poetic description of the abundance of the millennial kingdom.

In connection with Zebulun, Jacob predicted, "Zebulun will live by the seashore and become a haven for ships; his border will extend toward Sidon" (v. 13). Though Zebulun would not actually be bordered on the sea, it would be near enough so that they would benefit by seaborne trade.

Concerning Issachar, Jacob predicted, "Issachar is a rawboned donkey lying down between two saddlebags" (v. 14). He is pictured, however, as submitting to forced labor (v. 15).

Concerning Dan, Jacob predicted, "Dan will provide justice for his people as one of the tribes of Israel. Dan will be a serpent by the roadside, a viper along the path, that bites the horse's heels so that its rider tumbles backwards" (vv. 16-17). The name "Dan" means "a judge," implying fair and equal justice. Instead of that, Dan is described as a snake that bites at a horse's heels, resulting in the rider tumbling off his horse. Implied in this prediction is that Dan does not come up to the expectation of his name. Some believe the fact that idolatry appeared first among the sons of Jacob in the tribe of Dan (Jud. 18:30) is a reason for this. The tribe of Dan is also omitted in the description of the 144,000 of Israel (Rev. 7:4-8), implying that it was not an outstanding tribe.

Jacob inserted a plea for God's deliverance before continuing his prophecy, "I look for your deliverance, O LORD" (Gen. 49:18). As Jacob contemplated the difficulties which the tribes of Israel would encounter, he recognized that only God could deliver.

In connection with Gad, Jacob predicted, "Gad will be attacked by a band of raiders, but he will attack them at their heels" (v. 19). The name "Gad" means "attack," and there is a play on words in this prediction where Gad, the attacker, is attacked, but the prophecy indicates that Gad will counterattack. The surprise attacks from enemies were common, and the prophecy may refer to this (cf. 1 Chron. 5:18-19).

Jacob predicted concerning Asher, "Asher's food will be rich; he will provide delicacies fit for a king" (Gen. 49:20). The tribe of Asher was located in an area in Canaan with rich soil, able to provide much food, and possibly the prediction relates to this.

Jacob prophesied concerning Naphtali, "Naphtali is a doe set free that bears beautiful fawns" (v. 21). The tribe of Naphtali settled northwest of the Sea of Galilee in a mountainous area and is pictured here like a deer that is free. Deborah in her song pictured both the people of Zebulun and Naphtali as risking their lives "on the heights of the field" (Jud. 5:18).

Jacob gave a long prediction concerning Joseph, "Joseph is a fruit-ful vine, a fruitful vine near a spring, whose branches climb over a wall" (Gen. 49:22). Joseph is pictured as a fruitful vine in keeping with the meaning of his son Ephraim's name, which means "fruitful." Jacob predicted that Joseph would be attacked: "With bitterness archers attacked him, they shot at him with hostility. But his bow remained steady, his strong arm stayed limber, because the hand of the Mighty One of Jacob, because of the Shepherd, the Rock of Israel, because of your father's God, who helps you, because the Almighty, who blesses you with blessings of the heavens above, blessings of the deep that lies below, blessings of the breast and womb" (vv. 23-25). Joseph is pictured as strong and able to defend himself against all attacks because he is under the blessings of God.

Jacob goes on, "Your father's blessings are greater than the bless-ings of the ancient mountains, than the bounty of the age-old hills. Let all these rest on the head of Joseph, on the brow of the prince among his brothers" (v. 26). The extensive prophecies concerning Joseph indicate Jacob's particular interest and concern for him, and Jacob predicted great blessings on Joseph in the midst of his brethren.

Jacob concluded with a prophecy concerning Benjamin, "Benjamin is a ravenous wolf; in the morning he devours the prey, in the evening he divides the plunder" (v. 27). Benjamites were great war-riors and are here described as being powerful like a wolf.

In general, the prophecies that Jacob bestowed on his children were fulfilled in their subsequent history. In his prophecies Jacob was realistic, picturing the bad as well as the good, and estimating effectively and accurately the character of his sons. As the Scriptures indicate, each was given "the blessing appropriate to him" (v. 28). Following his prophecy, Jacob breathed his last.

### Other Prophecies Related to the Abrahamic Covenant

The promise of the land is prominent throughout the Book of Genesis and supports the conclusion that God meant literally the future land of Israel. Other aspects of the Abrahamic Covenant were also fulfilled. Coupled with the promise of the land was the continued promise of descendants to Abraham. Though all the children of Abraham fulfilled the promise that his descendants would be like the stars of the heaven and the sands of the sea in number, the narrative was clear that the promise of the land was limited to a particular line of descendants—Isaac, Jacob, and his twelve sons.

The promise that kings would descend from Abraham would be subject to later fulfillment, especially in the history of Israel when Saul, David, and Solomon were made kings. The promise that Abraham would be a great man was certainly fulfilled in the many chapters devoted to him and his descendants in the Book of Genesis. Taken as a whole, the Book of Genesis confirms that God made literal promises to Abraham which would be literally fulfilled in time and in eternity.

## PROPHECY IN EXODUS

Four books were dedicated to the Exodus from Egypt, the years of wandering in the wilderness, and the death of Moses. Though mainly historical books, numerous prophecies were revealed throughout this portion of the history of Israel. In most cases the prophecies described events that were to be fulfilled soon.

### Moses Called to Deliver His People

*Exodus 3:1–4:31; 6:1-8.* God as the Angel of the Lord appeared to Moses at the burning bush and revealed to Moses that he was to be the deliverer of the Children of Israel from Egypt. This experience was described in 3:5-12. The sign promised Moses (v. 12) was fulfilled (17:6).

Moses was reluctant to accept this challenge as described in 4:1-31, even though God promised to perform miracles (vv. 21-23). After his contest with Pharaoh (Ex. 5) Moses was given confirmation of his prophetic role of leading the Children of Israel out of Egypt (6:1-8). Subsequent history, of course, confirmed these prophetic promises (cf. 12:37-50).

## Ten Plagues on Egypt

*Exodus 7:1–12:36.* The ten plagues were inflicted on the Egyptians in fulfillment of prophecy: (1) water was turned to blood (7:14-24); (2) the plague of frogs (8:1-15); (3) the plague of gnats (vv. 16-19); (4) the plague of flies (vv. 20-30); (5) the plague on livestock (9:1-7); (6) the plague of boils (vv. 8-12); (7) the plague of hail and fire (vv. 13-35); (8) the plague of locusts (10:1-20); (9) the plague of darkness (vv. 21-29); (10) the plague of the death of the firstborn (11:1-10; 12:29-30).

At each of these plagues Pharaoh was warned of the next plague. In each case, except the final plague, Pharaoh resisted letting the Children of Israel go. And in each case the prophecy of the plague was fulfilled. It is noteworthy that all of these prophecies were simple, factual prophecies of events of the future which were literally fulfilled.

*Exodus 12:46; cf. Numbers 9:12.* The Passover lamb was a type of Christ. The fact that no bones were broken is a foreshadowing of Christ's sacrifice without a bone being broken (John 19:36).

## The Exodus Begun

*Exodus 12:31-36.* After the tenth plague Pharaoh allowed the Children of Israel to leave and they were delivered from Egypt as God had prophesied to Moses. The Israelites were able to take silver and gold and other plunder from the Egyptians because the Egyptians were eager to see them leave after the tenth plague (vv. 33-36). The Exodus from Egypt was the most important move in Israel's history until the twentieth-century movement of Israel back to the Promised Land.

## Deliverance through the Red Sea

*Exodus 14:1-31.* Biblical history recorded Pharaoh pursuing the Israelites to prevent their departure. God intervened and protected the Israelites. Then, miraculously, God prepared a way for them through the Red Sea. The Egyptians tried to follow, but they were thwarted by the waters returning and drowning all of them.

## Victory over the Amalekites

*Exodus 17:8-15.* Israel was attacked by the Amalekites but was able to overcome them. God predicted the Amalekites would be destroyed (v. 15; 1 Chron. 4:43).

## The Preliminary Promise of the Covenant with Moses

*Exodus 19:1-13.* The favored status of the people of Israel in the world was revealed (vv. 1-6). In connection with the giving of the covenant, the Children of Israel were warned not to approach Mount Sinai (vv. 11-13).

### Prophetic Promise of Guidance for Israel.

*Exodus 23:20-31.* God directed Israel to follow the guidance of the Angel of the Lord who would go ahead of them and lead them to the Promised Land. God promised to establish their borders from the Red Sea to the Sea of the Philistines and from the desert to the Euphrates River. The leading of the Lord was mentioned again in 33:15; 34:10-12.

# PROPHECY IN LEVITICUS
## Promises Relating to Their Laws

The Book of Leviticus is a summary of many laws and regulations which governed Israel's religious life. Promises are often attached to a regulation indicating blessing for obedience or judgment for disobedience. Promises of forgiveness are frequently found (5:13, 16; 6:7; 19:22). Certain rites would make things or people holy (6:18, 27). Some rituals resulted in ceremonial cleansing (14:20; 15:22; 16:30; 17:15). Some offerings were declared unacceptable (7:18). Certain acts of disobedience would result in individuals being cut off from Israel (7:27; 17:9; 23:29). Some acts of disobedience would result in death (10:6).

### The Feasts of the Lord

Though no major prophecies were revealed, Leviticus 23 outlines the feasts of the Lord which are typically prophetic of future events. The Passover pointed to the sacrifice of Christ (vv. 4-5). The Feast of Unleavened Bread represents the holiness of communion with Christ as represented by the absence of leaven (vv. 6-8). The Feast of the Firstfruits anticipates Christ's resurrection as the firstfruit from the dead (vv. 9-14). The Feast of Weeks, also known as Pentecost — fifty days after the Feast of Firstfruits — represents the coming of the Holy Spirit at Pentecost (vv. 15-22). The Feast of Trumpets anticipates the future regathering of Israel (vv. 23-25).

The Day of Atonement was a feast held on the tenth day of the seventh month (cf. Lev. 16), recognizing the sacrifice of atonement offered by the high priest that day and anticipating the repentance of Israel at the Second Coming (23:26-32). The final feast, that of Tabernacles, is a memorial of Israel's redemption from Egypt and is prophetic of her regathering and restoration at the Second Coming (vv. 33-44).

### Conditions for Blessing and Warnings of Curses

Leviticus 26 reveals the conditions for blessing and the warning of cursing. They are commanded not to make idols, to observe the Sabbath, and to reverence the sanctuary (vv. 1-2).

Conditions of blessing and resulting disobedience include bounteous crops, peace, triumph over enemies, increase in their numbers, and God's presence among them (vv. 3-13).

An extended statement of the curses for disobedience are revealed, similar to the warnings of Moses (Deut. 28:15-68). They were promised distress (vv. 16-17), drought (vv. 18-20), wild animals (vv. 21-22), plagues (vv. 23-26), famine (vv. 27-31), and worldwide dispersion (vv. 32-39).

Israel was promised forgiveness if their sins were confessed. The Abrahamic Covenant was reaffirmed as being certain of fulfillment even if they sinned (vv. 40-45).

## PROPHECY IN NUMBERS

### Prophecy at Kadesh Barnea

*Numbers 14:20-34.* The people of Israel failed to follow the Lord or to trust that He would lead them into the Promised Land. The Lord predicted that none of the adult population of men who left Egypt, except for Caleb and Joshua, would be allowed to enter the Promised Land. This was fulfilled in history (26:63-65). God also predicted that the children whom they said would be taken as plunder would be the ones who would conquer the Promised Land.

*Numbers 21:8-9.* The serpent made of bronze and elevated on a pole is a type of Christ crucified (John 3:14-15).

### The Prophecies of Balaam

*Numbers 22:1–24:25.* Balak, who was king of Moab, attempted to hire Balaam, a prophet, to curse Israel. Balaam was induced to attempt to prophesy curses on Israel. He was kept from doing so and, instead, prophesied blessing upon them as recorded in 23:7-10; 23:18-24; 24:3-9, 15-19, 20-24. This prophetic utterance described the greatness of Israel, her power as a nation, the blessing of God upon her land, and the prediction that she would conquer the Moabites. This was fulfilled in history.

### The Prophetic Command of God to Drive Out
### the Inhabitants of the Land

*Numbers 33:51-66.* God directed Israel to drive out the inhabitants of the land and prophesied that those they allowed to remain "will become barbs in your eyes and thorns in your sides. They will give you trouble in the land where you will live. And then I will do to you what I plan to do to them" (vv. 55-56; cf. 25:1-3; Josh. 9:1-26; 13:2-7; Judges 1:21, 28-36; 2:11-23).

# PROPHECY IN DEUTERONOMY

In Moses' summary of the history of Israel and his final word to the Children of Israel as recorded in Deuteronomy additional promises of prophetic nature were given.

### Prophecy of the Inheritance of the Land

*Deuteronomy 3:21-22.* The promise of the land being inherited by Israel was repeated once again. This prophecy will be fulfilled (Ezek. 45–48; Amos 9:14-15).

*Deuteronomy 4:25-31.* Israel was warned not to make idols or sin morally because God would judge them and drive them out of the land. They were promised restoration if they return to the Lord. This was fulfilled in history.

### The Coming of a Great Prophet

*Deuteronomy 18:15-18.* The coming of a great Prophet was revealed who would be like Moses. They should listen to Him or God would hold them to account. This was fulfilled by Christ (John 1:21-45; 6:14; Acts 3:22-23; 7:37).

*Deuteronomy 21:23.* The fact that one hanging on a tree is under divine curse is symbolic of Christ's dying on a tree bearing the sins of the world (Gal. 3:13).

### Promises of Blessing and Cursing

*Deuteronomy 28:1-68.* In this sweeping prophetic revelation of Israel's future, God promised to bless them if they obey the Law but to curse them if they do not. To some extent this chapter charts the course of Israel's history from here on. The closing verses of Deuteronomy described the worldwide dispersion of the Children of Israel, "Just as it pleased the LORD to make you prosper and increase in number, so it will please Him to ruin and destroy you. You will be uprooted from the land you are entering to possess. Then the LORD will scatter you among all nations, from one end of the earth to the other. There you will worship other gods — gods of wood and stone, which neither you nor your fathers have known. Among those nations you will find no repose, no resting place for the sole of your foot. There the LORD will give you an anxious mind, eyes weary with longing, and a despairing heart. You will live in constant suspense, filled with dread both night and day, never sure of your life. In the morning you will say, 'If only it were evening!' and in the evening, 'If only it were morning!' — because of the terror that will fill your hearts and the sights that your eyes will see. The LORD will send you back in ships to Egypt on a journey I said you should never make again. There you will offer yourselves for sale to your enemies as male and female slaves, but no one will buy you" (Deut. 28:63-68).

As brought out in many other passages, their ultimate restoration is assured (Jer. 23:5-8; 30:8-11; Ezek. 39:25-29). The worldwide dispersion predicted in Deuteronomy 28 has been literally fulfilled. So also their ultimate regathering already begun in the twentieth century will be brought to fulfillment at the Second Coming.

### Promise of Restoration of Israel

*Deuteronomy 30:1-10.* God promised to restore His people when they turn to Him in repentance and submission. This was fulfilled in history.

### Blessing Pronounced on Israel

*Deuteronomy 31:23.* Joshua was promised God's blessing as they entered the Promised Land. This was fulfilled (Josh. 21:43-45).

*Deuteronomy 33:1-29.* Final blessing on the people of Israel was recorded by Moses before his death. Throughout history the blessings and curses pronounced by Moses continued to be fulfilled.

# 2

# PROPHECY IN
# THE BOOKS OF HISTORY

# PROPHECY IN JOSHUA, JUDGES, AND RUTH

The Books of Joshua and Judges are the historical link between Moses and David. The Book of Ruth added its historical record of the line of the Messiah leading up to David. Prophecies in these books are relatively short and connected with the historical narrative.

### The Promise of the Land Given to Joshua

*Joshua 1:1-9.* After the death of Moses (Deut. 34:5; Josh. 1:1) God announced to Joshua His purpose of giving the Promised Land to Israel. The Lord said, "I will give you every place where you set your foot, as I promised Moses. Your territory will extend from the desert to Lebanon, and from the great river, the Euphrates — all the Hittite country — to the Great Sea on the west. No one will be able to stand up against you all the days of your life. As I was with Moses, so I will be with you; I will never leave you nor forsake you" (vv. 3-5). The prophecies concluded, "Have I not commanded you? Be strong and courageous. Do not be terrified; do not be discouraged, for the LORD your God will be with you wherever you go" (v. 9). The rest of the Book of Joshua recorded how Israel conquered most of the land. At the time of Joshua it is important to note that the promises of the land were still considered literal promises. The promises were partially fulfilled in Joshua's lifetime (21:43-45).

### The Conquest of Jericho

*Joshua 6:1-5.* In keeping with this promise to Joshua, when they came to Jericho God said, "See, I have delivered Jericho into your hands, along with its king and its fighting men. March around the city once with all the armed men. Do this for six days. Have seven priests carry trumpets of rams' horns in front of the ark. On the seventh day, march around the city seven times, with the priests blowing the trumpets. When you hear them sound a long blast on the trumpets, have all the people give a loud shout; then the walls of the city will collapse and the people will go up, every man straight in" (vv. 2-5).

*Joshua 6:6-27.* As Joshua obeyed the command concerning the manner of conquest, the promise was fulfilled and they conquered Jericho, saving only Rahab, her father and mother and brothers (vv. 23, 25). After the conquest of Jericho, according to the Scriptures, "Joshua pronounced this solemn oath: 'Cursed before the LORD is the man who undertakes to rebuild this city, Jericho: At the cost of

42

his firstborn son will he lay its foundation; at the cost of his youngest will he set up its gates' " (v. 26). This was fulfilled as recorded in 1 Kings 16:34, "In Ahab's time, Hiel of Bethel rebuilt Jericho. He laid its foundations at the cost of his firstborn son Abiram, and he set up its gates at the cost of his youngest son Segub, in accordance with the word of the LORD spoken by Joshua son of Nun." The prophecy was literally fulfilled.

### The Conquest of Ai

*Joshua 7:1–8:29.* After Israel's disobedience recorded in Joshua 7, God instructed Joshua how Ai should be taken, "Then the LORD said to Joshua, 'Do not be afraid; do not be discouraged. Take the whole army with you, and go up and attack Ai. For I have delivered into your hands the king of Ai, his people, his city and his land. You shall do to Ai and its king as you did to Jericho and its king, except that you may carry off their plunder and livestock for yourselves. Set an ambush behind the city' " (8:1-2).

In the course of the Conquest the Lord instructed Joshua, "Hold out toward Ai the javelin that is in your hand, for into your hand I will deliver the city" (v. 18). The verses that follow God's command described the fall of Ai and Joshua's carrying out the commands of the Lord.

### The Prophecy at Gibeon

*Joshua 10:1-28.* After Israel's failure to inquire of the Lord, they were deceived into a covenant with Gibeon. The enemies of the Gibeonites attacked Gibeon with the result that Joshua had to march against Gibeon's enemies.

At that time, "The LORD said to Joshua, 'Do not be afraid of them; I have given them into your hand. Not one of them will be able to withstand you' " (v. 8). The Scriptures which follow recorded the fulfillment as the armies were totally destroyed.

### The Destruction of the Northern Kings

*Joshua 11:1-15.* When the kings in the north of the land conspired to attack Israel with a large number of horses and chariots, Scriptures recorded the message of the Lord to Joshua, "Do not be afraid of them, because by this time tomorrow I will hand all of them over to Israel, slain. You are to hamstring their horses and burn their chariots" (v. 6). The prophecy was fulfilled and Joshua fulfilled this command. The reason for hamstringing the horses was that God did not want Joshua to trust in chariots and horses for his strength.

*Joshua 11:11-23.* A summary of the conquest of Joshua was recorded, fulfilling the promise that the Lord had given Joshua in Joshua 1. Though the Lord was said to have fulfilled all His promises, as the Book of Judges makes clear, much of the territory had not yet been possessed (Josh. 13:1–19:51). But God had given them every portion of the land that they had set their foot on (cf. 1:3).

*Joshua 21:43-45.* The interpretation of verses 43-45 must be considered in the light of the later revelation. Scriptures state, "So the LORD gave Israel all the land He had sworn to give their forefathers, and they took possession of it and settled there. The LORD gave them rest on every side, just as He had sworn to their forefathers. Not one of the enemies withstood them; the LORD handed all their enemies over to them. Not one of all the LORD's good promises to the house of Israel failed; every one was fulfilled" (vv. 43-45). The Lord had not failed to keep His promise even though Israel had failed by faith to conquer all the land. The amillennial view sometimes advanced that this fulfilled the promise of the land given to Abraham is without scriptural foundation as later promises picture a future possession of the land because the Children of Israel had not possessed all the land (Jud. 1:19, 21, 27, 29-34; 2:1-3, 20-23; 3:1-4).

### The Promise of Victory over the Canaanites
*Judges 1:1-8.* After Joshua's death the Lord gave instruction for the continued battle to obtain the land, "Judah is to go; I have given the land into their hands" (v. 2). The Simeonites assisted Judah in conquering the land. Important in their conquest was the destruction of Jerusalem which was set on fire (v. 8).

### Prophecy of God's Chastening Israel for Disobedience
*Judges 2:1-3.* The familiar picture of Israel's failure in the time of Judges was described in God's statement to Israel, "Yet you have disobeyed Me. Why have you done this? Now therefore I tell you that I will not drive them out before you; they will be thorns in your sides and their gods will be a snare to you" (vv. 2-3).

*Judges 2:20-23.* Further revelation was given concerning the Lord's anger with Israel: "Therefore the LORD was very angry with Israel and said, 'Because this nation has violated the covenant that I laid down for their forefathers and has not listened to Me, I will no longer drive out before them any of the nations Joshua left when he died. I will use them to test Israel and see whether they will keep the way of the LORD and walk in it as their forefathers did.' The LORD had allowed those nations to remain; He did not drive them out at once by giving them into the hands of Joshua" (vv. 20-23).

### Prophecy about Deborah and Barak

*Judges 4:1-11.* Deborah and Barak, fourth and fifth judges of Israel, were promised victory over Sisera. This prophecy was fulfilled and Sisera killed (vv. 12-24).

### Prophecy Given to Gideon

*Judges 6:11-24.* Scriptures record God's selection of Gideon as a judge over Israel. In verse 14 it was recorded, "The LORD turned to him [Gideon] and said, 'Go in the strength you have and save Israel out of Midian's hand. Am I not sending you?' "

*Judges 7:1-25.* The 300 warriors chosen by God attained a decisive victory over Midian, fulfilling the prophecy literally.

### Prophecy of Deliverance from
### the Ammonites and Philistines

*Judges 10:13-14.* Because the Children of Israel forsook the Lord, God told them that He would not heed their cry, "But you have forsaken Me and served other gods, so I will no longer save you. Go and cry out to the gods you have chosen. Let them save you when you are in trouble!" (vv. 13-14)

*Judges 11:1-40.* Because of their willingness to come back to God, however, God allowed Jephthah to be raised up as the ninth judge of Israel, and he delivered Israel from their enemies.

### Prophecy Related to Samson

*Judges 13–16.* The story of Samson is one of the enigmatic stories of the Bible. His birth was announced by the Angel of the Lord to his father Manoah. Early feats of strength and departures from God were described (14:1–16:19). God's promise to Samson's mother concerning her child that "he will begin the deliverance of Israel from the hands of the Philistines" (13:5) was nevertheless fulfilled.

After Samson was captured by the Philistines, blinded, and shackled to grind grain in prison, his strength returned, and in destroying the pillars on which the temple was built he was able to kill more in his death than in his life (16:23-31).

The Books of Joshua and Judges set the stage for the coming of Samuel, the last of the judges and the first of the prophets. In contrast to the Book of Judges, which is one of moral and physical defeat, the Book of Joshua is largely one of victory.

Nestled between Judges and 1 Samuel, however, is the Book of

Ruth which, though it contains no prophecies of the future, is itself a reminder that God has the purpose of fulfilling the promise of a coming Messiah. The lovely story of Ruth is one of the links leading up to David.

# PROPHECY IN FIRST SAMUEL

As the last of the judges and the first of the prophets, the ministry of Samuel was an important link between the time of the judges and the reign of David. Two chapters of 1 Samuel introduced the birth and life of Samuel as one of the great prophets of Scripture.

### Hannah's Prayer

*1 Samuel 1:1–2:11.* As one of the two wives of Elkanah, Hannah had to bear the embarrassment of not having a son in contrast to the other wife of Elkanah. Though her husband treated her kindly, Scriptures record her bitterness and her prayer at the doorpost of the temple, "In bitterness of soul Hannah wept much and prayed to the LORD. And she made a vow, saying, 'O LORD Almighty, if You will only look upon Your servant's misery and remember me, and not forget Your servant but give her a son, then I will give him to the LORD for all the days of his life, and no razor will ever be used on his head' " (1:10-11).

Eli thought that Hannah was drunk and rebuked her. When she explained that she had been praying with great anguish and grief, Eli replied, "Go in peace, and may the God of Israel grant you what you have asked of Him" (v. 17). In due time Samuel was born, his name meaning "heard of God," in recognition that he was an answer to prayer. After he was weaned, Hannah brought him to Eli to remain in the temple for the rest of his life along with a sacrifice of a bull and an ephah of flour and a skin of wine (vv. 24-28).

The second chapter of 1 Samuel recorded the inspired prayer of Hannah and recognized the greatness of God in answering her prayer and manifesting His supernatural strength.

### The Curse on Eli's Family

*1 Samuel 2:12-17.* In contrast to God's blessing on Hannah and Samuel, the sons of Eli proved to be very wicked.

*1 Samuel 2:27-34.* A man of God came to Eli and informed him that though God intended to bless the house of Eli forever, because of their sin, He was going to cut off the house of Eli, "so that there will not be an old man in your family line and you will see distress in My dwelling" (vv. 31-32).

As a sign of the fulfillment of this promise to Eli, the man of God told him, "And what happens to your two sons, Hophni and Phinehas, will be a sign to you—they will both die on the same day" (v. 34).

### Promise of a Future Faithful Priest

*1 Samuel 2:35-36.* In contrast to the unfaithfulness of Hophni and Phinehas, God declared, "I will raise up for Myself a faithful priest, who will do according to what is in My heart and mind. I will firmly establish his house, and he will minister before My anointed one always" (v. 35). The priesthood was taken away from Abiathar who had descended from Eli and instead was given to Zadok who was a descendant of Eleazar, a son of Aaron (1 Kings 2:27, 35). This prophecy, however, seems to go beyond the immediate line of priests and was partially fulfilled by Samuel. It ultimately will be fulfilled by Jesus Christ who will be a Priest forever (Ps. 110; Heb. 5:6; Rev. 19:16).

### Curse on Eli's Family Revealed to Samuel

*1 Samuel 3:1-21.* The beginning of Samuel's ministry as a prophet revealed that Samuel was called by the Lord. God said to Samuel in the night, "And the LORD said to Samuel: 'See, I am about to do something in Israel that will make the ears of everyone who hears of it tingle. At that time I will carry out against Eli everything I spoke against his family—from beginning to end. For I told him that I would judge his family forever because of the sin he knew about; his sons made themselves contemptible, and he failed to restrain them. Therefore, I swore to the house of Eli, "The guilt of Eli's house will never be atoned for by sacrifice or offering" ' " (vv. 11-14). The prophecy was fulfilled in the deaths of Hophni and Phinehas, and Eli died when their deaths were reported (4:11, 17-18). Later, Abiathar, a descendant of Eli's, was deposed from the priesthood (1 Kings 2:27).

### Prophecy of the Ark's Return

*1 Samuel 6:1–7:2.* The ark had been captured when the Philistines defeated Israel in war. The ark proved, however, to be a catastrophe to the Philistines, causing a series of disasters. Finally they decided to return the ark to Israel. When they asked their own priests and prophets concerning what they should do, they were told to prepare various gifts, to have a new cart be drawn by two cows who had not been yoked (6:7). Their own prophets told them, "Take the ark of the LORD and put it on the cart, and in a chest beside it put the gold objects you are sending back to Him as a guilt offering. Send it on its way, but keep watching it. If it goes up to its own territory, towards Beth Shemesh, then the LORD has brought this great disaster on us. But if it does not, then we will know that it was not His hand that struck us and that it happened to us by chance" (vv. 8-9). The Scriptures describe how the ark was drawn to Beth Shemesh, but God judged the men of Beth Shemesh because they had looked into the ark (v. 19). They sent messages to the people of Kiriath Jearim, asking them to come and take the ark. The ark remained with those at Kiriath Jearim for twenty years (v. 21; 7:1-2).

### Samuel's Promise of Deliverance

*1 Samuel 7:3-13.* Samuel challenged the house of Israel to return to the Lord, "And Samuel said to the whole house of Israel, 'If you are returning to the LORD with all your hearts, then rid yourselves of foreign gods and Ashtoreths and commit yourselves to the LORD and serve Him only, and He will deliver you out of the hand of the Philistines' " (v. 3).

Following this return to the Lord, Israel had a great military victory over the Philistines (vv. 10-13), fulfilling literally the prophecy given to Samuel.

### Prophecy Concerning Israel's Kings

*1 Samuel 8:1-22.* Samuel's sons, however, did not follow in his way and were dishonest (vv. 3-4), and the Children of Israel demanded of Samuel that a king be appointed. This greatly displeased Samuel, but as he prayed to the Lord, the prophetic revelation came to him from the Lord, "Listen to all that the people are saying to you; it is not you they have rejected, but they have rejected Me as their King. As they have done from the day I brought them up out of Egypt until this day, forsaking Me and serving other gods, so they are doing to you. Now listen to them; but warn them solemnly and let them know what the king who will reign over them will do" (vv. 7-9).

Samuel therefore warned the Children of Israel about what a king would do for them, "He said, 'This is what the king who will reign over you will do: He will take your sons and make them serve with his chariots and horses, and they will run in front of his chariots. Some he will assign to be commanders of thousands and commanders of fifties, and others to plow his ground and reap his harvest, and still others to make weapons of war and equipment for his chariots. He will take your daughters to be perfumers and cooks and bakers. He will take the best of your fields and vineyards and olive groves and give them to his attendants. He will take a tenth of your grain and of your vintage and give it to his officials and attendants. Your menservants and maidservants and the best of your cattle and donkeys he will take for his own use. He will take a tenth of your flocks, and you yourselves will become his slaves. When that day comes, you will cry out for relief from the king you have chosen, and the LORD will not answer you in that day' " (vv. 11-18). This was fulfilled (1 Kings 12:2-15).

### Saul Chosen and Anointed as King

*1 Samuel 9:1–10:27.* Saul had been seeking his father's lost donkeys and in the process contacted Samuel to see if he could help them. The Lord told Samuel "About this time tomorrow I will send you a man from the land of Benjamin. Anoint him leader over My people Israel; he will deliver My people from the hand of the Philistines. I have looked upon My people, for their cry has reached Me" (9:16). Subsequently Samuel invited Saul to a feast (vv. 19-24).

After the feast with Samuel, Saul was returning to his home and Samuel requested that Saul's servant go on ahead to permit Saul and Samuel privacy. "Then Samuel took a flask of oil and poured it on Saul's head and kissed him, saying, 'Has not the LORD anointed you leader over His inheritance? When you leave me today, you will meet two men near Rachel's tomb at Zelzah on the border of Benjamin. They will say to you, "The donkeys you set out to look for have been found. And now your father has stopped thinking about them and is worried about you. He is asking, 'What shall I do about my son?' " ' " (10:1-2)

Samuel also predicted other events that would occur to him while he was on his way home (vv. 3-13), including that the Spirit of the Lord would come upon him. This was fulfilled (vv. 10-11). Saul did not announce his anointing as king, but Samuel called a public meeting of the people of Israel and introduced them to Saul (vv. 17-27).

*1 Samuel 11:1-15.* After Saul was introduced as king, he led the people of Israel in a great military victory over the Ammonites (vv. 1-12). This confirmed the prophecy that Saul would be their king.

### The Kingship Confirmed

*1 Samuel 12:1-25.* In rehearsing his headship, Samuel reminded the people of Israel of his complete integrity. Nevertheless, they had asked for a king. Then Samuel told them, "Now here is the king you have chosen, the one you asked for; see, the LORD has set a king over you. If you fear the LORD and serve and obey Him and do not rebel against His commands, and if both you and the king who reigns over you follow the LORD your God—good! But if you do not obey the LORD, and if you rebel against His commands, His hand will be against you, as it was against your fathers" (vv. 13-15). After further exhortation, Samuel said, "But be sure to fear the LORD and serve Him faithfully with all your heart; consider what great things He has done for you. Yet if you persist in doing evil, both you and your king will be swept away" (vv. 24-25).

*1 Samuel 13:1-14.* Because Saul foolishly offered an offering to the Lord which Samuel should have done, Saul was informed that his kingdom would not endure. This was fulfilled when David succeeded him (2 Sam. 5:1-4). Nevertheless, Saul won many military victories over Israel's enemies (14:1-48).

### Prophecy Concerning the Amalekites

*1 Samuel 15:1-23.* Samuel had instructed Saul to attack the Amalekites and not to spare any men, women, children or cattle, sheep, camels, and donkeys (vv. 1-3). In obedience, Saul attacked the Amalekites but spared the best of the sheep, cattle, and lambs and other things that were good (vv. 8-9).

Though the Amalekites were defeated and killed as prophesied, Saul was rebuked for not carrying out God's command completely in destroying the cattle and sheep and the things which they took (vv. 12-21). Samuel replied, however, with the important truth that obedience is more important than offerings and sacrifices (vv. 22-23). Though Saul confessed his sin, he was not forgiven by God.

### Saul to Lose the Kingdom of Israel

*1 Samuel 15:24-35.* After Saul's disobedience, Samuel told him, "The LORD has torn the kingdom of Israel from you today and has given it to one of your neighbors—to one better than you. He who is the Glory of Israel does not lie or change His mind; for He is not man, that He should change His mind" (vv. 28-29).

### David Anointed King

*1 Samuel 16:1-23.* Samuel was sent by the Lord to anoint a new king over Israel. David, the son of Jesse, was chosen (vv. 12-13). Though David was anointed king, there was no public acceptance of this fact until much later. Saul, not knowing of David's anointing, requested that David be in his court as David played the harp for him (vv. 21-23). The prophetic anointment of David as king was, of course, the beginning of a long life in which David served the Lord as king over Israel.

## David and Goliath

*1 Samuel 17:1-58.* War had broken out between the Philistines and Israel. The Philistines had chosen Goliath, the giant, to be their champion and challenged Israel to choose someone to fight Goliath, with the agreement that if the champion were killed, the other nation would triumph. After some time, no one volunteered to challenge Goliath. David, visiting his brothers and bringing supplies to them, however, could not understand how they feared Goliath. He raised the question of why Goliath was not challenged.

This information reached Saul and after some hesitation David was allowed to approach Goliath. David declared prophetically to Goliath, "You come against me with sword and spear and javelin, but I come against you in the name of the LORD Almighty, the God of the armies of Israel, whom you have defied. This day the LORD will hand you over to me, and I'll strike you down and cut off your head. Today I will give the carcasses of the Philistine army to the birds of the air and the beasts of the earth, and the whole world will know that there is a God in Israel. All those gathered here will know that it is not by sword or spear that the LORD saves; for the battle is the LORD's, and He will give all of you into our hands" (vv. 45-47).

As Scripture records, David triumphed over Goliath, using his sling and stunning him with a stone. When David cut off the head of Goliath with his own sword, the men of Israel pursued the Philistines and had a great victory (vv. 51-54). These events confirmed the prophecy that David was to be king over Israel.

## Prediction of Victory Over the Philistines at Keilah

*1 Samuel 23:1-13.* Though Saul attempted to kill David and was seeking his life, David continued to be protected by God (18:1–22:23). After inquiring from the Lord, David learned that the Philistines were fighting Keilah, a city about thirty miles southwest of Jerusalem. When David inquired of the Lord, he was instructed to attack the Philistines. The attack against the Philistines was very successful, and he inflicted heavy losses on them. However, Saul also heard about it and began a plan to surround the city of Keilah in order to capture David. When David inquired of the Lord, he was informed that if he stayed, the citizens of Keilah would surrender him to Saul. Accordingly, he left Keilah and went into the desert (23:10-13).

### Prediction that Saul and His Sons Would Die

*1 Samuel 23:14–28:15.* In protecting David, God continued to give prophetic revelations (28:1-25), prophesying to Saul that he and his sons would die the next day and Israel would be defeated (28:16-19; cf. 31:1-6).

*1 Samuel 28:16-19.* Because of Saul's disobedience, Samuel tells him that he and his sons would die.

### The Prediction that David Would Conquer the Amalekites

*1 Samuel 30:1-20.* A closing incident in the Book of 1 Samuel records how the city of Ziklag, where David and his men had placed their families, had been attacked by the Amalekites, the city burned, and the people carried off captive. When David inquired of Abiathar the priest whether he should pursue the Amalekites, he was told to pursue them. In keeping with this prophecy, he caught up with the Amalekite raiders, recovered everything, and killed the Amalekite raiders, except for 400 young men (vv. 9-20), and fulfilled the prophecy.

*1 Samuel 31:1-6.* The closing chapter of 1 Samuel records the death of Saul and Jonathan which prepared the way for David to begin assuming his role as king in fulfillment of prophecy.

Though the Book of 1 Samuel is mainly historical, the prophecies in this book with confirming historical material provide an important lesson in how to interpret prophecy. Many prophecies were fulfilled in the immediate future after the prophecy was given. A few of the prophecies reached beyond the immediate future, as illustrated in the prophecy concerning Samuel as being a faithful priest which was partially fulfilled in the life and ministry of Samuel, but also looked forward to Jesus Christ as the ultimate Prophet.

# PROPHECY IN SECOND SAMUEL AND FIRST KINGS
## The Prophetic Anointing of David as King

Long before Saul was killed, Samuel was instructed to anoint David as the future king of Israel (1 Sam. 16:12-13). Though the anointing itself was not a prophecy, it was nevertheless prophetic of the future reign of David which began only after years of fleeing from Saul who wanted to kill David to prevent his assuming the throne. Once Saul was dead, the men of Judah recognized David as their king (2 Sam. 2:3-4), but the remaining tribes recognized Ish-Bosheth, a son of Saul. It was recorded in 2:12–4:12 that a divided kingdom continued for seven years, but after Ish-Bosheth's death

(4:1-12), David was able to assume control over all twelve tribes of Israel.

According to 5:1-2, representatives of the eleven tribes came and made a pact with David and anointed him king over all Israel. When they came to David, they recited the prophecy, apparently given to David when he was anointed, "You will shepherd My people Israel, and you will become their ruler" (v. 2).

In 2 Samuel 5:19-25 the Lord predicted David's victory over the warring Philistines (cf. 1 Chron. 14:10-16). In connection with David bringing the ark to the City of David (2 Sam. 6:12-23), a psalm of thanksgiving was written by David (1 Chron. 16:7-36). The prediction was also given that David would have a great name (2 Sam. 7:9).

### Background of the Davidic Covenant

The Davidic Covenant is one of a few major biblical covenants directly related to prophecy in its fulfillment. Like the Abrahamic Covenant, interpretation of the Davidic Covenant is determined largely by the decision to interpret it literally or nonliterally. In the case of the Abrahamic Covenant, most of its provisions have already been literally fulfilled, and little room is given to question its literal interpretation.

The major factor still debated in connection with the Abrahamic Covenant is the question whether the land promised to Israel was a literal prophecy, subject to future fulfillment, or whether this is not the correct interpretation. Amillenarians tend to negate the Abrahamic Covenant either on the basis that the promise will not be fulfilled because of Israel's failure or that the promise is fulfilled nonliterally, interpreting the land as a reference to heaven. In the case of the Abrahamic Covenant, this question of interpretation has been answered by premillenarians interpreting the promise of the land literally and by amillenarians who interpret the promise in a nonliteral sense or at least not fulfilled literally. The Davidic Covenant, likewise, has the same problem.

In connection with the promises given to Abram, God informed Abraham concerning Sarah, "I will bless her and will surely give you a son by her. I will bless her so that she will be the mother of nations; kings of peoples will come from her" (Gen. 17:16). The same promise was mentioned in Genesis 17:6, where God informed Abraham, "I will make you very fruitful; I will make nations of you, and kings will come from you." The promise of inheriting the general Abrahamic blessings was later narrowed to Isaac, not Ishmael, and then to Jacob, not Esau (Gen. 26:2-6; 28:13-15). The promise of kings was further limited in Genesis 49:10 with Jacob's prophetic statement of the future of his sons, "The scepter will not depart from Judah, nor the ruler's staff from between his feet, until He comes to whom it belongs and the obedience of the nations is His."

With the background of prophecies concerning the future kingdom of Israel in Genesis, the Abrahamic Covenant was given more specific fulfillment in the covenant God made with David (2 Sam. 7:5-16; 1 Chron. 17:3-15). The subject of the Davidic Covenant became, therefore, a major aspect of prophecy throughout the Old Testament.

*2 Samuel 7.* The Scriptures record that David conferred with Nathan the prophet, expressing David's concern that he lived in a magnificent house made of cedar and that the temple of the Lord was simply a tent (vv. 1-2). Without consulting God, Nathan told David to proceed (v. 3).

That night, however, God corrected Nathan's approval of David's plan (vv. 4-16). Even a prophet needs to have his decisions confirmed by God. In His instructions to Nathan, God pointed out that He had never asked the people of Israel to build a house of cedar for Him.

God first rehearsed how He had taken David from being a shepherd to being a king with great fame. God promised Israel would have a homeland (v. 10). Then God went beyond the plan of building a physical temple to that of establishing the house of David forever, "The LORD declares to you that the LORD Himself will establish a house for you: When your days are over and you rest with your fathers, I will raise up your offspring to succeed you, who will come from your own body, and I will establish his kingdom. He is the one who will build a house for My Name, and I will establish the throne of his kingdom forever. I will be his Father, and he will be My son. When he does wrong, I will punish him with the rod of men, with floggings inflicted by men. But My love will never be taken away from him, as I took it away from Saul, whom I removed from before you. Your house and your kingdom will endure forever before Me; your throne will be established forever" (vv. 11-16). The reference to the house of David was to his physical descendants who would occupy the throne of David.

### Specific Provisions of the Davidic Covenant in 2 Samuel 7

Though not specifically called a covenant here, elsewhere it was called a covenant (2 Sam. 23:5; Ps. 89:3, 28, 34, 39; cf. Ps. 132:11). At least four major provisions were involved in the Davidic Covenant according to 2 Samuel 7. (1) David was promised a son, not yet born, who would succeed David on his throne (v. 12). Actually, this was fulfilled by Solomon. (2) This son would build the temple (v. 13). This was later fulfilled by Solomon (1 Kings 6:37-38; 7:1-51; 2 Chron. 3:1–5:14). (3) The throne of Solomon's kingdom would continue forever (2 Sam. 7:13). If Solomon did wrong, God would punish him, but He would not take away the kingdom (vv. 10-15; 1 Kings 11:34). (4) David's descendants and David's kingdom would endure forever (2 Sam. 7:16). The promises of the Davidic Covenant in 2 Samuel 7 were repeated precisely in 1 Chronicles 17:3-15 (cf. also 2 Sam. 7:19-29; 1 Chron. 17:15-27; 2 Chron. 6:7-10).

In attempting to interpret the Davidic Covenant, certain facts stand out. (1) David understood that the promises had to do with his physical descendants or "house." (2) The prophecy is accurate in details as indicated by the fact that though Solomon's throne was promised to continue forever, his descendants were not given this promise as ultimately the line of Solomon was deposed (Jer. 22:28-30). (3) The ultimate Person to sit on the throne of David would be Jesus Christ. Mary's genealogy (Luke 3:23-38) was traced to Nathan, the son of David, instead of Solomon (v. 31). By contrast, Joseph's genealogy was traced to Solomon (Matt. 1:2-16) whose line was cursed, but Joseph provided the legal basis for Jesus Christ to claim the throne of David. (4) The language of the covenant in 2 Samuel 7 and 1 Chronicles 17, as it was certainly understood by David, referred to his physical lineage and to his political kingdom, not to an entity such as the elect, the saved, or the church. Premillenarians generally interpret the prophecy literally and find it fulfilled in the future millennial kingdom which will occur after the second coming of Christ.

A leading opposing view, however, is advanced by the amillenarians who interpret the prophecy nonliterally as referring to Christ, not in His reign over Israel or over the world but to Christ as the Head of the church. In the amillennial interpretation, the throne of David is equated with the throne of God in heaven, and the reign of Christ is usually related to the present age or Christ's spiritual reign in the hearts of believers. Some amillenarians, however, refer the fulfillment to the new heaven and the new earth in eternity. New light would be cast on the problem of interpretation by details confirming the covenant found later in Scripture.

### The Davidic Covenant in Psalm 89

*Psalm 89:1-4.* The entire contents of this long Psalm provide an exposition of the Davidic Covenant. The opening four verses state that the fulfillment of the covenant was related to the oath of God: "You said, 'I have made a covenant with My chosen one, I have sworn to David My servant, "I will establish your line and make your throne firm through all generations" ' " (vv. 3-4).

*Psalm 89:5-18.* The faithfulness and power of God who made the covenant was the theme of this Psalm. God's faithfulness, power, righteousness, and justice, as well as His love and faithfulness, assured the fulfillment of the covenant. The covenant was gracious and unconditional as to its ultimate fulfillment.

*Psalm 89:19-29.* The central character of David in the covenant and his anointing by sacred oil was brought out. David was declared to be "the most exalted of the kings of the earth" (v. 27). God asserted, "I will maintain My love to him forever, and My covenant with him will never fail. I will establish his line forever, his throne as long as the heavens endure" (vv. 28-29).

*Psalm 89:30-37.* The people of Israel, however, were warned that if they sinned God would punish them, "If his sons forsake My Law and do not follow My statutes, if they violate My decrees and fail to keep My commands, I will punish their sin with the rod, their iniquity with flogging" (vv. 30-32). In spite of the possibility of Israel's sin, God promised that this would not alter the covenant, "But I will not take My love from him, nor will I ever betray My faithfulness. I will not violate My covenant or alter what My lips have uttered. Once for all, I have sworn by My holiness—and I will not lie to David—that his line will continue forever and his throne endure before Me like the sun; it will be established forever like the moon, the faithful witness in the sky" (vv. 33-37).

*Psalm 89:38-52.* The psalmist then pointed out Israel's sins and God's chastening of them. The psalmist called on God to fulfill His promise (vv. 38-52).

The contribution of Psalm 89 cannot be overestimated. On the one hand, it confirmed a literal interpretation of the promises to David. It repeated the specific promises that God gave in the original revelation of the Davidic Covenant. The question whether the covenant was conditional or whether the covenant was nonliteral, views which have been adopted by some amillenarians, was answered because the Psalm firmly declared that the covenant was sure regardless of Israel's faithfulness. Accordingly, God will punish Israel for their sins, but He will not cancel His promises made in grace to David. It is important to note that this covenant was made in grace and is not subject to the conditional character of the Mosaic Covenant.

The meaning of the Davidic Covenant, as explained in Scripture in 2 Samuel 7 and 1 Chronicles 17 and amplified by Psalm 89, is relatively easy to understand. God entered into solemn covenant with David, promising that both his throne and his lineage would continue forever. Because such an expectation was contrary to ordinary history, David himself raised the question in 2 Samuel 7:18-19 about the unusual longevity to the promise. But it is clear that David understood the promise to extend to his political rule over Israel and to succession on the throne of those descended from David. Such an interpretation seems natural to the scriptural record of the Davidic Covenant.

### Amillennial Interpretation of the Davidic Covenant

Because theology is divided on the subject of a future Millennium, the literal fulfillment of this promise to David has been questioned, especially by those who deny a future Millennium.

The denial of a future Millennium by amillenarians makes it necessary for them to have fulfillment of the Davidic Covenant before the second coming of Christ. Amillenarians are not agreed as to how to explain this covenant, but, generally speaking, the majority of them try to find fulfillment in the present age with Christ reigning on the throne of the Father in heaven and the church being governed by Christ on earth.

Contemporary amillenarians, however, offer several other solutions, such as, that the Millennium is fulfilled in the intermediate state or that the Millennium is fulfilled in the new heaven and new earth revealed in Revelation 21–22. Obviously, this view requires reinterpretation of the Davidic Covenant and the terms of the promise. Amillenarians tend to justify their denial of literal fulfillment by turning to the New Testament which emphasizes the present rule of Christ as Head of the church.

Premillenarians, however, point out that not only the major pas-

57

sages in 2 Samuel 7 and 1 Chronicles 17 and Psalm 89 clearly reveal that a literal fulfillment was expected, but there are numerous confirmations, both in the Old Testament and in the New Testament, which support this concept of literal fulfillment.

One of the major messianic prophecies of the Old Testament included the expectation that Christ would sit upon the throne of David, "For to us a Child is born, to us a Son is given, and the government will be on His shoulders. And He will be called Wonderful Counselor, Mighty God, Everlasting Father, Prince of Peace. Of the increase of His government and peace there will be no end. He will reign on David's throne and over His kingdom, establishing and upholding it with justice and righteousness from that time on and forever. The zeal of the LORD Almighty will accomplish this" (Isa. 9:6-7). The prophecy concerns Jesus Christ and states plainly that He would reign on David's throne. Because Christ is One who has died and was resurrected, He is able to be related to the Davidic throne forever.

In this passage, as in other references to the throne of David, clear distinction should be maintained between the Davidic throne and the Father's throne in heaven. Obviously, David never sat on the throne in heaven where Christ is now enthroned. David's throne was a political throne which dealt with the earth and specifically the people of Israel. Accordingly, there is nothing that corresponds to this in the present reign of Christ on the throne of the Father. Rather, Christ is waiting for His second coming and the establishment of Christ's reign on the earth as brought out in Psalm 110:1-3. The announcement in Isaiah 9 of the coming birth of the Son of David was clearly linked to a work of God rather than a work of man. It stated, "The zeal of the LORD Almighty will accomplish this" (Isa. 9:7).

*Jeremiah 23:5-8.* The Prophet Jeremiah, likewise, predicted the coming of a King who would be a Descendant of David, " 'The days are coming,' declares the LORD, 'when I will raise up to David a righteous Branch, a King who will reign wisely and do what is just and right in the land. In His days Judah will be saved and Israel will live in safety. This is the name by which He will be called: The LORD Our Righteousness' " (vv. 5-6).

Reference to a future King obviously was to the Lord Jesus Christ, declared to be a Descendant of David in verse 5. His reign will be specifically over the land of Israel. Under His domain as

King, Judah (the two-tribe kingdom) and Israel (the ten-tribe kingdom), will dwell together in peace and safety.

This promise will be fulfilled in connection with the regathering of Israel from all over the earth in the Millennium. It was predicted that Israel will dwell in their land under the reign of their King (vv. 5-8). Comparing this to the present age reveals no fulfillment though some Israelites have returned to the land in the twentieth century. No earthly throne of David has been set up; no complete regathering of the Children of Israel from all over the world has been accomplished. These events are related in the context of the establishment of the future Davidic kingdom and the second coming of Christ.

*Jeremiah 30:1-9.* Jeremiah continued this theme in other passages. A similar prophecy was given in verses 1-9, "This is the word that came to Jeremiah from the LORD: 'This is what the LORD, the God of Israel, says: "Write in a book all the words I have spoken to you. The days are coming," declares the LORD, "when I will bring My people Israel and Judah back from captivity and restore them to the land I gave their forefathers to possess," says the LORD.' These are the words the LORD spoke concerning Israel and Judah: 'This is what the LORD says: "Cries of fear are heard—terror, not peace. Ask and see: Can a man bear children? Then why do I see every strong man with his hands on his stomach like a woman in labor, every face turned deathly pale? How awful that day will be! None will be like it. It will be a time of trouble for Jacob, but he will be saved out of it. In that day," declares the LORD Almighty, "I will break the yoke off their necks and will tear off their bonds; no longer will foreigners enslave them. Instead, they will serve the LORD their God and David their king, whom I will raise up for them." ' "

*Jeremiah 30:10-11.* In Jeremiah 30 it was predicted again that Israel and Judah would be brought back from the Captivity and installed in their land (vv. 10-11). Jeremiah pointed out that prior to this there would be a time of great trouble but that Israel will be delivered from it (vv. 5-9). After the regathering and deliverance from the time of tribulation, Jeremiah prophesied that they would be ruled by "David their king" (v. 9). This passage introduced a new factor that David himself will be resurrected to participate with Christ to rule over the earth (cf. Ezek. 34:23-24; 37:24). The resurrection of David is related to the second coming of Christ, not to any earlier period or event. Accordingly, the fulfillment of this passage awaits the future coming of Christ.

An additional confirmation was revealed in Jeremiah 33:14-17 where the familiar promises of a Descendant of David reigning over Israel were repeated. Many other Old Testament prophecies relating to this subject could be cited. In Ezekiel 37, in connection with the revival of Israel, the prophecy was given that the two kingdoms of Judah and Israel would once again be united under one king (v. 22). In verse 24 the prophecy of Jeremiah concerning David's resurrection and reign as king was confirmed. David's role as king will be that of a "prince." Though Christ is King of kings and Lord of lords, David will have an honored role as prince.

As history unfolded the role of Israel, there was obviously an interruption of the reign of David's descendants on the throne during the Babylonian Captivity. This was anticipated, however, in the Old Testament prophecies as given in Hosea 3:4-5, "For the Israelites will live many days without king or prince, without sacrifice or sacred stones, without ephod or idol. Afterward the Israelites will return and seek the LORD their God and David their king. They will come trembling to the LORD and to His blessings in the last days."

The fact that the throne was not occupied during this period does not mean that there was no rightful candidate for it. Ultimately, the Gospel of Matthew answers this question by showing that Christ has a legal right to the throne. Christ will not occupy this role, however, until His second coming to the earth.

One of the important prophecies in the Old Testament concerning the revival of Israel and the Davidic Covenant was revealed in Amos 9:11-15. Though the Book of Amos was largely a condemnation of Israel for their sin and an affirmation that God was disciplining them, the last five verses of the book turned to the bright future when Israel will be restored. Restoration was referred to as a restoration of "David's fallen tent" (v. 11). It was to be restored to the glory it once had. Obviously, this was a declaration of the restoration of the Davidic kingdom. In keeping with this future restoration of Israel, the productivity of Israel in the restored land was pictured in verses 13-15. Her cities will be rebuilt, vineyards will be planted, gardens will produce fruit. But the most important promise was given in verse 15, " 'I will plant Israel in their own land, never again to be uprooted from the land I have given them,' says the LORD your God." The restoration of Israel to their land under Christ their King will result in the evident restoration of Israel as a nation, never to be scattered again (v. 15).

### Other Old Testament Confirmations
### of the Davidic Covenant

*2 Samuel 12:1-12.* David himself was to experience God's chastening because of his sin of adultery and murder in connection with Uriah and Bathsheba. In verses 1-12 Nathan the prophet rebuked David and predicted that the sword would continue to plague the house of David (vv. 9-10).

Though the promise was given that David's house would reign forever as fulfilled by Christ, Solomon was warned that his descendants would occupy the throne only as long as they obeyed God. Solomon was told, "If your descendants watch how they live, and if they walk faithfully before Me with all their heart and soul, you will never fail to have a man on the throne of Israel" (1 Kings 2:4). Though Solomon's descendants failed God, the Davidic Covenant was fulfilled by David's descendants through his son Nathan.

*1 Kings 3:11-14; 6:11-13; 9:4-9.* In 3:11-14 God promised to bless Solomon in keeping with the Davidic Covenant and give him riches, wisdom, and honor. These prophecies were literally fulfilled (cf. 2 Chron. 1:11-12). In 6:11-13 God reiterated His promise which He gave to David concerning Solomon. In 9:4-9 God repeated His promise as given to David, but also warned that if the Children of Israel did not obey the Law they would certainly be driven out of the land.

*2 Chronicles 7:11-22.* This prophecy was literally fulfilled in the seventh and sixth centuries B.C. A similar conditional promise was given on the occasion of the completion of the temple. Solomon was warned, "When Solomon had finished the temple of the LORD and the royal palace, and had succeeded in carrying out all he had in mind to do in the temple of the LORD and in his own palace, the LORD appeared to him at night and said: 'I have heard your prayer and have chosen this place for Myself as a temple for sacrifices. When I shut up the heavens so that there is no rain, or command locusts to devour the land or send a plague among My people, if My people, who are called by My name, will humble themselves and pray and seek My face and turn from their wicked ways, then will I hear from heaven and will forgive their sin and will heal their land. Now My eyes will be open and My ears attentive to the prayers offered in this place. I have chosen and consecrated this temple so that My Name may be there forever. My eyes and My heart will always be there. As for you, if you walk before Me as David your father did, and do all I command, and observe My decrees and laws, I will establish your royal throne, as I covenanted with David your father when I said, "You shall never fail to have a man to rule over Israel." But if you turn away and forsake the decrees and commands I have given you and go off to serve other gods and worship them, then I will uproot Israel from My land, which I have given them, and will reject this temple I have consecrated for My Name. I will make it a byword and an object of ridicule among all peoples. And though this temple is now so imposing, all who pass by will be appalled and say, "Why has the LORD done such a thing to this land and to this temple?" People will answer, "Because they have forsaken the LORD, the God of their fathers, who brought them out of Egypt, and have embraced other gods, worshiping and serving them — that is why He brought all this disaster on them" ' " (vv. 11-22).

In David's charge to Solomon to build a house for the Lord, he reminded Solomon that though it was in David's heart to build the temple, God had declared that because David was a man of war who had shed much blood his son would be charged with this responsibility. Solomon was named by God. Though Solomon was promised that his throne would continue forever (1 Chron. 22:6-10), he was not promised, as God promised David, that a descendant of Solomon would sit on the throne.

This was explained later in Jeremiah 36:30 because of the curse on the line coming from Solomon. In the New Testament lineage of Mary, she was declared to be a descendant of a son of David by the name of Nathan (Luke 3:31). Though Christ is a descendant of David, He is not a descendant of Solomon. The place of Solomon was again the subject of prophecy in 1 Chronicles 28:4-7. David prophesied that Solomon would sit on his throne and that his kingdom will continue forever (1 Chron. 28:5), but the Bible says nothing about Solomon's descendants.

### Predicted Judgment on David
*2 Samuel 12:10-12.* Because of David's sin with Bathsheba, Nathan predicted the sword would not depart from David's house and his wives would be violated. This was fulfilled in 2 Samuel 15–20.

### Bathsheba's Child to Die
*2 Samuel 12:13-23.* Because of David's sin, his child by Bathsheba would die. This was fulfilled in verses 18-23.

### Birth of Solomon

*2 Samuel 12:24-25.* The promise of a son who would sit on David's throne and build the temple was fulfilled (cf. 1 Kings 2:12; 6:37).

### Solomon Promised Wisdom, Riches, and Honor

*1 Kings 3:5-15.* In a dream Solomon was told by God to ask what he willed about his kingdom. Solomon asked for wisdom to govern Israel (vv. 7-9). In reply God promised Solomon not only wisdom but honor and riches (vv. 10-15).

### Solomon's Conditional Promise of the Throne

*1 Kings 9:1-9.* Solomon was promised that his descendants would sit on his throne if they obeyed God. If they did not, they would be cut off and the temple would be destroyed. This was fulfilled in 2 Chronicles 36:14-21. The throne of David would survive, but Solomon's descendants would not sit on it.

*1 Kings 11:11-39.* God confronted Solomon because of his departure from the Lord and predicted that the kingdom would be taken from his descendants. God assured Solomon that this would not happen in his lifetime. In keeping with this, a prophet of God appointed Jeroboam to be the future king of ten tribes of Israel (vv. 29-39).

*1 Kings 13:1-3.* A prophecy was revealed concerning Josiah of the house of David: "By the word of the LORD a man of God came from Judah to Bethel, as Jeroboam was standing by the altar to make an offering. He cried out against the altar by the word of the LORD: 'O altar, altar! This is what the LORD says: "A son named Josiah will be born to the house of David. On you he will sacrifice the priests of the high places who now make offerings here, and human bones will be burned on you." ' That same day the man of God gave a sign: 'This is the sign the LORD has declared: The altar will be split apart and the ashes on it will be poured out' " (vv. 1-3). The prophecy of the split altar was immediately fulfilled. The prophecy of priests' bones being burned on the altar was fulfilled later (2 Kings 23:15-17).

*1 Kings 13:8-26.* The account of a disobedient prophet who died because he did not obey God was recorded (vv. 23-26).

*1 Kings 14:1-16.* It was revealed that the house of Jeroboam would be destroyed because of Jeroboam's sins against the Lord. Judgment was likewise pronounced on Baasha, king of Israel, for forsaking the Lord (vv. 1-4). Further chastisement of Israel was prophesied in 17:1-4 as God predicted the drought in Israel. Elijah was to be cared for by the widow of Zarephath (vv. 8-16). Rain would return to Israel only at the word of Elijah as brought out in 18:19, 41, 45.

*1 Kings 16:1-4, 11-13; 17:1, 7-16; 18:35-45; 20:13-14, 18-22, 26-30, 35-36, 42; 21:17-20, 23; 22:13-28, 34-38; 2 Kings 9:30-37; 2 Chron. 18:16-27, 33-34.* Many other prophecies were revealed and fulfilled quickly. The line of Baasha was to be destroyed (1 Kings 16:1-4, 11-13). Drought was to plague Israel (1 Kings 17:1; 18:36-45). The meal and the oil of the widow would not fail (1 Kings 17:7-16). Ahab was to have victory over Syria (1 Kings 20:13-14, 18-21). The attack on Syria was to be renewed (1 Kings 20:22, 26-30). The disobedient prophet was to die (1 Kings 20:35-36). Ahab and his people would suffer because he spared Ben-Hadad (1 Kings 20:42; 22:34-35). Ahab was to shed his blood and die in the same place where he killed Naboth (1 Kings 21:17-20; 22:37-38; 2 Chron. 18:33-34). Jezebel would be eaten by dogs (1 Kings 21:23; 2 Kings 9:30-37). Ahab was to be defeated (1 Kings 22:13-28, 34-38; 2 Chron. 18:16-27).

Prophecies again and again confirmed the method of interpretation that requires literal fulfillment of prophecy and relate to the discipline that God exerted over the people of Israel because of their sins. It is significant that in none of these prophecies was the covenant with David canceled or annulled.

### Confirmation of the Davidic Covenant
### in the New Testament

One of the major arguments of those who reject a future reign of Christ on earth is the contention that the New Testament does not support this concept. It is true that the New Testament does not repeat all the promises in the Old Testament, as to do so was not necessary because the Old Testament is the Word of God. The New Testament, however, is in constant agreement with the expectation of the people of Israel for the future restoration and the reign of Christ over them when He returns.

Confirmation of the Davidic Covenant is found in the words of the angel to Mary, announcing that she would be the mother of Jesus, "Do not be afraid, Mary, you have found favor with God. You will be with Child and give birth to a Son, and you are to give Him the name Jesus. He will be great and will be called the Son of the Most High. The Lord God will give Him the throne of His father David, and He will reign over the house of Jacob forever; His kingdom will never end" (Luke 1:30-33). In addition to the general promise that Jesus would be her son, the specific promises were given that He would occupy the throne of His father David and that His reign and His kingdom would never end.

If it is true, as advocates of amillennialism contend, that the Old Testament has been misunderstood and that a literal fulfillment of the Davidic Covenant should not be expected, why would God instruct His angel to use such terminology for Mary? Certainly, for a Jewish maiden living in a time of expectation of a coming Messiah for Israel, there would be no problem in accepting the promise as very literal. On the contrary, it would be most strange if what God intended to reveal was that her son was to be head of the church composed of both Jews and Gentiles. It is true that believers in the Church Age were called "children of Abraham" (Gal. 3:6-9) based on the Abrahamic promise of blessing on "all peoples of the earth" (Gen. 12:3), but the church was never related to Jacob. The reference to the house of Jacob must be a reference to the physical descendants of Jacob, that is, the people of Israel.

As Christ instructed His disciples on various scriptural truths, it was quite clear that the disciples themselves, after being taught by Jesus for more than three years, expected such a fulfillment of the Old Testament promises. In the incident recorded in Matthew 20:20-23, when the mother of James and John requested of Christ that her sons would share His throne, she certainly did not have in mind occupying the throne of the Father in heaven. It was rather that she anticipated the Davidic throne that would be on earth. Later Christ confirmed their expectation in promising them that they would sit on thrones judging the twelve tribes of Israel in the promised period of restoration (Matt. 19:28). This promise was confirmed later in Luke 22:30 when Christ met with His disciples for the Passover the night before His crucifixion. Again, they were assured that they would sit on thrones and judge the twelve tribes of Israel.

Even at the time of the ascension of Christ, the disciples were not clear how this promise of Christ's earthly kingdom would be fulfilled. Accordingly, in Acts 1:6 they asked the question, "Lord, are You at this time going to restore the kingdom to Israel?" They did not anticipate the present age, though Christ had instructed them concerning it in John 13–16. Their question was not whether Christ would bring in the kingdom but rather *when* He would bring it in. If this were a wrong concept on the part of the disciples, there should have been correction from the lips of Christ Himself. Instead, He told them that it was not for them to know the time. In stating this, in effect, Christ confirms their hope but does not reveal when this will occur. Later New Testament passages such as Revelation 19 make it clear that the reign of Christ on earth will begin with His second coming.

The disciples obviously had difficulty in understanding that prior to the restoration of Israel the present age would be fulfilled in which Gentiles would be prominent. This question came up in the Council of Jerusalem as recorded in Acts 15. In solving the problem, James quoted the prophecy of Amos 9:11-12. James concluded that scriptural prophecy indicated that there would be a time of Gentile blessing and prominence *preceding* the restoration of Israel. This, of course, is exactly what has occurred in the present age. James urged them, therefore, not to make it difficult for Gentiles by expecting them to maintain Jewish rites and ceremonies even though they should avoid needless irritation of the Jews who still hold to the old ceremonies. At the conclusion of the conference they suggested that Gentiles should abstain from "food sacrificed to idols, from blood, from the meat of strangled animals, and from sexual immorality" (Acts 15:28-29).

In coming to this conclusion, on the one hand, they reaffirmed God's present purpose of calling out a people to His name from the Gentiles as being fulfilled in the present Church Age. At the same time, they reaffirmed their expectation that after the present age a time of restoration and fulfilled promises would be given to the people of Israel in the period following the second coming of Christ.

Further light is cast on this in the dramatic presentation of the second coming of Christ in Revelation 19 and the millennial kingdom in Revelation 20. Accordingly, the assertion of amillennial scholars that the millennial kingdom is found only in Revelation 20 and therefore should not be accepted is not an adequate explanation of the constant theme of Scripture from 2 Samuel 7 until Revelation 20 concerning a future kingdom on earth which would continue the Davidic kingdom. The clarity of the promises and their interpretation as literal prophecy to be fulfilled is sustained by an examination of all the passages of Scripture involved. Only premillenarians are able to take these Scriptures in their natural meaning and find a clear record of their future fulfillment.

### Prophecy of Micaiah

Some prophecies are recorded in 1 Kings that are not related to the Davidic Covenant. One is the prophecy of Micaiah.

The question had been raised by King Jehoshaphat whether he should join with King Ahab in a military conquest of Ramoth Gilead. The lying prophets of Ahab urged them to go to battle (1 Kings 22:5-12; 2 Chron. 18:5-11). Jehoshaphat distrusted these prophets. When Micaiah prophesied he predicted they would lose the war (1 Kings 22:13-28; 2 Chron. 18:12-27). They went to battle and were defeated and Ahab was killed (1 Kings 22:37-38; 2 Chron. 18:33-34).

## PROPHECY IN SECOND KINGS, FIRST AND SECOND CHRONICLES

### Prophecy of the Death of Ahaziah

*2 Kings 1:4, 16-17.* In the Book of 2 Kings numerous prophecies are revealed with their fulfillment also recorded. Elijah prophesied that Ahaziah would die because he sent men to consult Baal-Zebub instead of the true God (v. 4). His death was recorded as fulfilled prophecy in verses 16-17.

### Prophecy Related to Elijah

*2 Kings 2:1-14.* A series of prophecies were revealed relating to Elijah being taken up to heaven in a whirlwind. In fulfillment of Elisha's request, a double portion of the Holy Spirit was given to him.

### Prophecy Related to Elisha

*2 Kings 3:15-27.* Elisha predicted that the kings of Israel and Judah would be able to conquer the Moabites. They were instructed to make ditches which the Lord would fill with water so that both men and animals could drink. The prophecy was literally fulfilled (vv. 21-27).

*2 Kings 4:5-6, 38-44.* The prophecy that the widow's jars would be filled with oil was fulfilled. Elisha predicted that the stew cooked in the large pot would not harm the company of the prophets, even though poisonous gourds were used (vv. 38-44). This was fulfilled.

*2 Kings 5:1-19.* The familiar story of Naaman's healing of leprosy is recorded. Naaman was instructed to wash in the Jordan, and when he did so, he was miraculously healed (vv. 10, 14).

*2 Kings 5:19-27.* By contrast, Elisha's prediction concerning Gehazi, his servant, that the leprosy of Naaman would afflict him because of his duplicity in asking a reward from Naaman was fulfilled.

*2 Kings 6:8-23.* When surrounded by soldiers of Aram, Elisha was miraculously delivered. The army was blinded and led to Samaria where it was released and abandoned the war.

*2 Kings 7:1-2.* In the time of famine in Israel, Elisha predicted their deliverance. The king's officer who questioned the prophecy was told by Elisha, " 'You will see it with your own eyes,' answered Elisha, 'but you will not eat any of it!' " (v. 2), a prophecy which was immediately fulfilled (v. 17).

*2 Kings 8:1-15.* The seven-year famine that was to come on Israel was predicted (vv. 1-6) and was fulfilled (v. 2). Elisha prophesied that Ben-Hadad, king of Aram, would recover from his illness, but that as a matter of fact he would die, which was literally fulfilled (v. 15).

*2 Kings 8:13-15.* Elisha also predicted that Hazael would become king of Aram, which was fulfilled (v. 15). Elisha also predicted that Hazael would kill many Israelites, men, women, and children (v. 12). Later, Scripture recorded the fulfillment of these prophecies (10:32; 12:17-18; 13:3, 22-25; 2 Chron. 22:5-6).

*2 Kings 9:1-10.* Elisha predicted that Jehu would be king over Israel.

*2 Kings 9:14-28.* Fulfillment of the prophecy concerning Jehu as king was recorded later.

*2 Kings 9:30-37.* The prophecy of Jezebel being killed was also fulfilled in keeping with the prophecy made in 1 Kings 21:23.

*2 Kings 10:1-11, 17.* The predicted judgment falling on the house of Ahab was recorded, fulfilling the prophecy of Ahab's death in 1 Kings 21:20-22.

*2 Kings 10:30.* The prophecy that the descendants of Jehu would sit on the throne of Israel to the fourth generation was recorded as fulfilled in 15:12.

*2 Kings 13:14-19.* Elisha predicted that Israel would defeat Aram three times. This was fulfilled in verse 25.

*2 Kings 14:25.* An unrecorded prophecy of Jonah that Jeroboam would possess the territory of Israel was fulfilled.

### Prophecy Related to Hezekiah

*2 Kings 19:5-7.* Hezekiah was informed that the Assyrian army besieging Israel would leave and that the king of Assyria would be assassinated.

*2 Kings 19:20-36.* Further prediction of Israel's deliverance from Assyria was revealed and the fulfillment recorded in verses 35-36.

*2 Kings 20:1-19.* At the time of Hezekiah's illness, he was informed that fifteen years would be added to his life during which he would be protected from the attacks of the king of Assyria (vv. 1-11). Isaiah the prophet, however, predicted that the Babylonian Captivity would not begin until after Hezekiah's death (vv. 16-19).

### Prophecy Related to Manasseh, Josiah, and Jehoahaz

*2 Kings 21:10-15.* The downfall of Manasseh was predicted and was fulfilled in 2 Chronicles 33:10-11. Manasseh's return to the Lord and his renewed reign was recorded in 2 Chronicles 33:12-20.

*2 Kings 22:1-20.* In response to Josiah's request of the Lord for direction after the Book of the Law was found and read (vv. 8-10) and in view of the sins of the people of Israel, the prophecy was given to Huldah the prophetess that God would bring disaster on Israel (cf. 2 Chron. 34:22-28). Because Josiah's heart was responsive and because he humbled himself before the Lord, this would not occur until after Josiah's death (2 Kings 22:15-20).

*2 Kings 23:1-30.* Though Josiah did what he could to eliminate false worship and made an attempt to fulfill the Law of Moses and though it is recorded that he "turned to the LORD as he did—with all his heart and with all his soul and with all his strength, in accordance with all the Law of Moses" (v. 25), God predicted that He would deal with Judah as He had with Israel and that He would reject Jerusalem and the temple (vv. 26-27). The death of Josiah was recorded (vv. 29-30), and Jehoahaz succeeded him as king, but reigned only three months. Pharaoh Neco put him in chains.

The closing chapters of 2 Kings recorded the prophesied judgment of God on Israel, both at the hands of Pharaoh and at the hands of Nebuchadnezzar, king of Babylon. The judgment of God begun by Pharaoh was completed by Nebuchadnezzar when he took Jerusalem captive.

### Battle with Edom

*2 Chronicles 20:15-17.* Jahaziel prophesied to King Jehoshaphat that the vast army coming against him from Edom would be destroyed without Jehoshaphat having to fight a battle (2 Chron. 20:15-17). He was instructed to order his troops to march against them, but was told that God would give them the victory without a fight.

*2 Chronicles 20:20-25.* Literal fulfillment was pointed out. Scripture recorded that the army against them began fighting among themselves and fled, leaving their equipment behind them. Jehoshaphat's venture in shipbuilding was to fail, however (v. 37).

### Prophecy of Elijah

*2 Chronicles 21:12-20.* At Jehoshaphat's death his son Jehoram assumed the throne, but because of his wickedness, Elijah the prophet predicted God's judgment on them (vv. 12-15). He predicted that God would deal in judgment with his family and that Jehoram himself would die of a lingering disease. This was fulfilled when Jehoram's family was carried off captive (vv. 16-17) and the death of Jehoram was described in verses 18-20.

### Prophecy of Zechariah

*2 Chronicles 24:20-22.* Zechariah, the son of Jehoiada the priest (actually, his grandfather), stood before King Joash and predicted that because he had not obeyed the Lord's command, the Lord had forsaken him. As a result, Zechariah was stoned to death because of his message, a fact to which Christ referred in His lament over Jerusalem in Matthew 23:35. In 2 Chronicles 25:15-17 God sent a prophet to Amaziah, predicting that God would destroy him because he had not listened to God's counsel. The result was recorded in verse 27 where Amaziah was assassinated.

# PROPHECY IN EZRA, NEHEMIAH, AND ESTHER

### Prophecy in Ezra

In the Book of Ezra, only one passage is prophetic. The priests and the Levites on the occasion of laying the foundation of Zerubbabel's temple, in voicing their praise and thanksgiving, sang, "He is good; His love to Israel endures forever" (Ezra 3:11).

### Prophecy in Nehemiah

Nehemiah also has only one prophetic passage. In answering those who ridiculed Israel's rebuilding the wall, Nehemiah answered, "The God of heaven will give us success. We His servants will start rebuilding, but as for you, you have no share in Jerusalem or any claim or historic right to it" (Neh. 2:20). Nehemiah recorded the literal fulfillment of this prophecy (6:15-16).

### Prophecy in Esther

The Book of Esther is unique in Scripture as it does not have any direct reference to deity, God's worship, prayer, sacrifice, or prophecy. Nevertheless, the book confirmed what was explicitly prophesied in other Scriptures that God would give His unfailing care to Israel and perpetuate them as a nation (Jer. 30:8-11; 31:23-40).

# 3

# PROPHECY IN
# THE BOOKS OF POETRY

## PROPHECY IN JOB

The Book of Job presented an unusual problem in prophetic interpretation in that much of it recorded the speeches of Eliphaz, Bildad, and Zophar. The Lord specifically declared in Job 42:7 that Eliphaz, Bildad, and Zophar "have not spoken of Me what is right, as My servant Job has." The Lord, however, did not condemn Elihu and He declared that Job said "what is right" (v. 7). Likewise, in the speech of Eliphaz in 5:17-26 there was general prophetic truth, but its accuracy is subject to question concerning its application to Job. The prophecy of Bildad (8:20-22) was faulty as Bildad attempted to prove that Job was suffering because of his sins.

*Job 11:14-20.* Zophar spoke prophetically that if Job would put away sin God would bless him. But his prophecy was marred by applying a general prophecy of judgment of the wicked to Job.

*Job 19:25-27.* Job himself gave utterance to one of the great prophecies of the Old Testament when he stated, "I know that my Redeemer lives, and that in the end He will stand upon the earth. And after my skin has been destroyed, yet in my flesh I will see God; I myself will see Him with my own eyes—I, and not another. How my heart yearns within me!" It was remarkable that Job, living in a time before any Scripture was written, nevertheless had firmly in mind the prophetic truth that his Redeemer was living at that time and that He would someday stand upon the earth. Job declared his faith that even though his body would be destroyed, he would see God when Job himself would be resurrected.

*Job 23:10-11.* This utterance of Job likewise stands as one of the great prophecies of the Old Testament, "But He knows the way that I take; when He has tested me, I will come forth as gold. My feet have closely followed His steps; I have kept to His way without turning aside."

*Job 36:8-12.* Elihu declared that those who repent and obey God "will spend the rest of their days in prosperity and their years in contentment" (v. 11). On the contrary, those who refused to listen will perish. This statement of the overall justice of God is true inasmuch as the Lord did not include Elihu in His condemnation (42:7).

## PROPHECY IN THE PSALMS

Though the Book of Psalms recorded the worship, prayers, and experiences of the psalmists, it was only natural that faith in God would anticipate the prophetic future. Prominent in the expectation of the Lord's people was the future care and faithfulness of God (1:1-3), the reward of the righteousness and judgment on the wicked (1:4-7; Rev. 20:11-15), the expectation of the coming Messiah, the hope of the reign of Christ in His future kingdom (Ps. 2), and confirmation of the Abrahamic (105:8-11) and Davidic (89:11-37) Covenants. These prophecies are all fulfilled in history and prophecy.

In addition to Scriptures that were specifically prophetic of a future situation were many passages that are in the present tense which anticipated a future situation. Whether or not these passages are classified as prophecy, they, nevertheless, provided support and illustration of the joyous hope of the saints for a glorious future.

### God's Loving Care and Faithfulness

*Psalm 12:7.* One of the major themes of the Psalms was the worship of God for His loving care and faithfulness as it will be fulfilled in the future. The psalmist declared, "O LORD, You will keep us safe and protect us from such people forever" (v. 7). This is fulfilled in history and prophecy.

*Psalm 27:1-14.* David expressed his confidence in God and His protecting care against David's enemies. In the opening three verses David declares, "The LORD is my light and my salvation—whom shall I fear? The LORD is the stronghold of my life—of whom shall I be afraid? When evil men advance against me to devour my flesh, when my enemies and my foes attack me, they will stumble and fall. Though an army besiege me, my heart will not fear; though war break out against me, even then will I be confident" (vv. 1-3). David declared his trust in the Lord that in the time of trouble he would be hidden and that he would be exalted over his enemies (vv. 5-6). He also expressed his faith that even if his father and mother forsook him, the Lord would receive him (v. 10). He expressed his confidence that not only in the future but in the present as well, he would witness the Lord's goodness (v. 13). This was fulfilled in David's lifetime (1 Kings 2:10-11).

*Psalm 28:1-9.* God cared for David as a shepherd cares for his sheep. This was fulfilled in David's life.

*Psalm 32:7-8.* David declared that the Lord was his hiding place (v. 7). David also assumed the role of a teacher in instructing and counseling them "in the way you should go" (v. 8). Some interpret

73

this as God speaking to David. This prophecy was fulfilled in David's lifetime.

*Psalm 37:1-40.* David declared his delight in the Lord and expressed his confidence that as one commits his way to the Lord, he will receive what his heart desires (vv. 4-6). He spoke also of the future revelation of the righteousness and justice of his cause (v. 6).

David predicted judgment on the wicked and that the meek would inherit the land (vv. 9-11). David predicted also that the wicked would perish in contrast to the Lord upholding the righteous (vv. 20-24). David expressed his faith that the Lord would protect His own and give them the land for an inheritance in contrast to the wicked who would be cut off (vv. 27-29). This theme was continued in verse 34 and verses 37-38. This was fulfilled in history and will be fulfilled in the Millennium (Amos 9:15).

*Psalm 41:1-13.* God's protection was assured His own, even in times of sickness and when friends desert them.

*Psalm 50:7-15.* God rebuked Israel for their keeping the letter of the Law without keeping the spirit of the Law and reminded them that their offering should be presented in true devotion to God. They then would be able to call on God in the time of distress and experience His deliverance.

*Psalm 50:22.* David promised that hypocrites would be judged by God and would have none to rescue them. This is fulfilled in history and prophecy.

*Psalm 59:9-17.* God will be a fortress and refuge in time of trouble. This was fulfilled in David's lifetime.

*Psalm 71:20-21.* The psalmist assured his readers that though they would have many troubles, God would deliver them and give them honor and comfort.

*Psalm 73:24-25.* The psalmist declared, "You guide me with Your counsel, and afterward You will take me into glory. Whom have I in heaven but You? And earth has nothing I desire besides You." In this life as well as in the life hereafter God cares for His own.

*Psalm 91:1-16.* This was a dramatic statement of God's care of His own. The psalmist declared that God was his "refuge" and "fortress" (v. 2), God will deliver "from the deadly pestilence" (v. 3), and will give refuge "under His wings" (v. 4). Though many others will fall, God will protect His own (vv. 5-7). By contrast the wicked will be punished (v. 8). In verses 9 and 12 he declared, "If you make the Most High your dwelling—even the LORD, who is my refuge—then no harm will befall you, no disaster will come near your tent. For He will command His angels concerning you to guard you in all your ways; they will lift you up in their hands, so that you will not strike your foot against a stone." This passage was misquoted by Satan in his temptation of Christ. He omitted "in all Your ways" (Matt. 4:5-6; Luke 4:10-11). The psalmist concluded that the Lord will protect His own in times of trouble and honor them and give them long life (Ps. 91:13-16), fulfilled in time and eternity.

*Psalm 92:8-15.* The enemies of God were assured of divine punishment (vv. 8-11). By contrast, the righteous will flourish, bearing fruit even in old age (vv. 12-15).

*Psalm 94:12-15.* The man whom God disciplines will be blessed. He will experience "relief from days of trouble" (v. 13). This is fulfilled in time and eternity.

*Psalm 94:22-23.* The psalmist declared that the Lord is his fortress and his rock who will destroy the wickedness of his enemies. This is fulfilled in time and eternity.

*Psalm 100.* In the psalmist's worship of God, the people of God were exhorted to enter into the Lord's courts with praise and thanksgiving in recognition of the fact that the Lord's "love endures forever; His faithfulness continues through all generations" (v. 5). This is fulfilled in time and eternity.

*Psalm 102:25-28.* The eternity of God, present and future, was expressed in this psalm. The objects of creation which God has brought into being "will all wear out like a garment" (v. 26). By contrast to the created world, the servants of God will live in His presence forever (v. 28). This is fulfilled in eternity.

*Psalm 103:1-18.* The Son of God will be with the righteous forever. This is fulfilled in time and eternity.

*Psalm 103:19-20.* The Lord has established His throne in heaven but will rule over all creation. This will be fulfilled in the Millennium and eternity.

*Psalm 118:1-29.* The love of God as enduring forever was expressed in repetition (vv. 1-4). This is fulfilled in time and eternity.

The psalmist predicted that "the stone the builders rejected" will become "the capstone" (v. 22). This will be accomplished by the Lord Himself (vv. 23-24). This passage anticipated the rejection of Christ (Matt. 21:42; Mark 12:10; Luke 20:17) and His later exaltation. The historical context of this passage may have been failure to recognize a king or the nation Israel for their victories.

*Psalm 121:1-8.* God's faithfulness in watching over His own was promised (vv. 1-4). Likewise, the Lord will be their protection from harm and His faithfulness will continue forever (vv. 5-8). This is fulfilled in history and prophecy.

*Psalm 130:7-8.* The Lord who was the unfailing hope of Israel will be their Redeemer. This is fulfilled in history and prophecy.

*Psalm 136:1-26.* The great truth that God's love "endures forever" was stated in each verse of the psalm. In keeping with this, the psalmist thanked God as the Creator of the sun, moon, and stars and as the One who "struck down the firstborn of Egypt" (v. 10). God was exalted as the One who "divided the Red Sea asunder" (v. 13), rid Israel from Pharaoh (v. 15), "led His people through the desert" (v. 16), and struck down Israel's enemies (vv. 17-20). God gave Israel the land as their inheritance (vv. 21-22), "freed us from our enemies" (v. 24), and continues to provide "food to every creature" (v. 25). The prophecy is fulfilled in history and prophecy.

*Psalm 138:8.* The enduring love of God was extolled with the faith that "The LORD will fulfill His purpose for me." This is fulfilled in history and prophecy.

*Psalm 145:13.* David declared, "Your kingdom is an everlasting kingdom, and Your dominion endures through all generations." This is fulfilled in prophecy.

Throughout these many verses referring to God's love and faithfulness, the certainty of God continuing His loving care was assured.

## Judgment on the Wicked

In contrast to the promises of reward for the righteous, the Psalms frequently spoke of the destiny of the wicked.

*Psalm 1:1-6.* The contrast between the blessed man who delights in the Law of God and the wicked was introduced. The wicked were compared to the chaff blown away by the wind (v. 4). The wicked will not stand in the time of judgment (v. 5). By contrast, the Lord's blessing will be on the righteous, "the way of the wicked will perish" (v. 6). This is fulfilled in history and prophecy.

*Psalm 6:8-10.* The wicked were promised that in their future they will be ashamed and dismayed and disgraced. This is fulfilled in history and prophecy.

*Psalm 9:1-20.* God will judge the righteous and govern the people with justice which will involve a judgment on the wicked (Rev. 19:15; 20:11-15). This is fulfilled in history and prophecy.

*Psalm 10:16.* After recounting the sins of the wicked, the psalmist declared that "the nations will perish from his land" (v. 16). This is fulfilled in history and prophecy.

*Psalm 11:6.* God "will rain fiery coals and burning sulphur" on the wicked, and "a scorching wind will be their lot" (Rev. 20:11-15).

*Psalm 21:8-13.* The judgment on the wicked was described: "In His wrath the LORD will swallow them up, and His fire will consume them. You will destroy their descendants from the earth, their posterity from mankind" (vv. 9-10). The psalm closed extolling the Lord's might (v. 13). The destruction of the nations was fulfilled in history and will be in prophecy.

*Psalm 25:3.* The wicked "will be put to shame who are treacherous without excuse." This is fulfilled in history and prophecy.

*Psalm 27:1-14.* David extolled the Lord as his salvation. He declared, "When evil men advance against me to devour my flesh, when my enemies and my foes attack me, they will stumble and fall" (v. 2). In the time of trouble God will keep him safe (v. 5). He was confident that he will see the goodness of God (v. 13). This was fulfilled in David's lifetime (1 Kings 2:10-11).

*Psalm 28:1-9.* David implored the Lord to come to his aid. He declared concerning the wicked, "Since they show no regard for the works of the LORD and what His hands have done, He will tear them down and never build them up again" (v. 5). As a shepherd, the Lord will carry His people forever (v. 9). This is fulfilled in history.

*Psalm 34:1-22.* David prophesied, "Evil will slay the wicked; the foes of the righteous will be condemned" (v. 21). Judgment on the wicked was certain, but the righteous will be delivered (v. 19). This is fulfilled in history and prophecy.

*Psalm 37:1-40.* David declared, "For evil men will be cut off, but those who hope in the LORD will inherit the land" (v. 9). One of the important promises given Israel was possession of the land. David again declared judgment on the wicked, "But their swords will pierce their own hearts, and their bows will be broken" (v. 15). David stated, "But the wicked will perish: The LORD's enemies will be like the beauty of the fields, they will vanish — vanish like smoke" (v. 20). That the wicked will be cut off because of their sin is repeated in this psalm (vv. 22, 28, 38). This is fulfilled in history and prophecy.

*Psalm 50:1-23.* In the psalmist's indictment of the wicked (vv.

16-22), God declared, "But I will rebuke you and accuse you to your face" (v. 21). God will deliver the righteous in time of trouble (v. 15). This is fulfilled in history and prophecy.

*Psalm 52:1-9.* David declared that God would bring the wicked "to everlasting ruin" (v. 5), that God "will uproot you from the land of the living" (v. 5) and make the wicked the ridicule of the righteous (vv. 6-7). Their judgment will be in contrast to the reward of the righteous.

*Psalm 55:16-23.* David declared that God "will bring down the wicked into the pit of corruption; bloodthirsty and deceitful men will not live out half their days" (v. 23). But God will sustain the righteous (v. 22). This is fulfilled in history and prophecy.

*Psalm 59:9-17.* David expressed his confidence that God will bring down the wicked because of their sins and will manifest His power "to the ends of the earth" (v. 13). God was his fortress and refuge in time of trouble (vv. 16-17). This was fulfilled in David's lifetime.

*Psalm 60:12.* David declared his confidence, "With God we will gain the victory, and he will trample down our enemies" (v. 12). This was fulfilled in David's lifetime.

*Psalm 63:9-11.* David declared that God would judge His enemies, "They who seek my life will be destroyed; they will go down to the depths of the earth. They will be given over to the sword and become food for jackals" (vv. 9-10). This was fulfilled in David's lifetime.

*Psalm 64:7-10.* David predicted that God would shoot down his enemies with arrows and bring his enemies to ruin (vv. 7-8). The righteous would rejoice and take refuge in God (vv. 9-10). This was fulfilled in David's lifetime.

*Psalm 68:21.* God will "crush the heads of His enemies, the hairy crowns of those who go on in their sins" (v. 21).

*Psalm 69:22-28.* David predicted that his enemies would incur the wrath of God (v. 24). David prayed, "May they be blotted out of the Book of Life and not be listed with the righteous" (v. 28). This was fulfilled in David's lifetime and will be in eternity (Rev. 20:11-15).

*Psalm 72:1-4.* Judgment on the wicked in the future kingdom was prophesied, "He will judge your people in righteousness, your afflicted ones with justice" (v. 2). God will "crush the oppressor" (v. 4). This will be fulfilled in the Millennium.

*Psalm 73:27.* Judgment will fall on the unfaithful, "Those who are far from You will perish; You destroy all who are unfaithful to You" (v. 27). This is fulfilled in history and in prophecy (Rev. 20:11-15).

*Psalm 89:1-4.* Christ as the Son of David will possess His throne forever. This will be fulfilled in the Millennium and eternity.

*Psalm 89:30-37.* God will crush the foes of David. He declared that He will punish the sons of David who sin against God (vv. 30-32). God declared, "I will not take My love from him, nor will I ever betray My faithfulness" (v. 33). God's purpose to fulfill the Davidic Covenant was declared explicitly (vv. 34-37). This is fulfilled in history and will be fulfilled in the Millennium.

*Psalm 91:1-8.* God will protect the righteous but will cause the wicked to perish. This is fulfilled in history.

*Psalm 92:7-15.* God declared that the wicked will be destroyed forever (vv. 7, 9, 11), but the righteous will flourish. This is fulfilled in eternity.

*Psalm 94:11-23.* The armies of the wicked will be destroyed. This is fulfilled in history and prophecy.

*Psalm 108:13.* This psalm declared that God would be victorious over the enemies of Israel. This is fulfilled in history and prophecy.

*Psalm 110:1-7.* The ultimate judgment of Christ on the nations of the world, particularly at His second coming, was prophesied, "The Lord is at your right hand; He will crush kings on the day of His wrath. He will judge the nations, heaping up the dead and crushing the rulers of the whole earth" (vv. 5-6). This will be fulfilled in the Millennium (Rev. 19:11-15).

*Psalm 125.* This psalm of worship declared, "But those who turn to crooked ways the LORD will banish with evildoers" (v. 5). This is fulfilled in history and prophecy.

*Psalm 145:1-21.* God is the refuge of the righteous. David declared, "The LORD watches over all who love Him, but all the wicked He will destroy" (v. 20). This is fulfilled in history and prophecy.

*Psalm 147:6.* A similar thought was declared, "The LORD sustains the humble but casts the wicked to the ground." This is fulfilled in history and prophecy.

### The Reward for Righteousness

*Psalm 1:1-6.* The contrast between the future of the righteous and the wicked was a constant theme of Psalms. Beginning with Psalm 1, the blessed man was one who delighted in the Law of the Lord

(v. 2), but the wicked were destined to be judged (v. 5). Frequently the psalmist spoke of the present joys of walking with the Lord, but coupled with this were prophecies of future reward (v. 3). This is fulfilled in history and prophecy.

*Psalm 15:1-5.* David stated that the one who walks with the Lord and has a righteous life "will never be shaken" (v. 5). This is fulfilled in history.

*Psalm 18:1-50.* The Lord was a fortress (v. 2) and a support for the righteous (v. 18). The Lord's "unfailing kindness to His anointed, to David and his descendants forever" is another statement of God's ultimate fulfillment of the Davidic Covenant (v. 50). This is fulfilled in history and prophecy.

*Psalm 25:1-22.* The godly man was promised "days in prosperity" and that "his descendants will inherit the land" (v. 13). No one who trusts the Lord will "be put to shame" (v. 2). This is fulfilled in history and will be fulfilled in the Millennium.

*Psalm 37:1-40.* Blessings on the "meek" included inheriting the land and enjoying peace (v. 11). The inheritance of the righteous "will endure forever" (v. 18). Also stated was that "the righteous will inherit the land and dwell in it forever" (v. 29). This is fulfilled in history and will be fulfilled in the Millennium (Amos 9:15).

*Psalm 55:16-19, 22.* David exhorted the distressed to "cast your cares on the LORD and He will sustain you; He will never let the righteous fall" (v. 22). This is fulfilled in history.

*Psalm 62:12.* David declared that the Lord will reward those who have served Him well (v. 12). This is fulfilled in history and prophecy.

*Psalm 73:24.* Asaph expressed confidence that he would receive guidance in his present life and "afterward You will take me into glory." This is fulfilled in history and prophecy.

*Psalm 121:1-8.* The unfailing care of the Lord and His watchfulness over the righteous was promised, "The LORD will keep you from all harm—He will watch over your life; the LORD will watch over your coming and going both now and forevermore" (vv. 7-8). This is fulfilled in history and prophecy.

### Messianic Prophecy and the Kingdom

Messianic prophecy usually included the psalms that are specifically messianic, such as Psalms 2, 16, 22, 40, 45, 69, 72, 89, 110, and 118. Some psalms not included formally in the messianic psalms nevertheless may refer to Christ. Among these are the eschatological psalms, 96–99, which refer to the enthronement of the King.

*Psalm 1:1-6.* The Book of Psalms opened in Psalm 1 with a general contrast between the blessed man who will be blessed in time and eternity and the wicked man who will be judged and perish. This theme is carried throughout the Book of Psalms. This is fulfilled in history and prophecy.

*Psalm 2:1-12.* Immediately following this introductory psalm, Psalm 2 described God's purpose to put His Son as King on Mount Zion. The opening verses prophesied the rebellion of the world against the Lord. In response, "The One enthroned in heaven laughs; the Lord scoffs at them" (v. 4). This described the attitude of God toward worldly power today. In God's prophetic purpose, however, He rebuked them in His anger and terrified them in His wrath, saying, "I have installed My King on Zion, My holy hill" (v. 6). The Lord also declared His eternal decree (vv. 7-9). God the Father was revealed as saying to the Son, "You are My Son; today I have become Your Father" (v. 7). This will be fulfilled in the Millennium.

This passage has been variously interpreted by biblical scholars because it refers to the sonship of Christ. The best interpretation is that Jesus Christ has always been a Son in relation to the Father but that the declaration of this was made in time. Some scholars have advanced other views such as that Christ became the Son by incarnation, by baptism, or by resurrection. The interpretation also relates to the question as to whether Christ was a Son eternally by eternal generation. In John 3:16 God is declared to have given "His only begotten Son" (KJV). Because the word "generation" implied beginning in time, it seemed a contradiction of eternal sonship. Probably the best solution is to hold that it referred to His eternal sonship with the thought of having the life of the Father without complicating it with the concept of a beginning. Isaiah 9:6 referred to Christ as "a Son" who "is given." Because the decree of God which declared Christ a Son is eternal, evidence seems to support the concept that He is eternally His Son but that the revelation of this fact is made in time.

Important to this purpose of God is the fact that God will subdue all things under the Son, "I will make the nations Your inheritance and the ends of the earth Your possession. You will rule them with an iron scepter, You will dash them to pieces like pottery" (Ps. 2:8-9). The fact that Christ will rule as an absolute monarch is supported by other prophecies. Revelation 19:15 declared, "Out of His mouth comes a sharp sword with which to strike down the nations. 'He will rule them with an iron scepter.' " In interpreting this passage, it is quite clear that Christ did not accomplish this at His first coming and that the premillennial interpretation that He will accomplish this after His second coming fits the prophetic Scriptures on this subject. The messianic psalms generally pictured Christ on the throne of the Father now awaiting His future triumph when He will subdue the earth and sit on the throne of David.

In view of this coming judgment, kings and rulers were exhorted to "serve the LORD with fear and rejoice with trembling. Kiss the Son, lest He be angry and you be destroyed in your way, for His wrath can flare up in a moment. Blessed are all who take refuge in Him" (Ps. 2:11-12).

Early in the Book of Psalms this general theme of the coming King was made a central revelation. In the Davidic Covenant David was declared to be a son of God (2 Sam. 7:14). How much more is the eternal Son of God the rightful King who will reign on the throne of David.

*Psalm 8:1-4.* This is considered one of the messianic psalms because verses 4-6 were quoted in Hebrews 2:6-8. The psalm itself considered Creation as a work of God, "When I consider Your heavens, the work of Your fingers, the moon and the stars, which You have set in place" (v. 3). In view of God's great work as Creator, man, by comparison, was insignificant. Psalm 8:4, which was quoted in Hebrews 2, stated, "What is man that You are mindful of him, the son of man that You care for him?" This is fulfilled in Christ (Heb. 2:6-8, 10).

*Psalm 8:5-8.* The habitation of Christ on earth is compared with the glory which He had when he returned to heaven, "You made Him a little lower than the heavenly beings and crowned Him with glory and honor" (v. 5). As the Book of Hebrews continues to treat this revelation, it was summarized in Hebrews 2:8, "In putting everything under Him, God left nothing that is not subject to Him. Yet at present we do not see everything subject to Him." Christ now has not realized subjection of the whole world, suffering death on the cross and being made "perfect through suffering" (Heb. 2:10). His right to rule was affirmed, "You made Him ruler over the works of Your hands; You put everything under His feet; all flocks and herds, and the beasts of the field, the birds of the air, and the fish of the sea, all that swim the paths of the seas" (Ps. 8:6-8).

The contrast of Psalm 8 was between Christ and Adam. It was God's intent that Adam should rule the world, but this was interrupted by the entrance of sin into the situation. Now Christ has fulfilled what was originally Adam's responsibility. Having suffered on earth and gone through the humiliation of death, Christ now has been exalted to heaven, and it is God's purpose ultimately for Him to rule over the earth. This Scripture will be completely fulfilled when Christ comes back in His second coming.

*Psalm 9:1-20.* Though this psalm was not considered a messianic psalm, nevertheless, it anticipated the coming rule of Christ, "The LORD reigns forever; He has established His throne for judgment. He will judge the world in righteousness; He will govern the peoples with justice" (vv. 7-8). Though this passage goes beyond judgment in the millennial kingdom to the universal judgment of all men, it has a particular fulfillment in Christ's reign on earth (Rev. 19:11-15; 20:11-15). This will be fulfilled in the Millennium (Rev. 19:15; 20:11-15).

*Psalm 10:1-18.* In verse 16 the statement was made, "The LORD is King forever and ever; the nations will perish from His land." This anticipated the future reign of Christ on earth. This will be fulfilled in the Millennium.

*Psalm 14:7.* The future restoration of Israel was predicted, stating that when this occurs at the time of the Second Coming, "Jacob" will "rejoice and Israel be glad!" This will be fulfilled at the Second Coming.

*Psalm 15:1-5.* The one who walks with the Lord will not be shaken. This is fulfilled in history.

*Psalm 16:1-11.* This psalm was considered one of the messianic psalms because verses 8-11 were quoted by Peter (Acts 2:25-28), and verse 10 was quoted by Paul at Antioch (Acts 13:35). David expressed his faith that he would not be abandoned to the grave (Ps. 16:10), referring to himself, but he added that God "will not let Your Holy One see decay" (v. 10). This was fulfilled by Christ as David's body did decay. David would continue in the grave but in his resurrection he would experience "the path of life" (v. 11).

As used by Peter and Paul, Psalm 16:10 referred to Christ's resurrection and was quoted by Peter and Paul as proof that the resurrection of Christ was predicted. Others today can enjoy fellowship with God as long as they live and have the assurance that when they die, though their bodies may be placed in the grave, they are subject to future resurrection and meanwhile will enjoy fellowship with God in heaven.

*Psalm 18:1-50; cf. 62:12.* David enjoyed God's wonderful deliverance from his enemies and praises God for His goodness.

*Psalm 22:1-31.* This psalm is considered one of the messianic psalms because some of the expressions in the psalm go far beyond any sufferings which David himself experienced. There was no known incident in the life of David that exactly corresponded to what the psalm stated. What may have been true of David as a type of one suffering was literally fulfilled by the sufferings of Christ.

The opening verse of Psalm 22, "My God, my God, why have You forsaken me? Why are You so far from saving me, so far from the words of my groaning?" was quoted by Christ as recorded in Matthew 27:46 and Mark 15:34.

In his distress David reassured himself that his God was "enthroned" (Ps. 22:3). The scorn and mocking of men and their insults mentioned in verses 6-8 was similar to what those mocking Christ on the cross expressed, not realizing they were quoting Scripture (cf. Matt. 27:39, 42-44). Those who surrounded the cross were compared to bulls and roaring lions (Ps. 22:12-13). His "strength is dried up like a potsherd" (v. 15).

There was an obvious reference to the Crucifixion, "Dogs have surrounded me; a band of evil men has encircled me, they have pierced my hands and my feet" (v. 16). The "dogs" were evil men.

Rude stares and the casting of lots for His clothing were described in verses 17-18. David's personal deliverance was indicated in verses 22-24, but it may also refer to Christ in His postresurrection ministry. The ultimate result was predicted in verses 27-28, "All the ends of the earth will remember and turn to the LORD, and all the families of the nations will bow down before Him, for dominion belongs to the LORD and He rules over the nations." The psalm closed in verses 29-31 with a note of victory and praise which in the case of David referred to this life, but in the case of Christ referred to His postresurrection triumph.

*Psalm 23:1-6.* This shepherd psalm is not usually included among the messianic psalms, but the role of the Lord as David's shepherd anticipated the role of Christ as the Good Shepherd who would care for His flock in this present life.

David declared, "I shall lack nothing" (v. 1), that his soul would be restored (v. 3), and that he could "walk through the valley of the shadow of death" (v. 4) without fearing evil. The Lord's goodness will follow him all the days of his life, and he has the hope of dwelling in the house of the Lord forever (vv. 5-6). Psalm 23 paralleled the experience of believers in the present age who are nourished spiritually and restored, are led by the Lord in their walk, and are protected by Him in times of danger.

*Psalm 24:1-10.* This psalm also is not considered a messianic psalm, and yet the wording of the psalm goes far beyond anything which David experienced. Some believe that it was written in connection with the ark being brought into Jerusalem and placed in the temple (2 Sam. 6). The importance of "clean hands and a pure heart" was essential to receiving the blessing from God (Ps. 24:4-5). The references to the "King of Glory" (vv. 7, 9-10) obviously went beyond the experience of David as king of Israel and anticipated the Lord's coming to claim the earth in His second coming.

*Psalm 27:12.* False witnesses would be brought against Christ (Matt. 26:59-61; Mark 14:57-59). This also is mentioned in Psalm 35:11.

*Psalm 31:1-24.* This was another psalm which was not considered messianic, but verse 5 stated, "Into Your hands I commit My spirit." Christ repeated these precise words when He was on the cross (Luke 23:46). Peter expresses the same thought in 1 Peter 4:19.

*Psalm 34:20.* In the sacrifice of Christ no bones were to be broken in contrast to the treatment of the two thieves (John 19:36).

*Psalm 35:19.* Christ was to be hated without a cause (John 15:24-25; cf. Ps. 69:4).

*Psalm 38:11.* Friends stay far away (Matt. 27:55; Mark 15:40; Luke 23:49).

*Psalm 40:6-10.* This is considered a messianic psalm largely because verses 6-8 were quoted in Hebrews 10:5-7 as fulfilled. As stated in the psalm, these verses referred to David's praise to the Lord and his expression of desiring to do the will of God. This, however, also anticipated prophetically Christ's perfect obedience and His sacrifice as superior to the sacrifices of the Mosaic Law. The argument of Hebrews 10 was that Christ in His perfect sacrifice supplied that which the Law could not do with its temporary sacrifices. Key words in the psalm are "righteousness" (vv. 9-10), "faithfulness," "salvation," "love," and "truth" (v. 10).

*Psalm 41:1-13.* God protects His own, fulfilled in history.

*Psalm 41:9.* Christ was to be betrayed by a friend (v. 9), which was fulfilled in His lifetime (Matt. 26:14-16, 47, 50; Mark 14:17-21; Luke 22:21-23; John 13:18-19; cf. Ps. 55:12-14).

*Psalm 45:1-17.* This was classified as a messianic psalm because verses 6-7 referred to David's throne as eternal (2 Sam. 7:16), and these verses were quoted in Hebrews 1:8-9 regarding the ultimate rule of Christ on earth. As the Scripture stated, God's "throne . . . will last forever and ever" (Ps. 45:6), and His rule will be characterized by righteousness and justice. Verses 8-9 picture the king on his wedding day. The beauty of the bride was described in verse 11, "The king is enthralled by your beauty; honor him, for he is your lord." The bride was further described in verses 13-14. Her garments were "interwoven with gold" (v. 13) and were beautifully "embroidered" (v. 14). Future children of the bride were described as princes, and their memory will be perpetuated (vv. 16-17).

Though the psalm seemed to refer to a wedding of David, it is remarkably similar to the concept of Christ and His bride. The Apostle John may have had this passage in mind in Revelation 19:6-21. The psalm as a whole, therefore, was typical of Christ as the King and Son of David and will be fulfilled in the Rapture.

*Psalm 46:4-10.* Here there was reference to God's making wars cease and being exalted among the nations (vv. 9-10). This will not be literally fulfilled until Christ returns in His second coming.

*Psalm 68:18-19.* Christ would lead captivity captive in His ascension (Eph. 4:8). He would also crush the hands of His enemies. This was fulfilled in David's lifetime and will be fulfilled in Christ at His second coming (Rev. 19:11-15).

*Psalm 69:1-36.* Often considered a messianic psalm, portions of this psalm detailing David's cry for help paralleled the sufferings of Christ. Those who hated David were similar to those who hated Christ, as stated in verse 4, "Those who hate me without reason outnumber the hairs of my head." The zeal of David in verse 9, "for zeal for Your house consumes me," was related by the disciples to Christ in explaining Christ's cleansing of the temple (John 2:17). In Psalm 69:21 David stated, "They put gall in my food and gave me vinegar for my thirst." This related to the vinegar given to Christ on the cross (Matt. 27:48; Mark 15:36; Luke 23:36). Though not a direct prophecy, these passages can be interpreted typically as relating to Christ.

*Psalm 72:1-20.* This obviously qualifies as a messianic psalm. Generally speaking, this psalm predicted that the righteous will prosper and the wicked will be judged. According to the inscription, it was written by Solomon and is one of two psalms which he wrote (cf. Ps. 127). It began with a prayer for the king and then prophesied his successful reign (vv. 1-3; cf. 2 Chron. 9:1-28).

As the psalm unfolded, however, it went far beyond anything which Solomon himself could fulfill. In Psalm 72:5 the King was predicted to "endure as long as the sun, as long as the moon, through all generations." Likewise, in verse 7 he stated, "In His days the righteous will flourish; prosperity will abound till the moon is no more." These obviously went beyond the reign of Solomon and anticipated the reign of Christ in the Millennium and ultimately His eternal reign (Isa. 2:1-5).

The fact that all kings will be under Him, as stated in Psalm 72:11, was relatively fulfilled by Solomon because the kings in his area bowed to him but, obviously, this did not include the whole globe. Of both Christ and Solomon it could be said, "May his name endure forever; may it continue as long as the sun" (v. 17). Though Solomon would not live forever, his good name has been perpetuated by the Scriptures which described his reign. The final prayer anticipated that "the whole earth" will "be filled with His glory" (v. 19), to be fulfilled in the Millennium.

The final verse of the psalm stated, "This concludes the prayers of David son of Jesse" (v. 20). However, according to the inscriptions, David was the author of other psalms, such as Psalms 86, 101, 103, 108–110, 122, 124, 131, 133, 138–145. This psalm supported the premillennial interpretation of Scripture as it does not find fulfillment in history. The scene was earth, not heaven, and its identification of the Euphrates River (v. 8) made clear that it will not be the new earth of Revelation 21–22.

*Psalm 78:2.* The coming Messiah will speak in parables and will reveal things formerly hidden.

*Psalm 89:1-37.* This also was clearly one of the messianic psalms. God declared, "I have made a covenant with My chosen one, I have sworn to David My servant, 'I will establish your line forever and make your throne firm through all generations' " (vv. 3-4). This psalm confirmed the Davidic Covenant revealed in 2 Samuel 7:11-16 (cf. discussion of Davidic Covenant).

The psalmist also declared that God's love for David will continue forever, that His covenant will never fail, and that His throne will endure as long as the heavens do (Ps. 89:28-37; Jer. 23:5-8). The contingency of disobedience on the part of his descendants was faced. God promised that if they forsook His covenant and His commands, He would punish them, but He would not reverse the covenant, "but I will not take My love from him, nor will I ever betray My faithfulness. I will not violate My covenant or alter what My lips have uttered. Once for all, I have sworn by My holiness—and I will not lie to David—that his line will continue forever and his throne endure before Me like the sun; it will be established forever like the moon, the faithful witness in the sky" (Ps. 89:33-37).

Any interpretation which takes these words in their normal meanings relating these promises to the Davidic Covenant and to the kingdom on earth will find that the only possible complete fulfillment will be by Christ Himself following His second coming.

Amillenarians take various approaches to this passage, but generally do not treat it literally, finding fulfillment in the present age in the grace of God extended to the church or referring to the reign of Christ on the heavenly throne.

*Psalm 96:1-13.* Psalms 96–99, though not generally considered messianic psalms, by their content justify consideration as messianic. The psalmist anticipated the time when the Lord will reign over the earth and judge people with justice (96:10-13). It was a time described as one of joy on earth. The psalmist concluded, "He comes to judge the earth. He will judge the world in righteousness and the peoples in His truth" (v. 13). This will be fulfilled in the Millennium.

*Psalm 97:1-12.* The opening verse declared that the Lord was reigning. The psalm as a whole described the millennial blessings of Christ when He will come to reign over the earth. This will be fulfilled in the Millennium.

*Psalm 98:1-9.* This psalm spoke of the joy on earth when the Lord reigns and concluded, "Let the rivers clap their hands, let the mountains sing together for joy; let them sing before the LORD, for He comes to judge the earth. He will judge the world in righteousness and the peoples with equity" (vv. 8-9). This will be fulfilled in the Millennium.

*Psalm 99:1-9.* Starting in a similar way, this psalm stated, "The LORD reigns, let the nations tremble" (v. 1). The Lord was pictured as King in Zion, as One who loves justice (vv. 2-4). Moses and

Aaron ministered as priests and "Samuel was among those who called on His name" (v. 6). This will be fulfilled in the Millennium.

*Psalm 102:12-28.* This psalm referred to the future kingdom on earth, "The nations will fear the name of the LORD, all the kings of the earth will revere Your glory. For the LORD will rebuild Zion and appear in His glory" (vv. 15-16). This will be fulfilled in the Millennium.

*Psalm 105:5-11.* The covenant that the Lord made with Abraham, Isaac, and Jacob will continue forever, "He is the LORD our God; His judgments are in all the earth. He remembers His covenant forever, the word He commanded for a thousand generations, the covenant He made with Abraham, the oath He swore to Isaac. He confirmed it to Jacob as a decree, to Israel as an everlasting covenant: 'To you I will give the land of Canaan as the portion you will inherit' " (vv. 7-11). As another reference to the Abrahamic Covenant, this psalm confirmed that the fulfillment will be literal and certain and that the promise was destined for fulfillment in the millennial kingdom.

*Psalm 110:1-7.* This is classified as a messianic psalm because it clearly referred to Jesus Christ as King. His present position was described in Psalm 110:1, "The LORD says to my Lord: 'Sit at My right hand until I make your enemies a footstool for your feet.' " Christ is declared "a Priest forever, in the order of Melchizedek" (v. 4). His judgment in the millennial kingdom was mentioned, "The Lord is at your right hand; He will crush kings on the day of His wrath. He will judge the nations, heaping up the dead and crushing the rulers of the whole earth" (vv. 5-6). This obviously was a reference to the beginning of the millennial kingdom after the second coming of Christ. This is fulfilled in history and prophecy.

*Psalm 118:2-29.* This psalm was a direct prophecy concerning Christ, "The stone the builders rejected has become the capstone; the LORD has done this, and it is marvelous in our eyes. This is the day the LORD has made; let us rejoice and be glad in it" (vv. 22-24). Christ as the rejected King in His second coming will be the Capstone, that is, He will fulfill what was anticipated in His authority as King of kings in ruling the entire earth.

*Psalm 132:11-18.* The oath that God made to David was declared, "A sure oath that He will not revoke" (v. 11). The psalmist continued, "One of your own descendants I will place on your throne — if your sons keep my covenant and the statutes I teach them, then their sons will sit on your throne forever and ever" (vv. 11-12). This is fulfilled in history and prophecy.

*Psalm 145:13-14.* God will fulfill His promises and possess His kingdom forever. This will be fulfilled in the Millennium and in eternity.

## PROPHECY IN PROVERBS, SONG OF SONGS, AND ECCLESIASTES

The Book of Proverbs, dealing with contemporary truths of a general nature, does not have any statement which may be interpreted prophetically.

The same can be said of the Song of Songs. One prophecy is found in the Book of Ecclesiastes, "Now all has been heard; here is the conclusion of the matter: Fear God and keep His commandments, for this is the whole duty of man. For God will bring every deed into judgment, including every hidden thing, whether it is good or evil" (12:13-14). This will be fulfilled in the final judgment (Rev. 20:11-15).

# 4

# PROPHECY IN ISAIAH

# PROPHECY IN ISAIAH

The Book of Isaiah was often regarded as the greatest of the prophetic books of the Old Testament. Isaiah prophesied in the reigns of Kings Uzziah, Jotham, Ahaz, and Hezekiah, kings of Judah, in the period from 790 to 686 B.C. According to tradition, Isaiah was martyred in the reign of King Manasseh, following the reign of King Hezekiah.

The unity of the Book of Isaiah has been upheld by solid scholarship. The book does have two important themes. The first thirty-nine chapters dealt generally with judgment on sin, and chapters 40–66 emphasized comfort and restoration. Isaiah dealt mainly with the sins of the people in his generation and revealed God's judgment on them which resulted in the Assyrian captivity of the ten tribes in his lifetime and later, after his death, the Captivity of Judah and Benjamin by Babylon. His prophetic vision, however, went far beyond his time to the ultimate judgment of God and the ultimate establishment of righteousness on earth.

## Judah's Sinfulness

*Isaiah 1:1-31.* As a basis for His prophecy of judgment God presented the evidence of sin and rebellion. Judah was a nation "loaded" with guilt (vv. 1-4). Her observance of the offerings was meaningless because her "hands are full of blood" (vv. 5-17). God will judge and purge Judah of her sins (vv. 18-25) and restore judges who will be righteous (vv. 26-31). This is fulfilled in history (2 Chron. 36:14-21; Jer. 23:5-8; Ezek. 20:33-38).

## The Future Messianic Kingdom

*Isaiah 2:1-11.* Isaiah predicted the future kingdom of the Messiah. He wrote, "In the last days the mountain of the LORD's temple will be established as chief among the mountains; it will be raised above the hills, and all nations will stream to it" (v. 2; Zech. 14:16). Jerusalem was described as the capital of the world in a time of peace rather than war, a time when the Lord will teach His ways (Isa. 2:3-5). This will be fulfilled in the Millennium.

## Judah's Humbling in the Day of the Lord

Isaiah predicted, however, that in the day of the Lord, Judah in spite of her wealth would be judged. He stated, "The eyes of the arrogant man will be humbled and the pride of men brought low; the LORD alone will be exalted in that day" (v. 11). The thought of humbling men in judgment was repeated in the verses which follow. This is fulfilled in history and will be fulfilled in the Millennium.

## Coming Judgment on Judah and Jerusalem

*Isaiah 3:1-26.* Isaiah predicted further judgments on Jerusalem and Judah (vv. 1-7). Isaiah described it, "Jerusalem staggers, Judah is falling; their words and deeds are against the LORD, defying His glorious presence. The look on their faces testifies against them; they parade their sin like Sodom; they do not hide it. Woe to them! They have brought disaster upon themselves" (vv. 8-9). The same theme that judgment will come on Jerusalem and Judah was predicted in detail (vv. 10-26). This prophecy was fulfilled in the Babylonian Captivity (2 Chron. 36:15-21).

*Isaiah 4:1.* The judgment of God killed so many men that Isaiah predicted, "In that day seven women will take hold of one man and say, 'We will eat our own food and provide our own clothes; only let us be called by your name. Take away our disgrace!' " (v. 1; 2 Chron. 36:15-21) This was fulfilled in the Babylonian Captivity.

## The Glory of the Kingdom

*Isaiah 4:2-6.* The expression "in that day" sometimes referred to the contemporary scene, sometimes to the future Millennium, as determined by the context. In Isaiah 4:2-6 the beauty of the millennial reign was described, "In that day the Branch of the LORD will be beautiful and glorious, and the fruit of the land will be the pride and glory of the survivors in Israel. Those who are left in Zion, who remain in Jerusalem, will be called holy, all who are recorded among the living in Jerusalem" (vv. 2-3).

Isaiah predicted cleansing of the bloodstains of Jerusalem and the presence of the Lord over Mount Zion signified by a cloud of smoke by day and fire by night (v. 5). In the millennial kingdom the day will come when Israel will be cleansed from sin and her glory restored (Zeph. 3:14-20).

## Israel as God's Vineyard

*Isaiah 5:1-30.* Isaiah compared God's tender dealings with Israel as a vinekeeper caring for a vineyard. But Israel did not produce true fruit, and the result will be that she will be made a wasteland and judgment will fall on those who increase their wealth and don't serve God (v. 8). Isaiah predicted that her mansions will be left vacant and her vineyards will be fruitless (vv. 9-10). Israel's sins were described in verses 11-23. Their time of judgment will come, however. Isaiah predicted graphically the coming invasion of those who would carry off Judah into Captivity (vv. 26-30). This was fulfilled in the Babylonian Captivity (2 Chron. 36:15-21).

## Isaiah's Commission

*Isaiah 6:1-13.* Isaiah was commissioned by the Lord to deliver the message of the coming desolation of Judah, but Judah would not heed the message (vv. 9-10). This was fulfilled in the Babylonian Captivity (2 Chron. 36:15-21).

## The Sign of Immanuel's Birth

*Isaiah 7:1-17.* The attack on Judah by Ephraim will not be successful (vv. 1-9). This was fulfilled in the events which followed. Isaiah recorded that "the LORD spoke to Ahaz, 'Ask the LORD your God for a sign, whether in the deepest depths or in the highest heights' " (v. 10). God promised that a sign would be given to Israel, "Therefore the Lord Himself will give you a sign: The virgin will be with child and will give birth to a Son, and will call Him Immanuel. He will eat curds and honey when He knows enough to reject the wrong and choose the right. But before the boy knows enough to reject the wrong and choose the right, the land of the two kings you dread will be laid waste. The LORD will bring on you and on your people and on the house of your father a time unlike any since Ephraim broke away from Judah — He will bring the king of Assyria" (vv. 14-17). Isaiah predicted the invasion of the king of Assyria and the destruction of the land (vv. 18-25).

The prophecy concerning a virgin with child has been variously considered by conservative scholars. Some believe it referred to a contemporary situation where a young woman, still a virgin, was about to be married and would bear a child, fulfilling the prophecy. Another point of view is that the prophecy is exclusively messianic and refers to the fact that Mary, while still a virgin, would be the mother of Christ (Matt. 1:18, 25), which according to Matthew 1:21-23 was a fulfillment of the prophecy of Isaiah. Still others consider this prophecy as referring to both, that is, a contemporary reference to a child whose birth is mentioned in Isaiah 8 and whose ultimate prophetic fulfillment is the birth of Christ.

*Isaiah 7:18-25.* Isaiah predicted that the Assyrians would make desolate the land which was fulfilled in the Assyrian captivity of the ten tribes (2 Kings 17:1-18).

## Summary of Messianic Prophecies in Isaiah

The prophecy concerning the virgin birth of Christ should be considered in the context of other messianic prophecies in the whole Book of Isaiah. Major future messianic prophecies in Isaiah include the reign of Christ in the kingdom (2:3-5), the virgin birth of Christ

(7:14), the joyful reign of Christ (9:2, 7), the rule of Christ over the world (v. 4), Christ as a Descendant of Jesse and David (11:1, 10), Christ to be filled with the Spirit (v. 2; 42:1), Christ to judge with righteousness (11:3-5; 42:1, 4), Christ to rule over the nations (11:10), Christ to be gentle to the weak (42:3), Christ to make possible the New Covenant (v. 6; 49:8), Christ to be a light to the Gentiles and to be worshiped by them (42:6; 49:6-7; 52:15), Christ to be rejected by Israel (49:7; 53:1-3), Christ to be obedient to God and be subject to suffering (50:6; 53:7-8), Christ to be exalted (52:13; 53:12), Christ to restore Israel and judge the wicked (61:1-3).

### The Assyrian Invasion and Israel's Coming Distress

*Isaiah 8:1-22.* The prophecy that a maiden who was then a virgin would later conceive and give birth to a son was fulfilled. He was given the name Maher-Shalal-Hash-Baz. The name means "quick to the plunder, swift to the spoil." The prophecy then was that before this child would become age two or three or when he would know the difference between good and evil, the Assyrians would conquer Samaria. This revelation was enlarged in the prophecies of verses 5-10 in which God prophesied that Israel (the ten tribes) would be defeated. Isaiah was instructed to fear God and not the people, and further prophesied Israel's defeat and suffering (vv. 11-22). Judah would be delivered from Assyrian domination (37:33-38). This illustrates the future deliverance when her Messiah will come. This prophecy is fulfilled in history and prophecy (2 Kings 17:1-18; Jer. 23:3-8)

The Lord will be a rock of offense to unbelievers (Isa. 8:13-15; Rom. 9:32-33).

### The Coming Son of David

*Isaiah 9:1-7.* In contrast to the past humiliation of Zebulun and Naphtali when they were under the rule of Assyria, the area known as "Galilee of the Gentiles" (v. 1) will be the scene of her great deliverance, referring to the birth of Christ. Though He was actually born in Bethlehem, His home was in Nazareth in the area related to Zebulun and Naphtali.

The coming of the Messiah was compared to a time when a great light would shine (v. 2) and be a time of joy and rejoicing (v. 3). The time was pictured as a great victory for Israel (vv. 4-5).

The great prophecy of the coming of Christ was recorded in verses 6-7, "For to us a Child is born, to us a Son is given, and the government will be on His shoulders. And He will be called Wonderful Counselor, Mighty God, Everlasting Father, Prince of Peace. Of the increase of His government and peace there will be no end. He will reign on David's throne and over His kingdom, establishing and upholding it with justice and righteousness from that time on and forever. The zeal of the LORD Almighty will accomplish this."

This passage was one of the great messianic prophecies of the Old Testament describing Christ as possessing the attributes of God. He will be "Everlasting Father" (v. 6), not in the sense of being God the Father, the first Person of the Trinity, but in the sense that He will be like a father in His government over Israel in the millennial kingdom. The peace of that period was indicated in the title "Prince of Peace" (v. 6).

As God promised David, his kingdom would go on forever, being fulfilled by the millennial kingdom. God will continue to be sovereign over creation throughout eternity to come. The prophecy specified that His throne would be David's throne (v. 7) in fulfillment of the Davidic Covenant indicating that this throne, like David's kingdom, would be on earth, not in heaven. This kingdom will be distinguished as one of justice and righteousness (cf. 11:3-5). The kingdom will be realized by the power of God—"The zeal of the LORD Almighty will accomplish this" (9:7).

These prophecies, as interpreted in their normal literal sense, predicted fulfillment of the expectation of a kingdom on earth after the second coming of Christ in keeping with the premillennial interpretation of Scripture. There was nothing in this passage that corresponded to the present reign of Christ on earth or the present position of Christ in heaven, the interpretation of amillenarians. In this passage, as in many passages in the Old Testament, the first and second coming of Christ were not distinguished and the Child who was born (v. 6) in Bethlehem in His first coming will be the same Person described as the Everlasting King who will reign forever (v. 7). The theme of the future kingdom of Christ on earth was a familiar subject of the prophecies of Isaiah (11:4; 16:5; 28:5-6, 17; 32:16; 33:5; 42:1, 3-4; 51:5).

### The Captivity of the Ten Northern Tribes of Israel

*Isaiah 9:8–10:4.* Immediately following this glorious picture of the future reign of Christ, the prophetic revelation returns to the contemporary situation in Israel. Isaiah prophesied the future captivity of the ten tribes of the kingdom of Israel (9:8–10:4). The ten tribes, the kingdom of Israel, were warned of God's judgment on them for their pride (9:8-17). They were described as already on the way to disaster. Though they claimed they would repair the "bricks" that "have fallen down" with "dressed stone" (v. 10), actually, their enemies were going to conquer them. God predicted judgment on their leaders, "the elders and prominent men" (v. 15) as well as their "prophets who teach lies" (v. 15). Their time of judgment would be one when there would be no pity for orphans and widows (v. 17).

Her increasing wickedness was described as a great fire that burns not only "briers and thorns" but "the forest thickets" as well (v. 18). God would respond in His wrath, scorching the land and destroying the people (v. 19). God predicted, "Each will feed on the flesh of his own offspring" (v. 20).

Further prediction of her coming disaster was made, but even this judgment would not turn away God's wrath (10:1-4). This was fulfilled in the Assyrian captivity.

### Divine Judgment on Assyria

*Isaiah 10:5-34.* God's judgment, however, would fall on Assyria whom God used to judge Israel as well as on Israel herself (vv. 5-19). God's judgment on Assyria was described in detail. The prophecy made clear that after God used the Assyrians to judge Israel, He would then judge the Assyrians, "When the Lord has finished all His work against Mount Zion and Jerusalem, He will say, 'I will punish the king of Assyria for the willful pride of his heart and the haughty look in his eyes' " (v. 12). God will destroy their "sturdy warriors" (v. 16) and their "forests and fertile fields" (v. 18).

After Assyria had been destroyed, God would restore "the remnant of Israel, the survivors of the house of Jacob" (v. 20). A remnant of Israel would return to their land (v. 21). In graphic language, Assyria was described as cut down like a tree whose limbs are cut off (vv. 33-34). A partial return of Israel to their land from Assyria was accomplished after Nineveh fell to the Babylonians (612 B.C.). The complete regathering of Israel will be fulfilled in relation to the second coming of Christ.

### The Future Glorious Kingdom of Israel

*Isaiah 11:1–12:6.* Isaiah predicted that Israel would enjoy the future glorious kingdom. Having cut down Assyria as a tree is cut down (10:33-34), now God would raise up a new "Shoot" which "will come up from the stump of Jesse" (11:1). This Branch which came from the root of Jesse, or David's line, "will bear fruit" (v. 1). This was fulfilled by the birth of Jesus Christ in His first coming.

The passage, however, revealed primarily Christ's position as King and Judge at the time of His second coming. It was prophesied that the Holy Spirit would rest on Him and that He would have wisdom, power, and knowledge (v. 2). His judgment will be with justice (vv. 3-4). He "will slay the wicked" (v. 4) and "righteousness" and "faithfulness" will characterize His rule (v. 5). These passages, of course, will be fulfilled at the time of the second coming of Christ and do not refer to God's present rule on earth.

The future kingdom reign of Christ will be characterized by peace among animals as well as among men. Wolf and lamb will live together and "the leopard will lie down with the goat, the calf and the lion and the yearling together" (v. 6). The peacefulness of nature was summarized in verse 9, "They will neither harm nor destroy on all My holy mountain, for the earth will be full of the knowledge of the LORD as the waters cover the sea." It should be obvious that any literal fulfillment of this passage requires a millennial kingdom after the second coming of Christ. Even in a nonliteral sense, this does not describe the present age. To apply it to heaven or to the new heavens and the new earth, as some amillenarians hold, again does not fit the picture provided in other Scriptures of heaven and of the new earth.

The restoration of Israel in the time when Christ reigns on earth will follow His second coming (vv. 10-16). The "Root of Jesse," referring to Christ, will be One to whom the nations rally (v. 10). Israel will be regathered from the nations to which Israel was scattered (vv. 11-12). The animosity between the kingdom of Judah and the kingdom of Israel will vanish, and Ephraim and Judah will be at peace. Together they will bring into subjection their former enemies (v. 14). To assist the regathering of Israel, "the gulf of the Egyptian Sea" may "dry up" and the Euphrates River will not be a formidable water barrier (v. 15). While this may be supernatural, Russia has already built a number of dams across the Euphrates River, and when these are closed, the Euphrates River dries up in several sections. The drying up of the Euphrates River will permit people to cross easily (cf. Rev. 16:12).

Because of their great victory, Israel will praise the Lord (Isa. 12:1-6). The glorious restoration of Israel and their joy in the future kingdom was anticipated in the Abrahamic Covenant (Gen. 12:1-3;

15:18-21; 17:7-8; 22:17-18), the Davidic Covenant (2 Sam. 7:16), and the New Covenant (Jer. 31:33-34). The glorious future millennial kingdom of Israel will be in contrast to the predicted fall of Babylon and Assyria (Isa. 10:5-19; 13:1-22).

### God's Judgment on Babylon

*Isaiah 13:1-22.* Isaiah, who was living at the time that Assyria conquered the ten tribes (722 B.C.), also predicted the future destruction of Babylon which would occur long after his death. The prophecy against Babylon and her destruction was described as occurring in "the day of the LORD" (v. 6). The prophecy of Babylon's destruction was partially fulfilled in 539 B.C. when the Medes and the Persians captured the city of Babylon. The prophecy concerning Babylon, however, looked far into the future to view the final fall of Babylon in the judgments related to the second coming of Christ (Rev. 18). The description of the Day of the Lord as a time of terror and God's wrath was not completely fulfilled at the fall of Babylon (539 B.C.) and described the great Tribulation, the three-and-a-half years that will precede the Second Coming.

The victory of the Medes over Babylon anticipated the fall of the city of Babylon as well as the religion and political power of Babylon. Babylon would be destroyed like Sodom and Gomorrah (Isa. 13:19). The city would be so destroyed that it would never be inhabited again (vv. 20-22). Historically, the city of Babylon was not destroyed in 539 B.C. or in the centuries which followed. Even in the beginning of the Christian era, Babylon was still an important city with a large colony of Jews. Instead of a sudden destruction, it was gradually destroyed by the forces of nature.

In Revelation 18 Babylon again was described as a city to experience sudden destruction by earthquake and fire. Though some understand that this will not be a literal city and not the literal city of Babylon, the realistic description of Revelation 18 fits perfectly into the concept of a major city to be rebuilt in the end time but to be destroyed by earthquake and fire as a judgment from God at the Second Coming.

### Israel's Blessing after the Destruction of Babylon

*Isaiah 14:1-8.* Babylon is today being partially rebuilt and is still inhabited. Israel was described as being the object of the Lord's compassion, a nation victorious over their enemies. Israel will taunt Babylon in the time of her destruction (vv. 3-11). The oppression of Babylon will end in the time of millennial peace (v. 7).

### The Destiny of the Wicked

*Isaiah 14:9-23*. The leaders were described as being in the realm of the spirits of the dead (vv. 9-11). The prophecy concerning Babylon here went beyond the literal Babylon of history or prophecy. The king of Babylon (v. 3) is usually identified as Sennacherib (705–651 B.C.). Sennacherib was actually the king of Assyria, but when he conquered Babylon, he also was related to Babylon. If he was the one in view (v. 12), he would be described like the falling of the morning star which suddenly disappears once the dawn arrives. He had been a great conqueror of the many nations about Israel. He now would be laid low and killed by assassination. His desire was to be greater than God (vv. 13-14).

Some interpreters consider these verses as referring to more than Sennacherib and actually a description of the fall of Satan in the prehistoric world. Satan, originally created as a holy angel, rebelled against God and was condemned to perpetual judgment of God. The wording of verses 13-14 would describe very accurately the viewpoint of Satan in his desire to be raised above all other rulers and made "like the Most High" (v. 14). This form of revelation is often found in prophecy. In addition to the historical reference, there is here reference to the larger struggle between Satan and God. Sennacherib was described as one who had been killed without proper burial (vv. 16-20). God predicted that Babylon would be cut off (v. 22) and would become a place of desolation (v. 23).

### Assyria to Be Judged

*Isaiah 14:24-27*. The destruction of Assyria was predicted again (v. 25). Historically, this was fulfilled in 612 B.C. when the Assyrian armies were defeated by the Babylonian armies. Nineveh, its capital, was destroyed. The same area once conquered by Assyria will be subject to Christ after His second coming.

### Judgment on the Philistines

*Isaiah 14:28-32*. Another prophecy was revealed against the Philistines who were Israel's constant enemies. They came out to rejoice over temporary victories over Israel, but they were destined for complete destruction themselves. This was partially fulfilled in history but also will be fulfilled in relation to Jesus Christ as the ultimate Victor at His second coming.

### Prophecy against Moab

*Isaiah 15:1–16:13*. The future destruction of Moab, another traditional enemy of Israel, was predicted (15:1-4). At the time of Isaiah's writing, some of the Moabite cities had already been destroyed such as Ar and Kir, located in the area in the southern part of the Dead Sea. Dibon, one of their principal cities, was close to the Dead Sea. Other principal cities were also destined for destruction along with cities such as Nebo and Medeba. Fugitives from Moab fled as far as Zoar to the south and west. The destruction of the Moabites was given graphic prediction (vv. 5-9).

The Moabites instead of fleeing to the south should have gone to the north to Israel and sent lambs as a tribute (16:1). Ultimately, this warfare would end and a man would sit on the throne of the house of David (v. 5), a prophecy to be fulfilled in the future Millennium. A lament of Moab and her grief was described (vv. 7-12). An immediate fulfillment of the destruction of Moab was predicted to come within three years (vv. 13-14). This prophecy was fulfilled either about 732 B.C. when the Assyrian armies pressed south or in a later invasion in 701 B.C. as led by Sennacherib, the king of Assyria.

### Prophecy against Damascus

*Isaiah 17:1-8.* The coming destruction of Damascus, one of the ancient cities of the Middle East, the capital city of Aram, was predicted (vv. 1-2). Damascus was allied with Israel in fighting the Assyrians, but it would all be to no avail because the Assyrians would triumph. Jacob would be like a person with a fat body that wasted away (v. 4). The destruction of Damascus was fulfilled in history and prophecy.

As a result of their discipline by the conquering Assyrians, Israel would turn from their false gods and Asherah poles to the true God (vv. 7-8).

*Isaiah 17:9-14.* Strong cities would be abandoned and become desolate (v. 9). The reason for their judgment was that they had forgotten God (v. 10). The raging of the nations against each other and against God is described, but in the end, God will be the One who triumphs (vv. 12-14).

### Prophecy against Cush

*Isaiah 18:1-7.* This prophecy concerned the destruction of Cush, or Ethiopia, referred to as "the land of whirring wings" (v. 1). The territory involved northern Ethiopia, the Sudan, and southern Egypt. The "whirring wings" represented either the invaders or locusts with their wings. They were described as a fearsome people, "tall and smooth-skinned" and an "aggressive nation" (v. 2).

The Lord promised to remain with them "like shimmering heat in the sunshine" (v. 4), but in due time God would punish the Assyrian invaders. After Assyria was destroyed, the people would bring gifts to Israel (v. 7). This prophecy about Cush is fulfilled in history and will be fulfilled at the Second Coming (Ezek. 38:5; Rev. 16:14-21).

### Prophecy against Egypt

*Isaiah 19:1-25.* Isaiah predicted that the Egyptians would fight each other (v. 2) and would "consult the idols and the spirits of the dead" (v. 3). They would be conquered by "a fierce king" (v. 4). The Nile River would dry up and "the reeds and rushes will wither" (v. 6). God's continued judgment on the Egyptians, the destruction of their economy, and their lack of wisdom were spelled out (vv. 8-15). With their internal problems as well as lack of crops and lack of water, Egypt would be brought to desolation.

The prediction that Judah would rule over the Egyptians (vv. 16-17) may refer to the future Millennium as it does not seem to correspond to any event in history. Some of the cities in Egypt will use the language of Canaan (v. 18). In the time of the future kingdom, prophecy indicated that Egypt would turn to the Lord and worship Him. As a result, He would heal them from the plague (vv. 19-22).

Reference was also made to the highway from Egypt to Assyria (v. 23) which will be in use in the future kingdom. God's blessing will rest on Israel as well as on Egypt and Assyria in that day (vv. 24-25). The prophecies are fulfilled in history and will be fulfilled in the Millennium.

### Cush as Well as Egypt to Be Conquered

*Isaiah 20:1-6.* Isaiah was instructed to walk about "stripped and barefoot" (v. 2) as a sign that not only Israel but Egypt and Cush as well would be conquered by Assyria and be led off as captives. This was fulfilled in history.

### Prophecy against Babylon

*Isaiah 21:1-10.* Isaiah prophesied some of the battles that would revolve around Babylon. Though some trace this to the final downfall of Babylon in 539 B.C., it may refer to earlier battles resulting from revolts against Assyria, with the revolt finally being put down about 702 B.C. Isaiah warned Israel that though there were temporary rebellions against Assyria, they should not trust in this victory, for Assyria would continue to be a strong power. Though details of the prophecy are not entirely clear, the message was given, "Babylon has fallen, has fallen! All the images of its gods lie shattered on the ground!" (v. 9) When Babylon was captured in 539 B.C. there was no extensive destruction as was described here, but the final fulfillment will occur at the Second Coming (Rev. 18).

### Prophecy against Edom

*Isaiah 21:11-12.* A brief prophecy was given concerning Dumah, probably a reference to Edom. The "watchman" reported that morning would come and also the night, meaning that prophetic judgments will eventually be fulfilled.

### Prophecy against Arabia

*Isaiah 21:13-17.* God's judgment was pronounced on Arabia. As a nation, they would be invaded by the Assyrians, and the Arabians would have to flee the Assyrian armies. The time of this event was fulfilled probably about 715 B.C.

### Judgment on Jerusalem

*Isaiah 22:1-14.* Jerusalem was the theme of this prophecy. It is not entirely clear which attack on Jerusalem by the Assyrians was mentioned, but it probably was a reference to the invasion of Sennacherib in 701 B.C. which was described later in Isaiah 36–37. On that occasion God marvelously delivered Jerusalem. Sennacherib had conquered a number of cities of Judah and taken many of the leaders of Judah. Jerusalem was probably meant by the reference to "the Valley of Vision" (22:5). Jerusalem can be variously described as a mountain, such as the expression, the Mount of Zion, but there also is a valley between Jerusalem and the Mount of Olives marked by the brook Kidron. The walls of Jerusalem were described as having many breeches (v. 9). The deliverance came supernaturally from the Lord, but the people foolishly gave themselves to revelry instead of praising the Lord (vv. 12-13).

### Prophecy against Shebna

*Isaiah 22:15-25.* A prophetic indictment was given against Shebna, who apparently was a high official in the palace in Jerusalem (v. 15). He joined with others in their revelry instead of honoring the Lord as their Deliverer. Isaiah prophesied that Shebna would be deposed from his office (v. 19). This was fulfilled (22:19; 36:3).

It was prophesied that Eliakim would replace Shebna. He was a leader in Israel and had Israel's respect. It was probable that he participated in the negotiations between Israel and Sennacherib when the Assyrian armies still surrounded Jerusalem (cf. 2 Kings 18:18, 26, 37; Isa. 36:3, 11, 22; 37:2). He would perform his work well, but eventually he too would fall (22:23-25). This is fulfilled in history.

## Judgment of Tyre

*Isaiah 23:1-18.* This prophecy of the destruction of Tyre (vv. 1-14) resulted in the city being in eclipse for about seventy years after which it would recover (vv. 15-18).

Tyre did well in the eighth century when the Assyrian Empire was gaining strength. The seventy years referred to may be the seventy years from 700 to 630 B.C. During this period the power of Assyria gradually declined, ending in its destruction in 612 B.C. This would allow Tyre to regain strength.

The prophecy pictured the whole Mediterranan world sorrowing at the destruction of Tyre. The merchants of Sidon (v. 2) as well as the Egyptians (v. 3) mourned Tyre's distress. Even Tarshish, located by some in Spain, was affected because their trade was hindered. From Isaiah's viewpoint, what was predicted was yet to be fulfilled.

At the end of the seventy years (v. 17) Tyre would again be restored and their trade restored. The fortunes of Tyre went up and down through the centuries, but the final blow came when Alexander besieged the city in 332 B.C. As the city was on an island, he built a causeway, scraping all the remains of the mainland city to fill in the space. The result of this may be seen today. Though the city was revived later, it was almost completely destroyed by Alexander. What was true of Tyre in Isaiah 23 will be true also of the earth as a whole.

## The Coming Destruction of the Earth

*Isaiah 24:1-23.* The destruction of the earth, which will occur in the Day of the Lord, will be a judgment over the entire face of the earth. This chapter does not have any fulfillment in history, but anticipated the coming Great Tribulation and the destruction of the earth by great earthquakes, fire from heaven, and other disasters. The time of the earth's future disaster, however, will be climaxed by the second coming of Christ and the bringing in of His kingdom of righteousness and peace.

## The Coming Glorious Kingdom

*Isaiah 25:1–27:13.* These three chapters predicted God's triumph and His peoples' praise of God for His omnipotent deliverance of His people. These prophecies to some extent have been fulfilled in the past but will have their ultimate and complete fulfillment in

God's future millennial kingdom. In that future time, those who have trusted God will be honored and those who are God's enemies will be brought down (25:12).

*Isaiah 26.* This is another long psalm of praise, recognizing the Lord's faithfulness in caring for His people. The future kingdom will be a time of peace (v. 12). It will also be a time of resurrection of the dead, "But your dead will live; their bodies will rise. You who dwell in the dust, wake up and shout for joy. Your dew is like the dew of the morning; the earth will give birth to her dead" (v. 19). The deliverance of the righteous in resurrection at the beginning of the Millennium refers to the Old Testament saints (cf. Dan. 12:1-2). In Isaiah 26:19 and Daniel 12:1-2 the most important prophecies of resurrection of the Old Testament saints were revealed.

In Isaiah 27 the praise of God and prediction of the deliverance of Israel were given further revelation. The future will fulfill this time of judgment on the enemies of God, but it will also record a time of restoration and revival of Israel and their possession of the land from the Euphrates River to the Wadi of Egypt, a brook forming the borderline between Egypt and Canaan (Isa. 26:12-13; Gen. 15:18-21).

### Ephraim and Judah Warned of Coming Destruction

*Isaiah 28:1-29.* The theme of judgment on the enemies of God was resumed and prophecies were revealed concerning Ephraim's future judgment of God at the time of the Assyrian invasion. The theme of judgment continues from Isaiah 28 to Isaiah 33. Whether the enemies of God were from Israel, and in this case from Ephraim, or whether they were Gentiles, in either case God would deal with them in judgment (28:29).

### The Precious Cornerstone

In the midst of these statements of coming judgment, revelation was given concerning Jesus Christ as "a stone in Zion, a tested stone, a precious cornerstone for a sure foundation; the One who trusts will never be dismayed" (v. 16; cf. Eph. 2:20; 1 Peter 2:6). This is fulfilled in Christ.

### Jerusalem Warned

*Isaiah 29:1-24.* Judgment was pronounced on the city of Jerusalem, here called Ariel. Jerusalem has been destroyed many times in history (2 Chron. 36:15-21) but was destined to be the capital of the millennial kingdom (cf. Isa. 2:3-5). God declared that the reason for His judgment was that the hearts of the people were far from Him

(29:13). Out of the judgment of Israel and Jerusalem, however, will come the ultimate triumph (vv. 17-24). These specific prophecies await fulfillment in the millennial kingdom.

## Judah Warned about Alliance with Egypt

*Isaiah 30:1–31:9.* The Lord denounced the tendency of Israel to rely on Egypt for their help. God declared the help of Egypt "utterly useless" (30:7). The reason that the Children of Israel go to Egypt is that they are a "rebellious people, deceitful children, children unwilling to listen to the LORD's instruction" (v. 9). God declared that their judgment would come like "a high wall, cracked and bulging, that collapses suddenly, in an instant" (v. 13). In verses 15-18 God called on His people to come and put their trust in Him as "the LORD longs to be gracious to you" (v. 18). Though there will be a time of judgment, there also will be a time of restoration and mercy from the Lord (vv. 19-26). Sorrow will be turned to joy when the Lord undertakes for them (vv. 27-33).

A further indictment pronounced on those who depend on Egypt, "Woe to those who go down to Egypt for help, who rely on horses, who trust in the multitude of their chariots and in the great strength of their horsemen, but do not look to the Holy One of Israel, or seek help from the LORD" (31:1). The Lord promised ultimate deliverance of Israel and Mount Zion (vv. 4-5). On the basis of this, Israel was exhorted to return to the Lord (v. 6). In time the hosts of Assyria "will fall by a sword that is not of man" (v. 8).

## The Coming of Christ, the Righteous King

*Isaiah 32:1-20.* Israel will have "a King" who "will reign in righteousness and rulers will rule with justice" (v. 1). Isaiah predicted that Israel at that time would listen to His exhortation (vv. 2-8). Israel was promised severe judgment from God but ultimate restoration and deliverance (vv. 9-20). The passage concluded, "how blessed you will be, sowing your seed by every stream, and letting your cattle and donkeys range free" (v. 20). This will be fulfilled in the Millennium (Jer. 23:5-8; Rev. 19:11-15).

## Israel's Distress and God's Deliverance

*Isaiah 33:1-24.* Future judgment was pronounced on Israel. This would be followed, however, by Israel's restoration (vv. 5-6). The judgment of God on those who disobey God, however, was described in graphic terms (vv. 7-14). By contrast, those who were righteous will be blessed of the Lord (vv. 15-18). They "will see the King in His beauty and view a land that stretches afar" (v. 17).

The future restoration of Israel and the deliverance of the people of Israel was predicted by Isaiah (vv. 20-24). This will be ultimately fulfilled in the Millennium.

### The Coming Day of Vengeance on the Nations

*Isaiah 34:1-17.* The "day of vengeance" on the nations (v. 8) was described in graphic terms in verses 1-15. By contrast, those who follow the Lord will be blessed (vv. 16-17). This is fulfilled in history and will be fulfilled at the Second Coming (Rev. 16:18-21).

### Kingdom Blessings

*Isaiah 35:1-10.* Those who have been redeemed from their enemies and blessed by the Lord in the future millennial kingdom will rejoice (vv. 1-2). It will be a time of great rejoicing when the desert will burst into bloom. In that time God will come and bring vengeance on the wicked but deliverance for the righteous (v. 4). The abundant blessings of the millennial kingdom were described in verses 5-7, "Then will the eyes of the blind be opened and the ears of the deaf unstopped. Then will the lame leap like a deer, and the mute tongue shout for joy. Water will gush forth in the wilderness and streams in the desert. The burning sand will become a pool, the thirsty ground bubbling springs. In the haunts where jackals once lay, grass and reeds and papyrus will grow." Reference was made again to the international highway that will come through Israel (vv. 8-10).

### Sennacherib Threatens Jerusalem

*Isaiah 36:1-22.* The threat of Sennacherib, king of Assyria, was described graphically in this passage. Sennacherib urged the people of Israel to surrender and to avoid military capture of Jerusalem. He challenged them not to listen to King Hezekiah who was trusting in the Lord (vv. 13-22; cf. 2 Kings 18–19).

### God's Deliverance of Jerusalem

*Isaiah 37:1-38.* The marvelous deliverance of Jerusalem from her enemies was recorded here. Isaiah the prophet declared, "Do not be afraid of what you have heard—those words with which the underlings of the king of Assyria have blasphemed Me. Listen! I am going to put a spirit in him so that when he hears a certain report, he will return to his own country, and there I will have him cut down with the sword" (vv. 5-7).

Sennacherib, however, renewed his attack on Israel, challenging them to surrender. He sent Hezekiah a letter, stating that they had conquered other countries, why could they not conquer Jerusalem? (vv. 9-13) Upon receipt of the letter, Hezekiah went to the temple and spread out the letter before the Lord (v. 14). In response to Hezekiah's prayer, Isaiah sent a message to Hezekiah, "This is what the LORD, the God of Israel, says: Because you have prayed to Me concerning Sennacherib king of Assyria, this is the word the LORD has spoken against him" (v. 21).

In the following poetic section, God predicted that they would be delivered from Assyrians (vv. 22-29). He gave Hezekiah a sign, predicting that Israel would continue to sow their crops and bear fruit in the land of Judah (vv. 30-32). Isaiah concluded that Assyria would not be able to conquer Jerusalem, and they would return by the way in which they came (vv. 33-35).

Scripture then recorded the death of 185,000 men in the Assyrian camp which precipitated the Assyrian withdrawal and ultimately the assassination of Sennacherib (vv. 36-38).

### Hezekiah's Illness and Healing

*Isaiah 38:1-22.* Hezekiah was told that his life would soon be ended, though he was comparatively a young man. Hezekiah asked the Lord to extend his life and God added fifteen years to his life (v. 5). As proof of the prophecy, he made the shadow cast by the sun to go back ten steps (vv. 7-8). In the poetic section which follows Hezekiah rejoiced in the deliverance that God has given him (vv. 9-20). Isaiah had predicted, "Prepare a poultice of figs and apply it to the boil, and he will recover" (v. 21; cf. 2 Kings 20:1-11).

### Envoys from Babylon

*Isaiah 39:1-8.* Hezekiah showed envoys from Babylon all of his treasures (vv. 1-2). Isaiah chided him for this (vv. 3-4). Isaiah predicted to Hezekiah that all of his treasures would be carried off to Babylon, including some of his descendants, but that it would not occur in his lifetime (vv. 5-8). Though it was not recorded by Isaiah, in the fifteen years which God gave him, Manasseh was born, one of the most wicked kings of the kingdom of Judah. Humanly speaking, it would have been far better for Hezekiah to have died before the fifteen added years.

### The Coming Restoration of Israel

*Isaiah 40:1-31.* The final major section of the Book of Isaiah (40–66) begins here. There is ample evidence that Isaiah wrote this as well as the first thirty-nine chapters, but the prophetic emphasis changes. In keeping with the purpose of God's revelation, a major change in theme of this section was God's plan for restoration and deliverance of His people. This will primarily be fulfilled after the second coming of Christ in the millennial kingdom. At that time Israel not only will receive blessings which she did not deserve, but judgment will fall on Babylon because of her sins. In view of Israel's glorious future, she was exhorted to live righteously before the Lord.

The prophet began with a message of comfort for the people of God. He assured them that their time of trial was about over, and that she would receive from "the Lord's hand double for all her sins" (v. 2), which indicated forgiveness. Prophecy was revealed concerning the voice of one preceding the Messiah, "A voice of one calling: 'In the desert prepare the way for the Lord; make straight in the wilderness a highway for our God. Every valley shall be raised up, every mountain and hill made low; the rough ground shall become level, the rugged places a plain. And the glory of the Lord will be revealed, and all mankind together will see it. For the mouth of the Lord has spoken' " (vv. 3-5).

All four Gospels quoted this passage as applying to John the Baptist as the forerunner of Christ (Matt. 3:1-4; Mark 1:1-4; Luke 1:76-79; John 1:23). In this passage the entire nation Israel was pictured as in a desert place (Isa. 40:3), but anticipating the glorious deliverance of God. Leveling the ground was a way of preparing for the coming of a king, and this passage anticipated the millennial kingdom. "And the glory of the Lord will be revealed" (v. 5).

Another voice reminded Israel, "A voice says, 'Cry out.' And I said, 'What shall I cry?' " (v. 6) The answer to this question was the fact of man's temporary character like the grass of the field (vv. 6-8). In contrast to the everlasting character of God, the human race was like grass which quickly withers and falls away. By contrast, also, "the Word of our God stands forever" (v. 8).

Those who brought the message to Zion were exhorted to raise their voice and declare God's purpose of restoration (vv. 9-11). The Lord would come with His reward, which will be fulfilled at the Second Coming. The power of God in Creation was described in verses 12-14. By contrast, men individually were inadequate as compared to the power of God. God was described as enthroned and the people were described as grasshoppers (vv. 21-24). The greatness of God was compared to the starry heavens (vv. 25-26). God never grows weary and He gives strength to those who put their trust in Him (vv. 28-31).

### God's Power and Deliverance

*Isaiah 41:1-29.* The omnipotence of God was compared to the limitation of man and nature (vv. 1-4). Idols cannot deliver (vv. 5-7) like the omnipotent God. This is fulfilled in history as well as prophecy.

God was able to direct Israel and viewed them as His servants (vv. 8-10). The ultimate destruction of the enemies of God and the triumph of God was described (vv. 11-16). God can relieve the thirst of the parched and needy (vv. 17-20). The limitations of the human race (vv. 21-24) and the inadequacy of men in comparison to the omnipotence of God was also brought out (vv. 25-29).

*Isaiah 42:1-13.* Isaiah presented the revelation concerning the Servant of the Lord. This passage described Christ Himself, "Here is My Servant, whom I uphold, My chosen One in whom I delight; I will put My Spirit on Him and He will bring justice to the nations. He will not shout or cry out, or raise His voice in the streets. A bruised reed He will not break, and a smoldering wick He will not snuff out. In faithfulness He will bring forth justice; He will not falter or be discouraged till He establishes justice on earth. In His law the islands will put their hope" (vv. 1-4; cf. partial quotation of this in Matt. 12:18-21). This is the first presentation of Christ as "the Servant" in contrast to Israel as the servant of God (Isa. 41:8; 42:19; 43:10; 44:1-2, 21; 45:4; 48:20). The "Servant" in this section is none other than Christ Himself, though some regard it as a reference to Israel. This is the first of four songs presenting the Servant as Christ (42:1-9; 49:1-13; 50:4-11; 52:13–53:12).

Israel was a blind servant, in contrast to Christ as the One who will bring justice and restoration to the world (42:19). God as the Creator would be the One who gives life to His people (v. 5). God promised to take Israel by the hand, regard them as a covenant people, and make them "a light for the Gentiles" (v. 6). The fact that Christ will be a light to the Gentiles (v. 16) was mentioned in Luke 1:79. God will not only deliver the people as a whole but open individual eyes that were blind and free captives of sin. In keeping with this, in Isaiah a voice of praise to the Lord was recorded, and the Lord's ultimate victory was described (vv. 10-13). This was fulfilled in Christ's first coming and will be fulfilled in His second coming.

### Israel Blind and Deaf

*Isaiah 42:14-25.* God's judgment on the world for its sin was predicted (vv. 14-17). Those who worshiped idols would be ashamed

(v. 17), and those who were deaf and blind to the Word of God would pay for their sin because they paid no attention to the Word of God (v. 23). The Lord declared that He Himself had handed Jacob (Israel) over to her enemies to be looted (vv. 23-25). In spite of her being disciplined by the Lord, she would not understand and would not return to the Lord. In order to bring Israel back to the Lord, God would send His Servant (vv. 1-4) and God would deal with her in mercy. This is fulfilled in history and will be fulfilled in millennial judgments (Ezek. 20:33-38).

### Israel to Be Restored

*Isaiah 43:1-28.* The God who had created Israel would be with her through the deep waters as well as the fires of their affliction (vv. 1-2). The ultimate purpose of God was to bring the people of Israel back to the Holy Land from being scattered all over the world (vv. 3-7). This was only partially fulfilled in return of the captivities and awaits its complete fulfillment at the second coming of Christ (Ezek. 39:26-28). In supernaturally restoring Israel, God will make Israel a testimony to His own deity and power (Isa. 43:8-13).

In the immediate future God would deliver them from Babylon (vv. 14-21). In spite of God's goodness to them, Israel would not respond (vv. 22-24). God reminded her that only He would be able to blot out her transgressions or punish her for her sins (vv. 25-28). This prophecy will be fulfilled in the millennial kingdom.

### The Promise of the Spirit and the Impotence of Idols

*Isaiah 44:1-23.* God again declared His purpose to redeem Israel, to restore her, like "streams on the dry ground" (v. 3). God would pour out His Spirit on her so that she would confess that she belonged to the Lord (v. 5). Israel was reminded that idols were nothing and only God could help her (vv. 6-23). This prophecy will be fulfilled at the Second Coming.

### Prophecy about Cyrus

*Isaiah 44:24-28.* The unusual prophecy was made that Jerusalem would be inhabited, its ruins restored, and that "Cyrus" would authorize the rebuilding of the temple after the Captivity. This prophecy in Isaiah was written 150 years before its fulfillment. Cyrus, king of Medo-Persia, who conquered Jerusalem in 539 B.C., in the following year gave the Jews permission to return to their land and build a temple. It is entirely possible that Daniel, who had a high position in the government of Cyrus, could have influenced this decision. The prophecy is unusual in that the name of the person is given before he was born. This was also true of Jesus (Matt. 1:21) and Maher-Shalal-Hash-Baz (Isa. 8:1-4).

*Isaiah 45:1-13.* Cyrus was again named as the one who would conquer all that is before him. In doing so the Lord would be acknowledged before the world. A further reference was made to Cyrus, "I will raise up Cyrus in My righteousness: I will make all his ways straight. He will rebuild My city and set My exiles free, but not for a price or reward, says the LORD Almighty" (v. 13).

### Israel's Restoration

*Isaiah 45:14-25.* The prophecies which followed went beyond what would happen to Cyrus and anticipated the coming of the Lord in His millennial kingdom. Accordingly, the prophecies of this section as a whole await future fulfillment.

### Exhortation to Israel and Babylon to Recognize God

*Isaiah 46:1-13.* Bel, one of the deities of Babylon, was described as bowing down, and Nebo, another deity, "stoops low" (v. 1). The Babylonians carried images of these gods in some of their triumphant festivals, but by contrast, God carried Israel (vv. 3-4). Israel was urged to remember God as the One who declared the end from the beginning (vv. 8-10), whose purpose would be fulfilled (v. 10). God would bring salvation to Israel (vv. 11-13).

### The Gods of Babylon

*Isaiah 47:1-15.* The destruction of Babylon, the "Virgin Daughter of Babylon," was predicted (v. 1). Babylon was compared to a woman, made a slave, grinding flour with the millstones (vv. 2-4). The judgment of God on Babylon was painted in graphic terms (vv. 5-15). Their astrologers would not be able to save her (vv. 13-15).

### God Keeps His Promises

*Isaiah 48:1-22.* Israel would resist acknowledging God and would break her oaths given to Him (vv. 1-6). God promised to continue to refine Israel (vv. 7-11). God again asked Israel to remember how much greater He is than any idol and prophesied that God would fulfill His purpose (vv. 12-15). In exhorting her to leave Babylon and return to her Promised Land, God reminded her of all He had done for her but predicted that unless she followed Him, she would not find peace (vv. 16-22). These prophecies are fulfilled in history and prophecy.

### Israel's Coming Redemption

The general theme of Isaiah 49–57 is that the Servant of the Lord would ultimately be Israel's Protector and Deliverer. In these chapters, in some cases the servant referred to Israel herself, but in other instances to Jesus Christ as the Servant of the Lord who would be Israel's deliverer.

*Isaiah 49:1-7.* The Servant was described as called by the Lord before He was born (v. 1). The ministry of the Servant will be to bring Israel back to God (vv. 5-6). In the prediction of the coming salvation by the Servant, He was also declared to be "a light for the Gentiles" (v. 6), referred in Luke 1:79; 2:32; cf. Isa. 42:6. Though "despised and abhorred by the nation" in His first coming (49:7), Israel will be brought back to God in the Millennium.

*Isaiah 49:8-13.* The prediction was made that the Servant would be triumphant in fulfilling God's covenant with His people (v. 8; cf. Jer. 31:31-34). Israel would come from all directions to be restored to their Promised Land (Isa. 49:12). This is fulfilled in history and prophecy.

### The Certainty of Israel's Restoration
*Isaiah 49:14-26.* In spite of these prophecies, however, Israel will feel she was forsaken (v. 14). God assured her that this was not the case and that He would not forget her (vv. 15-18). Though Israel returning from Babylon was a small nation, when finally regathered by Christ at His second coming, she will be a large nation (vv. 19-21). Then her land will seem too small for her (v. 20). The return of the children from the Captivity, however, fore-shadows the ultimate gathering of the nation as a whole, an event which is yet future (v. 20). The triumph of Israel will be recognized by the Gentiles (vv. 22-24). In the process of her deliverance and God's judgment on her oppressors, God will reveal Himself as Israel's "Redeemer, the Mighty One of Jacob" (v. 26). This is fulfilled in history and prophecy.

### The Servant Obedient in Humiliation
*Isaiah 50:1-11.* God described Himself as a husband who had temporarily divorced his wife because of sin (v. 1). Israel was referred to as one sold as a slave. The one who was speaking was the Servant of the Lord. God's power was such that He could redeem them out of any situation (v. 2). The submission of the Servant to the will of God led to being rejected and mocked by Israel (v. 6; Matt. 27:28-30; Mark 14:65; 15:19-20; Luke 22:63). Those who want to follow the Servant of the Lord in obeying God should trust in the Lord instead of in their own light (Isa. 50:10-11). This prophecy was fulfilled in the first coming of Christ.

### God Able to Fulfill His Promises to Israel

*Isaiah 51:1-23.* Israel was exhorted to look to Abraham and Sarah and to the Lord as the One who would fulfill her promises of blessing. The description of the situation corresponds to the millennial kingdom when there will be universal joy and righteousness (vv. 3-5). God's salvation will last forever (v. 6). God was extolled as the One who would be able to bring the ransomed back to Zion (v. 11). God who is her Creator will comfort Israel (v. 12). His power is greater than the power of Israel's oppressor (vv. 12-15). The cup of God's wrath drunk by Israel will be given to her oppressor (vv. 17-23). This prophecy is fulfilled in history and prophecy.

### The Coming Salvation of God

*Isaiah 52:1-6.* Though God had dealt with trouble in this way, Israel was exhorted to look forward to God's restoration. When restored, Israel will know that the Lord has done it. This will be fulfilled in the Millennium.

*Isaiah 52:7-12.* The scene described goes beyond the restoration of Israel after the captivities and envisions the millennial earth and Jerusalem as its central city (vv. 8-10). This will be done for all the nations to see.

### The Suffering Servant to Be Exalted

*Isaiah 52:13–53:12.* In the process, the Servant of the Lord will suffer (52:13), a prediction of the sufferings of Christ in connection with His crucifixion. The result will be, however, that blessings will extend to many nations (v. 15; cf. Rom. 15:21).

The great messianic prophecy of Isaiah 53 was devoted to the description of the death of Christ. Portions of this section of Isaiah were quoted in the New Testament. Israel's rejection of Him was pictured (v. 1; cf. John 12:38; Rom. 10:16). He had no outward beauty and He was despised and not esteemed (Isa. 53:2-3). Those in Israel who understood that Christ had died for them will recognize that He took their infirmities on Himself (vv. 4-6; cf. Matt. 8:17). The Servant was afflicted because of Israel's transgressions. The truth was summarized in Isaiah 53:6, "We all, like sheep, have gone astray, each of us has turned to his own way; and the LORD has laid on Him the iniquity of us all." The Servant was compared to a lamb being brought to the slaughter because He did not open His mouth. His death made it impossible for Him to have physical descendants (vv. 7-8; Acts 8:32-33). His "grave" was "with the wicked" but also "with the rich" (Isa. 53:9; 1 Peter 2:22). The Servant died in the will of God because "His life" was made "a guilt offering" (Isa. 53:10). This prophecy was fulfilled in Christ's death with the blessing to be fulfilled in the Millennium (Mark 15:3-4, 27-28; Luke 23:1-25; John 1:29; 11:49-52; Acts 8:28-35; 10:43; 13:38-39; 1 Cor. 15:35; Eph. 1:7; 1 Peter 2:21-25; 1 John 1:7-9).

His spiritual offspring would spring from His death and resurrection (Isa. 53:10). His ultimate victory over the wicked was described in verses 11-12 (cf. Luke 22:30).

## The Future Glory of Israel

*Isaiah 54:1-17.* In graphic language the future glory of Israel and Jerusalem was portrayed. She was compared to a barren woman who nevertheless has many children (v. 1). She was told to spread out and settle in various cities because of her increased descendants. God described Himself as her "Husband—the LORD Almighty is His name—the Holy One of Israel is your Redeemer" (v. 5). Though Israel was abandoned for a moment, God promised to keep His everlasting covenant and shower her with everlasting kindness and compassion (vv. 7-8). His treatment of Israel will be like His treatment of Noah and His "unfailing love for you will not be shaken" (vv. 9-10). The fact that God will not need to rebuke Israel again (v. 9) described her millennial kingdom.

Jerusalem will be as a city built of precious stones (vv. 11-12) which is similar to the description of the New Jerusalem in Revelation 21–22. The reference was, however, to the city of Jerusalem in the Millennium rather than the eternal state (Isa. 54:11-12). In the closing verses of the chapter Israel was declared to be free from tyranny and terror, and God Himself will be her defender against attack (vv. 14-17).

## The Promise of Salvation

*Isaiah 55:1-13.* An invitation was extended to all who were thirsty and who had no money to come and partake of wine and milk without price or cost (vv. 1-2). God will make an everlasting covenant with Israel as He did with David (v. 3). In the enforcement of this invitation, God reminded Israel that she should listen and seek the Lord while He may be found (vv. 3-7). The closing verses of the chapter continue to set forth the wonder of God's care in nature as well as in the proclamation of His Word which will not return empty (vv. 8-11). The prophecy promised that Israel would have great joy in the coming kingdom. All nature will join in rejoicing at God's blessing (vv. 12-13).

All of the blessings described in this chapter were related in verse 3 to "an everlasting covenant with you, My faithful love promised to David." Just as the promises of David and the promises of his kingdom are everlasting and sure to be fulfilled, so Israel's expectation of her restoration and joy in the future millennium was prophesied.

### Salvation for the Gentiles

*Isaiah 56:1-8.* God promised to include among the blessed those who were not Jews but who kept His sabbaths and loved and served the Lord. Their offerings would be accepted and they would have joy in the house of prayer (v. 7). The statement that "My house will be called a house of prayer" (v. 7) was quoted by Christ as a rebuke of Israel's desecration of the temple (Matt. 21:13). This is fulfilled in history and will be fulfilled in the Millennium. Isaiah 56 closed with a severe indictment on the wicked in contrast to the blessings pronounced on those who serve the Lord.

### Condemnation of the Wicked Contrasted
### to Comfort for the Righteous

*Isaiah 57:1-21.* After the preceding sweeping indictment on sin (vv. 1-13), comfort was promised to those who turn to the Lord (v. 14). Though the Lord will bring peace to the righteous, the wicked will have no comfort or peace (vv. 14-21). This is fulfilled in history and prophecy.

### True Fasting to Be Rewarded

*Isaiah 58:1-14.* The Lord exhorted them to true fasting and to doing good deeds, such as loosing the chains of injustice (v. 6), sharing food with the hungry (v. 7), and clothing the naked (v. 7). When they called on the Lord and served Him in this way, God would hear and would come to their help (vv. 7-10). The promise was renewed that God would guide them (v. 11) and that they would rebuild the ancient ruins (v. 12). Special blessing was pronounced on those who did not break the Sabbath and who found their joy in the Lord (vv. 13-14). This is fulfilled in history and will be fulfilled in the Millennium.

### The Promised Redeemer to Come in Spite of Israel's Sins

*Isaiah 59:1-21.* This graphic description of Israel's sins called for confession and restoration. God declared her sins had separated her from God (vv. 1-4). Her acts of violence (v. 6) and injustice (vv. 8-14) demanded a divine answer to Israel as well as to her enemies (v. 18). The Redeemer will come out of Zion to those who repent of their sins (v. 20). God promised that His Spirit would be speaking through them forever (v. 21). This was fulfilled in the first coming and will be fulfilled in the Second Coming.

### The Glory of Zion in the Kingdom

*Isaiah 60:1-22.* God's future redemption of Israel will bring a glorious future. The glory will come from God Himself, and the nations will respond and come to the light (vv. 1-3). The wealth of the world will accrue to them (vv. 4-7). Herds of camels will cover the land (v. 6) and abundant offerings will be offered on the altar (v. 7). These predictions have not been fulfilled in history and anticipate the future millennial kingdom. In that day the ships of Tarshish will bring silver and gold to honor the Lord.

The glories of Jerusalem will exceed anything realized in the past (vv. 10-12). "Foreigners will rebuild your walls, and their kings will serve you" (v. 10). The wealth of the nations will come to them (v. 11). The future glory of Israel and its possessions will include their enemies bowing down before them (vv. 13-14).

Their ultimate blessings and God's wonderful care for them was described in detail (vv. 15-22). They will have gold instead of bronze (v. 17). "No longer will violence be heard in your land, nor ruin or destruction within your borders" (v. 18). The prophecy anticipated the eternal state when it predicted, "The sun will no more be your light by day, nor will the brightness of the moon shine on you, for the LORD will be your everlasting light, and your God will be your glory" (v. 19; cf. Rev. 21:23; 22:5).

### The Two Advents of Christ

*Isaiah 61:1-11.* The Servant of the Lord, who is Christ Himself, will have the anointing of the Holy Spirit. "The Spirit of the Sovereign LORD is on Me, because the LORD has anointed Me to preach good news to the poor. He has sent Me to bind up the brokenhearted, to proclaim freedom for the captives and release from darkness for the prisoners, to proclaim the year of the LORD's favor and the day of vengeance of our God, to comfort all who mourn" (vv. 1-2). His anointing, like that of Saul and David, will set Him apart as King because the title "Christ" has the meaning of being anointed (cf. Matt. 3:16-17). In Luke 4:18-19 Christ quoted Isaiah 61:1 and part of verse 2 in connection with Himself. Significantly, He stopped the quotation before the mention of "the day of vengeance of our God" (v. 2). The previous verses will harmonize with His first coming, but the day of vengeance referred to His second coming. By this,

Christ signified the difference between the two events and their prophetic fulfillment.

As in other millennial passages, the reconstruction of the cities of Israel was prophesied (vv. 4-6). Not only will the material places be restored but also the people of Israel will be restored as a nation and aliens will be serving as servants to them. Israel herself will live as "priests of the LORD" (v. 6).

Her prosperity included that she would be forgiven her sins and would have a double portion of her inheritance and everlasting joy. To the nations her prosperity will be a token of the Lord's blessings. The prophet himself describes his joy in the Lord and enumerates the blessings that God has showered on him (vv. 10-11). These prophecies will be fulfilled primarily in the Millennium.

### Preparing the Way for the King

*Isaiah 62:1-12.* Another beautiful picture prophetic of the future kingdom was revealed as following the second coming of Christ. At that time her salvation will be evident to all (v. 1). The nations about Israel will observe her righteousness and glory (v. 2). Israel was compared to a crown or a royal diadem (v. 3). Though she once was described as desolate, now she will be called "Hephzi-bah," meaning "My delight is in her," and her land "Beulah," meaning "married one," for "the LORD will take delight in you, and your land will be married" (v. 4). Her restoration was described as a joyful marriage.

Israel will never have to surrender to foreigners her new wine or her crops (vv. 6-9). Israel was challenged to prepare the road for the King (vv. 10-11). The people of Israel themselves will be described as "the Holy People" (v. 12).

### The Coming Day of Judgment and Redemption

*Isaiah 63:1–64:12.* The Lord will come as a victorious Conqueror coming from Edom with garments stained with crimson. This predicted a coming day of judgment on Edom (63:1), a nation which often opposed Israel and was located to the southeast of Israel. The passage described Christ as treading a winepress of the judgment of God with blood spattering His garments (vv. 2-3). It will be "the day of vengeance" (v. 4). Christ's coming will be at a time of deliverance of Israel and her restoration, but it will be a time of judgment on those who are not right with God (vv. 3-6). Israel's many past blessings were contrasted to her future glory. Israel will recall then how God had blessed her in the days of Moses (vv. 7-

14), even though Israel rebelled against God (v. 10).

Israel petitioned God to judge the wicked who opposed her even though she was conscious of her own sins (64:1-7). Israel deplored her destruction by her enemies, the desolation of Jerusalem, and her temple destroyed by fire (vv. 8-11).

## Blessing for the Righteous Contrasted to
## Destruction of the Wicked

*Isaiah 65:1-16.* After Israel's sins were enumerated (vv. 1-7), God predicted her future blessings (v. 10). By contrast, the wicked will be judged (vv. 11-12). In God's future dealings with Israel He will supply all the needs of His servants but will judge those who reject Him (vv. 13-16).

*Isaiah 65:17-25.* A glorious picture was presented of the ultimate new heavens and new earth (vv. 17-19). The prophet then returned to the theme of Jerusalem in the millennial kingdom in which there will be longevity but also death. One who will die at 100 years will be considered still in one's youth. The millennial earth will provide Israel with security. "They will build houses and dwell in them; they will plant vineyards and eat their fruit" (v. 21). By contrast, the wicked will not take possessions away from the people of Israel, "My chosen ones will long enjoy the works of their hands" (v. 22). Israel's children will not be "doomed to misfortune" (v. 23). Tranquility in nature will also occur, "The wolf and the lamb will feed together, and the lion will eat straw like the ox, but dust will be the serpent's food. They will neither harm nor destroy on all My holy mountain" (v. 25; cf. 11:6-7). These prophecies do not fit the eternal New Jerusalem but relate to the Millennium.

In expressing Israel's future hope, the Old Testament often mingled prophecies of the millennial kingdom with that of the New Jerusalem in eternity. The distinctions are made clear when the details are observed. Here, obviously, the millennial kingdom was being described because in the New Jerusalem there will be no death, no sin, and no judgment. In the millennial kingdom it will be a time of great joy and rejoicing and deliverance for the people of God, but death and sin will still be present.

## Judgment on the Wicked Contrasted to the
## Eternal Hope of the Righteous

*Isaiah 66:1-24.* This chapter described the millennial kingdom following the second coming of Christ. Because heaven is God's throne, it follows that earth is "My footstool" (v. 1). Accordingly, no temple can really contain God. God declared that her sacrifices would be of no use unless her heart was with Him. God promised to judge with justice those who were not living in right relationship to Him (vv. 4-6).

Israel's restoration will be like a child born before his time. Israel will be delivered and restored quickly (vv. 8-9). God commanded her to rejoice (v. 10). In the future Millennium God also promised to care for His people like a mother caring for a baby (vv. 11-13). Israel "will flourish like grass" (v. 14). But the wicked will see God coming on them in judgment (vv. 15-17). Even the nations will come to see the glory of God and those not of the nation of Israel will be brought to Jerusalem to worship God (vv. 19-21).

In the closing verses of Isaiah the promise was repeated that God will care for His own forever in contrast to those who experience eternal punishment (vv. 22-24). The close of the Book of Isaiah was a stern warning to those who reject God and a word of assurance to those who put their trust in Him. These prophecies will be fulfilled in the Millennium.

# 5

# PROPHECY IN JEREMIAH

# PROPHECY IN JEREMIAH CONCERNING JUDAH

Jeremiah, though the son of a levitical priest, Hilkiah, ministered as a prophet from approximately 625 to 582 B.C. His prophecies were delivered in a time of great distress and apostasy for the people of Israel. His prophecies concerning Judah and the nations revealed more detail and concerned more peoples than any other book of Scripture. Jeremiah lived to see many of his prophecies literally fulfilled, but some stretched to the end of the age. His prophecies concerning Judah were revealed from Jeremiah chapter 1 through chapter 45.

### General Prophecies of Divine Judgment on Judah.

*Jeremiah 1:13-19.* Jeremiah reported this prophecy of the Lord, " 'What do you see?' 'I see a boiling pot, tilting away from the north,' I answered. The LORD said to me, 'From the north disaster will be poured out on all who live in the land. I am about to summon all the peoples of the northern kingdoms,' declares the LORD" (vv. 13-14).

In the verses that follow God declared that the kings who would conquer Jerusalem would set up their thrones in the gates of Jerusalem. God pronounced judgments on the people because of their wickedness (vv. 15-16).

God further instructed Jeremiah not to be terrified but to take his stand against the enemies of God. Jeremiah was informed, " 'They will fight against you but will not overcome you, for I am with you and will rescue you,' declares the LORD" (v. 19). These prophecies were fulfilled in the Babylonian Captivity.

*Jeremiah 2:35-37.* After a stinging indictment declaring that Israel was guilty of spiritual harlotry, God declared His purpose to judge her, "But I will pass judgment on you because you say, 'I have not sinned' " (v. 35). God informed her that though she would turn away from Egypt as well as from Assyria, "You will also leave that place with your hands on your head, for the LORD has rejected those you trust; you will not be helped by them" (v. 37). The reference of this prophecy is that though Israel declared her independence of Assyria as well as Egypt, she would be carried off as prisoners under the Babylonian Captivity which would follow the Assyrian period (2 Chron. 36:15-21).

### Blessings to Follow Judgment

*Jeremiah 3:11-18.* Declaring that Judah had been unfaithful to the Lord, the Lord urged her to return. He promised that she would be received in mercy (v. 12). God will "give you shepherds after My own heart, who will lead you with knowledge and understanding" (v. 15). God pictured Jerusalem at the time of her restoration in the Millennium, "At that time they will call Jerusalem The Throne of the LORD, and all nations will gather in Jerusalem to honor the name of the LORD. No longer will they follow the stubbornness of their evil hearts. In those days the house of Judah will join the house of Israel, and together they will come from a northern land to the land I gave your forefathers as an inheritance" (vv. 17-18).

### Disaster to Come on Israel

*Jeremiah 4:1-31.* The Lord beseeched Israel to put away her idols (v. 1) and to "Circumcise yourselves to the LORD, circumcise your hearts, you men of Judah and people of Jerusalem, or my wrath will break out and burn like fire because of the evil you have done — burn with no one to quench it" (v. 4). Instead of being blessed (v. 2), she would be punished by the Lord.

God declared that she would be invaded from the north (vv. 5-9). Judah was challenged to flee to her fortified cities (v. 5) because God was "bringing disaster from the north, even terrible destruction" (v. 6). The verses which follow pictured the cities lying in ruins and the people in sackcloth (vv. 7-9). With this revelation Jeremiah was distressed, telling the Lord that He had spoken of peace when actually "the sword is at our throats" (v. 10). In dramatic fashion God predicted how the enemy would advance (vv. 11-17). The verses which follow (vv. 18-20) declared that this had been brought on her by her conduct which resulted in "the whole land" lying "in ruins" (v. 20). The destruction of Judah was also predicted (vv. 21-31). This was fulfilled in the Babylonian Captivity.

### Divine Reasons for Judging Israel

*Jeremiah 5:1-19.* Because of her sins Judah would be attacked by the lion, the wolf, and the leopard (v. 6). God described the devastation of their vineyards because "they have lied about the LORD; they said, 'He will do nothing! No harm will come to us; we will never see sword or famine' " (v. 12). Because her "prophets are but wind" (v. 13), God will do precisely to her what she said would not be done.

God would come on the nation of Israel and bring "a distant nation against" them (v. 15). They would devour everything before them, but God promised, " 'I will not destroy you completely.' And when the people ask, 'Why has the LORD our God done all this to us?' you will tell them, 'As you have forsaken Me and served foreign gods in your own land, so now you will serve foreigners in a land not your own' " (vv. 18-19). This was fulfilled in the Babylonian Captivity.

*Jeremiah 6:1-30.* After a graphic description of Israel's judgment because of her sins, God declared, "Hear, O earth: I am bringing disaster on this people, the fruit of their schemes, because they have not listened to My words and have rejected My Law" (v. 19). He declared her offerings were not acceptable (v. 20). A great army would come from the north (v. 22) which would show no mercy to Judah. She was exhorted to put on sackcloth and roll in ashes (v. 26). This was fulfilled in the Babylonian Captivity.

### Israel's Sin and Idolatry

*Jeremiah 7:1-29.* After calling Israel's religion worthless because it did not change their lives (vv. 2-11), God declared He "will thrust you from My presence, just as I did all your brothers, the people of Ephraim" (v. 15).

After rebuking Israel for her sins and idolatry, the Lord declared, "My anger and My wrath will be poured out on this place, on man and beast, on the trees of the field and on the fruit of the ground, and it will burn and not be quenched" (v. 20). In verses 21-29 God continued to plead with Israel and promised He would be her God if she would walk in God's ways (vv. 22-23). This was fulfilled in the Babylonian Captivity.

*Jeremiah 7:30-34.* God declared that the Valley of Ben Hinnom would become the Valley of Slaughter (vv. 31-32). The dead would be so high in number that they would not have room to bury them (v. 32), and "the sounds of joy and gladness" and "the voices of bride and bridegroom" (v. 34) will no longer be heard. This was fulfilled in the Babylonian Captivity.

*Jeremiah 8:1-3.* Those who have dishonored God by worshiping idols would have their bones removed from their graves and exposed to the sun and moon as a token of God's judgment. This was fulfilled (2 Kings 23:4-16).

### Judgment because of Sin

*Jeremiah 8:9-22.* Because of Israel's rejection of the word of the Lord, it was prophesied that her wives would be given to other men and her fields to new owners. She would be brought down and punished (vv. 9-12).

Their harvest would be taken away (v. 13). When she fled to

fortified cities, she would be doomed to perish (v. 14). The enemy would come to devour the land (v. 15). God would send poisonous snakes among them (v. 17). These prophecies were fulfilled in the Babylonian Captivity.

*Jeremiah 9:11-26.* Jerusalem as well as the towns of Judea would be laid waste (v. 11). The people of Israel would be scattered among the nations. Her women would wail with tears (vv. 18-19). Death would cut off her young people as well as the children (vv. 21-22). God's judgment would extend not only to Israel but to Egypt, Edom, Ammon, Moab and others who lived in the desert (vv. 25-26). This was fulfilled in the Babylonian Captivity.

*Jeremiah 10:17-25.* Those who lived in the land would be captured (v. 18). Their families as well as their tents would be destroyed (v. 20). Jeremiah prays, "Pour out Your wrath on the nations that do not acknowledge You, on the peoples who do not call on Your name. For they have devoured Jacob; they have devoured him completely and destroyed his homeland" (v. 25). The desolation of the land was fulfilled (2 Chron. 36:21).

### The Covenant of Moses Broken

*Jeremiah 11:1-8.* The covenant of Moses that God made with the people of Israel had not been kept, though God fulfilled His promise of giving her the "land flowing with milk and honey—the land you possess today" (v. 5), and she had not obeyed the Law or listened to the Lord. Therefore, God would bring the curses of the covenant on her (v. 8).

*Jeremiah 11:9-14.* Because the Children of Israel had not followed the Lord, just as her fathers ignored God and worshiped other gods, so God would not hear her cry when disaster struck (vv. 11-13). Jeremiah was instructed not to pray for this people because God would not listen (v. 14).

*Jeremiah 11:15-17.* Though Israel may worship in the temple, because she was wicked, God would punish her (v. 15). God intended her to be an "olive tree with fruit beautiful in form. But with the roar of a mighty storm He will set it on fire, and its branches will be broken" (v. 16). Disaster was decreed on her because she had burned incense to Baal (v. 17). These prophecies were fulfilled at the time of the Babylonian Captivity.

### The Plot against Jeremiah

*Jeremiah 11:18-23.* The men of Anathoth were plotting to kill Jeremiah because they did not like his prophecies. God assured Jeremiah that He would punish them with death (v. 21). The famine as well as the sword which would devour her sons and daughters would result in the judgment that "not even a remnant will be left to them" (v. 23). These prophecies were fulfilled in the Babylonian Captivity.

### Why the Wicked Prosper

*Jeremiah 12:1-17.* Jeremiah's complaint about the wicked prospering was temporarily true. God in His time would give them into the hands of their enemies (v. 7). Their land would be laid waste (vv. 10-12), and they would reap thorns not wheat (v. 13). Those who punish Israel and seize their inheritance would in turn be uprooted (vv. 14-15). Those who would not listen to God would be completely destroyed (v. 17). These prophecies were fulfilled in the Babylonian Captivity.

### Jeremiah's Belt and the Wineskins

*Jeremiah 13:1-11.* Jeremiah was instructed by the Lord to take a belt and hide it in the rocks. Later the belt was ruined by this exposure. In like manner God "will ruin the pride of Judah and the great pride of Jerusalem" (v. 9). Those who refuse to worship God and follow wickedness would be completely useless like the belt of Jeremiah (vv. 10-11).

*Jeremiah 13:12-14.* As wineskins are filled with wine, so the Lord would cause the people of Israel to be drunk with wine and would destroy them. These prophecies were fulfilled in the Babylonian Captivity.

### The Coming Captivity

*Jeremiah 13:15-27.* When they asked why this was happening to them, God would declare, "All Judah will be carried into exile, carried completely away" (v. 19). "If you ask yourself, 'Why has this happened to me?'—it is because of your many sins" (v. 22). This was fulfilled in the Babylonian Captivity.

### Israel to Experience Drought, Famine, and the Sword

*Jeremiah 14:1-6.* The cities of Judah would mourn and the cry would come up from Jerusalem (vv. 1-2). Their cisterns would be empty (v. 3). They would have no rain (v. 4). Their animals would die (vv. 5-6).

*Jeremiah 14:10-12.* Though God loved the people of Judah, He would punish them for their sins (v. 10). God would not pay heed to their fasts nor accept their offerings, but they would be destroyed "with the sword, famine and plague" (v. 12).

*Jeremiah 14:13-16.* The prophets who prophesied lies that God's judgment would not come, "Those same prophets will perish by sword and famine. And the people they are prophesying to will be thrown out into the streets of Jerusalem because of the famine and sword. There will be no one to bury them or their wives, their sons or their daughters. I will pour out on them the calamity they deserve" (vv. 15-16). These prophecies were fulfilled in the Babylonian Captivity.

### *Judgment Inevitable but True Repentance*
### *Will Bring Restoration*

*Jeremiah 15:1-4.* Even though Moses and Samuel would intercede, God would nevertheless punish His people. They would be destined to death by the sword, others by starvation, others by captivity (v. 2). Four kinds of destroyers would attack them, the sword, the dogs, the birds, and the beasts of the earth (v. 3). Even the nations would abhor them because they followed the sins of Manasseh (v. 4). This was fulfilled in the Babylonian Captivity.

*Jeremiah 15:5-21.* No one would pity Jerusalem in her day of distress because she had rejected the Lord (vv. 5-6). There would be many widows, more than the sands of the sea (v. 8). These survivors would be put to the sword (v. 9). God promised to deliver Jeremiah in the time of distress. Their wealth would be plundered and they would be enslaved to their enemies. Jeremiah was promised that if he was a worthy spokesman of God, he would be like "a fortified wall of bronze" (v. 20). God promised to save him from the hand of the wicked (v. 21). These prophecies were fulfilled in the Babylonian Captivity.

### *The Coming Disaster*

*Jeremiah 16:1-13.* Jeremiah was instructed not to marry or have sons and daughters because they would be destined to die like others by the sword and by the famine.

Jeremiah was also told not to join in the funeral meal or to show pity for those in bereavement because God had withdrawn His pity from this people, and they were destined for a sad end. No more would the bride and the bridegroom celebrate with joy.

Jeremiah was instructed to tell the people that a great disaster was coming because not only they but their fathers had forsaken the Lord (vv. 10-12). They would be carried captive to a strange land and there would serve other gods (v. 13). These prophecies were fulfilled in the Babylonian Captivity and in Jeremiah's experience.

### God's Ultimate Purpose to Restore Israel

*Jeremiah 16:14-15*. Though the near prospect for Israel was that of disaster and removal from the land, God affirmed even in this context of apostasy that He would restore them to the land, " 'However, the days are coming,' declares the LORD, 'when men will no longer say, "As surely as the LORD lives, who brought the Israelites up out of Egypt," but they will say, "As surely as the LORD lives who brought the Israelites up out of the land of the north and out of all the countries where He had banished them." For I will restore them to the land I gave their forefathers.' "

Two things may be noted about this prophecy: 1. It was delivered in times of apostasy when Israel certainly did not deserve this promise; 2. The promise of the land was still understood as a literal promise as it is all through the Old Testament. Just as Israel was being carried off into captivity literally from her land to another land, so literally she will be brought back from other lands to her homeland. The time of fulfillment will be at the second coming of Christ when Israelites will come "out of all the countries where He had banished them" (v. 15). Her regathering will enable her to participate in the millennial kingdom following the Second Advent.

### Captivity to Precede Restoration

*Jeremiah 16:16-18*. In contrast to the merciful regathering of Israel mentioned in the preceding verses, this prophecy described hunting down the Israelites who would be carried off into Captivity. This would be a time when Israelites who were hidden would be searched out, and they would suffer for their sins and the sins of their forefathers. This was fulfilled in the Babylonian Captivity.

### Gentiles also to Be Saved

*Jeremiah 16:19-21*. God, who had been the refuge of those who turned to Him, would eventually bring to Himself those from all nations who trust in the Lord (v. 19). When they return to the Lord, the Lord will teach them of His "power and might" and "they will know that My name is the LORD" (v. 21). This is fulfilled in God's program of salvation.

### The Wicked and the Righteous Contrasted

*Jeremiah 17:1-18*. The sin of Judah was inscribed indelibly on her heart, causing God to punish her (vv. 1-2). Her wealth would be taken from her (v. 3), she would lose her inheritance (v. 4), and would be enslaved (v. 4). God pronounced a curse on those who trusted in man and described him as a bush in the desert (vv. 5-6).

By contrast, the blessed man "will be like a tree planted by the water that sends out its roots by the stream. It does not fear when heat comes; its leaves are always green. It has no worries in a year of drought and never fails to bear fruit" (v. 8). Israel at the time, however, was like a desert bush, not a righteous person drawing from an abundant supply of water. The problem with Israel and Judah was that her heart was deceitful (v. 9), and this resulted in God's forsaking her and putting her to shame (v. 13). Because Jeremiah's persecutors would not believe him, Jeremiah called on God to bring on her the judgment he had prophesied (vv. 14-18).

### Keeping the Sabbath

*Jeremiah 17:19-27.* Jeremiah's plea with the Children of Israel to keep the Sabbath went unheeded. God offered her a conditional promise. If she would keep His Sabbath and observe His Law, He would bless her; if they would not, "then I will kindle an unquenchable fire in the gates of Jerusalem that will consume her fortresses" (v. 27).

### Sign of the Potter's House

*Jeremiah 18:1-10.* Using the illustration of a pot of clay being shaped which was marred in the potter's hands, God declared to Jeremiah that He could do what the potter did as they were clay in His hands. God declared that if a nation under the curse of His judgment would repent of its evil, God would relieve them of the disaster (v. 8). If on the other hand He announced blessing on the nation or kingdom but it did evil, then God would "reconsider the good I had intended to do for it" (v. 10). Blessing under the Mosaic Law was conditioned on obedience. This prophecy is fulfilled in the history of Israel.

### Disaster Predicted

*Jeremiah 18:11-23.* In the light of this, God declared, " 'Look! I am preparing a disaster for you and devising a plan against you. So turn from your evil ways, each one of you, and reform your ways and your actions.' But they will reply, 'It's no use. We will continue with our own plans; each of us will follow the stubbornness of his evil heart' " (vv. 11-12). God charged Israel with a "most horrible thing" (v. 13). Israel had forgotten God and had been burning incense to idols that were worthless (v. 15). As a result, "Their land will be laid waste, an object of lasting scorn; all who pass by will be appalled and will shake their heads" (v. 16). Jeremiah asked God to fulfill His plans of punishment of Israel because she was making plots against Jeremiah himself.

### Sign of the Broken Pot

*Jeremiah 19:1-15.* Jeremiah was instructed to buy a clay jar from the potter and then pronounce judgment on Israel because of her sins (vv. 1-5). Instead of calling the place "Topheth or the Valley of Ben Hinnom," they would call it "the Valley of Slaughter" (v. 6). God described the terrible judgment on Israel which would devastate her cities and even cause them to eat the flesh of her children (vv. 7-9). Jeremiah then broke the jar and declared that God "will smash this nation and this city just as this potter's jar is smashed and cannot be repaired. They will bury the dead in Topheth until there is no room" (vv. 10-11). God will defile Jerusalem just as He defiled Topheth (vv. 12-13).

Jeremiah repeated his judgment that God would bring disaster on Jerusalem and the surrounding villages because "they were stiff-necked and would not listen to My words" (v. 15). This judgment was fulfilled in the Babylonian Captivity.

*Jeremiah 20:1-6.* After Jeremiah was beaten by Pashhur the priest (vv. 1-2), Jeremiah repeated the prophecy of the destruction of Jerusalem (v. 4). He declared that they would see their friends fall by the sword and see the treasures of Jerusalem being taken to Babylon (vv. 4-5). He predicted that Pashhur himself would go into exile in Babylon and would die and be buried there (v. 6). This was fulfilled in the Babylonian Captivity (2 Chron. 36:15-21).

### Judah's Kings Warned

*Jeremiah 21:1-7.* After Jeremiah complained that the Lord was allowing him to be rejected (20:7-18), Jeremiah received an invitation from King Zedekiah to ask the Lord about Nebuchadnezzar and his attack on Babylon (vv. 1-2). Jeremiah replied, however, that Jerusalem would be conquered (vv. 3-4), God was against them (v. 5), and both man and animals will die "of a terrible plague" (v. 6). Zedekiah himself and his officials as well as the people of the city would be handed over to Nebuchadnezzar who would put many of them to the sword and not show pity or compassion (v. 7). This was fulfilled in the Babylonian Captivity (2 Chron. 36:15-21).

### Jerusalem to Be Destroyed

*Jeremiah 21:8-14.* Jeremiah delivered God's message that those who stayed in the city would "die by the sword, famine or plague" (v. 9). By contrast, "whoever goes out and surrenders to the Babylonians who are besieging you will live; he will escape with his life" (v. 9). The city of Jerusalem itself would be destroyed by fire

(v. 10). The destruction of Jerusalem was again prophesied, and those who think they will have refuge there will be punished because of their evil deeds (vv. 11-14). This was fulfilled in the Babylonian Captivity (2 Chron. 36:15-21).

### Judah's Kings to Be Destroyed

*Jeremiah 22:1-30.* Jeremiah was instructed to go to the palace of the king and urge the officials to rule righteously (vv. 2-3). Jeremiah promised that if they obeyed the Lord they would continue to reign on the throne of David (v. 4). If they did not obey, the palace would be ruined (v. 5).

Jeremiah described the destruction of the temple in graphic terms (vv. 6-7). He prophesied that people from other nations would ask why Jerusalem was destroyed, and the answer would be that they had forsaken God's covenant (vv. 8-9). Jeremiah declared that they should not weep for the dead but rather weep for the fact that they were exiled and no longer would come back to their native land (v. 10). What was true of many of the captives was especially true of Shallum, son of Josiah, who succeeded his father who was king of Judah. Shallum is another name for Jehoahaz who was carried off captive.

Jeremiah described the judgment of God on those who built a palace and would not pay the workmen (vv. 13-14). Jeremiah pointed out that the king's father did better than he in defending the poor. God charged Shallum with being dishonest and shedding innocent blood (v. 17). Just as Shallum (Jehoahaz) forsook the example of his father Josiah and as a result was carried off captive to Egypt, so Jehoiakim, another son of Josiah who succeeded him, acted corruptly in trying to build a big palace at the expense of the laborers (vv. 13-14). Jeremiah records the judgment of God on him, "They will not mourn for him: 'Alas, my brother! Alas, my sister!' They will not mourn for him: 'Alas, my master! Alas, his splendor!' He will have the burial of a donkey — dragged away and thrown outside the gates of Jerusalem" (vv. 18-19). The judgment of God would not only fall on Jehoiakim but on his people (vv. 20-23).

God pronounced judgment also on Jehoiachin (also known as Coniah, and also as Jekoniah). The prophecy that he would be handed over to Nebuchadnezzar of Babylon and die in a strange country (vv. 25-27) was fulfilled (cf. Jer. 24:1; 29:2). He will be considered childless and his children would not sit on the throne (vv. 29-30).

The question was raised why Jehoiachin was thus cast out of the land. God declared, "Record this man as if childless, a man who will not prosper in his lifetime, for none of his offspring will prosper, none will sit on the throne of David or rule anymore in Judah" (v. 30). Actually, Jehoiachin had many children (cf. 1 Chron. 3:17-18), but none would sit permanently on the throne of David. His son Zerubbabel (1 Chron. 3:17-19; Matt. 1:12) became a governor of Judah but not king. Jehoiachin was therefore the last to sit on the Davidic throne as king until Christ. Actually, Zedekiah, another son of Josiah, sat on the throne for a period after Jehoiachin because he was not a son of Jehoiachin. The Scriptures which state that none of his offspring would reign was fulfilled. Zedekiah, because of his rebellion against Nebuchadnezzar, ultimately saw his two sons killed and then was blinded and carried off to Babylon (Jer. 52:9-11).

The accuracy of these prophecies may be noted by comparison to the genealogies of Christ in Matthew 1 and Luke 3. The line of Joseph came through Jehoiachin, called Jekoniah in Matthew 1:12 (cf. 1 Chron. 3:17). If Joseph had been the actual father of Christ, the lineage would have been disqualified because of the prophecy that none of Jehoiachin's heirs would sit on the throne. Instead, Luke's genealogy presents the physical line of Christ through Mary and did not come under the curse of Jehoiachin (cf. Matt. 1:2-17; Luke 3:24-38). These prophecies are fulfilled in history and prophecy.

### Judgment on Israel's Shepherds

*Jeremiah 23:1-4.* God pronounced judgment on the shepherds, the spiritual leaders of Israel, because they had led His people astray and had scattered the flock (vv. 1-2). God announced, however, that He Himself would "gather the remnant of My flock out of all the countries where I have driven them and bring them back to their pasture, where they will be fruitful and increase in number" (v. 3). God declared that then He would have shepherds to care for them who would properly tend the sheep (v. 4). These prophecies were related to the second coming of Christ and speak of the millennial situation.

### The Promise of a Righteous King

*Jeremiah 23:5-8.* In this passage God revealed His long-range program to restore Israel and declared that He would restore the Davidic monarchy (v. 5). The references to Christ's coming as the King of Israel was clearly predicted (vv. 5-6). God promised that in that day both Judah, the two tribes, and Israel, the ten tribes, "will live in safety" (v. 6). The reference to Christ was made evident by the fact that He was called "the LORD Our Righteousness" (v. 6). No such event has been fulfilled in history, and it must be related like many other passages to the second coming of Christ.

### The Coming Regathering of Israel

As this prophecy would be fulfilled, God predicted, " 'So then, the days are coming,' declares the LORD, 'when people will no longer say, "As surely as the LORD lives, who brought the Israelites up out of Egypt," but they will say, "As surely as the LORD lives, who brought the descendants of Israel up out of the land of the north and out of all countries where He had banished them." Then they will live in their own land' " (vv. 7-8).

In keeping with many other prophecies, God predicted the restoration and regathering of Israel from all over the world to their ancient land, a movement which has begun in the twentieth century but will be fulfilled completely following the second coming of Christ. Though Israel was restored to her land after the years in Egypt and returned from the Babylonian and Assyrian captivities, and though a portion of them have returned to the land in the twentieth century, this prophecy has not been fulfilled and is subject to future fulfillment in connection with the Second Advent. This important passage is a clear support for the premillennial interpretation of prophecy.

### Judgment on the Lying Prophets

*Jeremiah 23:9-40.* Having declared the sure prophecy of the restoration of Israel, God who does not lie continued His judgment on the lying prophets. The wickedness of those in the land was revealed by the fact that "The land is full of adulterers" (v. 10), " 'Both prophet and priest are godless; even in My temple I find their wickedness' declares the LORD" (v. 11). The description of their wickedness, their worship of Baal, their adultery, and lies which made them like Sodom and made Jerusalem like Gomorrah is detailed (vv. 12-14). God predicted their judgment would lead to their drinking poisoned water (v. 15). Their prophecies gave "false hopes" (v. 16). The coming judgment was pictured like a storm about to break on them (v. 19). God's anger will continue until His judgment is complete (vv. 20-24). He continued to denounce their dreams from which they prophesy falsely (vv. 25-32). They were false prophets speaking false oracles (vv. 33-37). Instead of fulfilling their promises, God would bring on them everlasting disgrace (vv. 39-40). These prophecies were fulfilled in the Babylonian Captivity (2 Chron. 36:11-15).

## The Two Baskets of Figs

*Jeremiah 24:1-10.* God showed Jeremiah two baskets of fruit, one very good and the other very bad (vv. 1-2). These were used as illustrations. The good figs represented those carried off into exile to Babylon. God promised to watch over them, protect them, and eventually bring them back to their land (vv. 5-7).

By contrast, the bad figs represented those left in the land with Zedekiah as their king. Whether they remained in the land or went to Egypt, God promised to destroy them (vv. 8-10). This is fulfilled in history.

## Seventy Years of Captivity

*Jeremiah 25:1-14.* Jeremiah reminded them that they had turned away from the prophets, and even though God promised that He would bless them if they turned from their evil way (v. 5), God declared that they had not listened to Him (v. 7). Because they had not listened to God, Nebuchadnezzar, the king of Babylon, would completely destroy them, and the songs of joy and gladness would no longer be heard (vv. 9-10). The result would be that the whole country would become waste, and they would serve the king of Babylon seventy years (v. 11).

This prophecy of seventy years of Captivity is very important prophetically because it gives the chronology of the Captivity. Sixty-seven years later Daniel would read this portion of Jeremiah and would be led to pray for the return of the people of Israel (Dan. 9). It is illuminating that Daniel took the prophecy as literal years and the promise of the return to the land as a literal promise.

God promised that after the seventy years He would judge Babylon and "will make it desolate forever" (Jer. 25:12). This prophecy has never been fulfilled. When the Medes and the Persians took over Babylon, they did not destroy the city. As a matter of fact, Babylon continued for hundreds of years, even after Christ, and gradually became the desolate place it is today. Some scholars believe Babylon will be rebuilt in the last days and destroyed summarily by Jesus Christ at His second coming as may be indicated in Revelation 18 and other Scriptures. Some rebuilding of Babylon is already in progress to make it a tourist attraction. Though God used the Babylonians as a disciplining agency for the people of Israel,

God in due time will judge the Babylonians for their wickedness and enslave them also as they enslaved Israel (Jer. 25:13-14).

## The Cup of Divine Wrath

*Jeremiah 25:15-29.* God instructed Jeremiah to take "the wine of My wrath and make all the nations to whom I send you drink it" (v. 15). When they drank it, they will "stagger and go mad because of the sword I will send among them" (v. 16). Though Jeremiah obviously could not make the nations drink of the symbolic cup, it described the fact that Jerusalem would be the first to be judged (vv. 17-18). After Jerusalem would be judged, other nations would be judged as well as those itemized in the verses which follow (vv. 19-26). These nations are the ones the Babylonians had conquered, but their judgment would continue after Babylon was destroyed. Sheshach has been taken by some to be a reference to Babylon. God's judgment would bring disaster first on Jerusalem, but then on the others who lived wickedly (v. 29). These prophecies are fulfilled in history and prophecy.

## Poetic Description of the Coming Judgment

*Jeremiah 25:30-38.* This poetic section described God as coming from heaven with a mighty roar and bringing judgment on all mankind, a judgment that will not occur until the second coming of Christ.

A graphic description was also given of those who were killed in judgment by God. The wicked will be shattered like fine pottery (v. 34). The Lord will be destroying shepherds as well as their pasture (vv. 35-37). The coming of the Lord was compared to a lion leaving his lair (v. 38).

## Jeremiah Threatened

*Jeremiah 26:1-24.* Jeremiah was commanded by God to stand in the courtyard of the Lord's house and deliver God's message of coming judgment unless they repented (vv. 2-6). However, the people would not heed Jeremiah's warning. Instead of the people following Jeremiah's prophecy, they declared that Jeremiah himself must die (vv. 7-8). The matter was presented formally to the officials of Judah (vv. 10-11).

Jeremiah asserted that the prophecies he gave were those commanded by the Lord. If they kill him, they would be guilty of innocent blood (vv. 12-15). After Jeremiah's reply, his word was recognized as coming from the Lord (v. 16).

The prophecy of the Lord, given in the time of Hezekiah, that

135

Jerusalem would be destroyed was heard and believed by Hezekiah (Isa. 37:1-7), and the result was that the disaster did not fall on them (Jer. 26:17-19). When Uriah delivered the same prophecies as Jeremiah, even though he fled to Egypt, he was brought back and killed (vv. 20-23). But Jeremiah was delivered through the influence of Ahikam and not put to death (v. 24). His prophecies were fulfilled in the Babylonian Captivity.

### Jeremiah Commands King Zedekiah to Submit to Babylon

*Jeremiah 27:1-22.* Using the symbolism of a yoke and crossbars such as are used on oxen, Jeremiah informed the kings of Edom, Moab, Ammon, Tyre, and Sidon that God "will hand all your countries over to My servant Nebuchadnezzar king of Babylon; I will make even the wild animals subject to him. All nations will serve him and his son and his grandson until the time for his land comes; then many nations and great kings will subjugate him" (vv. 6-7).

God predicted that any nation that would not bow to Nebuchadnezzar would be punished "with the sword, famine, and plague" (v. 8). Accordingly, Jeremiah warned them not to listen to prophets or interpreters of dreams that told them not to serve Babylon (v. 9). Nations that bowed to Babylon would be allowed to stay in their own countries, but those who resisted Nebuchadnezzar would be carried off (vv. 10-11).

The same message previously given to other nations was delivered to Zedekiah, king of Judah. Jeremiah warned him that he should serve Babylon or be consumed by sword, famine, and plague (vv. 12-13). Accordingly, Zedekiah should not have listened to prophets who told him not to serve Babylon (vv. 14-15).

Jeremiah told the prophets that they were prophesying lies when they urged the king to resist Nebuchadnezzar. Instead, Nebuchadnezzar would take away the remaining treasures in the palace and in the house of God and would take them to Babylon (vv. 16-22). Jeremiah's prophecies were fulfilled in the Babylonian Captivity.

### The False Prophecies of Hananiah

*Jeremiah 28:1-17.* The Prophet Hananiah predicted that the yoke of Babylon would be broken (vv. 1-2) and that within two years the articles taken by Nebuchadnezzar king of Babylon would be brought back to Jerusalem and the control of Babylon over Jerusalem would be broken (vv. 3-4). Hananiah continued his prophecy that the yoke of Babylon would be broken, but Jeremiah replied that the test would be if the prediction came true (vv. 9-11).

God told Jeremiah that instead of Babylon's yoke breaking, He would put "an iron yoke on the necks of all these nations to make them serve Nebuchadnezzar king of Babylon, and they will serve him. I will even give him control over the wild animals" (vv. 13-14).

Jeremiah denounced Hananiah as a false prophet and predicted that Hananiah would die within the year (vv. 15-16). In the seventh month of that year Hananiah died (v. 17). The prophecies of Jeremiah were fulfilled in connection with the Babylonian Captivity.

### Jeremiah's First Letter to the Exiles: The Captivity to Last Seventy Years

*Jeremiah 29:1-23.* Jeremiah sent word to the surviving elders and priests and prophets, who had been carried off by Babylon into exile, to make the best of their new home, build houses, marry, and increase in number (vv. 4-7). They were told not to listen to prophets who prophesied otherwise (v. 9).

The Lord revealed to Jeremiah a very important prophecy that after seventy years of captivity in Babylon the people of Israel would be allowed to return (v. 10). God promised then to bless them and to hear their prayers (vv. 11-12). God would then bring them back from their Captivity, gather them from the various nations to which they had gone, and bring them back to the place from which they were carried off into exile (v. 14). The seventy years of Captivity was an important prophecy of Israel's future.

In regard to those who remained in the land and were not carried off to Babylon, God predicted that they would suffer "the sword, famine and plague" (v. 17), and that He would make them like "poor figs" (v. 17). God would not bless those who remained in the land during the captivities. God predicted that those who were prophesying contrary to God's truth would be put to death for their wickedness and for their lies (vv. 21-23). These prophecies are fulfilled in the history of the Captivity.

### Shemaiah, the False Prophet, to Be Punished

*Jeremiah 29:24-32.* Shemaiah complained to Zedekiah and to some priests about what Jeremiah had told the captives in Babylon that they would be there a long time (vv. 24-28). Zephaniah the priest, however, read the letter of Shemaiah to Jeremiah (v. 29). Jeremiah replied that God "will surely punish Shemaiah the Nehelamite and his descendants." They would be cut off and not have a posterity because he had preached false prophecies (vv. 31-32). This prophecy was fulfilled (2 Chron. 36:11-15).

137

### The Restoration of Israel to Their Land

*Jeremiah 30:1-11.* This section is a far-reaching prophecy from Jeremiah concerning the ultimate regathering of Israel and the restoration to their land (vv. 2-3). In particular, the Lord prophesied a time of distress for Israel such as she had never experienced before (vv. 4-7; cf. Matt. 24:15-30). God assured Israel, however, that "he [Jacob] will be saved out of it" (Jer. 30:7).

God further predicted that Israel's slavery would end, and instead of serving foreigners she would serve God and David her king (vv. 8-9). The timing of this prophecy is of great significance because it was linked to the resurrection of "David their king whom I will raise up for them" (v. 9). David's resurrection will be connected with the second coming of Christ and will be part of the resurrection of Old Testament saints which will also occur at the time of the Second Coming (cf. Dan. 12:2-3). This prophecy has never been fulfilled and was part of the revelation contained in many Old Testament passages concerning the restoration of Israel to their land. This prophecy supports the chronology of pretribulationists that Israel must undergo an unprecedented time of trouble before the Second Advent, will be rescued by Christ at His coming, coinciding with David's resurrection, and will enjoy deliverance and blessing in the time period following the Second Coming.

God exhorted Israel not to be dismayed (v. 10) because God would surely save her out of a distant place, including her descendants from the land of her exile (v. 10). God promised that Jacob would have peace and security, and there would be no one to make him afraid (v. 10). God promised to save Israel. Even though He completely destroys the other nations, He would never destroy Israel (v. 11). He would, however, discipline her and not leave her unpunished (v. 11).

### Israel's Judgment Inevitable

*Jeremiah 30:12-15.* In regard to the generation of Israel living at the time of Jeremiah, God declared her wounds incurable (v. 12). He declared that Israel's guilt and sin were so much that it made necessary God's judgment on her (vv. 13-15). This was fulfilled in the Babylonian Captivity.

### Another Promise of Restoration

*Jeremiah 30:16-24.* God promised also to judge those who have attacked Israel but, by contrast, God would restore Israel to health (vv. 16-17).

God promised ultimately to restore Israel as a nation and to rebuild the city and the palace (v. 18). God predicted that there would be thanksgiving and rejoicing and honor for Israel in those days (vv. 19-20). God also promised to raise up a ruler who would bring her close to God (v. 21). The fact that Israel had a special relationship to God was mentioned in many Old Testament passages (Lev. 26:12; Deut. 7:6; 26:16-19; Jer. 7:23; 11:4; 24:7; 31:1, 33; Ezek. 11:20; 14:11; 34:30; 36:28; 37:23, 27; Hosea 2:23; Zech. 8:8; 13:9).

Jeremiah added his confirming word to what the Lord had said, that God would come like a storm and judge the wicked, and His fierce anger would not depart until He accomplishes His purpose. These prophecies are fulfilled in history and prophecy.

### Israel's Future Blessings

*Jeremiah 31:1.* Summarizing the preceding chapter, God declared that He would be Israel's God and she would be His people.

*Jeremiah 31:2-30.* This entire section describes Israel's future blessings, her return to the land, her joy in serving the Lord, and the fact that she would be gathered from all over the earth (vv. 1-9). This theme continued to be unfolded in the fact that God will gather Israel from distant places and she will return in prosperity and joy and will experience the bounty of the Lord (vv. 10-14). This will follow the Second Advent.

In the midst of her joy, however, there also will be weeping, a passage quoted in Matthew 2:18 in regard to Herod's killing of the infants of Bethlehem (v. 16). God exhorted her, however, to restrain from weeping and to look forward to the wonderful hope she has in Christ. Her discipline and her problems were part of her being brought back to the Lord, but God actually had great compassion for Israel (Jer. 31:16-20).

God exhorted individual Israelites to return to the land of Israel from their wanderings (vv. 21-22). Jeremiah left with them, a prophecy difficult to understand, "The LORD will create a new thing on earth — a woman will surround a man" (v. 22). Normally a man courts a woman, but in this case the woman will be Israel who will attempt to come back to God.

Another description was given of the blessings on Israel when she returns to her land in the Millennium. It will be a time when the Lord refreshes the weary and satisfies the faint (vv. 23-25).

In verse 26 Jeremiah spoke of awaking from sleep after sleep has been pleasant. Though the significance of this is not clear, it is possible that the preceding passage was given to him when he was in a trance or in a dream. Another promise of the restoration of Israel after her time of trouble was given (vv. 27-30).

### The New Covenant

*Jeremiah 31:31-40.* God declared He would make a New Covenant with Israel (v. 31). This would be in contrast to the Mosaic Covenant which He gave them in Egypt (v. 32). In the New Covenant God declared, " 'I will put My Law in their minds and write it on their hearts. I will be their God and they will be My people. No longer will a man teach his neighbor, or a man his brother, saying, "Know the LORD," because they will all know Me, from the least of them to the greatest,' declares the LORD. 'For I will forgive their wickedness and will remember their sins no more' " (vv. 33-34).

This is one of the great prophecies in the Old Testament that described the New Covenant that God will make, a gracious covenant stemming from the death of Christ, making it possible for God to forgive Israel as well as the Gentiles who come to Him. Though God in grace has saved and blessed Israel in the past, the major fulfillment for Israel will be after the Second Coming when she will be regathered to her land.

The absolute certainty of the New Covenant was described in verses 35-36. The New Covenant would be as sure as the natural laws that move the moon and the stars and stir up the sea. As long as these laws of nature continue, God would continue His promises to Israel. This covenant would not be a conditional covenant like the Mosaic Covenant.

Just as Israel will be graciously forgiven under the New Covenant, so also the church in the present age receives grace. All grace systems stem from the death of Christ, whether applied to Israel or other peoples. Hence, the church in the present age also participates in a New Covenant. This can best be explained as one New Covenant of grace made possible by the death of Christ, whether applied to Israel as in Jeremiah or the church as in the New Testament. All grace has its origin in the new promise of grace which has various applications. Jeremiah makes its application to Israel which will largely be fulfilled in connection with the coming kingdom on earth following the Second Coming.

The second reassuring pledge of the Lord declared that only if the heavens can be measured and the earth be searched out beneath would He reject the descendants of Israel (v. 37). As a matter of fact, even modern man with his great telescopes has not been able to find the end of the universe. The continuation of the sun and moon is a constant reminder that God is still keeping His promises to Israel and preserving her as a nation. The New Covenant is a major prophetic revelation given further treatment in the New Testament, and its gracious promises will continue forever.

In the time related to the future kingdom, God declared that Jerusalem "will be rebuilt for Me from the Tower of Hananel to the Corner Gate. The measuring line will stretch from there straight to the hill of Gareb and then turn to Goath. The whole valley where dead bodies and ashes are thrown, and all the terraces out to the Kidron Valley on the east as far as the corner of the Horse Gate, will be holy to the LORD. The city will never again be uprooted or demolished" (vv. 38-40).

This remarkable prophecy, given by Jeremiah almost 2,500 years ago, has seen modern fulfillment in the recapture of Jerusalem. Modern Jerusalem has built up this precise area, and today there are lovely apartments and streets in a location formerly used as a place for garbage heaps and dead bodies. In spite of the fact that Jerusalem has been demolished many times, God declared that this section will not be demolished but will continue to be holy to the Lord until the Second Coming. This prophecy is one of the signs that the coming of the Lord may be near.

### Jeremiah Commanded to Buy a Field

*Jeremiah 32:1-41.* Jeremiah was confined to the courtyard of the guard in the royal palace because Zedekiah, king of Judah, heard Jeremiah's prophecy that the city would be captured by the Babylonians (v. 3). He also had heard that the Lord had announced that "Zedekiah king of Judah will not escape out of the hands of the Babylonians but will certainly be handed over to the king of Babylon, and will speak to him face to face and see him with his own eyes" (v. 4). Jeremiah's prophecy further declared that Zedekiah would be taken to Babylon and that if Israel fought against the Babylonians they would not succeed (v. 5).

As a token of the promise of God that Israel would come back to the land, Jeremiah was instructed to buy a piece of land from Hanamel, his cousin (vv. 6-7). In obedience to God, Jeremiah bought the land and had it properly registered (vv. 8-12). Then Jeremiah instructed Baruch to take the documents and place them in a clay jar so that they would last for a long time. Jeremiah predicted, "For this is what the Lord Almighty, the God of Israel, says: 'Houses, fields and vineyards will again be bought in this land' " (v. 15).

After this transaction Jeremiah prayed concerning God's dealings with Israel in the past, her present siege by the Babylonians, and predicted that the city will be handed over to them (vv. 17-25).

God repeated the prophecy that He would hand over the city of Jerusalem to the Babylonians (vv. 26-28). The Babylonians would capture the city and burn it because the people of Judah had provoked God to anger by offering incense to Baal (v. 29).

The reasons for God's judgment on Israel were detailed as Israel had provoked God to wrath, had set up idols, and worshiped heathen gods (vv. 30-35). In spite of Israel's sins and God's punishment of her, He promised, "I will bring them back to this place and let them live in safety. They will be My people, and I will be their God" (vv. 37-38). God promised an everlasting covenant of grace, and God would continue to do them good (vv. 39-40).

God reiterated His plan to bring Israel back to her land where fields would be sold and deeds would be signed. God promised to restore her fortunes (vv. 42-44). This was fulfilled after the Babylonian Captivity.

### Restoration to Follow the Babylonian Captivity
*Jeremiah 33:1-26.* God predicted that Babylon would conquer Jerusalem and that her houses would be filled with dead bodies (vv. 4-5).

Just as God brought judgment on Israel for her sins, so God would extend in grace the healing ministry for His people in the future. Both Israel and Judah would come back from their captivity (vv. 6-7). God would cleanse them from sin and forgive their rebellion (v. 8). Once again they would have renown, joy, honor, and abundant prosperity (vv. 8-9). These promises of future blessing would result in their offering praise to God (vv. 10-11). God reiterated His promise to restore Israel. Her pastures would have shepherds and flocks (vv. 12-13).

In the future restoration of Israel in the Millennium God will raise up a Descendant from David (v. 15). In His days Jerusalem and Judah will be safe, and His name is called "The Lord Our Righteousness" (v. 16). God promised that the house of David would never fail to have a man who is qualified to sit on the throne, and the same would be true of the priests and the Levites (vv. 17-18). This will be fulfilled by Christ. Here God confirmed His covenant with Israel as one that cannot be broken. God promised that His people would be countless as the stars and measureless as the sand (vv. 19-22; cf. Gen. 15:5; 26:4; 28:14).

The report that God had completely rejected the kingdom of Israel and the kingdom of Judah was not true. God declared He had established His covenant with them as well as the laws that govern day and night.

### Warning to Zedekiah and Judah's Leaders

*Jeremiah 34:1-22.* God announced through Jeremiah that Zedekiah, the king of Judah, would be taken to Babylon, that Jerusalem would be burned down, and that Zedekiah would speak face-to-face with Nebuchadnezzar (vv. 2-3; cf. 32:4-5). God promised that Zedekiah would die peacefully (v. 4) and would be honored in his death (v. 5). These facts were reported to Zedekiah (v. 6).

Because the Children of Israel had failed to keep the law of freedom of slaves, for when they did temporarily free them they enslaved them again, God prophesied that He would judge them (vv. 8-16). As they had not obeyed God in freeing slaves, so God would free them "to fall by the sword, plague and famine" (v. 17). The result would be that the leaders of Jerusalem and those who participated in this would be handed over to the enemy and killed (vv. 18-20). As previously prophesied, Zedekiah would be handed over to the king of Babylon and the city would be burned (vv. 21-22). This was fulfilled in history (2 Kings 24:18–25:8).

### The Faithfulness of the Recabites

*Jeremiah 35:1-19.* This chapter records the faithfulness of the family of the Recabites to obey their forefather and not build houses, plant crops, or drink wine. They had fully obeyed their father.

In recognition of this, God revealed to Jeremiah, "Go and tell the men of Judah and the people of Jerusalem, 'Will you not learn a lesson and obey My words?' declares the LORD. 'Jonadab son of Recab ordered his sons not to drink wine and this commandment has been kept. To this day they do not drink wine, because they obey their forefather's command. But I have spoken to you again and again, yet you have not obeyed Me. Again and again I sent all My servants and prophets to you. They said, "Each of you must turn from your wicked ways and reform your actions; do not follow other gods to serve them. Then you will live in the land I have

143

given to you and your fathers." But you have not paid attention or listened to Me. The descendants of Jonadab son of Recab have carried out the command their forefather gave them, but these people have not obeyed Me' " (vv. 13-16).

Because of the record of Judah and Israel in rebelling against God, God promised to bring on them all the disasters He had predicted. In recognition of the family of Recab and their faithfulness, God promised, "Jonadab son of Recab will never fail to have a man to serve Me" (v. 19).

## Destruction of Jeremiah's Writing

*Jeremiah 36:1-26.* In obedience to the command from the Lord, Jeremiah dictated all his prophecies to Baruch who wrote them on a scroll (vv. 1-4). Jeremiah then instructed Baruch to read the scroll before the house of the Lord to the people gathered there in hope that they would repent (vv. 5-7). In keeping with the command of God, Baruch read the prophecies of Jeremiah (vv. 8-10).

When it became known that Jeremiah had had his scroll read, Jehudi instructed Baruch to bring him the scroll (vv. 11-14). When it was read (vv. 15-18), the officials told Jeremiah and Baruch to hide where they could not be found (v. 19).

When the scroll was read in the presence of the king, he cut it in pieces and threw it in the fire until it was burned (vv. 20-23). Though some protested, most of them did not (v. 24). The king commanded that Baruch and Jeremiah be arrested (v. 26).

## Jeremiah Ordered to Write Another Scroll

*Jeremiah 36:27-32.* Jeremiah was instructed by God to take another scroll and write what he had written before and additional words. God also pronounced judgment on Jehoiakim and his posterity, "He will have no one to sit on the throne of David; his body will be thrown out and exposed to the heat by day and frost by night. I will punish him and his children and his attendants for their wickedness; I will bring on them and those living in Jerusalem and the people of Judah every disaster I pronounced against them, because they have not listened" (vv. 30-31; cf. 22:30). In obedience to God, Jeremiah took another scroll and dictated his prophecies and additional words to Baruch. These prophecies are fulfilled in history.

## Jeremiah's Imprisonment

*Jeremiah 37:1-17.* None of the king's attendants or the people paid any attention to the prophecies of Jeremiah (vv. 1-2). Zedekiah, however, sent word to Jeremiah to pray for him (v. 3). Because

Pharaoh's army had come from Egypt and attacked the Babylonians, the Babylonian siege of Jerusalem was lifted (vv. 4-5).

Jeremiah instructed the king that when Pharaoh's army would go back to Egypt, the Babylonians would return, attack the city, and burn it down (vv. 7-8). God stated through Jeremiah that they should not be deceived, that Babylon would certainly come and destroy them (vv. 9-10).

When Jeremiah attempted to leave Jerusalem, he was arrested, beaten, and imprisoned (vv. 11-15). Jeremiah, however, was brought in secret to King Zedekiah in order that he might know whether there was a word from God. " 'Yes,' " Jeremiah replied, 'You will be handed over to the king of Babylon' " (v. 17). This prophecy was fulfilled (2 Kings 25:5-7).

### Jeremiah Delivered from Prison

*Jeremiah 37:18-21.* Jeremiah's request to be taken out of the dungeon and be given bread was heard by King Zedekiah, and he ordered him to remain in the courtyard of the guard.

### Jeremiah Thrown in a Cistern

*Jeremiah 38:1-13.* When Jeremiah continued to repeat the prophecy of God that Babylon would capture the city, he instructed those to leave the city because those who remain would die "by the sword, famine or plague, but whoever goes over to the Babylonians will live. He will escape with his life; he will live" (v. 2). These prophecies were fulfilled in connection with the Babylonian Captivity.

The officials complained to the king that Jeremiah should be put to death because he was discouraging the people. The king allowed them to do what they wished. The result was that Jeremiah was placed in a cistern where, ultimately, he would have died (vv. 5-6).

Ebed-Melech, an official in the palace, went to the king and reported that Jeremiah had been thrown in the cistern and the king commanded that he be taken out (vv. 7-10). So Jeremiah was taken out and remained in the courtyard of the king (vv. 10-13).

### Zedekiah Again Warned

*Jeremiah 38:14-28.* Called in by Zedekiah to give a word from God, Jeremiah reported that if he surrendered to Babylon, he would be spared and the city not burned. If he did not, he would not be spared and Jerusalem would be burned down (vv. 14-17). Zedekiah revealed to Jeremiah that he was afraid of the Jews, but Jeremiah urged him to obey the Lord and it would go well with him (vv. 19-21).

Jeremiah predicted that the women in the palace would be brought out to the Babylonians (v. 22). They would say that Zedekiah had been betrayed by his trusted friends. When Zedekiah's feet would be sunk in the mud, he would find that his friends had deserted him (v. 22). The prophecy was repeated that those who go to the king of Babylon would be rescued, and if they did not go to the Babylonians the city would be burned down (v. 23). Zedekiah urged Jeremiah not to tell anyone what he had told the king (vv. 24-26). Jeremiah did not reveal what he had told the king (v. 27), and he remained in the courtyard until Jerusalem was captured (v. 28). Jeremiah's prophecies were fulfilled.

### The Fall of Jerusalem

*Jeremiah 39:1-18.* These prophecies were literally fulfilled. When the Babylonians finally conquered Jerusalem, Zedekiah and many others attempted to flee, but they were overtaken by the Babylonians (vv. 1-5). Zedekiah's sons were killed before his eyes as well as the nobles of Judah. Then they blinded Zedekiah, bound him with bronze shackles, and took him to Babylon (vv. 6-7). The sad results of ignoring prophecy were graphically portrayed in these incidents. The Babylonians set fire to the city and the palaces, took the people of the city in Captivity to Babylon but left the poor of the land behind (vv. 8-10).

Jeremiah was given favorable treatment by the Babylonians and was allowed to remain with his people. Jeremiah sent word, however, to Ebed-Melech, the Cushite, that the Lord would protect him from destruction and rescue him because he had put his trust in the Lord. Ebed-Melech had been the one who caused Jeremiah to be rescued from the cistern (38:7-9).

### Jeremiah Freed

*Jeremiah 40:1-6.* Jeremiah had been chained along with other prisoners to go to Babylon, but when he was located he was released and allowed to choose whether to go to Babylon or not (vv. 1-4). Jeremiah elected to remain behind (v. 5). Jeremiah then stayed with Gedaliah and others who stayed behind (v. 6).

### Gedaliah Assassinated

*Jeremiah 40:7–41:18.* Many people who had run away came back and began to settle down in the land. Gedaliah was warned about a plot to assassinate him but did not believe it. In keeping with the warning, Ishmael, the son of Nethaniah of royal blood, assassinated Gedaliah (41:1-3). Those who came to Gedaliah, bringing their offerings, not knowing he had been killed, were slaughtered by Ishmael, except for some who claimed to have treasure (vv. 4-9). The rest were made captives (v. 10). Jeremiah's prophecy was fulfilled.

Ishmael, however, was overthrown and had to flee for his life (vv. 11-15). Those who had participated in the overthrow of Ishmael were afraid that the Babylonians would punish them, and so they escaped to Egypt (vv. 16-18).

### Officers of the Army Go to Egypt

*Jeremiah 42:1-22.* The people who were left came to Jeremiah and asked him to pray to the Lord to find out what they should do (vv. 1-3). They promised to obey the Lord (vv. 4-6). Jeremiah prayed for them and the Lord answered (v. 7). They were told to remain in the land with Jeremiah and God would bless them. If they would not stay in the land and go to Egypt, they would be destroyed (vv. 13-18). Jeremiah warned them, because they were disobeying God and going to Egypt anyway, that God would destroy them (vv. 19-22).

### Jeremiah Taken to Egypt

*Jeremiah 43:1-13.* In disobedience to God the people went to Egypt. Jeremiah delivered the prophecy of God that Nebuchadnezzar would pursue them into Egypt and destroy them in fulfillment of this prophecy (vv. 8-13).

### The Continued Rebellion of Israel

*Jeremiah 44:1-14.* Jeremiah delivered the word of the Lord to those in Egypt, that God's anger would be against them and that they would be the object of cursing and reproach. They would all perish by sword, famine, or plague. This was fulfilled in history.

### Idolatry in Egypt

*Jeremiah 44:15-30.* The Jews rejected the warning of Jeremiah and announced that they would worship the gods of Egypt (vv. 15-19). Jeremiah reminded them how God had punished the people of Israel. When they refused to listen (vv. 20-24), Jeremiah reminded them that God would cause them to perish and that He would give them a sign that He would punish them in this place, that is, that Pharaoh Hophrah, king of Egypt, would be handed over to Nebuchadnezzar, the king of Babylon. This prophecy as well as Ezekiel 29:19-20, which was given in 571 B.C., indicated the invasion was still future and it probably was fulfilled between 571 and 567 B.C.

### Jeremiah's Message to Baruch

*Jeremiah 45:1-5.* In the fourth year of Jehoiakim, Jeremiah told Baruch, who was overwhelmed by the tragedies that had overtaken his people, that he himself would escape the disaster that would overtake his people. Baruch had been the stenographer who wrote at Jeremiah's dictation (36:4, 32). The many prophecies about the destruction of Jerusalem were literally fulfilled.

# PROPHECY IN JEREMIAH CONCERNING THE NATIONS
### Egypt's Downfall

*Jeremiah 46:1-12.* Prophecies about the nations began with the prediction of Egypt's downfall to the armies of Babylon. One of the most important battles in the ancient world occurred at Carchemish in 605 B.C. The Babylonian armies decisively defeated Egypt and ended any Egyptian claim to influence the Holy Land. The Babylonian army had lifted its siege of Jerusalem in order to fight the Egyptians (cf. Jer. 37:4-13). After defeating the Egyptians, they came back and conquered Jerusalem. Jeremiah in this Scripture prophesied very graphically how the Egyptian army fell before the Babylonians. Egypt would never rise to great power again.

### Invasion of Egypt

*Jeremiah 46:13-26.* After the defeat of the Egyptians, the Babylonian armies later invaded Egypt. This was in keeping with earlier prophecies of Jeremiah that God would pursue the Israelites who fled to Egypt and would search them out and deliver them to the Babylonians (cf. 42:13-22). Jeremiah's prophecy not only predicted the invasions but pictured Egypt being laid waste and lying in ruins. It would be their day of disaster (46:21). God would use the Babylonians to bring judgment on the gods of Egypt (v. 25). Though the destruction of Egypt was to be extensive, later Egypt would resume her normal life (v. 26).

### The Later Restoration of Israel

*Jeremiah 46:27-28.* In contrast to the destruction brought on Egypt, God reassured Israel that she would ultimately be restored to her land and made safe and secure (v. 27). Though God would deal severely with those Israelites who had fled to Egypt, ultimately the nation would be restored. God declares, "Though I completely destroy all the nations among which I scatter you, I will not completely destroy you. I will discipline you but only with justice; I will not let you go entirely unpunished" (v. 28). This same thought is declared in Jeremiah 30:11. This is fulfilled in history and will be fulfilled in the Millennium.

PROPHECY IN JEREMIAH

### Prophecy about the Philistines

*Jeremiah 47:1-7.* The second nation to be destroyed according to Jeremiah's prophecy was the land of the Philistines. They occupied an area along the coast of Judah and periodically would rise in power to attack Israel and other nations. Many such incidents were recorded in Scripture (cf. Jud. 3:1-4, 31; 13–16; 1 Sam. 7:2-17; 1 Sam. 13:1–14:23; 28:1-4; 29:1-2, 11; 31:1-10; 2 Sam. 5:17-25; 8:1; 2 Chron. 21:16-17; 28:16-18). This section described a battle between Philistia and Pharaoh Neco, king of Egypt (cf. 2 Kings 23:29-30). This event probably occurred about 609 B.C.

Ashkelon, which was described as being destroyed (Jer. 47:5), was conquered by the Babylonians in 604 B.C. Though Ashkelon was rebuilt numerous times in its history after the seventh century B.C., the ancient ruins which are visible today are dramatic proof of God's judgment on it. The ruined city of Ashkelon is a testimony to fulfilled prophecy, and alongside it is the modern city of Ashkelon as one of the five most important cities of Philistia. Ashkelon was mentioned often in Scripture (Jud. 1:18; 14:19; 1 Sam. 6:17; 2 Sam. 1:20; Jer. 25:20; Amos 1:8; Zeph. 2:4, 7; Zech. 9:5).

### Prophecy about Moab

*Jeremiah 48:1-47.* The destruction of Moab was described as complete (v. 8). The Moabites were descendants of Lot's elder daughter (Gen. 19:36-37). Nebo and Kirjathaim were cities originally possessed by the tribe of Reuben but were conquered by the Moabites. Heshbon, another city once owned by the tribe of Reuben, also was to be destroyed. Other prophecies in Scripture related also to Moab (Isa. 15–16; Ezek. 25:8-11; Amos 2:1-3; Zeph. 2:8-11). From available evidence, scholars believe that Moab was destroyed in 582 B.C. by the Babylonians. The god of the Moabites, Chemosh, would no longer have her worship or honor.

Jeremiah described the word from the Lord as a prophecy of the further destruction of Moab (Jer. 48:11-12). They would be ashamed of Chemosh her God (v. 13). Her finest young men would be killed (v. 15).

Judgment was declared on the main cities of Moab which are named (vv. 20-24). Though once they scorned Israel, they would have to abandon their cities and live among rocks (v. 28).

Moab's pride, which had been so evident in her boasting in times past, now would be turned to weeping (vv. 29-33). Her cries of distress would be heard from Heshbon to Elealeh and Jahaz (v. 34).

No longer would she bring offerings to her gods (v. 35). Her wealth would be gone (v. 36). Moab would be shattered like a piece of pottery and the object of ridicule (vv. 37-39).

In concluding his predictions concerning Moab, the Lord indicates that her destruction would be complete (vv. 40-44). It would be a country destroyed by fire (v. 45), and her sons and daughters would be taken into exile (v. 46). At the conclusion of the prediction, however, God predicted the future restoration of Moab (v. 47; cf. 49:39).

## Prophecy about Ammon

*Jeremiah 49:1-6.* A devastating invasion and destruction of the land of the Ammonites was described in this prophecy that Jeremiah received from the Lord. The Ammonites were descendants of Lot's younger daughter (Gen. 19:38). Its capital city, Rabbah, would "become a mound of ruins" (Jer. 49:2). Ai, mentioned as destroyed (v. 3), is not the Ai in Joshua 7, but its location is unknown. Like his prophecy concerning Moab, though the destruction was extensive, God promised to "restore the fortunes of the Ammonites" (Jer. 49:6).

## Prophecy about Edom

*Jeremiah 49:7-22.* The Edomites, who lived in the area east of the Dead Sea, were descendants of Esau and traditional enemies of Israel. Throughout Israel's history there was constant conflict with the Edomites (cf. Num. 20:18-21; 1 Sam. 14:47; 2 Sam. 8:13-14; 1 Kings 11:14-23; 2 Chron. 20:22). The Edomites were denounced by later prophets (Isa. 34:5-8; 63:1-4; Lam. 4:21; Ezek. 25:13-14; Amos 1:11-12; Obad. 8-10).

Here the prophecy described the disaster that would fall on the Edomites as bringing on them ruin and horror (v. 13). The nations were urged to attack Edom (Jer. 49:14-15). "Edom will become an object of horror; all who pass by will be appalled and will scoff because of all its wounds" (v. 17). It was described as being overthrown like Sodom and Gomorrah (v. 18). The enemy was described like a lion (v. 19) and a swooping eagle (v. 22). No prophecy was given here concerning Edom's restoration. The Edomites disappeared from history after the destruction of Jerusalem in A.D. 70.

## Prophecy about Damascus

*Jeremiah 49:23-27.* Damascus, one of the oldest cities in the Middle East, was described here as being destroyed by fire. It was first mentioned in Scripture in Genesis 14:15 and continued to be an important city throughout biblical history. Though destroyed by the Assyrians, it was later rebuilt before Jeremiah's time. Here it was destroyed once again. Its destruction here prophesied in Jeremiah was predicted also in Isaiah 7:8; 8:4; 17:1-3. In New Testament times it again was a flourishing city. The home of Ananias in Damascus, where Paul went after his conversion, has been identified. Damascus, referred to as "the city of renown" (Jer. 49:25), was described here as suffering defeat of its soldiers and fire on its walls.

### Prophecy about Kedar and Hazor

*Jeremiah 49:28-33.* The Babylonian attack on Kedar and Hazor was predicted (v. 28). Kedar was a tribe descending from the Ishmaelites (Gen. 25:13). She was renowned for her excellence in archery (Isa. 21:16-17) and for her sheep (60:7) which were declared destroyed in this attack on them (Jer. 49:29). The reference to Hazor is not to the city by that name in Israel but a city apparently located somewhere in the Arabian desert. The destruction of these cities was along with the other conquests of the Babylonians in the period of Nebuchadnezzar's power.

### Prophecy concerning Elam

*Jeremiah 49:34-39.* The prophecy concerning Elam referred to an area east of Babylon, known today as Iran. The destruction of Elam was described as breaking her bow, for, like Kedar, Elam was noted for archery. The complete destruction of Elam does not seem to have been fulfilled in history and may have its final chapter in the future in connection with judgments at the second coming of Christ. Elam was promised, however, restoration (v. 39).

### Prophecy about Babylon

*Jeremiah 50:1–51:64.* The final two chapters of Jeremiah relate to Babylon and its future destruction. The prophecy revealed that a great nation from the north would attack her (50:3), probably referred to Medo-Persia and its conquest of Babylon described in Daniel 5. Because Babylon continued to figure in biblical history and prophecy until the time of the second coming of Christ, some of these prophecies may have their ultimate fulfillment at that time (cf. Rev. 17–18).

Prophecies concerning Babylon, stated extensively in these final chapters of Jeremiah, confirmed many other prophecies concerning Babylon's destruction (cf. Isa. 13:1–14:23; 21:1-9; Jer. 25:10-14, 26). The Scriptures are plain on the destruction of Babylon, "Babylon will be captured; Bel will be put to shame" (Jer. 50:2), referring to the god of Babylon (51:44; cf. Isa. 46:1). Marduk was an important deity of Babylon. According to the prophecy, "Marduk" will be "filled with terror. Her images will be put to shame and her idols filled with terror" (Jer. 50:2). The nation "from the land of the north" mentioned in verse 9 was also mentioned in verse 3. The invader will "lay waste her land. No one will live in it; both men and animals will flee away" (v. 3). As this, like the prophecies of Isaiah 13:1-16, was not completely fulfilled in history, it may relate to the final destruction of Babylon at the second coming of Christ (cf. Rev. 18). In the midst of the description of judgment on Babylon, reassurance was given Israel that ultimately she would be restored and forgiven (Jer. 50:4-5).

In this prophecy the complete destruction of Babylon was described in detail (vv. 11-16). As this and the preceding prophecies of the destruction of Babylon did not occur when the Medes and the Persians conquered Babylon, there seems to be another reference here to the final destruction of Babylon at the time of the Second Coming.

In the midst of these prophecies concerning Babylon, prophetic revelation was given concerning Israel. Though crushed both by Assyria and Babylon, God promised to punish Israel's oppressors. The day would come when Israel's guilt would be forgiven and Israel would be brought back to her own land (vv. 18-20).

Babylon was described as the nation completely destroyed (v. 26). Her enemies were charged with letting none escape (v. 29) and instructed to silence her soldiers (v. 30). Babylon's punishment was great because she was "arrogant" (vv. 31-32). Though God would again deal with Israel in mercy, He would not deal with Babylon in this way (vv. 33-34).

God called for a sword against Babylon, against her false prophets, against all other Babylonians (vv. 35-38). Babylon was described as a city which "will never again be inhabited or lived in from generation to generation. As God overthrew Sodom and Gomorrah along with their neighboring towns" (vv. 39-40), God declared, "so no one will live there; no man will dwell in it" (v. 40). Like other prophecies in connection with the destruction of Babylon, these punishments have never been completely fulfilled and seem to indicate a future destruction of Babylon in connection with the second coming of Christ (Rev. 17:18).

The army from the north was again mentioned (v. 41). Babylon would be in anxiety and anguish when they hear reports of the coming army. Again, a complete destruction of Babylon was described (v. 45).

The prophetic revelation concerning Babylon continued as Babylon's destruction was described (51:1-10). "Leb Kamai" is an unusual expression apparently meaning "the heart of my attackers." Those who came to Babylon as foreigners would devastate her completely (v. 2). Her young would not be spared and her army would be completely destroyed (v. 3). Though Babylon would be destroyed, Israel and Judah would not be forsaken (v. 5). Babylon was declared to fall suddenly and be broken (v. 8).

In this passage (vv. 11-14) the attackers were described as "the kings of the Medes" who actually conquered Babylon in 539 B.C. In the conquering of Babylon this promise was fulfilled. The prophetic message was based on the fact that God is sovereign, that He created the world and is able to control its events (vv. 15-16). By contrast, the people of Babylon were "senseless and without knowledge" (v. 17). Her idols "are a fraud; they have no breath in them" (v. 17). God is not like these idols. He is the Lord Almighty (v. 19).

God declared that He would "shatter nations, with you I destroy kingdoms" (v. 20). He would also shatter their horses, their chariots, men and women, old men and youth, shepherd and flock, farmer and oxen, governors and officials (vv. 21-23). God said that He was repaying Babylon "for all the wrong they have done in Zion" (v. 24). Again God declared that Babylon "will be desolate forever" (v. 26).

God revealed that He would summon Ararat, Minni and Ashkenaz to fight against Babylon (v. 27). These people were all warlike and apparently had part in the battle against Babylon. "The kings of the Medes" again were fighting Babylon (v. 28). The destruction of Babylon and her warriors was described in graphic terms (vv. 29-32). Babylon was "like a threshing floor at the time it is trampled; the time to harvest her will soon come" (v. 33).

Just as Nebuchadnezzar had devoured Israel, so God would devour Babylon (vv. 34-35). Her destruction was described in graphic terms (vv. 36-39). Babylon was being led "like lambs to the slaughter, like rams and goats" (v. 40). The complete destruction of Babylon would leave it like "a dry and desert land, a land where no one lives" (v. 43). Bel, the god of Babylon, will be punished and "the wall of Babylon will fall" (v. 44).

Babylon would be destroyed by attackers from the north, resulting in their idols being punished and the whole land being disgraced. The destruction of Babylon was a result of their cruel dealing with Israel. God declared " 'But days are coming,' declares the LORD, 'when I will punish her idols, and throughout her land the wounded will groan. Even if Babylon reaches the sky and fortifies her lofty stronghold, I will send destroyers against her,' declares the LORD" (vv. 52-53). The destruction of Babylon was caused by "a God of retribution; He will repay in full" (v. 56). Even though Babylon's walls were thick, they would be leveled and her gates set on fire (v. 58).

In this passage Jeremiah delivered a message to Seraiah, the son of Neriah, at the time when he went with Zedekiah to Babylon (v. 59). Nebuchadnezzar had summoned his vassal kings to Babylon for a conference, attempting to avoid insurrection. Seraiah was instructed to read the prophecies of Jeremiah concerning the destruction of Babylon (v. 62), apparently a copy of the prophecies from the larger manuscript. After the scroll was read, he was instructed, "Tie a stone to it and throw it in the Euphrates River. Then say, 'So will Babylon sink to rise no more because of the disaster I will bring upon her. And her people will fall' " (v. 64). Jeremiah stated that this was the end of his prophecies. The final chapter was appended by someone else.

### The Fall of Jerusalem and Beginning of the Captivity of Judah

*Jeremiah 52:1-34.* Jeremiah chapter 52 is clearly similar to 2 Kings 24:18–25:30. The opening portion of Jeremiah 52 recorded Zedekiah's rebellion against Babylon, with the result that Nebuchadnezzar marched against Jerusalem and destroyed it (vv. 1-8). Zedekiah saw his sons killed before his eyes and he saw the execution of all the officials of Judah. Then he was blinded and taken to Babylon, bound with bronze shackles (vv. 10-11; cf. 39:6-7). This was a literal fulfillment of the prophecies given to Zedekiah.

"In the nineteenth year of Nebuchadnezzar king of Babylon" the temple, the royal palace, and all the houses of Jerusalem were destroyed by fire (52:12-13). This occurred in 586 B.C., nineteen years after Babylon first conquered Jerusalem. Jerusalem's walls were destroyed and many were carried captive (v. 15). Only the poorest of the people were left behind (v. 16). Various articles and

154

decorations of the temple were broken down and taken away to Babylon (vv. 17-23).

The important leaders of Jerusalem were carried off and later executed (vv. 24-27). All of this constituted fulfillment of the many prophecies of Jeremiah concerning the destruction of Jerusalem.

Those who were carried into Captivity were enumerated, including 4,600 people in all.

The concluding note of the Book of Jeremiah concerned the release of Jehoiachin in 561 B.C. when Evil-Merodach was king of Babylon after Nebuchadnezzar's death. Jehoiachin was taken out of prison, given a seat of honor, and treated as a king at the king's table for the rest of his life (vv. 31-34).

The Book of Jeremiah, containing hundreds of prophecies, is a dramatic proof that biblical prophecy is subject to literal fulfillment. The idea that prophecy is fulfilled in a nonliteral way is almost entirely absent in Jeremiah.

# 6

# PROPHECY IN EZEKIEL

## PROPHECY OF JUDGMENT ON JUDAH IN EZEKIEL

Predicted judgments on the kingdom of Judah occupy the first twenty-four chapters of Ezekiel. This is followed by judgment on the Gentile nations in Ezekiel 25–32 and prophecy of blessings on Israel (Ezek. 33–48).

Ezekiel himself was a priest who had been carried off in the Babylonian Captivity. He and the other captives had settled "by the Kebar River in the land of the Babylonians" (1:2). It was a canal to the east of Babylon which connected one point in the Euphrates River to another point lower down. This forms the geographical background of this prophetic book. As the revelation unfolds, further facts are given about Ezekiel.

### Preparation of Ezekiel as a Prophet

*Ezekiel 1:1–3:15.* Though not strictly prophetic in themselves, the opening chapters of Ezekiel prepared the prophet for the series of revelations and visions that he would experiece as recorded in this book.

Though Ezekiel was in exile far from Jerusalem and the temple, he received a vision of the glory of God. In particular, he saw "four living creatures" (1:5), somewhat like a man but with four faces. The first face was of a man, the second the face of a lion, the third the face of an ox, and the fourth the face of an eagle (v. 10). Interpreters differ as to their interpretation, but it would seem reasonable to equate the face of a man with intelligence, the face of a lion as the king of beasts, representing man as a ruler, the ox representing power, and the eagle as the most noble of birds, man in his nobility.

Though explanations of the revelation to Ezekiel may differ, it obviously was intended to represent the glory of God, referred to many times in the book (1:28; 3:12, 23; 8:4; 9:3; 10:4, 18-19; 11:22-23; 39:21; 43:2, 4-5; 44:4). In response to this glorious revelation, Ezekiel fell on his face and heard the voice of the one mentioned in 1:25.

Though Ezekiel was a priest on the basis of his human lineage, he was now given the special call of a prophet from God. He was told that he was being sent to a people who would be "obstinate and stubborn" (2:4). He was instructed to deliver his message whether they would listen or not (v. 7). A scroll was also handed to him and unrolled containing "written words of lament and mourning and woe" (v. 10).

In chapter 3 Ezekiel was instructed to "eat this scroll; then go and speak to the house of Israel" (v. 1). He was informed again that the people to whom he would speak would be "unyielding and hardened" (v. 8).

After this revelation he was lifted up by the Spirit (v. 12) and taken away so that he could go to the exiles living near the Kebar River (v. 15). The next seven days he sat silent, overwhelmed (v. 15).

*Ezekiel 3:16-27.* In these verses Ezekiel recorded his subsequent experience as he prepared to be a prophet. He was told that he would be held responsible if he did not warn the Israelites in exile (vv. 17-21).

Ezekiel was told to "Get up and go out to the plain, and there I will speak to you" (v. 22). When the Holy Spirit came to him he was told to shut himself inside his house (v. 24) and that he would not be able to speak until the Lord opened his mouth (v. 27). He was further instructed, "Whoever will listen let him listen, and whoever will refuse let him refuse; for they are a rebellious house" (v. 27). These opening chapters gave a prophetic background for Ezekiel's message as a message from God to His people Judah.

## Prophetic Warning of Judgment on Jerusalem

*Ezekiel 4:1-17.* The first prophecy was symbolized by Ezekiel taking a clay tablet on which was drawn the city of Jerusalem (v. 1). Then Ezekiel built what represented a ramp against Jerusalem and camps around about (v. 2). Then Ezekiel, following instructions, took an iron pan which was used as a wall between Ezekiel and the city of Jerusalem. This was to indicate that Jerusalem would be under siege, and what he did was to be a sign to the house of Israel (v. 3).

Ezekiel was instructed to lie on his left side for 390 days, symbolizing the number of years Israel had sinned against God since the time of Solomon (vv. 4-5). Then he was to lie on his right side for 40 days, symbolizing each year by a day (v. 6), possibly referring to the wicked reign of Manasseh (2 Kings 21:11-15; 23:26-27; 24:3-4; 2 Chron. 33:12-13).

Then Ezekiel was told to take for food "wheat and barley, beans and lentils, millet and spelt" (Ezek. 4:9). He was instructed to weigh out twenty shekels of food for each day and "a sixth of a hin of water and drink it at set times" (v. 11). By this symbolic act he was to prophesy that the supply of food in Jerusalem would be cut off, that they would ration food and water as they would be scarce (vv. 16-17). This was fulfilled in the Babylonian Captivity (2 Chron. 36:11-15).

### The Symbol of Ezekiel's Sharp Sword

*Ezekiel 5:1-17.* Ezekiel was told to shave off the hair of his head and his beard (v. 1). Then he was instructed to burn a third of his hair with fire inside the city. He was to take a third of the hair and strike it with a sword and then scatter a third to the wind. A few strands of hair were to be put in the folds of his garment (v. 3). In addition, a few hairs were to be thrown in the fire. Prophetically, Ezekiel was told, "A fire will spread from there to the whole house of Israel" (v. 4).

This symbolism was explained as relating to Jerusalem which would be destroyed because of her rebellion against God (vv. 5-6). Her sins exceeded the sins of the Gentile nations about her (v. 7). Because of her idolatry He would do to Jerusalem what He had not done before (v. 9). Fathers in Israel would eat their own children and children would eat their fathers (v. 10). Following this He would scatter the survivors to the winds. Just as Ezekiel divided the hair into thirds, so a third of the people would die by plague or famine, a third by the sword, and a third would be scattered (v. 12).

God would make her an object of horror to the nations (v. 15) and would destroy her with famine, wild beasts, plague, and bloodshed (vv. 15-17).

### Prophecy of Destruction against the Mountains of Israel

*Ezekiel 6:1-14.* God predicted destruction against the mountains of Israel as well as the ravines and valleys (vv. 1-3). Israel was supposed to worship in the temple in Jerusalem, but heathen idolatry caused her to build shrines for high places throughout the land. God predicted that these altars would be smashed and that her dead bodies would be in front of her idols and their cities would be laid waste (vv. 5-7).

Those who escaped would be able to remember why God judged her as she lived in a strange land, and she would know the power of God (vv. 8-10). Because of her sins, her land would lie waste (vv. 11-14). This was fulfilled in the Babylonian Captivity (2 Chron. 36:11-15).

### The Coming Day of God's Judgment

*Ezekiel 7:1-27.* God had been patient with Israel for many years, but now the end of His patience had come. He would unleash His anger against her and would not spare her (vv. 1-4).

Throughout the land of Israel there would be panic as the day of God's wrath was poured on her. She would know that the Lord was the one who was punishing her (vv. 5-9). The day of her judgment had come, much like the time when a flower is in full bloom. Neither the buyer of land nor the seller would possess the land (vv. 11-14).

In the time of destruction the Israelites would put on sackcloth, shave their heads, and throw their silver and gold into the streets. All this would be useless (vv. 15-20). Their plunder would go to foreigners who would take their wealth and desecrate their "treasured place" (v. 22). Sorrow and destruction would extend to all the people, resulting in not only kings and princes mourning but the people as a whole being filled with terror (vv. 23-27). This was fulfilled in the Babylonian Captivity.

### Idolatry Revealed in the Temple

*Ezekiel 8:1-18.* Ezekiel was taken by the Spirit to the north gate of the temple (vv. 1-4). Ezekiel was then brought to the entrance of the court and told to look through a hole in the wall. He "saw portrayed all over the walls all kinds of crawling things and detestable animals and all the idols of the house of Israel. In front of them stood seventy elders of the house of Israel, and Jaazaniah son of Shaphan was standing among them. Each had a censer in his hand, and a fragrant cloud of incense was rising" (vv. 10-11).

Ezekiel was then at the entrance of the north gate of the temple where he saw women mourning for Tammuz, a Sumerian god related to vegetation. Worshipers of this idol believed that when drought came in the summer Tammuz would die but in the spring would come out and bring rain (vv. 14-15).

When Ezekiel was brought into the inner court of the temple, he witnessed twenty-five men with their backs toward the temple and bowing toward the sun (v. 16). As a result of their desecration of the temple and turning to heathen gods, God would bring judgment on them and He would not show pity (vv. 17-18). This was fulfilled in the Babylonian Captivity (2 Chron. 36:11-15).

### God Commands Idolaters to Be Killed

*Ezekiel 9:1-11.* God instructed six guards to go about the city and mark all "who grieve and lament over all the detestable things that are done in it" (vv. 1-4).

God then told others to kill everyone who did not have the mark, whether old or young, but not to touch those who had the mark, indicating that they detested idol worship (vv. 5-7).

When Ezekiel questioned whether the Lord was going to pour out His wrath on Jerusalem, God replied that the time of judgment had come because of her wickedness and that God "will not look on them with pity or spare them, but I will bring down on their own heads what they have done" (vv. 8-11). This was fulfilled in the Babylonian Captivity (2 Chron. 36:11-15).

### The Glory Departs from the Defiled Temple

*Ezekiel 10:1-22.* In a vision that is similar but not identical to what Ezekiel saw earlier (1:1-28), Ezekiel saw another vision of the glory of God. God was in a chariot throne with wheels and containing burning coals (10:1-3). As God entered the temple, the temple was filled with the glory of God (vv. 4-5).

God then instructed a man clothed in linen, probably an angel, to take fire from the coals in the chariot and scatter them over the city of Jerusalem (vv. 2, 6-7).

The four wheels were described as sparkling like chrysolite (v. 9). The cherubim described had four faces similar to the four faces mentioned in 1:4-10, but somewhat different because one of the faces instead of being the face of an ox had the face of a man (10:14).

Ezekiel identified the living creatures as those he saw by the Kebar River (v. 15, 20; 1:1). The main point of this revelation was that "the glory of the LORD departed from over the threshold of the temple and stopped above the cherubim" (10:18). Another picture of the cherubim was given in verses 20-22. This was fulfilled in the Babylonian Captivity (2 Chron. 36:11-15).

### Coming Judgment on the Wicked Leaders of Israel

*Ezekiel 11:1-15.* Ezekiel was given another vision of twenty-five leaders of Israel who were plotting evil and were wicked (vv. 1-4). Those who had been already killed in the city were only the beginning as God was going to drive them out and inflict punishment on them in keeping with their sins (vv. 5-12). The death of Pelatiah, one of the leaders, was a foreshadowing of death that would destroy the others (v. 13). In contrast to the destruction of the leaders of Israel was the remnant of Israel, the fellow captives of Ezekiel (vv. 13-15). God reassured Ezekiel that ultimately the land would be given for the possession of Israel (v. 15). This was fulfilled in the Babylonian Captivity, and the restoration of the land will be fulfilled in the millennial kingdom.

## Israel to Be Restored to Their Land

*Ezekiel 11:16-25.* Just as God had scattered them among the heathen, so God would bring her ultimately back to their land (vv. 16-17). This promise, repeated so often, must be taken in the same literal sense as the destruction which followed that fell on her because of her sins. Such restoration was partially fulfilled in the return from the Babylonian and Assyrian captivities but ultimately will be fulfilled by the complete regathering of Israel at the time of the second coming of Christ.

When she returns there will be a new spirit among her which will cause her to remove the idols. God promised to "put a new spirit in them; I will remove from them their heart of stone and give them a heart of flesh" (v. 19). At that time God declared, "Then they will follow My decrees and be careful to keep My laws. They will be My people, and I will be their God" (v. 20). Those who have been wicked and departed from God will bring judgment on their own heads. In closing this episode of Ezekiel's image, he saw the glory going from within the city and stopping in the mountain to the east of Jerusalem (v. 23). Ezekiel recited to his fellow exiles what he had seen (vv. 24-25). This will be fulfilled in the Millennium (Jer. 23:3-8).

## The Captivity Symbolized

*Ezekiel 12:1-28.* God gave Ezekiel instructions to act out going into exile (vv. 1-6). In obedience to what God commanded, Ezekiel packed his things, as if going into exile, dug a hole through the wall, and at dusk carried out his things on his shoulders while the people watched (v. 7).

God instructed him that if they asked what he was doing, he should tell them that it symbolized the whole house of Israel going into exile (vv. 8-11). God described "The prince among them" (v. 12) doing the same thing as Ezekiel. Zedekiah's departure from Jerusalem, however, would only result in his being caught and brought to Babylon (vv. 12-13). The prediction was made that while he was going to Babylon he would not see it, a prophecy fulfilled by Nebuchadnezzar (Jer. 52:10-11). Because Zedekiah was blinded, he was unable to see Babylon even though he was taken to it.

The dispersion of Israel among the nations of the world was predicted (Ezek. 12:15-16). This prediction was not completed by the Babylonian or Assyrian captivities but was fulfilled in the dispersion of Israel after the destruction of Jerusalem in A.D. 70.

Ezekiel was instructed to eat and drink but to "shudder in fear" (v. 18). By this means, symbolically, he was to represent what would happen in Jerusalem as in their despair they saw the land stripped of everything and their cities destroyed (vv. 17-20). God promised to fulfill without delay the visions and revelations of their destruction (vv. 25-28). This was fulfilled in the Babylonian Captivity (2 Chron. 36:11-15).

### Condemnation of False Prophets

*Ezekiel 13:1-23.* Having delivered two messages that judgment was near (12:21-25; 26-28), the third message of judgment to come concerned the false prophets who had encouraged Israel to believe that she would not go into captivity (13:1-3). God declared, "Their visions are false and their divinations a lie" (v. 6). She would be destroyed and would not be able to return to the land of Israel (v. 9).

God compared Israel's false prophets to "a flimsy wall" covered "with whitewash" (v. 10). God predicted that rain, violent winds, and hailstones would destroy the wall (vv. 10-13). God declared, "I will tear down the wall you have covered with whitewash and will level it to the ground so that its foundations will be laid bare. When it falls, you will be destroyed in it; and you will know that I am the LORD" (v. 14). God also declared judgment on "the women who sew magic charms on all their wrists and make veils of various lengths for their heads in order to ensnare people" (v. 18). God declared that He would judge them for their wicked behavior (vv. 19-22). These false prophets and the women "will no longer see false visions or practice divination" (v. 23). This was fulfilled in the Babylonian Captivity (2 Chron. 36:11-15).

### Judgment on Idolaters

*Ezekiel 14:1-23.* Those who practiced idolatry and then went to a prophet would be judged by the Lord (vv. 1-5). God exhorted them, "Turn from your idols and renounce all your detestable practices!" (v. 6)

If an Israelite served idols and sought a prophet, God would destroy him and also the prophet if the prophet would not resist the enticement to utter a prophecy (vv. 7-11). God declared that His judgment on Israel could not be avoided even if Noah, Daniel, and Job would intercede (vv. 13-14). The reference to these historical characters is very significant. Noah and Job lived many years before Ezekiel, but Daniel was a contemporary. Though liberal scholars have attempted to destroy the historicity of Daniel, this reference is a significant confirmation that Daniel was in Babylon serving King Nebuchadnezzar during the time of the Captivity. The arbitrary declaration of some scholars that this reference cannot be taken at face value is without justifiable reason. As an important Babylonian official, it would be natural for Ezekiel to have heard of him.

After God amplified His declaration that these three notable men could not save Israel, God declared that if wild beasts went through the land even these men would not be able to save their own sons and daughters, that they only would be saved (vv. 15-16). He stated the same thing concerning the sword passing through the land or plague (vv. 17-20). The names of the three men were repeated (v. 20). Then God declared that judgment against Jerusalem would be terrible, including sword, famine, wild beasts, and plague (v. 21). There would be some survivors, but most of the people would be destroyed (v. 22). This was fulfilled in the Babylonian Captivity (2 Chron. 36:11-15).

### Jerusalem as Useless as a Fruitless Vine

*Ezekiel 15:1-8.* In the revelation given to Ezekiel, signs had been used to indicate the coming disaster (12:1-20), then a series of five messages followed (12:21–14:23). This chapter is the first of three parables confirming the fact that Israel could not escape her coming judgment. By its nature a vine is useful only as it is fruitful. As wood, it is useful for nothing (vv. 1-5). Because of this God would cast the vine into the fire and consume it and "will make the land desolate because they have been unfaithful" (v. 8). This was fulfilled in the Babylonian Captivity (2 Chron. 36:11-15).

### Jerusalem as an Unfaithful Wife

*Ezekiel 16:1-63.* Jerusalem was described as an unwanted baby cast out to die (vv. 1-6) but rescued by God. Eventually the baby became a beautiful woman. Having grown up to be a beautiful woman, God declared that He cared for her, dressed her in fine linen and beautiful jewelry. Her beauty was such that she became a queen (vv. 8-14).

Having received all these favors, Jerusalem became a prostitute and used her jewelry to make idols. The food that God gave her was offered as incense to idols. The sons and the daughters that were born were sacrificed to idols (vv. 15-21).

Because of these detestable things, God declared judgment on Jerusalem (vv. 22-29). Even the heathen nations of Babylon and

Egypt were shocked at her adultery. Because of her continued brazen conduct, God would judge not only her but those who committed adultery with her (vv. 30-38). Her lovers would destroy her shrines, strip her clothes and fine jewelry, and leave her naked (v. 39). "They will bring a mob against you, who will stone you and hack you to pieces with their swords. They will burn down your houses and inflict punishment on you in the sight of many women. I will put a stop to your prostitution, and you will no longer pay your lovers. Then My wrath against you will subside and My jealous anger will turn away from you; I will be calm and no longer angry" (vv. 40-42).

God declared that Jerusalem had become like her mother who was described here as a Hittite with her father an Amorite (v. 45). Her older sister was compared to Samaria and her younger sister to Sodom (v. 46). According to God, Jerusalem became more depraved than any others (vv. 47-52).

God promised to restore Sodom and Samaria, but Jerusalem would be scorned by Edom and the Philistines (vv. 53-58). God declared, " 'This is what the Sovereign LORD says: I will deal with you as you deserve, because you have despised My oath by breaking the covenant' " (v. 59).

God promised, however, to remember the everlasting covenant He made with Israel (v. 60). But as she received God's grace, she would be ashamed of their conduct (vv. 61-63).

### The Parable of the Two Eagles and the Vine

*Ezekiel 17:1-24.* This third parable setting forth God's judgment on Israel described a situation in Israel when Zedekiah was ruling (about 592–591 B.C.). God described a great eagle that cut off the top of a cedar and carried it to a distant land where it prospered with abundant water (vv. 1-5). It became a spreading vine (v. 6).

God then described another eagle which attracted the vine to send out its roots and branches toward the second eagle. God declared that the vine would not prosper.

Explaining the parable, God compared the first eagle to Babylon which conquered Jerusalem in 605 B.C. and carried off many of its leaders and inhabitants in 597 B.C. After this Zedekiah was placed by Babylon over Israel left in the land. The second eagle described the enticement of Egypt which caused Zedekiah to rebel against Nebuchadnezzar and rely on the armies of Egypt (vv. 9-15). Jeremiah had warned Zedekiah that it would result in disaster if he rebelled against Babylon (Jer. 38:17-28). When Zedekiah tried to escape, he was caught by the Babylonians and had to watch as his sons and nobles were killed. Then Nebuchadnezzar blinded Zedekiah and took him to Babylon (Jer. 52:10-11). This corresponded to the word of the Lord in Ezekiel (Ezek. 17:11-21).

Following Zedekiah's downfall in 586 B.C., in fulfillment of this prophecy of Jeremiah, God declared in Ezekiel that He Himself would take a shoot from the top of the cedar, plant it on the mountains of Israel, and it would grow and prosper (vv. 22-24). Ezekiel, who had been carried off captive, probably in 597 B.C. recorded this prophecy which was fulfilled in the fall of Jerusalem in 586 B.C. Again and again in Isaiah, Jeremiah, and Ezekiel the literal fulfillment of prophecy was illustrated.

### Judgment on Those Who Sin

*Ezekiel 18:1-32.* God asked the question about their interpretation of the proverb, "The fathers eat sour grapes, and the children's teeth are set on edge" (vv. 1-2). The point of this prophecy seems to be that the Children of Israel were claiming that their punishment was because of their fathers' sins, not their own. God declared by way of rebuttal, " 'As surely as I live,' declares the Sovereign LORD, 'you will no longer quote this proverb in Israel. For every living soul belongs to Me, the father as well as the son — both alike belong to Me. The soul who sins is the one who will die' " (vv. 3-4). The proverb which God repeated was also quoted by Jeremiah (Jer. 31:29-30). In the Ten Commandments the principle was indicated that punishment sometimes goes to the third and fourth generation (cf. Ex. 20:5; 34:6-7; Deut. 5:9).

In the present case, however, God was declaring that He was judging the children themselves for their sinfulness and urged them to repent to avoid His judgment (Ezek. 18:3-4).

God itemized the sins of the wicked (vv. 5-9) and declared that if a righteous man would not do these things, he would live (v. 9). By contrast, the wicked person who does these things would not live (vv. 10-13).

If one was a son of such a wicked person, however, and would not follow in his wickedness, God declared, "He will not die for his father's sin; he will surely live" (v. 17). In the particular case of Israel with whom God was dealing in judgment, a son would not inherit the sins of the father nor the righteousness of the father, but each would be judged on the basis of his own actions (vv. 18-24).

God defended His actions as being just in contrast to the charge of some that He was unjust (vv. 25-29).

The final appeal of the Lord was for Israel to "repent!" (v. 30) God declared, " 'For I take no pleasure in the death of anyone,' declares the Sovereign LORD. 'Repent and live!' " (v. 32) This was fulfilled in the Babylonian Captivity (2 Chron. 36:11-15).

### A Lament for the Princes of Israel

*Ezekiel 19:1-14.* In a way similar to prophecy and fulfillment being pictured by symbols in the previous chapters, this was a formal dirge such as was customarily used for a funeral. In this case the prophet used it as a dirge for the nation Israel and Jerusalem.

A lioness was pictured as rearing a cub who became strong but was trapped and taken to the land of Egypt (vv. 1-4). This probably referred to Jehoahaz who was taken in captivity to Egypt (cf. 2 Kings 23:31-34; Jer. 22:11-12).

The second cub probably referred to Zedekiah who was carried off to Babylon (Ezek. 19:5-9; cf. 2 Kings 25:7). At the time Ezekiel wrote, the reference to Zedekiah was still a prediction which was later fulfilled in 586 B.C.

Israel, or Jerusalem, was then pictured as a vine, fruitful because of abundant waters that had strong branches (Ezek. 19:10-11). The vine, however, "was uprooted in fury and thrown to the ground. The east wind made it shrivel, it was stripped of its fruit; its strong branches withered and fire consumed them" (v. 12). It was then portrayed as being planted in the desert and its branches consumed by fire (vv. 13-14). It should be noted that though the prophecy was given in symbolic form, it had a literal reference to prophecy or history as the case may be.

### Israel's Past Rebellion

*Ezekiel 20:1-29.* When the elders of Israel came to inquire of the land, God instructed Ezekiel to tell them that first they had to review their many sins. God then recited their rebellion in the wilderness, their failure to keep God's laws (vv. 8-10), and their desecration of the Sabbaths (vv. 12-13).

God declared, however, that He wanted to fulfill His promise of bringing them to the Promised Land (vv. 14-20).

Though God did not destroy Israel in the desert, He did predict that they would be scattered among the nations because of their sins (vv. 21-26). When they got to the Promised Land, they used the high places for offering of sacrifices to idols (vv. 27-29).

## Restoration after Judgment

*Ezekiel 20:30-44.* God indicated that the time would come when He would judge them and the righteous would enter into the Promised Land. This restoration, however, would not be extended to the elders who came to Ezekiel (vv. 30-32).

In the prophecy which follows (vv. 33-38) the far-reaching promise that God will regather Israel and restore them permanently to the land was detailed. This was a prophecy which was not fulfilled in the return from the Babylonian and Assyrian captivities.

God declared, " 'As surely as I live,' declares the Sovereign LORD, 'I will rule over you with a mighty hand and an outstretched arm and with outpoured wrath. I will bring you from the nations and gather you from the countries where you have been scattered—with a mighty hand and an outstretched arm and with outpoured wrath. I will bring you into the desert of the nations and there, face to face, I will execute judgment upon you. As I judged your fathers in the desert in the land of Egypt, so I will judge you,' declares the Sovereign LORD. 'I will take note of you as you pass under My rod, and I will bring you into the bond of the covenant. I will purge you of those who revolt and rebel against Me. Although I will bring them out of the land where they are living, yet they will not enter the land of Israel. Then you will know that I am the LORD' " (vv. 33-38).

This important prophecy was never fulfilled in the history of Israel and is connected to the judgments at the Second Coming. At that time all Israelites still living in the world will be gathered, but only those who belong to the godly remnant will be allowed to enter the land (vv. 36-38). The purpose of God to bring Israel eventually to their Promised Land and permanently settle them there is one of the great lines of prophecy, beginning with Genesis 12:7 and continuing throughout the Old Testament. This passage, however, was unique in describing in detail the purging separation of the saved from the unsaved at the beginning of the millennial kingdom and the regathering and planting of Israel in their ancient land. After Israel will be regathered, they will remember their sins and serve the Lord (vv. 40-44). This future regathering of Israel will be in keeping with the New Covenant revealed in Jeremiah 31:31-37.

## Prophecy against the South

*Ezekiel 20:45-49.* Prophecy here is directed against Jerusalem and Israel which was viewed as being toward the south. When the

Babylonians came, they would come from the north and attack Israel to the south.

The south, here called the Negev, is now a desert but was pictured here as being a forest which will be consumed by fire (vv. 45-47). Whether considered a literal fire or a symbolic prophecy of the destruction of Israel, God declared, "Everyone will see that I the LORD have kindled it; it will not be quenched" (v. 48). Ezekiel complained, however, that the people were saying that he was speaking in parables that they did not understand (v. 49). The truth of the matter was they did not want to understand. This passage of judgment against the south was introductory to the prophecies of judgment in chapter 21. This prophecy of judgment was fulfilled in the Babylonian Captivity (2 Chron. 36:11-15).

### Babylon as the Sword of Divine Judgment

*Ezekiel 21:1-27.* God first declared that He had drawn a sword against Israel (vv. 1-7). This sword was described as sharpened and polished and made ready to kill (vv. 8-17).

Ezekiel was informed that God would supernaturally direct Babylon toward Jerusalem, giving them an omen to go in that direction (vv. 18-23).

God informed the king who was addressed, "O profane and wicked prince of Israel" (v. 25) that he should take off his crown because the leaders of Israel would be brought low and the lowly would be exalted. This was fulfilled in the Babylonian Captivity (2 Chron. 36:11-15).

### Prophecy against Ammon

*Ezekiel 21:28-32.* The next prophecy was against Ammon because of their insults (vv. 28-29). God would pour out His wrath on them and they would be as fuel for fire (vv. 31-32).

The Ammonites were mentioned again in Ezekiel 25:1-10 but were not mentioned in Scripture after the sixth century B.C. Today nothing remains of the Ammonite civilization except archeological ruins, and no one identified as an Ammonite lives today.

### Jerusalem's Many Sins

*Ezekiel 22:1-31.* In almost every possible way Jerusalem and its inhabitants had sinned against God. They had been guilty of shedding blood (vv. 1-4). Their objects of worship had been idols (v. 4). Because of their many sins they had become "an object of scorn to the nations and a laughingstock to all the countries" (v. 4).

Their princes had shed blood, treated father and mother con-

170

temptuously, and had "oppressed the alien and mistreated the fatherless and widow" (v. 7).

They had been guilty of despising the Sabbath and despising holy things (v. 8). They had been guilty of slander, worshiping at idolaters' shrines, and committing lewd acts (v. 9). They had been guilty of many sexual sins (vv. 10-11). They had accepted bribes and charged usury and excessive interest and made unjust gains by extortion (v. 12). As a result of her many sins, God predicted that they would be dispersed among the nations (v. 15).

God compared the house of Israel to dross, the material left over after the refining of copper, tin, iron, and lead. He declared, "They are but the dross of silver" (v. 18). God predicted that He would gather them into Jerusalem just as men gather metals and put them in a furnace to melt them (vv. 19-20). "As silver is melted in a furnace, so you will be melted inside her, and you will know that I the LORD have poured out My wrath upon you" (v. 22).

Their drought had been declared a day of wrath because their rulers had behaved wickedly like a roaring lion. They had stolen treasures and precious things and made many widows (v. 25). The priests also violated the Law and profaned sacred things (v. 26). They did not distinguish between clean and unclean and did not keep the Sabbath (v. 26). Her officials were described as if they were wolves who kill people (v. 27). Her prophets were accused of whitewashing their deeds (v. 28). Extortion and robbery and oppression characterize the people of the land (v. 29). When God looked for a man to stand in the gap to prevent Israel from being destroyed, He could find none (vv. 30-31).

The Word of God clearly described these sins as absolutely forbidden in the Law (cf. Lev. 18:7-20; 20:10-21; Deut. 22:22-24, 30; 27:22). There were few sins which Israel had not committed. Jerusalem was judged in the Babylonian Captivity (2 Chron. 36:11-15).

## The Two Sinful Sisters

*Ezekiel 23:1-48.* Ezekiel was given a special revelation concerning two women. Described as daughters of the same mother, they became prostitutes. The older was named Oholah and her sister Oholibah (vv. 1-4). Oholah represented Samaria and Oholibah represented Jerusalem.

Oholah was described as a prostitute who sought Assyrian lovers. Her prostitution had begun in Egypt (vv. 5-8). Eventually the Assyrians stripped her and killed her with the sword (vv. 9-10).

Oholibah, representing Jerusalem, was even worse. She not only sought Assyrian lovers but sent to Babylon to seek lovers from the Babylonians (vv. 14-21).

The Lord predicted that the Chaldeans whom she sought would come against Jerusalem and destroy her (vv. 22-24). They would mutilate her noses and ears and would take away her sons and daughters (v. 25) and would strip her of her fine clothes and take her jewelry (v. 26). In judging her, God would "put a stop to the lewdness and prostitution you began in Egypt" (v. 27). God predicted that He would turn her over to her enemies (vv. 28-31).

In poetic form God declared that Oholibah would "drink your sister's cup, a cup large and deep" (v. 32). They would bear the consequences of their sins (v. 35). God's judgment would put an end to her many flagrant sins and would demonstrate that God is sovereign (vv. 48-49). These judgments were fulfilled in the Assyrian and Babylonian captivities.

### The Sign of the Cooking Pot

*Ezekiel 24:1-27.* Ezekiel was commanded to record the date because on that date the king of Babylon would begin the siege of Jerusalem (vv. 1-2). This date was in the ninth year of King Jehoiachin. The tenth month and the tenth day may be computed as January 15, 588 B.C. This significant date was mentioned elsewhere in Scriptures (2 Kings 25:1; Jer. 39:1; 52:4). The city was not immediately conquered and was not destroyed until 586 B.C.

Ezekiel was told to enact another parable. He was instructed to put on a cooking pot and add meat and the best pieces. He was to put wood under it and bring the water to a boil (Ezek. 24:3-5).

In the verses that follow, the city of Jerusalem was compared to the pot. What was in her would be emptied piece by piece (v. 6). The pot would be cooked and finally emptied (vv. 9-10). Ezekiel was then instructed to put the empty pot on the fire until its impurities were melted (v. 11). But the fire did not remove the deposit (v. 12). God declared that this deposit was a picture of their lewdness (v. 13). Though God attempted to clean away the impurity, it would not be cleansed until His wrath had been expressed (v. 13). God declared that He would not show pity and they would be judged according to their sins (v. 14).

In support of this sign God told Ezekiel that his wife would die. He was not to lament or do the various things that were normally associated with mourning for the dead (vv. 15-17). In keeping with

172

this prediction his wife died that evening.

When Ezekiel did not follow the usual customs of mourning, he declared to Israel the message from God that He was about to desecrate her sanctuary. Her sons and daughters would be killed, and when this happened she too would not mourn. Ezekiel was a sign to her of what was going to happen (v. 24).

Ezekiel was told that when this event took place and Jerusalem was destroyed he would receive the news and at that time also God would speak to him (2 Chron. 36:11-15).

# PROPHECY OF JUDGMENTS ON THE NATIONS IN EZEKIEL

### The Prophecy against Ammon

*Ezekiel 25:1-7.* This section begins the prediction of coming judgment on the Gentiles. In keeping with previous prophecy against Ammon, this further word was recorded here. Ezekiel was told to prophesy against Ammon (vv. 1-2). Because Ammon rejoiced when Israel's temple was destroyed and the people of Israel were led captive, God would give them also "to the people of the East as a possession" (v. 4). The reference to "the people of the East" apparently refers to nomadic tribes who lived east of Ammon. Some think this refers to Nebuchadnezzar and his army (cf. 21:31). The destruction of this ancient people led to their disappearance in the history. For earlier prophecies concerning Ammon, see Jeremiah 9:25-26; 25:21; 49:1-6; Ezekiel 21:28-32.

### The Prophecy against Moab

*Ezekiel 25:8-11.* The Moabites were a traditional enemy of Israel, beginning when they opposed Moses leading the Children of Israel to the Promised Land (Num. 22–24). In the time of the Judges, Eglon, king of Moab, oppressed Israel. They also figured in the opposition to Saul, but David later conquered the Moabites, and they continued under Israel's power until Solomon's death. Moab had also attacked Judah during the reign of Jehoshaphat. God predicted judgment on Moab because of their contempt for Israel. Like the Ammonites, they would be conquered by "the people of the East as a possession" (v. 10). This was fulfilled by the Babylonians who attacked Moab.

### The Prophecy against Edom

*Ezekiel 25:12-14.* Israel's conflict with Edom goes back to the time of the Exodus when they opposed the path of the Children of Israel.

Saul fought them (1 Sam. 14:47) and David made them subject to his reign (2 Sam. 8:13-14). After gaining freedom from Israel, however, Edom became subject to Babylon after Nebuchadnezzar's defeat of Egypt (605 B.C.). Her sin was that she took vengeance on the house of Judah. She will be punished for her opposition to God and to Israel. Edom was mentioned as subject to God's judgment in other Scriptures (Isa. 11:14; 63:1; Jer. 9:26; 49:7-22; Joel 3:19; Mal. 1:4-5). This was probably fulfilled by the attack by the Babylonians.

### The Prophecy against Philistia

*Ezekiel 25:15-17.* Israel's conflict with the Philistines also had a long history, and here God pronounces judgment on her. From the time of the Exodus the Philistines opposed Israel and attempted to control her territory in the time of the Judges. David finally conquered her, and she remained under Israel's control until the death of Solomon. The contest between Philistia and the divided kingdom was finally settled when Babylon established control over her. Because Philistia had acted in malice against Israel, God judged her for her attempt to destroy Israel, and especially Judah. Like many other ancient nations, Philistia disappeared in the period before Christ and became merged with other people.

### The Prophecy against Tyre

*Ezekiel 26:1-21.* The prophecy against Tyre occupies three long chapters of Ezekiel. Tyre was judged because she rejoiced in Judah's destruction, thinking that it would bring further business to them (vv. 1-2). God predicted that Tyre would be destroyed and the rubble of her city would be scraped away to bare rock. On the ocean side of Tyre where she formerly had great commerce there would be fishnets (vv. 4-6).

This prophecy was given "In the eleventh year, on the first day of the month" (v. 1), the time when Jerusalem was in imminent danger of collapse or capture by Babylon. At this time of tension God spoke to Ezekiel concerning Tyre. God pronounced judgment on her because she rejoiced in Judah's fall (v. 2). God predicted that Tyre herself would be destroyed, her walls pulled down, and ruins scraped away down to the bare rock (vv. 3-4). Where they formerly had commerce, on the seashore fishermen would spread their nets. "Ravaged by the sword" (v. 6), Tyre would not be rebuilt. Though Tyre had gloated over Jerusalem's fall, she herself was to experience the devastation of the Babylonian armies and later the invasion of the armies of Alexander the Great.

In 332 B.C. the armies of Alexander destroyed the city on the shore and scraped the debris into the sea to make a causeway to the island fortress. The bare ground where Tyre once stood is testimony today of the literal fulfillment of this prophecy. Tyre never regained power after this attack. Further details concerning the prophecy of Tyre's complete destruction were recorded in the rest of this chapter (vv. 15-21).

*Ezekiel 27:1-36.* Unlike Jerusalem which was rebuilt many times, Tyre was not to survive and so her rich trading enterprise would cease. Her customers included Lebanon (v. 5), Egypt (v. 7) Elishah, an ancient name for Cyprus (v. 7), Persia, Lydia, and Ceball, an ancient name for Byblos (vv. 8-10), Greece, Tubal, and Meshech (v. 13), Rhodes, Togarmah, and Aram (vv. 14-16), Judah, Israel, and Damascus (vv. 17-18), Greece and Arabia (vv. 19-24), and many others. Her ships were renowned for their rich merchandise (vv. 25-27). Her destruction, however, would cause mourning on behalf of those who traded with her (vv. 27-36). God declared that she would "come to a horrible end and will be no more" (v. 36).

### The Prophecy against the King of Tyre

*Ezekiel 28:1-19.* God pronounced judgment on the "ruler of Tyre" (vv. 1-2) because of his pride and that he claimed to be God (v. 2). God asked the question, "Are you wiser than Daniel?" (v. 3) This was Ezekiel's third reference to Daniel (cf. 14:14, 20) who at this time was a prominent ruler in Babylon. As the man immediately under King Nebuchadnezzar, he was known for his wisdom as he helped in the government of the vast empire. The question implied that Daniel, who did not claim any wisdom except from God, was actually wiser than the ruler of Tyre who claimed to be God.

The ruler of Tyre had collected gold and silver and other things that belonged to wealth (28:4-5), but God would bring "foreigners against you, the most ruthless of nations; they will draw their swords against your beauty and wisdom and pierce your shining splendor" (v. 7). He would die a violent death, and God challenged him to claim that he was God in the presence of his executioners (vv. 8-10). In the foregoing section of this chapter the ruler of Tyre was not called a king, as Ezekiel rarely uses the word king. In the verses which follow, however, a message was addressed to "the king of Tyre" (vv. 11-12).

Interpreters differ in their understanding of this passage because it seems to go beyond the attributes of the ruler of Tyre. Some claim it refers to his god, but the description given does not relate to a heathen god, and Ezekiel would not recognize such a claim. According to the passage, he was declared to be, "the model of perfection, full of wisdom and perfect in beauty. You were in Eden, the garden of God" (vv. 12-13).

This ruler of Tyre was described as having every precious stone set in gold (v. 13). Reference was made to "the day you were created" (v. 13). Here the passage seems to transcend anything that would correspond to the ruler of Tyre or his heathen gods. In verse 14 God declared, "You were anointed as a guardian cherub, for so I ordained you. You were on the holy mount of God; you walked among the fiery stones. You were blameless in your ways from the day you were created till wickedness was found in you" (vv. 14-15).

Because of the unusual description of this king of Tyre, from the church fathers to modern time some expositors conclude that this was a reference to Satan rather than to a man. This would explain the fact that he was created (v. 13) and that he was "a guardian cherub" (v. 14). It would also explain how he was "on the holy mount of God" (v. 14) which implied he was permitted to be in God's holy presence. Further, in verse 15, he was declared to be "blameless in your ways from the day you were created" (v. 15). This state of holiness, however, was lost when "wickedness was found in you" (v. 15).

Though the Bible does not give much specific information concerning the origin of Satan, theologians for centuries have long held that Satan was originally created as a holy angel and fell from that position long before man was created. Some relate this passage to Isaiah 14:12-15 as another reference to the fall of Satan from a state of holiness to a state of sin. These references to the origin of Satan and the origin of his present sinful condition harmonize with what the Bible teaches about Satan. Here he was described as the real power behind the ruler of Tyre and actually the king over the ruler of Tyre.

The further description of him as being driven from the mount of God and as a guardian cherub who was expelled because of his pride (vv. 16-17) also seems to go beyond anything that the ruler of Tyre experienced (vv. 18-19), or it may be interpreted as having a double reference to both the ruler of Tyre and Satan.

## The Judgment on Sidon

*Ezekiel 28:20-24.* Located about twenty miles north of Tyre, Sidon was a city with a long history. Sidon was a son of Canaan, and later a city was founded in his name (Gen. 10:15, 19). The history of Sidon continued to the time of Christ and for hundreds of years thereafter and is now the modern city of Saida. Because Sidon was a traditional enemy of Israel, God promised He would inflict punishment on her and her streets would flow with blood. Then she would know that God is the Lord (Ezek. 28:21-23). After her fall, Israel would have Sidon removed as "painful briers and sharp thorns" (v. 24) which formerly afflicted her.

*Ezekiel 28:25-26.* Following the prophecy against Sidon, God again predicted that He would regather His people Israel (v. 25) and that they would live in safety in their own land (vv. 25-26). This will be fulfilled in the Millennium (Jer. 23:5-8).

## The Prophecy against Egypt

*Ezekiel 29:1-21.* The nation of Egypt was the subject of many prophecies in the Old Testament. In Ezekiel 29 God declared Himself against Pharaoh and described her destruction (vv. 1-6). Egypt, first mentioned in Genesis 12:10, is the subject of hundreds of prophecies throughout the Old Testament and frequent references in the New Testament as well. Egypt was the land where Israel grew from a family to a nation, where Christ spent His early years, where Moses was born, and from which the Children of Israel left for the Promised Land. At the time of Ezekiel's prophecy, Hophra was Pharaoh of Egypt and reigned from 589 to 570 B.C. Part of Zedekiah's problem was that he depended on Egypt to protect him from Babylon which proved a fatal mistake.

Egypt was declared to be "a staff of reed for the house of Israel" (Ezek. 29:6). As a weak plant she was not capable of supporting weight, as Israel learned when she relied on Egypt (v. 7).

God declared that He would make Egypt "a desolate wasteland" (v. 9) and would kill both her men and animals (v. 8).

God predicted forty years of desolation for Egypt (vv. 10-12). Some interpret the forty years as a symbolic picture of trial. Though history does not record a deportation of Egypt to Babylon, Nebuchadnezzar conquered Egypt (cf. Jer. 43:8-13; 46:1-25; Ezek. 29:17-21), and it would be natural for him to take Egyptian captives. When the Persians defeated Babylon, however, Egyptian captives were allowed to return to their land just as Israel was allowed to return to Jerusalem. Forty-three years elapsed between Nebuchadnezzar's conquering Egypt and Babylon falling to the Persians, the period could easily be referred to as approximately forty years. In this passage there is no need to expect a future fulfillment.

In any event, God promised to return Egyptians to their ancient land from their being scattered, much as He promised Israel that she would be returned to her land (vv. 13-14). However, Egypt will never rise to be a great nation again (vv. 15-16).

The Lord declared to Ezekiel that God was going to give Egypt to Nebuchadnezzar so that he could carry off its wealth as payment for destroying Tyre where he had no reward (vv. 17-20). The reference to a horn (v. 21) probably is a symbolic indication that Israel will once again have authority and power in the day of her restoration to her land, probably fulfilled in the return from Babylon.

### The Lament for Egypt

*Ezekiel 30:1-26.* A poetic description of the Egyptian fall was recorded in Ezekiel 30. Her day of destruction would be a time of judgment when not only Egypt but other nations would fall by the sword (v. 5). The nations mentioned were allies of Egypt, and when Egypt fell, they would as well. Cush designated the area of southern Egypt and what is today northern Ethiopia (Es. 1:1; Jer. 46:9). Put corresponded to modern Libya (Isa. 66:19; Jer. 46:9; Ezek. 27:10). Lydia formed a part of the western coast of Asia Minor (cf. v. 10). Arabia normally designated the large peninsula between the Red Sea and the Persian Gulf. The reference to "the people of the covenant land" may refer to those in Israel who fled to Egypt to escape from Nebuchadnezzar. The reference to "from Migdol to Aswan" (30:6) described Egypt from north to south. Their cities would be ruined and their buildings set on fire (v. 8). The destruction of Egypt was related to the invasion of Nebuchadnezzar (v. 10). In the process of destroying Egypt, God would also destroy her idols and images (v. 13).

Memphis was one of the large cities of Egypt, originally its capital. Pathros probably referred to Upper Egypt. The destruction would be as far as upper Egypt (v. 14). Zoan was a city in the delta of the Nile (cf. Ps. 78:12, 43; Isa. 19:11, 13). Thebes, another prominent city of Egypt, was located several hundred miles south of Cairo, an area featuring modern Karnak and Luxor frequently visited by tourists today. Some of these cities were destroyed by the Assyrians when they invaded Egypt in 663 B.C. They were probably rebuilt by the time the Babylonians invaded Egypt.

The reference to Heliopolis was the area in Egypt just below the Nile delta. Bubastis, referred to only by Ezekiel in Scripture, for a time served as the capital of Egypt and was located northeast of Cairo. Tahpanhes was in eastern Egypt near the present Suez Canal and was the location of one of the Egyptian palaces. Jeremiah predicted her destruction (Jer. 2:16; cf. 43:7-8). As a result of her destruction, Egypt would know that the God of Israel is the true God (Ezek. 30:19).

In the closing verses of Ezekiel 30, God declared that He would break both arms of Pharaoh and strengthen the arms of the king of Babylon (vv. 20-25). When Nebuchadnezzar conquered Egypt he would disperse the Egyptians and scatter them through the countries. This would cause them to know that the Lord is God (v. 26).

**The Coming Destruction of Egypt and Her Allied Nations**
*Ezekiel 31:1-18.* In Ezekiel 31 the prophecy concerning the destruction of Assyria illustrated the destruction of Egypt. The nation of Assyria, which was destroyed suddenly after her defeat by the Babylonians in 612 B.C., was compared to a beautiful cedar tree that was cut down (vv. 1-9). God had destroyed Assyria by handing her over to "the most ruthless of foreign nations" (v. 12). It was described as an event which caused many nations and even the natural world to mourn (vv. 15-17). What happened to Assyria would also happen to Egypt.

The nation that would destroy Egypt and her allies was Babylon led by Nebuchadnezzar. The Assyrians earlier had destroyed some of the major cities of Egypt in 663 B.C. (Nahum 3:8-10). The destruction of Egypt following the destruction of Assyria probably occurred about 571 B.C. when armies of Babylon invaded Egypt.

The widespread destruction of Egypt was indicated by the mention of these cities scattered throughout Egypt. Not only the country and its cities were destroyed but also its armies, referred to as "all his hordes" (Ezek. 31:18). Ezekiel frequently refers to the hordes of the Gentiles and in this case Egypt (cf. Isa. 29:5, 7-8; Ezek. 30:10, 15; 31:2, 18; 32:12, 16, 18, 20, 24-26, 31-32; 38:7, 13; 39:11). The loss of thousands of soldiers was characteristic of the warfare of that day.

**The Lament for Pharaoh**
*Ezekiel 32:1-32.* This chapter recorded a long lament for Pharaoh (vv. 1-16). The captives had heard of the fall of Jerusalem in 586

B.C., and this prophecy was dated a year later. Prophesying the destruction of Egypt, this lament recorded the certainty of this destruction in the future. Previously, Ezekiel had recorded laments similar to a funeral dirge for Judah (Ezek. 19), Tyre (26:17-18; 27), and the king of Tyre (28:12-19). The lament was divided by the expression, "This is what the Sovereign LORD says" (32:3, 11). A preliminary statement was given in verse 2.

Egypt was compared to a lion and a monster (v. 2). The lion would be caught in a net (v. 3), exposed to the birds of the air and the beasts of the earth (v. 4). The land would be drenched with blood (v. 6). Even the heavens would respond by dimming the light of the sun and moon and darkening the stars (vv. 7-8). People of the world would be appalled by the destruction of Egypt (vv. 9-10).

The prophecy specifically refers to the "sword of the king of Babylon" (v. 11). The Egyptian soldiers and those that they hired would be cut down (v. 12). Her cattle would be killed (v. 13) and Egypt would be left desolate (v. 15). The world would join in the lament (v. 16). When they were killed they would lie down with the uncircumcised (vv. 19, 21). This referred to a disgraceful death of being killed by the sword. The slain of Egypt would join the slain of Assyria in Sheol (vv. 22-23).

Other nations such as Elam would also be in Sheol (v. 24). They were a people who settled east of Babylon and later were absorbed by the Persian Empire. They were conquered by both Assyria and Nebuchadnezzar (Jer. 49:34-39). The thought of their dying with the uncircumcised, a disgraceful death, was mentioned frequently in this passage (Ezek. 32:19, 21, 24-30). Meshech and Tubal are also in Hades (v. 26), referring to a people probably originally living in the area north of Turkey. They later became the subject of prophecy in Ezekiel 38–39. In addition to all the people mentioned, Pharaoh would join them in Sheol. Also there would be the Sidonians, described as "All the princes of the north" (v. 30), probably located north of Egypt. The concluding prophecy was that Pharaoh and his army would be there as well, having been killed by the sword. This was fulfilled in 663 and 571 B.C.

# PROPHECY OF FUTURE BLESSINGS
# ON ISRAEL IN EZEKIEL

In previous chapters of Ezekiel, prophecies had been directed against Israel and revealed her future judgments because of her sin.

These prophecies had been confirmed because Jerusalem had now fallen to the Babylonians and had been destroyed. Because of the literal fulfillment of these prophecies, it gave credence to prophecies yet unfulfilled.

In Ezekiel 25–32 judgments had been pronounced on the various nations surrounding Israel. Many of these were yet subject to future fulfillment.

Beginning with Ezekiel 33, the prophet predicted future blessing on Israel, some blessings to come relatively soon and others referring to the far distant restoration of Israel at the end of the Great Tribulation.

### Ezekiel Commissioned as a Watchman

*Ezekiel 33:1-20.* Ezekiel was warned to deliver the message of judgment to Israel just as a watchman would announce the coming of an enemy (vv. 1-6). Accordingly, Ezekiel was charged to warn the wicked of their coming judgment. If he did not, he would be held accountable.

God instructed Ezekiel to tell Israel that God does not take pleasure in judging them. What He wants them to do is to turn from their evil ways.

God will honor the wicked who turn to the Lord if he turns from his wickedness and He will judge the righteous who turn from their righteousness to sin. In effect, God offered forgiveness to all those who come to Him in sincere repentance (vv. 13-16).

If Israel blamed God saying that He was not just, they would be judged for her sin (vv. 17-20). This was fulfilled in Ezekiel's lifetime.

### Report of Jerusalem's Fall

*Ezekiel 33:21-22.* Several months after Jerusalem fell in 586 B.C. word of its destruction reached Ezekiel (v. 21). Following this, the Lord who had been keeping Ezekiel somewhat silent "opened my mouth before the man came to me in the morning. So my mouth was opened and I was no longer silent" (v. 22).

### Judgment Pronounced on Those Who Remain in the Land

*Ezekiel 33:23-33.* Those who remained in the land likened their possession of the land to Abraham possessing the land when he came from Ur of Chaldees (Gen. 11:31; 12:1-5). God informed the people who were remaining in the land that their case was not the same as Abram because Abram was a righteous man while they were still disobeying the Law, worshiping idols, eating meat with blood, and committing immorality (Ezek. 33:23-26). God warned the people left in the land that they would perish by the sword, by wild animals, by plague, and they would experience the judgment of the Lord (vv. 27-29).

God evaluated Ezekiel's ministry to them, indicating that the people heard what He had to say but they did not practice what they heard (vv. 30-33; James 1:22-25). This was fulfilled after the fall of Jerusalem.

## Israel's Faithless Shepherds Contrasted to Her Future True Shepherd

*Ezekiel 34:1-10.* Israel had been led astray because she had false shepherds who did not care for her but "ruled them harshly and brutally" (v. 4). No one had attempted to find the sheep who were scattered (v. 6).

God declared that He was going to hold the shepherds accountable for their failure to tend to the sheep of Israel (vv. 7-10). This was fulfilled in the Babylonian Captivity. God promised to rescue them in her future restoration (v. 10).

*Ezekiel 34:11-16.* God declared that He Himself would search for His sheep and rescue them from where they had been scattered (vv. 11-12). God promised, "I will bring them out from the nations and gather them from the countries, and I will bring them into their own land. I will pasture them on the mountains of Israel, in the ravines and in all the settlements in the land" (v. 13). This prediction of the future regathering of Israel from all over the world is still an unfulfilled commitment that will be fulfilled when the coming millennial kingdom begins.

God will especially care for those who are weak or injured and will bring them to rich pastures and will shepherd them with justice (vv. 14-16). This will be fulfilled in the Millennium (Jer. 23:5-8).

*Ezekiel 34:17-31.* God promised special care for those who were weak and who had been trampled by the stronger sheep. He will serve as a judge "between the fat sheep and the lean sheep" (v. 20).

Central to God's plan of restoration for Israel will be the resurrection of David as a true shepherd who will serve as a prince under Christ as King of kings and Lord of lords (vv. 23-24). This places the fulfillment at the Second Coming when Old Testament saints will be resurrected (Dan. 12:1-3).

God also promised that this will be a time of peace when the wild beasts will not afflict them, when they will receive showers to water the land, and trees will bear their fruit (Ezek. 34:25-27).

God also promised to keep them in safety, no longer allowing the nations to plunder them and would deliver them from famine (vv. 28-29). As a result of God's work in restoration of Israel, " 'Then they will know that I, the LORD their God, am with them and that they, the house of Israel, are My people,' declares the Sovereign LORD. 'You My sheep, the sheep of My pasture, are people, and I am your God,' declares the Sovereign LORD" (vv. 30-31). This will be fulfilled in the Millennium (Jer. 23:5-8).

### Prophecy against Edom

*Ezekiel 35:1-15.* The prophecy against Mount Seir predicted destruction of the Edomites, descendants of Esau, who lived in that area. Though Ezekiel had predicted earlier the destruction of the Edomites (25:12-14), this prophecy apparently was representative of all the nations that opposed Israel who will be judged in the future. The Edomites seemed to have participated with the Babylonians in the destruction of Jerusalem and had part in the cruelty which those in Jerusalem experienced.

The long history of the animosity of the descendants of Esau against Israel called for many prophecies in the Bible in addition to those mentioned by Ezekiel (Isa. 34:5-8; 63:1-4; Jer. 49:17; Lam. 4:21; Amos 1:11, 12; Obad. 8, 10).

Though the Edomites had rejoiced in the destruction of Jerusalem, she in turn would be made desolate (Ezek. 35:1-9). God would fill her mountains as well as her valleys and ravines with the slain (v. 8). Her towns would be destroyed and never inhabited (v. 9).

Edom had rejoiced in the fall of both Israel (the ten tribes) and Judah (the two tribes) which had led to the destruction of Jerusalem in 586 B.C. (v. 10). She then thought that she would be able to take possession of all twelve tribes of Israel. Instead, God was going to cause her devastation (vv. 11-15).

Actually, Edom continued for another four centuries before she gradually disappeared from history. In God's time the prophecies were literally fulfilled.

### The Future Restoration of Israel to Her Land

*Ezekiel 36:1-7.* Just as the people of Edom and other nations had hounded Israel, destroyed her cities, and plundered them, so God promised He would destroy the nations, including Edom, who had done this to Israel (vv. 1-7).

*Ezekiel 36:8-36.* But to Israel, however, God gave the wonderful promise of her restoration. She will be restored like a tree producing branches and fruit (v. 8). God will increase the number of the house of Israel, and her cities will once again be inhabited and her ruins rebuilt (v. 10). Even animals will be more plentiful and the land will become fruitful (v. 11). God not only promised that the Children of Israel would walk on her ancient land and possess it, but "you will never again deprive them of their children" (v. 12), referring to the fact that Israel would be permanently established in her land when her final restoration takes place (Amos 9:15). God declared that never again will the Children of Israel be destroyed and suffer taunts from the nations (Ezek. 36:13-15).

God reminded the Children of Israel, however, of her wickedness and how she was judged and dispersed among the nations because she had sinned against God (vv. 16-18). God declared that Israel would be "scattered through the countries; I judged them according to their conduct and their actions" (v. 19).

God would not restore her because she deserved it but because of His desire to show her His righteousness and His holiness (vv. 22-23). In her restoration God would cleanse her and give her His Holy Spirit, "For I will take you out of the nations; I will gather you from all the countries and bring you back into your own land. I will sprinkle clean water on you, and you will be clean; I will cleanse you from all your impurities and from all your idols. I will give you a new heart and put a new spirit in you; I will remove from you your heart of stone and give you a heart of flesh. And I will put My Spirit in you and move you to follow My decrees and be careful to keep My laws" (vv. 24-27). The Holy Spirit will indwell them in that day in contrast to the Mosaic dispensation when only a few were indwelt.

In that day as the Israelites would live in her Promised Land, she will belong to God and God will be her God (v. 28). God will make her grain plentiful and she will no longer have famine (vv. 29-30). When God will prosper her in her day of the restoration she will think back to her wickedness and know that God has shown her His grace.

The land was described as resettled, rebuilt, no longer desolate, but like the Garden of Eden (vv. 33-35). This will be a testimony to the nations that God has restored Israel (v. 36). Most important, Israel will know that the Lord is her God and that He has restored her.

This entire chapter requires a future millennial kingdom after the second coming of Christ for its complete and literal fulfillment (Jer. 23:5-8). Just as the prophecies of judgment were literally fulfilled in connection with Israel and the nations, so her future restoration will be literally fulfilled and she will experience the marvelous grace of God.

### Division of the Dry Bones: The Restoration of Israel

*Ezekiel 37:1-10.* Ezekiel was given a vision of a valley filled with dry bones. The Lord asked him the question, "Son of man, can these bones live?" (v. 3) Ezekiel was cautious in replying, indicating that only the Lord would know (v. 3).

Ezekiel then was instructed to prophesy that these dry bones would come to life, that the bones would come together, and that the flesh would cover them, and finally that they would have the breath of life much like Adam (Gen. 2:7).

Then God spoke to Ezekiel, "Prophesy to the breath; prophesy, son of man, and say to it, 'This is what the Sovereign Lord says: "Come from the four winds, O breath, and breathe into these slain, that they may live" ' " (Ezek. 37:9).

When Ezekiel obeyed the Lord and prophesied, "breath entered them; they came to life and stood up on their feet—a vast army" (v. 10).

*Ezekiel 37:11-14.* Having given Ezekiel the vision, the Lord now interpreted it for him. In the interpretation Ezekiel was informed that the bones represented Israel. Her hopeless, dried condition illustrated Israel's hopelessness of ever being restored. In response to this God promised to bring her back from death and to the land of Israel. God would put His Holy Spirit in her and she would be settled in her own land.

The Lord said, "Son of man, these bones are the whole house of Israel. They say, 'Our bones are dried up and our hope is gone; we are cut off.' Therefore prophesy and say to them: 'This is what the Sovereign Lord says: "O My people, I am going to open your graves and bring you up from them; I will bring you back to the land of Israel. Then you, My people, will know that I am the Lord, when I open your graves and bring you up from them. I will put My Spirit in you and you will live, and I will settle you in your own land. Then you will know that I the Lord have spoken, and I have done it," declares the Lord' " (vv. 11-14).

In biblical interpretation today many affirm that Israel will never

185

be restored. They share the hopelessness that gripped Israel at this time as they were scattered from their land and many of them were in Assyria and Babylon. Contradicting this hopeless situation, God promised to restore Israel, and in the strongest possible terms indicated that He would bring new life to her, that she would be restored as a nation, that she would be indwelt by the Holy Spirit, and she would settle in her own land in safety.

The prediction that she would be brought up from the grave is partly symbolic in that the nation seems to be dead and will be restored to physical life. But it is also to be considered literally because, according to Daniel 12:1-3, at the close of the Great Tribulation when Christ returns in His second coming, there will be a resurrection of Old Testament saints. Both figuratively and literally Israel will be restored and given new life. Those who have died who were saved will be resurrected to share in the millennial kingdom as resurrected saints.

The promise that His Holy Spirit would be in her goes beyond her experience under the Law when the Holy Spirit was with her but not necessarily in her (John 14:17). Beginning on the Day of Pentecost (Acts 2) all genuinely saved people were indwelt by the Holy Spirit, a situation that will continue until the Rapture of the church. Though there is no clear revelation of what will be true between the Rapture and the Second Coming, this and other Scriptures make clear that the Holy Spirit will indwell the saints in the millennial kingdom (Ezek. 37:14; Jer. 31:33).

### Sign of the Two Sticks
*Ezekiel 37:15-17.* Ezekiel was commanded, "Son of man, take a stick of wood and write on it, 'Belonging to Judah and the Israelites associated with him.' Then take another stick of wood, and write on it, 'Ephraim's stick, belonging to Joseph and all the house of Israel associated with him.' Join them together into one stick so that they will become one in your hand" (vv. 15-17).

The situation being addressed is that of the divided kingdom. After Solomon, the ten tribes following Jeroboam became the kingdom of Israel, the two remaining tribes in Jerusalem, Judah and Benjamin, became the kingdom of Judah. The ten tribes were carried off to Assyria in 722 B.C., and the two remaining tribes were carried off by Babylon between 605 and 586 B.C. The situation where these two kingdoms were divided will end, and as this and other prophecies predict, the two kingdoms will become one nation (cf. Jer. 3:18; 23:5-6; 30:3; Hosea 1:11; Amos 9:11). No fulfillment has ever been recorded in history, and the future regathering of Israel will occur in the Millennium.

*Ezekiel 37:18-23.* Ezekiel was instructed to answer the questions of those who asked the meaning of the two sticks and he was to tell them, "This is what the Sovereign LORD says: 'I am going to take the stick of Joseph—which is in Ephraim's hand—and of the Israelite tribes associated with him, and join them to Judah's stick, making them a single stick of wood, and they will become one in My hand' " (v. 19).

God then further interpreted this, saying, "I will take the Israelites out of the nations where they have gone. I will gather them from all around and bring them back into their own land. I will make them one nation in the land, on the mountains of Israel. There will be one king over all of them and they will never again be two nations or be divided into two kingdoms" (vv. 21-22). God promised He would keep Israel from defiling herself as she has done in the past, and God declared, "I will save them from all their sinful backsliding, and I will cleanse them. They will be My people, and I will be their God" (v. 23). This will be fulfilled in the millennial kingdom.

*Ezekiel 37:24-25.* As predicted in 34:23-24, so here again the prophecy was given, "My servant David will be king over them, and they will all have one shepherd. They will follow My laws and be careful to keep My decrees. They will live in the land I give to My servant Jacob, the land where your fathers lived. They and their children and their children's children will live there forever, and David My servant will be their prince forever" (37:24-25).

Though some have attempted to take this prophecy in less than its literal meaning, the clear statement is that David, who is now dead and whose body is in his tomb in Jerusalem (Acts 2:29), will be resurrected. This will occur at the Second Coming (Dan. 12:1-3), indicating plainly that the restoration of Israel will be subsequent to, not before, the Second Coming. This required Christ's coming before the Millennium or in fulfillment of the premillennial promises. The promise that David would be her prince forever must be interpreted as being fulfilled in the 1,000-year reign. Actually, the word "forever" is a translation of an expression "to the ages" which may be interpreted as forever or until eternity begins.

*Ezekiel 37:26-28.* As Jeremiah stated, God predicted here a covenant of peace with Israel which will be "an everlasting covenant" (v. 26). Though announced in the Old Testament, it will replace the Mosaic Covenant and will have its primary fulfillment for Israel at the time of the Second Coming when Israel is restored nationally and spiritually.

Scholars have puzzled over the precise meaning of the New Covenant, earlier announced by Jeremiah (Jer. 31:31-34). Probably the simplest explanation is that in dying on the cross, God made possible a covenant of grace for those who would trust the Lord. This covenant of grace was the basis for the salvation of every individual, from the time of Adam to the last person who is saved. It has been preeminently illustrated in the present age when God saves the church by grace and the Lord's Supper commemorates the New Covenant. The New Covenant as applied here to Israel primarily has a prophetic meaning which was indicated here as being fulfilled in the peace, righteousness, and restoration which will characterize the millennial kingdom.

At the time of the fulfillment of this covenant the numbers of Israelites in the land will increase greatly, especially during the millennial kingdom. A preliminary prophecy that God will provide a sanctuary (Ezek. 37:28) referred to a millennial temple which will be described later in Ezekiel (40–48).

God promised to be with Israel and dwell among her in the millennial kingdom (v. 27). This will also be true in the new earth in eternity.

The restoration of Israel will be a sign to the world so that the nations will know that it will be accomplished by the holy Lord who is able to cleanse Israel and make her holy.

### Prophecy against Gog

*Ezekiel 38:1–39:24.* Included in the section dealing with Israel's blessing is the description of the deliverance of Israel from the invaders from the north in Ezekiel 38–39 led by Gog.

The prophecy against Gog is one of the most dramatic predictions of Ezekiel. Many details of the prophecy are not entirely clear, but the main thrust of the prediction is not difficult to understand. The passage predicted an invasion of Israel by a great army that will attack Israel from the north.

In order to understand this prophecy, some background in the prophetic foreview of the end of the age is necessary.

This passage is a part of the predictions of the great world conflict which will characterize the years just before the Second Coming. Though Bible expositors have differed as to when this fits into the prophetic picture, it is plausible that preceding this event the predictions of the revived Roman Empire, a ten-nation confederacy, will be fulfilled. This will be considered in the prophecies of Daniel 2 and Daniel 7.

A political leader will arise who will head up the ten nations and makes the Mediterranean Sea a Roman lake as it was in New Testament times. He was referred to in 9:26 as "the ruler who will come." This ruler will be associated with the people who destroyed the city of Jerusalem in A.D. 70, that is, the Roman people and, accordingly, he will fulfill the role of a Roman leader in the end time as heading up this ten-nation confederacy. This ruler will be featured in the first of three major phases of prophetic fulfillment, climaxing in the second coming of Christ. His rise and the formation of the ten-nation confederacy will set the stage for what will follow.

The second phase of this struggle with a duration of three-and-one-half years was described by Ezekiel in these two chapters. Though variously interpreted, it may be the forerunner and major event that leads up to the world government predicted for the last three-and-a-half years leading up to the Second Coming. As the battle described here is a disaster for the invading countries, it may change the political power structure to such an extent that it will be possible for the Roman leader of the ten nations to become a world dictator.

The third phase of the period leading up to the Second Coming will be this world-empire stage, including all nations of the world (Dan. 7:23; Rev. 13:7-8). The third phase, ending in the Second Coming, will be a time of the Great Tribulation. The Great Tribulation also records another mammoth world war (Dan. 11:40-45; Rev. 16:12-16) which will occur just before the Second Coming. This should be distinguished from the war described in Ezekiel 38–39 which is not a world conflict but a war between a select group of nations attacking Israel.

In the quarter of a century since World War II Russia has risen to be one of the great military powers of the modern world. To a far greater extent than ever before Russia has become a prominent nation, especially in its influence on the Middle East. The possibility of Russia attacking Israel is a modern concern of the United States and other nations. With both Russia and Red China constituting a major political bloc, the question of a future war between Russia and Israel becomes a possibility.

The word "Russia" never occurs in Scripture, but the description of this war connects these two important chapters of Ezekiel with the future outcome of Russia as a world power.

If Ezekiel 38–39 is studied carefully, it reveals a future invasion of the land of Israel by the armies of Russia and five other nations. Though sometimes confused with the battle of Armageddon, which will be a world conflict before the Second Coming, this war will be distinct, both in its objectives, its character, and its outcome. According to Scripture the invaders will be totally destroyed which, undoubtedly, will have an effect on the world power struggle in which Russia now is a major factor. As this prophecy was written 2,500 years ago, the question remains whether this has ever been fulfilled in the past.

A search of history finds no such battle or outcome. Accordingly, as illustrated in countless other passages, prophecy that has not been fulfilled is subject to future fulfillment just as literally as the prophecies were fulfilled in the past. Accordingly, though it may leave some questions unanswered, the study of these two chapters supplies an important segment of prophecy as it relates to the end-time period leading up to the second coming of Christ.

The point of view adopted here places this war in the first half of the last seven years, probably toward its close. Other views have been advanced which should be compared to this interpretation.

A few have advanced the theory that this war must occur before the Rapture. The situation described here does not come to pass until after the Rapture. The scene is one of peace which has its best explanation with the seven-year covenant enacted by the ruler of the ten-nation confederacy. This can only occur after the restraint of the presence of the Holy Spirit has been removed at the Rapture (cf. 2 Thes. 2:6-8). Further, it would contradict the doctrine of the imminency of the Rapture.

Another view combines the war with Russia with the battle of Armageddon (Rev. 16:13-16). The war centering in Armageddon is one which involves all the nations of the world. The Russian war is predominantly Russia with six allies. The Armageddon struggle covers all the Holy Land, but the war with Russia is settled on the northern mountain of Israel. Armageddon is the climax of the Great Tribulation, a time of persecution for Israel. Ezekiel 38 describes

190

Israel at peace and in prosperity. For these reasons, Ezekiel 38–39 do not fit Armageddon.

Some have suggested the war will take place at the beginning of the Millennium. This will be a time of peace which will follow the Second Coming. But all the unsaved are executed in the judgments at the Second Coming, and believers in Christ would not support a war against Israel and Jerusalem.

Still another suggestion is that it will occur at the end of the Millennium. The fact that Gog and Magog are mentioned both in Ezekiel 38:1, 6 and in Revelation 20:7 indicates to some a connection. However, Gog is a human leader and Magog are a people in Ezekiel 38, but their meaning is not defined in Revelation 20. In other respects the scene is different. In Ezekiel life goes on after the war, requiring months to bury the dead. The war in Revelation 20 is followed immediately by the destruction of the earth and the creation of the new heaven and new earth. The war in Revelation 20 concerns Jerusalem. The war of Ezekiel does not touch Jerusalem. The scenes are different.

*Ezekiel 38:1-6.* In the opening portion of this great prophecy six nations are mentioned, the most important of which was called Gog (v. 2), identified as a ruler of Magog. He was further described as "the chief prince of Meshech and Tubal" (v. 2). The leader described as Gog apparently will lead a force from the land of Magog (v. 2). Magog was mentioned in Genesis 10:2 as one of the sons of Japheth, a fact repeated in 1 Chronicles 1:5. In addition to the two references in Ezekiel 38–39 (38:2; 39:6), Magog was also mentioned in Revelation 20:8 where it seems to refer to a totally different situation. The most plausible explanation is that Gog is the ruler and Magog are the people. In the description of Gog as "the chief prince of Meshech and Tubal," the *American Standard Version* translates this expression, "the prince of Rosh" which some connect with the root consonants of the modern term "Russia." They were an ancient people located to the north of Israel (Ezek. 27:13; 32:26).

Tubal (38:2) was also mentioned as a son of Japheth (Gen. 10:2; 1 Chron. 1:5). Though originally located south of the Holy Land area, they eventually went north and have been identified as the ancient Scythian tribe which at one time occupied Asia Minor. The leading thought on these identifications is that it verifies that the invaders come from the north of Israel.

The prediction pictured God as putting hooks into the jaws of Gog and leading him and his army from the north against Israel (Ezek. 38:4). Persia (v. 5) has been easily identified as related to modern Iran which could easily supply an army, attacking Israel from the north, even though located to the east.

The identity of Cush (v. 5) is uncertain, but it has often been referred to as the area east of Egypt and west of the Red Sea. This would require them to go around, possibly by sea, to join the army from the north attacking Israel.

The identity of Put (v. 5) also is uncertain, but some have placed it immediately south of Cush in Africa.

Gomer (v. 6) was usually associated with the ancient Cimmerians, some who were located in Asia Minor and others in Eastern Europe.

Beth Togarmah (v. 6) has been identified with Armenia located to the north of Israel. Though all the nations were not located to the north of Israel, it is not too difficult to understand their participation in the major invasion from the north dominated by Russia.

Any nation that attacks Israel is doing so in disregard of God and the Bible, and this fits the political background of Russia whose leadership is largely atheistic. Some also point to the fact that Meshech has some similarity to the modern name of Moscow in its consonant structure, and Tubal is similar to one of the prominent provinces of Russia — Tobolsk.

When all the facts are put together, it indicates that linguistically, geographically, and theologically, the identity of the invading nations is sufficiently clear to identify them as a great force coming from the north.

Probably the most convincing explanation is the fact that the invaders, especially Gomer and Magog (vv. 2-3), invade the land from the "far north" (vv. 6, 15; 39:2). The only nation that the description "far north" would fit would be Russia which, of course, is immediately to the north of Israel, with Moscow being directly north of Jerusalem. Though some attempt to question the identification, because Russia extends more than six thousand miles east and west any reference to a nation to the far north of Israel would have to be Russia because of the geographic facts involved.

As early as 38:4 the prophecy revealed that the army will come mounted on horses with the horsemen fully armed (v. 4). The horsemen are armed with shields and swords and helmets (vv. 4-5) with additional weapons, including bows and arrows and war clubs and spears (v. 9).

Much speculation has arisen from the fact that these are ancient weapons contemporary with Ezekiel but not describing modern warfare. Some regard these ancient weapons as simply typical or figurative of modern warfare. Others attempt to explain these weapons on the basis that they are quickly and readily made and possibly may be used in the period where other weapons have been subject to disarmament. The final answer to explain the weapons is unknown. The fact that they are on horses, however, is not strange as Russia today has troops on horses as a part of their military operation.

*Ezekiel 38:7-9.* The army was described as a great horde which will invade a land that has been restored from previous desolation (vv. 7-8). The people were described as those who have been "gathered from many nations to the mountains of Israel, which had long been desolate" (v. 8). They were further described as coming from the nations and living in safety (v. 8). The attack therefore was unexpected and was imposed on a people who were not prepared militarily to defend themselves. The invaders were described as so great in number that they look like a "cloud covering the land" (v. 9).

*Ezekiel 38:10-13.* The invaders were quoted as saying, "I will invade a land of unwalled villages; I will attack a peaceful and unsuspecting people—all of them living without walls and without gates and bars" (v. 11).

The scene described is a modern scene where walls are no longer necessary to protect a village, confirming the idea that it is a sneak and unexpected attack. The people of Israel in the land are described as "a peaceful and unsuspecting people—all of them living without walls and without gates and bars" (v. 11). The people of Israel were described as living in "the resettled ruins" (v. 12), and they were described as "gathered from the nations, rich in livestock and goods, living at the center of the land" (v. 12).

Sheba, Dedan, and the merchants of Tarshish ask the question whether they have come to seize plunder (v. 13). Sheba probably refers to the kingdom from which the Queen of Sheba had come to see Solomon (1 Kings 10:1-13; 2 Chron. 9:1-12). It was located in southwestern Arabia mentioned by Isaiah (21:13), Jeremiah (Jer. 25:23; 49:8), and Ezekiel (25:13; 27:15, 20; 38:13) and probably referred to a tribe that had intermarried with the Cushite people. Tarshish was probably related to an area where oil was mined in Spain, though some identify it also at a location in southern Arabia where ore was also smelted. In a word, these were the merchants who were acquainted with the wealth of Israel.

*Ezekiel 38:14-16.* Ezekiel was instructed to prophesy that this event would take place. Israel was described as "living in safety" (v. 14), and their safety was mentioned also in verse 8 and 39:6. This reference should make clear that it was not describing Israel today which is an armed camp and living in fear of its neighbors. The nature of the attack was summarized by God, "You will come from your place in the far north, you and many nations with you, all of them riding on horses, a great horde, a mighty army. You will advance against My people Israel like a cloud that covers the land. In days to come, O Gog, I will bring you against My lands, so that the nations may know Me when I show Myself holy through you before their eyes" (38:15-16).

These verses summarized what has been said earlier in the chapter that the attack will come when Israel will be living in safety, that the invaders will come from the far north, that they will be riding on horses, that they will be numerous like a cloud, and that God will bring them against the people of Israel so that by their destruction He can show His own holiness and power.

*Ezekiel 38:17-23.* God reminded the invaders of what was predicted "in former days by My servants the prophets of Israel" (v. 17). The specifics of this prophecy had not been previously mentioned, but many chapters in the prophets dealt with the nations about Israel and God bringing judgment upon them. Accordingly, what was about to be revealed was in keeping with God's previous prophecies.

God declared His reaction to the attack against Israel, " 'When Gog attacks the land of Israel, My hot anger will be aroused,' declares the Sovereign LORD. 'In My zeal and fiery wrath I declared that at that time there shall be a great earthquake in the land of Israel' " (vv. 18-19).

The remarkable aspect of this prophecy is that the Scriptures do not reveal any opposing army attacking the invaders. Rather, it will be a time when God Himself by supernatural actions destroys the army. The first step will be a great earthquake in the land of Israel. The effect of this earthquake will be felt by all of God's creatures on earth, "The fish of the sea, the birds of the air, the beasts of the field, every creature that moves along the ground, and all the people on the face of the earth will tremble at My presence. The mountains will be overturned, the cliffs will crumble and every wall will fall to the ground" (v. 20).

The second great judgment that God will bring on the invaders will be that they will fight among themselves, " 'I will summon a sword against Gog on all my mountains,' declares the Sovereign LORD. 'Every man's sword will be against his brother' " (v. 21). Because of the disruption brought about by the earthquake and the fact that the army will be composed of various peoples coming from various nations, it is easy to understand how through misunderstanding they can start fighting among themselves, thinking that the others were a defending people.

The next form of judgment will be by plague and bloodshed (v. 22). In addition to their being destroyed by the sword, they will experience a plague, a means God has often used to attack the enemies of Israel (cf. Isa. 37:36).

The next judgment speaks of "torrents of rain, hailstones and burning sulphur on him and on his troops and on the many nations with him" (Ezek. 38:22). The floods caused by torrents of rain would obviously hinder an invading army and cause more confusion in communications and properly accounts for the fact that they will be fighting each other. The hailstones also being supernatural may be destructive of human life. The burning sulphur which will fall on them will be a reminder of how God destroyed Sodom and Gomorrah. The nature of these judgments demonstrated to all that God will fight the invading army and pour His judgment on them. This was brought out in the closing verse of the chapter, "And so I will show My greatness and My holiness, and I will make Myself known in the sight of many nations. Then they will know that I am the LORD" (v. 23).

*Ezekiel 39:1-6.* In repeating aspects of the prophecy of their destruction, God noted again that the invasion of the land was caused by God bringing them into this conflict, "I will turn you around and drag you along. I will bring you from the far north and send you against the mountains of Israel" (v. 2). The geographic origination of the invasion was again said to be "the far north" (v. 2).

God further declared, "Then I will strike your bow from your left hand and make your arrows drop from your right hand" (v. 3).

Earlier he had mentioned other weapons, but this passage for the first time mentioned bows and arrows which were standard weapons in the time Ezekiel lived. Though bows and arrows are usually characterized as primitive weapons, they actually have played a part in modern warfare and were used extensively, for instance, in the war in Vietnam. Because an arrow going through the air did not give away the location of the one who shot the arrow, it therefore was good for use in jungle situations. No final answer can be given why primitive weapons are specified. Though the outcome of the battle was clearly prophesied, Scripture does not offer any explanation why the weapons described were primitive.

Because of the various judgments of God mentioned earlier, God declared that the invading army will fall on the mountains of Israel (v. 4). God stated, " 'I will give you as food to all kinds of carrion birds and to the wild animals. You will fall in the open field, for I have spoken,' declares the Sovereign LORD" (vv. 4-5). From these Scriptures it is clear that the entire invading army will be wiped out. In the KJV Ezekiel 39:2 was translated, "And I will turn thee back, and leave but the sixth part of thee." This translation is inaccurate, and from the NIV it is clear that the entire invading force will be wiped out as indicated in the expression, "All your troops and the nations with you" (v. 4).

In addition to wiping out the army that will be invading Israel, a judgment of fire will also be inflicted on Magog and "those who live in safety in the coastlands" (v. 6), indicating that a special judgment will be visited also on the land from which the Russian army troops came.

*Ezekiel 39:7-8.* The purpose of the destruction of the armies will be to give notice to the nations that they will no longer be able to profane the holy name of the Lord (v. 7). God reaffirmed the certainty and literalness of this event, declaring, "It is coming! It will surely take place" (v. 8).

*Ezekiel 39:9-10.* The extent of the destruction was indicated by the amount of weapons that will be accumulated from the victory over the invading army. They will be used for fuel and include " 'the small and large shields, the bows and arrows, the war clubs and spears. For seven years they will use them for fuel. They will not need to gather wood from the fields or cut it from the forests, because they will use the weapons for fuel. And they will plunder those who plundered them and loot those who looted them,' declares the Sovereign LORD" (vv. 9-10).

The theory that these weapons were simply figurative and not representing real weapons of wood was countered by the fact that they will be used for fuel, indicating that the weapons will be actually as described. Also, the fuel will be of such large amount that they will be able to use it for seven years for their fires.

The figure of seven years introduces some problems as it affects the location of this war in the end-time events because it pictures Israel at peace and in safety (38:8; 39:6). The burning of the fuel is not a prophetic event but only a statement of the amount of debris. A number of expositors have located this war in the first half of the last seven years leading up to the Second Coming. The first half of the seven years will be a period of peace because of the covenant entered into between Israel and the Gentile ruler of that period (Dan. 9:27). The problem of the fuel lasting seven years, however, is not a real prophetic problem because even after the Lord returns they will still need fuel for fires in the millennial kingdom as life goes on. Accordingly, the seven-year figure should not be considered an obstacle to placing the war somewhere in the middle of the last seven years with the possibility that it may occur earlier in the seven-year period and justify the approximate figure of seven years.

*Ezekiel 39:11-16.* The thousands of soldiers killed in the war were described as requiring seven months to bury them in order to cleanse the land (vv. 11-13). After the seven months there still will be other bodies located, and according to the prophecy some will be permanently employed to search out the dead and bury them (vv. 14-16).

*Ezekiel 39:17-20.* Immediately after the battle, before the burial takes place, God invited the birds and wild animals to feast on the dead bodies. God pointed out how the dead will include riders, some of whom were important people, and also their horses (vv. 17-20).

*Ezekiel 39:21-24.* The judgment on the invaders was designed to display the power of God (v. 21). God had previously judged the people of Israel because of her unfaithfulness and many of them had died (vv. 23-24).

### The Restoration of Israel

*Ezekiel 39:25-29.* God here announced the restoration of Israel as has been predicted in many other passages in the Old Testament. God declared, "I will now bring Jacob back from captivity and will have compassion on all the people of Israel, and I will be zealous for My holy name. They will forget their shame and all the unfaithfulness they showed toward Me when they lived in safety in their land with no one to make them afraid" (vv. 25-26). This prediction of restoration was just as literal as the prediction of the battle, and both will take place in the future.

God, having previously predicted His judgments on Israel, here made a special point of how they will be gathered completely from the various foreign lands from which they were scattered. This had been described in Ezekiel 38. Now God makes a specific and sweeping prediction, " 'When I have brought them back from the nations and have gathered them from the countries of their enemies, I will show Myself holy through them in the sight of many nations. Then they will know that I am the LORD their God, for though I sent them into exile among the nations, I will gather them to their own land, not leaving any behind. I will no longer hide My face from them, for I will pour out My Spirit on the house of Israel,' declares the Sovereign LORD" (39:27-29). Not only will God restore Israel to the land, but He promised to gather all of them from their scattered position and bring them back to the land. This will occur in the opening period of the millennial kingdom. It will not be an option to the Children of Israel, but she will be commanded to come to her Promised Land. This is a sweeping and dramatic prediction and supports the doctrine of a glorious future for Israel in the Millennium.

Early in Ezekiel 20:33-38 God had declared His purpose to regather Israel but will purge out the rebels or the unsaved so that only righteous Israel will be allowed to possess her ancient land. An important point in biblical interpretation is to treat these prophecies in the literal sense as are the other prophecies which have been fulfilled. If so, it requires a coming of Christ before the thousand-year reign of Christ or the premillennial return of the Lord.

### The Millennial Temple

*Ezekiel 40:1–43:27.* Beginning in Ezekiel 40 the specifications for the millennial temple and its system of worship were described. Scholars have differed over the question whether these prophecies should be taken literally or in some figurative sense. Some suggest the plans were for a temple to replace Solomon's which had been destroyed. But no such temple was built. Others find it a symbolic picture of the church, but leave unanswered why such specific details were revealed. Further, those who adopt the figurative interpretation have not agreed as to the meaning of this temple. Inasmuch as the specifications are very specific and imply a literal temple and inasmuch as having a temple in the Millennium would coincide with a period of joy and peace and worship of the Lord, it would seem best to consider this temple a literal temple though problems of interpretation remain.

Ezekiel recorded how the Lord in a vision took him to a high mountain where he was introduced to a man who seemed to be made of bronze. The man said to him, "Son of man, look with your eyes and hear with your ears and pay attention to everything I am going to show you, for that is why you have been brought here. Tell the house of Israel everything you see" (40:4).

In the introduction of a millennial temple and its worship in the Millennium, Ezekiel was continuing his discussion of the restoration of Israel spiritually which was incorporated in the predictions of Ezekiel 33–39. In the first three chapters of the section concerning the temple (40–43) the new temple was described as the center of worship. This was followed by revealing the characteristics of worship in chapters 44–46 and the final division of the land for Israel in chapters 47–48.

As the detailed picture of the temple was unfolded, it was obvious that it cannot be explained as plans for the temple built by the returning exiles from Babylon. The temple they built was totally different in its structure. Also, it is unexplainable if you take this in a symbolic sense because the details given were not necessary for a symbolic temple. Accordingly, those who believe in interpreting prophecy in a literal sense believe this will be an actual temple that will be built in the millennial kingdom. There may be a previous temple built on different specifications in the period of the Great Tribulation before the Second Coming as a sacrificial system of offerings was restored and then stopped by the political developments, but it will not be the temple that was described here in Ezekiel.

Before considering the details of the temple, the question may be fairly asked: Why is the millennial temple revealed with so many details? The answer seems to be that it will be the symbol of God's presence with His people as He promised to be with them at the time of the Millennium. As stated earlier in 37:26-27, God declared, "I will establish them and increase their numbers, and I will put My sanctuary among them forever. My dwelling place will be with them; I will be their God, and they will be My people. Then the nations will know that I the LORD make Israel holy, when My sanctuary is among them forever."

The sanctuary in their midst will be also an assurance of God's presence in their midst as God will indwell the millennial temple much as He did the temple of God and the tabernacle before it. The glory of God had left Solomon's temple as described in Ezekiel 8–11. The restoration of Israel as a nation will feature God's presence reentering a temple and being with His people visibly. In keeping with the promise of the New Covenant (37:26), the temple will be the visible evidence of God's presence. Such a large temple is in keeping with the other promises of God's presence and blessing in the millennial kingdom and Israel's restoration to their land.

Though the details of the construction of the temple were not in themselves of prophetic significance, putting these details together involves a description of a building that has never been built in the past and which will be the centerpiece of God's plan for the kingdom when Christ returns. Its size far exceeds anything that was known in previous temples.

As described in Ezekiel (40:5–42:20), the outer dimensions of the temple complex will form a square 875 feet (500 cubits) across and in length. The temple faces east as did the tabernacle and the temples of Solomon and of the Exile. The south, east, and north sides have an outer wall. Thirty rooms were also built on the second and third levels. The temple itself was projected from inside the western wall of the temple complex toward the east, and, except on the western wall, it had outer courts on three sides — south, east, and north, 175 feet in width. The rooms inside the temple area were assigned to their respective uses, including the temple proper in the center with an inner court in front of it extending to the east. The details, while not prophetic in themselves, together give a tremendous vision of the central place of worship in the millennial kingdom.

Ezekiel, who recorded this vision of the temple, was given what amounted to a tour which prompted the detailed description. He was led by an angel described as "a man whose appearance was like bronze"(40:3).

The measuring rod used by the angel was six cubits long (v. 5), with a rod being approximately twenty-one inches in length. The

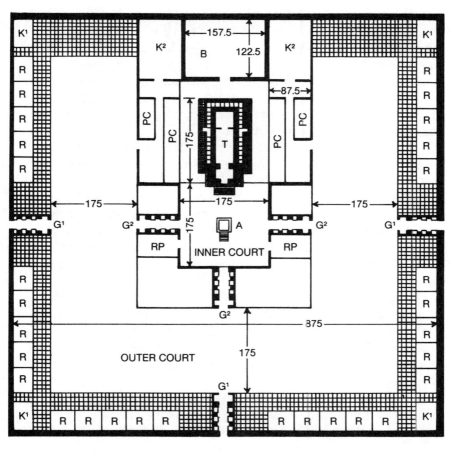

**THE MILLENNIAL TEMPLE**
(Dimensions are in feet.)

A    Altar (43:13-17)
B    Building (function not explained) (41:12)
G¹   Outer gates (40:6-17, 20-27)
G²   Inner gates (40:28-37)
K¹   Kitchens for people's sacrifices (46:21-24)
K²   Kitchens for priests (46:19-20)
PC   Priests' chambers (42:1-14)
R    30 rooms in outer court (40:17)
RP   Rooms for ministering priests (40:44-47)
T    Temple proper (40:48–41:11, 13-14, 16-26)

From *The Bible Knowledge Commentary,* Old Testament (Victor Books, 1985), p. 1303. Used with permission.

total measuring rod therefore was about ten feet six inches. Ezekiel entered through the eastern gate (v. 6); there was also one gate on the south and one on the north, corresponding to the gates of the outer court. Solomon's temple had only a gate on the east.

As Ezekiel comprehended what he was seeing, he was informed concerning the measurements which were mentioned in the Scriptures. After the outer court was measured, Ezekiel recorded that the angel measured the inner court (vv. 28-37). Each of the gates had tables set up on either side of the entrance for the purpose of slaughtering the sacrifices, with eight tables, four on each side, being available in each of the three gates.

One of the exegetical problems of Ezekiel's temple is the fact that sacrifices will be offered in the Millennium. This has often been considered a contradiction of the fact that Christ is the one sacrifice that takes away sin inasmuch as His sacrifice caused the Mosaic Law of sacrifices to be abolished. Why then is the sacrificial system predicted here?

Though some have attempted to explain this by symbolic explanations, actually, the explanation of a literal interpretation is quite clear. First of all, it should be observed that the sacrifices in the Old Testament did not take away sin. They were prophetic, looking forward to the death of Christ which was the final sacrifice. In the Millennium, apparently, sacrifices will also be offered, though somewhat different than those required under the Mosaic Law, but this time the sacrifices will be memorial, much as the Lord's Supper is a memorial in the Church Age for the death of Christ.

Though it is objectionable to some to have animal sacrifices in the millennial scene, actually, they will be needed there because the very ideal circumstances in which millennial saints will live will tend to gloss over the awfulness of sin and the need for bloody sacrifice. The sacrifices offered will therefore be a reminder that only by the shedding of blood and, more specifically, the blood of Christ, can sin be taken away. Ezekiel was not alone in referring to a sacrificial system in the Millennium (cf. Isa. 56:7; 66:20-23; Jer. 33:18; Zech. 14:16-21; Mal. 3:3-4). The prophets therefore seem to be united in referring to literal sacrifices in connection with a literal temple in the Millennium.

It is natural that a future sacrificial system in the Millennium should raise objections. Bloody sacrifices are offensive to modern culture. Their use in the Mosaic Covenant and before was, howev-

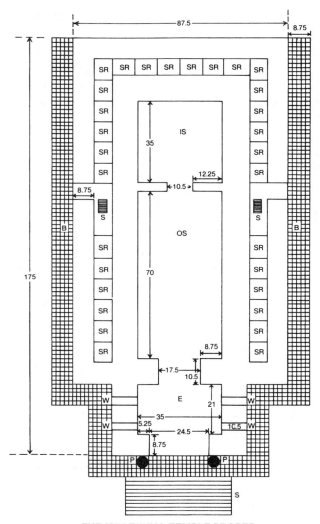

**THE MILLENNIAL TEMPLE PROPER**
(Dimensions are in feet.)

B    Base surrounding temple (41:11)
E    Entrance to temple (portico; 40:48-49; 41:2a, 26)
IS    Inner Sanctuary (41:3-4)
OS    Outer Sanctuary (41:2b, 21)
P    Pillars (40:49b)
S    Steps (40:49b; 41:7b)
SR    Side Rooms (41:5-11)
W    Windows (41:26)

From *The Bible Knowledge Commentary,* Old Testament (Victor Books, 1985), p. 1306. Used with permission.

er, ordered by God Himself as a typical religious rite that pointed to Christ. Any attempt to spiritualize the temple as well as the millennial sacrifices runs into major difficulties with the details revealed as no satisfactory explanation can be offered which accounts for the details of the prophetic revelation. If bloody sacrifices were proper as typical illustration of redemption in the Old Testament, they are also proper as a memorial to the death of Christ.

Two rooms were mentioned specifically (Ezek. 40:44) which were designated for the use of priests (vv. 44-46).

The angel also measured the most holy place and also the inner sanctuary, into which Ezekiel could not enter. Various other details were mentioned concerning the most holy place, the interior and the rear buildings (41:1-26).

As recorded in Ezekiel 42, the chambers of the priests and the temple itself were measured. The total dimensions of the temple were tremendous and exceeded by far any previous temple that had been built for Israel.

Climaxing the tour of the temple, Ezekiel prophetically saw the return of the Lord and the glory of the Lord filling the temple (43:1-5). God declared that this temple will be His residence and His throne (vv. 6-7). God promised that the temple would be kept holy (vv. 8-9). Ezekiel was instructed to describe the temple to the people of Israel, including its various aspects of design, that they may be faithful in building the temple when the time comes (vv. 10-11). The area around the temple was also going to be declared "most holy" (v. 12). Details concerning the altar of sacrifice were also described by Ezekiel (vv. 13-17).

A detailed program of how to consecrate the priests and the people was also described by Ezekiel (vv. 18-27). A seven-day period of offering bull, goats, and rams would sanctify the priests and the temple, somewhat similar to how the tabernacle was consecrated by Moses (Ex. 40:2-33) and Solomon consecrated his temple (2 Chron. 7:8-9).

Following the burnt offerings presented for the people, fellowship offerings (peace offerings) would also be offered. The meaning of this was that God was renewing His fellowship with the people of Israel and these sacrifices would point back to Christ as the One who was the supreme sacrifice for sin and who made it possible for them to approach God the Father (Heb. 10:19-25).

As brought out previously, there is no good reason for under-

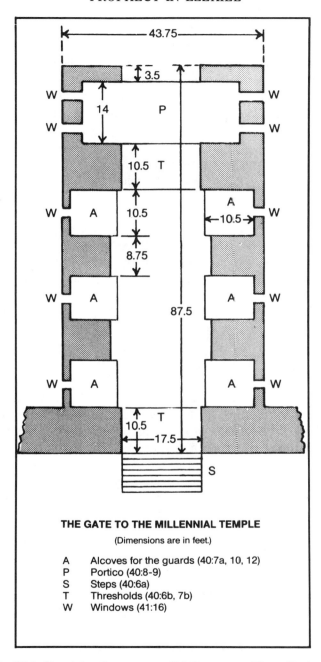

**THE GATE TO THE MILLENNIAL TEMPLE**

(Dimensions are in feet.)

A  Alcoves for the guards (40:7a, 10, 12)
P  Portico (40:8-9)
S  Steps (40:6a)
T  Thresholds (40:6b, 7b)
W  Windows (41:16)

From *The Bible Knowledge Commentary,* Old Testament (Victor Books, 1985), p. 1305. Used with permission.

standing this passage in other than its literal sense. The offerings here do not take away sin any more than the offerings under the Mosaic Covenant, but they point back to the one offering of Christ on the cross just as the Old Testament offerings pointed forward to the death of Christ. Because the Lord's Supper will no longer be observed, the sacrificial system, somewhat different than the Mosaic system, was reinstituted but with similar intent to point people to Christ.

### New Life and Worship in the Millennial Kingdom

*Ezekiel 44:1–46:24.* The temple as the center of Israel's religious life will bring about changes in their forms of worship and in the regulations concerning the use of the temple. Ezekiel was informed that the eastern gate was to be kept closed because through it "the LORD, the God of Israel" would enter (44:2). David was identified as "the prince himself," resurrected to serve as a prince under Christ in the millennial kingdom (v. 3; 34:23-24; 37:24-25). David will be resurrected at the Second Coming and the kingdom will follow this event as held by premillenarians. The outer wall of the temple had three gates facing south, east, and north leading into the outer court. Because the prince would enter the eastern gate, the gate itself would be closed except for him, and all others would enter either through the north or the south gate.

In the present wall about the city of Jerusalem, including the wall that is near the temple site, there is only one gate on the eastern wall which has been closed for many centuries. This probably is to be distinguished from the eastern gate which led into the outer court of Solomon's temple. The eastern gate of the outer court will be opened and will lead to the eastern gate of the temple (44:1-3). The present gate in the wall of Jerusalem does not correspond to the gate of the millennial temple, but it will undoubtedly be open to the Lord when He comes.

The angel, referring to "the man" who had been showing Ezekiel the temple (40:3-4) brought Ezekiel to the front of the temple through the north gate (44:4). Ezekiel then witnessed "the glory of the LORD filling the temple of the LORD" (v. 4), causing Ezekiel to fall on his face. God instructed Ezekiel to communicate to Israel that she was not to defile the temple as she had defiled the temple of Solomon by bringing in foreigners and wrong practices and not observing the laws concerning the sacrifices (vv. 5-8). All foreigners were excluded from entering the sanctuary (v. 9).

In observing the worship of the future temple, the Levites are limited in their service in the sanctuary to having charge of the gates, slaughtering the burnt offerings, and similar tasks, but are not to serve as priests or come near to holy things or the holy offerings (vv. 10-14).

The priests who descended from Zadok, the godly line of priests from Aaron, and Levites, who were descendants of Zadok, will be the ones entrusted with the sacred ministry and will be allowed to enter the sanctuary and minister to the Lord (vv. 15-16).

They were instructed not to wear woolen garments lest they perspire and were to use linen garments instead. When they go out into the outer court of the temple, however, they were to put on other clothes (vv. 17-19).

Further instructions were given that they should not shave their heads or let their hair grow long, not to drink wine when they enter the inner court, not to marry widows or divorced women, for they are to teach the people of Israel the difference between holy and that which is not holy (vv. 20-24).

As was true also under the Mosaic code, the priest was not to defile himself by coming near a dead body. If this became necessary, he was to cleanse himself for seven days before again offering offerings to the Lord (vv. 25-27).

The priests were not given an inheritance but were to be supported by the offerings which the people brought which would be food for them (vv. 28-31).

These regulations relating to the use of the temple and its worship can only be taken in their literal sense as any symbolic interpretation does not fit any other chronological period. The detailed regulations outlined in Ezekiel would not make sense unless taken in their ordinary sense as applied to this future kingdom.

Though the priests were not allowed to have a personal inheritance, they were given a special section of land (45:1-5).

In addition to the land allocated to the priests as a place for them to live which included the temple itself, the city will also be provided with a portion of the land next to the sacred area which would belong to Israel as a whole (v. 6).

The prince will also have a portion of land extending both east and west from this central block of land, and it will go all the way from the area allotted to the priests in the city to the Mediterranean to the west and to the Jordan River on the east. Further division of the land is outlined in Ezekiel 47–48.

On the basis of God's plan for them to be a holy people in a holy land, Ezekiel was to exhort the people of Israel to be honest in their present situation, not giving themselves to violence or oppression but being just and honest in their dealings (vv. 9-12).

Details were given concerning a special gift in their offerings (vv. 13-16). The prince will also provide various offerings during times of observance of the new moons and sabbaths and at other appointed feasts (v. 17).

Special sacrifices were to be offered in the first month and the first day (vv. 18-19). This offering should be repeated on the seventh day of the month (v. 20).

The Passover feast will also be observed in the first month on the fourteenth day to be followed by the seven-day feast of unleavened bread (vv. 21-25).

Special regulations governed the worship and service of God on the Sabbath Day and other special feast days (46:1-8). The people coming from outside the temple into the outer court should enter by the north gate and exit by the south gate, or if they enter by the south gate they exit at the north gate (v. 9). Further details on their offerings were outlined for various occasions (vv. 11-15).

The laws of inheritance as it relates to the prince and also the people were outlined by Ezekiel with the view that each one should receive his inheritance from his own property and not be dispossessed by the prince (vv. 16-18).

Ezekiel was also shown the sacred rooms which belonged to the priests and where they could cook the guilt offering and sin offering and also where they could bake the grain offering (vv. 19-20). Ezekiel was also shown the other features of rooms related to the outer court (vv. 21-24).

### The Promised Land in the Millennium

*Ezekiel 47:1–48:35.* In the last two chapters of Ezekiel attention is directed to the river which will flow from the temple and to the various boundaries and divisions of the Promised Land. The river will flow from the south side of the temple (47:1). The river was pictured as one of considerable volume, so much so that he could not wade across (vv. 3-6).

On the banks of the river trees will grow (vv. 7-9), and living creatures and fish were related to the river. This river will flow into what is now the Dead Sea and will restore its water without salt

(v. 8). The river will reach the ocean to the south of Israel and flow into the Gulf of Aqabah. Though the Dead Sea itself will no longer be salt but will be characterized by fresh water, marshes will be left which have salt, an important ingredient in the mineral world which will be for the benefit of Israel.

The boundaries of the land were outlined for Ezekiel's information as they will exist in the millennial kingdom. Though some of the geographic places mentioned are not certain, it is quite clear the northern boundary will run beyond Sidon from the Mediterranean north of Damascus and then come southwest to the Jordan River below the Sea of Galilee and hence down to the Dead Sea where a portion of the land south of the Dead Sea will reach the River of Egypt. The Mediterranean will be the western boundary of Israel.

As outlined by Ezekiel, the land will be distributed from north to south, giving Dan a portion, then Asher, Naphtali, Manasseh, Ephraim, Reuben, and Judah. Judah's southern boundary will be marked out as the prince's and priests' portion. South of this will be Benjamin, Simeon, Issachar, Zebulun, and Gad. There is no reason to question that these are literal places and situations. These prophecies have never been fulfilled in the past but will be fulfilled in the future millennial kingdom after the second coming of Christ.

The millennial Jerusalem is also described as a glorious city with twelve gates, three on each side. The gates will bear the names of the twelve tribes of Israel, the northern gates bearing the name of Reuben, Judah, and Levi, the eastern gates being named for Joseph, Benjamin, and Dan, the southern gates named after Simeon, Issachar, and Zebulun, and the western gates named after Gad, Asher, and Naphtali (vv. 30-34).

Notably different than the present state of Jerusalem will be the fact that Jerusalem will in the Millennium have the glorious presence of God (v. 35). The return of the visible glory of God to the city indicated God's blessing on Israel and Jerusalem in the millennial state. The millennial Jerusalem is much smaller than the New Jerusalem in the new earth which will be the eternal city (Rev. 21:15-17).

Though many attempts have been made to symbolize the prophecies of Ezekiel as if they were past or present, obviously, the simplest and best interpretation in keeping with the way the prophecy was presented is to take it in its literal form as a prophecy of future events.

# 7

## PROPHECY IN DANIEL

# INTRODUCTION TO THE BOOK OF DANIEL

Among prophetic biblical books, Daniel has a special place that sets it apart as a unique and distinctive contribution. Written by Daniel, a Jewish captive carried off from Jerusalem to Babylon in 605 B.C., the book records not only illuminating experiences of Daniel himself but also the remarkable prophecies which God gave to him which provide a chronology both for the times of the Gentiles and for the future of Israel up to the second coming of Christ. Daniel himself lived longer than the seventy years of the Captivity and was still a prominent character in 536 B.C. in the third year of Cyrus the Persian. Though the death of Daniel was not recorded, he probably lived to about 530 B.C. which gave him ample time to complete the writing of the Book of Daniel.

Though some have attacked the Book of Daniel as not genuine Scripture, it is clear that the book itself claims to be a product of Daniel as he is referred to in the first person in numerous passages in the second half of the book (7:2, 15, 28; 8:1, 15, 27; 9:2, 22; 10:2, 7, 11-12; 12:5). Daniel is also mentioned in Ezekiel (14:14, 20; 28:3) which would be quite natural as Ezekiel was a contemporary of Daniel who, as a primary official of the Babylonian Empire would, no doubt, be known by Ezekiel.

The authenticity of the Book of Daniel went unchallenged from the time of its writing, before 530 B.C., until the third century of the Christian era, or almost 900 years. A pagan and atheistic writer by the name of Porphyry (third century A.D.) raised the question whether the Book of Daniel was a genuine biblical prophecy on the premise that prophecy of the future is impossible. Porphyry found that the Book of Daniel was so accurate in describing future events that it must have been written after the event. He advanced the theory that the book was a forgery, written in the Maccabean period, about 175 B.C. His attack on the Book of Daniel aroused immediate opposition and caused Jerome (A.D. 347–420) to write his own commentary on Daniel in which he answered Porphyry in detail.

For another 1,300 years Daniel was considered as a genuine book by orthodox Christians and Jews until modern liberalism arose in the seventeenth century. Critics of the Bible as the inspired Word of God picked up Porphyry's idea and attempted to prove that Daniel was not a genuine book of the Bible. Their objections have been answered in full by many conservative scholars. The discovery of a

Book of Daniel in the Dead Sea Scrolls (ca. 100 B.C.), on the basis of premises entertained by the liberals themselves, proved that it was impossible for the book to have been written in the second century B.C. and that it clearly was written many years before. Both Jewish and Christian scholars have attested to the genuine character of the Book of Daniel, and the proof includes recognition by Christ Himself of "Daniel the prophet" (Matt. 24:15).

Daniel is found in the Hebrew Bible in what is known as "The Writings" rather than "The Prophecy." This has been explained by the fact that Daniel professionally was a government official rather than a prophet, and because his book was so different compared to other prophetic writings. However, the prophetic character is recognized in the Septuagint and the Vulgate, and Luther classified Daniel as one of the major prophets. Early in the history of the church Josephus put Daniel with the other prophetic books of the Old Testament.

The Book of Daniel is often classified as apocalyptic from the Greek *apokalypsis* (meaning, to uncover, to unveil) because many of its prophecies were revealed in symbolic form. However, the Book of Daniel itself usually explained the symbols and gave them plain meaning. Other apocalyptic books such as Ezekiel and Zechariah take their place along with the Book of Revelation in the New Testament.

The Book of Daniel, unlike most Old Testament books, was written in two languages, beginning with Hebrew and then changing to Aramaic, beginning in 2:4 and ending at 7:28. As Aramaic was the standard language of Babylon, it was natural for this portion of the book that deals with Gentiles to be written in the language that was currently used among the Gentiles in Daniel's time.

The Book of Daniel has been often divided into the first section, Daniel 1–6 as primarily history though it included prophetic revelation, and Daniel 7–12 as prophetic because in these chapters Daniel recorded visions which he himself had. Another approach has been to recognize chapter 1 as Daniel's personal background, chapters 2–7 as dealing with the times of the Gentiles, and chapters 8–12 as dealing with Gentile history as it relates to Israel.

The Book of Daniel, more so than any other book in the Old Testament, revealed very specific prophecies concerning the future, so specific that those who believed that prophecy of the future was impossible have been forced to try to put the record of

Daniel after the event. However, even a second-century Daniel could not explain some prophecies which are yet to be fulfilled. An outstanding illustration of detailed prophecy is Daniel 11:1-35, containing over 100 specific prophecies, all of which have been fulfilled.

Because so many of Daniel's prophecies have already been literally fulfilled, it gives substantial basis for faith that the prophecies not yet fulfilled will have the same literal fulfillment in God's time. Accordingly, the Book of Daniel is not only important as a key to understanding the past in God's sovereign control of both Gentile and Jewish history but also gives insight concerning the future, and in particular helps to understand the symbolism in the Book of Revelation.

In most respects, Daniel gave the most comprehensive and detailed picture of the times of the Gentiles of any book of the Bible as well as the future history of Israel from Daniel's time to the second coming of Christ. Accordingly, the Book of Daniel is the key to prophetic interpretation, and proper understanding of its revelation would do much to help the interpretation of other prophetic portions. For a commentary by the author on Daniel, see *Daniel*, Moody Press, 1971.

## PROPHECY OF THE TIMES OF THE GENTILES IN DANIEL

*Daniel 1:1-21.* The Book of Daniel began with the explanation of how Daniel and his companions were carried off to Babylon, there to be schooled in the religion and history of Babylon in order to become servants of the king. Though Daniel 1 was not prophetic in itself, it justified the claim that Daniel was himself a prophet, and his interpretation of the prophetic vision of Nebuchadnezzar formed the basis for later, more detailed prophecy concerning the times of the Gentiles. The fact that Daniel stood the test of obeying the Law of Israel rather than giving in to the dietary customs of the Babylonians made it possible for God to use him as a pure instrument through whom He could reveal His truth. Daniel and his three companions stood out as those who are true to God when other Jewish captives undoubtedly compromised, and their names were lost to history.

### Nebuchadnezzar's Prophetic Image

*Daniel 2:1-16.* King Nebuchadnezzar had a series of dreams which deeply troubled him so that he could not sleep (v. 1). Even though it may not have been during an hour when the court was in session, he required his "magicians, enchanters, sorcerers and astrologers" to appear before him to interpret the dream (v. 2). When they were assembled, they asked the natural question of the king about the content of the dream (v. 4). He informed them, however, that he was not going to tell them the dream, and if they would not tell him the dream and its interpretation, they would be "cut into pieces and your houses turned into piles of rubble" (v. 5). This was no idle threat as ancient monarchs were known for cruel, unusual punishments.

Scholars are divided as to whether Nebuchadnezzar purposefully withheld knowledge of the dream or did not remember the dream well enough to communicate it to his counselors. There was a possibility that Nebuchadnezzar, a young ruler, who had inherited these counselors from his father, was somewhat impatient with their claims to supernatural powers and knowledge and wanted to test them.

Though the counselors pled with the king to inform them concerning the dream (v. 7), the king reaffirmed that if they did not tell him the dream and its interpretation the penalty would be inflicted (vv. 8-9). When the astrologers protested that this was a request that no king had ever demanded of his subjects (vv. 10-11), the king was so angry that he ordered their immediate execution. Daniel and his three companions, though classified as wise men, were apparently not in the company, but they were sought out for execution along with the others (v. 13).

When the commander of the king's guard, Arioch, informed Daniel of the decree, "Daniel went in to the king and asked for time, so that he might interpret the dream for him" (v. 16). Apparently Nebuchadnezzar had cooled down, and the thought of this young servant, not yet twenty years of age, being able to interpret the dream, no doubt intrigued him and set Daniel apart from the fawning counselors with whom he had dealt first.

*Daniel 2:17-18.* Daniel shared his problem with his three companions, Hananiah, Mishael, and Azariah (v. 17), and together they turned to the Lord in prayer that they might have the secret revealed to them.

*Daniel 2:19-23.* Daniel had the secret revealed to him in a night vision (v. 19) and immediately gave praise to the Lord in a remarkable poetic utterance.

*Daniel 2:20-23.* Daniel's praise to the Lord revealed his spiritual maturity, careful choice of words, and fitting recognition of the wisdom and power of God and His mercy in revealing to Daniel the secret of the dream.

*Daniel 2:24.* Daniel reported to Arioch that he would interpret the dream, and Arioch immediately, hoping to gain favor from the king, went into Nebuchadnezzar and stated, "I have found a man among the exiles from Judah who can tell the king what his dream means" (v. 25).

*Daniel 2:25-28.* Having been given immediate audience with Nebuchadnezzar, Daniel in his answer to the king's question was careful to attribute the revelation to God rather than to any human intelligence. He told Nebuchadnezzar, "No wise man, enchanter, magician or diviner can explain to the king the mystery he has asked about, but there is a God in heaven who reveals mysteries. He has shown King Nebuchadnezzar what will happen in days to come. Your dream and the visions that passed through your mind as you lay on your bed are these" (vv. 27-28).

*Daniel 2:29-35.* Daniel described the vision and said it was like "a large statue—an enormous, dazzling statue, awesome in appearance" (v. 31). The vision apparently was larger than the normal stature of a man, and the statue stood close to the bed of Nebuchadnezzar in a situation that would cause Nebuchadnezzar to respond with fear. Daniel further explained that the head of the statue was of "pure gold," and that the upper part of the body, "its chest and arms," were of "silver." He further described the lower part of the body and the thighs as made of "bronze" (v. 32). The legs were made of "iron" and the feet "partly of iron and partly of baked clay" (v. 33).

Daniel recorded how in the dream Nebuchadnezzar saw "a rock was cut out, but not by human hands" and that it "struck the statue on its feet of iron and clay and smashed them" (v. 34). The result of the impact of the rock on the statue was that the whole statue broke up into fine pieces and became like chaff on a threshing floor (v. 35). He then saw the chaff blown away so that all the debris of the statue disappeared. Finally, Daniel recorded that he saw the "rock that struck the statue became a huge mountain and filled the whole earth" (v. 35).

No doubt, the recital of Daniel of the details of the vision either reminded the king of the dream he had or confirmed what he re-

## WORLD EMPIRES OF THE BIBLE IN THE HISTORY OF ISRAEL

| EGYPT | ASSYRIA | BABYLON | MEDO-PERSIA | GREECE | ROME | MILLENNIAL KINGDOM FINAL WORLD EMPIRE |
|---|---|---|---|---|---|---|
| Gen. 46–Deut. 34 | 722 B.C.–605 B.C. | 605 B.C.–539 B.C. | 539 B.C.–331 B.C. | 321 B.C.–63 B.C. | 63 B.C.–A.D. 70 | |
| Jacob and Family in Egypt Until Exodus | 10 Tribes of Israel in Captivity | 2 Tribes in Captivity | Captives of Israel Return 536 B.C. | Israel under Control of Syria | Israel under Rome | |
| | | | | | Jerusalem Destroyed A.D. 70 | |
| | | | | | Decline of Rome in Church Age | |
| | | | | | Rome to Be Revived after the Rapture | |

membered. In any case, he was astounded that Daniel would tell him the dream.

*Daniel 2:36-45.* Having told the dream, Daniel explained its meaning (v. 36). He reminded Nebuchadnezzar that he was a great king and that God had given him a great dominion and glory, not only over men but beast as well (vv. 37-38). He declared to Nebuchadnezzar, "You are that head of gold" (v. 38).

Daniel explained that the upper part of the body represented another kingdom that was inferior to the kingdom of Babylon (v. 39) and that it would be followed by "a third kingdom, one of bronze, will rule over the whole earth" (v. 39). Later in Daniel these kingdoms are named Medo-Persia and Greece (8:20-21).

Then Daniel defined the meaning of the fourth kingdom represented by the iron legs and the feet part of iron and part of pottery. He declared, "Finally, there will be a fourth kingdom, strong as iron — for iron breaks and smashes everything — and as iron breaks things to pieces, so it will crush and break all the others" (2:40). A separate explanation is given of the feet and toes which were partly of baked clay and partly of iron which Daniel explained as representing "the divided kingdom" (v. 41). It would have the strength of iron but the weakness of clay pottery (v. 42). Daniel explained the mixture of clay and iron as representing the mixture of people who were not united (v. 43).

In the vision there remained the explanation of the rock that destroyed the image and then grew to be a mountain. Daniel explained this: "In the time of those kings, the God of heaven will set up a kingdom that will never be destroyed, nor will it be left to another people. It will crush all those kingdoms and bring them to an end, but it will itself endure forever. This is the meaning of the vision of the rock cut out of a mountain, but not by human hands — a rock that broke the iron, the bronze, the clay, the silver and the gold to pieces" (vv. 44-45). The kingdom represented by the rock is the kingdom which Christ will inaugurate at His second coming. It will destroy all previous kingdoms.

Daniel summarized the whole vision as God showing "the king what will take place in the future" (v. 45).

This prophetic revelation makes clear that the kingdom from heaven is not a spiritual kingdom which by spiritual processes will gradually conquer the earth, but rather a sudden catastrophic judgment from heaven destroying the political kingdoms of the Gentiles.

This will pave the way for a political millennial kingdom which will begin with the second coming of Christ. The revelation gives no support to either the amillennial view that the kingdom is a spiritual kingdom now on earth or to the postmillennial view that the kingdom will gradually gain control over the earth spiritually in a thousand years or more. The destruction of the Gentile world powers is an event, not a process and will be fulfilled by Christ in the Second Coming.

*Daniel 2:46-49.* The interpretation of the dream left Nebuchadnezzar overwhelmed, and he "fell prostrate before Daniel and paid him honor and ordered that an offering and incense be presented to him" (v. 46). His reaction to Daniel's revelation was profound. He said to Daniel, "Surely your God is the God of gods and the Lord of kings and a revealer of mysteries, for you were able to reveal this mystery" (v. 47). If Nebuchadnezzar was searching for truth about the God of heaven, he had a dramatic introduction.

As a result of Daniel's interpretation of the dream, even though he was probably yet a teenager and either was nearing or just finished his educational period with Nebuchadnezzar, he was given the high rank of "ruler over the entire province of Babylon" and was placed "in charge of all its wise men" (v. 48). This was especially remarkable because Daniel was a Jew, a foreigner, not a Babylonian.

Daniel was not unmindful of the part that Hananiah, Mishael, and Azariah had in the prayer which led to the revelation of the dream and asked that they be appointed over the province of Babylon (v. 49), but Daniel himself remained in the court of the king (v. 49). In one brief day Daniel, having interpreted Nebuchadnezzar's dream, was raised from the position of a lowly slave along with hundreds of others to a unique place where he, even though a Jew, was placed in charge over "the entire province of Babylon" and "in charge of all its wise men" (v. 48). Up to this time no comprehensive prophecy had been given concerning the times of the Gentiles which began with Nebuchadnezzar and will end with the second coming of Christ. Daniel continued to serve the king as an executive administrator until Nebuchadnezzar's death in 562 B.C.

### The Golden Image of Nebuchadnezzar

*Daniel 3:1-30.* In response to the revelation in Daniel 2 that Nebuchadnezzar would be the head of gold, Nebuchadnezzar ordered the building of an image entirely of gold. No doubt, this served to reflect his thinking that he did not want anyone to succeed him.

Strictly speaking, Daniel 3 is not prophecy as it does not anticipate a specific future, but the events of the chapter to some extent support the general idea of God restoring and saving His people.

As recorded in Daniel 3, Nebuchadnezzar set up an image near Babylon that was plated with gold, 90 feet high and 9 feet wide. The image itself was probably built on a platform which raised its height. At the sound of the trumpet everyone was commanded to bow down to the image (vv. 4-6). In the Babylonian religion the power of the emperor was part of their worship of the Babylonian gods, and the two concepts were intertwined.

While the whole multitude bowed down at the sound of the music, Daniel's three companions, whose Babylonian names were Shadrach, Meshach, and Abednego, stood erect and did not bow down to the image. The king's followers noted this and reported it to Nebuchadnezzar.

In a rage Nebuchadnezzar brought the men before him, reminded them of the command, and told them if they did not bow down they would be thrown immediately into the blazing furnace (vv. 13-15).

Shadrach, Meshach, and Abednego, however, told the king that they could not do this because they served the true God, and they told the king that their God was able to rescue them, but even if He did not, they would not bow down before the image (vv. 16-18).

Nebuchadnezzar ordered the furnace heated seven times hotter than normal and had the three men cast into the fire with their clothes on and bound with rope.

As Nebuchadnezzar watched, he was astonished to see four men walking in the fire, unbound and unharmed, and he said that the fourth "looks like a son of the gods" (v. 25). The fourth figure may have been Christ as the Angel of Yahweh or an angel. Approaching the furnace, Nebuchadnezzar asked the men to come out. Then he saw that the flames had not harmed them, their hair was not singed, their robes were not scorched, and there was not even a smell of fire on them (vv. 26-27). Their marvelous deliverance prompted Nebuchadnezzar to issue a decree that anyone who would say anything against the God of Israel would be cut in pieces. Shadrach, Meshach, and Abednego were promoted in their positions in the province of Babylon.

Though the chapter is entirely history, to some extent it anticipates the ultimate restoration of Israel in spite of the wrath of the

Gentile world in the Great Tribulation at the time of the second coming of Christ. It was also an important chapter in the progress of Nebuchadnezzar in understanding the power and glory of the God of Israel.

### Nebuchadnezzar's Dream of the Great Tree

Though Daniel 4 is largely a historical record of what happened to Nebuchadnezzar, it also contained prophecy in its fulfillment as related to Nebuchadnezzar. The chapter was most unusual in that it is in the form of a decree of the king that was circulated throughout the empire. It is possible that Daniel had a part in framing the document on behalf of Nebuchadnezzar.

*Daniel 4:1-3.* The opening of Daniel 4 is a greeting recognizing the greatness of God, its marvelous signs and wonders, and the fact that He was an eternal God.

*Daniel 4:4-8.* As in Daniel 2, Nebuchadnezzar had a dream and what he saw terrified him. As in chapter 2, he called in the magicians, enchanters, astrologers, and diviners, but they could not interpret the dream even though he told them what he had seen. As a last resort Nebuchadnezzar called in Daniel because of his previous experience in having him interpret the dream of Daniel 2 many years before.

*Daniel 4:9-17.* As recorded in Daniel 4, Nebuchadnezzar in his dream saw a great tree of enormous height and size which was visible to the whole earth. It bore beautiful fruit and lovely leaves. Beasts found shelter under it, and the birds of the air lived in its branches (vv. 9-12).

As Nebuchadnezzar saw the tree, however, he heard "a messenger, a holy one" coming from heaven and calling with a loud voice to cut down the tree and trim off its branches and scatter those that were being sheltered by it (vv. 13-14). Instruction was given, however, that the stump should be bound with iron and bronze (v. 15).

The messenger from heaven also said that he should live among the animals and be given the mind of an animal and be drenched with the dew of heaven until "seven times pass by for him" (v. 16). Nebuchadnezzar reported that he was told that the fulfillment of his dream would make clear that God was the Most High God and able to set over kingdoms "the lowliest of men" (v. 17). As he recited the dream to Daniel, he asked Daniel to interpret.

*Daniel 4:19-23.* Daniel was reluctant, however, to interpret the dream because he realized it was going to be a catastrophe for

Nebuchadnezzar. Daniel summarized the image and then proceeded to the interpretation.

*Daniel 4:24-27.* Daniel informed the king that the vision meant that the king would lose his mind; he would be driven away from his palace, would live like a wild animal, eating grass, and would act like the cattle of the field (vv. 24-25). The length of the trial would be seven times, meaning seven years. The fact that the stump had a band around it Daniel interpreted as revealing that he would be restored to his kingdom ultimately. On the basis of this prophecy, Daniel pleaded with the king, "Therefore, O king, be pleased to accept my advice: Renounce your sins by doing what is right, and your wickedness by being kind to the oppressed. It may be that then your prosperity will continue" (v. 27).

*Daniel 4:28-32.* As the vision had indicated, twelve months later as Nebuchadnezzar was walking on the roof of his royal palace in Babylon, he said to himself, "Is not this the great Babylon I have built as the royal residence, by my mighty power and for the glory of my majesty?" (v. 30) As Nebuchadnezzar said these words, he heard a voice from heaven indicating the time had come to fulfill the prophecy of the vision.

*Daniel 4:33.* Nebuchadnezzar, according to the decree, was then driven away and ate grass like cattle. He lived outdoors with his body drenched with dew. His hair was allowed to grow, and his nails became like "the claws of a bird" (v. 33). His rare illness has been identified as *insania zoanthropica* or boanthropy, in which an individual thinks of himself as an ox.

*Daniel 4:34-35.* At the end of the seven years Nebuchadnezzar's sanity was restored and he expressed in the decree his praise of God, declaring that God's dominion was eternal, that all people were under His authority, that He could do what He pleased and no one could tell Him to hold back His hand (vv. 34-35).

*Daniel 4:36-37.* Subsequent to his restoration of sanity, he was immediately returned to his former glory as the king of the empire. It is probable that Daniel was instrumental in maintaining the kingdom during the seven years of the king's insanity and also assuring the king's court that when he came to the end of the period he would be restored. Ordinarily, if something like this had happened, his enemies would have had a conspiracy and killed the king. Nebuchadnezzar closed his decree with this statement, "Now I, Nebuchadnezzar, praise and exalt and glorify the King of heaven, because everything He does is right and all His ways are just. And those who walk in pride He is able to humble" (v. 37). This chapter makes clear that Gentile power is subject to the will of God and will eventually be destroyed.

On the basis of this experience, the question has been raised whether Nebuchadnezzar ever placed faith in the God of Israel. Though opinions vary, he does seem to have had a growing consciousness that the God of Daniel was the true God as illustrated in the revelation of the four kingdoms of the image in Daniel 2, his experience with the companions of Daniel in Daniel 3, and now this personal experience where God made it clear to Nebuchadnezzar that all his power and grandeur was subject to God's bestowal. It may be that in answer to Daniel's prayers over many years Nebuchadnezzar put his faith in the God of Daniel.

### Belshazzar's Feast and the Fall of Babylon

When Nebuchadnezzar died in 562 B.C., his son Evil-Merodach succeeded him. He turned out to be a poor leader and was assassinated by Neriglisar after he had reigned two years. Neriglisar occupied the throne for four years when he died and was succeeded by his son Lavorosoarchod who was only a child. He occupied the throne for only nine months when he was beaten to death by a group of conspirators who made Nabonidus king. Nabonidus reigned from 556 B.C. to 539 B.C. when Babylon was conquered by the Medo-Persians. Belshazzar who was named as king of Babylon in Daniel 5 was appointed by Nabonidus after he had reigned for three years, and Belshazzar assumed this position of coregent in 553 B.C. and principally governed the city of Babylon because Nabonidus lived elsewhere.

Liberal scholars have long attacked the historicity of Belshazzar because his name had not been discovered in any secular history. However, with the discovery of the Nabonidus Cylinder in which Belshazzar was mentioned, liberals no longer can attack the historicity of Belshazzar even though they were slow in acknowledging their previous mistake.

The beginning of Belshazzar's service as coregent with Nabonidus in 553 B.C. became important because it was in that year that Daniel had the first of his four visions in Daniel 7. Actually, Daniel 7 and Daniel 8 both occur in the time period between Daniel 4 and Daniel 5 and are out of chronological order, possibly because Daniel desired to give the final chapter of history on Babylon and the resulting incident of Daniel in the lions' den before turning to prophetic analysis of the four empires in chapter 7 with additional information in chapter 8.

Perhaps more important was the fact that Daniel had received the revelation of chapter 7 and 8 before he came to Belshazzar's feast. The revelation of Daniel 7–8 reinforced the earlier information given in Daniel 2 when Daniel prophesied the downfall of Babylon. The message on the wall which Daniel was to interpret supported Daniel's opinion that this was the night of destiny when Babylon would fall.

The situation which King Belshazzar faced at the time of the banquet was that the Medes and the Persians had already conquered all of the empire of Babylon except the city of Babylon itself. Babylon was built to withstand a siege of twenty years, and according to the account of Herodotus, it was a tremendous city fourteen miles square, the outer walls of the city were 87 feet thick and 350 feet high with 100 great bronze gates in the walls. There was also a system of inner and outer walls with a water moat between which made the city even more secure. The wall was so strong and broad that chariots could parade on top of the wall four abreast. Herodotus also pictured hundreds of towers which reached 100 feet in the air above the wall.

Most contemporary scholars believe, however, that Herodotus greatly exaggerated the size of the city, and archeology seems to confirm that it was much smaller than Herodotus claimed. Actually, it may have been about a third of the size of Herodotus' description.

One of the important facts, however, was that the Euphrates River flowed through the middle of the city in a general direction from north to south, the water going underneath the outside walls and the riverbank itself with walls on each side. Even with the reduced dimensions, Babylon was the greatest city of the ancient world with many tall buildings, some as high as the Temple of Bel, eight stories high. The king's palace which has been excavated corresponds to what Scripture records. The river was crossed both by a bridge and by a tunnel. In recent years efforts have been made to restore some of the buildings, including the king's palace, for the sake of tourist trade. Thousands of visitors come to Babylon each year. Because more than 10,000 clay tablets have been found and inscriptions reciting various aspects of Babylon's history, a great deal is known about the city and its history. Because of Babylon's great construction and wall system, Belshazzar and his fellow rulers in Babylon felt safe even though the city had been surrounded for some time.

There was cause for alarm, however. Nabonidus had already been captured, and the fact that the city was surrounded did not speak well for her future history. The banquet was designed to reassure the leaders and the people of Babylon of the superiority of their god Bel and the certainty of their victory over their enemies.

*Daniel 5:1-4.* The opening verses of Daniel 5 reveal that a thousand Babylonian nobles had been assembled for this great feast, probably meeting in the throne room itself which archeologists believe they have identified in contemporary Babylon. It was a typical orgy with the drinking of wine until many of them were drunk. Not only nobles but their wives and concubines drank with them (vv. 1-2). Because of his desire to attribute his future victory to their god Bel, Belshazzar gave orders to bring the gold and silver goblets, taken from the temple in Jerusalem, and use them to drink to their god. This was particularly an act of blasphemy against the true God. This was probably the first time that they had been so used. Scripture recorded, "As they drank the wine, they praised the gods of gold and silver, of bronze, iron, wood and stone" (v. 4).

*Daniel 5:5-6.* In the smoke-filled banquet room lit only by torches and resounding with the noise of the banquet, something happened that almost immediately stilled conversations and the revelry that was going on. As Daniel recorded it, "Suddenly the fingers of a human hand appeared and wrote on the plaster of the wall, near the lampstand in the royal palace. The king watched the hand as it wrote. His face turned pale and he was so frightened that his knees knocked together and his legs gave way" (vv. 5-6). This was obviously a message from God because while the hand was writing on the plastered wall there was no arm or body connected to it. No doubt, there swept through Belshazzar's mind some of the supernatural feats attributed to Daniel and his three companions as outlined in chapters 2 and 3 and also Nebuchadnezzar's experience as recorded in Daniel 4.

*Daniel 5:7-8.* Just as Nebuchadnezzar had done in chapter 2 and 4, so Belshazzar "called out for enchanters, astrologers and diviners with a view to having them interpret the writing. He promised "Whoever reads this writing and tells me what it means will be clothed in purple and have a gold chain placed around his neck, and he will be made the third highest ruler in the kingdom" (5:7). As Nabonidus was number one ruler and Belshazzar was number two, he was offering the most he could by making the interpreter number three in the kingdom of Babylon.

When the wise men came, however, they were unable to interpret the dream any more than they could in Daniel 2 and Daniel 4. This left Belshazzar all the more in a panic, his face grew more pale, and his nobles did not know what to say (5:8).

*Daniel 5:10-12.* Daniel recorded that the queen, hearing of the problem, came into the banquet hall. Scholars are uncertain as to whom this was. She could have been the wife of Nebuchadnezzar who might still be living; she could have been the wife of Nabonidus; she could have been a daughter of Nebuchadnezzar; or she might have been the wife of Belshazzar, whether or not she was a daughter of Nebuchadnezzar. In effect, she said to Belshazzar, "Pull yourself together; there is a solution to your problem." Daniel recorded, "The queen, hearing the voice of the king and his nobles, came into the banquet hall. 'O king, live forever!' she said. 'Don't be alarmed! Don't look so pale! There is a man in your kingdom who has the spirit of the holy gods in him. In the time of your father he was found to have insight and intelligence and wisdom like that of the gods. King Nebuchadnezzar your father — your father the king, I say — appointed him chief of the magicians, enchanters, astrologers and diviners. This man Daniel, whom the king called Belteshazzar, was found to have a keen mind and knowledge and understanding, and also the ability to interpret dreams, explain riddles and solve difficult problems. Call for Daniel, and he will tell you what the writing means' " (vv. 10-12).

The reference to Nebuchadnezzar the father of Belshazzar can be explained as he may have been his grandfather, in which case Belshazzar was his grandson, or possibly it could be used simply in a successor sense of one who succeeded Nebuchadnezzar. In any case she addressed Belshazzar to remind him that there was one in the kingdom who could interpret the dream. The fact that the queen was allowed to enter and speak so freely was characteristic of the ancient world which honored parents particularly (Ex. 20:12; 1 Kings 2:13-20; 2 Kings 24:12-15).

*Daniel 5:13-16.* When Daniel was brought before the king, the king informed him that he understood that he was able to interpret dreams and therefore would be able to read the writing which was on the wall. Belshazzar promised, "If you can read this writing and tell me what it means, you will be clothed in purple and have a gold chain placed around your neck, and you will be made the third highest ruler in the kingdom" (v. 16).

The appearance of Daniel, a venerable man of possibly eighty years of age, was in contrast to the drunken nobles who with their wives and concubines occupied the banquet hall. It was as if God was there to challenge their wickedness.

*Daniel 5:17-21.* Daniel disavowed any interest in the gifts or positions offered him and assured Belshazzar that he would read the writing.

Daniel reminded Belshazzar, "the Most High God gave your father Nebuchadnezzar sovereignty and greatness and glory and splendor" (v. 18). Daniel pointed out how Nebuchadnezzar was an absolute ruler who would promote or demote as he wished. However, as Belshazzar already knew, Nebuchadnezzar had his period of insanity when he acted like one of the beasts (vv. 19-21). Only when Nebuchadnezzar "acknowledged that the Most High God is sovereign over the kingdoms of men and sets over them anyone He wishes" (v. 21) did he have his sanity restored.

*Daniel 5:22-23.* Daniel then reminded Belshazzar that he knew all these things but did not humble himself before the Most High God. Instead, he had blasphemed God as they had taken the goblets from the sacred temple of Israel and had used them in praise of their own gods "of silver and gold, of bronze, iron, wood, and stone" (v. 23). Daniel reminded him that their gods could not hear or understand. But the important fact was that Belshazzar had honored his Babylonian gods instead of the true God.

*Daniel 5:24-28.* Daniel then interpreted, "This is the inscription that was written: MENE, MENE, TEKEL, PARSIN" (v. 25).

Only the consonants of these words appeared on the wall, making it even more difficult to discern what was meant. The word *mene* meant "numbered," "God has numbered the days of your reign and brought it to an end" (v. 26). The repetition of the first word made it all the more certain.

The word *tekel* meant "weighed," "You have been weighed on the scales and found wanting" (v. 27). *Peres,* the singular of *parsin,* meant "divided," "Your kingdom is divided and given to the Medes and Persians" (v. 28). The inscription meant that his kingdom had been numbered, weighed, divided.

*Daniel 5:29-31.* In keeping with his promise, Belshazzar put purple clothing around Daniel and a gold chain around his neck and proclaimed him the third highest ruler in the kingdom. All this, however, was empty because as Daniel recorded, "That very night Belshazzar, king of the Babylonians, was slain, and Darius the Mede took over the kingdom, at the age of sixty-two" (v. 30).

The sudden end of the Babylonian Empire which came on that fateful night is typical of the end of Gentile power at the second coming of Christ. Though the city of Babylon was not destroyed in 539 B.C. when the Medo-Persian Empire took over political power, at the second coming of Christ even Babylon the city will be suddenly destroyed (Rev. 18). This prophecy and its fulfillment provides further proof that literal fulfillment of prophecy is normal as illustrated in hundreds of instances in the Old Testament. Daniel's prophecy of an empire which would follow Babylon was fulfilled by the Medes and Persians conquering Babylon.

### Daniel in the Lions' Den

*Daniel 6:1-28.* The familiar account of Daniel being thrown in the lions' den (Dan. 6) is not prophecy in itself but provided an important background for the Lord's dealings with Daniel. In subsequent chapters Daniel received four prophetic visions that add a great deal of detail and confirmation to the previous prophetic revelation.

Daniel 6 was important in testifying to the continued fidelity of Daniel even though tested to the extreme in this chapter. Daniel's enemies, in plotting the downfall of Daniel, had secured from Darius a decree that anyone praying to God or man for thirty days, except to Darius, would be thrown in the den of lions. Daniel's enemies were sure Daniel would continue praying. Darius was easily trapped in this predicament as the Medes and Persians believed a decree once signed could not be reversed.

Daniel, however, continued his prayer life which he had practiced three times a day for many years. He had his windows opened toward Jerusalem and no attempt was made to hide his continued devotion to his God. Darius, when confronted with Daniel's disobedience, very much against his desire, had Daniel thrown in the lions' den. But Darius himself, showing his extreme love for Daniel, was hoping that the God of Daniel would deliver him.

On the following morning when Daniel was rescued, Darius had no compunction against ordering the conspirators, their wives, and children, all to be cast into the den of lions where they had intended

Daniel to be cast. Daniel 6 closes with another decree, possibly written by Daniel himself in which the king ordered that everyone must fear and reverence the God of Daniel.

In the decree Darius showed remarkable understanding that God is eternal and that His kingdom and dominion will never end (v. 26). He attributes to God the ability to perform "signs and wonders in the heavens and on the earth" (v. 27). The decree closed with the statement, "He has rescued Daniel from the power of the lions" (v. 27).

The whole chapter is remarkable for a number of reasons. Daniel was then about eighty years of age and had been in obscurity for some years since Nebuchadnezzar's death twenty-three years before. Daniel had emerged from retirement at the feast of Belshazzar. Now the Persians recognized his genius in administration, and he prospered for the remaining years of his life. In the midst of a difficult situation politically and living in a land that worshiped another god, Daniel continued to remain untouched by the immorality and idolatry of those about him and had a testimony among all men of his faithfulness to his God. Prophetically the events of the chapter spoke of the rescue of the godly remnant of Israel at the Second Coming.

### Daniel's Vision of Future World History

*Daniel 7:1-7.* The vision of this chapter occurred, according to Daniel, "In the first year of Belshazzar king of Babylon" (v. 1), probably the year 553 B.C. or fourteen years before the Medes and the Persians conquered Jerusalem. This vision already was past when Belshazzar held his feast in chapter 5.

Daniel recorded seeing this vision of "the four winds of heaven churning up the great sea" (7:2). The four beasts, described later, came up out of the sea (vv. 2-3).

The first beast was compared to a lion having the wings of an eagle (v. 4). As Daniel watched, the wings were torn off and the eagle was lifted several feet off the ground, and "the heart of a man was given to it" (v. 4).

Daniel then had a vision of a second beast described as "like a bear. It was raised up on one of its sides, and it had three ribs in its mouth between its teeth. It was told, 'Get up and eat your fill of flesh!' " (v. 5)

A third beast was revealed. It resembled a leopard with four wings such as a bird would have and four heads. This beast also "was given authority to rule" (v. 6).

The fourth beast revealed to Daniel was by far the most important and the most frightening. Daniel described it as being very powerful. "It had large iron teeth; it crushed and devoured its victims and trampled underfoot whatever was left. It was different from all the former beasts, and it had ten horns" (v. 7).

*Daniel 7:8-10.* As Daniel continued to watch, he saw an eleventh horn "a little one, which came up among them; and three of the first horns were uprooted before it. This horn had eyes like the eyes of a man and a mouth that spoke boastfully" (v. 8).

The vision then shifted from the four beasts emerging from the great sea to a scene in heaven. Daniel saw one described as "the Ancient of Days" (v. 9). The clothing and hair of the one he saw was white and His throne "was flaming with fire, and its wheels were all ablaze" (v. 9). Further, as he looked at the scene "A river of fire was flowing, coming out from before Him. Thousands upon thousands attended Him; ten thousand times ten thousand stood before Him. The court was seated, and the books were opened" (v. 10).

*Daniel 7:11-14.* Daniel continued to watch the vision of heaven until he saw "the beast was slain and its body destroyed and thrown into the blazing fire" (v. 11). This referred to the fourth beast or the last of the four. He witnessed also, however, that the first three beasts "had been stripped of their authority, but were allowed to live for a period of time" (v. 12).

The climax of the vision was when he saw "one like a Son of man, coming with the clouds of heaven. He approached the Ancient of Days and was led into His presence. He was given authority, glory and sovereign power; all peoples, nations and men of every language worshiped Him. His dominion is an everlasting dominion that will not pass away, and His kingdom is one that will never be destroyed" (vv. 13-14).

If Daniel 7 had closed with verse 14, based on other Scripture, one could almost understand a portion of the vision. Like the image in chapter 2, the four beasts represented four kingdoms (cf. chart of World Empires in the Bible at Dan. 2).

The first kingdom with characteristics of a lion and an eagle represented Babylon. This kingdom had the regal splendor of the empire of Babylon as represented by the lion, the king of beasts, and the eagle, king of birds. The heart of a man given to it referred to Nebuchadnezzar's experiences in Daniel 4 when he was humbled before God.

The second kingdom represented the Medo-Persian Empire which conquered Babylon in 539 B.C. (Dan. 5). Like a bear it had great power but not the regal characteristics of Babylon. The greater power of Persia as compared to the Medes was revealed in the bear raising up on one side. The three ribs in its mouth probably referred to the three provinces of Babylonia, Persia, and Media.

The third kingdom represented Greece, identified in 8:21, and the rapid conquests of Alexander the Great who conquered all of Western Asia were the fulfillment of the leopard. The leopard is a beast capable of great speed like Alexander's conquests. The four winds also represented speed of conquest. When Alexander the Great died in Babylon in 323 B.C. his empire was divided among his four generals, represented by the four heads and four wings. They were Lysimachus who was given Thrace and Bithynia; Cassander who was given Macedonia and Greece; Seleucus who was given Syria, Babylonia, and land to the east; and Ptolemy who was given Egypt, Palestine, and Arabia Petrea. The kingdoms of Medo-Persia and Greece were named in verses 20-21.

The fourth kingdom was not named but was historically fulfilled by the Roman Empire. As described in 7:7, it crushed and devoured the countries which it conquered. The ten horns represented a future Roman Empire which will reappear in the end time.

The little horn represented a ruler who would come up last in the fourth kingdom who would be a world conqueror. Just as the image was destroyed in Daniel 2, so the fourth beast was destroyed by fire (7:11). The first three beasts were distinguished from the fourth in that instead of being cut off, they were allowed to continue for a time, that is, each was absorbed in the kingdom that followed in contrast to the fourth kingdom which will be suddenly destroyed (v. 12).

The coming of the Son of man (v. 13) could be understood to refer to the coming of Jesus Christ as the Messiah in His second coming, as Christ Himself used this expression "a Son of man" in many references to Himself in the New Testament (Matt. 8:20; 9:6; 10:23; 11:19; 12:8, 32, 40; etc.).

This passage referred to Jesus Christ in His incarnation approaching "the Ancient of Days" (Dan 7:13), an obvious reference to God the Father. The reference to giving Him complete authority over all peoples would be fulfilled in His millennial kingdom which, as far as dominion is concerned, will continue forever (v. 14).

*Daniel 7:15-22.* Daniel did not immediately understand the image, and he approached one standing by, probably an angel, and asked the meaning of the vision (vv. 15-16). Daniel was told, "The four great beasts are four kingdoms that will rise from the earth. But the saints of the Most High will receive the kingdom and will possess it forever—yes, forever and ever" (vv. 17-18).

Daniel was particularly concerned about the meaning of the fourth beast which was given special emphasis in the vision. Daniel wrote, "Then I wanted to know the true meaning of the fourth beast, which was different from all the others and most terrifying, with its iron teeth and bronze claws—the beast that crushed and devoured its victims and trampled underfoot whatever was left. I also wanted to know about the ten horns on its head and about the other horn that came up, before which three of them fell—the horn that looked more imposing than the others and that had eyes and a mouth that spoke boastfully" (vv. 19-20).

Before Daniel had an opportunity to hear the answer, he wrote, "As I watched, this horn was waging war against the saints and defeating them, until the Ancient of Days came and pronounced judgment in favor of the saints and the Most High, and the time came when they possessed the kingdom" (vv. 21-22).

*Daniel 7:23-28.* Daniel was given this explanation, "The fourth beast is a fourth kingdom that will appear on the earth. It will be different from all the other kingdoms and will devour the whole earth, trampling it down and crushing it. The ten horns are ten kings who will come from this kingdom. After them another king will arise, different from the earlier ones; he will subdue three kings. He will speak against the Most High and oppress his saints and try to change the set times and the laws. The saints will be handed over to him for a time, times and half a time" (vv. 23-25).

In this interpretation Daniel was told that the final kingdom described by the fourth beast will "devour the whole earth, trampling it down and crushing it" (v. 23). This was an advance over anything that had been revealed before. In the vision in chapter 2 the stone destroyed the image but it did not go into detail concerning the end-time form of the empire as this did.

Daniel was told that the ten horns represented ten kings (7:24). The little horn, representing "another king" (v. 24), will differ from the ten horns and will, in fact, conquer three of the horns (v. 24). He will not only be a world ruler who eventually will conquer the whole earth (v. 23), but he will also speak against God and will oppress His saints (v. 25). He will attempt to change long-accepted laws and times (v. 25), and for a time he will be able to persecute saints.

The time factor was represented as "time, times and half a time" (v. 25). Though this time factor was not transparent, by comparing this with other Scriptures it was evident that what he was talking about was a period of three-and-a-half years, a time representing one year, the plural "times" representing two, and then adding "half a time" (v. 25) representing a half a year. This will be seen to correspond to the last half of the seven-year period described in Daniel 9:27, the forty-two months described in Revelation 13:5, and the 1,260 days spoken of in Revelation 11:3. The fact that the word "time" represented a year was also illustrated in Daniel 4:16, 23, 25, 32. The similar expression "a time, times and half a time" was indicated in Revelation 12:14, also representing three-and-a-half years. In all these cases the probability was that it referred to the last three-and-a-half years preceding the second coming of Christ to the earth.

The description of the final ruler as one that ruthlessly "crushed and devoured its victims and trampled underfoot whatever was left" (Dan. 7:19) was characteristic of the Roman Empire historically and was here applied to its final form when it comes to the status of a world dictatorship in the last three-and-a-half years before the Second Coming.

The minute description given here of the end time, the fourth beast, and the ten horns followed by the eleventh horn that gained control of three has never been fulfilled in history. Some expositors have attempted to find ten kings of the past and the eleventh king who would arise to somehow fulfill this prophecy, but there is nothing corresponding to this in the history of the Roman Empire. The ten horns do not reign one after the other, but they reign simultaneously. Further, they were not the world empire, but they were the forerunner to the little horn which after subduing three of the ten horns will go on to become a world ruler (v. 23; Rev. 13:7).

It is obvious to many expositors that the first three kingdoms have come and gone in history, represented by Babylon, Medo-Persia, and Greece. The fourth empire, though not named here, has been identified as the Roman Empire as it was historically. The last stage of the Roman Empire, described here as the ten-horn stage and becoming a world empire, has never been fulfilled. In fact, the whole present age intervenes between the Roman Empire and this future world empire, a factor characteristic of the Old Testament in revealing the future. The present age is passed over in its foreview.

This parenthetical period of the present age has many parallels in Scripture. In the Old Testament frequently the first and second coming of Christ are referred to in the same verse without respect to the almost 2,000 years that have elapsed between the First and Second Coming. The Old Testament foreview simply did not anticipate the present age of the church composed of Jews and Gentiles on an equal standing, baptized into the body of Christ and becoming one.

As far as the Old Testament prophecies are concerned, the end time would immediately follow the first coming of Christ. The Old Testament prophets did not know or anticipate that there would be this long period of time between the two advents. In view of the fact that prophecy is fulfilled literally in other respects, it is understandable how many scholars hold that this future aspect is still ahead and, in fact, may be fulfilled in the relatively near human history. Those who would place the Rapture as before the end-time Tribulation believe that the Rapture will occur first before these end-time prophecies will be fulfilled, including the ten-nation group and the world empire led by the eleventh horn, or ruler.

Daniel concluded his prophetic picture of this dramatic series of events by saying, "But the court will sit, and his power will be taken away and completely destroyed forever. Then the sovereignty, power and greatness of the kingdoms under the whole heaven will be handed over to the saints, the people of the Most High. His kingdom will be an everlasting kingdom, and all rulers will worship and obey Him" (Dan. 7:26-27). As Daniel concluded this episode, he declared, "I, Daniel, was deeply troubled by my thoughts, and my face turned pale, but I kept the matter to myself" (v. 28).

It is clear that Daniel did not understand the prophecy he recorded. Those living today, because of the fulfillment of so much of this prophecy, can understand this prophecy better than Daniel did. Some interpreters of this prophecy have attempted to find fulfillment in the past. The amillennial interpretation which holds there is no millennial kingdom after the Second Coming often claims fulfillment of this chapter completely in history. A complete fulfillment, however, would require first, a ruler who would rule the entire earth, and second, a ten-nation confederacy in which the ruler conquered three of the ten kings. No ruler in the past has singled out a period of three-and-a-half years to be the persecutor of Israel and to bring in the special period that in the Old Testament was placed before the Second Coming. If such a ruler could be identified, he and his rule would have to be destroyed forever by God Himself and would need to be supplanted by a kingdom of God.

Attempts to interpret the little horn as the Roman papacy is also faulty as no king or pope can be identified in history fulfilling these prophecies. Papal power is still active in the world and not limited to three-and-a-half years, and the papacy has not been destroyed by the Second Coming. In other words, if this prophecy is to be understood in its literal fulfillment, it must be interpreted parallel to chapter 2 where the prophecy of the destruction of the feet of the image and the whole image itself has not been fulfilled. In this prophecy the final ruler has not emerged, and the various circumstances surrounding his rule have not been fulfilled in history. In view of the fact that prophecies up to the time of the end have been fulfilled so literally, a literal climax is also the only satisfactory approach, and this holds that there is yet a future time when the end-time prophecies will be fulfilled.

## PROPHECY OF ISRAEL IN THE TIMES OF THE GENTILES IN DANIEL
### Daniel's Second Vision: Persia and Greece

*Daniel 8:1-4.* The second vision of Daniel in the third year of Belshazzar, which can be dated approximately 550 B.C., also preceded the final destruction of Babylon in 539 B.C. The prophecy in this vision, however, has to do with the second and third kingdoms implied in the image of Daniel 2 as the upper part of the body and the arms of silver and the lower part of the body and thighs of brass. Little detail was given in either Daniel 2 or Daniel 7 about the second and third kingdoms though their presence is recognized.

Daniel here recorded a vision that gave in detail how the second and third kingdoms would come on the scene.

Daniel described his vision as occurring while he was in Susa (biblical Shushan) in the province of Elam, a Persian capital about 200 miles from Babylon. Daniel was not involved in the kingdom

235

reign of Belshazzar, and why he was in Susa was not explained. Later, after the Medo-Persians had conquered Babylon, Xerxes built a great palace in this city which was the scene of the Book of Esther and where Nehemiah served as King Artaxerxes' cupbearer (Neh. 1:11).

In his vision Daniel saw himself alongside the Ulai Canal. The Ulai River flowed from 150 miles north of Shushan to the Tigris River to the south. The location of the vision is important only as implying the background of the vision dealing with Medo-Persia and Greece.

As Daniel described the vision, he writes, "There before me was a ram with two horns, standing beside the canal, and the horns were long. One of the horns was longer than the other but grew up later. I watched the ram as he charged toward the west and the north and the south. No animal could stand against him, and none could rescue from his power. He did as he pleased and became great" (Dan. 8:3-4).

Later in the vision Daniel identified the ram, "The two-horned ram which you saw represents the kings of Media and Persia" (v. 20).

The ram clearly corresponded to the empire of the Medes and the Persians because, having two horns representing Media and Persia, the longer horn represented the greater power of Persia. They were able to destroy everything that was before them going to the west, north, and south (v. 4). This included the conquest of Babylon as well as other countries to the west of Persia. The Persian power historically reached its biblically significant triumph when Babylon was conquered in October 539 B.C. Until Alexander the Great came on the scene 200 years later, Persian power was predominant. Though Daniel was alive and observed the fulfillment of prophecies surrounding the destruction of Babylon and the coming of the Medes and the Persians in his lifetime, he did not live long enough to see the outcome of Persian rule as this prophecy will reveal.

*Daniel 8:5-8.* As Daniel was watching the ram conquering all before it, he wrote, "Suddenly a goat with a prominent horn between its eyes came from the west, crossing the whole earth without touching the ground. He came toward the two-horned ram I had seen standing beside the canal and charged him in great rage. I saw him attack the ram furiously, striking the ram and shattering his two horns. The ram was powerless to stand against him; the goat knocked him to the ground and trampled on him, and none could rescue the ram from his power. The goat became very great, but at the height of his power his large horn was broken off, and in its place four prominent horns grew up toward the four winds of heaven" (vv. 5-8).

As Daniel later declared, "The shaggy goat is the king of Greece, and the large horn between his eyes is the first king" (v. 21).

As Daniel plainly stated, the goat represented Greece, a country that was small and insignificant when Daniel lived but was destined to rule the Middle East in the time of Alexander the Great. Instead of two horns which would be normal for a goat, only one large horn was placed between the eyes of the goat who was declared to be "the first king" (v. 21).

The whole vision concerning Greece was most appropriate as describing the conquest of Alexander the Great who with rapid marches of his army conquered the whole Middle East and went as far as India. No conqueror preceding Alexander ever covered more territory so quickly. Accordingly, the fact that the goat was pictured as not touching the ground but flying through the air would correspond to Alexander's rapid conquest. This was implied also in Daniel 7 where the third empire, Greece, was compared to a leopard, a very swift animal that in Daniel's vision was described as having four wings, implying great speed (7:2).

The prediction that the large horn, representing Alexander the Great, would be broken off at the peak of his power was literally fulfilled in Alexander the Great's death in Babylon as he and his armies had returned from a conquest of India to Babylon to celebrate. Alexander the Great died in 323 B.C. at thirty-three years of age, a man who could conquer the world but could not conquer himself.

After Alexander's death his conquests were divided among four generals as indicated by the four horns. Cassander was given Macedonia and Greece; Lysimachus was given Thrace, Bithynia, and most of Asia Minor; Seleucus was given Syria and the area east of Syria, including Babylon; Ptolemy was given Egypt and probably Palestine and Arabia Petrea. Though another leader under Alexander, Antigonus, attempted to gain power, he was easily defeated. It was another testimony to the accuracy of Daniel's prophetic vision that the conquests of Alexander the Great were divided into four sections, not three or five. The accuracy was so clear that liberal scholars want to consider this as history written later after the fact and by one who assumed the name of Daniel but actually was not the sixth-century B.C. character described in the Bible.

*Daniel 8:9-12.* As Daniel continued to observe the vision, he saw a little horn come up in addition to the four prominent horns (v. 8), and this little horn "grew in power to the south and to the east and toward the Beautiful Land" (v. 9). The prophecies are very accurate as to direction. The ram, the Medo-Persian Empire, went largely to the west and not to the east in keeping with what the Medo-Persian Empire did. The goat instead, coming from Greece in the west, attacked the Middle East from the west (v. 5) in keeping with the conquests of Alexander the Great that were always east of Greece. The little horn, however, mentioned here manifested his power to the south and to the east and toward the "Beautiful Land," referring to the Holy Land.

There is an obvious distinction between the little horn which is mentioned here and the little horn of Daniel 7:8. The little horn of Daniel 7 came out of the fourth empire and in its final stage which, properly interpreted, still refers to the future. By contrast, the little horn of Daniel 8 came out of the third kingdom, the goat, and refers to prophecy that has already been fulfilled.

Daniel reported further on the vision, "It grew until it reached the hosts of the heavens, and it threw some of the starry host down to the earth and trampled on them. It set itself up to be as great as the Prince of the host; it took away the daily sacrifice from Him, and the place of His sanctuary was brought low. Because of rebellion, the host of the saints and the daily sacrifice were given over to it. It prospered in everything it did, and truth was thrown to the ground" (8:10-12).

The difficulty in understanding this portion of Scripture has given rise to a number of theories of interpretation. As mentioned earlier in the introduction of Daniel, liberal scholars held that the Book of Daniel was forgery written in the second century because they held that prophecy of the future was impossible. This conclusion is contradicted by the finding of the Qumran scrolls in which a complete copy of Daniel was found. Even liberal scholars on the basis of their own presuppositions have difficulty in harmonizing this archeological find with the idea that a pseudo-Daniel wrote the Book of Daniel in the second century when what was presented as prophecy was already history. Conservative scholars reject this, of course, and accept the inspiration and authority of the Book of Daniel as it was held for many years throughout the Old Testament period and for hundreds of years in the Christian era.

A second interpretation holds that this prophecy has already been fulfilled in the person of Antiochus Epiphanes, a ruler of Syria (175–164 B.C.). In general, conservative interpreters, whether premillennial or amillennial, agree on this interpretation.

A third view is that this prophecy was fulfilled historically in the second century B.C., but typically represented the future world ruler of the Great Tribulation before the Second Coming. This is supported by the reference to the "time of the end" (vv. 17, 19).

The best approach is to accept this as primarily fulfilled prophecy as Antiochus Epiphanes met the requirements set down in this prophecy though this may typically picture the time of the end.

According to history, Antiochus Epiphanes set himself up as God, thus disregarding "the starry host" (v. 10) or the powers of heaven. He set himself up as the "Prince of the host" (v. 11) in the sense of making himself great. Antiochus took away and stopped the daily sacrifices offered by the Jews in the temple and desecrated their sanctuary (v. 13), turning it into a pagan temple. He fulfilled the requirements of throwing truth to the ground (v. 12). History has recorded that Antiochus by taking the name Epiphanes, which means glorious one, assumed that he was God, much as the little horn of Daniel 7 will do in the future Great Tribulation. His role is similar to the future role of the coming world dictator.

*Daniel 8:13-14.* Daniel reported hearing two described as "holy" (v. 13), apparently angels, discussing how long it would take for this vision to be fulfilled (v. 13), defined as "the vision concerning the daily sacrifice, the rebellion that causes desolation, and the surrender of the sanctuary and of the host that will be trampled underfoot" (v. 13).

Daniel was told by the angel, "It will take 2,300 evenings and mornings; then the sanctuary will be reconsecrated" (v. 14).

If there were some agreement that the earlier verses refer to Antiochus Epiphanes, verse 14 adds additional revelation which has caused a number of differing points of view.

Many of the details referred to in the preceding verses were recorded in the historical book of 1 Maccabees which described the desecration of the temple, the persecution of the Jewish people, and the so-called Maccabean revolt of the Jews. Thousands of Jews were killed by Antiochus Epiphanes in the attempt to stamp out the Jewish religion, but it was all to no avail.

The statement that it would take 2,300 evenings and mornings, however, before the sanctuary could be reconsecrated has caused many different opinions because it is not entirely clear what it means. Seventh-Day Adventists understand 2,300 days to refer to 2,300 years, and on the basis of this expected culmination of the Second Coming in the year 1884. History, of course, has demonstrated that this was not the proper answer. Others have taken it that the 2,300 days, including evening and morning sacrifices, were actually 1,150 days, that is, 2,300 evenings and mornings. This view is difficult to harmonize with the history of the period.

Probably the best interpretation goes back to the fact that in the year 171 B.C. Onias III, who was the reigning high priest, was assassinated and another line of priests assumed power. This, of course, was the beginning of the desecration, but the temple itself was not desecrated until December 25, 167 B.C. when the sacrifices were forcibly stopped, a Greek altar was placed in the temple, and a Greek statue representing a pagan god was erected.

If the period from 171 B.C. to 164 B.C., when Antiochus died, is considered that period, the total of 2,455 days would be reduced to 2,300 days if the parts of the first and last years be subtracted. This would account for the 2,300 days as a round number. The history of the case does not provide enough detail to determine exactly how the fulfillment was accomplished. Taking everything into consideration, it is best to consider the 2,300 days as fulfilled at that time in the second century B.C. and not subject to prophetic fulfillment in the future.

*Daniel 8:15-22.* Daniel, as he was watching the vision, recorded that the one stood beside him was "like a man" but probably was an angel (v. 15). Daniel also heard a man's voice instructing Gabriel, an angel, to give Daniel the interpretation of the dream (v. 16). This was the first mention of the Angel Gabriel in Scripture. He is also mentioned in 9:21; Luke 1:19, 26. While angels were given numerous titles in apocryphal literature, the Bible only names one other angel, Michael (Dan. 10:13, 21; 12:1; Jude 9; Rev. 12:7). When the Angel Gabriel came to him Daniel fell prostrate before this holy angel (Dan. 8:17).

Daniel was addressed as "Son of man" and instructed to "understand that the vision concerns the time of the end" (v. 17). The encounter with the angel caused Daniel to go into "a deep sleep," but Gabriel raised him to his feet (v. 18).

Gabriel then confirmed the interpretation of the ram and the goat and the details of the vision. He stated, "I am going to tell you what will happen later in the time of wrath, because the vision concerns the appointed time of the end. The two-horned ram that you saw represents the kings of Media and Persia. The shaggy goat is the king of Greece, and the large horn between his eyes is the first king. The four horns that replaced the one that was broken off represent four kingdoms that will emerge from his nation but will not have the same power" (vv. 19-21). As Gabriel's interpretation has been confirmed by history, it is comparatively easy to find a consensus of conservative interpreters relating this passage as referring to Medo-Persia and to Greece.

*Daniel 8:23-26.* This portion has been the subject of endless discussion and difference of opinion following several interpretations: (1) the idea that this has already been completely fulfilled in history by Antiochus Epiphanes; (2) that this represents a period entirely future, referring to the final world ruler; (3) that it is a prophecy concerning Antiochus Epiphanes, but that in some sense it has a double fulfillment because of the similarity between him and the end-time world ruler.

Daniel described the wicked king of this prophecy as "a stern-faced king, a master of intrigue" (v. 23). It was stated that "He will become very strong, but not by his own power. He will cause astounding devastation and will succeed at whatever he does. He will destroy the mighty men and the holy people. He will cause deceit to prosper, and he will consider himself superior. When they feel secure, he will destroy many and take his stand against the Prince of princes. Yet he will be destroyed, but not by human power" (vv. 24-25).

The description given here of this wicked ruler is very similar to what history and the Bible record concerning Antiochus Epiphanes. He did have great power over the Holy Land and Syria and for a time had power in Egypt until he had to withdraw because of Roman Empire pressure. He devastated the Hebrew worship and desecrated the temple. He killed thousands of Jews who attempted to continue their worship in opposition to him. He considered himself above others; in fact, he claimed to be God, indicated by his title "Epiphanes" which means "glorious one." He obviously opposed

Christ as "the Prince of princes" (v. 25). Antiochus died, however, in 164 B.C. while on a military campaign, but his death was by natural causes, indicating that "he will be destroyed, but not by human power" (v. 25). Daniel had been instructed in verse 17 that "the vision concerns the time of the end." He was further instructed that the vision was true, "but seal up the vision, for it concerns the distant future" (v. 26).

This passage, though fulfilled by Antiochus, was also typical of the description of the future role of the coming Antichrist, the man of sin, the dictator of the whole world during the last three-and-a-half years before the Second Coming. Some believe that this also has prophetic overtones and anticipates the climax of the ages. While the controversy cannot be completely settled, it can be understood that this prophecy is certainly an illustration in history of what would take place in prophecy in the yet-future Great Tribulation. Like Antiochus, the final world ruler will claim to be God, will persecute Jews, will stop Jewish sacrifices, and will be an evil character.

*Daniel 8:27.* Daniel, who had been brought through tremendous emotional strain in the course of receiving this vision, wrote, "I, Daniel, was exhausted and lay ill for several days. Then I got up and went about the king's business. I was appalled by the vision; it was beyond understanding" (v. 27). What was prophecy for Daniel in the sixth century B.C. is now understandable because of the history of the second century B.C., and the Scriptures here can be construed as being literally fulfilled. Because, however, they approximate so nearly the character, the stopping of sacrifices, and other qualities of the final world ruler, many feel that this is a shadow of things yet to be fulfilled.

### Introduction to the Prophecy of the Seventy Sevens

Daniel the prophet was not only revealing the tremendous prophecies concerning the times of the Gentiles, embracing the four great empires, beginning with Babylon and ending with Rome, and the final destruction of Gentile power by the second coming, but also Daniel received in his third vision in the next chapter a detailed chronology of Israel's future, culminating in the Second Coming of Christ. Because of the revelation given through Daniel, both concerning the times of the Gentiles and the program of God for Israel, the prophecies of Daniel are the key to understanding the major prophecies of Scripture in both the Old and New Testaments.

In Daniel 9 three important segments are presented: first, the approaching fulfillment of Israel's return to the land (vv. 1-2); second, the remarkable prayer of Daniel in view of the approaching fulfillment of prophecy (vv. 3-19); and third, the important prophecy concerning the seventy sevens of Israel's future, culminating in the Second Coming.

The events of this chapter followed the earlier two visions of Daniel in 553 B.C. and 550 B.C. and the downfall of the Babylonian Empire in Daniel 5 (539 B.C.). The experience of Daniel in the lions' den (6:1-24) was not clearly before or after the vision of Daniel 9 as the vision was not dated.

The great prophecies given to Nebuchadnezzar as well as to Daniel and the fulfillment of the downfall of Babylon must have given Daniel a great sense of the sovereignty of God and the certainty of prophecy being literally fulfilled. It was with this background that Daniel reported his discovery of the prophecy of Jeremiah concerning the seventy years of Israel's Captivity.

## Daniel's Prayer for Restoration of Jerusalem

*Daniel 9:1-2.* Daniel recorded that the early events of Daniel 9 occurred "In the first year of Darius son of Xerxes" (v. 1), which was probably the year 539–538 B.C. Daniel for the first time comprehended the prophecies of Jeremiah the prophet concerning the seventy years of Israel's Captivity. It may be that he had not read the prophecy or it had not come into his possession before this event.

According to the Book of Jeremiah, these prophecies were written before the downfall of Jerusalem in 586 B.C., at least fifty-seven years before the events of this chapter. Jeremiah himself had been carried off to Egypt against his will and apparently died there and was buried in a strange land (Jer. 43:4-13). How the prophecies of Jeremiah, probably taken with him to Egypt, found their way to Babylon and into the hands of Daniel remains unknown. Because of the high position of Daniel in the government of the Medes and the Persians, it would be natural to refer this manuscript to him when it reached Babylon.

Upon reading the prophecies of Jeremiah, Daniel concluded that the time was about to come when Israel could go back and claim their ancient city Jerusalem. In Jeremiah 25:11-12 Jeremiah had written, " 'This whole country will become a desolate wasteland, and these nations will serve the king of Babylon seventy years. But when the seventy years are fulfilled, I will punish the king of Babylon and his nation, the land of the Babylonians, for their guilt,' declares the LORD, 'and will make it desolate forever.' "

As the Captivity of Israel began in 605 B.C., seventy prophetic years of 360 days each would bring it approximately to the time of the fall of Babylon in 539 B.C. Actually, the Medo-Persians did not destroy Babylon. In fact, it went on for many hundreds of years and never became a desolation until modern time. For this reason some believe that Babylon will be rebuilt in the end time and destroyed at the time of the Second Coming (Isa. 13:1-22; Rev. 18:1-24). Though the fall of Babylon occurred in 539 B.C., the complete destruction of Babylon as described in this passage has not been fulfilled in history.

Daniel also read Jeremiah 29:10-14, "This is what the LORD says: 'When seventy years are completed for Babylon, I will come to you and fulfill My gracious promise to bring you back to this place. For I know the plans I have for you,' declares the LORD, 'plans to prosper you and not to harm you, plans to give you hope and a future. Then you will call upon Me and come and pray to Me, and I will listen to you. You will seek Me and find Me when you seek Me with all your heart. I will be found by you,' declares the LORD, 'and will bring you back from captivity. I will gather you from all the nations and places where I have banished you,' declares the LORD, 'and will bring you back to the place from which I carried you into exile.' " The reason that Daniel was excited at this prophecy was that approximately sixty-seven years had already passed since Jerusalem fell in 605 B.C. As Daniel believed in the literal fulfillment of prophecy based on his own experience, the prophecy was a tremendous revelation to him.

In the events of Daniel 6 when Daniel was cast in the lions' den, the Scripture reveals that it was Daniel's practice to pray three times a day with his windows open toward Jerusalem. Ever since he was led away to Babylon as a teenager he had been praying that Jerusalem might be restored and the people might return. There would be no message more welcomed or more stimulating to Daniel than the assurance from the Word of God that after seventy years they would be able to return. It was noteworthy that Daniel took the prophecy literally. He knew that God would do exactly what Jeremiah had prophesied. This led to the remarkable prayer which follows.

Some interpreters point out that there is a difference between the seventy years of Captivity and the seventy years of Israel's desolation. In Jeremiah 29:10 reference is made to the period of the captivities which began in 605 B.C. and would end at approximately 533 B.C. This is what prompted Daniel to pray and to ask God to fulfill this prophecy.

In Jeremiah 25:12 Jeremiah is considering the desolations of Babylon. The fact is the desolations of Babylon did not take place after 539 B.C. and may still be projected to the future end of the Inter-advent Age.

Likewise, the desolation of Jerusalem did not begin until 586 B.C. when Jerusalem was destroyed, and it extended seventy years. It ended at approximately 516 or 515 B.C. Accordingly, some conclude that because the seventy-year Captivity ended in 538 B.C., Ezra was authorized to go back to Jerusalem. The actual rebuilding of Jerusalem was delayed, including the rebuilding of the temple, until approximately 515 B.C. in order to allow Jerusalem to lie desolate for seventy years from the date of its destruction in 586 B.C. In view of the fact that the desolations of Jerusalem are somewhat different than the Captivity of Jerusalem in date and circumstance, this distinction may serve to explain the sequence in events in fulfillment. Though the major deportation of captives from Jerusalem to Babylon took place in 597 B.C., Daniel was probably in the first contingent which was taken soon after the fall of Jerusalem in 605 B.C. Accordingly, Daniel would date the time of the conclusion of the seventy years of the Captivity to be fulfilled approximately seventy years after he himself was carried captive.

In trying to reconstruct the prophecy and fulfillment, it should be borne in mind that a prophetic year is 360 days, not 365 and, accordingly, the years were somewhat shorter than in the modern calendar. Though the seventy years were literal, it is obvious that the Bible does not attempt to prove that it was to the exact day or even to the exact year, but that it was approximately in round numbers seventy years, not an indefinite period of time.

Scholars attempting to reconstruct the chronology of this period also bear in mind that the capture of Babylon was in October 539 B.C. when Darius was appointed as ruler. However, Cyrus, the king of Persia, issued his decree permitting captives to return to Jerusalem in the first full year of his reign over Babylon which did not begin until March 538 B.C. as fractions of years were not counted.

245

Accordingly, the return of the captives could be from 538 B.C. to 537 B.C. The discovery of Jeremiah's prophecies, however, moved Daniel to one of the remarkable prayers of the Bible.

*Daniel 9:3-16.* Daniel's prayer is a model for those seeking to move God in prayer. Daniel first of all prepared himself spiritually through fasting, sackcloth, and ashes (v. 3). While this was not necessary, Daniel did everything he possibly could to put himself in a favorable spiritual position for prayer.

As he prayed he reminded God of His greatness and the fact that He keeps His covenants, especially for those whom He loves (v. 4). Daniel does not dodge the fact, however, that the Captivity was caused by the sins of Israel. In his prayer he declared, "We have sinned and done wrong. We have been wicked and have rebelled; we have turned away from Your commands and laws. We have not listened to Your servants the prophets, who spoke in Your name to our kings, our princes and our fathers, and to all the people of the land" (vv. 5-6).

Though Daniel himself was never identified with any sinful act in the Book of Daniel, it is significant that Daniel identifies himself with his people. Though he did not participate in their rebellion against God, he recognizes he was a part of the nation, and the nation as a whole was punished by God. Daniel was saying their Captivity was justified as a righteous judgment from a righteous God.

Daniel goes on to point out that God is righteous which brings out all the more the awfulness of sin. He declared, "Lord, You are righteous, but this day we are covered with shame—the men of Judah and people of Jerusalem and all Israel, both near and far, in all the countries where you have scattered us because of our unfaithfulness to you. O LORD, we and our kings, our princes and our fathers are covered with shame because we have sinned against You. The Lord our God is merciful and forgiving, even though we have rebelled against Him; we have not obeyed the LORD our God or kept the laws He gave us through His servants the prophets. All Israel has transgressed Your law and turned away, refusing to obey You" (vv. 7-11).

In this model prayer Daniel not only emphasized the necessity for spiritual preparation but also made an honest confession of the sins of which we may be guilty personally or corporately.

Daniel pointed out how the very judgments brought on the people of Israel were a fulfillment of prophecy, "Therefore the curses and sworn judgments written in the Law of Moses, the servant of God, have been poured out on us, because we have sinned against You. You will fulfill the words spoken against us and against our rulers by bringing upon us a great disaster. Under the whole heaven nothing has ever been done like what has been done to Jerusalem. Just as it is written in the Law of Moses, all this disaster has come upon us, yet we have not sought the favor of the LORD our God by turning from our sins and giving attention to Your truth. The LORD did not hesitate to bring the disaster upon us, for the LORD our God is righteous in everything He does; yet we have not obeyed Him" (vv. 11-14).

In confessing his sins and the sins of the people of Israel, Daniel was laying the proper groundwork for confidence that God will still accomplish His prophecy. Just as there was prophecy of Israel's judgment, so there was prophecy of Israel's restoration, and his prayer now turns to this aspect of Jeremiah's prophecy.

*Daniel 9:17-19.* Daniel then offered his petition that God would hear and answer prayer and fulfill the prophecy He had made (v. 17). It is noteworthy that in this prayer Daniel not only petitions God but he petitions that God would answer prayer for that which concerns Him, that is, that His sanctuary is lying desolate. Accordingly, Daniel was pleading that God would glorify Himself by fulfilling His prophecy, "Give ear, O God, and hear; open Your eyes and see the desolation of the city that bears Your Name. We do not make requests of You because we are righteous, but because of Your great mercy. O Lord, listen! O Lord, forgive! O Lord, hear and act! For Your sake, O my God, do not delay, because Your city and Your people bear Your Name" (vv. 18-19).

Daniel's prayer in many ways is a remarkable model for all prayer. Daniel first of all made personal spiritual preparation; then Daniel confessed the sins of the people of Israel; Daniel pointed out how God was righteous in fulfilling the prophecies of judgment; the result was that Jerusalem and the temple lay in ruins and the people were in Captivity. On the basis of this, however, Daniel then presented his petition, arguing in the same way as he stated that prophecy was fulfilled in their judgment. So now he presents to God the need of fulfilling the prophecy of mercy and doing that which was necessary to return His people to Jerusalem and to bring about the rebuilding of the temple and the city. Daniel pleaded with God on the basis of His mercy, the fact that He is a forgiving God, and prayed that God would not delay the answer further after these many years of the desolation of Jerusalem and the temple.

As revealed so often in both prophecy and fulfillment, God not only dealt with Israel in judgment on their sins in fulfillment of prophecy but He also desired to restore them in fulfillment of prophecy, and the restoration of the people to the land this time was in keeping with the prophecy given through Jeremiah. During the time of Daniel's prayer the verses which follow reveal that the Angel Gabriel was sent at the beginning of Daniel's prayer.

Undoubtedly, the prayer of Daniel actually was much longer than was recorded in the Book of Daniel, and what was revealed was a condensation as was often the case in Scripture. It seems evident that the prayer ended close to the time of the evening sacrifice though actually no sacrifices had been offered since the temple was destroyed in 586 B.C.

*Daniel 9:20-23.* Daniel summarized these prophetic facts in these words, "While I was speaking and praying, confessing my sin and the sin of my people Israel and making my request to the LORD my God for His holy hill — while I was still in prayer, Gabriel, the man I had seen in the earlier vision, came to me in swift flight about the time of the evening sacrifice" (vv. 20-21). In referring to his previous contact with Gabriel, Daniel was referring to the contact he had with Gabriel the angel more than eleven years before (8:15). In Scripture Gabriel was frequently related to important messages from God delivered to His people (Luke 1:19, 26).

Upon arrival and contact with Daniel, Gabriel informed him, "Daniel, I have now come to give you insight and understanding. As soon as you began to pray, an answer was given, which I have come to tell you, for you are highly esteemed. Therefore, consider the message and understand the vision" (Dan. 9:22-23).

### Daniel's Third Vision: The Seventy Sevens of Israel: The Place of Israel in the Times of the Gentiles

*Daniel 9:24-27.* In the verses which follow Daniel recorded one of the most comprehensive and yet concise prophecies to be found in the Bible concerning what is called "seventy sevens." This revelation should be placed alongside prophecy concerning Gentiles outlined previously in Daniel. The chronology and sequence of events in the times of the Gentiles, like Israel's seventy sevens, climaxes in the Second Coming. Daniel was informed concerning how Israel related chronologically to this same Gentile period of time.

# SEVENTY SEVENS OF DANIEL
## DANIEL 9:24-27

| Babylonian Captivity 605–444 B.C. | Decree to Build Jerusalem 444 B.C. Neh. 1:5-8 | | Messiah Cut Off A.D. 30-33 Dan. 9:26 | Church Age Pentecost to Rapture | Rapture 1 Thes. 4:13-18 | Period of Preparation 10-Nation Kingdom | Seven-year Covenant Signed 7 Years—70th Seven Dan. 9:27 | | Second Coming Resurrection Tribulation Saints Rev. 20:1-6 | New Heaven New Earth New Jerusalem Rev. 21–22 |
|---|---|---|---|---|---|---|---|---|---|---|
| | 49 Years 7 Sevens Dan. 9:25 | 434 Years 62 Sevens Dan. 9:25 | After 62 Sevens | Jerusalem Destroyed A.D. 70 | | | 3½ Years of Peace | 3½ Years Great Tribulation / Covenant Broken / World Government / Armageddon Rev. 16:16 | Millennium Rev. 19:11-20 / Judgment of Unbelievers | Judgment of Great White Throne |

Gabriel declared, "Seventy 'sevens' are decreed for your people and your holy city to finish transgression, to put an end to sin, to atone for wickedness, to bring in everlasting righteousness, to seal up vision and prophecy and to anoint the Most Holy" (v. 24). Gabriel first presented the prophecy as a whole, covering a period he declares as "seventy sevens."

### The Seventy Sevens: Liberal Interpretation

The prophecy, because of its precision, has aroused great opposition from liberal expositors who attempt to explain it away as somehow a garbled restatement of the seventy years of Israel's Captivity. Most liberals also hold that Daniel was a forgery written by a person in the second century B.C. instead of the sixth century B.C. and, accordingly, they are opposed to anything that would constitute a prophetic vision of the future. In other words, liberals attempt to say that this was not prophecy at all, at the same time realizing that they have a difficult passage to explain. Actually, they themselves admit that they have no reasonable interpretation.

### Seventy Sevens as 490 Years

Unfortunately, even conservative scholars have not all agreed on the interpretation of the "seventy sevens," most of the trouble being the determination of the beginning date of the series. Conservatives generally feel the time units are years; in other words, seventy sevens add up to 490 years. Conservative scholars, particularly those who are amillennial, resist the idea that this is a literal 490 years because they have difficulty in finding fulfillment that is satisfactory to their other views.

Even liberal commentators, however, agree that the units were years, not days of twenty-four hours as 490 days would not constitute a comprehensive prophecy. Conservative scholars generally have recognized that seven was often used in relation to some great work of God. Orthodox Jews have not done any better in their interpretation in believing that the prophecy was fulfilled in A.D. 70 which does not give literal fulfillment to the passage. Proceeding, however, on the concept that the units are years, a number of interpretations challenge any united understanding of this passage.

### Seventy Sevens: Christological or Non-Christological

In general, interpretations divide between christological and non-christological explanations. Those who reject a christological meaning do not take Scripture as literal prophecy. Those who believe that these prophecies relate to Jesus Christ and the ultimate fulfillment of the Second Coming usually regard the first sixty-nine years as literal years. Amillenarians usually follow the same procedure, but there is considerable difference of opinion on whether the last seven years have been or will be fulfilled literally. This is the crux of the problem.

### Seventy Sevens: Major Events

According to Daniel 9:24, six major events characterize the 490 years: (1) "to finish transgression," (2) "to put an end to sin," (3) "to atone for wickedness," (4) "to bring in everlasting righteousness," (5) "to seal up vision and prophecy," and (6) "to anoint the Most Holy" (v. 24). As none of the six achievements were explained, it leaves the expositor to find a plausible explanation.

The accomplishment defined as "the finished transgression" most probably refers to Israel's tendency to apostasy which must be brought to a close as Israel is brought to restoration and spiritual revival at the time of the Second Coming. Practically all premillennial expositors agree that the terminus of this prophecy is before the future millennial kingdom. The restoration of Israel spiritually and the return to Jerusalem as mentioned by Daniel in prayer, of course, has already been fulfilled, but the ultimate restoration of Israel awaits their regathering at the time of the Second Coming. Obviously, the Old Testament sacrifices could not bring Israel to this important milestone, and it required the death of Christ on the cross establishing grace as a method of divine dealing with Israel. The fulfillment of many details of the New Covenant for Israel (Jer. 31) would not begin until the Second Coming. Eschatologically, Israel will be restored because God will deal with them in grace rather than what they deserve.

The objective, "put an end to sin," may be understood either as bringing sin to its point of forgiveness or it could mean bringing sin to its final judgment. A variation in the text also permits a translation "to seal up sin." The total explanation apparently includes all of these elements of bringing sin to its end, bringing sin into judgment, and extending forgiveness for sins already committed. It is obviously God's program to bring sin into judgment and to bring forgiveness to those who receive grace.

The third achievement, "to atone for wickedness," refers both to the death of Christ on the cross which is the basis for all grace and the application of this, especially to Israel, at the time of the Second Coming. The expression "to atone" literally means "to cov-

251

er." The death of Christ deals with sin in the final way that the sacrifices of the Old Testament could only illustrate temporarily. When Christ died on the cross He brought in permanent reconciliation for those who would turn to Him in faith (2 Cor. 5:19).

The fourth achievement, "to bring in everlasting righteousness," was made possible by the death of Christ on the cross. The application of this to Israel individually and nationally relates to the Second Coming. As stated in Jeremiah 23:5-6, " 'The days are coming,' declares the LORD, 'when I will raise up to David a righteous Branch, a King who will reign wisely and do what is just and right in the land. In His days Judah will be saved and Israel will live in safety. This is the name by which He will be called: The LORD Our Righteousness.' " The time of this is the Second Coming, the same time as David will be resurrected to be a regent under Christ (30:9). Righteousness is one of the outstanding characteristics of the millennial kingdom in contrast to previous dispensations.

The fifth objective of the 490 years is "to seal up vision and prophecy." This expression refers to completion of the inspired Bible with the writing of the New Testament. The figure of "seal" refers to the sealing of a letter after it is completed and closed and now rendered safe by the seal. In like manner, God has completed the inspiration of the Bible, and no additional books will be written.

The sixth achievement, "to anoint the Most Holy," has brought a variety of interpretations, some relate it to the dedication of the temple built by Zerubbabel (516 B.C.), others to the sanctification of the temple altar in the Maccabean period after it had been desecrated by Antiochus Epiphanes (165 B.C.) (cf. 1 Macc. 4:52-56), or in the distant future to the dedication of the New Jerusalem (Rev. 21:1-27). Still others refer it to the millennial temple described by Ezekiel (Ezek. 40–42). Because the prophecy is not entirely clear, probably the best conclusion is that its complete fulfillment is still future and refers to the New Jerusalem which will be God's temple in eternity. Because the other items of prophecy concluded with the Second Coming, there was no clear event at that time relating to the temple. The anointing of the Most Holy will, however, be in keeping with other facets of the 490 years that have to do with judgment of sin, atonement, forgiveness, and spiritual restoration.

### Seventy Sevens: Date of Its Beginning

Another important decision in interpretation of this passage is the question of the beginning of the 490 years. This is described in

Daniel 9:25, "Know and understand this: From the issuing of the decree to restore and rebuild Jerusalem until the Anointed One, the Ruler, comes, there will be seven 'sevens,' and sixty-two 'sevens.' " Daniel was instructed, "Know and understand this," but it is questionable whether he understood it. If students of Scripture today, after much of Daniel has been fulfilled, have difficulty pinpointing the beginning of the 490 years, it is obvious that Daniel would have the same problem.

Amillenarians tend to adopt a view which, essentially, does not give the prophecy literal fulfillment. One suggestion is that the period begins in 586 B.C. when Jerusalem was destroyed. The decree then is a command of God, something that the text does not support, and its fulfillment falls far short of being literal.

If the decree refers to a political decree, four different decrees have been suggested: (1) the decree of Cyrus that the temple be rebuilt in 538 B.C. (2 Chron. 36:20-23; Ezra 1:1-4; 6:1-5); (2) the decree of Darius confirming the decree of Cyrus (Ezra 6:6-12); (3) the decree of Artaxerxes (Ezra 7:11-26); and (4) the decree of Artaxerxes given in Nehemiah authorizing the rebuilding of the city (Neh. 2:1-8). Though it is clear that the decree of Cyrus authorized the rebuilding of the temple, there is question whether he authorized the rebuilding of the city. The later decrees in Ezra apparently deal only with the temple. In any case, the city wall and the city were not rebuilt until the time of Nehemiah (445–444 B.C.). Scholars differ as to whether the exact date is the last month of 445 B.C. or the first month, 444 B.C. Though scholars continue to differ on the subject, the most plausible explanation is the 444 B.C. date because this works out precisely to the fulfillment of the prophecy and also coincides with the actual rebuilding of the city. This interpretation provides the most literal explanation without disregarding some of the specifics of the prophecy.

Amillenarians, who in general have taken this prophecy in less than its literal sense, in many instances tend to avoid the 444 B.C. date in favor of having fulfillment at the time of Christ's first coming. Under this projection the decree was issued at an earlier date than 445 B.C., and the first half of the last 7-year period, according to their interpretation, was fulfilled in the life of Christ, culminating in His crucifixion which they place at the middle of the last 7 years. This, however, provides no realistic fulfillment of the prophecy of the first 3½ years and certainly no fulfillment of the last 3½ years.

As in the interpretation of many other prophecies, a literal or normal interpretation requires a future fulfillment, in this case fulfillment of the last 7 years of the 490 years of prophecy.

### Seventy Sevens: Date of Culmination

If 444 B.C. is accepted as the beginning date of the 490 years, the 483 years would culminate in the year A.D. 33 where recent scholarship has placed the probable time of the death of Christ. In interpretation the Bible authorizes the use of the prophetic year of 360 days. The 360 days are multiplied by 483 years, or the 490 years minus seven. The computation comes out at A.D. 33. The concept that the prophetic year is 360 days is confirmed by the 1,260 days (Rev. 11:3; 12:6), with the forty-two months (11:2; 13:5), and with a time, times and half a time, or 3½ years (Dan. 7:25; 12:7; Rev. 12:14). This interpretation permits the 483 years to run their course. The intervening time between the 483 years and the last 7 years was provided in the prophecy itself as would be seen in examination of Daniel 9:26-27.

### Seventy Sevens: First Seven Years

The 490 years is divided into three parts. First, a 7-year period, then sixty-two times seven, or 434 years, and then the final seventieth seven, or the last 7 years.

## The 483 Years in the Jewish and Gregorian Calendars

| Jewish Calendar (360 days per year*) | Gregorian Calendar (365 days a year) |
|---|---|
| $(7 \times 7) + (62 \times 7)$ years = 483 years | 444 B.C. to A.D. 33 = 476 years† |
| 483 years<br>$\times$  360 days<br>173,880 days | 476 years<br>$\times$  365 days<br>173,740 days<br>+  116 days in leap years‡<br>+   24 days (March 5–March 30)<br>173,880 days |

*See comments on Daniel 9:27b for confirmation of this 360-day year.
†Since only one year expired between 1 B.C. and A.D. 1, the total is 476, not 477.
‡A total of 476 years divided by four (a leap year every four years) gives 119 additional days. But three days must be subtracted from 119 because centennial years are not leap years, though every 400th year is a leap year.

From *The Bible Knowledge Commentary,* Old Testament (Victor Books, 1985), p. 1363. Used with permission.

According to verse 25, in the first seven years the streets and a trench will be built in times of trouble. This period of forty-nine years described the aftermath of Nehemiah building the wall of Jerusalem and requiring one out of ten in Israel to build a house in Jerusalem which was fulfilled in the fifty years after the building of the wall. This was in complete fulfillment of the first seven times seven years.

### Seventy Sevens: Next 62 Sevens, 434 Years

The second segment of sixty-two sevens, or 434 years, was added to the first 49 years, bringing the total to 483 years.

### Seventy Sevens: Events between
### Sixty-Nine and Seventy Sevens

In this period the Anointed One, or the Messiah, is born and is cut off after the conclusion of the 483rd year as stated in verse 26, "After the sixty-two 'sevens,' the Anointed One will be cut off and will have nothing."

A further prophecy is given of an event after the sixty-ninth seven and before the seventieth seven, "The people of the ruler who will come will destroy the city and the sanctuary. The end will come like a flood: War will continue until the end, and desolations have been decreed" (v. 26).

Two major events mark the difference between the ending of the sixty-ninth "seven" and the beginning of the seventieth "seven," meaning that the Messiah would be cut off approximately A.D. 33 and that the city of Jerusalem would be destroyed in A.D. 70. Obviously, if the fulfillment of the last seven years immediately followed the preceding period, there would be no time in which to consider the destruction of Jerusalem as part of the fulfillment which would precede the last seven years. Again, a literal interpretation, as held by premillenarians, is preferable to the amillennial explanation that this has already been fulfilled in one sense or another. The end came for Jerusalem in its destruction in A.D. 70, and following that, war continues with its desolations as history has confirmed.

### Seventy Sevens: Seventieth Seven

The final revelation in Daniel 9:27 states, "He will confirm a covenant with many for one 'seven,' but in the middle of that 'seven' he will put an end to sacrifice and offering. And one who causes desolation will place abominations on a wing of the temple until the end that is decreed is poured out on him."

### Seventy Sevens: Amillennial Interpretation
### of Seventieth Seven

Daniel 9:27 brings to a head the various interpretations of this passage. Amillenarians, in opposition to the premillennial interpretation which considers this last 7 years still future, have offered at least four other points of view: (1) liberal amillenarians find fulfillment in the second century B.C. in the Maccabean time of persecution during the reign of Antiochus Epiphanes; (2) Jewish scholars find the seventieth week related to the destruction of Jerusalem in A.D. 70; (3) amillenarians who are conservative hold the seventieth week, particularly the last half, as an indefinite period; (4) amillenarians also consider 7 literal years beginning with the 3½ years of Christ's ministry, climaxing in His death and followed by the last 3½ years of the 490-year period for which they have no specific interpretation.

The amillenarian views, as well as that of the Jewish scholars, all have the problem of not explaining the prophecy in its normal, literal sense. No specific fulfillment can be found for major elements of the prophecy, particularly the last half of the seventieth week which, according to the Scriptures, climax in the Second Coming.

### Seventy Sevens: Premillennial View
### of Seventieth Seven

Premillenarians confirm its future fulfillment by the identification of "the ruler who will come" of verse 26 with the "he" of 9:27, the future world ruler. By contrast, some amillenarians hold that the one confirming the covenant in verse 27 was Christ Himself with reference to the New Covenant, but this covenant is obviously longer than seven years in duration.

The interpretation of "he" which begins verse 27 is crucial to understanding this prophecy in its fulfillment. In normal laws of reference a pronoun refers back to the last preceding person mentioned. In this case it is the "ruler who will come" of verse 26 rather than "the Anointed One" of the earlier portion of that verse. Because the fulfillment was never literally accomplished by Christ in His first coming, and even the New Covenant which they claim is referred to here cannot be related to a seven-year covenant because it is eternal, leaves the identification of the covenant-maker as the future world ruler, or Antichrist of the end time, a Roman related to the people who destroyed the city.

This is in keeping with other prophecy which indicates that he will stop sacrifices in the middle of the last seven years, the conclusion confirmed later in Daniel 12:7 in reference to the last three-and-a-half years and the revelation of daily sacrifices being abolished and the abomination set up in verse 11.

The concept that there is a time gap between 9:26 and verse 27, though opposed by many amillenarians, has a great deal of scriptural confirmation. One of the most important confirmations was the fact that the Old Testament presents the first and second coming of Christ as occurring at the same time as Isaiah 61:1-2. If the entire Inter-advent Age can be interposed between references to the first and second coming of Christ in the Old Testament, it certainly sets a precedent for having a time gap between the sixty-ninth "seven" and the seventieth "seven" of Daniel 9:24-27.

As in other problems in prophecy, so much of the difficulty comes when interpreters fail to take note of the particulars of the prophecy. Once it is understood that prophecy needs to be fulfilled literally and completely, many of the problems disappear.

### Seventy Sevens: Covenant with World Ruler

If the covenant of Daniel 9:27 is not the covenant of grace made possible by the death of Christ as amillenarians suggest, to what can this be referred? The best explanation is that this refers to the coming world ruler at the beginning of the last seven years who is able to gain control over ten countries in the Middle East. He will make a covenant with Israel for a seven-year period. As Daniel 9:27 indicates, in the middle of the seven years he will break the covenant, stop the sacrifices being offered in the temple rebuilt in that period, and become their persecutor instead of their protector, fulfilling the promises of Israel's day of trouble (Jer. 30:5-7). The temple of that future day will be desecrated much as Antiochus desecrated the temple in his day in the second century B.C., stopping the sacrifices and putting the temple to pagan use.

Just as Antiochus Epiphanes in the second century B.C. desecrated the temple in Jerusalem by offering a sow on the altar and setting up an idol of a Greek god, so in the end time the final world ruler, who will claim to be God, will set up an image of himself and constitute the abomination of the temple as was described in Daniel 9:27. The establishment of such an image was mentioned in Revelation 13:14-15. This will be accomplished by the beast out of the earth, the religious ruler who will be affiliated with the beast out of the sea who will be the world ruler (vv. 11, 14). The beast out of the earth "ordered them to set up an image in honor of the beast who was wounded by the sword and yet lived. He was given power to give breath to the image of the first beast, so that it could speak and cause all who refused to worship the image to be killed" (vv. 14-15). The fact that the final world ruler was presented as God was also mentioned in 2 Thessalonians 2:4, "He opposes and exalts himself over everything that is called God or is worshiped, and even sets himself up in God's temple, proclaiming himself to be God."

### Seventy Sevens: Best Interpretation

Accordingly, the best explanation of the 490 years is that the 483 years were fulfilled just before the time of Christ's crucifixion, that an interval time between Christ's crucifixion and the destruction of Jerusalem of more than thirty-five years will occur, fulfilling Daniel 9:26, with both events occurring in that period.

The final seven years, however, will begin when the ruler of the ten nations in the Middle East, who yet will appear, will fulfill the description as being a ruler related to the people who destroy the city of Jerusalem, that is, the Roman people. He will begin the final seven-year period by making a covenant of peace with Israel which will be broken after the first three-and-a-half years. This approach has the advantage of giving literal fulfillment to the prophecy and harmonizing it with any other prophecies of the end time.

Other interpretations simply do not fit the passage. Some have suggested Antiochus Epiphanes as the person who would fulfill this in the second century B.C. However, there is nothing in history that corresponds to a seven-year covenant following Antiochus. Only those who believe that Daniel is a forgery, written in the second century B.C., offer any support for this point of view.

Taken as a whole, the "seventy sevens" of Daniel's prophecy present the whole history of Israel from the time of Nehemiah in 444 B.C. until the Second Coming. Interposed is the present age not revealed in the Old Testament, which often prophesied the First Coming as the same event as the Second Coming and did not take into consideration the present age between the two events.

In Daniel's vision, then, he not only covered the sweep of Gentile prophecy terminating in the Second Coming, but he revealed that the "seventy sevens" of Israel will conclude with the same event, the Second Coming. The fact that Israel is already back in the land, that a world movement toward world government is also current, and that there is already a world religious movement combine to indicate that the time of fulfillment of end-time events may not be distant.

### Daniel's Fourth Vision: His Experience

*Daniel 10:1-3.* The fourth and final vision given to Daniel was recorded in Daniel 10–12. This was Daniel's final vision given "In the third year of Cyrus king of Persia" (the year 536 B.C.) (v. 1). Daniel was assured that the vision presented the truth and that its main vision related to a "great war" (v. 1).

Apparently in response to the fact that a vision was to be given, Daniel prepared by fasting for three weeks (v. 2). This does not mean that he completely abstained from food or drink but that as he expressed it, "I ate no choice food; no meat or wine touched my lips; and I used no lotions at all until the three weeks were over" (v. 3). At the time this vision came to Daniel, he was about eighty-five years of age.

Though Daniel did not mention it, he had occasion for distress because the Israelites who had returned to the Promised Land and were attempting to build the temple had run into hard times. The period of his fast included the time of the Passover which normally occurred on the fourteenth day of the first month and was followed by seven days in which unleavened bread was eaten. The three-week period, obviously, were weeks of days in contrast to the "seventy sevens" of Daniel 9, referred to here as "three sevens of day." The fact that the word "day" was used made clear that Daniel was speaking of a literal twenty-four-hour day.

Word had come back from Jerusalem concerning the plight of the Jews who had attempted to build the temple and had laid the foundation only to be stopped by the opposition of the people who already lived in the land (Ezra 4:1-5, 24). This was considered a great difficulty by Daniel as one of the primary reasons for going back to Jerusalem was to rebuild the temple and reinstitute the sacrificial system. Actually, the temple was delayed about twenty years. As has been explained before, the difference was between the seventy years of the Captivity which began in 605 B.C. and the seventy years of the desolation of Jerusalem which began in 586 B.C. The temple construction was delayed twenty years and the temple was completed in 515 B.C., seventy years after the temple was destroyed in 586 B.C. From a human standpoint it was delayed; from a divine standpoint it was on time. The period of fasting, however, gave opportunity for further revelation from God.

*Daniel 10:4-6.* The beginning of the three weeks of fasting was not indicated in the Bible, but it apparently was completed by the twenty-fourth day of the first month. This would allow time for the two-day festival of the beginning of the year and the beginning of the new moon which was a time of joy and, accordingly, not a suitable time for Daniel to fast (1 Sam. 20:18-19, 34). Apparently, Daniel's period of fasting began immediately afterward or on the fourth day of the new month, and it continued through the Feast of the Passover and the Feast of Unleavened Bread which had concluded before the vision was given.

Daniel recorded that the vision came to him: "As I was standing on the bank of the great river, the Tigris" (Dan. 10:4). In Daniel 8 he had a vision "beside the Ulai Canal" (8:2), but that could be interpreted as being there in vision, not actually there in body. Here the implication was that he was actually at the Tigris and standing on its bank when the vision begins. The fact that Daniel was beside the River Tigris answers the question why he did not go back to Jerusalem with the returning pilgrims. Apparently, this was impossible for Daniel, partly due to his age and partly due to his occupation as one of the administrators of the empire. He may have been there on some business for the empire. The Tigris River was approximately thirty-five miles to the northeast of Babylon, and being there did not require a great deal of travel.

Daniel recorded that in his vision he saw a glorious figure in the form of a man, "I looked up and there before me was a man dressed in linen, with a belt of the finest gold around his waist. His body was like chrysolite, his face like lightning, his eyes like flaming torches, his arms and legs like the gleam of burnished bronze, and his voice like the sound of a multitude" (10:5-6).

Scholars have wrestled with the question as to whether this man is a theophany (appearance of God) or a glorious angel. Because of the similarity of this vision to the one found in Revelation 1:11-16, many regard this first revelation as that of Christ Himself appearing as the Angel of the Lord. If so, it was in contrast to the person described in Daniel 10:10-14 or Michael mentioned in verse 13 because they were clearly angels. What Daniel saw was in keeping with the glorious vision of God.

The general clothing of the man was linen, which seemed to characterize heavenly visitors (Ezek. 9:2-3, 11; 10:2, 6-7) as well as the garments of priests (Ex. 28:39-43). Angels frequently appear in long white garments, whether linen or not, and sometimes brilliant in color (Mark 16:5; Luke 24:4; John 20:12; Acts 1:10). The belt, or girdle, was probably made of linen embroidered with the finest gold (Dan. 10:5). In the *King James Version* the "girdle" was described as having "fine gold of Uphaz." A similar reference was found in Jeremiah 10:9, but it is unknown what the meaning of this phrase was except that it intimates that it was of very fine gold.

The glorious appearance of the body of the man was said to be "like chrysolite," also translated as beryl (NASB). Some think it was like a topaz. This jewel was mentioned also in Exodus 28:17 and Ezekiel 1:16; 10:9. Because in the Hebrew it was called *tarshish*, the implication was that it originated in Spain and possibly was yellow in color.

The face of the man was described to be "like lightning, his eyes like flaming torches," similar to the description of Christ in Revelation 1:14-16. The arms and legs were described as "burnished bronze," similar to the description of Christ in Revelation 1:15, "His feet were like bronze glowing in a furnace." As in Revelation 1:15, the voice of Christ was described "like the sound of rushing waters," so here Daniel hears a sound "like the sound of a multitude" (Dan. 10:6).

*Daniel 10:7-9.* Though Daniel saw the vision which overwhelmed him with terror, those who were with him did not see the vision but sensed that something awesome was happening and "they fled and hid themselves" (v. 7). Daniel, however, after gazing on the image declared, "I had no strength left, my face turned deathly pale and I was helpless. Then I heard him speaking, and as I listened to him, I fell into a deep sleep, my face to the ground" (vv. 8-9). Daniel's experience is similar to that of Paul on the road to Damascus when the men with Saul heard a sound but did not see anyone and did not understand what was being said (Acts 9:7;22:9). The fact that the men with Daniel did not see the vision corroborates the conclusion that he was actually at the River Tigris geographically. How he knew that his face was "deathly pale" was not stated, but apparently he sensed that he was very weak. He then fell into a deep sleep. The account illustrates how men in their mortal bodies, even godly men like Daniel, cannot stand the glorious presence of God. Also illustrated is Paul's response to the vision of Christ on the road to Damascus (Acts 9:4).

*Daniel 10:10-11.* In his weakness Daniel recorded, "A hand touched me and set me trembling on my hands and knees" (v. 10). Daniel was told the vision was given to him because he was a man "highly esteemed," and Daniel was instructed to "consider carefully the words I am about to speak to you, and stand up, for I have now been sent to you" (v. 11). In response to this Daniel said he "stood up trembling."

*Daniel 10:12-14.* The person talking to him said, "Do not be afraid, Daniel. Since the first day that you set your mind to gain understanding and to humble yourself before your God, your words were heard, and I have come in response to them. But the prince of the Persian kingdom resisted me twenty-one days. Then Michael, one of the chief princes, came to help me, because I was detained there with the king of Persia. Now I have come to explain to you what will happen to your people in the future, for the vision concerns a time yet to come" (vv. 12-14).

If the man described in verses 4-6 were a theophany, a revelation of Christ Himself, it was made clear that the first man described here was an angel and not Christ because he was said to be less than omnipotent and resisted by "the prince of the Persian kingdom" for "twenty-one days" (v. 13). He was then assisted by Michael the archangel who helped him (v. 13). The angel declared to Daniel that "the vision concerns a time yet to come" (v. 14). The revelation of the conflict between the angels and the demon world described in this passage is similar to other indications of this conflict that goes on without ceasing (Eph. 6:10-17).

*Daniel 10:15-19.* The revelation left Daniel "speechless" (v. 15) and he bowed toward the ground. Again Daniel was touched by "one who looked like a man" (v. 16). It was not clear whether this refers to an angel or to the theophany, but more probably to the angel mentioned in the preceding verses. Daniel who tried to talk stated, "My strength is gone and I can hardly breathe" (v. 17).

Daniel was again touched and given strength, and the angelic being stated, " 'Do not be afraid, O man highly esteemed,' he said. 'Peace! Be strong now; be strong' " (v. 19). In response to this Daniel declared, "I was strengthened and said, 'Speak, my lord, since you have given me strength' " (v. 19).

*Daniel 10:20–11:1.* The angelic figure told Daniel, "Do you know why I have come to you? Soon I will return to fight against the prince of Persia, and when I go, the prince of Greece will come;

262

but first I will tell you what is written in the Book of Truth. (No one supports me against them except Michael, your prince. And in the first year of Darius the Mede, I took my stand to support and protect him.)" This referred to the prophetic vision given to Daniel in chapter 8 where the ultimate triumph of Greece over Medo-Persia was prophesied. The angel indicated, however, that he supported Darius the Mede when he took charge of Babylon.

### Daniel's Fourth Vision:
### Prophecy of Kings before Antiochus IV

*Daniel 11:2-35* provided the most detailed prophecy to be found anywhere in Scripture. The interpreter is faced with the question as to whether God is omniscient, that is, He knows all events of the future and also whether God reveals in detail future events.

The Book of Daniel was held as genuine Scripture written by Daniel the prophet in the sixth century B.C. for at least 800 years without anyone questioning the validity of this prophecy.

As previously discussed, in the third century of the Christian era, about 800 years after Daniel, an atheistic philosopher by the name of Porphyry in studying the Book of Daniel concluded that the prophecies of Daniel 11:2-35 were extremely accurate describing the historical period which it covered. Because he did not believe in God or believe that God was omniscient, he had to find some way to account for this extraordinary piece of writing. He concluded that whoever wrote it must have lived after the events described. Accordingly, he offered the theory that Daniel was not written by Daniel the prophet in the sixth century B.C. but rather in the Maccabean period, about 175 B.C., by a man who claimed to be Daniel and actually wrote the book as a forgery.

Until modern times no others undertook to support Porphyry. When liberal scholars began to emerge they were faced with the same problem as Porphyry had in attempting to interpret this passage. Because they did not believe in supernatural revelation and they even questioned whether God was omniscient, they adopted the view of Porphyry with little change and argued that the book must be a forgery of the second century after the events described. Up to the present time this is the position of the liberal scholars.

The finding of a complete manuscript of Daniel among the Qumran papers, which was hundreds of years earlier than the oldest copy of Daniel previously found, served to undermine this liberal position because it brought the Book of Daniel back to the second century B.C. but in comparatively modern Hebrew instead of ancient Hebrew. According to the liberal theologians' own position, this would require a couple of centuries between this copy and the original which, of course, would put it back into Daniel's lifetime or at least before the events described in Daniel 11. Liberals have been largely silent about this discovery, but a new generation of liberals will have to face the fact that their old theory no longer holds and that Daniel is a genuine prophecy.

The details offered in Daniel 11:2-35 included the major events and personalities beginning with the major rulers of the Persian Empire and then continuing into the major events of the Alexandrian period, culminating in the prophecy about Antiochus Epiphanes (175–164 B.C.). Beginning with verse 36, the prophecy leaped ahead of events which have followed Antiochus to the time of the end which is yet future from the viewpoint of our present twentieth century.

*Daniel 11:2.* The prophecy began by describing four kings of Persia (v. 2). Daniel writes: "Now then, I tell you the truth: Three more kings will appear in Persia, and then a fourth, who will be far richer than all the others. When he has gained power by his wealth, he will stir up everyone against the kingdom of Greece" (v. 2).

In attempting to identify the four kings, it is probable that Daniel excluded Darius the Mede and Cyrus II (550–530 B.C.). The four kings probably are Cambyses (529–522 B.C.) who was not mentioned in the Old Testament, Pseudo-Smerdis (522–521 B.C.), Darius I Hystaspes (521–486 B.C., Ezra 5–6), Xerxes I (486–465 B.C., Ezra 4:6).

As Daniel indicated, Xerxes I was the ruler who attempted to conquer Greece at the time of the greatest power of the Persian Empire. Xerxes I had gathered an army of several hundred thousand and began a war against Greece (580 B.C.) in which his fleet as well as his troops were defeated. Persia never rose to great power after this. Many identify Ahasuerus, who chose Esther as his queen, as this Xerxes I. The disastrous expedition against Greece probably occurred between Esther 1 and Esther 2. Daniel did not give many details on the Persian Empire as additional facts were furnished in Ezra, Nehemiah, and Esther, supplemented by Haggai, Zechariah, and Malachi. As Daniel probably died about 530 B.C., his life ended before these events took place, and therefore it had to be genuine prophecy.

*Daniel 11:3-4.* Daniel prophesied the coming of Alexander the Great, "Then a mighty king will appear, who will rule with great power and do as he pleases. After he has appeared, his empire will be broken up and parceled out towards the four winds of heaven. It will not go to his descendants, nor will it have the power he exercised, because his empire will be uprooted and given to others" (vv. 3-4). This prophecy anticipated the rise of Alexander the Great and his conquering the Persian Empire. As history records, when Alexander the Great died in 323 B.C. his conquest was divided among his four generals. The same events were prophesied in verses 5-8 interpreted by Daniel in verses 21-22. At the time Daniel wrote this prophecy Greece was a small and relatively insignificant nation.

*Daniel 11:5-6.* Daniel continued with a prophecy even more detailed than the previous prophecies. He wrote, "The king of the South will become strong, but one of his commanders will become even stronger than he and will rule his own kingdom with great power. After some years, they will become allies. The daughter of the king of the South will go to the king of the North to make an alliance, but she will not retain her power, and he and his power will not last. In those days she will be handed over, together with her royal escort and her father and the one who supported her" (vv. 5-6).

As intimated in verse 5, the passage concerned struggles between Syria as the king of the North and Egypt as the king of the South. Though Syria was not mentioned because it did not exist as a nation at that time and Egypt was referred to only as the king of the South, it was nevertheless quite clear how this corresponds to history. Ptolemy I Soter (323–285 B.C.) is the king of the South. The one who is stronger than he is in reference to Seleucus I Nicator (312–281 B.C.). In the historic background of these events there is evidence that Seleucus had left Antigonus in Babylon and for a brief time was associated with Ptolemy I in Egypt. They together had defeated Antigonus which made it possible for Seleucus to control in a military way the large area from Asia Minor to India, and he became stronger than Ptolemy who ruled Egypt. This explains verse 5, "one of his commanders will become even stronger than he and will rule over his kingdom with great power." The two areas of strength in this period were Egypt, led by Ptolemy, and Seleucus as the ruler of Syria. It is also indicated, "After some years, they will become allies" (v. 6).

It would be normal to have intermarriage between these two rulers, and this is referred to in verse 6, stating, "The daughter of the king of the South will go to the king of the North to make an alliance, but she will not retain her power, and he and his power will not last. In those days she will be handed over, together with her royal escort and her father and the one who supported her" (v. 6). The daughter mentioned here was Berenice who was the daughter of Ptolemy II Philadelphus (285–246 B.C.) who was king of Egypt. At that time the king of Syria, or "the king of the North" was Antiochus II Theos (261–246 B.C.). However, the alliance did not last as a former wife of Antiochus by name of Laodice joined a conspiracy in which both Berenice and Antiochus were killed and her father, who was Ptolemy, also died at that time. The verses are accurate in describing the future events of that period.

*Daniel 11:7-9.* A later king of Egypt, Ptolemy III Euergetes (246–222 B.C.), was able to conquer the Northern Kingdom, seizing a great deal of booty as is described by Daniel, "One from her family line will arise to take her place. He will attack the forces of the king of the North and enter his fortress; he will fight against them and be victorious. He will also seize their gods, their metal images and their valuable articles of silver and gold and carry them off to Egypt. For some years he will leave the king of the North alone" (vv. 7-8). Ptolemy III Euergetes in commemorating his victory over the kingdom of the North erected a monument named *Marmor Adulitanum* in which he recorded his boast that he had conquered a large area, including Mesopotamia, Persia, Media, Susiana, and other countries. After this victory apparently he ceased invading the North.

In the history which followed this period there were attacks from the North and from the South as they fought each other at various times. Verse 9 indicated an attack of the king of the North against the king of the South which occurred about 240 B.C. and was led by Seleucus II Callinicus. He, however, was defeated and returned without conquering the land of Egypt.

*Daniel 11:10-12.* His older son was killed while on a military campaign in Asia Minor. Later, the younger son, Antiochus III, attacked Egypt with some success. As ruler of the kingdom of the North, Antiochus III had several successful campaigns against Egypt during a period when the Egyptian ruler, Ptolemy Philopator

(221–203 B.C.) did not raise sufficient defense against him.

In a later battle in 217 B.C. Antiochus the Great challenged an Egyptian army with about 70,000 soldiers on each side which resulted in Egypt destroying the entire army of Antiochus as indicated in verses 11-12.

*Daniel 11:13-16.* In the verses which follow, however, additional invasions of Egypt carried on by the king of the North are mentioned, "For the king of the North will muster another army, larger than the first; and after several years, he will advance with a huge army fully equipped. In those times many will rise against the king of the South. The violent men among your own people will rebel in fulfillment of the vision, but without success. Then the king of the North will come and build up siege ramps and will capture a fortified city. The forces of the South will be powerless to resist; even their best troops will not have the strength to stand. The invader will do as he pleases; no one will be able to stand against him. He will establish himself in the Beautiful Land and will have the power to destroy it" (vv. 13-16).

These prophecies correspond precisely to the history of the period which described these wars and the success of the kingdom of the North. The conquering of a fortified city (v. 15) was fulfilled when the Egyptian armies were defeated at Paneas at the headwaters of the Jordan River with the result that Antiochus III was able to take Sidon which was captured 199–198 B.C. The result was that Syria controlled all the Holy Land as far south as Gaza.

Subsequently, Egypt attempted to conquer Syria, and armies led by the Egyptians Eropas, Menacles, and Damoyenus failed to dent the Syrian power.

*Daniel 11:17-20.* At this time, however, Rome began to exert its power in the eastern Mediterranean, and it seemed best for Antiochus to make peace with Egypt by marrying his daughter Cleopatra to Ptolemy V Epiphanes. This was described by Daniel, "He will determine to come with the might of his entire kingdom and will make an alliance with the king of the South. And he will give him a daughter in marriage in order to overthrow the kingdom, but his plans will not succeed or help him" (v. 17).

Antiochus, having settled things with Egypt, attempted to conquer Greece but was defeated in 191 B.C. at Thermopylae and in 189 B.C. again was defeated at Magnesia southeast of Ephesus, this time by Roman soldiers. This fulfilled what Daniel wrote, "Then he will turn his attention to the coastlands and will take many of them, but a commander will put an end to his insolence and will turn his insolence back upon him. After this, he will turn back toward the fortresses of his own country but will stumble and fall, to be seen no more" (vv. 18-19). Though Antiochus was a great ruler, his failure to conquer Greece left him a broken man at the time of his death which occurred when he attempted to plunder a temple in Elam.

### Daniel's Fourth Vision: Antiochus IV

Daniel's prophecy now turns to two other rulers, Seleucus IV Philopator (187–175 B.C.), and Antiochus IV Epiphanes (175–164 B.C.) who was the famous persecutor of the Jews previously mentioned in Daniel 8:23-25 and referred to as the little horn mentioned in Daniel 8:9-14. Seleucus IV Philopator was indicated by Daniel 11:20, "His successor will send out a tax collector to maintain the royal splendor. In a few years, however, he will be destroyed, yet not in anger or in battle" (v. 20). The necessity for raising taxes was caused by the tribute he had to pay to Rome of 1,000 talents each year.

*Daniel 11:21-35.* The tax collector he appointed was named Heliodorus (2 Macc. 3:7). Some believe that Seleucus IV Philopator was killed by poison and his death set the stage for the final ruler of this period that Daniel mentioned described in Daniel 11:21-35. In verses 21-35 a comparatively insignificant ruler of Syria, known as Antiochus IV Epiphanes, next appears. The importance of this man to Daniel and to God was his persecution of the Jewish people during the period of his reign 175–164 B.C.

In comparison to the earlier rulers of the Northern Kingdom, he was described by Daniel as "a contemptible person who has not been given the honor of royalty" (v. 21). He secured the throne by a series of intrigues and murders of other possible candidates as Daniel described, "He will invade the kingdom when its people feel secure, and he will seize it through intrigue" (v. 21).

The path by which he came to the throne is rather complicated. There were several possible legitimate rulers at the death of his predecessor, Seleucus IV Philopator. The younger son of Seleucus IV was Demetrius and probably was the most legitimate successor to the throne, but at that time he was in prison in Rome as a hostage. A younger son, Antiochus, was still a baby. The brother of Seleucus IV was Antiochus IV who at the time his brother died was living in Athens. There he heard Heliodorus had murdered his brother Seleucus as prophesied in Daniel 11:20. Antiochus IV Epiphanes went to Antioch and somehow secured the throne. Andronicus helped this by murdering the baby Antiochus but in turn was put to death by Antiochus IV. Heliodorus who had murdered Seleucus IV apparently faded from history. For a prophecy to predict accurately such a tangled history can only be explained by the inspiration of the Holy Spirit.

Antiochus IV began a very troubled life, struggling against Egypt the kingdom of the South and the rising power of Rome. His ascendancy to power was described in verse 21. Antiochus IV added the title of Epiphanes which means "glorious one." Because of his various intrigues he was nicknamed by others as "Epimanes," meaning madman. Antiochus was attacked by a large army, probably from Egypt, but somehow Antiochus was able to defeat the army as Daniel states, "Then an overwhelming army will be swept away before him" (v. 22). The further reference that "a prince of the covenant will be destroyed" probably referred to the fact that the deposed Onias III the high priest had begun his persecution of the Jews.

Some of his military successes were described in the verses which follow, "After coming to an agreement with him, he will act deceitfully, and with only a few people he will rise to power. When the richest provinces feel secure, he will invade them and will achieve what neither his fathers nor his forefathers did. He will distribute plunder, loot and wealth among his followers. He will plot the overthrow of fortresses — but only for a time" (vv. 23-24).

Having consolidated his political power through victories by arms, he then attempted what others had done before him, to attack Egypt. Daniel wrote, "With a large army he will stir up his strength and courage against the king of the South. The king of the South will wage war with a large and very powerful army, but he will not be able to stand because of the plots devised against him. Those who eat from the king's provisions will try to destroy him; his army will be swept away and many will fall in battle" (vv. 25-26).

This war occurred approximately five years after he took the throne. A large Egyptian army met the forces of Antiochus at Pelusium near the Nile delta and were defeated by Antiochus. After the battle the two attempted to establish a peace covenant which Daniel described, "The two kings, with their hearts bent on evil, will sit at the same table and lie to each other, but to no avail, because an end will still come at the appointed time. The king of the North will return to his own country with great wealth" (vv. 27-28). Though the conference was an attempt at arriving at a peace, both conspirators were trying to get the best of the other, and the result was that peace was not achieved.

Antiochus, now with apparent success over Egypt, was irritated by the Jews' failure to support him actively. Accordingly, Daniel wrote, "But his heart will be set against the holy covenant. He will take action against it and then return to his own country" (v. 28). Antiochus was very much opposed to the Jewish religion and against the "holy covenant." He desecrated their temple, offering a sow on the altar and installing a statue of a Greek god. This precipitated the Maccabean revolt in which thousands of Jews were killed, including men, women, and children, some being hurled from tops of buildings to their deaths, in the vain effort to stamp out the Jewish religion.

The desecration of the Jewish temple as described in verses 31-32 followed another attack on Egypt which was unsuccessful. The problem now was that Rome was beginning to extend its power, and Antiochus did not think it was safe to attempt to conquer Egypt under the circumstances. Accordingly, as Daniel wrote, "At the appointed time he will invade the South again, but this time the outcome will be different from what it was before. Ships of the western coastlands will oppose him, and he will lose heart. Then he will turn back and vent his fury against the holy covenant. He will return and show favor to those who forsake the holy covenant" (vv. 29-30).

The attempt of Antiochus to destroy the Jewish religion was described by Daniel in these words, "His armed forces will rise up to desecrate the temple fortress and will abolish the daily sacrifice. Then they will set up the abomination that causes desolation. With flattery he will corrupt those who have violated the covenant, but the people who know their God will firmly resist him" (vv. 31-32). This had been anticipated in Daniel 8:9-12, 23-25. The time of persecution of Israel was described further by Daniel: "Those who are wise will instruct many, though for a time they will fall by the sword or be burned or captured or plundered. When they fall, they will receive a little help, and many who are not sincere will join them. Some of the wise will stumble, so that they may be refined, purified and made spotless until the time of the end, for it will still come at the appointed time" (11:33-35).

These intricate prophecies describing in detail the relationship between the empires of Persia and Greece with the Jewish people can only be explained by divine inspiration. The details were such that even a person living at the time might have difficulty putting all the facts together in proper relationship and conclusion. Regarding the fact that unbelievers have attacked Daniel on the basis of this prophecy is in itself an admission that the prophecies were accurate, and the supporting data indicated that it was written by Daniel in the sixth century B.C.

### Daniel's Fourth Vision: The Time of the End

The reference to "the time of the end" referred to in the remaining prophecy beginning in verse 36 was not the immediate outcome of the reign of Antiochus IV Epiphanes. The chronological gap between Antiochus IV Epiphanes (vv. 21-35) and the end time (vv. 36-45) was common in the Old Testament as many prophecies concerning the first and second coming of Christ though presented together were separated by thousands of years in their fulfillment.

*Daniel 11:36-45.* The detailed prophecies of Daniel 10:1–11:35 were entirely prophetic from Daniel's viewpoint in the sixth century B.C. and have now all been fulfilled. From Daniel's standpoint it was all future, but beginning with verse 36, prophecies given by Daniel have not yet been fulfilled and, in fact, relate to the period just before the Second Coming.

The final world ruler was described by Daniel, "The king will do as he pleases. He will exalt and magnify himself above every god and will say unheard-of things against the God of gods" (v. 36). Some interpreters have attempted to relate this king to Antiochus IV mentioned in the earlier verses of this chapter. However, the evidence of history is that Antiochus IV died shortly after fulfilling the preceding verses in the year 164 B.C. Some think he was insane at the time of his death. In any event he did not fulfill any of the events described in the latter part of this chapter, beginning in verse 36.

A more plausible explanation is that this ruler referred to the little horn of Daniel 7:8, 21-24 as well as to the beast out of the sea (Rev. 13:1-10). In this identification he will be the future world ruler and a Gentile.

Some expositors hold that the final king will be an apostate Jew, possibly not the world ruler but one who arises in Palestine and cooperates with the final Gentile power.

For many reasons the identification of this king as the final Gentile ruler is a superior interpretation. According to Daniel himself, he will be a willful king who will consider himself above every god as well as above every king. This would not fit a Jewish king who was not the supreme ruler in the times of the Gentiles. It would also be incredible that this ruler would be a Jew inasmuch as he persecuted Jews.

This ruler was also described by Daniel, "He will be successful until the time of wrath is completed, for what has been determined must take place" (Dan. 11:36). This was in keeping with Daniel 7:27-28 and also the destruction of the final world ruler in Revelation 19:20. He will fulfill the prophecy of speaking "against the God of gods" (Dan. 11:36) as mentioned also in Revelation 13:5-7.

The future ruler was described in an unusual way by Daniel, "He will show no regard for the gods of his fathers or for the one desired by women, nor will he regard any god, but will exalt himself above them all" (Dan. 11:37). On the basis of this verse some have considered this ruler a Jew because of the familiar phrase, "the gods *(Elohim)* of his fathers." In the KJV "gods" is translated in the singular "God." The usual expression regarding the God of Israel as the God of their fathers is *Yahweh* which is unmistakably the God of Israel. The fact that Daniel used *Elohim* is significant because *Elohim* is used both of the true God and of false gods and is a general word like the English word *God.* Further, *Elohim* is a natural plural, and though it was sometimes translated in the singular, its more accurate translation in this case would be in the plural, referring to heathen gods. The point of the passage is not simply that he will reject the God of Israel, but he will disregard all deities as indicated in the preceding verse where he considered himself greater than any god. The passage included the fact that he will not regard "the one desired by women" (v. 37). From the Jewish perspective, the desire of women was to fulfill the promise given to Eve of a coming Redeemer to be born of a woman. Undoubtedly, many Jewish women hoped that one of their sons would fulfill this prophecy. Accordingly, "the one desired by women" is the Messiah of Israel. What this passage accordingly predicted was that he, as a Gentile, will have a total disregard for Scripture and its promise of a coming King of kings.

In keeping with verse 36, Daniel declared, "Nor will he regard any god, but will exalt himself above them all" (v. 37). This reinforced the concept that he rejected not simply the God of Israel but all gods, whether pagan or the true God. In other words, he will be an atheist and will consider himself deity.

Daniel went on to describe him, however, as hardly an object of worship, "Instead of them, he will honor a god of fortresses; a god unknown to his fathers he will honor with gold and silver, with precious stones and costly gifts" (v. 38). As the preceding verses made clear, he did not recognize any person as God, but in place of worship of God he will place material things which will enable him to increase his power militarily and politically. It is similar to the modern concept of "the god of war" which is a personification of the desire to wage war.

His military endeavors will be successful for a time as Daniel stated, "He will attack the mightiest fortresses with the help of a foreign god and will greatly honor those who acknowledge him. He will make them rulers over many people and will distribute the land at a price" (v. 39). His reign will be connected with the concept of deity, and he apparently will use belief in deities as a stepping-stone to bringing people to believe in him as God. He will be successful in this as is confirmed by Revelation 13:8, "All inhabitants of the earth will worship the beast—all whose names have not been written in the Book of Life belonging to the Lamb that was slain from the creation of the world." All religions of whatever character will be merged into the final worship of this world ruler who is Satan's substitute for Christ as King of kings and Lord of lords. He will reward those who have been supportive by making them rulers and will distribute wealth in a way that will help his reign.

The final verses of Daniel 11, beginning with verse 40, described the final world war which will occur in the period just before the Second Coming. According to Revelation 13:7, the king will have achieved his goal of being over every nation in the world. But as the events of the Great Tribulation transpire with its wholesale destruction of people, dissatisfaction with his reign develops, and the result is that various portions of the world begin to revolt against this world ruler and attack him.

The Holy Land will be the battlefield, and armies from all over the world will converge. Daniel described this, "At the time of the end the king of the South will engage him in battle, and the king of the North will storm out against him with chariots and cavalry and a great fleet of ships" (Dan. 11:40). Prophecy is not entirely clear how to classify these various people, but apparently a great army from Africa described as coming from the South and a great army from Europe, probably including Russia and other European nations, will attack him from the North. Daniel stated, however, "He will invade many countries and sweep through them like a flood" (v. 40). This prophesies that the world ruler will be triumphant against these invading forces. It states, "He will also invade the Beautiful Land" which refers to the Holy Land (v. 41). Daniel declared, "Many countries will fall," but there are exceptions which Daniel described, "but Edom, Moab and the leaders of Ammon will be delivered from his hand. He will extend his power over many countries; Egypt will not escape. He will gain control of the treasures of gold and silver and all the riches of Egypt, with the Libyans and Nubians in submission" (vv. 41-43).

Though he will be very successful in the war, the world leader of the future will hear reports of additional armies coming from the East and the North. This apparently refers to the great army from the East described in Revelation 16:12 as "the kings from the East." Some connect this also with 9:13-16 which states the army is 200 million. This will probably not only include the armies which will fight but also supporting personnel behind them. It is significant in connection with this that China today boasts a militia of 200 million men.

Scriptures are clear that apparently the world ruler will continue to dominate the situation right up to the time of the Second Coming. As Daniel summarized it, "He will pitch his royal tents between the seas at the beautiful holy mountain. Yet he will come to his end, and no one will help him" (Dan. 11:45). The final destruction of Gentile power had been anticipated earlier in 7:11, "Then I continued to watch because of the boastful words the horn was speaking. I kept looking until the beast was slain and its body destroyed and thrown into the blazing fire."

At the Second Coming the world ruler will be captured and cast into the "fiery lake of burning sulphur" (Rev. 19:20).

Though Daniel was not given prophecies concerning the present age between the first and second coming of Christ, more than any other prophet he described the sequence of prophetic events that embraced Israel to the time of the Second Coming as well as those that included Gentile rule. Further details are given in Daniel 12.

*Daniel 12:1-3.* In the preceding chapter Daniel was informed about the Great Tribulation and the world war that will come at its conclusion. Naturally, he would be concerned about the people of Israel. In answer to this natural question concerning the destiny of his people, he was informed, "At that time Michael, the great prince who protects your people, will arise. There will be a time of distress such as has not happened from the beginning of nations until then. But at that time your people — everyone whose name is found written in the Book — will be delivered" (v. 1).

According to other prophecies, many of the Jews as well as Gentiles will turn to Christ in the period after the Rapture but will be martyrs. In Revelation 7:1-8 the Apostle John was informed that 144,000 of the people of Israel, 12,000 from each of the twelve tribes enumerated, would be sealed and would go through the Great Tribulation unscathed. In 14:1 they are seen standing on Mount Zion intact.

In 7:9-17 many others will be martyred from every country and race. They are pictured in heaven triumphant, but they have gone to heaven from the Great Tribulation because they will be put to death by the world ruler who will demand that everyone worship him at the pain of death (cf. Rev. 13:15). Daniel was assured that while individuals may perish, the nation of Israel as such will be protected and continue to exist through the Great Tribulation and enter the millennial kingdom when Jesus Christ, their Messiah, comes in His second coming.

### Daniel's Fourth Vision: Resurrections of the End Time

Daniel was informed that many who die will be resurrected, "Multitudes who sleep in the dust of the earth will awake: some to everlasting life, others to shame and everlasting contempt" (Dan. 12:2). This prophecy concerns the fact of resurrection. In reconstruction of the order of resurrection, it is clear that all will not be resurrected at the same time. Also mentioned in relation to Christ's resurrection was the token resurrection of a small number of saints (Matt. 27:51-53). At the Rapture of the church at the end of the present age, members of the body of Christ, Christians who died since Pentecost, will be raised out from among the dead. A special resurrection also was revealed concerning the two witnesses (Rev. 11:3-13) who will be raised and caught up to heaven at the conclusion of their witness (v. 12). All of these resurrections precede the resurrection at the time of the Second Coming (Dan. 12:2-3). The resurrection of some to shame and everlasting contempt (v. 2) will not occur until the end of the Millennium as is made clear in Revelation 20:4-6, 11-15. The resurrection here extended to all the saved of the Old Testament, whether Jews or Gentiles, all who were not resurrected at the time of the Rapture. They will be given resurrection life and new bodies and will enter the millennial kingdom as resurrected people. Tribulation saints will also be raised (v. 4). At the beginning of the Millennium the only ones remaining in the grave will be the unsaved.

The time of resurrection will be a time of reward as well, and Daniel was told, "Those who are wise will shine like the brightness of the heavens, and those who lead many to righteousness, like the stars forever and ever" (Dan. 12:3). Just as those who are raptured will be judged and rewarded at the Judgment Seat of Christ, so all other saints who have died will be resurrected at the time of the Second Coming and, in like manner, be rewarded for what they have done for God.

### Daniel's Fourth Vision: Outcome of the End Time

*Daniel 12:4.* Though Daniel had been a faithful recorder of the prophecies received from God, Daniel only partially understood what he was writing. Then Daniel was instructed, "But you, Daniel, close up and seal the words of the scroll until the time of the end" (v. 4). Those who will profit most by the prophecies of Daniel will be those who will be living in the end time. Even today, before the climactic events take place that will follow the Rapture, it is possible to interpret most of Daniel's prophecies and find fulfillment of these prophecies in history. Those not fulfilled will yet be fulfilled. The age leading up to the end was characterized in the final words, "Many will go here and there to increase knowledge" (v. 4). The implication is that they will rush around trying to increase knowledge. Our modern world is certainly characterized by this, and there is more scientific discovery in one year now than there used to be in a century. But the sad fact is that most of this knowledge does not pertain to eternal values and does not prepare a person for the coming of the Lord. Too often in an intellectual world the Scriptures, which are the fountain of all truth about God and His plan for the universe, are neglected.

*Daniel 12:5-13.* In receiving further revelation Daniel was still standing on the bank of the Tigris (10:4), and now he saw two others, one on one side of the river and one on the other side. He hears them conversing, "One of them said to the man clothed in linen, who was above the waters of the river, 'How long will it be before these astonishing things are fulfilled?' " (12:6) The Scriptures record that the other man also replied, "The man clothed in linen, who was above the waters of the river, lifted his right hand and his left hand toward heaven, and I heard him swear by him who lives forever, saying, 'It will be for a time, times and half a time' " (v. 7). The expression "time, times and half a time" (cf. 7:25; Rev. 12:14) is the final three-and-one-half years before the Second Coming. In connection with the Great Tribulation, the woman, referring to the nation of Israel, was declared to be protected "for a time, times and half a time" from the persecution of Satan (v. 14). Though many Israelites will be killed in the Great Tribulation (7:9-17), the nation as such will survive, will be regathered (Ezek. 20:33-38), and will be judged, and only those who are saved will be allowed to enter the millennial kingdom. Because the period of the Great Tribulation was declared to be forty-two months (cf. Dan. 9:27; Rev. 13:5), the expression is best understood as being that a "time" is one year, "times"—two years, and "a half a time" a half a year, adding up to three-and-one-half years.

Daniel was also informed that "When the power of the holy people has been finally broken, all these things will be completed" (v. 7). As indicated in many Scriptures such as Revelation 13:7, the people of Israel as well as Gentiles who become Christians will be subject to purging judgments at the hand of the world ruler at the end time who will attempt to exterminate all Christians and all Jews. Scriptures are clear that sometimes God has permitted martyrdom, but on other occasions He delivered His people from martyrdom, as illustrated in the 144,000 of Revelation 7.

Daniel again declared that he does not understand the prophecy and that he asked, "My Lord, what will the outcome of all this be?" (Dan. 12:8)

The angel replied, "Go your way, Daniel, because the words are closed up and sealed until the time of the end" (v. 9). Daniel was further instructed that in the end time some will be purified by their persecution but that the wicked will continue to be wicked, "Many will be purified, made spotless and refined, but the wicked will continue to be wicked. None of the wicked will understand, but those who are wise will understand" (v. 10).

The climax of the time of the end is summarized by the angel, "From the time that the daily sacrifice is abolished and the abomination that causes desolation is set up, there will be 1,290 days. Blessed is the one who waits for and reaches the end of the 1,335 days" (vv. 11-12).

This brief summary of the end time of approximately three-and-a-half years is confirmed by other Scriptures. The beginning of the three-and-a-half years of the Great Tribulation will feature the abolishment of the daily sacrifices and the setting up of an abomination in the temple (7:25; 9:27; Rev. 11:2-3). The time in view will be the Great Tribulation, the last three-and-a-half years leading up to the second coming of Christ. This will be a terrible time of divine judgment as well as governmental persecution as brought out in Revelation 6:1–18:24. Because three-and-a-half years of 360 days each, commonly used as a prophetic year, did not explain the addition of 30 days in the figure 1,290, two explanations remain possible. It may be that the announcement of the stopping of the sacrifices will occur 30 days before the middle of the last seven years, allowing for the remaining 1,260 days to climax in the second coming of Christ. Another explanation is that when Christ comes back there will be a time gap before the Millennium as Christ begins to deal with judgments which may not all take place in a few days. In that case the 30 days would be a period in which Christ begins to bring to bear His judgment on the world before the Millennium begins.

In any case, at the time of the Second Coming the wicked will be brought to trial. The sheep will be rescued and will enter the kingdom, but the goats will be put to death (Matt. 24:36-41; 25:31-46). These passages seem to refer to Gentile judgment particularly, but the Jews will experience a similar purging judgment (Ezek. 20:33-38). In these judgments all adult unbelievers, whether Jew or Gentile, will be purged out, and only believers will be allowed to enter the millennial kingdom, with children who are not old enough to make a decision apparently exempted from judgment. Accordingly, anyone who lives to the end of the 1,335 days will be saved because the purging judgments have taken place of all the unsaved before this time is reached. Accordingly, those who remain will be allowed to enter the millennial kingdom.

Daniel obviously did not understand these prophecies, though today with the perspective of history and many prophecies being fulfilled, interpreters can understand it better than Daniel could. But Daniel was told simply that he would go on his way, that is, he would die, and then at the end of days, namely, at the time of the second coming of Christ, he would be resurrected, "As for you, go your way till the end. You will rest, and then at the end of the days you will rise to receive your allotted inheritance" (Dan. 12:13).

### The Great Scope of Daniel's Prophecies

The tremendous scope of Daniel's prophetic revelation can hardly be overemphasized. Only Daniel gives us the sweep of Israel's history in 490 years with the present age interjected between the 483rd year and the 490th year. Likewise, Gentile prophecy, describing the empires of Babylon, Medo-Persia, Greece, and Rome, have the same course, beginning at 605 B.C. when Nebuchadnezzar conquered Jerusalem and extending to the second coming of Christ when Gentile power will be destroyed and the world ruler cast into the lake of fire.

Like the panoramic view of Israel, Gentile prophecies relating to the kingdoms will be interrupted by the present age, extending from the first coming of Christ to the period just before His second coming and excluding the period from Pentecost to the Rapture of the church. The revelation of Daniel is not only essential to understanding Old Testament prophecy but it is in a particular sense the key to understanding the Book of Revelation. The Book of Daniel supports the point of view that the Book of Revelation from chapter 4 to the end is future from our present point of view like the end times of the times of the Gentiles in Daniel and the end times in the course of Israel's prophetic future.

# 8

# PROPHECY IN
# THE MINOR PROPHETS

## THE PROPHECY IN HOSEA

*Hosea 1:1.* Little is known concerning Hosea the prophet, except the biographical information given in the first verse of the book. He was described as the son of Beeri and his ministry was during the reign of four kings of Judah, Uzziah, Jotham, Ahaz, and Hezekiah, and seven kings of Israel (the ten tribes), Jeroboam, the son of Jehoash, Zechariah, Shallum, Menahem, Pekahiah, Pekah, and Hoshea. Hosea's ministry was primarily to the ten tribes of Israel. Four of the kings of Israel were assassinated in office. He lived in the period 750–722 B.C. that was leading up to the captivity of the ten tribes in 722 B.C., and his prophecies generally were a warning to Israel as well as warnings to the two tribes (Judah) of coming judgment from God for their sins.

Though the work of Hosea may be outlined in various ways, it is probably most clarifying to consider his prophetic ministry as revolving around three themes: the sins of Israel and Judah, the punishment from God because of their sins, and their ultimate spiritual and political restoration. Accordingly, the sins and resulting judgment recognized in 1:2-9 will be followed by restoration (1:10–2:1). A second series of indictments for the sins of Israel and Judah was described in 2:2-13 and resulting restoration and deliverance in 2:14–3:5. A third series of indictments was recorded in 4:1–5:14 followed by prophecies of restoration in 5:15–6:3. A fourth period of indictments was revealed in 6:4–11:7 followed by restoration prophesied in 11:8-11. The final prophecies concerning judgments to come for their sins was given in 11:12–13:16 followed by a prophecy of restoration found in chapter 14.

Throughout the book the marriage relation between Hosea and his adulterous wife Gomer provided the unifying thread through the prophecies of Hosea and typically represented the relationship of Yahweh and the twelve tribes of Israel viewed as an adulterous wife. Though, no doubt, there was actual physical idolatry involved with the sins of Israel and Judah, the prophecies predominantly take up spiritual adultery, that is, unfaithfulness to God and love of the world.

### The First Cycle of the Sins of Israel
### and Her Restoration

*Hosea 1:2–2:1.* In the first cycle of condemnation, judgment, and ultimate restoration, Hosea was instructed to marry "an adulterous wife" because "the land is guilty of the vilest adultery in departing from the LORD" (v. 2). Of the three children born to the union, probably genuine children of Hosea rather than children of adultery, the first was given a name "Jezreel" as significant of the coming judgment of God on the ten tribes of Israel because of "the massacre at Jezreel" (v. 4). This referred to the slaughter by Jehu of the descendants of Ahab and Jezebel which had first been prophesied by Elijah (1 Kings 21:21-24), then commanded by Elisha (2 Kings 9:6-10) and approved by the Lord Himself (10:30). The question arose as to why this judgment was predicted. The answer is probably found in the fact that Jehu had gone beyond the Lord's instructions and had also killed Joram (9:24), Ahaziah of the kingdom of Judah (vv. 27-28), and had also killed many of Ahaziah's relatives (10:12-14), who were not part of the original command.

The prophecy of judgment on Jehu's line was fulfilled later at the assassination of Zechariah, a king who descended from Jehu (15:10), thus cutting off the line of Jehu to any succession to the throne. The fulfillment of this prophecy also brought in focus the fact that Assyria would capture the ten tribes, beginning rule over them in 734 B.C. and ending in the captivity of the ten tribes in 722 B.C.

The second child born to Hosea and Gomer was a daughter named "Lo-Ruhamah" (Hosea 1:6), meaning "not loved," referring to the house of Israel. The third child was named "Lo-Ammi" (v. 9), meaning "not My people." The prophecy of destruction, however, was not fulfilled because of the promise that Judah will be saved (v. 7) and that the twelve tribes of the kingdom of Israel also will again be called "sons of the living God" (v. 10). The prophecy also states, "The people of Judah and the people of Israel will be reunited, and they will appoint one leader and will come up out of the land, for great will be the day of Jezreel" (v. 11). This prophecy will have prophetic fulfillment at Christ's return to occupy the throne of David (2 Sam. 7:11-16; Isa. 3:5; 9:6-7; Amos 9:11; Micah 5:2). The reference to "the land" (Hosea 1:11) is probably referring to the land in which they were exiled. The section closes with reference to Israel and Judah as " 'My people,' and of your sisters, 'My loved one' " (2:1).

### The Second Cycle of Judgment of Israel and Her Restoration

*Hosea 2:2–3:5.* The second cycle of judgment on sin and ultimate restoration began with a rebuke of Gomer as representing Israel. It was predicted that she would be stripped naked, made like a desert without water, and disgraced (2:2-6). Her lovers would leave her, but God declared that He would judge her and punish her (vv. 7-13). After the time of judgment, however (v. 13), she would be restored to her husband (vv. 14-20). At that time she would be planted in the land (v. 23), be beloved by her husband, God would declare her "My people" and God would become her God (v. 23).

In keeping with this prophecy, Hosea was ordered by the Lord to reclaim his wife as he would buy a slave (3:1-3). She was to stay at home and not continue her adulterous life (v. 3).

The prophetic significance of this was stated, "For the Israelites will live many days without king or prince, without sacrifice or sacred stones, without ephod or idol. Afterward the Israelites will return and seek the LORD their God and David their king. They will come trembling to the LORD and to His blessings in the last days" (vv. 4-5). This will be fulfilled at the Second Coming.

### The Third Cycle of Judgment of Israel
### and Her Restoration

*Hosea 4:1–6:3.* The third cycle of judgment followed by restoration began with judgment on Israel, "no faithfulness, no love, no acknowledgment of God in the land," but, "only cursing, lying and murder, stealing and adultery . . . bloodshed follows bloodshed" (4:1-2). God predicted that though priests would increase in number, they would only sin against God (v. 7). The people of Israel would be like them, "They will eat but not have enough; they will engage in prostitution but not increase" (v. 10). They will make offerings to idols and engage in spiritual prostitution (vv. 11-14).

The indictment continued with charges of Israel's rebellion, corruption, and arrogance (5:1-5). Because of her sins she "will be laid waste on the day of reckoning" (v. 9). Judgment was pronounced on "Ephraim," representing the ten tribes of Israel. God predicted that they would be carried off captives (v. 14).

Though Israel was unrepentant, God promised that the day would come when "they will seek My face; in their misery they will earnestly seek Me" (v. 15). God promised to restore them like the rain restores the earth (6:1-3). Ultimate restoration will be fulfilled at the Second Coming.

### The Fourth Cycle of Judgment of Israel
### and Her Restoration

*Hosea 6:4–11:11.* The fourth cycle of judgment and restoration began with a series of indictments. God charged them, "Your love is like the morning mist, like the early dew that disappears. Therefore I cut you in pieces with My prophets, I killed you with the words of My mouth; My judgments flashed like lightning upon you" (vv. 4-5). She was guilty of being unfaithful (v. 7), they "murder on the road to Shechem, committing shameful crimes" (v. 9).

The indictment continued that her sins were engulfing her (7:2), and she was like "all adulterers, burning like an oven whose fire the baker need not stir from the kneading of the dough till it rises" (v. 4). She was filled with passion (v. 6), and Ephraim was declared to be "a flat cake not turned over" (v. 8). Ephraim was compared to a dove, calling to Egypt and then to Assyria, both of whom would betray Israel (v. 11). They gathered to drink wine but turned away from God (v. 14). They had broken their covenant with God (8:1), and had "rejected what is good" (v. 3). They worshiped a calf instead of the true God (vv. 4-6).

God was going to come on Israel like a whirlwind (v. 7), and she would become "a worthless thing" (v. 8). Her altars would only become places for sinning (vv. 11-13). Because Israel had forgotten her God and Judah had attempted to fortify her cities, God would consume her with fire.

God predicted that she would not remain in the land of Israel (9:3) but would go to Egypt where she would be destroyed and her treasures taken away (vv. 3-6). God predicted the time of her punishment was coming (v. 7), and God would punish her for her wickedness (vv. 7-9). She would be bereaved of her children (v. 12) and would be like a plant "blighted, their root is withered, they yield no fruit" (v. 16).

Israel was described as "a spreading vine" (10:1), which led her to build more altars, but God would demolish them (v. 2). Her idols would be carried away to Assyria, and she would be disgraced (vv. 5-6). As she becomes conscious of the wrath of God, "they will say to the mountains, 'Cover us!' and to the hills, 'Fall on us!' " (v. 8)

God will plead with her, "Sow for yourselves righteousness, reap the fruit of unfailing love, and break up your unplowed ground"; but they will not respond (vv. 12-13). As a result, "your fortresses will be devastated—as Shalman" will devastate "Beth Arbel" in battle (v. 14). Beth Arbel was a small city. As Beth Arbel was destroyed, so would Beth Aven be destroyed, referring to Bethel as the house of God. "Beth Aven" means "house of wickedness," while Bethel had formerly been known as the house of God. God predicted that mothers will be "dashed to the ground with their children" (v. 14), and "the king of Israel will be completely destroyed" (v. 15).

God rehearsed how He had led the Children of Israel out of Egypt in love (11:1-4). Some interpret the reference to a son a prophecy that Christ would come out of Egypt (v. 1; Matt. 2:15). Israel was determined to turn away from God (Hosea 11:7).

God promised, however, to bring about her ultimate restoration, "How can I give you up, Ephraim? How can I hand you over, Israel? How can I treat you like Admah? How can I make you like Zeboiim?" (v. 8) God declared that His compassion was aroused (v. 8), and ultimately the Children of Israel would come back to her land and be settled in her homes (v. 11). This will be fulfilled at the Second Coming.

### The Fifth Cycle of Judgment of Israel
### and Her Restoration

*Hosea 11:12–14:9.* The fifth and final cycle of judgment followed by restoration declared that "Ephraim has surrounded me with lies, the house of Israel with deceit. And Judah is unruly against God, even against the faithful Holy One" (11:12).

Ephraim was condemned because of her attempt to make alliances with both Egypt and Assyria (12:1). As Jacob struggled with God, God "found him at Bethel" (v. 4). God declared He brought her out of Egypt and she lived in tents. God predicted that she would live in tents again (v. 9). God promised to repay Israel for her guilt and "will repay him for his contempt" (v. 14).

The condemnation of Ephraim continued, "Now they sin more and more; they make idols for themselves from their silver, cleverly fashioned images, all of them the work of craftsmen" (13:2). She was charged with offering human sacrifice (v. 2). God reminded her how He had brought her out of Egypt (v. 4) and cared for her in the desert (v. 5), but she forgot God (v. 6). Accordingly, God would bring judgment on her like a lion or leopard lurking in a person's path or like a bear robbed of her cubs (vv. 7-8). Her kings could not save her (vv. 9-10).

God stated, "I will ransom them from the power of the grave; I will redeem them from death. Where, O death, are your plagues? Where, O grave, is your destruction?" (v. 14) This was applied by the Apostle Paul (1 Cor. 15:55-56) to the victory of believers over death. But here it was an appeal to death and the grave to overtake her because of her sin. God stated that Israel would shrivel like a dry east wind coming from the desert (Hosea 13:15). The Lord predicted, "They will fall by the sword; their little ones will be dashed to the ground, their pregnant women ripped open" (v. 16).

In the final chapter of Hosea the theme turns to Israel's ultimate repentance and restoration. The day will come when God will forgive her sins (14:1-3) and will love Israel freely (v. 4). Once again Israel will "blossom like a lily" (v. 5). She will prosper like an olive tree and have fragrance like a cedar of Lebanon (v. 6). The passages conclud- ed with a statement, "Who is wise? He will realize these things. Who is discerning? He will understand them. The ways of the LORD are right; the righteous walk in them, but the rebellious stumble in them" (v. 9).

Though God's judgment was clearly pronounced on Israel and her sins had already been judged in history by such things as the Assyr- ian captivity and later the Babylonian Captivity, the prophets were clear that there will come a time for ultimate restoration of Israel. While some of this will be partially accomplished when they come back from the Babylonian Captivity, the ultimate fulfillment will be when the Lord returns and David is resurrected and she will be regathered to her own land permanently.

# THE PROPHECY IN JOEL

Joel, the author of the book which bears his name, may have lived as early as the ninth century B.C. before the Assyrian and Babylonian captivities or as late as the sixth century B.C. after the captivities. The book itself does not relate directly to any historical event or situation.

The theme of the Book of Joel is the Day of the Lord (Yahweh), an expression found often in the Old Testament and also in the New Testament. The Day of the Lord refers to any period of time in which God deals directly with the human situation either in judgment or in mercy. The expression may refer to a specific day or to an extended period of time as in the Day of the Lord eschatologically which stretches from the Rapture of the church to the end of the millennial kingdom (1 Thes. 5:1-9; 2 Peter 3:10-13).

### The Plague of Locusts

Joel 1:1-14. What the prophet described was an invasion of locusts, a catastrophe greatly feared by those in the Old Testament. Some believe the locusts were a description of an invading army, but others consider it to be a literal invasion of locusts which destroys like an invading army. All plant life was consumed. The priests were called to mourning and fasting. The locusts were described in verse 4, descriptive of the coming destruction in the Day of the Lord. The prophecy was fulfilled in the immediate destruction of the locusts, but the ultimate fulfillment will be seen in the Great Tribulation when a similar destruction will take place.

*Joel 1:15-20.* In addition to the plague of locusts, the plague of drought was described, a divine judgment which often was experienced by Israel. The effect of all this on the pastures was described as fire devouring everything living. This could be literal fire but more probably refers to the effect of the locusts and drought as producing the same effect as a fire would cause. This foreshadowed the destruction of the future Great Tribulation.

### The Day of the Lord

*Joel 2:1-11.* Though some expositors consider the locusts in Joel 2 as literal locusts, it is probable that they described an army which devastates like the locusts did in chapter 1. It was typical of military invasions that they would ruin everything which they conquered. In any case, the destruction was described as an event of the Day of the Lord (v. 11). This was fulfilled in the Assyrian captivity.

### The Call to Repentance

*Joel 2:12-17.* On the basis of the power of God to bring judgment, Israel was exhorted to return to the Lord with fasting and weeping (v. 12). They were assured that God was gracious and compassionate and that He could bless them instead of cursing them. The prophet exhorted all people, the elders, the children, the bridegroom and bride, and the priests to come to the Lord in prayer and repentance. This was fulfilled after the Babylonian Captivity.

### The Promise of Restoration

*Joel 2:18-27.* In response to such repentance, the prophet promised that the Lord would answer, would send grain and wine and oil and drive away "the northern army far from you" (v. 20). Israel was described as a nation with plenty of food which would "repay you for the years the locusts have eaten" (v. 25). Out of this experience Israel would know "that I am the LORD your God, and that there is no other" (v. 27). This was fulfilled in their return to the land after the Babylonian Captivity.

### The Promise of the Holy Spirit

*Joel 2:28-32.* In addition to material blessings the prophet promised that God would pour out His Spirit in the Day of the Lord with the result that, "Your sons and daughters will prophesy, your old men will dream dreams, your young men will see visions. Even on My servants, both men and women, I will pour out My Spirit in those days" (vv. 28-29).

The Apostle Peter in his pentecostal sermon quoted from this passage (Acts 2:14-21). It was quite clear that the entire prophecy of Joel was not fulfilled, but what Peter was alluding to was the similarity of the situation. Just as in Joel's time the people of Israel were called to repentance in the hope that the Day of the Lord's blessing would come on them, so those who listened to Peter's pentecostal sermon were exhorted to turn to the Lord in anticipation that the promised blessings may follow.

The length of the present Church Age was unknown to Peter and to everyone else at the time of his pentecostal sermon. On the basis of existing Scripture he could rightfully expect the Rapture to occur and the events following to come about immediately. This would include the dark days of the Great Tribulation described in Joel 2:30-31 which would precede the second coming of Christ and a time of blessing would follow.

Accordingly, the Children of Israel should not have been surprised to see the outpouring of the Holy Spirit. At the same time it was a reminder that God could bless those in Israel who trusted in her Messiah.

Though many individual Jews accepted Christ as Saviour on the Day of Pentecost, the nation as a whole as well as her religious leaders had failed to come to the Lord. Her ultimate repentance was pictured in Scripture as occurring just before the second coming of Christ (Zech. 12:10-13).

The prophecy of Joel awaits complete fulfillment in relation to the second coming of Christ. It will include supernatural revelation, miraculous events in the heavens and earth, and opening the day of salvation to all who call on the name of the Lord (cf. Rom. 10:13).

### The Judgment of the Nations and Israel's Future Restoration

*Joel 3:1-3.* The future Day of the Lord will include judgment on the nations after the Second Coming (Matt. 25:31-46). The Valley of Jehoshaphat described the valley between Jerusalem and the Mount of Olives containing in modern times a small cemetery just outside the wall and the Brook Kidron. Whether the Valley of Jehoshaphat would literally be large enough to judge the nations, it is pictured as a place of judgment and the name Jehoshaphat itself means "the Lord judges." In this valley Jehoshaphat, who was king over Judah 875–850 B.C., experienced a military victory over his enemies, whom God caused to quarrel among themselves, so that Jehoshaphat did not need to fight them because they destroyed each other.

*Joel 3:4-8.* Judgment was declared on Tyre and Sidon for their treatment of the Children of Israel and the silver and gold and the other treasures that they carried off. God also judged them for selling the Children of Israel as slaves to Greece and promised that, in return, their sons and daughters would be sold to the people of Judah. This was fulfilled in the fourth century B.C. by Alexander the Great.

*Joel 3:9-15.* The prophet called for the armies of the nations to be roused and to assemble themselves for war in the Valley of Jehoshaphat where they would encounter the judgment of God. Joel declared that God "will sit to judge all the nations on every side" (v. 12). On the basis of these prophecies being fulfilled, Joel pleaded with the multitudes to recognize that the Day of the Lord was near (v. 14) and that it would be preceded by the darkening of the sun and the moon and the blotting out of the stars (v. 15). Ultimate fulfillment will be at the Second Coming.

*Joel 3:16-21.* In the preceding portion of the prophecy of Joel God was declared to turn from Zion and be a refuge for His people. God will judge the wicked but will redeem His people Israel. Abundance of food, wine, and water will characterize the period for Israel in contrast to Egypt and Edom which are described as desert wastes (vv. 18-19). When this restoration of Israel takes place, after the Second Coming, "Judah will be inhabited forever in Jerusalem through all generations" (v. 20). The prophet closes with the declaration that God will pardon Israel for their sins (v. 21). The prophecies of Joel are in harmony with the premillennial interpretation of Scripture because these events will take place before and after the second coming of Christ when Christ takes over as King of kings and Lord of lords.

## THE PROPHECY IN AMOS

Amos describes himself as coming from Tekoa, a town located about ten miles south of Jerusalem. His occupation was that of a shepherd, but because of the unusual word for shepherd which he uses, interpreters have judged him a supervisor not only of herds of sheep and goats but also as one who cultivated sycamore-fig trees (7:14). God called him, however, to be a prophet primarily to the ten tribes of the kingdom of Israel but also with some prophecy relating to the king of Judah.

The towns in which Amos lived were prosperous during the reigns of Uzziah (790–739 B.C.) in Judah and that of Jeroboam II (793–753 B.C.) in Israel as Amos mentioned in 1:1. The prosperity of Israel and Judah in this period had been predicted by Elijah forty years earlier (2 Kings 13:7-19), and Jonah also mentioned it (14:25). Though both kingdoms were prospering financially, they were guilty of social and moral failures, and their religious worship was in form but not in substance. Accordingly, the prophecies of Amos were in anticipation of the severe judgment God would inflict on Israel, beginning with the Assyrian captivity (722 B.C.) and later the Babylonian Captivity of Judah (beginning 605 B.C.). The prophecies of Amos were intended to jar Israel and Judah out of their complacency and self-satisfaction occasioned by their financial prosperity.

The time of the ministry of Amos was pinpointed by Amos himself as being two years before an earthquake which archeologists had established at approximately 760 B.C. To Amos, the earthquake was symbolic of God's power to judge the world. His prophetic ministry probably continued for about ten years, beginning in 762 B.C.

### Prophecy of Judgment against Israel's Neighbors

*Amos 1:1-5.* After introducing the prophecies, Amos delivered an indictment against the nations who were neighbors of Israel. The first prophecy was against Damascus which introduced the formula for later prophecies, "This is what the LORD says: 'For three sins of Damascus, even for four, I will not turn back My wrath' " (v. 3). The implication was that the many sins of Israel add up until they require judgment. The expression relating to three sins plus a fourth is found throughout the book (vv. 6, 9, 11, 13; 2:1, 4, 6). The designation of a certain number of sins plus one was characteristic of other biblical prophecies (cf. Prov. 6:16; 30:15, 18, 21, 29; Micah 5:5).

Damascus had been distinguished for its cruel treatment of Israel. The expression "sledges having iron teeth " (v. 3) referred to an instrument used in threshing which would cut up the grain and indicated how Damascus treated Israel. In judgment on Damascus,

God will break down the gate of Damascus and destroy "the house of Hazael" (v. 4), town of the king of Damascus, with fire.

*Amos 1:6-8.* A similar judgment was pronounced against Gaza because "she took captive whole communities and sold them to Edom" (v. 6). God would destroy her walls as well as her king and would also judge the Philistines as a whole.

*Amos 1:9-10.* In a similar way, God would judge Tyre because she likewise carried Israel to slavery and disregarded a previous "treaty of brotherhood" (v. 9). Tyre was to experience having her walls and her fortresses destroyed as well.

*Amos 1:11-12.* A similar judgment was pronounced against Edom because she had no compassion on Israel. Fire would also destroy their fortresses.

*Amos 1:13-15.* The people of Ammon likewise would be judged because they killed pregnant women and attempted to extend her borders at Israel's expense. Her walls would also be destroyed by fire and her kings would go into exile (vv. 14-15).

*Amos 2:1-3.* Moab was condemned because she deprived the king of Edom a decent burial. She also would be destroyed in war.

*Amos 2:4-5.* God's condemnation of the nations would be extended to the kingdom of Israel who would be judged and her fortresses consumed because she rejected the Law of the Lord and served false gods. These prophecies are fulfilled to some extent in history and complete fulfillment is prophesied for the future.

### Judgment against the Kingdom of Israel

*Amos 2:6-12.* Because of her sins of injustice and oppression of the poor and desecration of the temple, Israel will be judged (vv. 9-12). Though God had helped Israel in destroying the Amorites and bringing them out of Egypt and caring for them for forty years in the desert (vv. 9-10), Israel did not listen to the prophets that God raised up and she encouraged Nazarites to void their vows by drinking wine. She also attempted to stifle the prophets. This prophecy was fulfilled in the captivities.

*Amos 2:13-16.* The result will be judgment from God and Israel will be crushed, with even her bravest warriors fleeing naked (vv. 13-16). This was fulfilled in the captivities.

### Reasons for God's Judgment on Israel

*Amos 3:1-15.* The judgments would fall on Israel even though she was a chosen people. Though God had chosen Israel from all families of the earth, He promised to punish her for their sins (vv. 1-2).

Amos asked a series of questions, "Do two walk together unless they have agreed to do so?" (v. 3) A lion does not roar unless there is prey (v. 4). When the trumpet sounds, do not the people of the city tremble? (v. 6) The judgments of God were justified because God has revealed His plan through His servants the prophets (v. 7). Just as people fear when a lion roars, so she should fear when God speaks (v. 8). God promised, "An enemy will over-run the land; he will pull down your strongholds and plunder your fortresses" (v. 11). Israel will be saved only as a shepherd saves part of a lamb from the lion's mouth (v. 12). God predicted that as punishment He will "destroy the altars of Bethel" and "will tear down the winter house along with the summer house" (vv. 14-15). Her fancy houses and mansions will be demolished (v. 15). The prophecy was fulfilled in the captivities.

*Amos 4:1-13.* Illustrating how Israel had not turned to God, he described women referred to as "you cows of Bashan" (v. 1) and accused them of oppressing the poor, requiring their husbands to keep them well supplied with drinks. Instead of dominating their husbands, they were promised that they will be led away with hooks as slaves (vv. 2-3).

Her empty religion and worship of Bethel, where they brought sacrifices every morning and tithes every three years (v. 4), were not acceptable to God. Instead, He promised that she would have "empty stomachs" (v. 6). God would withhold rain from her (vv. 7-8). Her vineyards would be struck with mildew and locusts would devour her fragrant olive trees (v. 9). Even though God had sent plagues among them as He did to Egypt and killed their young men, she had not returned to the Lord (v. 10). God would deal with her in summary judgment as He overthrew Sodom and Gomorrah (vv. 11-13). This was fulfilled in the captivities.

*Amos 5:1-17.* God promised judgment on her armies which would decimate their troops (v. 3). Instead of journeying to Bethel or Gilgal to worship, she should seek the Lord in order to live (vv. 5-6). God accused her of casting righteousness to the ground (v. 7) which would unleash destruction on her strongholds (v. 9). Her trampling of the poor (v. 11) may result in her planting vineyards but not drinking the wine (v. 11). Her oppression of the righteous, taking bribes, and depriving the poor of justice will be judged (vv. 12-13). God described her mourning for her sins and God's judgment on her (vv. 14-17). This was fulfilled in the captivities.

*Amos 5:18-27.* The Day of the Lord would come on her, a day of darkness and not light (v. 18). It would overtake her because God despised her religious feasts and her burnt offerings (vv. 19-22). God said He would not listen to her music but would let righteous judgment fall on her. As a result of her sins, God would send her into exile beyond Damascus (v. 27). This was fulfilled in the captivities.

*Amos 6:1-14.* Her complacent and luxurious living would bring complete judgment on her. She may "lie on beds inlaid with ivory and lounge on your couches. You dine on choice lambs and fattened calves" (v. 4). She could listen to harps like David played and drink wine "by the bowlful" (vv. 5-6), but she would be among the first to go into exile where her feasting and luxurious living would end (v. 7).

God declared that He abhorred the pride of Jacob (v. 8). God declared that He would smash her great houses into pieces (v. 11). She had "turned justice into poison" (v. 12). Accordingly, God would stir up a nation against her (v. 14). This was fulfilled in the captivities.

### The Inescapable Character of Her Future Judgment

*Amos 7:1-17.* Her enemies would be like swarming locusts who strip the land clean (vv. 1-2). Though God had forgiven her some sins, eventually He could spare her no longer (v. 8). Her high places dedicated to idols "will be destroyed" (v. 9). Likewise, "the sanctuaries of Israel will be ruined" (v. 9).

Because Amos' prophecies were unwelcomed, Amaziah, the priest of Bethel, informed Jeroboam that Amos was conspiring against him (v. 10). In replying, Amos rejected the plea to stop prophesying and predicted that the wife of Amaziah would be a prostitute and that "your sons and daughters will fall by the sword" (v. 17). The people of Israel would die in a pagan country and go into exile (v. 17). This was fulfilled in the captivities.

*Amos 8:1-14.* As typical of Israel's judgment, a basket of ripe fruit was shown Amos as a token that the time was ripe for the judgment of Israel (vv. 1-3). Those who oppress the poor and give short measure would be judged (vv. 4-6). Judgment would fall on the land (v. 8) and the sun would be darkened (v. 9). Her religious feasts would result in mourning (v. 10). God promised to send famine through the land, not for food or drink but for hearing the words of God (v. 11). Amos predicted that she would be searching for the

Word of God but would not find it. Her "lovely young women and strong young men will faint because of thirst" (v. 13). This was fulfilled in the captivities.

## Israel to Be Destroyed

*Amos 9:1-10.* Israel would be judged and those who were left would be killed with the sword (v. 1). God would search her out regardless of where she would hide and she would be driven into exile by her enemies (vv. 2-4). God declared that His eyes were on Israel as a sinful nation (v. 8). But God promised, "I will not totally destroy the house of Jacob" (v. 8). Sinners among the people would die by the sword along with those who claimed that disaster would not overtake her (v. 10). This was fulfilled in the captivities.

## The Restoration of Israel

*Amos 9:11-15.* After the recital of the many sins of Israel and God's certain judgment on them, the last five verses of Amos described the ultimate restoration of Israel which will follow the times of God's judgment. The prophecies of Israel's complete restoration have never been fulfilled. Amos declared, however, "In that day I will restore David's fallen tent. I will repair its broken places, restore its ruins, and build it as it used to be" (v. 11). This reference was made to the restoration of the Davidic kingdom with David resurrected from the dead to reign as king under Christ in the future kingdom following the Second Coming (Jer. 30:9; Ezek. 34:23-24; 37:24). God promised that she will "possess the remnant of Edom" (Amos 9:12).

The time of prosperity was described for the kingdom, "when the reaper will be overtaken by the plowman and the planter by the one treading grapes" (v. 13).

God promised to "bring back My exiled people Israel; they will rebuild the ruined cities and live in them. They will plant vineyards and drink their wine; they will make gardens and eat their fruit" (v. 14). While this had partial fulfillment in the restoration of the people of Israel in the fourth and fifth centuries B.C., its ultimate fulfillment will be related to the coming of Christ and her permanent restoration.

The certainty of Israel's restoration, her being regathered to her land, and again being blessed by the Lord was summarized, " 'I will plant Israel in their own land, never again to be uprooted from the land I have given them,' says the LORD your God" (v. 15). This prophecy has obviously not been fulfilled as Israel was scattered after A.D. 70 and Jerusalem was destroyed. In the twentieth century a partial restoration has been fulfilled with the first of Israel returning to her land, beginning the process of her ultimate complete restoration. This process of returning to the land is in stages, with the first stage already fulfilled in the twentieth century. A second stage will be fulfilled after the covenant is signed with the Middle East ruler. The third stage will be fulfilled when Israel goes through her period of trouble in the Great Tribulation. The final stage will occur when she will be rescued at the second coming of Christ, and the prophecies of verses 11-15 will be completely fulfilled.

Because Israel has already returned to the land and formed a capital state, the biggest return since the time of Moses, the events of the twentieth century seem to anticipate that God will fulfill the other aspects of Israel's restoration which many believe will follow the rapture of the church which is still an imminent event. The Prophet Amos on the one hand approves the righteousness of God by His judgment on the people of Israel and, on the other hand, manifests the grace of God who restores Israel to her land in fulfillment of His ultimate promises to Abram and his descendants. Once restored, Israel will never be scattered again (v. 15).

## THE PROPHECY IN OBADIAH

The Book of Obadiah, the shortest book in the Bible, was written by an obscure prophet about whom very little is known. Obadiah was a common name and refers to at least twelve Old Testament characters. But little is known concerning Obadiah the prophet except that his name means "worshiper of Yahweh." Scholars differ as to when the book was written as there is no clear indication of date in the book itself, some dating it as early as the reign of Jehoram (848–841 B.C.) or as late as after the destruction of Jerusalem in 586 B.C.

The prophecies of Obadiah were largely concerned with the nation of Edom, who descended from Esau and were traditional enemies of Israel. The conflict between Edom and Israel went back to the conflict between Esau and Jacob and included the incident where the Edomites refused passage to Israel going from Egypt to the Promised Land (Num. 20:14-21). Edom is the object of many predicted judgments, and more is said about Edom than many other foreign nations (Isa. 11:14; 34:5-17; 63:1-6; Jer. 9:25-26; 25:17-26;

49:7-22; Lam. 4:21-22; Ezek. 25:12-14; 35; Joel 3:19; Amos 1:11-12; 9:11-12; Obad.; Mal. 1:4). Edom epitomizes the arrogance of the enemies of Israel who were often used to chastise Israel for her sins but, nevertheless, were considered accountable to God as those who attack His chosen people.

### Edom's Destruction Predicted

*Obadiah 1.* The nations surrounding Edom were called on to rise up and attack this nation with a view to destroying it.

*Obadiah 2-9.* The prophet predicted that Edom will be "utterly despised. The pride of your heart has deceived you" (vv. 2-3). Though the Edomites thought they were safe in their homes in clefts of the rocks (v. 3), God declared that she would be brought down to the ground even if she made her nest among the stars (vv. 3-4).

Esau would not simply be robbed as a robber would take what he desired, but she would be completely ransacked and her treasures pillaged (vv. 5-6). Her friends would forsake her (v. 7), and God declared, "Will I not destroy the wise men of Edom, men of understanding in the mountains of Esau?" (v. 8)

*Obadiah 10-14.* The prophet predicted that Esau would be annihilated (v. 9) as a judgment of God, "Because of the violence against your brother Jacob, you will be covered with shame; you will be destroyed forever" (v. 10).

Edom was described as standing off and allowing strangers to loot Jerusalem and rejoicing in Israel's downfall. Edom was judged because she not only observed but also participated in the looting of Israel.

*Obadiah 15-21.* In the prophetic future in the Day of the Lord, Edom's sins will be brought back on themselves, but on Mount Zion the house of Jacob will have deliverance and possess its inheritance (vv. 15-17). Israel will be like a fire and the house of Esau as stubble to be consumed by fire with no survivors (v. 18). The land of the Edomites will be possessed by others, principally Israel (vv. 19-21).

Many of these prophecies have already been fulfilled as the Edomites were crushed by a series of military disasters and were almost completely wiped out by Titus the Roman general in connection with the subduing of Israel in A.D. 70.

The prophecies of Obadiah in capsule form, on the one hand, voice the judgment of God on the enemies of God and the enemies of Israel and, on the other hand, assure that Israel in spite of her sins and difficulties would ultimately be restored to her land.

## THE PROPHECY IN JONAH

The account of Jonah's unusual experience is one of the more familiar stories of the Old Testament, probably written by Jonah. He described himself only as the son of Amittai from Gath Hepher (2 Kings 14:25) located in Zebulun (Josh. 19:10, 13). Jonah had received a command to go to preach to Nineveh and had attempted to flee from the Lord only to be deterred by the great storm on the ship bound for Tarshish (probably Spain). After being rescued by the great fish and cast on shore, he preached his message to Nineveh only to be disappointed by her amazing repentance. If Jonah's ministry occurred about 150 years before the fall of Nineveh (612 B.C.), the book recorded a unique situation where God spared a Gentile city for more than a century because of her immediate repentance in response to the preaching of Jonah.

The Book of Jonah, being essentially a narrative, contained only a few prophecies except those immediately fulfilled. When the storm engulfed the ship, Jonah rightly prophesied that if they threw him overboard, the storm would cease, " 'Pick me up and throw me into the sea,' he replied, 'and it will become calm. I know that it is my fault that this great storm has come upon you' " (1:12). Then the sailors threw Jonah overboard after hestitating to take his life. The sea immediately became calm and was proof to the men that Jonah's God was a real God (vv. 15-16).

The prophecy that Nineveh would be destroyed in forty days was conditional. After her repentance, her judgment was deferred for 150 years to Jonah's displeasure. The narrative gave remarkable insight into Israel's lack of ministry to the Gentile world.

The principal prophetic significance of Jonah, however, was the fact that Christ Himself referred to Jonah and his experience as a type of His own death and resurrection as stated in Matthew 12:39-40, "He answered, 'A wicked and adulterous generation asks for a miraculous sign! But none will be given it except the sign of the Prophet Jonah. For as Jonah was three days and three nights in the belly of a huge fish, so the Son of man will be three days and three nights in the heart of the earth.' "

In this statement Christ not only affirmed the historicity of Jonah himself but also the historicity of his strange experience of being swallowed by a great fish and eventually delivered safely to shore. The question has also been raised as to whether the three days and three nights automatically meant seventy-two hours. Some scholars believe that they may include only parts of three days and that a part of the day was counted as a whole frequently in the Bible. In the traditional view of Christ's crucifixion on Friday, the time span of His resurrection was less than that prophesied for Jonah unless it is understood to refer to parts of days. Some explain this by placing the death of Christ on Thursday or Wednesday.

In connection with the unbelief of the Pharisees and Sadducees who were seeking signs, Christ stated, "A wicked and adulterous generation looks for a miraculous sign, but none will be given it except the sign of Jonah" (Matt. 16:4; cf. Luke 11:29-32).

Though some have doubted the story of Jonah because it was an unusual event truly supernatural, it is not more strange than many other supernatural acts of God. The events of Jonah must be taken as historical and their application prophetically by Christ is confirmation of the veracity and inspiration of the Book of Jonah. The possibility of a great fish swallowing a man or another live object and later the man being rescued alive is not without historical precedents. Obviously, additional supernatural factors were in view with the great fish prepared to swallow Jonah and later deliver him to the dry land. The major factor, however, of confirmation is the word of Christ Himself that the story of Jonah was true, illustrating the supernatural character of His own death and resurrection.

## THE PROPHECY IN MICAH

The Prophet Micah, the author of the book bearing his name, according to his own statement, was from the town of Moresheth, a Judean town about twenty-five miles southwest of Jerusalem. His name is an abbreviation of a longer name, Micaiah, which means "Who is like Yahweh?" He ministered in the period from 750 to 686 B.C. according to his own statement in the reigns of Kings Jotham, Ahaz, and Hezekiah (1:1; cf. Jer. 26:18). He was a contemporary of Isaiah and Hosea and was quoted as one who predicted the doom of Jerusalem. Micah 3:5 was quoted by those who were defending the predictions of Jeremiah (Jer. 26:18). They argued that Hezekiah had listened to Micah and God was merciful to him, securing the safety of Jeremiah from destruction (vv. 19-24).

Micah was notable for predicting the fall of the Northern Kingdom of the ten tribes of Israel in 722 B.C. He alternated between prophecies of doom and destruction to prophecies of restoration and forgiveness. In the process he attacked the social ills and the moral ills of his day. His bright picture of the future glory of Israel, however, tended to soften the prophecies of doom which had to be fulfilled first.

### Impending Judgment on Israel

*Micah 1:2–3:12.* After the brief introduction of the book, Micah pleaded with the people to listen.

Micah pictured the Lord as coming down to tread the high places of the earth with the result that the mountains would melt and the valleys would split apart (1:3-4). The cause for this divine judgment were the sins of Israel and ultimate judgment on Judah. Micah predicted that Samaria would be "a heap of rubble" (v. 6). He stated, "All her idols will be broken to pieces; all her temple gifts will be burned with fire; I will destroy all her images" (v. 7).

Micah pictured himself like Samaria, walking about "barefoot and naked" (v. 8). Micah called the people to mourning because of her shame and declared, "Disaster has come from the LORD, even to the gate of Jerusalem" (v. 12). He promised that a conqueror would come against her (v. 15). Her "children in whom you delight . . . will go from you into exile" (v. 16).

Micah denounced those who "plan iniquity" (2:1). He stated, "They covet fields and seize them, and houses, and take them. They defraud a man of his home, a fellowman of his inheritance" (v. 2). As a result, Micah quoted the Lord as saying, "I am planning disaster against this people, from whom you cannot save yourselves. You will no longer walk proudly, for it will be a time of calamity. In that day men will ridicule you; they will taunt you with this mournful song: 'We are utterly ruined; my people's possession is divided up' " (vv. 3-4).

Micah denounced their false prophets who declared God's judgment would not come on her. Instead, her sins will result in the people being deprived of her houses (vv. 6-11).

In the midst of these prophecies of judgment, Micah also predicted the future restoration of Israel when her king will come to open the way before her (vv. 12-13). This will be fulfilled in the Second Coming.

Micah denounced her leaders because they "hate good and love evil" (3:2). Because of her sins when they "cry out to the LORD,"

God will not listen to them (v. 4). The prophets who predicted peace will be ashamed and disgraced (vv. 5-7). By contrast to the false prophets, Micah declared, "I am filled with power, with the Spirit of the Lord, and with justice and might" (v. 8).

Because of this, he was able to condemn the unrighteous and prophesy their disaster (vv. 9-10). Because of their sins, Micah declared, "Zion will be plowed like a field, Jerusalem will become a heap of rubble, the temple hill a mound overgrown with thickets" (v. 12). These prophecies were fulfilled in the captivities.

### The Future Glorious Kingdom

*Micah 4:1-8.* In describing the glorious future kingdom, Micah declared, "In the last days the mountain of the Lord's temple will be established as chief among the mountains; it will be raised above the hills, and peoples will stream to it" (v. 1). The first three verses of chapter 4 are almost identical to Isaiah 2:2-4. The glorious temple was declared to be established "in the last days" (Micah 4:1). This has its fulfillment in the Millennium when Ezekiel's temple (Ezek. 40–44) will be built. As far as Micah's foreview was concerned, the temple could be established very soon as he does not contemplate the intervention of the present age of the church. People from all over the world will come to visit the Lord's temple.

Even the Gentiles will seek to come to the temple. They will say, "He will teach us His ways, so that we may walk in His paths" (v. 2). Zion and Jerusalem will be the center from which the Law goes forth. The contemporary situation in the kingdom will be one of peace because, "They will beat their swords into plowshares and their spears into pruning hooks. Nation will not take up sword against nation, nor will they train for war anymore" (v. 3). The people will be at peace and "Every man will sit under his own vine and under his own fig tree, and no one will make them afraid, for the Lord Almighty has spoken" (v. 4). In this kingdom period the Lord will rule them in Mount Zion (v. 7) and will restore the governmental dominion of Zion (v. 8). These prophecies will be fulfilled in the millennial kingdom.

*Micah 4:9-13.* In the near view Micah predicted the Babylonian Captivity (v. 10) and stated that the nations would welcome the destruction of Israel (v. 11). Micah predicted, however, that in the end the nations would be broken into pieces and their wealth would be devoted to the Lord (v. 13). This was fulfilled in the Babylonian Captivity.

*Micah 5:1-4.* In contrast to predictions of judgment (v. 1), the future ruler of Israel, referring to Christ, will come to Bethlehem, "But you, Bethlehem Ephrathah, though you are small among the clans of Judah, out of you will come for Me One who will be Ruler over Israel, whose origins are from of old, from ancient times" (v. 2). This is fulfilled in Christ. Until this future Ruler takes over, "Israel will be abandoned" (v. 3). When the Ruler comes, however, He will "stand and shepherd His flock in the strength of the LORD" (v. 4). He will cause Israel to dwell securely and live in peace (vv. 4-5).

*Micah 5:5-15.* Though Assyria would invade Israel's land and conquer her for a time (vv. 5-6), ultimately the people of Israel will prevail and be like a lion among the beasts of the forests (vv. 7-8). Micah predicted, "Your hand will be lifted up in triumph over your enemies, and all your foes will be destroyed" (v. 9). When that day comes, God will bring about the destruction of that which is evil in the midst of Israel, their chariots (v. 10), their witchcraft, their carved images (vv. 12-13), and the Asherah poles (v. 14). God's vengeance will be against Israel as well as the nations (v. 15). This will be fulfilled in the millennial kingdom.

### The Basis of the Condemnation of Israel

*Micah 6:1-8.* God stated His case against Israel. In spite of God's goodness to them in delivering them out of Egypt and from slavery, providing Moses, Aaron, and Miriam to lead them (v. 4), Israel had departed from His ways and laws. God was not pleased with her calves or rams (vv. 6-7). What God wanted was for her to "To act justly and to love mercy and to walk humbly with your God" (v. 8).

*Micah 6:9-16.* God called her to account for treasures she had stolen, for dishonest weights, for being violent, liars, and speaking deceitfully (vv. 9-12). God stated that she would not be satisfied with food (v. 14). She will plant but not be able to reap the harvest (v. 15). She will follow idolatrous worship such as performed by Ahab and his house (v. 16). Because of this, God will give her up to derision (v. 16). These prophecies are fulfilled in history and prophecy.

### The Ultimate Victory in the Kingdom

*Micah 7:1-20.* Micah called attention to the departure of Israel from the laws of God. He declared, "The godly have been swept from the land; not one upright man remains. All men lie in wait to shed blood; each hunts his brother with a net" (v. 2).

He described her hands as being "skilled in doing evil" (v. 3); "the ruler demands gifts, the judge accepts bribes, the powerful dictate what they desire—they all conspire together" (v. 3). Because of this, God is going to bring a time of confusion (v. 4). He declared, "For a son dishonors his father, a daughter rises up against her mother, a daughter-in-law against her mother-in-law— a man's enemies are the members of his own household" (v. 6; cf. Matt. 10:34-36).

By contrast, Micah instead of seeking evil looks in hope and waits for his Saviour with confidence that God will hear him, "But as for me, I watch in hope for the LORD, I wait for God my Saviour; my God will hear me" (Micah 7:7).

Micah pleaded with the enemy not to gloat over them (v. 8). Though it was true that Israel has sinned and will bear the wrath of God (vv. 9-10), the day will come when Israel will continue to build her walls and extend her boundaries (v. 11). God's judgment on that day will be on the nations instead of on Israel (vv. 12-13).

In Israel's future God will once again show her His miraculous wonders (v. 15), the world will see and be ashamed (v. 16). The world will turn in fear to God (v. 17). Micah asked rhetorically, "Who is a God like You, who pardons sin and forgives the transgression of the remnant of His inheritance?" (v. 18) Micah stated of God, "You do not stay angry forever but delight to show mercy. You will again have compassion on us; You will tread our sins underfoot and hurl all our iniquities into the depths of the sea" (vv. 18-19). In concluding his prophecy, Micah said of God, "You will be true to Jacob and show mercy to Abraham, as You pledged on oath to our fathers in days long ago" (v. 20). The future restoration of Israel will be based on the doctrine of grace rather than the doctrine of judgment and will fulfill the covenant with Abraham which God has pledged Himself to fulfill regardless of Israel's sins and shortcomings.

The mingled picture of prophecy, including Israel's condemnation and then glorification, is in keeping with the other Scriptures describing this process in which Israel will ultimately be regathered and blessed by God in the millennial kingdom.

## THE PROPHECY IN NAHUM

All that is known about the Book of Nahum is that Nahum the prophet is its author and that he lived in Elkosh whose location is unknown. Several suggestions have been made as the probable location of Elkosh, including that of Jerome (A.D. 340–420) who said it was in Galilee. This and other possible locations do not have any convincing evidence as the book was looking at Nineveh from the standpoint of Judah. Elkosh was probably located in southern Galilee.

Nahum recorded the downfall of Thebes, a common city of Egypt, conquered by the Assyrian king Ashurbanipal (663 B.C.). Nahum must have lived in the seventh century B.C. prior to the destruction of Nineveh which he predicted which was fulfilled in 612 B.C.

Mentioned in Scripture as early as Genesis 10:11-12, Nineveh was a frequent subject of prophecy. There Jonah delivered his message of warning which was heeded by the generation to whom he spoke, and the destruction of Nineveh was postponed. If Jonah's warning to Nineveh occurred during the reign of Jeroboam II (793–753 B.C.), Nineveh was protected from destruction for almost 150 years before it finally fell in 612 B.C.

During the time of Nineveh's power Azariah, king of Judah (790–739 B.C.) and Menahen, king of Israel (752–742 B.C.) paid tribute and recognized Nineveh's dominance. Nineveh had conquered the ten tribes in 722 B.C. but was prevented by God from conquering Jerusalem when 185,000 of Sennacherib's army were supernaturally killed while attempting to conquer Jerusalem. When the ten tribes went into captivity the tribes of Judah and Benjamin escaped. Nineveh fell to combined armies of the Medes and Scythians in the month of August in 612 B.C. Nineveh was so thoroughly ruined that it was lost to history until its ruins were discovered by archeologists in 1845.

*Nahum 1:1-11.* God was angry with Nineveh because of His own character. Nahum wrote, "The LORD is a jealous and avenging God; the LORD takes vengeance and is filled with wrath. The LORD takes vengeance on His foes and maintains His wrath against His enemies" (v. 2).

On the other hand, God had allowed Nineveh to go on relatively unchecked because "The LORD is slow to anger and great in power" (v. 3). He causes the mountains to quake and the rivers to run dry (vv. 4-5).

When God chooses to bring judgment on the wicked city of Nineveh, no one would be able to stand against Him (v. 6). Even though

"The LORD is good, a refuge in times of trouble" (v. 7), the time had come when Nineveh should bear God's wrath for her sins (vv. 8-11). This was fulfilled in 612 B.C.

*Nahum 1:12-15.* Nahum predicted that Nineveh would be cut down and lose her political power; her temples and idols would be destroyed and her people would go down to the grave (vv. 12-14). This was fulfilled in 612 B.C.

In contrast to His wrath and judgment on Nineveh, God will bless Judah, "Look, there on the mountains, the feet of one who brings good news, who proclaims peace! Celebrate your festivals, O Judah, and fulfill your vows. No more will the wicked invade you; they will be completely destroyed" (v. 15). This will be fulfilled in the millennial kingdom.

### Nineveh to Be Destroyed

*Nahum 2:1-13.* Nineveh's downfall had been predicted much earlier by other prophets. Isaiah who lived in the eighth century B.C., a hundred years before Nineveh was destroyed, predicted that Nineveh would come to its end (10:12-19; 14:24-25; 30:31-33; 31:8-9). Ezekiel also predicted Nineveh's fall (32:22-23), and it was mentioned in Zephaniah 2:13-15 and Zechariah 10:11.

As the armies of Babylon and the Medes approached, Nahum taunted Nineveh to put up protection which will prove to be futile, "Guard the fortress, watch the road, brace yourselves, marshal all your strength!" (Nahum 2:1) By contrast to the downfall of Nineveh, God referred to His restoration of Jacob, "The LORD will restore the splendor of Jacob like the splendor of Israel" (v. 2).

Nahum described the invading army as having red uniforms and shields of red who then stormed through the streets in their conquering of Nineveh (vv. 3-4). The fall of Nineveh was complete and sudden (vv. 5-7). The invaders were invited to "Plunder the silver! Plunder the gold! The supply is endless, the wealth from all its treasures" (v. 9). The result was stated in verse 10, "She is pillaged, plundered, stripped! Hearts melt, knees give way, bodies tremble, every face grows pale" (v. 10).

Nineveh was likened to a lions' den where formerly the lions killed enough for food with plenty to spare. But now there was nothing left. Nineveh no longer could be likened to the king of beasts (vv. 11-12).

God declared, " 'I am against you,' declares the LORD Almighty. 'I will burn up your chariots in smoke, and the sword will devour your young lions. I will leave you no prey on the earth. The voices of your messengers will no longer be heard' " (v. 13).

### Nineveh's Complete Destruction

*Nahum 3:1-19.* Nineveh, who once was irresistibly victorious over her enemies, now was going to experience the destruction that she brought on others. The many dead will pile up their carcasses without number. Her judgment is just because she had enslaved the nations (vv. 1-5). "I will pelt you with filth, I will treat you with contempt and make you a spectacle. All who see you will flee from you and say, 'Nineveh is in ruins — who will mourn for her? Where can I find anyone to comfort you?' " (vv. 6-7)

Nineveh's protecting walls would be of no avail. Just as Thebes was taken captive and went into exile, so her infants would be killed and her great men put in chains (v. 10).

Nineveh's fortresses were compared to a fig tree with ripe fruit which falls when shaken (v. 12). Nineveh's troops were compared to women, their gates are open to their enemies (v. 13).

Nineveh was taunted to prepare for the siege, draw her water, strengthen her defenses, repair the brickwork, but, neverthless, it would be devoured by fire and sword. Like grasshoppers, though they multiply, she would be of no avail (vv. 14-17).

The king of Assyria was informed that his people would be scattered like sheep with no one to gather them (v. 18). Her wound and injury would be fatal (v. 19). Those who hear of the fall of Nineveh would clap their hands with joy because of God's retribution on Nineveh for her endless acts of cruelty (v. 19).

In 612 B.C. Nineveh was so thoroughly destroyed that it was never rebuilt and soon became a pile of sand. For centuries the location of Nineveh was unknown, so completely had it been destroyed, but in 1845 it was located by archeologists. The lesson to be learned was that God's prophecies of judgment may be delayed in fulfillment but in God's time will be completely fulfilled.

# THE PROPHECY IN HABAKKUK

The Book of Habakkuk has the unusual feature of recording a dialogue between the author Habakkuk and God rather than the prophet acting as an instrument of God's communication to man.

Not much is known about Habakkuk personally, and even the meaning of his name is disputed. He describes himself as a prophet (1:1) which was unusual in the prophetic books of the Old Testament; only Haggai and Zechariah included the term "prophet" in their introductions.

The literary style of the book was similar to that of the Wisdom books and the Psalms. The book itself demonstrated that Habakkuk was properly recognized as a prophet and that he had both theological and liturgical training. In many ways the book was one of the most incisive approaches to the question of God's righteousness in dealing with human sin.

*Habakkuk 1:1-4.* Though the book itself does not date the time of its writing, from verse 6 which predicted the Babylonian invasion it may be concluded that he ministered in the seventh century B.C. Though some date the book as early as the reign of Manasseh (697–642 B.C.) or in the reign of Josiah (640–609 B.C.), it is more probable that he ministered closer to the date of the Babylonian invasion during the reign of Jehoiakim (609–598 B.C.). He therefore was not only a prophet of the fall of Jerusalem but also later on was a witness of the fulfillment of the prophecy. The date relating the prophecy to the Babylonian invasion of the kingdom of Judah was supported by the contents of the book which raised the question how a righteous God could use an unrighteous nation like Babylon to punish Judah for their sins. The fact that God allowed the Babylonians to be victorious in conquering Judah created theological problems for everyone who believed that the Children of Israel were a special people. It is this question of how God's justice relates to this situation that dominates the tone of the book and also leads to the answer.

### Why Are the Ungodly Not Judged?

Habakkuk lived in the time of apostasy just preceding the Babylonian Captivity. Though it was the time when Jeremiah was challenging Judah to return to God, there was little response. Habakkuk complained, "How long, O LORD, must I call for help, but You do not listen? Or cry out to You, 'Violence!' but You do not save? Why do You make me look at injustice? Why do You tolerate wrong? Destruction and violence are before me; there is strife, and conflict abounds" (vv. 2-3).

### The Lord's Answer

*Habakkuk 1:5-11.* Habakkuk was informed that God was raising up the Babylonians who would sweep through the land like the wind and conquer every city before it (vv. 5-11). God's answer was that judgment was on the way, but it was not yet time.

## Why Is God Going to Use a Wicked Nation
## Like Babylon to Conquer Judah?

*Habakkuk 1:12-17.* Habakkuk renewed his question now on why God uses Babylon, a nation that is utterly wicked and less righteous than Israel. How can God tolerate a nation like this that was allowed to conquer Israel in spite of Babylon's sinful state?

### The Lord's Answer

*Habakkuk 2:1-8.* Habakkuk wrote that he would wait to see what God had to say (v. 1). God answered that judgment awaited God's time, "For the revelation awaits an appointed time; it speaks of the end and will not prove false. Though it linger, wait for it; it will certainly come and will not delay" (v. 3).

The answer of God is summarized in verse 4, "But the righteous will live by his faith." This central statement of the book is repeated in Romans 1:17; Galatians 3:11; and Hebrews 10:38. This statement is not only the central theme of Habakkuk but of the entire Scripture.

Though Babylon will be victorious for the time being, the day will come that those who were plundered by Babylon will plunder Babylon, "Because you have plundered many nations, the peoples who are left will plunder you. For you have shed man's blood; you have destroyed lands and cities and everyone in them" (Hab. 2:8). The prophecy was fulfilled in 539 B.C. when Babylon was conquered by the Medes and the Persians.

*Habakkuk 2:9-20.* Four times God declared woe on Babylon (vv. 9, 12, 15, 19). God reassured Habakkuk that though the judgment may take time and not be swift from Habakkuk's point of view, the judgment of Babylon was inevitable and God would deal with her because of her many sins and her wickedness. God not only denounced her moral wickedness but also her idolatry, pointing out that an idol is lifeless wood or stone, and though it be covered with gold and silver, it was not alive (vv. 18-19). By contrast, God stated, "But the LORD is in His holy temple; let all the earth be silent before Him" (v. 20). This was fulfilled in 539 B.C. but also will be fulfilled at the Second Coming (Rev. 18).

### Habakkuk's Prayer

*Habakkuk 3:1-15.* In response to the tremendous revelation of God's ultimate righteousness in which He will judge every sin, Habakkuk broke out in prayer and worship, "LORD, I have heard of Your fame; I stand in awe of Your deeds, O LORD" (v. 2).

Habakkuk went on to describe God as an all-powerful conqueror who shakes the earth and makes the nations tremble (v. 6). God's power split the earth from the rivers (v. 9); "Sun and the moon stood still in the heavens" (v. 11). God in wrath deals with the nations and delivers His people (vv. 12-13).

*Habakkuk 3:16-19.* In response to this Habakkuk declared, "I heard and my heart pounded, my lips quivered at the sound; decay crept into my bones, and my legs trembled. Yet I will wait patiently for the day of calamity to come on the nation invading us" (v. 16). Habakkuk closed with the remarkable statement of his faith in the time of apostasy, "Though the fig tree does not bud and there are no grapes on the vines, though the olive crop fails and the fields produce no food, though there are no sheep in the pen and no cattle in the stalls, yet I will rejoice in the LORD, I will be joyful in God my Saviour" (vv. 17-18).

The perplexity of Habakkuk in asking God why the wicked continued to flourish and why God uses Babylon as an avenging instrument was replaced by Habakkuk's simple trust in God that was not based on what he saw but on the Word of God and His prophetic promise of ultimate justice and triumph for God.

The close of the book stated, "For the director of music. On my stringed instruments" (v. 19). Apparently, Habakkuk's prayer became part of the worship and service of God in the temple.

Though the Book of Habakkuk was not primarily prophetic, it assured believers that God in His time will bring justice to the world and will triumph over the wicked and deliver the righteous.

# THE PROPHECY IN ZEPHANIAH

The opening verse of Zephaniah introduced the author as the great-great-grandson of Hezekiah. Implied in this statement was that he had high social ranking and probably belonged to the royalty. His ministry was during the reign of King Josiah (640–609 B.C.). He probably was a distant relative of Josiah and was a contemporary of Jeremiah, Nahum, and probably Habakkuk.

The high point in the reign of Josiah was the recovery of the Law by Hilkiah in 622 B.C. (2 Kings 22–23; 2 Chron. 34). The discovery of the Law caused a revival of Israel spiritually. Baal worship was cut off (Zeph. 1:4), but otherwise Judah's moral condition justified the severe judgments which Zephaniah predicted.

The reign of Josiah was in a period when Assyria was losing

power, making it possible for the kingdom of Judah to expand and for Josiah to stop some of the religious practices of the Assyrians. A few years before Josiah died, Nineveh, the capital of Assyria, was destroyed in 612 B.C. Though some of the wicked practices introduced by King Manasseh who preceded Josiah were destroyed, even the spiritual revival did not bring about any deep-seated change in Judah.

As a result of the spiritual state of Judah, the Book of Zephaniah was largely dedicated to declaring the coming judgment of God, referred to as the Day of Yahweh or Day of the Lord to which references were made about nineteen times in this book.

The Day of the Lord is best understood as a time when God deals in direct judgment on the world though it may also be a time of unusual blessing as in the Millennium. The main burden of Scripture concerning the Day of the Lord pointed to the ultimate judgment in connection with the second coming of Christ. The period immediately before Judah was the Babylonian Captivity which was the Day of the Lord as far as she was concerned. This coming time of judgment, though extending to all the earth (1:2-3), was primarily on Judah and Jerusalem (1:4–2:3). Following judgment on Jerusalem, however, would be judgment on the surrounding nations (vv. 4-15). The book concluded with the ultimate restoration referring to the millennial kingdom which will take place after the second coming of Christ (3:9-12).

### The Ultimate Judgment of the Day of the Lord on the Entire Earth

*Zephaniah 1:1-3.* Speaking specifically of the ultimate judgment of God on the entire earth at the time of the second coming of Christ, Zephaniah declared the word of the Lord, " 'I will sweep away everything from the face of the earth,' declares the LORD. 'I will sweep away both men and animals; I will sweep away the birds of the air and the fish of the sea. The wicked will have only heaps of rubble when I cut off man from the face of the earth,' declares the LORD" (vv. 2-3).

### The Impending Judgment of the Day of the Lord on Judah and Jerusalem

*Zephaniah 1:4-18.* Zephaniah declared the word of the Lord against Judah and Jerusalem, "I will stretch out My hand against Judah and against all who live in Jerusalem" (v. 4). God particularly details that the "remnant of Baal" (v. 4) and the names of the idolatrous

310

priests would be judged, "I will cut off from this place every remnant of Baal, the names of the pagan and the idolatrous priests—those who bow down on the roofs to worship the starry host, those who bow down and swear by the LORD and who also swear by Molech" (vv. 4-5).

Judah was compared to a prepared sacrifice (v. 7) and on the Day of the Lord princes, king's sons, and those wearing foreign clothes would be especially the objects of His wrath (vv. 7-8).

Zephaniah declared the word of the Lord, "Wail, you who live in the market district; all your merchants will be wiped out, all who trade with silver will be ruined" (v. 11). Their houses would be taken over by others, their vineyards would provide wine for others, and their wealth would be plundered (vv. 12-13). The Day of the Lord was described in detail, "The great Day of the LORD is near—near and coming quickly. Listen! The cry on the Day of the LORD will be bitter, the shouting of the warrior there. That day will be a day of wrath, a day of distress and anguish, a day of trouble and ruin, a day of darkness and gloom, a day of clouds and blackness, a day of trumpet and battle cry against the fortified cities and against the corner towers. I will bring distress on the people and they will walk like blind men, because they have sinned against the LORD" (vv. 14-17). These prophecies are fulfilled in history and will be fulfilled at the Second Coming.

### Zephaniah's Plea to Repentance

*Zephaniah 2:1-3.* In the light of the prophecies soon to be fulfilled, Zephaniah pleaded with the people of Judah to repent and come to God before His anger was revealed to them. He stated, "Seek the LORD all you humble of the land, you who do what He commands. Seek righteousness, seek humility; perhaps you will be sheltered on the day of the LORD's anger" (v. 3).

### The Judgment of the Day of the Lord
### to Fall on Surrounding Nations

*Zephaniah 2:4-15.* The land of the Philistines would be destroyed, including Gaza and Ashkelon, Ashdod, and Ekron (vv. 4-5). The land of the Philistines would be so destroyed that it would become a place for flocks.

Moab and Ammon also would share in the judgment, " 'I have heard the insults of Moab and the taunts of the Ammonites, who insulted My people and made threats against their land. Therefore, as surely as I live,' declares the LORD Almighty, the God of Israel,

'Surely Moab will become like Sodom, and the Ammorites like Go-morrah—a place of weeds and salt pits, a wasteland forever. The remnant of My people will plunder them' " (vv. 8-9). The Cushites, referring to Ethiopia, also will bear God's judgment (v. 12). God finally would judge Assyria and leave Nineveh desolate (v. 13). Where formerly the city of Nineveh was situated, it would be a place for flocks and herds and the desert owl. The city itself would be abandoned (v. 14). These prophecies are fulfilled in history.

### The Apostasy of Israel Leading to Her Captivity

*Zephaniah 3:1-7.* Jerusalem was described under the indictment of Zephaniah, "Woe to the city of oppressors, rebellious and defiled! She obeys no one, she accepts no correction. She does not trust in the LORD, she does not draw near to her God" (vv. 1-2). Zephaniah denounced her officials, her prophets as arrogant, her priests as profane (vv. 3-4). God declared that not only Jerusalem but the cities and the nations would be destroyed with no one to inhabit them (vv. 6-7). The Day of the Lord will be a time when God's wrath is poured out on the entire earth (v. 8). These prophecies are fulfilled in history.

### The Coming Cleansing of the Nations

*Zephaniah 3:8-10.* Following the Day of the Lord will come a time when the nations will be cleansed and will once again worship the Lord, "Then will I purify the lips of the peoples, that all of them may call on the name of the LORD and serve Him shoulder to shoulder. From beyond the rivers of Cush My worshipers, My scattered people, will bring Me offerings" (vv. 9-10).

### Restoration of Israel

*Zephaniah 3:11-13.* Most important to God will be the restoration of the people of Israel in the Day of the Lord. God declared, "On that day you will not be put to shame for all the wrongs you have done to Me, because I will remove from this city those who rejoice in their pride. Never again will you be haughty on My holy hill. But I will leave within you the meek and humble, who trust in the name of the LORD. The remnant of Israel will do no wrong; they will speak no lies, nor will deceit be found in their mouths. They will eat and lie down and no one will make them afraid" (vv. 11-13). This will be fulfilled in the Millennium.

Though some spiritual revival took place in Israel when they returned from the Babylonian Captivity to Jerusalem, the ultimate fulfillment will be in the millennial kingdom following the second coming of Christ. Then there will be a true purging of that which is contrary to God and the nation Israel, and those who are left will be the true worshipers.

### The Blessing of God in Israel's Restoration

*Zephaniah 3:14-20.* Israel is exalted, "Sing, O Daughter of Zion; shout aloud, O Israel! Be glad and rejoice with all your heart, O Daughter of Jerusalem! The LORD has taken away your punishment, He has turned back your enemy. The LORD, the King of Israel, is with you; never again will you fear any harm" (vv. 14-15). It will be a time when God takes "great delight" in Israel (v. 17) and will take away her sorrows. The prophecy concluded, " 'At that time I will gather you; at that time I will bring you home. I will give you honor and praise among all the peoples of the earth when I restore your fortunes before your very eyes,' says the LORD" (v. 20).

The closing verse of Zephaniah summarized the promises of God of blessing Israel in the future, including the regathering to their Promised Land, being honored and praised by the nations, and restoration of their good fortunes in being returned to the land. In the Millennium the promises to Israel of ultimate possession of her land (Gen. 12:1-7; 13:14-17; 15:7-21; 17:7-8) and the coming of Christ as her Messiah and King will result in restoration of the Davidic kingdom, fulfilling the promises to David (2 Sam. 7:16; Ps. 89:3-4; Isa. 9:6-7; Dan. 7:27; Zeph. 3:15). The closing expression of the book, "says the LORD" (v. 20), is a reminder that what has been promised has been promised by the Lord who does not fail to fulfill His promises. These promises have ultimate fulfillment in the Millennium.

## THE PROPHECY IN HAGGAI

Little is known concerning Haggai except that he was the first prophet to speak to the house of Israel in the postexilic period. His book, the second shortest book of the Old Testament—only Obadiah is shorter—reported five messages relative to the rebuilding of the temple. Each message was dated in the year 520 B.C., the second year of Darius I. He was a contemporary of Zechariah whose ministry followed his and Ezra who recorded the first return to the land. Haggai 1:1-11 should be compared with Ezra 4:24–5:1; Haggai 1:12-15 should be compared with Ezra 5:2 and Zechariah 1:1-6; Haggai 2:10-23 should be compared with Zechariah 1:7–6:15; also, Ezra 5:3-17; 6:1-13 should be compared with Zechariah 7–8.

The messages which Haggai recorded were given to Zerubbabel who was governor of Judah and to Joshua the high priest. The theme of the messages was stated in Haggai 1:2, in which God rebuked the people for procrastinating on the rebuilding of the temple.

The pilgrims had returned to Jerusalem from the Babylonian Captivity in 538 B.C. and had attempted to build the temple, laying the foundation as recorded in Ezra 3. Adversaries, however, accused them of rebuilding the city and succeeded in getting an order from King Artaxerxes (465–424 B.C.) which had ordered them to stop building. When Haggai delivered his message, eighteen years had passed since the original start. King Artaxerxes had died, but no one apparently dared to proceed. The Book of Haggai recorded his rebuke of the people of Israel for not building the temple and the beginning of her undertaking to construct it.

### Haggai's Message of Rebuke

*Haggai 1:1-11.* The Prophet Haggai delivered the word of the Lord which raised the question why she was living comfortably in her own houses while the house of God was in ruin. Haggai reminded her that she was being chastened by God with her crops not bringing forth plentiful harvest because God was withholding His blessing.

### Haggai's Word of Encouragement

*Haggai 1:12-15.* When the people responded to Haggai's message and began rebuilding the temple, Haggai delivered the message of the Lord, encouraging them, " 'I am with you,' declares the LORD" (v. 13). Under the leadership of Zerubbabel who was governor of Judah and Joshua the high priest, work began on the temple.

### Haggai's Second Message of Encouragement

*Haggai 2:1-9.* The few who had seen the original temple saw, obviously, that the house they were building was far less glorious than that of Solomon's. But God, speaking through Haggai, exhorted them to be strong and continue building the temple (vv. 2-4). Haggai delivered the message of God, ""Be strong, all you people of the land,' declares the LORD, 'and work. For I am with you,' declares the LORD Almighty. 'This is what I covenanted with you when you came out of Egypt. And My Spirit remains among you. Do not fear' " (vv. 4-5).

In addition to encouraging the people of Israel, God reminded her of His ultimate purpose of bringing in the kingdom on earth when

Christ returns in His second coming. Haggai reported the word from God, "This is what the LORD Almighty says: 'In a little while I will once more shake the heavens and the earth, the sea and the dry land. I will shake all nations, and the desired of all nations will come, and I will fill this house with glory,' says the LORD Almighty" (vv. 6-7).

God also promised, " 'The glory of this present house will be greater than the glory of the former house,' says the LORD Almighty. 'And in this place I will grant peace,' declares the LORD Almighty" (v. 9).

In this prophecy God was predicting the far future where, before the second coming of Christ, the earth will be judged and Christ will return to take possession of the redeemed earth for the millennial kingdom. In this connection He will not only bless the temple that Israel was then building but also the future temples, one to be built in the period preceding the second coming of Christ, and the great temple described in Ezekiel 40–43 to be built after the Second Coming. God will glorify the millennial temple and will also glorify Himself in the temple that she was then building.

### Haggai's Second Message of Rebuke

*Haggai 2:10-19.* God delivered through Haggai the message concerning that which is defiled and that which is pure. The pure contacting the impure does not make the impure pure. Accordingly, what she had been doing and offering to the Lord was considered defiled. The result was that God had limited her harvests and not blessed her in a material way. Now that she was beginning the building of the temple, God declared, "From this day on I will bless you" (v. 19). This was fulfilled in the building of the temple.

### Haggai's Final Message of Encouragement

*Haggai 2:20-23.* The Lord instructed Haggai the prophet to deliver the message to Zerubbabel, stating, "Tell Zerubbabel governor of Judah that I will shake the heavens and the earth. I will overturn royal thrones and shatter the power of the foreign kingdoms. I will overthrow chariots and their drivers; horses and their riders will fall, each by the sword of his brother" (vv. 21-22). This referred to God's sovereign judgment on the various governments and peoples throughout history, and especially will be true of the final judgments preceding the second coming of Christ.

The message continued, " 'On that day,' declares the LORD Almighty, 'I will take you, My servant Zerubbabel son of Shealtiel,' declares the LORD, 'and I will make you like My signet ring, for I have chosen you,' declares the LORD Almighty" (v. 23).

The closing verse of Haggai was another confirmation of the restoration of Israel with a background of judgment of Gentile power in the world. God promised to honor Zerubbabel and make him like a signet ring, a token of royal authority. This was not to be fulfilled in Zerubbabel's lifetime but was symbolic of the coming of Messiah at which time Zerubbabel will be raised from the dead and share delegated authority with David in the millennial kingdom. In this revelation God was reassuring His people of His ultimate blessing on her and the ultimate fulfillment of the promises to David concerning his kingdom and his people.

## THE PROPHECY IN ZECHARIAH

Zechariah, the prophet whose book bears his name, was an outstanding postexilic prophet. The son of Berakiah and the grandson of Iddo, a priest (Zech. 1:1), he was born in Babylon during the time of the Babylonian Captivity (Neh. 12:4, 16). Both Ezra and Nehemiah described him as "a descendant of Iddo" (Ezra 5:1; 6:14; cf. Neh. 12:4, 16). He was both a prophet and a priest. His name, a common one shared by about thirty other individuals mentioned in the Old Testament, has the meaning, "The LORD remembers." Zechariah had returned to Jerusalem from Babylon with the first expedition of about 50,000 Jewish exiles. He was a contemporary of Haggai the prophet, Zerubbabel the governor, and Joshua the high priest (Ezra 5:1-2; Zech. 3:1; 4:6; 6:11).

After the return of the Jewish captives to Jerusalem, an altar had been built to renew the burnt sacrifices (Ezra 3:1-6), and the second year after they returned the foundation of the temple was laid (Ezra 3:8-13; 5:16). Because of the opposition of people of the land, however, the building of the temple was halted until 520 B.C. when the Children of Israel responded to the preaching of Haggai the prophet and began rebuilding (Ezra 5:1-2; Hag. 1:1). Haggai was not mentioned after the brief period in which he prophesied, but Zechariah picked up the prophetic ministry (v. 1; Zech. 1:1). Portions of Zechariah's prophecy which were dated were related to the rebuilding of the temple which was completed in 515 B.C. Undated prophecies, such as are found in Zechariah 9–14, may have been written later.

The important events, beginning with Haggai's first sermon until the temple was dedicated, form a chronological background for Zechariah's time and may be itemized as follows:

| | |
|---|---|
| August 29, 520 B.C. | First sermon of Haggai (Hag. 1:1-11; Ezra 5:1) |
| September 21, 520 B.C. | The rebuilding of the temple resumed (Hag. 1:12-15; Ezra 5:2) |
| October 17, 520 B.C. | Haggai's second sermon of encouragement (Hag. 2:1-9) |
| October–November 520 B.C. | Ministry of Zechariah begins (Zech. 1:1-6) |
| December 18, 520 B.C. | Haggai's second message of rebuke and third message of encouragement (Hag. 2:10-23) |
| February 15, 519 B.C. | Zechariah's eight visions (Zech. 1:7–6:8) |
| December 7, 518 B.C. | The delegation from Bethel with question about fasting (Zech. 7) |
| March 12, 515 B.C. | The temple dedicated (Ezra 6:15-18) |

The Book of Zechariah as a whole constituted one of the most compact apocalyptic prophetic books of the Old Testament. The Book of Zechariah included not only the eight prophetic dreams which were visions which occurred in one night (Zech. 1:7–6:8) but also apocalyptic descriptions which constituted eschatological revelation. Chapters 9–14 concluded the book with two prophetic oracles relating to Israel's future restoration. Though the apocalyptic sections are not easy to interpret, careful study will reveal the literal prophetic facts that are related to them.

### The Warning to Repent

*Zechariah 1:1-6.* As children of the captives of Israel, God warned them not to be like their forefathers, " 'Do not be like your forefathers, to whom the earlier prophets proclaimed: This is what the LORD Almighty says: "Turn from your evil ways and your evil practices." But they would not listen or pay attention to Me,' declares the LORD" (v. 4). The Children of Israel had repented, but it was too late. They were carried off into captivity.

### The First Vision: The Rider on the Red Horse

*Zechariah 1:7-17.* The date of the vision was declared to be the twenty-fourth day of the eleventh month, the month of Shebar in the second year of Darius. This was February 15, 519 B.C. This prophecy in verse 1 uses a Gentile ruler as dating the period,

317

a reminder that the Children of Israel were living in the times of the Gentiles and Jerusalem would be under control of the Gentiles and Israel would be scattered.

The man on the red horse (v. 8) was identified as the Angel of the Lord (v. 11) which was a theophany or an appearance of Jesus Christ in the Old Testament. The fact that the Angel of the Lord was the Lord Jesus Christ in the theophany was indicated in Zechariah 3:1-2 as well as many other Scriptures. The horses that were described were declared to be messengers of God sent throughout the earth (1:10) to find out what state the world was in. They reported to the Angel of the Lord, "We have gone throughout the earth and found the whole world at rest and in peace" (v. 11).

The fact that the nations were at peace when Israel was in Captivity resulted in the revelation that God was angry with the nations. The response of the Lord is that He would ultimately restore and bless Israel, "Proclaim this word: This is what the LORD Almighty says: 'I am very jealous for Jerusalem and Zion, but I am very angry with the nations that feel secure' " (vv. 14-15). The promise of the Lord was given for the restoration of Israel, "Therefore, this is what the LORD says: 'I will return to Jerusalem with mercy, and there My house will be rebuilt. And the measuring line will be stretched out over Jerusalem,' declares the LORD Almighty" (v. 16). The prophecy concluded with the statement that prosperity would extend to the towns around Jerusalem and that God would comfort the people of Israel (v. 17). In general, the vision indicated that God had in mind to restore Israel in the immediate future. The rebuilding of the temple will be part of their present restoration after the Babylonian Captivity.

### The Second Vision: The Four Horns and the Four Craftsmen

*Zechariah 1:18-20.* In the second vision Zechariah saw four horns which were described as scattering Judah, Israel, and Jerusalem (vv. 18-19). The four craftsmen were God's instrument in bringing judgment on the very nations that afflicted Israel, "the craftsmen have come to terrify them and throw down these horns of the nations who lifted up their horns against the land of Judah to scatter its people" (v. 21).

The four craftsmen may be identified as four judgments from God, the sword, famine, wild beasts, and the plague (cf. Ezek. 14:21; Rev. 6:1-8). The revelation was to the point that the nations that afflicted Israel would themselves be afflicted, a fact that has been well illustrated in the history of the nations that have afflicted Israel. Some have interpreted the four horns as relating to the four empires of Babylon, Medo-Persia, Greece, and Rome, but the scattering seems to refer to a period before Zechariah. In that case, the four empires might be Assyria, Egypt, Babylonia, and Medo-Persia. The principle was established, however, that God would ultimately judge those who judge Israel just as surely as He would restore Israel.

### The Third Vision: The Man Who Will
### Measure Jerusalem

*Zechariah 2:1-13.* Zechariah saw a man with a measuring line (v. 1). When asked where he was going, he said, "To measure Jerusalem, to find out how wide and how long it is" (v. 2). Interpreters of this Scripture have made several suggestions concerning who this man with the measuring line was. Some interpret it as an unidentified person whose identity was not known. Others think of it as Zechariah himself or the Angel of the Lord, Christ Himself in His Old Testament theophany. Actually, the Scriptures do not make it clear. The important point is that the revelation indicated that Jerusalem was to be rebuilt (cf. Ezek. 40:3-5). As such, the revelation would be an encouragement to those now building the temple though the city itself was still in ruin.

After the preliminary revelation, the angel to whom he was speaking left and another angel told him to run after the young man and declare, " 'Jerusalem will be a city without walls because of the great number of men and livestock in it. And I myself will be a wall of fire around it,' declares the LORD, 'and I will be its glory within' " (vv. 4-5).

This revelation, while it related to the rebuilding of Jerusalem, obviously extended beyond the building of the city that followed the coming of Nehemiah. God's ultimate purpose was to build Jerusalem in the millennial kingdom where it will be a large city without walls as described here.

In keeping with God's plan to restore Jerusalem and the people of Israel to her land, God invited her to come back from her scattering all over the world to the holy land (v. 6). He declared, " 'Come, O Zion! Escape, you who live in the Daughter of Babylon!' For this is what the LORD Almighty says: 'After he has honored Me and has sent Me against the nations that have plundered you — for whoever touches you touches the apple of His eye—I will surely raise My hand against them so that their slaves will plunder them. Then you will know that the LORD Almighty has sent Me' " (vv. 7-9). The passage goes on to describe the blessings of Israel in the millennial kingdom following the second advent of Christ (vv. 11-12).

### The Fourth Vision: Joshua the High Priest

*Zechariah 3:1-10.* This vision differed from the previous visions in that the actors were identifiable and the symbolic actions did not require the same extent of interpretation as provided by the angel in previous visions. The actors included Joshua the high priest (v. 1), the Angel of the Lord, a theophany of Christ (v. 1), and Satan the accuser standing to accuse Joshua (v. 1). Apparently, in addition to Zechariah himself who was part of the vision, there were angels in attendance (v. 4).

In the vision Joshua was pictured as standing before the Angel of the Lord (v. 3), implying that he was functioning as a priest (Deut. 10:8; 2 Chron. 29:11). The fact that the Angel of the Lord was Christ in His revelation as an Old Testament theophany was brought out in Zechariah 3:2 where He spoke to Satan and in verse 4 where He spoke as the Angel. Also, in verse 2 the Lord was distinguished from the Angel of the Lord speaking to Satan.

Because of Satan's accusation, the scene became a judicial judgment on sin rather than a portrayal of the priestly work of Joshua. Joshua was pictured as "a burning stick snatched from the fire" (v. 2), indicating that he had been rescued in order to be one who serves the Lord. The reference to the Lord's choosing Jerusalem (v. 2) indicated that Jerusalem has been chosen by the Lord for forgiveness and restoration.

The spiritual situation of Israel, however, was represented by Joshua and his filthy clothes (v. 3). The Angel of the Lord commanded that they take off his filthy clothes representing the act of God in taking away the sin of Israel and, instead, clothe him in the righteousness of God (v. 4).

Having been cleansed, Joshua then was exhorted by the Angel of the Lord to walk in the ways of the Lord and was promised that if he did, he "will govern My house" (v. 6), "have charge of My courts" (v. 6), and will be given a place of one representing the people of Israel (v. 6). The vision which represented Joshua being cleansed and recommissioned was declared to be "symbolic of things to come" (v. 8).

The ultimate cleansing and restoration of Israel will result from God's servant, the Branch, coming (v. 8), referring to the second coming of Christ to bring in His future kingdom and restore the people of Israel. Christ referred to here as "the Branch" (v. 8) indicated that He was a Descendant of David and will sit on David's throne (2 Sam. 7:8-16; Isa. 11:1). As the Branch, Christ will exercise supreme authority as King of kings as well as occupying the throne of David (Isa. 4:2; Jer. 23:5; 33:15; Zech. 6:12-13). As the Branch, He will also be the servant of the Lord who will do God's will (Isa. 42:1; 49:3-4; 50:10; 52:13; 53:11).

As the stone (Zech. 3:9; Ps. 118:22; Matt. 21:42; 1 Peter 2:6) He will bring purging judgment on the Gentiles (Dan. 2:44-45) and to Israel will be a stone of stumbling in their time of unbelief (Rom. 9:31-33). Ultimately, however, in the time of Israel's restoration He "will remove the sin of this land in a single day" (Zech. 3:9). The result of the second coming of Christ, the establishment of His kingdom on earth, and the restoration of Israel will be peace on earth, making it possible to fulfill the promise, " 'In that day each of you will invite his neighbor to sit under his vine and fig tree,' declares the LORD Almighty" (v. 10). The seven eyes referred to (v. 9) indicated the all-seeing eye of God who will have complete knowledge of what is going on in the world and will judge in the light of that infinite knowledge (Isa. 11:2-5). Taken as a whole, the vision reassured Joshua and the people of Israel that she should proceed in building the temple and promised the ultimate fulfillment of her restoration at the second coming of Christ.

## The Fifth Vision: The Gold Lampstand
## and Two Olive Trees

*Zechariah 4:1-14.* After the previous vision apparently the Angel of the Lord awoke Zechariah and asked him what he saw.

Zechariah answered, "I see a solid gold lampstand with a bowl at the top and seven lights on it, with seven channels to the lights. Also there are two olive trees by it, one on the right of the bowl and the other on its left" (vv. 2-3). The exact form of the lampstand was not indicated, but it probably was similar to the lampstands used in the tabernacle and the temple. Here, however, there were unusual features. A bowl was above the lampstand apparently with olive oil, and there were seven channels or pipes to each of the seven lights, making forty-nine channels in all, obviously an abundant provision for the flow of oil.

Zechariah asked the question concerning the two olive trees, one on the right and the other on the left. The answer was not immediately given, but Zerubbabel was informed that the main feature of this revelation was, " 'Not by might nor by power, but by My Spirit,' says the LORD Almighty" (v. 6). The revelation was that only God's power can accomplish God's purposes as indicated by the olive oil representing the Holy Spirit. Because the bowl containing the olive oil was connected to the two olive trees, there was a constant flow of oil in abundance for the seven lamps. The fact that the revelation was directed to Zerubbabel indicated recognition of him as the governor of Judah and God's instrument to fulfill God's goal in rebuilding the temple. In verse 7 it was declared that the "mighty mountain" will become level ground before Zerubbabel, indicating that all obstacles can be overcome by the power of God.

The word of the Lord came to Zechariah, "The hands of Zerubbabel have laid the foundation of this temple; his hands will also complete it. Then you will know that the LORD Almighty has sent me to you" (vv. 8-9). The building of the temple for which Zerubbabel laid the foundation and brought out the plumb line (vv. 9-10) will cause those who observe to rejoice as it symbolized God working once again and blessing His ancient people. A parenthetical thought was introduced in verse 10 with the seven eyes of God "which range throughout the earth," speaking as in 3:9 of God's omniscience in seeing all things and all events.

Because the previous question of 4:4 was not answered concerning the two olive trees, Zechariah asked the angel again, "What are these two olive trees on the right and the left of the lampstand?" (v. 11) He also wants to know about two olive branches and two gold pipes. The answer was given in verse 14, "These are the two who are anointed to serve the LORD of all the earth." Taken as a whole, the lampstand may be considered as representing Israel as a light to the world and the two olive trees as represented by Joshua and Zerubbabel who together represent both priest and king as portrayed in Christ in His second coming. All of this encouraged the returning captives to rebuild the temple. The abiding truth for all was that what was accomplished for God must be accomplished in the power of the Spirit.

### The Sixth Vision: The Flying Scroll

*Zechariah 5:1-4.* In the previous visions the emphasis was on the divine grace revealed in His forgiveness and plan to restore Israel as well as His power to accomplish for the returning captives the rebuilding of the temple. The sixth vision had to do with condemnation of sin. Zechariah saw a huge scroll, thirty by fifteen feet, flying through the air. This was interpreted to Zechariah, "This is the curse that is going out over the whole land; for according to what it says on one side, every thief will be banished, and according to what it says on the other, everyone who swears falsely will be banished" (v. 3). The vision as a whole portrayed the fact that God will judge sin, in part fulfilled in Israel's current experience, and to be completely fulfilled in the millennial kingdom when every sin will be judged and God's grace will be made manifest.

## The Seventh Vision: The Measuring Basket and the Women

*Zechariah 5:5-11.* The Angel, referring to the Angel of the Lord, asked Zechariah to tell what he saw. "He replied, 'It is a measuring basket.' And he added, 'This is the iniquity of the people throughout the land' " (v. 6). The measuring basket was used for dry measure by the Jews and would contain from five to ten gallons of contents. In the vision, however, the basket was enlarged in order to fulfill the description of the verses which follow. The basket, said to represent the wickedness of the people, has its lead cover raised and a woman is revealed sitting in the basket (v. 7). The Angel of the Lord informed Zechariah, " 'This is wickedness,' and he pushed her back into the basket and pushed the lead cover down over its mouth" (v. 8). The woman was wickedness personified in the vision, and the Angel of the Lord continued her confinement when he pushed the lead cover down.

In the vision Zechariah next saw two other women with large wings who carried off the basket (v. 9). Zechariah asked, " 'Where are they taking the basket?' I asked the Angel who was speaking to me. He replied, 'To the country of Babylonia to build a house for it. When it is ready, the basket will be set there in its place' " (vv. 10-11). Because Babylon was uniformly represented in Scripture as the source of much evil, the return of the basket and the woman in the basket symbolized that evil will be removed from Israel and returned to Babylonia where it will become part of their apostate religious system. The language indicating that the basket will be set in a place in the house probably means that it will be an object of worship as an idol in Babylon.

In the ultimate preparation of the world for the second coming of

Christ Babylon will be judged (Rev. 17–18), and its judgment will be preliminary for the revival of Israel and bringing in of the righteous kingdom of Christ in His second coming (Rev. 19–20).

### The Eighth Vision: The Four Chariots

*Zechariah 6:1-8.* In the first vision horses were seen going throughout the world to describe the scene in the world. Here they were represented as four chariots coming out from between two bronze mountains (v. 1). When Zechariah asked what this meant, the Angel stated, "These are the four spirits of heaven, going out from standing in the presence of the Lord of the whole world. The one with the black horses is going toward the north country, the one with the white horses toward the west, and the one with the dappled horses toward the south" (vv. 5-6).

Some believe the different colored horses have spiritual significance, with black referring to death and famine, red symbolizing war, and the dappled indicating pestilence and plagues. The white horse may symbolize the invincible power of God as in the second coming of Christ (Rev. 19). The two bronze mountains from which the four horses came (Zech. 6:1) indicated divine judgment against sin, usually associated with bronze (Rev. 1:15; 2:18).

The fact that the horses go north may indicate the former invasions of Israel by Babylon. The south seems to represent the invasions of Egypt which also affected Israel's history. Some interpret the horses toward the west in a different translation which would read, "The one with white horses after them." In other words, the white horse would follow the black horse to the north, leaving the two major directions of Israel's conquest in the north and the south in view. As a result of God's action on these countries, the Spirit will have rest in the land in the north (Zech. 6:8). The meaning may be that after divine judgments indicated in previous visions evil will have been judged and righteousness will be introduced as it will be primarily in the future millennial kingdom on earth.

The eight visions as a whole represented God's power and certainty of fulfillment of His promises for Israel, both in blessing and in judgment, and was intended to give her reassurance as she built the temple of God that she was operating under God's power and direction.

### The Crowning of Joshua

*Zechariah 6:9-15.* As a final revelation bringing together the eight visions, Zechariah was instructed to take silver and gold from three exiles, Heldai, Tobijah, and Jedaiah, and with the silver and gold make a crown to be set on the head of the high priest Joshua, the son of Jehozadak (vv. 9-11).

The fact that Joshua the high priest was crowned rather than Zerubbabel, the governor, would indicate that God was guarding against the idea that Zerubbabel was the fulfillment of God's promise for the Descendant of David to sit on a throne.

In the crowning of Joshua he was taken as Israel's representative of the coming Messiah. The prophecy was given, "Here is the man whose name is the Branch, and He will branch out from His place and build the temple of the LORD. It is He who will build the temple of the LORD, and He will be clothed with majesty and will sit and rule on His throne. And He will be a Priest on His throne. And there will be harmony between the two" (vv. 12-13).

As Joshua had relatively a minor role in the rebuilding of the temple, the fulfillment must go on to the Messiah, Jesus Christ, in His second coming when He will fulfill the prophecy completely and be both King (Isa. 9:7; Jer. 23:5; Micah 4:3, 7; Zeph. 3:15; Zech. 14:9) and priest (Heb. 4:15; 5:6; 7:11-21). A priest of the levitical order could not sit on a throne and reign, but Christ will be both King and Priest and will combine the two offices in His person and work.

In the situation of the rebuilding of the temple, the crown was given to Heldai, Tobijah, Jedaiah, and Hen to be a memorial in the temple when it was built. The vision closed with a promise that there will come help from many corners of the world to assist in the building of the temple (Zech. 6:15). Taken as a whole, the visions were reassuring to the people of Israel that they were in the will of God in building the temple and at the same time that God has in mind the ultimate restoration of Israel which is still future and will be fulfilled in the Millennium.

### The Question about Fasting

*Zechariah 7:1-3.* In the early part of the Babylonian Captivity to commemorate the destruction of Jerusalem and the temple, the Jews had inserted a ceremony of fasting in the fifth month. The people of Bethel, a town twelve miles north of Jerusalem, asked the priests in the house of the Lord whether they should continue this fast. The fast had been of human invention and not commanded by God and accordingly illustrated how ritual and ceremonial rites can take place without having any real meaning.

325

The answer to the question was given in four messages which follow in 7:4–8:23.

### The First Message

*Zechariah 7:4-7.* In the first message God asked the question, "Was it really for Me that you fasted?" (v. 5) The implication was that it was a mere ceremony without any real meaning. Accordingly, God rebuked them for their formalism. Though they had asked about the fast in the fifth month, actually they had also observed a fast in the seventh month (Lev. 16:29, 31; 23:26-32). The fast in the seventh month was in commemoration of the murder of Gedaliah, governor of Judea, connected with the fall of Jerusalem (Jer. 41:2). Their feast in the seventh month, like the one in the fifth month, was not divinely instituted and did not relate to the fast which they should have observed on the annual Day of Atonement.

### The Second Message

*Zechariah 7:8-14.* In the second message their hardness of heart and not listening to the word of God served to prove that their feasts were not observed in the right spirit. When God told them not to oppress the widow and the alien and the fatherless, they refused, "But they refused to pay attention; stubbornly they turned their backs and stopped up their ears. They made their hearts as hard as flint and would not listen to the Law or to the words that the LORD Almighty had sent by His Spirit through the earlier prophets. So the LORD Almighty was very angry" (vv. 11-12). The result was that God would not hear their prayers when they called, and the land was left desolate (vv. 13-14).

### The Third Message

*Zechariah 8:1-17.* The third message from God assured Israel of her ultimate restoration in fulfillment of God's purpose. The promise of restoration went far beyond the immediate future for Israel and looks forward to the millennial kingdom following the second coming of Christ. God revealed to them, "This is what the LORD says: 'I will return to Zion and dwell in Jerusalem. Then Jerusalem will be called the City of Truth, and the mountain of the LORD Almighty will be called the Holy Mountain' " (v. 3). In stating that God would return to Zion, he was referring to the name given the temple site in Jerusalem, though originally it referred to a fortress which David conquered in southwest Jerusalem. Accordingly, Zion was a synonym for Jerusalem (Ps. 2:6; Isa. 2:3; 4:3; 8:18; 33:20; Joel 2:1; Amos 1:2; Micah 3:10, 12). Zechariah referred to Zion as

Jerusalem frequently (Zech. 1:14, 17; 8:3; 9:9).

God promised that Jerusalem would be safe for older people as well as childen in the future golden age (8:4). What seemed marvelous to the people at the present time (v. 6) would be eclipsed by God's larger purpose to bring Israel back to her land, "This is what the LORD Almighty says: 'I will save My people from the countries of the east and the west. I will bring them back to live in Jerusalem; they will be My people, and I will be faithful and righteous to them as their God' " (vv. 7-8). In view of God's ultimate purpose to bless Israel, they were encouraged to rebuild the temple with the promise that God would bless them as they served Him (vv. 9-11). God would bless their crops and have the land bring forth abundantly (vv. 12-13). As God had brought them into judgment earlier, now He would pour out on them His blessings (v. 15). For in order to receive blessings, however, they should speak the truth and live honorably before God and man (vv. 15-16).

### The Fourth Message

*Zechariah 8:18-23.* The fourth message gave the final answer to their question about fasts, "This is what the LORD Almighty says: 'The fasts of the fourth, fifth, seventh and tenth months will become joyful and glad occasions and happy festivals for Judah. Therefore love truth and peace' " (vv. 18-19). In other words, their observance of fasts will have real meaning and be acceptable before God.

In further encouragement of the people of Israel, God promised that Jerusalem would be a great world city, "And many peoples and powerful nations will come to Jerusalem to seek the LORD Almighty and to entreat Him" (v. 22). In that day it will be recognized that the Jew is blessed of God, and people of other languages and nations will want to be associated with them (v. 23; 14:16-19; Isa. 2:3). This will be fulfilled in the millennial kingdom.

The four messages considered together were on the one hand a rebuke for ceremony without meaning and on the other hand were to be an encouragement to them in their rebuilding of the temple as well as in their hope for ultimate restoration and spiritual blessing on the people of Israel in the future kingdom.

### The Coming Judgment on the Nations Surrounding Israel

*Zechariah 9:1-8.* In contrast to the ultimate blessing of God on the people of Israel was the prediction of judgment on the nations and cities surrounding Israel (vv. 1-8). The future judgments include those on Damascus, the land of Hadrach (v. 1), Hanath, and

Tyre and Sidon (v. 2). Though Tyre was a stronghold with great wealth, the Lord will take away her possessions and destroy her (vv. 3-4). Likewise He would deal with the major cities of the Philistines such as Ashkelon, Gaza, and Ekron. God declared, "Gaza will lose her king and Ashkelon will be deserted" (v. 5). Foreigners would occupy Ashdod and conquer the Philistines (vv. 6-7).

Many of these prophecies were literally fulfilled when the Holy Land was invaded by Alexander the Great, after winning the Battle of Issus in 333 B.C. Though Alexander was the instrument, the result would be destruction on the cities that had oppressed Israel. Tyre, in particular, was subdued in a five-month siege and destroyed.

In the same period the armies of Alexander bypassed the city of Jerusalem without destroying it, a fulfillment of God's protection of the city. These judgments and the protection of Jerusalem in this situation in the fourth century B.C. foreshadow the ultimate protection of Israel and Jerusalem in the millennial kingdom.

### The Coming Deliverance of the Messiah

*Zechariah 9:9-17.* In contrast to the destruction of the enemies of Israel, Jerusalem would be blessed when her Messiah came. A particular prophecy was given concerning Christ entering Jerusalem in the triumphant procession, "Rejoice greatly, O Daughter of Zion! Shout, Daughter of Jerusalem! See, your king comes to you, righteous and having salvation, gentle and riding on a donkey, on a colt, the foal of a donkey" (v. 9). The announcement relates to the first coming of Christ (Isa. 9:5-7; Micah 5:2-4; Luke 1:32-33). His righteous character is revealed in both the Old and New Testaments (Ps. 45:6-7; Isa. 11:1-5; 32:17; Jer. 23:5-6; 33:15-16). He will come as a Deliverer having salvation, both in the sense of providing personal salvation for those who put their trust in Him and ultimately in delivering Israel from their enemies. The prophecy particularly described Christ in His first coming as "gentle and riding on a donkey, on a colt, the foal of a donkey" (Zech. 9:9). This was literally fulfilled as recorded in Matthew 21.

The prophecies which follow leap the present age and blend the first and second comings of Christ as if they were one event (Isa. 9:6-7; 61:1-2; Luke 4:18-21). The prophetic vision extends to the future kingdom on earth, "I will take away the chariots from Ephraim and the war-horses from Jerusalem, and the battle bow will be broken. He will proclaim peace to the nations. His rule will extend from sea to sea and from the River to the ends of the earth" (Zech. 9:10). This was not accomplished in His first coming but will be accomplished in His second coming. The millennial kingdom will be characterized as a time of peace (Isa. 2:4; Micah 4:3). The nation Israel will occupy the land as originally promised to Abram from the river of Egypt to the River Euphrates. The rest of the world will come under the rule of Christ as King of kings and Lord of lords.

In referring to "the blood of My covenant with you" (v. 11), the prophecy indicated the absolute certainty of the fulfillment of the covenant concerning the land sealed with blood (Gen. 15:7-17). The prisoners or captives in Babylon will return to the fortress, that is, Jerusalem where God will bless them (Zech. 9:12-13). Some interpreters consider verse 13 a reference to the Maccabean period (169–135 B.C.) when the Children of Israel were oppressed by Antiochus IV Epiphanes (cf. Dan. 11:32). Ultimately, they won the victory, cleansed their temple, and restored their worship. In picturesque language God was described as their ultimate leader who causes them to conquer over their enemies (Zech. 9:14-17).

### The Promise of Deliverance of Judah and Ephraim

*Zechariah 10:1-8.* God was described as the One who ultimately gave victory to Israel. God was the One who gave showers of rain (v. 1). He will punish her shepherds who do not properly care for the flock (vv. 2-3). He will raise up Judah as a power for God (vv. 4-6). The promise of blessing on the Ephraimites may have referred to the entire Northern Kingdom of the ten tribes (vv. 7-8).

### The Regathering of Israel

*Zechariah 10:9-12.* In addition to any blessing that will come to Israel before the kingdom on earth, though God will scatter them in distant lands (v. 9), they will survive and come back from Egypt, Assyria, and other parts of the world (v. 10). When they pass through the "sea of trouble" (v. 11) they will be strengthened in contrast to God's judgment on Assyria and Egypt (vv. 11-12). This was one of many prophecies which were yet to be fulfilled that pictured Israel's being scattered over the world but regathered at the time of the second coming of Christ in order to possess their Promised Land.

### The Rejection of Israel's Messiah
### and Its Consequences

*Zechariah 11:1-17.* Though previous Scriptures had anticipated the ultimate restoration of Israel, the long process before this was fulfilled was related to their rejection of their Messiah. Accordingly, the cedars of Lebanon, the oaks of Bashan, and the rich pastures of the land were all to be destroyed (vv. 1-3).

Zechariah was told to assume the role of a shepherd and pasture the flock of Israel (vv. 4-6). The religious leaders of Israel, represented by Zechariah, were not true shepherds and did not care for the sheep but, instead, will oppress them (vv. 4-6).

Zechariah, acting the part of a shepherd, took two staffs called "Favor" and "Union." It is not clear what Scriptures mean that state, "In one month I got rid of the three shepherds" (v. 8). The leaders of Israel occupied the offices of prophet, priest, and king, and it is possible it referred to this.

But the flock would not receive Zechariah as her shepherd. Accordingly, he broke the staff "Favor," indicating that she no longer was in favor with God. As a shepherd he asked for his pay (v. 12). Scriptures recorded, "So they paid me thirty pieces of silver" (v. 12). This was the price of a slave, but Zechariah, acting the role of the shepherd, threw the thirty pieces of silver into the house of the Lord for the potter (v. 13). By this means he then broke the second staff called "Union," representing the brotherly relation between Judah and Israel already fractured by the two kingdoms of Judah and Israel. This anticipated prophetically that Judas would be paid thirty pieces of silver to betray Christ (Matt. 26:14-16; 27:3-10).

Zechariah was then told to take the role of a foolish shepherd (Zech. 11:15), representing prophetically the Antichrist who will lead Israel in the end time and the false leader of Israel. Woe was pronounced on this restless shepherd (v. 17).

While all the details of this chapter prophetically were not clear, it generally indicates the reason why Israel's restoration did not take place sooner and points to her rejection of the Messiah in His first coming.

In spite of Israel's rejection of the Messiah at His first coming, it was God's settled purpose to enthrone Christ as the King of Israel. The statement of this purpose of God was set in the context of the military conflict which will precede His coming.

### The Future Deliverance of Israel from Her Enemies

*Zechariah 12:1-9.* God declared His purpose, " 'I am going to make Jerusalem a cup that sends all the surrounding peoples reeling. Judah will be besieged as well as Jerusalem. On that day, when all the nations of the earth are gathered against her, I will make Jerusalem an immovable rock for all the nations. All who try to move it will injure themselves. On that day I will strike every horse with panic and its rider with madness,' declares the LORD. 'I will keep a watchful eye over the house of Judah, but I will blind all the horses of the nations' " (vv. 2-4). The prophetic picture goes on to describe Jerusalem as standing against her enemies with God blessing the inhabitants in their defense against the nations. God declared, "On that day I will set out to destroy all the nations that attack Israel" (v. 9).

### The Repentance of Israel in That Day

*Zechariah 12:10-14.* In addition to the physical deliverance of the people of Israel, there will be spiritual restoration and repentance on the part of those delivered. God declared, "I will pour out on the house of David and the inhabitants of Jerusalem a spirit of grace and supplication. They will look on Me, the One they have pierced, and they will mourn for Him as one mourns for an only child, and grieve bitterly for Him as one grieves for a firstborn son" (v. 10). The passage goes on to speak of the weeping throughout the land (vv. 11-14). This prophecy will be fulfilled in preparation for the Second Coming.

### The Cleansing of the Remnant of Israel

*Zechariah 13:1-7.* In keeping with the spiritual preparation indicated by Israel in repentance, God promised, "On that day a fountain will be opened to the house of David and the inhabitants of Jerusalem, to cleanse them from sin and impurity" (v. 1). This will be fulfilled at the Second Coming.

### The Purging Judgments on Israel

*Zechariah 13:8-9.* The time of Israel's complete restoration will be preceded by a time of purging judgments. The Lord stated, " 'On that day, I will banish the names of the idols from the land, and they will be remembered no more,' declares the LORD Almighty. 'I will remove both the prophets and the spirit of impurity from the land. And if anyone still prophesies, his father and mother, to whom he was born, will say to him, "You must die, because you have told lies in the LORD's name." When he prophesies, his own parents will stab him" (vv. 2-3). The reference to "that day" refers to the Day of the Lord which at its beginning at the Rapture included the Great Tribulation before the second coming of Christ. The reference to "that day" occurs many times in the closing chapters of Zechariah (12:3-4, 6, 8-9, 11; 13:1, 4; 14:4, 6, 8-9, 13, 20-21).

Though the cleansing was provided by the death of Christ on the cross, Israel did not experience this until she turned to the Lord as portrayed in this passage. The banishing of idols (v. 2) is a reference to the fact that the world dictator will set up an idol of himself in the temple and will be worshiped as God (2 Thes. 2:3-4; Rev. 13:14-15). There will be many false prophets in that day, and God will judge them as well (v. 3). The false prophets will attempt to deny that they are prophets (vv. 4-5). As prophets sometimes had self-inflicted wounds which were in connection with idol worship, they will say that these were given them in the house of a friend (v. 6).

### The Prophecy of the True Prophet

In the poetic prophecy which follows the true Shepherd was declared to be struck, fulfilled in the crucifixion of Christ with the result that the sheep will be scattered (v. 7).

### The Purging Refinement of Israel

It was prophesied that two-thirds of Israel in the land will perish, " 'In the whole land,' declared the LORD, 'two-thirds will be struck down and perish; yet one-third will be left in it. This third I will bring into the fire; I will refine them like silver and test them like gold. They will call on My name and I will answer them; I will say, "They are My people," and they will say, "The LORD is our God" ' " (vv. 8-9). This prophecy will be fulfilled in the Great Tribulation when two out of three of the Jews in the land attempting to flee their persecutor, the future world leader, will perish, and only one-third will escape and be waiting for Christ when He comes. The 144,000 of Revelation 7 and Revelation 14 will be part of that remnant.

### The Triumphant Coming of Israel's Messiah
### and the Lord's Second Coming

*Zechariah 14:1-3.* The interpretation of this difficult portion was made clear by later revelation concerning the events of the end time leading up to the second coming of Christ.

The final drama of the Great Tribulation ending in the second coming of Christ was described in these verses, "The Day of the LORD is coming when your plunder will be divided among you. I will gather all the nations to Jerusalem to fight against it; the city will be captured, the houses ransacked and the women raped. Half of the city will go into exile, but the rest of the people will not be taken from the city. Then the LORD will go out and fight against those nations as He fights in the day of battle." This will be a stage in what is called in Revelation 16:14 "the battle on the great day of God Almighty," also commonly referred to as the Battle of Armageddon (Rev. 16:16).

### Physical Changes in the Holy Land

*Zechariah 14:4-8.* Attending the second coming of Christ will be cataclysmic events, including the division of the Mount of Olives into northern and southern halves with the great valley between, "On that day His feet will stand on the Mount of Olives, east of Jerusalem, and the Mount of Olives will be split in two from east to west, forming a great valley, with half of the mountain moving north and half moving south" (v. 4). Those who seek to escape Jerusalem will flee by this newly made valley which, apparently, will extend from Jerusalem down to the city of Jericho. This makes clear that the Second Coming is a future event as the Mount of Olives is still intact.

That day will also be unique in that apparently it will be a lengthened day, "On that day there will be no light, no cold or frost. It will be a unique day, without daytime or nighttime—a day known to the LORD. When evening comes, there will be light" (v. 6).

Other topological changes will take place which apparently will elevate Jerusalem so that waters flowing from Jerusalem will go half to the eastern sea, or the Sea of Galilee, and half to the western sea, or the Mediterranean (v. 8). There will be other unusual phenomena occurring in connection with the second coming of Christ (Isa. 11:10; 34:4; Joel 2:10, 30-31; 3:15; Matt. 24:29). A great many events are packed into a relatively short period of time.

### The Millennial Kingdom Established

*Zechariah 14:9-21.* The millennial kingdom will be distinguished by the fact that the Lord, Jesus Christ as the Messiah of Israel and King of kings, will rule over the entire earth (v. 9). Included in the topographical changes will be the elevation of Jerusalem as described in verse 10. From that day forward Jerusalem will be secure and never be destroyed again.

An indication of the rule of Christ as Kings of kings and Lord of lords is that He will judge the nations that fought against Jerusalem (vv. 12-13). A plague will seize man and beast alike, but in the results a great quantity of gold, silver, and clothing will accrue to Israel's benefit (v. 14).

Those who survive the purging judgments at the beginning of the millennial kingdom will be required to worship Christ annually (v. 16). If they do not worship Him as commanded, God will hold their rain (vv. 17-19). It will be a time when the holiness of God is especially revealed, and false elements like the Canaanites will be shut out (vv. 20-21). The partial revelation of the nature of the millennial kingdom as described here was amplified in many other Scriptures in both the Old and New Testaments.

## THE PROPHECY IN MALACHI

The Book of Malachi is a fitting climax to the Old Testament, carefully providing the last prophetic utterance until John the Baptist appeared in the New Testament. From references to the temple worship, it was clear that the temple had already been reconstructed and finished as in 515 B.C. It is probable that Malachi was a younger contemporary to Nehemiah whose ministry was either to the same generation as was addressed by Ezra and Nehemiah or to the next generation.

Malachi encountered the same sins of Israel that had been earlier met by Israel in 458 B.C. and by Nehemiah in 444 B.C. The situation included corruption of the priesthood as illustrated in Malachi's criticism of them (1:6–2:9). Intermarriages with Gentiles involving divorce from their previous wives was criticized by Malachi in 2:10, and a similar condition existed in Ezra 9:1-2; Neh. 13:1-3, 23-28. In a similar way there was lack of support of the priests and Levites (Mal. 3:10; cf. Neh. 13:10), and the poor were oppressed (Mal. 3:5; cf. Neh. 5:4-5). It is clear that these were recurring sins and probably Nehemiah's corrective did not last very long. The name Malachi appears to mean "My messenger," and as such he was the last prophet of the Old Testament.

The form of the book was not in a direct quotation of God but rather in the form of questions and answers as Malachi would ask questions of priests or other people, and there would be a dispute concerning the answer. Malachi in the process would offer proof that his charges and corrections are justified. Several centuries were to elapse between the ministry of Malachi and the coming of John the Baptist anticipated in Malachi 3:1. As the first verse of the book illustrated, the contents were a message from God given through Malachi. The revelation related to six oracles dealing with successive problems in Israel to which Malachi addressed the truth of God.

### The First Oracle: They Should Love God

*Malachi 1:1-5.* These verses show Israel's failure to respond to God's love. The discussion begins with the statement, " 'I have loved you,' says the LORD. 'But you ask, "How have You loved us?" ' " (v. 2) The Lord replied with the statement, "Yet I have loved Jacob, but Esau I have hated" (v. 2). As proof, God pointed out how the inheritance of Edom had been left a waste (v. 3). Though Edom may boast that they will rebuild, God declared that if they do He will demolish their building (v. 4).

In stating that God loved Jacob but hated Esau, it must be understood as a relative statement in the sense that God, choosing between the two, chose Jacob. Esau was the father of Edom and the Edomites (Gen. 36:1). Though he was the firstborn, Jacob was chosen even before he was born to be the heir of the messianic promise.

In subsequent history God had blessed Jacob and his descendants and had not blessed Edom though they were entitled to some promises which God had given Jacob. Edom had gradually been reduced until her last recognition as a separate people faded in history. By contrast, Israel was promised to be a nation forever (Jer. 31:35-37). As the chosen people, Israel should have recognized God's love for them and His purposes which should be fulfilled in eternity as well as time.

### The Second Oracle: They Must Honor God

*Malachi 1:6–2:9.* In spite of all that God had done for them, Israel had failed to honor God and the priests had been leaders in this lack of proper respect. Malachi pointed out that a son should honor his father and the servant his master (v. 6), and if God is their Father, where is the respect that is due Him? (v. 6) Then they asked how they had not honored His name. Malachi pointed out that they had offered "defiled food on My altar" (v. 7). Malachi pointed out how they had brought animals for sacrifice that were blind or crippled or diseased and challenged them to observe that they would not have dared do this to one of their political governors. How much more should they have avoided doing this to God (vv. 8-9).

Malachi declared that it would be better to shut the temple's doors and not have sacrifices on the altar at all if they were not going to do it according to the Law of God which demands perfect offerings (vv. 10-13). Malachi challenged them that if they did not correct their ways, God would curse them and defile their faces with offal from their sacrifices showing His contempt for them (2:1-3). Instead of being priests who did not honor the Lord, they should instead be the fountain of instruction in the truth of God (v. 7). Instead, they caused the people of Israel to stumble (v. 8). The result was that they themselves were despised by the people (v. 9). They should have known that they were doing wrong in bringing imperfect animals for sacrifice because the Law was clear (Lev. 22:18-25; Deut. 15:21). Instead of honoring God, they were defiling the table, probably a reference to the sacrificial offering. They had made the Lord's table the place of offerings contemptible to the people. These prophecies are fulfilled in history and prophecy.

### The Third Oracle: They Were to Be Thankful as God's Covenant People

*Malachi 2:10-16.* Not only had they sinned against God, but they sinned against each other in profaning the covenant that God had made with their forefathers (v. 10). Not only had they sinned against each other, but they had sinned against God as a group by desecrating His sanctuary and worshiping idols which Malachi referred to as "marrying the daughter of a foreign god" (v. 11). When God would not accept their offering and they wept because of it, it was because of their sins (v. 13). They had been guilty of breaking faith with their wives in order to enter into a union often with foreign women (v. 14). They should stop breaking faith with their wives and doing evil in the sight of the Lord (v. 17).

### The Fourth Oracle: Their Hope Should Be in God

*Malachi 2:17–3:6.* You have made the charge, " 'All who do evil are good in the eyes of the LORD, and He is pleased with them' or 'Where is the God of justice?' " (2:17) The problem of how the wicked may temporarily prosper, apparently without check from God, was a frequent subject of Scripture (Job 21:7-26; 24:1-17; Ps. 73:1-14; Ecc. 8:14; Jer. 12:1-4; Hab. 1:12-17).

The Scripture, however, made plain that while the wicked may prosper for a time, ultimately justice from God will come on them (Job 24:22-24; 27:13-23; Ps. 73:16-20; Ecc. 8:12-13; Jer. 12:7-17; Hab. 2:3; 3:2-19). Scriptures frequently referred to the fact that God will bring in His righteous kingdom as the climax to human history in the period following the second coming of Christ.

While they still may question whether God is just, God is going to send His messenger to prepare the way of the Lord, " 'See, I will send My messenger, who will prepare the way before Me. Then

336

suddenly the Lord you are seeking will come to His temple; the Messenger of the covenant, whom you desire, will come,' says the LORD Almighty" (Mal. 3:1). This reference was to John the Baptist, according to the New Testament (Matt. 11:10; Mark 1:2; Luke 7:27), but the phrase "the Lord you are seeking" was not quoted in the New Testament. It was true that when Christ came, He would come suddenly to His temple at His first coming. But the final second coming of Christ will be one of judgment, not of grace. As is so often true in the Old Testament, both the first and second comings of Christ are considered as one event. None of the prophets seem to have understood the separation of these events by a long period between. The messenger obviously was John the Baptist, however, and Christ was the One who will come suddenly both in His first and second comings.

The second coming of Christ will be preceded by the beginning of the Day of the Lord, including the judgments leading up to the second coming of Christ (Isa. 2:12; Joel 3:11-16; Amos 5:18-21; Zech. 1:14-18). In answer to the question of who can endure the day of His coming (Mal. 3:2), the answer was that no one, except by God's purification, can stand at that time. The figure was used of refiner's fire or a launderer's soap (v. 2). God will purify His people, including the Levites, and they will come to the Lord for cleansing, bringing their acceptable sacrifices in that day (vv. 3-4).

In the day of judgment those who are adulterers and perjurers and others who have sinned will be easily identified (v. 5). By contrast, God Himself will not change, and He will see to it that Jacob is not destroyed.

### The Fifth Oracle: The Command to Obey God

*Malachi 3:7-12.* God accused them that from their forefathers they had turned away from His commands and not kept them (v. 7).

Israel had a long history of disobedience to God (Ex. 32:7-9; Deut. 9:6-8, 13, 23-24; 31:27-29). Accordingly, God pleaded with them, " 'Return to Me, and I will return to you,' says the LORD Almighty" (Mal. 3:7). But they ask, "How are we to return?" (v. 7) Their pretense of being unaware of their waywardness illustrated how far they were from God. God bluntly accuses them of robbing God (v. 8).

When they asked how they had robbed Him, He replied, " 'In tithes and offerings. You are under a curse—the whole nation of you—because you are robbing Me. Bring the whole tithe into the

337

storehouse, that there may be food in My house. Test Me in this,' says the LORD Almighty, 'and see if I will not throw open the flood-gates of heaven and pour out so much blessing that you will not have room enough for it' " (vv. 8-10).

If they had been faithful in obeying God, He would have blessed their harvest and made them a nation obviously blessed, " 'Then all the nations will call you blessed, for yours will be a delightful land,' says the LORD Almighty" (v. 12). The promises of blessing and cursing are fulfilled in history and prophecy.

### The Sixth Oracle: The Command to Fear God

*Malachi 3:13–4:3.* Though God had abundantly blessed Israel, God charged Israel, "You have said harsh things against Me" (3:13). When they asked, "What have we said against You?" God charged them with saying, "It is futile to serve God. What did we gain by carrying out His requirements and going about like mourners before the LORD Almighty? But now we call the arrogant blessed. Certainly the evildoers prosper, and even those who challenge God escape" (vv. 14-15).

As always in times of apostasy, the majority may not serve God or honor Him, but there were always the godly few, in this case, a faithful remnant who were walking with God. They had written "a scroll of remembrance," listing those who feared the Lord and honored Him (v. 16). " 'They will be Mine,' says the LORD Almighty, 'in the day when I make up My treasured possession. I will spare them, just as in compassion a man spares his son who serves him. And you will again see the distinction between the righteous and the wicked, between those who serve God and those who do not' " (vv. 17-18).

The distinction between the righteous and the wicked will be a feature of the Day of the Lord which Malachi stated was coming (4:1). It will be a day that " 'will burn like a furnace. All the arrogant and every evildoer will be stubble, and that day that is coming will set them on fire,' says the LORD Almighty" (v. 1). Further, God said, "Not a root or a branch will be left to them" (v. 1). This does not promise annihilation of the wicked, but it does indicate that any who are so wicked will be excluded from the kingdom.

While the Day of the Lord will be a time of judgment on the wicked, it also will be a time when the righteous will be recognized, "But for you who revere My name, the sun of righteousness will rise with healing in its wings. And you will go out and leap like calves released from the stall" (v. 2). The wicked were represented as being trampled underfoot like ashes under a person's feet (v. 3). This answers completely the false statement of the wicked, but it does make a difference whether they serve God or not. In the ultimate judgment the righteous will flourish and the wicked will suffer. This is fulfilled in history and will be fulfilled at the Second Coming.

### The Final Word

*Malachi 4:4-6.* By way of conclusion to the entire book as well as by way of preparation spiritually for the coming days, God declared, "Remember the Law of My servant Moses, the decrees and Laws I gave him at Horeb for all Israel" (v. 4). The Law which God delivered through Moses was His word to the people of Israel, including the commands to do righteousness and the prohibition of evil. They were given the promise that they would be blessed if they kept the Law but cursed if they rejected it. History has well served to demonstrate the truth about this prediction.

The final word from Malachi predicted the coming of Elijah, "See, I will send you the Prophet Elijah before that great and dreadful Day of the LORD comes. He will turn the hearts of the fathers to their children, and the hearts of the children to their fathers; or else I will come and strike the land with a curse" (vv. 5-6).

Interpreters have differed as to whether this prophecy of Elijah was fulfilled by John the Baptist or not. According to Matthew 11:7-10, the messenger of Malachi 3:1 was specifically stated to be John the Baptist and as such one who prepared the way of the Lord in His first coming. It had been predicted before his birth that John would operate in the spirit and power of Elijah (Luke 1:17).

Though it is clear that John the Baptist prepared the way for the Lord (Isa. 40:3; Mal. 3:1), John the Baptist, however, expressed that he was not Elijah (John 1:21-23). Christ even called John, "the Elijah who was to come," with the stipulation, "if you are willing to accept it" (Matt. 11:14). The matter is further discussed in Matthew 17:11-12 where Christ affirmed, "Elijah comes and will restore all things" (Matt. 17:11). In other words, because Israel did not accept John the Baptist as Elijah, another Elijah is yet to come. But in Matthew 17:12 Jesus said, "Elijah has already come, and they did not recognize him."

It was clear that Elijah was a type of John and to some extent that John the Baptist fulfilled Elijah's role. But, predictively, it is difficult to determine whether the future one will come in the spirit and power of Elijah or be Elijah himself. Though some identify one of the two witnesses in Revelation 11:1-13 as Elijah, there is no scriptural evidence that this is the case. The Book of Malachi closes with a warning that if their hearts are not turned to the Lord, God will strike the land with a curse (Mal. 4:6).

So the Old Testament which began with the statement, "In the beginning God," ends with a possibility of a curse on the land followed by several hundred silent years when there was no prophet until John the Baptist appeared on the scene. Much of the Old Testament has already been fulfilled, but much also awaits future fulfillment in the last days.

# 9

# PROPHECY IN
# THE GOSPELS

# GENERAL PROPHECIES IN THE GOSPELS

Prophecies in the Gospels have a special character because most of them are prophecies made by Jesus Christ. The fact that Jesus is present in the Gospels also gives these prophecies a special significance because Jesus Himself is fulfilling prophecies in His person, His works, and His teachings. The prophecies of the Gospels form an important bridge between the Old Testament and the New Testament, and they present a prophetic revelation in contrast to the 400 years preceding during which there were no prophets. The events of the Gospels lay a new platform for the complete revelation in the New Testament.

Most of the prophecies in the four Gospels are general in nature and cover a wide variety of prophetic subjects. There are certain passages, however, which provide a special prophetic emphasis. The Sermon on the Mount (Matt. 5–7) has a special prophetic emphasis. Likewise, Matthew 13, dealing with prophecy concerning the present age, and the Olivet Discourse (Matt. 24–25) provide a special presentation of prophecies concerning the end of the age. Also emphasized in the Gospels are prophecies concerning the death and resurrection of Christ. These areas of special revelation will be considered after general prophecies in the Gospels are examined.

### The Prophecy of the Birth of John the Baptist

*Luke 1:5-25.* An introductory statement relating to the birth of John the Baptist provides an important prophetic introduction to the contents of the Gospel. Zechariah, a priest, had been chosen by lot to burn incense, representing his division of the priesthood. He had a good reputation as one who kept the Law. Zechariah and his wife were concerned because they were getting older and had no children (v. 7).

Zechariah, in performance of his duties in the temple, was confronted by an angel standing at the altar of incense (v. 11). Zechariah was informed by the angel, "Do not be afraid, Zechariah; your prayer has been heard. Your wife Elizabeth will bear you a son, and you are to give him the name John. He will be a joy and delight to you, and many will rejoice because of his birth, for he will be great in the sight of the Lord. He is never to take wine or other fermented drink, and he will be filled with the Holy Spirit even from birth. Many of the people of Israel will he bring back to the Lord their God. And he will go on before the Lord, in the spirit and power of

Elijah, to turn the hearts of the fathers to their children and the disobedient to the wisdom of the righteous – to make ready a people prepared for the Lord" (vv. 13-17; cf. Matt. 3:11; Mark 1:1-18; John 1:6-8, 15-37).

Because Zechariah and his wife were both old and childless, he asked for confirmation of this prophecy. "The angel answered, 'I am Gabriel. I stand in the presence of God and I have been sent to speak to you and to tell you this good news. And now you will be silent and not able to speak until the day this happens, because you did not believe my words, which will come true at their proper time' " (Luke 1:19-20; cf. vv. 63-64).

When Zechariah left the temple he was unable to speak to the people who were waiting for him (vv. 21-22). After he returned home, his wife became pregnant in fulfillment of the prophecy. In due time the prophecy was literally fulfilled in all of the details given to Zechariah and forms an important background to the birth of Christ Himself.

### Prophecy of the Birth of Jesus

*Luke 1:26-38.* Just as the Angel Gabriel had appeared to Zechariah, six months later he appeared to Mary, described as "a virgin pledged to be married to a man named Joseph, a descendant of David. The virgin's name was Mary" (v. 27).

The angel greeted her, "Greetings, you are highly favored! The Lord is with you" (v. 28).

Because Mary was troubled by this greeting, Scripture records the angel's announcement to Mary, "But the angel said to her, 'Do not be afraid, Mary, you have found favor with God. You will be with child and give birth to a Son, and you are to give Him the name Jesus. He will be great and will be called the Son of the Most High. The Lord God will give Him the throne of His father David, and He will reign over the house of Jacob forever; His kingdom will never end' " (vv. 30-33).

The prophecy was too extensive for her to grasp immediately. She probably could not comprehend why He should be called Jesus which means Saviour. He also was to be "Son of the Most High" (v. 32), meaning that He would be the Son of God. Though Mary was acquainted with the hope of Israel for a Messiah and a Redeemer, it is undoubtedly true that she did not comprehend completely the fact that her Son would have the throne of His father David, and that He would reign over this kingdom forever; His kingdom would never end (Ps. 89:36; Jer. 23:5-8). Only time would let her contemplate the full extent of the prohecy. She was concerned, however, with the question as to how she would have a Son when she was not yet married.

Accordingly, Mary asked the angel, "How will this be . . . since I am a virgin?" (Luke 1:34)

The angel responded, "The Holy Spirit will come upon you, and the power of the Most High will overshadow you. So the Holy One to be born will be called the Son of God. Even Elizabeth your relative is going to have a child in her old age, and she who was said to be barren is in her sixth month. For nothing is impossible with God" (vv. 35-37; cf. Isa. 7:14; Matt. 1:21-22, 25; Luke 2:1-8).

Mary's simple response was, "I am the Lord's servant. . . . May it be to me as you have said" (v. 38).

Most of the prophecies itemized by Gabriel were fulfilled in the lifetime of Christ. The prophecy concerning His reigning on the throne of David is related eschatologically to the second coming of Christ when the Davidic kingdom will be revived and will continue in some form forever.

Of particular importance to the subject of eschatology is the fact that Christ was predicted to reign on the throne of David. Because many have attempted to limit the prophecy of the Davidic kingdom to the Old Testament and to claim that the New Testament interprets the prophecy in a nonliteral sense as being fulfilled today, this is an important interpretive passage in the New Testament, reaffirming that the Davidic kingdom would be restored literally. This announcement established the hope of the revival of the Davidic kingdom as a New Testament prophecy and gave a basis for a belief in the premillennial return of Christ to be followed by the millennial kingdom and the Davidic kingdom. Apparently, the Davidic kingdom will be an aspect of the millennial kingdom of Christ and will concern Israel and her regathered situation in the Promised Land. Mary had the expectation, as did the people of Israel, of the coming of a future Messiah who would literally revive the Davidic kingdom. The angel confirmed this by asserting that Christ would reign on the throne of David. The literal political revival of Israel in relation to the second coming of Christ is not an erroneous interpretation into which the people of Israel had fallen but rather precisely what the Old Testament predicted and what the New Testament here confirms.

### Elizabeth's Prophecy concerning Jesus

*Luke 1:39-45.* Apparently, about the time that Mary realized that she was pregnant, she left Nazareth to visit Zechariah's wife. Upon her arrival in Zechariah's home, further confirmation of the angel's message to Mary was recorded, "When Elizabeth heard Mary's greeting, the baby leaped in her womb, and Elizabeth was filled with the Holy Spirit. In a loud voice she exclaimed: 'Blessed are you among women, and blessed is the Child you will bear!' " (vv. 41-42) Elizabeth continued, "But why am I so favored, that the mother of my Lord should come to me? As soon as the sound of your greeting reached my ears, the baby in my womb leaped for joy. Blessed is she who has believed that what the Lord has said to her will be accomplished!" (vv. 43-45)

### Mary's Song of Praise

*Luke 1:46-56.* Mary was greatly reassured by the greeting of Elizabeth which at once confirmed the prophecies concerning John and the prophecies concerning Jesus. In reply, Mary delivered a prophetic poem, often called the "Magnificat."

"And Mary said: 'My soul glorifies the Lord and my spirit rejoices in God my Saviour, for He has been mindful of the humble state of His servant. From now on all generations will call me blessed, for the Mighty One has done great things for me—holy is His name. His mercy extends to those who fear Him, from generation to generation. He has performed mighty deeds with His arm; He has scattered those who are proud in their inmost thoughts. He has brought down rulers from their thrones but has lifted up the humble. He has filled the hungry with good things but has sent the rich away empty. He has helped His servant Israel, remembering to be merciful to Abraham and his descendants forever, even as He said to our fathers' " (vv. 46-55).

The declaration of Mary, no doubt, was inspired by the Holy Spirit but also revealed in Mary an amazing spiritual maturity for a young woman and an intelligent faith in God that comprehended both the historic and the prophetic aspects of her experience.

In her declaration Mary stated that her rejoicing was in God because He had taken her from her humble state and now all generations will call her blessed. She stated that God's mercy extended to those who fear Him and that God performs mighty deeds, bringing down rulers and establishing others. He has filled the hungry and sent the rich away. Most important, He has remembered His promises to Abraham and his descendants. In this declaration Mary was calling attention to the fact that prophecies concerning Abraham and the Davidic kingdom may be expected to have literal fulfillment.

Mary stayed with Elizabeth until just before the birth of John and then returned to Nazareth.

### Prophecy concerning John's Birth Fulfilled

*Luke 1:57-66.* In fulfillment of the prophecy concerning John in due time Elizabeth gave birth and there was great rejoicing. When some wanted to name him after his father Zechariah, Scriptures record, "But his mother spoke up and said, 'No! He is to be called John' " (v. 60). Because no one in her family was named John, they were astonished; but when they asked Zechariah, he called for a tablet and wrote, "His name is John" (v. 63). Then for the first time since he received the announcement, he was able to speak and in his praise to God indicated that the birth of John was an important prophetic event.

### Zechariah's Prophetic Song

*Luke 1:67-80.* As the Scripture indicates, Zechariah, being filled with the Holy Spirit, delivered his prophetic message, "Praise be to the Lord, the God of Israel, because He has come and has redeemed His people. He has raised up a horn of salvation for us in the house of His servant David (as He said through His holy prophets of long ago), salvation from our enemies and from the hand of all who hate us — to show mercy to our faithers and to remember His holy covenant, the oath He swore to our father Abraham: to rescue us from the hand of our enemies, and to enable us to serve Him without fear in holiness and righteousness before all of our days. And you, my child, will be called a prophet of the Most High; for you will go on before the Lord to prepare the way for Him, to give His people the knowledge of salvation through the forgiveness of their sins, because of the tender mercy of our God, by which the rising sun will come to us from heaven to shine on those living in darkness and in the shadow of death, to guide our feet into the path of peace" (vv. 68-79).

In his prophecy Zechariah, referring to Christ, declared that God had raised up someone to bring deliverance through the house of David. He pointed out that the coming of Christ was in fulfillment of His solemn oath to Abraham (v. 73).

In regard to John, Zechariah predicted, "And you, my child, will be called a prophet of the Most High" (v. 76), and will serve as the forerunner to prepare the way for Christ (vv. 76-79). The prophecies through Zechariah, Elizabeth, and Mary were clearly a confirmation of the expectation of the Jews that a Son of David would literally appear and would literally deliver His people from their enemies and bring great blessing and salvation to Israel.

A brief statement concluded the narrative concerning John, indicating that he grew up to be a strong young man and that he lived in the desert until the time of his introduction of Christ (v. 80).

# BACKGROUND OF JESUS AS THE SON OF DAVID
## Matthew's Genealogy

*Matthew 1:1-17.* The Gospel of Matthew is unique in presenting both the life of Christ from a particular point of view and an explanation of why the Old Testament prophecies concerning the kingdom on earth were not fulfilled at the first coming of Christ. Unlike the Gospel of Luke, which is designed to set forth a true historical record of the facts concerning Christ (Luke 1:1-4), the Gospel of Matthew has the specific purpose of explaining to Jews, who expected their Messiah to be a conquering and glorious King, why, instead, Christ lived among men, died on the cross, and rose again. In keeping with this objective, the Gospel of Matthew provides a bridge between the Old Testament prophecies and expectation of the coming of the Messiah of Israel and its fulfillment in the birth and life of Christ.

Accordingly, in the Gospel of Matthew, the lineage of Jesus was traced back to Abraham and David. The genealogy of Matthew ended with Joseph the husband of Mary. Matthew made clear that Jesus was not the son of Joseph but that Mary was His mother (Matt. 1:16). By contrast, the genealogy of Mary was given in Luke 3:23-37 which assured that Christ is a genuine Descendant of David. The genealogy of Matthew supports the concept that Jesus is the legitimate heir to the throne of David through Joseph His father. Even though Joseph was not the human father of Jesus, nevertheless, the right of the royal throne was passed through Joseph to Jesus. Accordingly, Jesus fulfilled the Old Testament expectation that a Son of David would reign on the throne of David forever as Gabriel had announced to Mary (Luke 1:32-33).

A careful study of Matthew's genealogy reveals that it was not intended to be a complete genealogy as only fourteen generations were selected, from Abraham to David and from David to the Babylonian Exile and a third fourteen from the Exile to the time of the birth of Jesus. Matthew 1:13-15 records people in the genealogy of Jesus who are not listed in the Old Testament. Likewise, some names in the Old Testament are not included in the genealogy as in the case of Uzziah who was declared to be the son of Jehoram when actually he was the great-great-grandson of Jehoram (Matt. 1:9; cf. 2 Kings 8:25; 13:1–15:38; 2 Chron. 22–25). The fact that the New Testament includes some names not in the Old Testament and the Old Testament includes some names that are not in the New Testament is one of the reasons why it is impossible to take genealogies as a basis for determining the antiquity of the human race as the Scriptures themselves make plain that this was not the divine intent. On the other hand, it does not justify the point of view that the human race is many thousands of years older than the Scriptures seem to indicate.

Another unusual feature of the genealogies is the prominence of four women who would not normally be included in a genealogy. Each of them has a special background. Tamar (Matt. 1:3) actually got into the line by playing the harlot (Gen. 38:1-30). Rahab the harlot was protected by Joshua when Jericho was captured and became part of the messianic line (Josh. 2:1-6; 6:25). Rahab was declared to be the wife of Salmon the father of Boaz, and this was revealed only in the New Testament (Matt. 1:5). Only Ruth, who is the subject of a beautiful portrayal in the Book of Ruth, had an unspotted record, but even she was not an Israelite. Bathsheba the mother of Solomon, who had formerly been the wife of Uriah, had an adulterous relationship with David which resulted in the murder of her husband (2 Sam. 11:1–12:25). The fact that these women were in the genealogy also put a stop to any Jewish pride. Undoubtedly, Mary also had to withstand the burden of gossip concerning her Son, who was conceived before she was taken by Joseph as his bride.

### The Conception and Birth of Jesus

*Matthew 1:18-24.* When Mary returned from her visit to Elizabeth, she apparently was three months pregnant, and this became evident to Joseph. Not willing to make a public example of Mary by a public divorce, he had in mind divorcing her quietly. Matthew explained, however, that God communicated to Joseph the facts in the case, declaring, "an angel of the Lord appeared to him in a dream and said, 'Joseph son of David, do not be afraid to take Mary home as your wife, because what is conceived in her is from the Holy Spirit. She will give birth to a Son, and you are to give Him the name Jesus, because He will save His people from their sins' " (vv. 20-21). Matthew stated that this was in fulfillment of the prophecy of Isaiah 7:14, "All this took place to fulfill what the Lord had said through the prophet: 'The virgin will be with Child and will give birth to a Son, and they will call Him Immanuel' — which means, 'God with us' " (vv. 22-23).

The Scriptures are silent concerning Mary's anxiety in this whole situation as, apparently, she did not feel free to divulge to Joseph the facts in the case. Having received this instruction from God, however, Joseph "did what the Angel of the Lord had commanded him and took Mary home as his wife. But he had no union with her until she gave birth to a son. And he gave Him the name Jesus" (vv. 24-25). No doubt, both Joseph and Mary suffered malicious gossip concerning this whole matter and were unable to proclaim the truth. For Mary it was a great relief, however, to have Joseph take her home as his wife.

### The Prophecy of the Birth of Jesus Fulfilled

*Luke 2:1-7.* In condensed statement Luke recorded how Joseph and Mary had come back to their home city Bethlehem to be recorded for the tax. Luke took pains to pinpoint the time of the decree as being related to the first census under Quirinius governor of Syria. In simple, direct historical record Luke indicated how Mary gave birth to her Son and placed Him in a manger because the inn was full (vv. 5-7).

### The Angelic Announcement of the Birth of Jesus

*Luke 2:8-14.* The birth of Jesus had none of the trappings of modern publicity. He was born in an obscure town and was placed in a manger because even the innkeeper was unaware of the importance of His birth. The world's publicity would have had Jesus born in Jerusalem, attended by the religious leaders of the Jews, and his birth hailed as an important historic event. God chose to do this differently. Instead of revealing it to the religious hierarchy, the announcement was made to shepherds in a nearby field.

Luke pictured these shepherds in a nearby field to Bethlehem watching their flocks at night. It may well have been the traditional field east of Jerusalem where they were keeping their flocks. In the darkness of the night there suddenly was a glorious light as they saw the glory of the Lord (v. 9). Though they were terrified,

Scripture recorded, "But the angel said to them, 'Do not be afraid. I bring you good news of great joy that will be for all the people. Today in the town of David a Saviour has been born to you; He is Christ the Lord. This will be a sign to you: You will find a Baby wrapped in cloths and lying in a manger' " (vv. 10-12).

As the shepherds struggled to comprehend what was taking place, Scriptures recorded, "Suddenly a great company of the heavenly host appeared with the angel, praising God and saying, 'Glory to God in the highest, and on earth peace to men on whom His favor rests' " (vv. 13-14).

The great event of the birth of Jesus, though little publicized on earth, must have been a sensational development in heaven. One can only contemplate what the angels thought. They knew Jesus in His preincarnate glory in heaven. How could they understand His birth as a man and His lying like a babe in the manger? The unfolding of the life, death, and resurrection of Christ must have been an all-absorbing subject to the heavenly host. It was God's plan that the news should be received by lowly shepherds who witnessed the announcement of the fulfilled prophecy of Jesus being born in Bethlehem and now were contemplating the tremendous fact of the prophecy being fulfilled.

### The Shepherds Visit Jesus

*Luke 2:15-20.* The shepherds hurried into Bethlehem and apparently had little difficulty locating the inn and the manger where Jesus had been placed. Having seen with their own eyes, the shepherds then became the vehicle of announcement to others in Bethlehem that Jesus had been born, and the shepherds returned to their flocks, praising God for His marvelous revelation (v. 20). Mary, meanwhile, was struggling to comprehend the fulfillment of the prophecy that she would be the mother of Jesus, no doubt, wondering how all that she had heard and expected would be fulfilled (v. 19).

### The Prophecy of Simeon
### When Jesus Was Presented in the Temple

*Luke 2:21-35.* When Jesus was presented in the temple on the eighth day to be consecrated, they offered a sacrifice prescribed by the Law for those of very moderate circumstances, a pair of doves and two young pigeons (vv. 21-24). On the occasion of His presentation, Simeon was moved by the Holy Spirit to go into the temple. When Jesus was presented by His parents, Simeon took Him in his arms and praised God (vv. 25-28). His prophetic proclamation was comprehensive, Simeon saying, "Sovereign Lord, as You have promised, You now dismiss Your servant in peace. For my eyes have seen Your salvation, which You have prepared in the sight of all people, a light for revelation to the Gentiles and for glory to Your people Israel" (vv. 29-32). This comprehensive, prophetic vision included not only Jesus as the answer to the hope of Israel but also His revelation of God and His grace to the Gentiles.

Joseph and Mary marveled at what he had said (v. 33). Scripture recorded, "Then Simeon blessed them and said to Mary, his mother: 'This Child is destined to cause the falling and rising of many in Israel, and to be a sign that will be spoken against, so that the thoughts of many hearts will be revealed. And a sword will pierce your own soul too' " (vv. 34-35). This prophecy was to have fulfillment when Jesus died on the cross, something that Mary was unable to understand at the time.

According to Luke, to confirm Simeon's prophecy, Anna came to them at that moment and "gave thanks to God and spoke about the child to all who were looking forward to the redemption of Jerusalem" (v. 38).

### The Visit of the Magi

*Matthew 2:1-12.* The final immediate confirmation of the birth of Jesus as the future King of the Jews came from the visit of the magi who traveled all the way from Persia to find Jesus. The magi were known as people who studied the stars, and it was possible that they saw the light attending the glorious announcement of the angels. They were not without some information about the Messiah as there had been frequent contact between Jews and Persians in the years before the birth of Christ, and the idea that Israel was looking forward to a Messiah was apparently widely known.

There is no indication that the number of the magi was limited to three nor that they were kings though this is often the way they were referred to traditionally. They probably were a larger company. They had apparently sensed what had happened when Christ was born, and it took some months for them to organize and come to Israel to find the Baby Jesus. Because Jerusalem was the center of Jewish religion, the magi came asking, "Where is the One who has been born King of the Jews? We saw His star in the east and have come to worship Him" (v. 2). King Herod was much disturbed by this announcement as he saw in the birth of a Child, destined

destined to be King of the Jews, competition for his own rule. Accordingly, he called the leaders of Israel together to find out where Christ was to be born (vv. 3-4). They replied that He would be born in Bethlehem of Judea and quoted Micah 5:2 in support of their conclusion (Matt. 2:5-6). King Herod attempted to determine then when the star appeared as the time of the child's birth and told the magi to report to him when they found the child (vv. 7-8).

As the magi journeyed to Bethlehem, the star reappeared and led them to the place where the child was. This time it was not a manger but a house, and it is apparent, taking the whole narrative in consideration, that some weeks, if not months, had passed since the birth of Christ. They were overjoyed when they saw Mary and the Child and worshiped Him (vv. 9-11). In recognition of the honored Child, they brought gifts of gold, frankincense, and myrrh (v. 11). Though they probably were not conscious of the meaning of the gifts, obviously, the gold represented the deity of Christ; frankincense, the fragrance of His life; and the myrrh spoke of His sacrifice and death. The magi were warned in a dream not to return to Herod (v. 12).

*Matthew 2:13-15.* The Lord appeared to Joseph in a dream and told him to take the child and His mother to Egypt because of Herod's plot to kill the child (vv. 13-14). Matthew calls our attention to the fact that this was a fulfillment of prophecy, "Out of Egypt I called My Son" (v. 15; Hosea 11:1). Like the nation as a whole, Christ came out of Egypt to come back to the Promised Land.

*Matthew 2:16-18.* When Herod realized that the magi were not going to report to him, he was very angry and ordered that all boys two years old and under in the Bethlehem area should be killed. This resulted in the fulfillment of Jeremiah's prophecy, "A voice is heard in Ramah, weeping and great mourning, Rachel weeping for her children and refusing to be comforted, because they are no more" (v. 18; Jer. 31:15).

### The Return to Nazareth

*Matthew 2:19-23.* After Herod's death Joseph and Mary were able to bring Jesus back to Israel, but because Herod's successor, Archelaus, a son of Herod (v. 22), was also a cruel man, and being warned by God in a dream, they went to live in Nazareth, thus fulfilling the prophecy, "He will be called a Nazarene" (v. 23). This reference to Christ as a Nazarene may be connected to Isaiah 11:1 where Christ was spoken of as "a shoot . . . from the stump of Jesse."

The Hebrew for "shoot" is *"netzer"* which is here assigned a special meaning. As Matthew and Luke both indicated, the events leading up to the birth of Christ, His birth itself, and the events which follow all correspond to the prophetic foreview provided in the Old Testament.

*Luke 2:39-52.* Luke summarized the events following the birth of Christ, stating simply that Joseph and Mary returned to Nazareth and that Jesus grew as a Boy and "was filled with wisdom and the grace of God was upon Him" (vv. 39-40). Except for the brief reference to Jesus going with His parents to the Feast of the Passover in Jerusalem, no other mention was made of Jesus in His boyhood and early manhood (vv. 41-52).

## PROPHECIES IN THE LIFE OF JESUS
### The Ministry of John the Baptist
### as a Forerunner of Christ

*Matthew 3:1-12; Mark 1:2-8; Luke 3:1-18.* For 400 years there had been no prophet in Israel when John the Baptist began his prophetic ministry preaching in the wilderness of Judea. Many in Judea and Jerusalem went out to hear him. John himself made a spectacular appearance, living in rough clothing of camel's hair with a leather belt about his waist. His food was locusts and wild honey. His message was abrupt and unyielding. He urged them to confess their sins (Matt. 3:6; Mark 1:5). He denounced their religious leaders, especially the Pharisees and the Sadducees, calling them a "brood of vipers!" (Matt. 3:7) His message was one of repentance and baptism with water as a sign of their spiritual change. John predicted that after him would come the prophesied One, of whom he declared, "whose sandals I am not fit to carry" (v. 11).

His message was a practical one. If one had two coats, he should share one (Luke 3:11), and they should do likewise with their surplus of food. Publicans were exhorted not to extort taxes but only what was legal. Soldiers were told not to do that which was violent and not to exact anything which was not correct (vv. 13-14). Matthew, Mark, and Luke each viewed John as fulfilling the prophecies of Isaiah 40:3, "A voice of one calling in the desert, 'Prepare the way for the Lord, make straight paths for Him' " (Matt. 3:3; Mark 1:3; Luke 3:4; cf. Isa. 40:3-5). Though John the Baptist knew Jesus as an individual, he probably did not know that He was the prophesied Messiah until Jesus presented Himself for baptism. John made it clear that he was not the Messiah, but he also anticipated that the true Messiah might appear at any time.

### Jesus Baptized by John in the Jordan

*Matthew 3:13-17; Mark 1:9-11; Luke 3:21-22.* When John demurred at the thought of baptizing Jesus, he, nevertheless, was exhorted to do so. After Jesus was baptized, Matthew, Mark, and Luke all record the voice from heaven declaring that Jesus was the beloved Son of the Father. Luke declared that Jesus at His baptism had the Holy Spirit descending on Him as a dove and the voice from heaven speaking as God the Father, a clear indication of the Trinity, the Father, Son, and Holy Spirit. The commendation of Jesus by God the Father was anticipated in Psalm 2:7 and Isaiah 42:1.

### The Kingdom of God at Hand

*Matthew 4:17; Mark 1:14-15; Luke 4:14-15.* Upon His arrival in Galilee, Jesus preached His central message, "The time has come. . . . The kingdom of God is near. Repent and believe the good news!" This central aspect of His prophetic ministry persisted throughout the three years of His public preaching.

### The Danger of False Profession

*Matthew 7:15-27; Luke 6:46-49.* Jesus warned His disciples of those who profess faith but are not true believers. He declared that they were false prophets and were wolves not sheep (Matt. 7:15). Jesus predicted that the difference will be demonstrated in the fruit that they bear, as a good tree will bear good fruit and a bad tree will bear bad fruit (vv. 16-20). Jesus also predicted that those who are guilty of mere profession will not enter the kingdom of heaven (vv. 21-23).

Jesus illustrated this in the Parable of the Two Builders and the Two Houses. Those who build their house on a rock illustrate a wise man who is true in his faith in God and when a storm arises his house will not fail because it is founded on the rock (vv. 24-25). By contrast, those who profess faith but do not follow in real trust in God are like a house built on the sand which is destroyed when the storm comes (vv. 26-27).

### True Believers in Jesus to Enter the Kingdom of Heaven

*Matthew 8:5-13; Luke 7:1-10.* When Jesus entered Capernaum, a centurion approached Him, asking that He would heal his servant who was in terrible suffering at his home. Jesus responded that He would go and heal him (Matt. 8:5-7). The centurion replied, however, that it was not necessary for Him to go because He could command just as the centurion commanded his soldiers to do things and it would be done (vv. 8-9).

The Scriptures record, "When Jesus heard this, He was astonished and said to those following Him, 'I tell you the truth, I have not found anyone in Israel with such great faith. I say to you that many will come from the east and the west, and will take their places at the feast with Abraham, Isaac and Jacob in the kingdom of heaven. But the subjects of the kingdom will be thrown outside, into the darkness, where there will be weeping and gnashing of teeth' " (vv. 10-12). Then the Scriptures further recorded, "Then Jesus said to the centurion, 'Go! It will be done just as you believed it would.' And his servant was healed at that very hour" (v. 13).

### Judgment Pronounced on Korazin, Bethsaida, and Capernaum

*Matthew 11:20-24.* In the cities where most of His miracles had been performed, Christ declared them under God's righteous judgment because they should have responded in repentance. He stated, "Woe to you, Korazin! Woe to you, Bethsaida! If the miracles that were performed in you had been performed in Tyre and Sidon, they would have repented long ago in sackcloth and ashes" (v. 21). Jesus further declared, "It will be more bearable for Tyre and Sidon on the day of judgment than for you" (v. 22). Jesus declared that Tyre and Sidon would have repented if they had seen the same miracles as these cities had witnessed (v. 21).

A final judgment was pronounced on Capernaum. Jesus declared, "If the miracles that were performed in you had been performed in Sodom, it would have remained to this day. But I tell you that it will be more bearable for Sodom on the day of judgment than for you" (vv. 23-24; cf. Matt. 10:15).

Today Capernaum, in particular, is an eloquent witness of God's judgment on it for it stands in ruins at the north end of the Sea of Galilee in contrast to Tiberias on the west shore of Galilee which has never been destroyed.

### The Invitation to Rest in Christ

*Matthew 11:28-30.* In view of His rejection on the part of those who had seen the miracles, Christ extended the invitation to individuals to come and put their trust in Christ. He stated, "Come to Me, all you who are weary and burdened, and I will give you rest. Take My yoke upon you and learn from Me, for I am gentle and humble in heart, and you will find rest for your souls. For My yoke is easy and My burden is light" (vv. 28-30). In contrast to His addressing the nation as a group, Jesus now extended the invitation to personal faith and commitment to any individual who would come to Him in faith.

### Jesus in His Healing Ministry Would Fulfill Prophecy

*Matthew 12:9-20.* Because Jesus had healed on the Sabbath, the Pharisees plotted to kill Him (vv. 9-14). Knowing of their plots to kill Him, Jesus then quoted from Isaiah 42:1-4, the prophecy that was being fulfilled in His healing ministry. "Aware of this, Jesus withdrew from that place. Many followed Him, and He healed all their sick, warning them not to tell who He was. This was to fulfill what was spoken through the Prophet Isaiah: 'Here is My Servant whom I have chosen, the One I love, in whom I delight; I will put My Spirit on Him, and He will proclaim justice to the nations. He will not quarrel or cry out; no one will hear His voice in the streets. A bruised reed He will not break, and a smoldering wick He will not snuff out, till He leads to victory' " (Matt. 12:15-20).

As Isaiah prophesied, Jesus was a delight to God the Father, beloved and indwelt by the Holy Spirit. He would proclaim justice but would not quarrel or cry out. His would ultimately be the victory (vv. 18-20).

### Warning against Careless Words of Unbelief

*Matthew 12:32-37; Mark 3:28-30.* In reply to those who had accused Him of performing miracles by Beelzebub (Matt. 12:24), Jesus had pointed out how inconsistent this was as the devil would be fighting his own possessions. He warns, however, "And so I tell you, every sin and blasphemy will be forgiven men, but the blasphemy against the Spirit will not be forgiven. Anyone who speaks a word against the Son of man will be forgiven, but anyone who speaks against the Holy Spirit will not be forgiven, either in this age or in the age to come" (vv. 31-32).

This declaration of Christ has raised the question as to whether there are some sins that are not subject to pardon. The point is that if they reject the demonstration that Christ is the Son of God on the basis of the miracles He performs, they are denying what the Holy Spirit is using to bring conviction and faith; and as long as they do this, their sins are not subject to being pardoned. In the twentieth century this sin is no longer possible because no one is a witness to these miracles, but the principle abides that rejecting the ministry of the Holy Spirit to an individual can lead to his confirmed unbelief. The rejection of the very instrument which God uses to bring faith can only result in the penalty assigned to unbelievers.

## Condemnation of Those Seeking a Sign

*Matthew 12:38-45.* In reply to some of the Pharisees and teachers of the Law who demanded a miraculous sign, Jesus replied that they would receive no sign except the sign of Jonah, for just as Jonah was in the huge fish three days and three nights, so Jesus would be in the heart of the earth three days and three nights. Nineveh, who repented at the message of Jonah, would rise up in judgment against them (v. 41). The Queen of the South would also condemn them because she honored Solomon, and now One greater than Solomon has appeared (v. 42). Jesus described the worthlessness of moral renewal without real faith as one of inviting evil spirits to take up their abode. Jesus stated, "That is how it will be with this wicked generation" (v. 45).

## Warning concerning the Cost of Discipleship

*Matthew 10:24-42.* Jesus warned His disciples that if the Pharisees called Him Beelzebub (v. 25), they could expect similar treatment. He warned them, however, "So do not be afraid of them. There is nothing concealed that will not be disclosed, or hidden that will not be made known" (v. 26). Jesus also indicated that those who received a prophet as sent from God would be rewarded (v. 41). Jesus also said, "And if anyone gives even a cup of cold water to one of these little ones because he is My disciple, I tell you the truth, he will certainly not lose his reward" (v. 42).

*Matthew 12:41-42.* Nineveh as well as the Queen of the South would rise up to condemn their unbelief (vv. 41-42).

*Matthew 12:43-45; cf. Luke 11:24-26.* Self-reformation will lead only to a worse spiritual condition as it is not a permanent solution to the problem of sin.

## Jesus' Prediction of the Building of His Church and the Giving of the Keys of the Kingdom to the Disciples

*Matthew 16:17-19.* In His first prediction concerning the future prediction of the church, Jesus declared that it would be built upon Peter in the sense that he would belong to the first generation of Christians. Furthermore, He would give to Peter and the other disciples the keys of the kingdom of heaven which is the message of the Gospel that through Christ they can enter the kingdom of heaven (vv. 18-19).

### Jesus' Warning against the Danger of
### Being Ashamed of Him

*Matthew 16:24-27; Mark 8:34-38; Luke 9:23-27.* Jesus pointed out that following Christ involves taking up the will of God as their cross and following Him (Matt. 16:24). He promised to reward everyone according to his commitment to Jesus Christ (v. 27). The same truth is embodied in Luke's statement (Luke 9:23-27). Jesus further declared that some who were standing before Him would not taste death until they see the kingdom of God (Luke 9:27). This must have been fulfilled by the Transfiguration which immediately followed when the disciples saw in prophetic vision the future glory of Christ and the coming of His kingdom.

### Promise to Answer Prayer

*Matthew 18:19-20.* If two agree on earth as concerning a prayer request, their prayer will be answered. This was especially true for the twelve disciples.

### Warning against Mistreating a Brother

*Matthew 18:15-18, 21-35.* Jesus used an illustration of a servant who had been forgiven by his master but, nevertheless, inflicted punishment on one that owed him. Jesus warned, "This is how My Heavenly Father will treat each of you unless you forgive your brother from your heart" (v. 35; cf. Luke 17:3-4).

### Jesus' Denunciation of Those Who Reject
### the Seventy-Two Disciples

*Luke 10:1-24.* In connection with the seventy-two that were sent out to every town and place, He predicted that some would receive them and some would not, but that those who did not receive them would find it more bearable for Sodom in the final judgment than for them (cf. Matt. 11:20-24). The same is true where Christ performed miracles (vv. 13-14).

### Persistent Prayer Urged

*Luke 11:1-13; cf. Matt. 6:9-15.* In response to the disciples' request, He gave them what is known as the Lord's Prayer (Luke 11:2-4). Actually, it was the disciples' prayer, not the Lord's prayer. Jesus used the illustration of their need for bread. When a friend drops in and the host goes to his neighbor to ask for bread, the neighbor will get up and give it to the host. And so Jesus urged them, "So I say to you: Ask and it will be given to you; seek and you will find; knock and the door will be opened to you. For everyone who asks receives; he who seeks finds; and to him who knocks, the door will be opened" (vv. 9-10). He also assured them that what they receive will be a good gift (vv. 11-13).

### Warning against Hypocrisy and Unbelief

*Luke 12:1-12; cf. Matthew 16:6-12; Mark 8:14-21.* The disciples were warned to be on their guard against the yeast and leaven of the Pharisees (Luke 12:1) which is hypocrisy. Though hypocrisy can be concealed for a time, Jesus declared, "There is nothing concealed that will not be disclosed, or hidden that will not be made known. What you have said in the dark will be heard in the daylight, and what you have whispered in the ear in the inner rooms will be proclaimed from the housetops" (vv. 2-3). The hypocrisy of all unbelievers will be discerned and they will be judged at their final judgment.

Jesus declared that they have more value to God than sparrows and that the very hairs on their head are numbered (vv. 4-7). Jesus further declared that if men disown Him before men, they will be disowned before the angels of God (v. 9). He promised them also that when they are tried before the rulers of the synagogue that God would give them words to say (vv. 11-12).

### Warning against Materialism

*Luke 12:13-40.* Jesus declared that they should "Watch out! Be on your guard against all kinds of greed; a man's life does not consist in the abundance of his possessions" (v. 15). He used an illustration of a man who tears down his barn to build bigger ones (vv. 16-21) only to die unexpectedly. Jesus declared, "Therefore I tell you, do not worry about your life, what you will eat; or about your body, what you will wear. Life is more than food, and the body more than clothes. Consider the ravens: They do not sow or reap, they have no storeroom or barn; yet God feeds them. And how much more valuable you are than birds!" (vv. 22-24) He promised that those who seek the kingdom of God first will have treasure in heaven (vv. 31-33).

### Warning against Superficial Faith and His Lament over Jerusalem in Its Unbelief

*Luke 13:22-32.* Jesus warned them that it was necessary to have real faith as only a few people will be saved. It will not be enough to say, "We ate and drank with You, and You taught in our streets" (v. 26). They will see the saved—Abraham, Isaac, and Jacob and the prophets—going into the kingdom, but they themselves will be shut out (vv. 28-29).

### Warning of Judgment of Jerusalem

*Luke 13:33-35.* At the close of this section Jesus laments, however, over Jerusalem and its unbelief and rejection of the prophets, "O Jerusalem, Jerusalem, you who kill the prophets and stone those sent to you, how often I have longed to gather your children together, as a hen gathers her chicks under her wings, but you were not willing! Look, your house is left to you desolate. I tell you, you will not see Me again until you say, 'Blessed is He who comes in the name of the Lord' " (vv. 34-35; cf. Matt. 23:37-39).

### Warning against Rejecting the Invitation to the Lord's Banquet

*Luke 14:1-24.* Jesus recited how important it is to be invited to the banquet of God. He gave the illustration of preparing a banquet and inviting many guests who do not come. Each made one excuse after another (vv. 16-20). Upon hearing of their rejection, the master urges them to bring in the poor, crippled, blind, and lame (v. 21). He ended the discussion by saying, "I tell you, not one of those men who were invited will get a taste of My banquet" (v. 24).

### The Rewards of His Disciples

*Mark 10:28-31; Luke 18:28-30.* In regard to the disciples' question as to what they will receive in eternity, Jesus replied, "I tell you the truth . . . no one who has left home or brothers or sisters or mother or father or children or fields for Me and the Gospel will fail to receive a hundred times as much in this present age (homes, brothers, sisters, mothers, children and fields—and with them, persecutions) and in the age to come, eternal life. But many who are first will be last, and the last first" (Mark 10:29-31). In making these promises, Jesus was asserting that not only are there some rewards that are present for a believer and follower of Christ, but other rewards will be given abundantly in heaven.

### The Reward of Faithful Service

*Luke 19:11-27.* In the Parable of the Nobleman who gave three servants ten minas each to care for the workmen while he was gone, the two servants who were faithful and increased the lord's money by hard service were rewarded, but the one who hid his lord's money, perhaps thinking that his lord would not come back, was judged and the money taken from him and given to the one who had earned the ten minas. Jesus, in connection with this, stated, "I tell you that to everyone who has, more will be given, but as for the one who has nothing, even what he has will be taken away" (v. 26).

What the successful servant had was faith that his lord would come back and that he would reward faithful and obedient service. What was true of these servants is true of all who follow Jesus.

**Jesus' Answer to the Pharisees' Challenge of His Authority**
*Matthew 21:23–22:14; Mark 11:27–12:12; Luke 20:1-19.* The chief priests and the elders had come to Christ asking the question, " 'By what authority are You doing these things?' they asked, 'And who gave You this authority?' " (Matt. 21:23) Jesus replied by asking another question, "John's baptism—where did it come from? Was it from heaven, or from men?" (v. 25) The chief priests and the others were unable to answer because they did not recognize John as a prophet as the people had, but they did not dare say that he was not a prophet. Accordingly, Jesus replied that He would not answer their question either. He followed this conversation, however, with a series of parables to illustrate what He was talking about.

One son said he would not go but did go and work in the vineyard; the other said he would go but did not (vv. 28-31). On the basis of this illustration, Jesus told them, "I tell you the truth, the tax collectors and the prostitutes are entering the kingdom of God ahead of you. For John came to show you the way of righteousness, and you did not believe him, but the tax collectors and prostitutes did. And even after you saw this, you did not repent and believe him" (vv. 31-32).

This was followed by another parable about the owner of a vineyard who sent his servants to collect the rent, but the tenants beat some and killed others (vv. 33-35). Finally he sent his son, and the tenants took and killed him. Jesus raised the question, "Therefore, when the owner of the vineyard comes, what will he do to those tenants?" (v. 40) His listeners, of course, said that the owner would judge them for it. Jesus then made the application that He, like the stone which the builders rejected (v. 42), was going to be the capstone (v. 42). In other words, though they could reject Him now, the time would come when they would pay the price and Jesus would become the capstone of the building. Jesus predicted, "Therefore I tell you that the kingdom of God will be taken away from you and given to a people who will produce its fruit. He who falls on this stone will be broken to pieces, but he on whom it falls will be crushed" (vv. 43-44). The Pharisees caught on that He was talking about their rejecting Christ's message and their being subject to future punishment.

A final illustration was used by Christ to drive home His point in which He used the Parable of a Wedding Banquet. Those who were invited had one excuse after another and would not come, and he sent his servants to invite others, whomever they could. When the king came to the feast, Jesus said that one of them did not have a wedding garment, "But when the king came in to see the guests, he noticed a man there who was not wearing wedding clothes. 'Friend,' he asked, 'how did you get in here without wedding clothes?' The man was speechless" (Matt. 22:11-12). The point in this parable is that the guests were invited and the wedding garments were furnished by the one putting on the banquet, and there was no excuse for him not having a wedding garment. Accordingly, in the illustration Jesus had them cast the man into the outer darkness because he could not participate in the feast. Without salvation, it is impossible to go to heaven.

### Jesus' Answer to the Question of the Saducees about Resurrection

*Matthew 22:23-33; Mark 12:18-27; Luke 20:27-40.* Because the Sadducees did not believe in the resurrection of the body, they thought they could trap Jesus with a theoretical story of a woman who had seven husbands. They raised the question as to whose wife she would be in heaven. Jesus answered them. First of all, in regard to their particular question, Jesus said, "You are in error because you do not know the Scriptures or the power of God. At the resurrection people will neither marry nor be given in marriage; they will be like the angels in heaven" (Matt. 22:29-30). Jesus also took up the basic question about resurrection and added, "But about the resurrection of the dead — have you not read what God said to you, 'I am the God of Abraham, the God of Isaac, and the God of Jacob'? He is not the God of the dead but of the living" (vv. 31-32). The Sadducees, having been silenced, did not dare to ask further questions.

### Denunciation of the Scribes and the Pharisees

*Matthew 23:1-39; Mark 12:38-40; Luke 20:45-47.* Christ denounced the Pharisees first of all because they sought to exalt themselves instead of being servants (Matt. 23:1-11). Jesus predicted that those who humble themselves will be exalted but that the Pharisees would be shut out of the kingdom (vv. 12-13).

After the severe denunciation of the scribes and Pharisees (vv. 15-26), Jesus predicted, "You snakes! You brood of vipers! How will you escape being condemned to hell? Therefore I am sending you prophets and wise men and teachers. Some of them you will kill and crucify; others you will flog in your synagogues and pursue from town to town. And so upon you will come all the righteous blood that has been shed on the earth, from the blood of righteous Abel to the blood of Zechariah son of Berekiah, whom you murdered between the temple and the altar. I tell you the truth, all this will come upon this generation" (vv. 33-36). This solemn denunciation of the Pharisees was by way of preparation for the prophetic Olivet Discourse in Matthew 24–25; Mark 13:1-35; Luke 21:5-36.

### The Prophecies of Jesus at the Last Passover Feast

*Matthew 26:17-75; Mark 14:12-72; Luke 22:7-71.* In connection with the last twenty-four hours of Jesus' life on earth prior to His crucifixion, a number of prophecies were given in addition to the discourse in the Upper Room (John 13–17) which will be given separate treatment. Jesus announced that one of them would betray Him, "I tell you the truth, one of you will betray Me" (Matt. 26:21). When each of them disclaimed this, Jesus replied, "The one who has dipped his hand into the bowl with Me will betray Me. The Son of man will go just as it is written about Him. But woe to the man who betrays the Son of man! It would be better for him if he had not been born" (vv. 23-24). After this prediction Scriptures recorded that "Judas, the one who would betray Him, said, 'Surely not I, Rabbi?' Jesus answered, 'Yes, it is you' " (v. 25). Judas later that night betrayed Jesus.

While they were observing the institution of the Lord's Supper at the time of the Passover feast, Jesus declared, "I tell you, I will not drink of this fruit of the vine from now on until that day when I drink it anew with you in My Father's kingdom" (v. 29). Jesus was referring to the millennial kingdom when they would again be together following their resurrection.

After they had left the Upper Room and had gone on their way to the Mount of Olives, Jesus said to them, "This very night you will all fall away on account of Me, for it is written: 'I will strike the Shepherd, and the sheep of the flock will be scattered.' But after I have risen, I will go ahead of you into Galilee" (vv. 31-32). When Peter denied that he would do this, Jesus said, "I tell you the truth . . . this very night, before the rooster crows, you will disown Me three times" (v. 34; Mark 14:29-32; Luke 22:34; John 13:35-38). This prophecy, accordingly, was fulfilled later that night as well as the prophecy that all the disciples would flee.

In connection with His questioning before the Sanhedrin, He was asked by the high priest, "I charge you under oath by the living God: Tell us if You are the Christ, the Son of God" (v. 63). " 'Yes, it is as you say,' Jesus replied. 'But I say to all of you: In the future you will see the Son of man sitting at the right hand of the Mighty One and coming on the clouds of heaven' " (v. 64). The high priest took this as the same as claiming to be God and declared Him worthy of death (vv. 64-66).

### The Disciples Told to Meet Jesus in Galilee

*Matthew 28:7; Mark 16:7.* As the disciples gradually comprehended the fact Jesus was indeed raised from the dead, they were informed by the angel at the tomb that Christ would meet them in Galilee. Actually, He met them several times much sooner than that but did meet them in Galilee later (John 21:1).

## PROPHECY IN RELATION TO THE SERMON ON THE MOUNT

### The Ethical Character of the Sermon on the Mount

*Matthew 5–7; Mark 4:21-23; 10:2-12; Luke 6:20:49; 8:16-18.* The Jews, in their anticipation of their coming Messiah, had realized when He came that there would be political independence from their enemies and material blessings on the nation Israel. What they had overlooked, however, was that the future kingdom when Christ would reign would have certain spiritual principles as well which would characterize the period. Because of their one-sided emphasis on the political, the Sermon on the Mount was delivered by Christ to emphasize the ethical principles of the King.

Interpretations of the Sermon on the Mount have varied from the extreme of holding that it is entirely prophetic and not fulfilled before the Second Coming to the other extreme where it is taken as the Gospel message of the way of salvation for the present age. A careful reading of the Sermon on the Mount supports the conclusion that what Christ was dealing with were the ethical principles of the kingdom which will come into play in the future millennial kingdom but to some extent are applicable now. Accordingly, in the Sermon on the Mount there are frequent references to the present and how the principles He is annunciating should be applied. At the same time there is the distant view of the realization of these ethical principles when Christ will be reigning on earth.

## The Prophetic Character of the Beatitudes

*Matthew 5:1-12; Luke 6:20-23.* The Beatitudes are a good illustration of the ethical character of the kingdom, including present blessing but also future reward. Each of the Beatitudes speaks of present blessing and then the ultimate blessing in the kingdom. Accordingly, those who are "poor in spirit" will possess "the kingdom of heaven" (Matt. 5:3). Those who "mourn" are promised "they will be comforted" (v. 4). Those who are "the meek" are promised that "they will inherit the earth" (v. 5). Those at the present time "who hunger and thirst for righteousness" are promised that "they will be filled" (v. 6). Those who are "merciful" will have mercy shown them (v. 7). Those who are "pure in heart" are promised that "they will see God" (v. 8). Those who are "the peacemakers" are promised that they "will be called sons of God" (v. 9). Those who are "persecuted because of righteousness" are promised that "theirs is the kingdom of heaven" (v. 10). These Beatitudes are general in their promise to anyone who qualifies.

Immediately following, Jesus made an application to the disciples themselves. He declared, "Blessed are you when people insult you, persecute you and falsely say all kinds of evil against you because of Me. Rejoice and be glad, because great is your reward in heaven, for in the same way they persecuted the prophets who were before you" (vv. 11-12). What is true of the Beatitudes is true of other promises in the Sermon on the Mount. There is present application, and there is future promise of reward.

## The Truths of the Law or the Prophets
## to Be Fulfilled in the Future Kingdom

*Matthew 5:17-20.* The dispensation of the Mosaic Law was to be brought to its end in the earth by Christ, but its end would not be one of being abolished but one of being fulfilled. Accordingly, as Paul wrote in 2 Corinthians 3:13, "the radiance" of the Law "was fading away." Likewise, the Galatians were instructed, "Now that faith has come, we are no longer under the supervision of the Law" (Gal. 3:25). The Mosaic Law was limited in its application to the nation Israel and was limited as to its continuance because it was to be fulfilled by Christ and succeeded by another dispensation.

The spiritual and moral principles of the Law, however, continue, and Jesus declared, "I tell you the truth, until heaven and earth disappear, not the smallest letter, not the least stroke of a pen, will by any means disappear from the Law until everything is accomplished" (v. 18). Accordingly, though the Mosaic Law as a direct application was terminated, the moral and spiritual principles involved were to continue forever. In this statement Jesus was affirming the inspiration of Scripture extending not simply to the words but also to the smallest letter or the smallest part of a letter. The smallest Hebrew letter was *yod,* and the smallest part of a letter was probably *tittle* which refers to the smallest part of a letter being changed and affecting its meaning. An illustration in English is provided in the English capital letter "E." If the bottom horizontal line is removed, it becomes a capital "F." In the letter "E," the *tittle* is the bottom horizontal line.

Building on this revelation, Jesus declared that breaking the commandments and teaching others to do this will call for judgment, resulting in some not entering the kingdom. On the other hand, those who obey the Law and the moral principles of the kingdom "will be called great in the kingdom of heaven" (v. 19).

### The Law's Requirement of Reconciliation Before Sacrifice

*Matthew 5:21-26.* The Law was clear that one should not murder another, but the full application of the Law indicated that one should be careful even about foolish speaking, such as calling a person a fool (v. 22). If one was offering a sacrifice but had not settled things with his brother, one should settle things first with him and then bring one's sacrifice (vv. 23-26).

### The Law Applied to Adultery and Divorce

*Matthew 5:27-32.* Though divorce was easily accomplished in the Old Testament, looking at a woman in lust was adultery, and divorce should be granted only for marital unfaithfulness (vv. 28, 32).

### The Application of the Law to Oaths, Resisting Evil People, and Generous Giving as a Fulfillment of the Spiritual Character of the Law

*Matthew 5:33-42.* Careless oaths will bring trouble both in time and eternity (vv. 33-36). Retaliation of evil for evil is also forbidden (vv. 38-39). Likewise, one should not resist if another wants to rob him or take his cloak or ask to borrow money (vv. 40-42). These commands are illustrative of the ultimate character of the Law which, in these instances, will not be able to achieve full application until the millennial kingdom.

### Loving One's Enemies

*Matthew 5:43-48; Luke 6:27-36.* Though the Law instructed to love your neighbor, the highest application of the Law would be that of loving one's enemies (Matt. 5:43-45). Even worldly tax collectors love those who reward them (vv. 46-47). The perfect standard, of course, is God's love to us embodied in the exhortation, "Be perfect, therefore, as your Heavenly Father is perfect" (v. 48).

The Gospel of Luke, which also records this portion of the Sermon on the Mount, emphasized the need to love your neighbor (Luke 6:27-36). Likewise, we should not judge others but forgive them (v. 37). The Law provides that Jews should be generous and they would be blessed in proportion as they are generous to others (v. 38). Luke also enlarged on the need not to judge each other by using an illustration of a person who has a large obstacle in his own eye and attempts to take the speck out of his brother's eye. Instead, he should clear up his own eyesight first (Luke 6:41-42).

### The Life of Faith Forbids Hypocrisy

*Matthew 6:1-8.* When acting righteously, an individual should not display his act to be seen by men for this will prohibit his getting reward in heaven (v. 1). Our giving of our substance should be in secret lest we lose our eternal reward (vv. 2-4). Prayer should be devoid of hypocrisy and not be given in public in order to be heard by men (v. 5). Instead, the ideal is to pray in secret, avoiding vain repetition, recognizing that God knows our request before we give it (vv. 6-8).

### The Model Prayer

*Matthew 6:9-15; Luke 11:1-4.* This prayer, offered as a model by Christ to His disciples, has present application and also future fulfillment. It anticipates the future kingdom (v. 10). It exhorts to forgiveness now of those who sin against us in view of God's future forgiveness of us (v. 12). The promise was reiterated that if we forgive men, God will forgive us. This is on the family level rather than on the judicial level as, obviously, Christians are justified by faith and do not need forgiveness in the judicial sense.

### Hypocrisy Again Denounced

*Matthew 6:16-18.* When they fasted, they were instructed not to disfigure themselves or make it obvious that they were fasting. Rather, God should be considered as the witness to what they were doing, and reward was promised (vv. 17-18). Treasure in heaven is contrasted to treasure on earth.

### Treasures in Heaven

*Matthew 6:19-34.* Jesus reminded them that earthly treasures can be stolen or spoiled. Those who have their treasure in heaven have it in a safe place (vv. 19-21). Coveting money is also contrary to God's will (vv. 22-23). One cannot serve money and serve God at the same time (v. 24).

Proper understanding that earthly treasure is temporary does much to take away worry about this life (v. 25). Jesus used the illustration of birds that were fed by their Heavenly Father. If God feeds them, He also will take care of us (v. 26). After all, worry does not add anything to life (v. 27). This was illustrated by the lilies of the field and the grass of the field which are only temporary in their value (vv. 28-32). The basic law is stated, "But seek first His kingdom and His righteousness, and all these things will be given to you as well" (v. 33). In these exhortations, as many others in the Sermon on the Mount, the present is linked to future reward and future riches. The life of faith, as illustrated in Matthew 6, is impossible without realization of the real riches that are stored in heaven.

### Unjust Criticism Condemned
*Matthew 7:1-6; Luke 6:37-45.* Keeping the spiritual principles of the kingdom involves not being involved in judging others when we should be considering our own shortcomings (Matt. 7:1-5).

### Jesus' Encouraging His Disciples to Pray
*Matthew 7:7-11; cf. Luke 11:5-13.* Jesus again encouraged the disciples to pray for present blessings as well as future reward. Just as a father would not give his son a stone instead of bread (Matt. 7:9) or a snake instead of a fish (v. 10), like a good earthly father, God can give good gifts to His children.

### The Golden Rule
*Matthew 7:12; Luke 6:31.* The basic law of serving others well, as we would expect them to serve us, is the essence of the Law and the Prophets (Matt. 7:12), and what we do would have eternal reward.

### The Two Ways
*Matthew 7:13-27; Luke 6:43-49.* The Sermon on the Mount closed with emphasis on the fact that men constantly have to choose between two ways. The way to salvation is narrow, and only a few find it, often because they are not seeking it (Matt. 7:13-14). False prophets can be contrasted to true prophets and recognized by their fruit (vv. 15-20). Their fruit also will be a basis for judgment in eternity.

The contrast between true faith and false profession also will have its ultimate revelation (vv. 21-23).

The ultimate illustration of the two ways is presented as a contrast between true foundations and false foundations. A house constructed by a wise man will be built upon a rock (v. 24). The foolish man will build his house upon the sand (v. 26). When tested by the rain and the storm, the house on the rock endures; the house on the sand crumbles (vv. 25, 27). Even a life built on ethical principles will not survive unless it is built on true faith in God and reliance on His grace for salvation. Though some other exhortations will have their complete fulfillment in the millennial kingdom, many of the truths which are revealed here apply to the present life as well as to the future.

## THE MYSTERIES OF THE KINGDOM OF HEAVEN
### *The Purpose of God in the Revelation of the Parables*

Matthew 13, presenting seven parables of the kingdom of heaven, is a unique chapter in the Gospels because it deals with the kingdom of heaven in its mystery form, that is, the kingdom of heaven as it will be fulfilled in the present age before the Second Coming.

The Jews had expected their Messiah to deliver them politically from their oppressors and establish them as the leading nation of the world. It became increasingly obvious that Jesus was not going to fulfill this expectation. Accordingly, Matthew is presenting the truth to explain the real answer to this question to those among the Jews who were questioning the role of Jesus as the Messiah.

Earlier in the Gospel of Matthew the lineage of Jesus from David to Joseph, His legal father, constituted proof that Jesus was indeed qualified to be the Messiah. The record of His conception and birth, also presented in Matthew, made clear that Jesus was the One promised to be born of a virgin in Isaiah 7:14. The visit of the magi confirmed that Jesus was indeed the Messiah.

With the coming of John the Baptist, Jesus was baptized and had the further witness of John that He was indeed the promised One.

The problem with the Jews was that their expectation of their Messiah was one-sided. They had anticipated the political side of it only, that is, that Jesus would redeem them from their enemies. The Jews did not realize that the coming kingdom would also have demands on them in the way of spiritual life. To correct this, Jesus delivered the Sermon on the Mount as recorded in Matthew 5–7. Only Matthew recorded all these parables though Mark also re-

369

vealed the Parable of the Sower and the Parable of the Mustard Seed (Mark 4:1-9, 13-20, 30-32; Luke 8:5-15). The Parable of the Leaven, not found in Mark, is revealed in Luke 13:20-21.

The high ethical standards of the kingdom to come did not appeal to the Jewish people. In support of His revelation, Jesus performed many miracles, as described in Matthew 8–10, but, in general, the Jewish people rejected Jesus though many individuals became His followers. Because of this, Jesus turned to the individual rather than to the nation as a whole, inviting them to come to Him and find rest (Matt. 11:28-30). As the opposition of the Jews increased, Christ delivered His own denunciation of their unbelief and hardness of heart in Matthew 12.

In view of the fact that the Jews, for the most part, had rejected Christ, the moral standards of His kingdom, and the evidence that Jesus was indeed the Messiah, Jesus now turned to what would result, namely, that the kingdom would not come immediately but that, instead, a new form of the kingdom would be fulfilled that was not anticipated in Old Testament revelation.

The idea of a postponed kingdom has been opposed by some who view God as changing His mind and as nullifying the offer of Christ as Messiah and as King of the Jews. It should be understood that postponement of God's plan to bring in the kingdom is only from the human side. From the divine side, the plan of God included this contingency. God knew a rejection would take place and that His purpose concerning the present age would accordingly be fulfilled.

The comparison may be made between Israel at Kadesh Barnea and the followers of Jesus in the first century. At Kadesh Barnea the Children of Israel were promised the land if they would go in and possess it (Num. 13:26–14:25). The entrance of the Children of Israel into the Promised Land was delayed forty years because of their unbelief. This was anticipated, however, in the plan of God and does not represent a change of mind on the part of God, but rather a change in human expectation of fulfillment of God's purpose.

In Matthew 13, accordingly, Jesus answers the question as to what is going to happen before Christ comes back to set up His kingdom. Jesus does not reveal all the details of this period but rather the general character of the present age. What He reveals to them is in parables designed to be understood by the people of God but not by unbelievers. The truth that Jesus revealed is declared to be a mystery, "the secrets of the kingdom of heaven" (Matt. 13:11).

As defined in Scripture, a mystery is a truth that is not discerned simply by investigation, but a truth that requires revelation. Generally speaking, it refers to a truth hidden in the Old Testament and unknown to that period, but a truth which is now revealed. A definition is found in Colossians 1:26 where the mystery, or secret, is defined, "the mystery that has been kept hidden for ages and generations, but is now disclosed to the saints." Similar references can be found to mysteries throughout the New Testament (Rom. 11:25; 16:25; 1 Cor. 2:7; 4:1; 13:2; 14:2; 15:51; Eph. 1:9; 3:3-4, 9; 5:32; 6:19; Col. 1:27; 2:2; 4:3; 2 Thes. 2:7; 1 Tim. 3:16; Rev. 1:20; 10:7; 17:5, 7).

From these passages it becomes evident that a mystery is not a truth hard to understand but one that requires revelation before understanding is possible. Because the present age was largely hidden from the Old Testament, where Christ's first and second coming are often presented as the same event, truths to be fulfilled in the present age constitute mysteries or truth once not revealed but now revealed. The setting for the message on the mysteries of the kingdom was along the Lake of Galilee where Jesus sat in a boat and a large crowd stood on the shore hearing Him speak.

### The Parable of the Sower and Various Kinds of Soil

*Matthew 13:1-9; Mark 4:1-20; Luke 8:4-15.* In presenting the parables, Jesus used illustrations that referred to common aspects of life in Israel. In this first parable Jesus described how there was a variety of reception of the seed. Sometimes farmers would sow where they had not even plowed, and Jesus referred to the seed falling on a hard, beaten path where it would be unable to root and birds would eat the seed (Matt. 13:4). Some seed would fall on soil that thinly covered rock. Here too because the soil was shallow, the seed, though beginning to take root, would soon wither (vv. 5-6). Still other seed would fall on ground that was good ground but choked by weeds. It too would never grow well (v. 7). Some seed, however, would fall on good soil which would be receptive and produce up to a hundredfold (v. 8). Having delivered the parable, Jesus urged them, "He who has ears, let him hear" (v. 9).

In the interpretation of the parable, it should be remembered that the interpreters come from various points of view eschatologically. Those who are premillennial interpret this as referring to the present age preceding the second coming of Christ with the kingdom following for 1,000 years after Jesus returns. Amillenarians come to the passage and attempt to find fulfillment of the promise of the kingdom on earth in one sense or another. Postmillenarians attempt to find in this passage evidence that the Gospel is going to be ultimately triumphant and will, for all practical purposes, dominate the entire world.

It should be obvious from this parable that this does not anticipate the Gospel as a triumphant force in the world. Rather, it is only a small portion of the population who will receive the message of the Gospel and respond favorably and bring forth fruit. This as well as the other parables make clear that the Bible does not teach a world getting better and better, climaxing in the second coming of Christ. Rather, it portrays a dual fulfillment of good and evil which will be judged at the Second Coming.

This Parable of the Sower also does not correspond to amillennial interpretation that the millennial kingdom is being fulfilled now. Rather, there is emphasis on the rejection of the Gospel in a way that would not be true in fulfilling the prophecies of the kingdom on earth.

### Reasons for Revelation in the Form of Parables

*Matthew 13:10-17.* After the first parable the disciples came to Jesus asking, "Why do You speak to the people in parables?" (v. 10)

The secret of why parables are used is that those who have rejected Jesus Christ as presented without parables now are not entitled to understand the secrets that belong to those who are of faith. Accordingly, Jesus said, "Whoever has will be given more, and he will have an abundance. Whoever does not have, even what he has will be taken from him" (v. 12). What is lacking is the element of faith. In other words, those who refuse to accept a clear presentation of the Gospel are not going to be inducted into the secrets that are involved in spiritual truth.

As a result, Jesus characterized their hardness of heart in not accepting the truth in the words, "Though seeing, they do not see; though hearing, they do not hear or understand" (v. 13).

Jesus also quoted from Isaiah, who, as a prophet, anticipated the difficulty of people hearing the Word of God. Jesus also quoted from Isaiah 6:9-10, referring to Isaiah's statement of the people who were hard of hearing spiritual truth in his generation, "You will be ever hearing but never understanding; you will be ever seeing but never perceiving. For this people's heart has become calloused; they hardly hear with their ears, and they have closed their eyes. Otherwise they might see with their eyes, hear with their ears, understand with their hearts, and turn, and I would heal them" (Matt. 13:14-15). Deeper knowledge of the truth of God requires acceptance of earlier simpler truths without which the deeper truths will never be revealed. Jesus, however, commended the disciples as those who hear and stated that what they hear, "many prophets and righteous men longed to see what you see but did not see it, and to hear what you hear but did not hear it" (v. 17).

### The Parable of the Sower Interpreted

*Matthew 13:18-23.* With this background Jesus interpreted the Parable of the Sower. The seed on the hard path is immediately snatched away by the evil one because there is no receptivity (vv. 19-20). Seed falling on the rocky places indicates shallow reception that does not last long enough for the seed to grow effectively (vv. 20-21). The seed among thorns refers to one who is receptive but whose life is choked up with "the worries of this life and the deceitfulness of wealth" (v. 22), with the result that the seed is choked and does not bear fruit (v. 22). The seed that is productive, however, falls on good soil where the Gospel is understood, and it may produce as much as a hundredfold (v. 23). The Gospel, though rejected by many, will be received by a few.

### The Weeds among the Wheat

*Matthew 13:24-30, 37-43.* In contrast to the first parable that taught various types of reception of the seed, the second parable refers to the difference between true wheat seed and weeds. Jesus used the situation where a man sows good seed in his field (v. 24). However, after he has sown the good seed, his enemies come and sow weeds (v. 25). When both begin to grow up, it becomes evident that the wheat and the weeds are growing together. When servants ask whether they should try to pull up the weeds, they are told to wait until the harvest (vv. 28-30). At the time of the harvest the harvesters are instructed to collect weeds first and then the wheat (v. 30). As in the first parable of the kinds of soil, so here the parable does not support the postmillennial idea that the Gospel will be triumphant and bring in a golden age. Also, it does not support the concept that the present age is the fulfillment of the kingdom promises of Christ. Instead, it is an accurate portrayal of the present age where both the true Gospel and false gospels are proclaimed.

This parable is used by the posttribulationists as proving that the Rapture cannot be placed before the end-time events of the Great Tribulation because the weeds are gathered first. This would refute the pretribulationists who teach that the Rapture gathers out the saved first. Accordingly, they place the Rapture as an event preceding the second coming of Christ to the earth.

The answer to this is quite simple. First of all, the order of the gathering is not significant as illustrated in the final Parable of the Dragnet, as just the reverse is true when the good fish are gathered out first and the bad fish are thrown away (v. 48). The fact is that there will be a series of judgments at the Second Coming, and the order is not significant here.

However, the real answer is that the Rapture is not in view here. The period involved is the whole period between the first and second advents of Christ without special consideration of the Church Age as such from Pentecost to the Rapture.

The disciples did not readily understand the Parable of the Weeds in the Field, and Jesus explained it to them, stating, "The One who sowed the good seed is the Son of man. The field is the world, and the good seed stands for the sons of the kingdom. The weeds are the sons of the evil one, and the enemy who sows them is the devil. The harvest is the end of the age, and the harvesters are angels. As the weeds are pulled up and burned in the fire, so it will be at the end of the age. The Son of man will send out His angels, and they will weed out of His kingdom everything that causes sin and all who do evil. They will throw them into the fiery furnace, where there will be weeping and gnashing of teeth. Then the righteous will shine like the sun in the kingdom of their Father. He who has ears, let him hear" (vv. 37-43). Once explained, the parable is simple to understand and believe, but this parable, like others, requires interpretation.

### The Parable of the Mustard Seed

*Matthew 13:31-32; Mark 4:30-32.* Jesus used the mustard seed as an illustration of the rapid growth of the kingdom. The mustard plant is not the one used for condiments today, but a different variety. A single pod will often contain hundreds of small seeds, each of which could produce a plant. Jesus used this, therefore, as an illustration of the growth from little to much, stating, "Though it is the smallest of all your seeds, yet when it grows, it is the largest of garden plants and becomes a tree, so that the birds of the air come and perch in its branches" (Matt. 13:32). In general, this parable refers to the rapid growth of the church. The kingdom of heaven refers to a sphere of profession (those who only profess belief) that obviously grows fast, or it refers to a true kingdom of God, as in Mark 4:30-32, which also grows rapidly. Note is taken, however, of the fact that the birds of the air perch in its branches, referring to evil influences of those who are not even in a sphere of profession that relates to the church.

A question is sometimes raised about this statement because the passage declared that the mustard seed is "the smallest of all your seeds" (v. 32). Actually, the text in the Greek New Testament is a comparative *(mikroteron)* which means that it is smaller. Some hold that this is an error in Scripture because the seed of the orchid, for instance, is still smaller. This, however, is ruled out by the passage itself which limits the seeds under consideration to those that are planted in the Holy Land. The fact that smaller seeds are found elsewhere in the world is without significance.

This parable is especially significant because it is found only in Matthew's Gospel which reveals the mysteries of the kingdom of heaven as well as in Mark where the kingdom of God is related to this parable. Though most scholars consider the kingdom of heaven and the kingdom of God as reference to the same entity, in Matthew 13, in particular, the kingdom of heaven seems to include that which is not a genuine part of the kingdom but an area of mere profession in contrast to the kingdom of God which includes only saved men and angels. This parable is significant, however, as including both because it so happens that both the kingdom of heaven as a sphere of profession and the kingdom of God as a sphere of salvation (the true body of Christ) grow rapidly. It should be pointed out that the parables in Matthew 13 include a sphere of profession as in the case of the wheat and the weeds and later on in the case of the dragnet which gathers both good and bad fish. These parables are not used of the kingdom of God in the other Gospels.

### The Parable of the Yeast

*Matthew 13:33; Luke 13:20-21.* In preparing dough that was fermented and would rise, it was customary to keep out part of the dough in order to spread the ferment to the new batch. This was used by Christ to illustrate the penetrating quality of the truth concerning the kingdom of heaven, that is, it penetrates through the dough and because of the quality of yeast, it makes the dough look much larger than it really is without adding any food value.

Postmillenarians, because of their desire to prove the growing kingdom, tend to say that the leaven represents the Gospel permeating the whole world and eventually affecting the whole world. This, however, is not supported in other Scripture where leaven is universally used to represent evil. In the sacrifices no leaven was permitted in the unleavened bread representing holiness. However, in the fellowship offering (Lev. 7:11-13) the two loaves representing the professing church (23:15-18) contained leaven even as the kingdom of heaven contains a strain of evil here. Because the yeast tends to puff up the dough, it represents, as used by Christ, the externalism of the Pharisees, unbelief as illustrated in the Sadducees, worldliness as represented in the Herodians, and evil doctrine in general (Matt. 16:6-12; Mark 8:14-21). Paul, likewise, used leaven to represent evil (1 Cor. 5:6-8; Gal. 5:7-10). The fact that a certain amount of evil penetrates the professing church as well as the true church is a fact of life recognized in Scripture. The history of the church since the first century supports all too clearly the prevalence of externalism, unbelief, worldliness, and inaccurate doctrine.

### Parables in Fulfillment of Prophecy

In concluding the revelation of the previous parable, Jesus referred to parables as a fulfillment of prophecy and quoted Psalm 78:2, "I will open my mouth in parables, I will utter things hidden since the creation of the world" (Matt. 13:35).

### The Hidden Treasure

*Matthew 13:44.* Jesus compared the kingdom of heaven to a treasure hidden in the field (v. 44). He described the joy that comes when a man discovers it and sells all that he has and buys it (v. 44).

Postmillenarians, because of their desire to demonstrate that the world is getting better, attribute this to salvation as a case in which we must sell all that we have in order to buy the treasure which is Jesus. Though this is a common interpretation, it also is flawed because in salvation an individual has nothing with which to purchase the treasure but is spiritually bankrupt. A far more accurate explanation is to identify the man as Jesus Christ, the Saviour, who sells all that He has, that is, leaves behind the glories of heaven, and purchases the field.

Though the passage does not indicate it, inasmuch as this was addressed to Jews, they were very conscious of the fact that the

Old Testament pictured them as a treasure as far as God was concerned. Exodus recorded the message given to Moses to deliver to the Children of Israel, "Now if you obey Me fully and keep My covenant, then out of all nations you will be My treasured possession. Although the whole earth is Mine, you will be for Me a kingdom of priests and a holy nation. These are the words you are to speak to the Israelites" (Ex. 19:5). Also, in Psalm 135:4, it is declared, "For the LORD has chosen Jacob to be His own, Israel to be His treasured possession." From Scripture it is evident that Christ in His coming had as a primary purpose the redemption of Israel which was accomplished on the cross. Accordingly, correct interpretation of the Parable of the Treasure interprets it as representing Jesus selling all, in other words, dying on the cross in order to purchase the treasure (cf. Phil. 2:7-8; 1 Peter 1:18-19). Though Israel is obvious in the world today, it is not generally recognized that they are God's treasure, and this truth explained why the treasure is declared to be hidden in the field.

### The Parable of the Pearl

*Matthew 13:45-46.* A parable similar to that of the treasure is found represented by the pearl which was purchased by the merchant selling all that he had in order to buy it (vv. 45-46). Postmillenarian influence again has attempted to represent this as the believer selling everything that he has in order to buy the pearl which is Jesus Christ. Again, the problem is that unbelievers have nothing with which to pay for salvation. Only Jesus can provide salvation and pay the price of our redemption. Accordingly, here, as in the Parable of the Treasure, the merchant represents Jesus and the pearl represents the church.

The pearl has the unusual quality of being an organism growing out of the side of an irritated oyster. In an similar way, it can be viewed that the church grows out of the wounded side of Christ. Just as Christ died for Israel, so He died also for others, including those who are believers in the present age who are both Jews and Gentiles.

### The Parable of the Dragnet

*Matthew 13:47-50.* The Parable of the Dragnet, like the Parable of the Wheat and Weeds, represents the judgment that will take place at the second coming of Christ. The net described here is a long one, often as long as a half mile, and the catch would be far too great for a single boat to get in. Accordingly, it is brought to shore where what is in the net is sorted out, with the good fish being saved and the bad fish being thrown back into the sea (vv. 47-48). Jesus declared that this is a similar picture which will occur at the end of the age when the angels will separate the wicked who are in the net, the sphere of profession, throw them in the fiery furnace in contrast to the wheat which will be gathered and blessed (vv. 49-50). The order of the judgment may mean the wicked separated last and the righteous taken out first, which is the opposite order of the wheat and the tares, demonstrating that this is not significant in itself. Actually, at the Second Coming there will be a series of judgments which has the end result of separating the righteous and the wicked; but each judgment is described as a separate judgment, and the order is not significant.

In general, the seven parables describe the age between the first and second comings of Christ. This will be a period when some will respond to the truth and others will not. This will be an age when good and evil grow up side by side, with the good not conquering evil and the evil not conquering the good. Separation in judgment occurs at the end when the evil is gathered out and the good is allowed to go into the kingdom. On the one hand, it does not correspond to the postmillennial expectation of an age in which the good gradually overcomes the evil, nor does it fulfill the Old Testament promises of Christ reigning on earth. In fact, through the parables Jesus is seen as absent except where the references are to what He did in His first coming. This chapter, therefore, becomes an important one in filling in what the Old Testament did not reveal concerning the age between the first and second comings of Christ. It is further complemented and augmented by the Olivet Discourse, concerning the end of the age, and John 13–17, the discourse of Christ on the present age from the spiritual standpoint.

## PROPHECIES OF THE DEATH AND RESURRECTION OF JESUS IN THE GOSPELS

Jesus, having presented the great ethical principles of His kingdom and having supported His claim to be the Messiah by many miracles, had turned His appeal to individuals who would follow Him, as He did in Matthew 11:28-30. After condemning the unbelief and His rejection by the leaders of Israel, Jesus revealed the special character of the present age between the first and second comings of Christ. In so doing He assumed that He would be rejected, die, and be resurrected and ascended to heaven. After the revelation of the present age, which would be fulfilled after His departure into heaven, Jesus began to speak more plainly to His disciples concerning His death and resurrection.

### The First Predictions of His Death and Resurrection

*Matthew 16:21-28; Mark 8:31–9:1; Luke 9:21-27.* As recorded in three of the four Gospels, Jesus predicted His coming death and resurrection. Matthew recorded, "From that time on Jesus began to explain to His disciples that He must go to Jerusalem and suffer many things at the hands of the elders, chief priests and teachers of the Law, and that He must be killed and on the third day be raised to life" (16:21). Though Peter objected strenuously to this statement as something that would never happen, Jesus rebuked him and reminded him and the other disciples that there is a cross to be taken up in following Jesus. The principle is followed "For whoever wants to save his life will lose it, but whoever loses his life for Me will find it" (v. 25). Though He would need to die and be resurrected, He would return in power and glory from heaven (v. 27), and He also predicted that some of the disciples "will not taste death before they see the Son of man coming in His kingdom" (v. 28). This is most probably a reference to the Transfiguration which took place immediately afterward when Jesus was revealed in the glory that will be His.

### The Second Prophecy of Jesus concerning His Death and Resurrection

*Matthew 20:17-19; Mark 10:32-34; Luke 18:31-34.* The second prediction of Christ concerning His death and resurrection is recorded in three of the Gospels. The twelve disciples were on their way to Jerusalem, and Jesus took them apart from the multitude and told them, "We are going up to Jerusalem, and the Son of man will be betrayed to the chief priests and the teachers of the Law. They will condemn Him to death and will turn Him over to the Gentiles to be mocked and flogged and crucified. On the third day He will be raised to life!" (Matt. 20:18-19) Luke added, "The disciples did not understand any of this. Its meaning was hidden from them, and they did not know what He was talking about" (Luke 18:34).

### A Third Announcement of the Death and Resurrection of Jesus

*Matthew 26:2-5; Mark 14:1-9.* In the third announcement of His death, He did not mention the fact that He would also be raised from the dead. In Luke 22:1-6 mention is made of the plot of Judas to betray Jesus to the chief priests at an opportune time.

## PROPHECIES CONCERNING THE END
## OF THE INTER-ADVENT AGE
### *Prophecy on the Mount of Olives*

*Matthew 24–25; Mark 13:1-27; Luke 21:5-36.* The extensive prophecies of Christ in His sermon on the Mount of Olives were delivered to four of the disciples, Peter, James, John, and Andrew (Mark 13:3). His discourse was in response to the disciples' questioning, "Tell us, when will these things happen? And what will be the sign that they are all about to be fulfilled?" (v. 4) They had reference to the previous prediction of Christ that the magnificent temple would be destroyed which did not fit the disciples' expectation of the coming kingdom.

It is evident that the three Gospels recorded only a portion of this discourse, and the full picture is given by putting together the revelation in each of the three Gospels. This should be understood in light of the fact that Jesus had declared the moral principles of the kingdom in the Sermon on the Mount (Matt. 5–7) and had described the present age (Matt. 13). Now He was describing the period following His death and resurrection and ascension and extending to the end of the Tribulation period the time of His second coming. The disciples were still having a great deal of difficulty understanding how this fit in with their messianic expectations.

### *General Signs of His Second Coming*

*Matthew 24:1-14; Mark 13:5-13; Luke 21:5-19.* A sharp rebuke against the Pharisees and Sadducees for their hypocrisy and unbelief was delivered by Christ. This had come to a conclusion when Jesus lamented over Jerusalem for its long history of rejecting the prophets and killing those sent to them with the truth. He pronounced a solemn curse on Jerusalem, saying, "Look, your house is left to you desolate. For I tell you, you will not see Me again until you say, 'Blessed is He who comes in the name of the Lord' " (Matt. 23:38-39). A little later after He had left the temple, the disciples called His attention to the magnificence of the temple (24:1). Jesus came back, however, with a devastating prophecy, "I tell you the truth, not one stone here will be left on another; every one will be thrown down" (v. 2).

This prophecy had alarmed the disciples. Four of them, Peter,

380

Andrew, James, and John, in a private meeting with Jesus asked, " 'Tell us,' they said, 'when will this happen, and what will be the sign of Your coming and of the end of the age?' " (v. 3; Mark 13:3-4; Luke 21:7)

In answering the three questions, the answer to the first question concerning the destruction of Jerusalem was given in Luke 21:20-24. The second and third questions concerning signs of His coming and the end of the age actually were the same question because the age ends at the time of His coming. Matthew gives us the most complete answer to these two questions (Matt. 24:4-30).

Scholars interpret Matthew from several different points of view. Usually their interpretation of prophecy in general dictates the interpretation of this section. Amillenarians, who deny a literal millennial reign of Christ, tend to take these prophecies in more of a general than specific way and frequently attempt to find fulfillment in the first century. Accordingly, they attempt to relate most of the prophecies to the time when Jerusalem was destroyed in A.D. 70.

Postmillenarians have a different problem in that they want to support their view that the world is going to get better and better as the Gospel gradually triumphs; but this passage of Scripture does not support this and, in fact, predicts increasing evil with the climax at the Second Coming. Liberal interpreters, who do not accept legitimate prophecy of the future, tend to question that Christ actually taught what is valid in this passage and view it as a summary of His teachings plus later findings in the church. They feel the setting is the apocalyptic writings of that time which are outside the Scriptures.

Only the premillennial interpretation tends to interpret this prophecy as literal and specific. Even among premillenarians, however, variations can be observed. Some hold that this entire passage will be fulfilled in the future in connection with the Great Tribulation. Others believe that the break comes at verse 9 with the previous predictions being general in character and the particular prophecies, beginning with verse 9, being fulfilled in the Great Tribulation. Still another point of view which is presented in this writing is that the entire period described in verses 4-14 are general prophecies that can find fulfillment throughout the present age, with verses 15-30 fulfilled in the Great Tribulation. However, these same prophecies and the events predicted in verses 4-14 are repeated in the Great Tribulation when what was perhaps partially

# PREDICTED ORDER OF PROPHETIC EVENTS RELATED TO ISRAEL

1. The holocaust and suffering of Jews in Germany in World War II lead to worldwide sympathy for a homeland for the Jews.
2. United Nations recognizes Israel as a nation and allows 5,000 square miles of territory, excluding ancient Jerusalem in 1948.
3. Israel, though immediately attacked by those nations surrounding her, achieves increases in territory in subsequent wars.
4. Though Russia at the beginning was sympathetic to Israel, the United States becomes her principal benefactor and supplier of military aid and money.
5. Israel makes amazing strides forward in reestablishing her land, its agriculture, industries, and political power.
6. In the series of military tests, Israel establishes that she has a superior army to that of surrounding nations.
7. Arab power opposing Israel is sufficient to keep Israel from having peaceful coexistence with other nations in the Middle East.
8. Israel continues in the state of confusion and conflict until the church is raptured.
9. With the formation of the ten-nation confederacy by the Gentile ruler in the Middle East, Israel is forced to accept a seven-year peace settlement.
10. The world and the Jewish people celebrate what appears to be a permanent peace settlement in the Middle East.
11. Israel prospers and many return to Israel after the peace is settled.
12. Toward the close of the three-and-a-half years of peace, Russia accompanied by several other nations attempts to invade Israel but is destroyed by a series of judgments from God.
13. After three-and-a-half years of peace, the covenant is broken and the Middle East ruler becomes a world dictator and a principal persecutor of Israel.
14. The world dictator desecrates the temple of Israel and sets up an idol of himself to be worshiped.

15. Worldwide persecution of the Jews begins, and in the land two out of three perish.
16. A Jewish remnant emerges who puts their trust in Christ.
17. Though the world ruler massacres both Jews and Gentiles who fail to worship him as God, some survive from both Jews and Gentiles and are rescued by Christ.
18. The second coming of Christ rescuing persecuted Jews and Gentiles and bringing judgment upon all wickedness in the world and unbelievers.
19. The promised kingdom on earth with Jesus as Israel's Messiah and David as her regent prince begins with godly Israel being regathered from all over the world to inhabit her Promised Land.
20. For 1,000 years Israel experiences unusual blessing as the object of Christ's favor.
21. With the end of the millennial kingdom and the destruction of the present earth, godly Israel has its place in the eternal state and the new heaven and the new earth.
22. Those among Israel who are saved are placed in the New Jerusalem in the new earth.

fulfilled earlier then have a very literal and devastating fulfillment. The central question is whether the specific signs given in verses 15-26 are the future Great Tribulation. Under this interpretation the sign of the abomination will be the beginning of the last three-and-a-half years when the world ruler takes over and the Great Tribulation begins.

In the predictions that Christ made almost 2,000 years ago, He accurately portrayed the progress in the present age. In verses 4-14 He predicted at least nine distinctive features of the period: (1) false christs (vv. 4-5); (2) wars and rumors of wars (vv. 6-7); (3) famines (v. 7); (4) pestilence (v. 7, KJV); (5) earthquakes (v. 7); (6) many martyrs (vv. 8-10); (7) false prophets (v. 11); (8) increase in wickedness with love growing cold (v. 12); (9) worldwide preaching of the Gospel of the kingdom (vv. 13-14). Luke 21:8-24 records similar prophecies.

All of these situations have been fulfilled in history. In spite of advances in many areas, the world still suffers from war, famine, and pestilence. Earthquakes take on an increasingly serious role. As the density of population increases, the earthquakes become more destructive. Scripture, of course, predicts the greatest earthquake of all time in Revelation 16:18-20 when the cities of the world will apparently be leveled shortly before the second coming of Christ. It may be true that these signs are having fulfillment in the present age with growing intensity, but ultimately they will have even a greater and more literal fulfillment in the period of the Great Tribulation. The three-and-a-half-year period of the Great Tribulation will be climaxed by the second coming of Christ.

An important notation should be made at this point that the Rapture of the church and the close of the Church Age is nowhere mentioned in this prophecy. Some expositors have tried to bring in the Rapture of the church in Matthew 24–25, but this has only introduced confusion in the program. Matthew's Gospel is not discussing the Church Age as such but the whole Inter-advent Age from the first coming of Christ to His second coming and, therefore, deals with the Great Tribulation at the close of the present age.

The Church Age is a more limited period because it begins on the Day of Pentecost with the advent and baptism of the Holy Spirit and is concluded when the church is taken out of the world before the end-time prophecies are fulfilled. Though Matthew anticipates the church, in the statement to Peter (Matt. 16:18), there is no exposition of the Church Age such as is found later in John 13–17. The conclusion is safely reached that the Church Age and the Rapture are not introduced until 14:1-3.

Some problems have arisen from Matthew 24:13 where it states, "But he who stands firm to the end will be saved" (cf. Mark 13:13). A common interpretation that those who stand firm will endure to the end of the Tribulation is contradicted by the fact that thousands of Christians in the Great Tribulation will be martyred (Rev. 7:9-17). What is meant, then, by salvation at the end of the Tribulation?

This statement is best interpreted as physical deliverance, and it predicts that those who are still alive at the time of the second coming of Christ will have demonstrated their faith by standing with Christ through that period and will be delivered by Jesus, or saved, in the sense that they will be delivered from their persecutors. Accordingly, this verse does not have any bearing on the matter of eternal security or the question as to whether one once saved would always be saved but refers, rather, to physical deliverance of the righteous at the end of the Tribulation. By contrast,

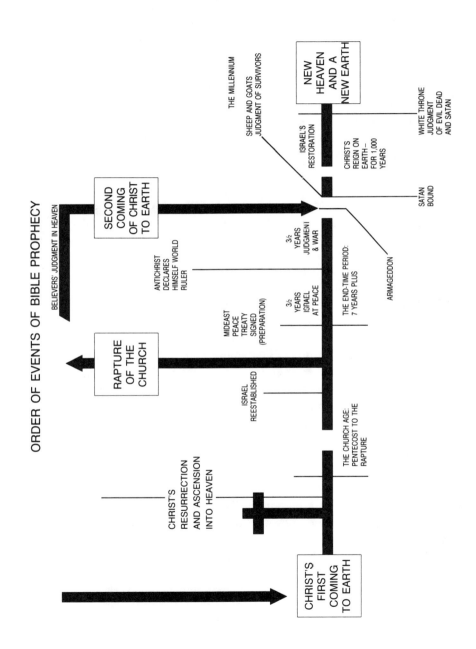

ORDER OF EVENTS OF BIBLE PROPHECY

many thousands will die who are also saved and will go to heaven but will not remain on earth until the time of the Second Coming.

In this section of Matthew 24:4-14, Matthew is answering the question concerning the signs of the end and of Christ's coming and presents the signs that are in general. Matthew does not deal, however, with the first question the disciples asked of when the destruction of Jerusalem would take place, as predicted by Christ in verse 2. This is answered, however, in Luke's Gospel.

### The Sign of the Destruction of Jerusalem

*Luke 21:20-24.* Luke stated that the sign of Jerusalem being surrounded by armies should alert them to the fact that its destruction is imminent, "When you see Jerusalem being surrounded by armies, you will know that its desolation is near" (v. 20). To the extent that they are able, they are urged to flee to the mountains and get out into the open country because it is going to be a terrible time of persecution for Israel (vv. 21-22). It will be a time especially difficult for pregnant women and nursing mothers for it will be a time of God's judgment on the land of Israel (v. 23). Jesus predicted that many in Israel will fall by the sword or be taken as prisoners (v. 24). Jerusalem will continue to be trampled underfoot by the Gentiles until the times of the Gentiles are fulfilled (v. 24).

The times of the Gentiles began in 605 B.C. when Nebuchadnezzar and his armies conquered Jerusalem and took the first captives to Babylon. Since then there have been times when Israel had possession of Jerusalem temporarily, but they did not have permanent possession. At the time Jesus was on earth, though Israel was in Jerusalem, it was under the control of the Gentiles. That has continued to the present time. Even today Israel controls Jerusalem because of military support from the United States.

According to Daniel's prophecies, the times of the Gentiles will not end until the end of the Great Tribulation which is future. The section of prophecy in Luke 21:20-24 should be distinguished from the other prophecies dealing with signs of the end because Luke 21:24 has already been literally fulfilled while the other aspects of its signs, as in Matthew 24 and Mark 13, are yet to see complete fulfillment. Only Luke gives the specific answer to signs of the destruction of Jerusalem.

### The Specific Signs of the End and of the Coming of Christ

*Matthew 24:15-26; Mark 13:14-25; Luke 21:25-28.* Jesus, having described the signs relating to the destruction of Jerusalem, which some of them would live to see, and the general signs of the progress of the present age, then reveals in detail the specific signs which will be unmistakable evidence that the second coming of Christ and the end of the age is near. It is important to note that the specific signs are entirely different than the signs for the destruction of Jerusalem, though there are some similarities. In both, Israel will be in time of trouble and tribulation. In both periods those in Judea are urged to flee to the mountains. In both cases Gentile power, at least at first, will be triumphant. But the specific signs of the end of the age and the coming of Christ do not occur in connection with the destruction of Jerusalem but await the future period leading up to the second coming of Christ which will be the specific sign of the end.

One of the sources of confusion among interpreters of the Olivet Discourse is their attempt to find complete fulfillment of the entire Olivet Discourse in connection with the destruction of Jerusalem. This is sometimes related to the attempt to avoid specific prophecy and the tendency to avoid details in prophecy as being accurate. Actually, Christ is painting a detailed and accurate picture of the Great Tribulation and its effect on the inhabitants of Jerusalem. As previously pointed out, Matthew's predictions do not relate to the Church Age as such, the Rapture of the church, or related events. Here, Matthew's Gospel, reporting the prophecies of Christ, focuses on the last three-and-a-half years leading up to the Second Coming. In that time there will be specific signs that will unmistakably identify the period as the time of the Great Tribulation.

Jesus first of all called attention to the specific sign of the appearance of " 'the abomination that causes desolation' spoken of through the Prophet Daniel" (Matt. 24:15). According to Daniel 9:26-27, the future world ruler, who will be in power in that period of three-and-a-half years, will desecrate the temple and cause the sacrifices to cease. This is called "an abomination that causes desolation" because it destroys the sacred character of the sacrificial altar and the temple that will be in existence at that time. A similar event, occurring in the second century B.C., is recorded in history as an act of Antiochus Epiphanes who stopped the sacrifices and desecrated the temple. This event fulfilled Daniel's prophecy, recorded in Daniel 11:31.

Matthew's account describes this event, which is still future, as a time when the temple will be desecrated in a similar way, "From the time that the daily sacrifice is abolished and the abomination that causes desolation is set up, there will be 1,290 days" (Dan. 12:11). This period of approximately three-and-a-half years will be the period of the Great Tribulation and will climax in the second coming of Christ. Accordingly, when the temple is desecrated by the future world ruler, it will be a specific sign of the imminent coming of Christ (cf. 2 Thes. 2:3-4; Rev. 13:11-15).

Just as the surrounding of Jerusalem by the Roman armies was a sign for them to flee to the mountains of Judea in A.D. 70, so when this temple is desecrated in the future, it will be a sign for Jews in Jerusalem to flee. It will be a very specific sign that will come on a certain day at a certain time. When they learn of it, Jesus urges them to flee immediately, not even bothering to go back to the house or to stop to get their cloak (Matt. 24:16-18). As it was in the case when Jerusalem was destroyed, so it will be difficult for pregnant women and nursing mothers to leave home and endure the hardships of escaping Jerusalem.

Jesus also said they should pray that they will not have to leave on the Sabbath because travel on the Sabbath Day would be an obvious sign that they were fleeing as normally they do not journey on the Sabbath (v. 20).

The initial sign of the desecration of their temple will be followed by the fearful fulfillment and the time of great trouble anticipated in the Old Testament (Jer. 30:4-7; Dan. 9:25-26). Jesus declared that "there will be great distress, unequaled from the beginning of the world until now—and never to be equaled again" (Matt. 24:21). This time of trouble will be so great that the period, if not limited to the three-and-a-half years duration as described in Scriptures, would destroy the human race. Jesus stated, "no one would survive, but for the sake of the elect those days will be shortened" (Matt. 24:22).

The Gospel of Mark stated essentially the same truths as that of Matthew 24 (Mark 13:14-17). Luke recorded Christ as saying, "There will be signs in the sun, moon and stars. On the earth, nations will be in anguish and perplexity at the roaring and tossing of the sea. Men will faint from terror, apprehensive of what is coming on the world, for the heavenly bodies will be shaken" (Luke 21:25-26).

All these events will be warnings that Christ is coming at the end of this period. Though they will not know the day nor the hour, they will be able to comprehend the approximate time because the length of the total period is forty-two months (Rev. 13:5). Taking all the Scriptures into consideration, and especially the graphic picture of the Great Tribulation provided in the Book of Revelation, it seems that the population of the world will be decimated and only a fraction of those that enter the period will still survive at the end. Jesus said, in fact, that if He did not stop the period by His second coming, there would be no human beings left on earth (Matt. 24:22). The idea of posttribulationists that survival through this time is a blessed hope is not tenable.

There will also be deceitful signs and reports that Christ has already appeared, "At that time if anyone says to you, 'Look, here is the Christ!' or, 'There He is!' do not believe it. For false christs and false prophets will appear and perform great signs and miracles to deceive even the elect—if that were possible" (vv. 23-24; cf. Mark 13:21-23). According to Matthew 24:26, there will be reports that Jesus has appeared in the desert or has been revealed in the inner room, but they are urged not to believe this.

The point is that the second coming of Christ will be a very visible event. Jesus described it as recorded in Matthew, "For as lightning that comes from the east is visible even in the west, so will be the coming of the Son of man" (v. 27). The Second Coming will be preceded by many supernatural events in the skies which are described in the Book of Revelation. Jesus, according to Matthew's Gospel, said, "Immediately after the distress of those days 'the sun will be darkened, and the moon will not give its light; the stars will fall from the sky, and the heavenly bodies will be shaken' " (Matt. 24:29; cf. Mark 13:24-25; Luke 21:25-26).

The final sign will be the appearance of Christ Himself in the sky in His return from heaven to the earth. As recorded by Matthew, Jesus said, "At that time the sign of the Son of man will appear in the sky, and all the nations of the earth will mourn. They will see the Son of man coming on the clouds of the sky, with power and great glory" (Matt. 24:30; cf. Mark 13:26; Luke 21:27). Revelation 19:11-16 described the scene in greater detail.

It should be noted that Matthew was not talking about the Rapture of the church, which is described in totally different language (cf. 1 Thes. 4:16). The final sign is the glory of Christ Himself in the skies in return to the earth. The nations will grieve because it is the time of judgment for rejection of Jesus as Saviour and Lord.

When Christ comes to earth He will send out His angels to assemble the elect, "And He will send His angels with a loud trumpet call, and they will gather His elect from the four winds, from one end of the heavens to the other" (Matt. 24:31). Mark described the same event as the assembling of the elect both from earth and heaven (Mark 13:27).

Some have taken the elect here to refer specifically to the elect living on earth, but it is more probable that this event will include all the elect, or the saved, including Old Testament saints, saved Israel, the church, and the saints of the Tribulation period leading up to the Second Coming. Some will need to be resurrected from the dead, such as the martyrs (Rev. 20:4-6) and the Old Testament saints (Dan. 12:2). The church was resurrected, or translated, earlier, at the time of the Rapture. At the second coming of Christ no child of God will be left unresurrected or unrestored, but all will share in the millennial kingdom.

Taken as a whole, the revelation of Matthew 24:4-31, with parallel passages in Mark and Luke, answers the questions that the disciples had raised, first, concerning the destruction of Jerusalem, which occurred in A.D. 70, and the second and third questions dealing with the end of the age and the coming of Christ. The event itself is preceded by the signs which Jesus described and are climaxed in the second coming of Christ at the beginning of His kingdom on earth.

Having answered their questions, Jesus next turned to illustrations and applications of the truths of these prophecies.

### The Parable of the Fig Tree

*Matthew 24:32-35; Mark 13:28-31; Luke 21:29-33.* Jesus first used the fig tree as an illustration of the signs of the Lord's coming. Jesus declared, "Now learn this lesson from the fig tree: As soon as its twigs get tender and its leaves come out, you know that summer is near. Even so, when you see all these things, you know that it is near, right at the door" (Matt. 24:32-33; cf. Mark 13:28-29; Luke 21:29-31). A common interpretation has been to interpret the fig tree as a type of Israel and the revival of Israel as the budding of the fig tree. The fig tree could very well be a type of Israel, but it does not seem to be so used in Scripture. Good and bad figs are mentioned in Jeremiah 24:1-8; the good figs are those carried off in captivity, and the bad figs, those who remain in the land of Israel.

Jeremiah 29:17 also mentioned figs. In Judges 9:1-11 fig trees are mentioned but not in relation to Israel. They are mentioned by Christ in Matthew 21:19-20 and Mark 11:12-14. There is no indication in the interpretation of Matthew 21:18-22, and Mark 11:12-14, 20-26 that relates the fig tree to Israel. Accordingly, though many have followed this interpretation, there is no scriptural basis.

A better alternative is the simple explanation that the fig tree is used as a natural illustration. Because the fig tree by its nature brings forth leaves late in spring, if one sees leaves on a fig tree, it is evidence that summer is very near. This illustration is carried over to the second coming of Christ. When the events described in the preceding verses occur, it will be a clear indication of the second coming of Christ being near. The sign in the passage is not the revival of Israel, which is not the subject of Matthew 24, but rather the details of the Great Tribulation which occur in the three-and-a-half years preceding the Second Coming. Accordingly, "all these things" (v. 33) refers not to the revival of Israel but to the events of the Great Tribulation. It is true, however, that Israel will have a measure of revival preceding the second coming of Christ, but this is based on other scriptural revelation rather than the revelation presented here.

### The Generation to See the Fulfillment

Jesus made a further comment on the situation in saying, "This generation will certainly not pass away until all these things have happened. Heaven and earth will pass away, but My words will never pass away" (Matt. 24:34-35). The normal use of the word "generation" is in reference to the time span between one's birth and the time when one becomes a parent. Obviously, the generation that lived in Christ's day did not see all the things described in the preceding context. Some have inferred from this that the term "generation" is a reference to Israel and have asserted that Israel will not pass away until all these things are fulfilled. However, Israel will never pass away. Still other scholars take "generation" as an indefinite period of time.

The most natural meaning, however, is to take it as normally used as a reference to a period of twenty-five to forty years. But instead of referring this to the time in which Christ lived, it refers back to the preceding period that is described as the Great Tribulation. As the Great Tribulation is only three-and-a-half years long, obviously, those who see the Great Tribulation will also see the coming of the Lord. Regardless of how it is interpreted, Christ affirmed, in support of the fulfillment of the prophecy, that His words will never pass away even though our present earth and heaven will ultimately be destroyed.

### The Time Preceding the Second Coming
### Compared to the Days of Noah before the Flood

*Matthew 24:36-42.* Though the time of the coming of the Lord may be recognized as about to happen, it is not given in such clarity that one can determine the day or the hour. Needless speculation concerning the time of the coming of the Lord would be spared if this verse were taken literally. Jesus said, "No one knows about that day or hour, not even the angels in heaven, nor the Son, but only the Father" (v. 36).

Jesus, of course, here is referring to His human intelligence, which is limited, not to His divine omniscience. The time leading up to the Second Coming is compared to the days leading up to the Flood. In both cases there are numerous signs of the approaching end. It should be noted that the signs are in relation to the second coming of Christ at the end of the Tribulation, not to the Rapture of the church which has no signs and is always imminent until it occurs. Noah took more than a hundred years to build the ark. In this time people carried on their normal activities, as Jesus mentioned (vv. 37-38). When the ark was finally finished, however, the situation suddenly changed. Now it would be possible for the Flood to come.

As Noah's neighbors observed, they saw a very strange sight — the animals walking in pairs in almost military precision, marching into the ark (Gen. 7:2-3). God also announced to Noah, "Seven days from now I will send rain on the earth for forty days and forty nights, and I will wipe from the face of the earth every living creature I have made" (v. 4).

After the animals had come safely into the ark, Moses recorded that Noah and his family, consisting of his wife and three sons and their wives, also entered the ark. Now the situation was entirely changed. Everything that preceded the Flood was now fulfilled. The door to the ark was shut, and then it began to rain. In a similar way, many prophecies have to be fulfilled leading up to the Second Coming. As the period of the Great Tribulation progresses, and those who understand the prophecies of the end time realize that approximately three-and-a-half years have passed, they will undoubtedly know and expect Christ to come even though the prophecies are not specifically detailed to allow them to know the day or the hour. They will know the year.

Jesus then compared the situation of the flood of Noah to the time of the Second Coming. He stated, "That is how it will be at the coming of the Son of man. Two men will be in the field; one will be taken and the other left. Two women will be grinding with a hand mill; one will be taken and the other left. Therefore keep watch, because you do not know on what day your Lord will come" (Matt. 24:39-42).

Because this event is somewhat similar to the Rapture in that some are taken and some are left, posttribulationists almost universally cite this verse as proof that the Rapture will occur as a part of the second coming of Christ after the Tribulation. However, a careful reading of the passage yields exactly the opposite result. At the Rapture of the church, those taken are those who are saved, and those who are left are left to go through the awful period, including the Great Tribulation. Here the situation is just in reverse. Those who are taken are taken in judgment, and those who are left are left to enter the millennial kingdom.

In spite of the obvious fact that the illustration has to be reversed in order to make an application to the Rapture, posttribulationists sometimes point out that the Greek word *airo,* used to express "took them all away" (v. 39), is a different word (Gr., *paralambano)* than used in verse 40 and in verse 41, "will be taken." Though admitting that in verse 39 at the time of the Flood those taken were taken in judgment, they claim the change in wording justifies reading the Rapture into verses 41-42. However, this conclusion is not only contrary to the text of Matthew 24 but does not take into consideration Luke 17 in its description of the Second Coming where Jesus said, "I tell you, on that night two people will be in one bed; one will be taken and the other left. Two women will be grinding grain together; one will be taken and the other left" (vv. 34-35). In Luke, however, the question is asked by the disciples, "Where, Lord?" (v. 37) In reply, Jesus said, "Where there is a dead body, there the vultures will gather" (v. 37). In other words, the ones taken are obviously put to death in judgment in contrast to what will happen at the Rapture when the one taken is taken to heaven. There is no scriptural basis for reading the Rapture into Matthew 24. The occasion is entirely different. At the Rapture, the church, composed of those who are saved, is taken to heaven. At the second coming of Christ, the saved remain on earth, and the unsaved are taken away in judgment at the beginning of the millennial kingdom. The very word used to describe those taken away in Matthew 24:40-41 is used of Christ being taken away to the cross, obviously being taken in judgment as used here (cf. John 19:16, "So the soldiers took charge of Jesus").

The conclusion for those living at the time of the Second Coming is similar to that of the time of Noah, "Therefore keep watch, because you do not know on what day your Lord will come" (Matt. 24:42). Though the passage is talking about the second coming of Christ and not the period preceding the Rapture, obviously, if those living in the period before the Second Coming, who are able to see signs of the Second Coming indicating its approach, should be watching, how much more should those waiting for the Rapture, which has no signs, live in constant expectation of the imminent return of Jesus for His church.

### Watchfulness Encouraged for the Owner of a House

*Matthew 24:43-44.* Jesus made the application of watchfulness as would be required of the owner of a house who did not know when a thief would break in (v. 43). Not knowing the exact hour, he would have to watch continuously. Jesus made this apply to those waiting for the Second Coming with the exhortation, "So you also must be ready, because the Son of man will come at an hour when you do not expect Him" (v. 44).

### Illustration of a Servant Put in Charge
### of His Master's House

*Matthew 24:45-50; Mark 13:33-37.* One who is waiting for the second coming of Christ is like a servant who is put in charge of his master's house. Not knowing when his master would return, the servant was urged to be faithful (vv. 45-47). If, however, the servant takes advantage of his master and abuses his fellow servants and lives the life of a drunkard, he will experience the judgment of his master when the master returns unexpectedly (vv. 48-50). Jesus stated that the unfaithful servant will be cut in pieces and placed with the hypocrites (v. 51). The implication of this passage is that belief in the second coming of Christ is linked to belief in the first coming of Christ. If one accepts what Christ was and did in His first coming, he will also accept what Christ will be and do at His second coming and, accordingly, will live in preparation.

## The Parable of the Ten Virgins

*Matthew 25:1-13.* As another illustration of the need for preparedness for the Second Coming, Christ described a familiar scene in Israel — that of the bridegroom claiming his bride. The normal procedure was for a wedding to have three stages. First, the parents of the bridegroom would arrange for the marriage with the parents of the bride and would pay the dowry. This was the legal marriage. The second stage, which often took place a year or more later, was fulfilled when the bridegroom, accompanied by his friends, would proceed from the home of the bridegroom at midnight and go to the home of the bride and claim her. The bride would know that he was coming and be ready with her maiden friends and would join the procession from the home of the bride to the home of the bridegroom. The third phase of the traditional wedding was a marriage feast following this which might take place for days and was illustrated in the wedding at Cana (John 2).

While the figure of bride/wife is used with more than one application in Scripture, normally, Israel is described as the wife of the Lord, already married, and the church is pictured as a bride waiting for the coming of the Bridegroom (2 Cor. 11:2). At the Rapture of the church the Bridegroom will claim His bride and take her to heaven.

The illustration that is used here is in reference to the attendants at the wedding. Each of the ten virgins took a lamp, but only the five wise virgins took oil with their lamps. Though the Scripture does not explain the spiritual meaning of these elements, frequently in the Bible the Holy Spirit is described as oil, as illustrated in the lamps burning in the tabernacle and in the temple. When the cry rang out that the bridegroom was coming (Matt. 25:6), the virgins all rose to light their lamps and meet the procession. The foolish virgins, however, had no oil at all, even in their lamps, and their wicks soon burned out. When they requested oil from the wise virgins, they were told to go buy some.

While they were out trying to make their purchase at midnight, which could have been difficult, the five wise virgins went with the procession to the home of the bridegroom, and Scripture recorded that then the door was shut (v. 10). When the five foolish virgins finally arrived, they were shut out because they were not watching for the coming of the bridegroom and his procession. As in all illustrations, the meaning of the illustration should not be pressed to the point where it becomes a basis for doctrine. In this case the main objective is clear. When the Second Coming occurs, it is going to be too late to get ready. Though some have viewed this incident as the Rapture of the church, there is really no justification for this because the context is entirely related to the second coming of Christ, and Jesus had not yet revealed any truth concerning the Rapture. He could hardly, therefore, expect His disciples to understand an illustration of a truth that had not been revealed.

It is significant also that the bride is not mentioned, but only the bridegroom. The ten virgins were not the bride but the attendants at the wedding, and this will apply, of course, to those who are waiting for the second coming of Christ. Though the interpretation relates to the Second Coming, obviously, there is an application of this truth to the Rapture in the sense that preparedness for the Rapture is just as necessary as preparedness for the Second Coming.

### The Parable of the Talents

*Matthew 25:14-30; cf. Luke 19:11-26.* While Jesus was still in the vicinity of Jericho and on His way to Jerusalem, He used the Parable of the Ten Minas to indicate the need for working while waiting for the return of the Lord (Luke 19:11-26). Luke recorded how the master gave his servants ten minas, one mina each to ten servants, and instructed them to invest this and use it to best advantage while he was gone to receive appointment as king. A mina was equivalent to three months' wages. Upon his return, one servant had gained ten minas, another five, and both were commended. The one who hid the mina, however, and had not done anything with it was condemned by his master because he had not taken advantage of the opportunity of making this money work for his lord.

The account in Matthew of the Parable of the Talents has the same illustration, somewhat changed, which Jesus used in connection with His Olivet Discourse. In the Parable of the Talents the master of the house gives to one five, another two, and another one talent and instructs them to work with this while he is gone. A talent was originally a weight of from 58 to 100 pounds. In modern value, a single silver talent is worth in excess of $2,000, and a gold talent in excess of $30,000. In today's inflated prices, gold and silver are worth much more. In Jesus' time, a day's wages amounted to sixteen cents. Accordingly, these sums represented an enormous value.

In the illustration which Christ used, He is referring to silver talents as illustrated in the word "money" (Matt. 25:18) which is literally silver. In the illustration the master gives one servant five talents, another two, and another one, according to his estimate of their abilities. The master is gone for a long period of time, but when he returns, he calls in his servants to give an account (v. 19). The five-talent man brought in an additional five talents, saying, " 'Master,' he said, 'you entrusted me with five talents. See, I have gained five more' " (v. 20). He was commended by his lord, "Well done, good and faithful servant! You have been faithful with a few things; I will put you in charge of many things. Come and share your master's happiness!" (v. 21) When the two-talent man reported, he, likewise, had doubled his money and received precisely the same commendation (vv. 22-23).

The one-talent man, however, had a different report, " 'Master,' he said, 'I knew that you are a hard man, harvesting where you have not sown and gathering where you have not scattered seed. So I was afraid and went out and hid your talent in the ground. See, here is what belongs to you' " (vv. 24-25).

The master judged his servant, saying, "You wicked, lazy servant! So you knew that I harvest where I have not sown and gather where I have not scattered seed? Well then, you should have put my money on deposit with the bankers, so that when I returned I would have received it back with interest" (vv. 26-27). The handling of the one-talent man is one of the major points of this illustration. Why was the master so hard on his servant? The answer is that the servant indicated he had serious questions as to whether the master would return. If he did not, the servant could keep the money and not report it as part of the estate of his master. If the master returned, he would be able to reproduce the talent and could not be accused of stealing. What the unprofitable servant displayed, however, was lack of faith in his master and a desire to have his master's money illegally.

The point is that those who reject the truth of the return of the Lord are, in effect, nullifying the fact of His first coming, as acceptance of one should lead to acceptance of the other. In the illustration the master declared, "Take the talent from him and give it to the one who has the ten talents. For everyone who has will be given more, and he will have an abundance. Whoever does not have, even what he has will be taken from him. And throw that worthless servant outside, into the darkness, where there will be weeping and gnashing of teeth" (vv. 28-30).

As brought out in 2 Peter 3:3-4, for one to question the literalness of His second coming raises questions as to whether he believed in the first coming. If Jesus is indeed the Son of God, then His coming again is both reasonable and to be expected. If He is not the Son of God, of course, He would not return. Accordingly, a lack of faith in the Second Coming stems from lack of faith in the First Coming. The one-talent man indicated outward profession of service to his master but without real faith.

### The Judgment of the Gentiles at the Second Coming

*Matthew 25:31-46.* This judgment relating to the Gentiles at the time of the Second Coming is revealed only here in Scripture. Premillenarians interpret this judgment as determining who among the Gentiles will enter the millennial kingdom. The basis for judgment is how they treated Christ's brethren, the Jews, as a token of their faith or lack of it. Amillenarians believe that the Second Coming ushers in the eternal state and interpret this judgment as determining who will enter into the new heaven and the new earth. The question of whether or not there is a Millennium after the second coming of Christ must be determined by other Scriptures as this passage in itself is not decisive.

Premillenarians contrast this judgment to several other judgments mentioned in Scripture such as the judgment of the church (2 Cor. 5:10), the judgment of Israel and the purging out of the rebels as a prelude to the millennial kingdom (Ezek. 20:33-38), and it is also different than the judgment of the wicked dead resurrected at the judgment of the Great White Throne (Rev. 20:11-15) which occurs at the end of the Millennium.

The time of this judgment is clearly stated in Matthew 25:31, "When the Son of man comes in His glory, and all the angels with Him, He will sit on His throne in heavenly glory." The judgment is not of all men but of living Gentiles (Gr., *ethne*). The Gentiles are described as either sheep or goats, and Jews are described as brothers of Christ.

Jesus described the situation, "All the nations will be gathered before Him, and He will separate the people one from another as a shepherd separates the sheep from the goats. He will put the sheep on His right and the goats on His left" (vv. 32-33). While sheep and goats look much alike, they are a different breed; and even though in ordinary life sheep and goats sometimes are in the same flock, at the proper time they could be separated.

The sheep, representing the saved, are addressed, "Then the King will say to those on His right, 'Come, you who are blessed by My Father; take your inheritance, the kingdom prepared for you since the creation of the world. For I was hungry and you gave Me something to eat, I was thirsty and you gave Me something to drink, I was a stranger and you invited Me in, I needed clothes and you clothed Me, I was sick and you looked after Me, I was in prison and you came to visit Me' " (vv. 34-36). When the sheep were surprised, and stated that they did not know that they had done this to Christ, Jesus said, "The King will reply, 'I tell you the truth, whatever you did for one of the least of these brothers of Mine, you did for Me' " (v. 40).

Likewise, the goats will be addressed, "Then He will say to those on His left, 'Depart from Me, you who are cursed, into the eternal fire prepared for the devil and his angels. For I was hungry and you gave Me nothing to eat, I was thirsty and you gave Me nothing to drink, I was a stranger and you did not invite Me in, I needed clothes and you did not clothe Me, I was sick and in prison and you did not look after Me' " (vv. 41-43). The goats, likewise, replied, saying that they had not been aware that they had neglected Christ, but He replied, "I tell you the truth, whatever you did not do for one of the least of these, you did not do for Me" (v. 45). The passage closes with the statement that the sheep will be declared righteous and have eternal life, and the goats will go into eternal punishment (v. 46).

Taken as a whole, this judgment fits naturally into the premillennial order of events before and after the second coming of Christ. This judgment related to the Gentiles is similar to the judgment relating to Israel (Ezek. 20:33-38). The contrast of Jews and Gentiles is a familiar one in Scripture as Gentiles are distinguished from the Jews in their outlook and hope (cf. Rom. 11:13; 15:27; 16:4; Gal. 2:12). They are contrasted to those who are considered Jews as in Romans 3:29 and 9:24.

This passage, however, has puzzled expositors because there is no preaching of the Cross, there is no statement of the Gospel as necessary for salvation, and all the passage speaks of is the contrast of the works of the sheep and the goats. The answer to this problem, however, is not a denial that salvation is based on faith and

# PREDICTED EVENTS
# RELATING TO THE NATIONS

1. United Nations organized as first step toward world government in 1946.
2. Israel is formed as a recognized nation in 1948.
3. Europe is rebuilt after World War II, setting stage for its role in future revival of the Roman Empire.
4. The rise of Russia as a world military and political power.
5. World movements such as the Common Market and the World Bank set the stage for future political and financial events.
6. Red China becomes a military power.
7. The Middle East and the nation of Israel become the focus of worldwide tension.
8. The Arab oil embargo in 1973 results in world recognition of the power of wealth and energy in the Middle East.
9. Lack of a powerful political leader prevents the Middle East from organizing as a political power.
10. The Rapture of the church removes a major deterrent to expansion of political and financial power of the Mediterranean world.
11. The rise of a new leader in the Middle East who later is identified as the Antichrist who secures power over first three, and then all ten nations, uniting them in a Mediterranean confederacy.
12. The new Mediterranean leader imposes a peace settlement for seven years on Israel.
13. Russian army accompanied by several other nations invades Israel and is destroyed by judgments from God.
14. Peace settlement in the Middle East is broken after three-and-a-half years.
15. Middle East ruler as the Antichrist becomes a world dictator.
16. Middle East ruler claims to be God and demands that all worship him at the pain of death.
17. Middle East dictator defiles the temple in Jerusalem.
18. The beginning of the terrible judgments of the Great Tribulation described in the seals, trumpets, and bowls of the wrath of God in the Book of Revelation.

19. Worldwide discontent at the rule of the Middle East ruler resulting from many catastrophes causing rebellion and gathering of the world's armies in the Middle East to fight it out with
Armageddon as the center of the conflict.
20. Second coming of Christ occurs accompanied by the armies
from heaven.
21. The armies of the world attempt to fight the armies from heav-
en but are totally destroyed.
22. Christ's millennial reign is established, climaxing judgments
on all the unsaved and the final disposition of Gentile political power.
23. Those saved from both Jews and Gentiles are placed in the
New Jerusalem in the earth where they will spend eternity.

grace alone (Rom. 3:10-12, 21, 28). The passage can be seen in the
light of James 2:26 which declares, "faith without deeds is dead."
What is here presented is not the ground of salvation but the fruit of
salvation.

In ordinary times it would be difficult to determine whether a
Gentile is saved or lost on the basis of his treatment of Jews. However, in the Great Tribulation preceding the Second Coming because of
worldwide anti-Semitism and the attempt to kill all the Jews, anyone
who opposes this and actually befriends a Jew and visits him in
prison or in the hospital is obviously declaring his faith in the Bible
and his recognition that the Jews are God's chosen people. Apart
from faith in Christ under these circumstances, no one would dare to
befriend a Jew. Though the sheep were different in nature than
goats, they are demonstrated as the saved by their works, and goats
are demonstrated by their lack of good works.

In the larger question as to whether the premillennial, amillennial,
or postmillennial views of the future are correct, it should be noted
that the passage gives no basis for hope for either amillennial or the
postmillennial point of view. While it fits naturally into the premillennial sequence of events, there is no evidence that this judgment is of
all men as it deals only with the living at the time of the Second
Coming in contrast to the demands of the amillennial concept of one
general judgment at the Second Coming.

This judgment is also quite different than the judgment of the

Great White Throne (Rev. 20:11-15) because there are no resurrected peoples here, but rather people living on earth. Further, the purpose of the judgment is to allow the righteous to enter the millennial kingdom. It should be noted that there is no resurrection related to this judgment such as would be true if it was the Rapture of the church.

The passage also tends to contradict the posttribulational view that the Rapture occurs at the end of the Tribulation at the time of the Second Coming. If such a Rapture had taken place in the process of Christ's coming from heaven to earth and believers were caught up to meet Him, as the Rapture is described, the sheep would have already been separated from the goats, and no judgment like this would be necessary. After Christ's kingdom is set up on earth, there is still the mingled picture of saved and unsaved. Living Gentile believers at this judgment prove that no posttribulational Rapture had taken place.

The Olivet Discourse takes its place among the great prophetic passages of Scripture. The judgment is explanatory of why Christ did not bring His kingdom in at His first coming because other prophecies had to be fulfilled first before the Second Coming could be fulfilled. Accordingly, while Christ is declared the King of Israel and the Saviour of the world, He was rejected at His first coming but will return in triumph, fulfilling literally the passage in the Old Testament that describes this victory.

The disciples were ill prepared to understand this, and they, no doubt, did not understand at the time as they asked the further question in Acts 1 concerning the time that Christ would bring in His kingdom. The early church was slow to respond and understand that there would be an extensive time period between the first coming of Christ and His second coming and that in it would be fulfilled God's program, unpredicted in the Old Testament, that God would call out a people, both Jews and Gentiles, to form a special body of believers for time and for eternity.

## PROPHECY IN THE GOSPEL OF JOHN

The Gospel of John is not primarily a book on prophecy as John himself states that the purpose of the book is to bring people to faith in Jesus Christ (John 20:30-31). Because of the special purpose of the Gospel of John, it deals more with history than prophecy. Written as it was in the last part of the first century, it is ministering to the second generation of the church which, of course, was primarily concerned with what would happen in the present age.

Accordingly, though the Gospel of John has numerous prophecies of a general nature, the major prophetic message is found in John 13–17, revealed the night before Jesus was crucified. The Upper Room Discourse found in this section takes its place along other major prophetic portions, such as Matthew 5–7, Matthew 13, and Matthew 24–25.

### The Testimony of John the Baptist Concerning Jesus

*John 1:15-17.* The ministry of John the Baptist as a forerunner of Jesus was prophesied in Isaiah 40:3-5. Matthew calls attention to this (Matt. 3:3, quoting Isa. 40:3). Luke quotes the whole passage of Isaiah 40:3-5 (Luke 3:4-6). John claimed that he was that prophet in connection with the baptism of Jesus (John 1:23). John had predicted, "This was He of whom I said, 'He who comes after me has surpassed me because He was before me' " (v. 15). John traced grace and all the blessing of God through Jesus, stating, "From the fullness of His grace we have all received one blessing after another. For the Law was given through Moses; grace and truth came through Jesus Christ" (vv. 16-17). John, in effect, announced that a new dispensation would be brought in by Jesus in which grace and truth would be its central feature. These statements are compatible only with the concept that Jesus Christ is the Son of God and the promised Messiah of Israel.

### John the Baptist Announces One Who Is Greater Than He

*John 1:26-27.* When John was asked whether he was Christ or Elijah or the Prophet, John disclaimed his identification with them. He stated instead that he baptized with water, but One after him is greater than he (1:24-27).

### John the Baptist Identifies Jesus as the Lamb of God

*John 1:29-34.* The day after John the Baptist announced that One was coming who was greater than he, he saw Jesus approaching, and John announced, "Look, the Lamb of God, who takes away the sin of the world! This is the One I meant when I said, 'A Man who comes after me has surpassed me because He was before me.' I myself did not know Him, but the reason I came baptizing with water was that He might be revealed to Israel" (vv. 29-31). Because Jesus was related to John the Baptist, no doubt he had met Jesus before but John did not know that He was the Messiah until that moment. The pronouncement that Jesus would be the Lamb of

God was a prediction that this would be His future ministry. John stated that one of the primary reasons for his ministry was to reveal Jesus to Israel.

John had been informed that when he met Jesus he would see a dove coming from heaven that would remain on Him, "Then John gave this testimony: 'I saw the Spirit come down from heaven as a dove and remain on Him. I would not have known Him, except that the One who sent me to baptize with water told me, "The Man on whom you see the Spirit come down and remain is He who will baptize with the Holy Spirit." I have seen and I testify that this is the Son of God' " (vv. 32-34). In Matthew's record of the same incident, Matthew recorded that after Jesus was baptized, "At that moment heaven was opened, and he saw the Spirit of God descending like a dove and lighting on Him. And a voice from heaven said, 'This is My Son, whom I love; with Him I am well pleased' " (Matt. 3:16-17). The record of John and the record of Matthew put together provide a remarkably clear demonstration of the doctrine of the Trinity. John saw the dove, symbolic of the Holy Spirit, remaining on Christ and, of course, Jesus was being baptized. At the same time the voice from heaven, recorded by Matthew, indicated God the Father. Luke, likewise, confirmed the fact that the Father's voice was heard (Luke 3:21-22).

### The Testimony of Nathanael

*John 1:40-51.* Andrew, who had been called to follow Jesus the day before, first went to find his brother Simon Peter and bring him to Jesus (vv. 40-42). The next day Philip was called (v. 43). Philip called Nathanael (v. 45), but Nathanael was concerned because he said no prophet comes from Nazareth (vv. 45-46). When Nathanael approached Jesus, Jesus said, "Here is a true Israelite, in whom there is nothing false" (v. 47). Nathanael was astounded that Jesus knew him and asked how He knew him (v. 48). Jesus' reply was, "I saw you while you were still under the fig tree before Philip called you" (v. 48). Nathanael recognized that the only way Jesus could know him, because he had been all alone, was that He was God, and he declared, "Rabbi, You are the Son of God; You are the King of Israel" (v. 49). In connection with the finding and call of Nathanael, Jesus made the pronouncement, "You believe because I told you I saw you under the fig tree. You shall see greater things than that" (v. 50). Then Jesus added, "I tell you the truth, you shall see heaven open, and the angels of God ascending and descending

404

on the Son of man" (v. 51). In this passage on the call of Nathanael, John was proving first of all that Jesus is omnipresent in His deity, which explains why He saw Nathanael under the fig tree, and also that He was omniscient—knowing things in the future.

### Jesus' Prediction of His Death and Resurrection

*John 2:13-22.* John recorded the first purification of the temple by Jesus (vv. 13-17). Jesus had driven the sheep and the cattle out of the temple area and scattered the tables of the money changers (v. 15). John recorded, however, "Then the Jews demanded of Him, 'What miraculous sign can You show us to prove Your authority to do all this?' " (v. 18) Jesus' reply was the prediction of His death and resurrection, "Destroy this temple and I will raise it again in three days" (v. 19). The Jews, of course, thought He was talking about the temple that Herod was building which had now been under construction for forty-six years (v. 20). John explained that the temple Jesus was talking about was His body (v. 21). At the time the disciples did not understand what Jesus said, but John recorded, "After He was raised from the dead, His disciples recalled what He had said. Then they believed the Scripture and the words that Jesus had spoken" (v. 22).

### Jesus Predicts His Crucifixion

*John 3:14-16.* When Jesus testified to Nicodemus concerning the difficulty of accepting spiritual truth, He stated, "Just as Moses lifted up the snake in the desert, so the Son of man must be lifted up, that everyone who believes in Him may have eternal life. For God so loved the world that He gave His one and only Son, that whoever believes in Him should not perish but have eternal life" (vv. 14-16). In alluding to Moses' lifting up the snake in the desert, Jesus was referring to Numbers 21:6-9. When the Children of Israel complained about not having food and water to their liking, Numbers recorded that God sent venomous snakes among the people and caused many to die (v. 6). When Israel confessed that they had sinned, the Lord instructed Moses to make a bronze snake, place it on a pole, and if they were bitten by the snake, they could look at the bronze snake and be healed (vv. 8-9).

Using this historical illustration, Jesus declared that He also "must be lifted up" (John 3:14). Just as in the case in Israel when they looked at the bronze serpent in faith and were healed, so Jesus predicted that when they looked at Him lifted up, they would believe and have eternal life (v. 15). In referring to being lifted up,

Jesus was referring to His crucifixion and the need for them to go to the cross in faith in order to have salvation through Christ. Jesus concluded this with the great affirmation that the gift of God's Son was an act of love but that "whoever believes in Him shall not perish but have eternal life" (v. 16). No doubt, the disciples did not understand what Jesus was referring to until after His death and resurrection.

### Necessity of Faith in Christ to Have Life

Coming as a summary of this important chapter, the Apostle John declares, "Whoever believes in the Son has eternal life, but whoever rejects the Son will not see life, for God's wrath remains on him" (3:36). This verse declared a marvelous prophecy that belief in Jesus as the Son assures an individual of eternal life in contrast to those who reject Jesus who not only do not receive life but are under God's wrath.

### Jesus' Testimony to the Samaritan Woman

*John 4:7-42.* The journey between Judea and Galilee required going through Samaria, the direct route which Jesus and His disciples used, or to go around by the east through Perea. After journeying all day, Jesus and His disciples came as far as Jacob's well located in Samaria, and the disciples went into the village to buy food. As Jesus sat by the well, a Samaritan woman came to draw water. Jesus, fully aware of her spiritual need, asked her for a drink (v. 7). The Samaritan woman, well aware of the antagonism between Samaritans and Jews, was surprised that He would have anything to do with her. When she questioned why Jesus was willing to ask for the drink, Jesus answered her, "If you knew the gift of God and who it is that asks you for a drink, you would have asked Him and He would have given you Living Water" (v. 10). The Samaritan woman replied, of course, that Jesus had nothing with which to draw water and, after all, His forefathers, Jacob and his sons, had drawn water from the well. Naturally, it raised the question as to how He could give her Living Water (vv. 11-12).

Jesus expounded on the living water, saying, "Everyone who drinks this water will be thirsty again, but whoever drinks the water I give him will never thirst. Indeed, the water I give him will become in him a spring of water welling up to eternal life" (vv. 13-14). When the Samaritan woman asked that she might have this water, Jesus told her, "Go, call your husband and come back" (v. 16).

406

In the resulting conversation, she said she had no husband, and Jesus said that was right, that though she had had five husbands, the one she was living with now was not her husband. The Samaritan woman, recognizing that she was talking to a prophet, brought up the Samaritan's familiar contention with the Jewish people as to where they could worship. She said, "Our fathers worshiped on this mountain, but you Jews claim that the place we must worship is in Jerusalem" (v. 20).

In His reply Jesus pointed out that worship is not a matter of place but a matter of true worship in spirit and in truth (v. 23). The Samaritan woman replied, "I know that Messiah" (called Christ) "is coming. When He comes, He will explain everything to us" (v. 25). Jesus then declared to her, "I who speak to you am He" (v. 26).

At this point in the narrative, the disciples had returned and were surprised that He would talk to a Samaritan woman but, nevertheless, did not ask Him why. When they urged Jesus to eat, He replied, "I have food to eat that you know nothing about" (v. 32). When the disciples could not understand this, He told them, " 'My food,' said Jesus, 'is to do the will of Him who sent Me and to finish His work' " (v. 34). Jesus then pointed out to them that the fields were white unto harvest, speaking, of course, of a spiritual harvest.

When the woman testified to the inhabitants of her village that Jesus had told her all she had ever done, because of her sinful life they naturally came out of curiosity to see One who knew all about her, and many believed (vv. 40-41). The Gospel of John, designed to lead people to faith in Christ that they may receive eternal life, had now added the Samaritan woman as a possible candidate for salvation along with Nicodemus, a Law-abiding Jew. In the process of leading the Samaritan woman to faith in Him, Jesus had demonstrated His omniscience and His capacity to give eternal life.

### Jesus Heals the Son of an Official at Capernaum

*John 4:43-53.* When the official sought Christ to come down and heal his son, Jesus replied simply, "You may go. Your son will live" (v. 50). In the verses which follow John recorded how the child was healed at that very hour, leading the entire household to believe in Jesus (vv. 52-53).

### Jesus' Claim of Equality with the Father, the Right to Judge, and the Ability to Give Eternal Life

*John 5:16-29.* Because Jesus had healed the invalid at the Pool of Bethesda on the Sabbath, the Jews persecuted Him (vv. 2-16). Because Jesus claimed God as His Father, the Jews all the more persecuted Him because they regarded this as a statement that He was equal with the Father (vv. 17-18).

In His exposition on His union with the Father, He declared that the Father loves Him (v. 20), that He has the power to raise the dead even as the Father does (v. 21), and that the Father had entrusted all judgment to the Son (vv. 22-23). Accordingly, he who does not honor the Son does not honor the Father (v. 23).

This led Jesus to declare, "I tell you the truth, whoever hears My word and believes Him who sent Me has eternal life and will not be condemned; he has crossed over from death to life" (v. 24).

Expanding further on His ability to save, Jesus said, "I tell you the truth, a time is coming and has now come when the dead will hear the voice of the Son of God and those who hear will live. For as the Father has life in Himself, so He has granted the Son to have life in Himself. And He has given Him authority to judge because He is the Son of man. Do not be amazed at this, for a time is coming when all who are in their graves will hear His voice and come out—those who have done good will rise to live, and those who have done evil will rise to be condemned" (vv. 25-29).

The broad prophecies which here are being revealed by the Saviour predict, first of all, the salvation of individuals who hear the facts about Christ and as a result of believing will live eternally. Just as Jesus has life in Himself from the Father, so He has authority to judge as the Son of man (v. 26). For further confirmation of Christ's ability, Jesus called attention to the fact that those in the grave, referring to those who have died physically, will someday hear His voice and come out of the grave with the result that they will be judged concerning their life on earth, whether good or bad (vv. 28-29). In asserting this fact of judgment, Christ Jesus is not teaching that all the resurrections will occur at the same time as other Scriptures make clear that there will be a series of resurrections, and the wicked will not be judged until all the righteous will be raised.

In these predictions and assertions, the Apostle John recorded one fact after another supporting his belief that Jesus is the Son of God and the only Saviour who can give eternal life.

### The Coming of a False Christ

*John 5:41-44.* John amasses additional proofs that Jesus is all that He claimed to be by summarizing the testimony of John the Baptist

(vv. 33-35), the evidence from the miraculous works which Jesus Himself had performed (v. 36), the testimony of God the Father Himself who had spoken from heaven concerning Jesus (vv. 37-38), and the Scriptures themselves (vv. 39-40).

In the light of these many evidences, unbelief in Jesus is unreasonable and is caused by their lack of love of God (vv. 41-42). Jesus then predicted that while He has come in His Father's name they have rejected Him, and later they will accept one who is a false christ (v. 43). He summarized it by saying that their unbelief leads them to accept the praise of men but not to make an effort to gain the praise of God (v. 44).

### Jesus as the Bread of Life

*John 6:30-59.* The crowds followed Jesus after He had fed the 5,000 (vv. 5-11). Jesus accused them, however, of following Him because He furnished them bread, not because they wanted eternal life (vv. 26-27). In contemplating the miracle of Christ, Jews had also recalled that they had manna from heaven which was more miraculous than the one instance of Christ's feeding them (vv. 30-31). Jesus did not deny that Moses gave them bread from heaven but stated, "It is My Father who gives you the true bread from heaven. For the Bread of God is He who comes down from heaven and gives life to the world" (vv. 32-33).

When they declared that they wanted this bread, Jesus expanded on the fact of being the Bread of Life, "I am the Bread of Life. He who comes to Me will never go hungry, and he who believes in Me will never be thirsty" (v. 35).

The Jews, however, found fault because Jesus said He was the Bread from heaven (v. 41). They said, "Is this not Jesus, the Son of Joseph, whose father and mother we know? How can He now say, 'I came down from heaven'?" (v. 42) Jesus went on to explain to them that He was not talking about physical manna or physical bread; He was talking about Himself. Their forefathers had eaten the manna and died. The one who eats of the Bread from heaven will live forever (vv. 50-51). The Jews did not understand, however, that when Christ spoke of eating His flesh and drinking His blood (v. 53), He was not talking about literally eating His flesh and blood but rather partaking of Christ by faith (vv. 53-57). Jesus asserted, "Our forefathers ate manna and died, but he who feeds on this bread will live forever" (v. 58). The Jews had difficulty understanding Jesus because they lacked faith in Him to begin with and were not ready for the assertions that exalted Jesus Christ as Saviour and God.

### The Necessity of the Father Enabling Men to Believe

*John 6:60-65.* The Jews were not able to accept Christ's teaching and were offended by it, so Jesus asked, "Does this offend you? What if you see the Son of man ascend to where He was before!" (vv. 61-62) He closed His discussion by reminding them once again, as He had earlier in this chapter, that apart from enablement of the Father, no one would believe in the Son (v. 65).

### Jesus' Prediction that He Will Leave Them
### but Will Send the Spirit

*John 7:33-39.* As the people were puzzled that Jesus had not been arrested, guards were sent from the temple to take Him into custody (vv. 26, 30-32). Jesus told the guards sent to arrest Him, "I am with you for only a short time, and then I go to the One who sent Me. You will look for Me, but you will not find Me; and where I am, you cannot come" (vv. 33-34).

John recorded Jesus' prediction of the coming of the Holy Spirit, "On the last and greatest day of the Feast, Jesus stood and said in a loud voice, 'If anyone is thirsty, let him come to Me and drink. Whoever believes in Me, as the Scripture has said, streams of Living Water will flow from within him.' By this He meant the Spirit, whom those who believed in Him were later to receive. Up to that time the Spirit had not been given, since Jesus had not yet been glorified" (vv. 37-39). In His prediction Jesus anticipated the coming of the Spirit on the Day of Pentecost and the Holy Spirit filling the disciples.

### Jesus as the Light of the World

*John 8:12-20.* Jesus announced, "I am the Light of the world. Whoever follows Me will never walk in darkness, but will have the light of life" (v. 12). When challenged by the Pharisees concerning this witness, Jesus pointed out that a matter is verified by two witnesses (v. 17). As Jesus testifies, so the Father also testifies, fulfilling the requirement of the two witnesses. Though Jesus is the Light of the world, the Pharisees did not receive the Light, and Jesus told them, "You do not know Me or My Father. . . . If you knew Me, you would know My Father also" (v. 19).

### Jesus' Prediction that the Pharisees Will Die in Their Sins
### and Where Jesus Was Going They Could Not Come

*John 8:21-30.* Jesus again announced that He would leave them but that the Pharisees would not come to Him because they will die in their sins (vv. 21-24). Jesus also declared that when He was lifted up, that is crucified, His claim to be able to forgive sins will be supported (v. 28; cf. Num. 21:6-9; John 3:14).

### Jesus Greater Than Abraham

*John 8:48-59.* In debating with the Jews whether they were legitimate sons of Abraham, Jesus called attention to their unbelief which indicated that they were not true children of Abraham, even though related to him physically. In the course of the argument, Jesus declared, "I tell you the truth, if anyone keeps My word, he will never see death" (v. 51). This caused the Jews to challenge Him whether He was greater than Abraham (v. 53). In reply, Jesus said, "Your father Abraham rejoiced at the thought of seeing My day; he saw it and was glad" (v. 56).

When the Jews asked Him how this could be because he was not that old, Jesus replied, "I tell you the truth . . . before Abraham was born, I am!" (v. 58) The Jews rightly viewed this as claiming to be God, and though they picked up stones to stone Him, Jesus was protected from them (v. 59). Throughout the passage what Jesus was asserting was that those who are true spiritual descendants of Abraham would recognize Jesus also for what He is.

### The Contrast between Natural Sight and Spiritual Sight

*John 9:39-41.* In the aftermath of Jesus' healing the one who was born blind (vv. 1-38), Jesus made the pronouncement, "For judgment I have come into this world, so that the blind will see and those who see will become blind" (v. 39). When the Pharisees asked whether they also were blind, Jesus replied, "If you were blind, you would not be guilty of sin; but now that you claim you can see, your guilt remains" (v. 41). Though the healing of the man who was naturally blind was a great miracle, it was also an evidence of the power of God that those who were once blind spiritually can see and that those who claim they can see spiritually often are blind.

### Jesus as the Good Shepherd

*John 10:5-18.* In expanding the fact that Jesus was the Good Shepherd and that His sheep would follow Him, Jesus stated, "But they will never follow a stranger; in fact, they will run away from him because they do not recognize a stranger's voice" (v. 5). When the disciples did not understand this, Jesus enlarged the explanation by declaring, "I tell you the truth, I am the gate for the sheep. All who ever came before Me were thieves and robbers, but the sheep did not listen to them. I am the gate; whoever enters through Me

411

will be saved. He will come in and go out, and find pasture. The thief comes only to steal and kill and destroy; I have come that they may have life, and have it to the full" (vv. 7-10). Jesus is declaring that He is the only Saviour and that those who are saved through Him will not only have life but will have pasture and God's care. They will have life and have life to the full (v. 10).

In expanding the declaration that He is the Good Shepherd, Jesus declared, "I am the Good Shepherd. The Good Shepherd lays down His life for the sheep" (v. 11). In contrast to false shepherds who flee when the wolf comes and abandons the sheep (vv. 12-13), Jesus declared, "I am the Good Shepherd; I know My sheep and My sheep know Me—just as the Father knows Me and I know the Father—and I lay down My life for the sheep" (vv. 14-15). As a Good Shepherd in dying on the cross, Jesus will die for His sheep.

In proclaiming that He is the Good Shepherd, Jesus added, "I have other sheep that are not of this sheep pen. I must bring them also. They too will listen to My voice, and there shall be one flock and one Shepherd" (v. 16). In this prophecy Jesus was anticipating the church, composed of both Jews and Gentiles, where the wall of partition between will be broken down and they will be one in Christ and be one flock and have one Shepherd.

Jesus then enlarged on His sacrifice of His life, declaring, "The reason My Father loves Me is that I lay down My life—only to take it up again. No one takes it from Me, but I lay it down of My own accord. I have authority to lay it down and authority to take it up again. This command I received from My Father" (vv. 17-18). In making this assertion, Jesus was anticipating His death on the cross when He would lay down His life for the sheep. In the case of Jesus, however, He not only had the power to lay down His life, but He had the power to take it again—something that had never been true of any previous person raised from the dead. This was to be the supreme proof of His deity which His disciples recognized. As a study of Christ's resurrection demonstrates, Jesus was not simply restored to the life He had before His death but was given a new body, the pattern of the resurrection body of the saints which they will receive at the time of the resurrection or Rapture.

### Jesus' Deity and His Power to Give
### Eternal Life to Those Who Trust Him

*John 10:19-39.* The sayings of Jesus divided His audience, and some claimed that He was demon possessed and others that, nevertheless, His miracles demonstrated that He was a genuine Prophet (vv. 19-21).

When the Jews addressed Him, "How long will You keep us in suspense? If You are the Christ, tell us plainly" (v. 24), Jesus replied that He had given them adequate proof. His miracles testified to His claim to be genuine (v. 25). The reason they were having trouble believing Him was that they were not His sheep (v. 26). Jesus declared, "My sheep listen to My voice; I know them, and they follow Me. I give them eternal life, and they shall never perish; no one can snatch them out of My hand" (vv. 27-28). This passage is another assertion that those who are once born again have received an eternal salvation in the eternal life that they receive. Jesus promised that they will never perish or fall from their exalted position. He said, "No one can snatch them out of My hand. My Father, who has given them to Me, is greater than all; no one can snatch them out of My Father's hand. I and the Father are One" (vv. 28-30).

As a double assurance of the certainty of their salvation, Jesus declared not only that they are in His hands but also in the Father's hands, and no one can take them out of the Father's hands. When He concluded with the statement, "I and the Father are One" (v. 30), the Jews recognized this as a claim to Deity and picked up stones to stone Him (v. 31). Jesus asked them why they were offended. They replied, "We are not stoning You for any of these . . . but for blasphemy, because You, a mere man, claim to be God" (v. 33).

When Jesus quoted from the Law to the effect that those who had received the word of God were "gods" (v. 34), He asked why they accused Him of blasphemy. In His use of the Law here, Jesus referred not only to the Pentateuch but here to the entire Old Testament.

The particular reference is Psalm 82 where men are appointed to judge on behalf of God, and God declared in verse 6, "I said, 'You are "gods"; you are all sons of the Most High.' " This psalm does not declare that men are gods except as appointed by God to act on His behalf as in this case. Jesus was arguing much like the Jews argue, pointing to this passage in the Old Testament that would widen the use of the word "gods." If ordinary men could be gods as in this psalm, they should not object to His claiming to be God in view of His credentials where He actually is God's Son. Jesus once again appeals to them to accept His word, but if they could not do that to at least believe because of the miracles which He performed (John 10:37-38). Once again they attempted to seize Him but were kept from succeeding (v. 39).

In the process of declaring that He rightly used the word "God" concerning Himself, Jesus also made a great pronouncement concerning the Scripture, "the Scripture cannot be broken" (v. 35). Here, as in other instances, Jesus gives full authority to the Bible as inspired of God, to the very words here but sometimes even the very letters and even to the smallest letter (Matt. 5:18). Because Jesus put His own stamp of approval on the concept that the Bible is inspired of the Holy Spirit and therefore without error, one who attacks the written Word must also attack the veracity of Jesus as the incarnate Word. If Jesus is right, then the Bible also is right.

### Jesus' Pronouncements concerning Lazarus and His Resurrection

*John 11:1-53.* This chapter, dealing with the death and resurrection of Lazarus, was an appropriate introduction of the death and resurrection of Christ which occurred not many days later. It centers in the great truth that in Jesus there is resurrection and life.

When Jesus heard of Lazarus' illness, He declared, "This sickness will not end in death. No, it is for God's glory so that God's Son may be glorified through it" (v. 4).

After learning of Lazarus' sickness, Jesus deliberately stayed two more days before beginning the return journey. When He announced to His disciples that He was returning to Judea (v. 7), they called His attention to the fact that the Jews were laying wait to kill Him, but Jesus answered, "Are there not twelve hours of daylight? A man who walks by day will not stumble, for he sees this world's light. It is when he walks by night that he stumbles, for he has no light" (vv. 9-10).

Jesus then announced to them that Lazarus had fallen asleep (v. 11). The disciples, thinking of natural sleep, thought this was a sign that he was getting better (v. 12), but, as the Scripture informs us, Jesus said to them, "Lazarus is dead, and for your sake I am glad I was not there, so that you may believe. But let us go to him" (vv. 14-15). Led by Thomas, they would return at his exhortation, "Let us also go, that we may die with Him" (v. 16).

Upon the return of Jesus and His disciples to Bethany, they learned that Lazarus had been in the tomb for four days. Martha, who went out to greet Him, said, as no doubt they had said many times in His absence, "Lord . . . if You had been here, my brother would not have died. But I know that even now God will give You whatever You ask" (vv. 21-22). Though she did not expect Jesus to raise Lazarus, she did assert that He had the power to do it.

This gave occasion to Jesus to discuss resurrection with her, and Jesus said to Martha, "Your brother will rise again" (v. 23). Martha in her reply asserted her faith that all would be resurrected eventually. Jesus went on to affirm more than the hope of all for resurrection, and said to Martha, "I am the resurrection and the life. He who believes in Me will live, even though he dies; and whoever lives and believes in Me will never die. Do you believe this?" (vv. 25-26) Martha in her reply came back to the basic fact that she believed that Jesus was the Christ, the Son of God (v. 27).

Martha then called Mary. When Mary met Jesus, the Scriptures recorded, "She fell at his feet and said, 'Lord, if You had been here, my brother would not have died' " (v. 32). When Jesus saw that she wept along with the Jews who were there, Scripture recorded, "He was deeply moved in spirit and troubled" (v. 33). Then He asked to see the place where Lazarus was entombed. Some of the Jews who were there agreed with Mary and Martha that if Jesus had been there while Lazarus was still alive, there was no question He could have healed Him. But it was beyond the faith of most of them that Jesus could raise Lazarus, even at this point. When they came to the tomb, which was a cave, Jesus said to them, "Take away the stone" (v. 39). When Martha objected that there would be a bad odor because he had been dead for four days, Jesus replied to her, "Did I not tell you that if you believed, you would see the glory of God?" (v. 40) Jesus then prayed to God the Father, "Father, I thank You that You have heard Me. I knew that You always hear Me, but I said this for the benefit of the people standing here, that they may believe that You sent Me" (vv. 41-42).

Then Jesus, speaking with a loud voice, said, "Lazarus, come out!" (v. 43) To the astonishment of those who observed, Lazarus came out of the tomb with his graveclothes. Jesus ordered them to take the graveclothes from him and to let him go (v. 44).

The obvious great miracle that occurred influenced many others to put their trust in Jesus (v. 45), but the chief priests and the Pharisees were upset by this demonstration of the power of God, and they said, "Here is this Man performing many miraculous signs. If we let Him go on like this, everyone will believe in Him, and then the Romans will come and take away both our place and our nation" (vv. 47-48).

The utter blindness of the Pharisees to the significance of what had happened at the tomb of Lazarus and their selfish desire to maintain their own place of leadership are a constant reminder of the blindness of the human heart untouched by the grace of God when faced with the facts of Jesus Christ. John does record that Caiaphas, who was high priest, spoke up, "You know nothing at all! You do not realize it is better for you that one man die for the people than that the whole nation perish" (vv. 49-50). What Caiaphas meant was that it was better for Jesus to die than for the whole nation to be misled. But as John reminded us, Caiaphas unwittingly delivered a true prophecy, which was exactly what was going to happen, that Jesus was going to die, and the result would be the nation would be saved. John stated, "He did not say this on his own, but as high priest that year he prophesied that Jesus would die for the Jewish nation, and not only for that nation but also for the scattered children of God, to bring them together and make them one" (vv. 51-52). From this time on, as Scripture stated, the Jews actively plotted His death (v. 53).

### Jesus Anointed by Mary of Bethany

*John 12:1-11; Matthew 26:6-13; Mark 14:3-9.* Jesus and His disciples had returned to Bethany to have a dinner in Jesus' honor. While reclining at the table, John recorded, "Then Mary took about a pint of pure nard, an expensive perfume; she poured it on Jesus' feet and wiped His feet with her hair. And the house was filled with the fragrance of the perfume" (John 12:3). John recorded that Judas Iscariot objected to what he thought was a waste of the perfume and that it should have been sold and the money given to the poor (vv. 4-5). John, however, recorded that the real concern of Judas Iscariot was that he was the treasurer, and the money would have come into his possession and he would profit by it as he was a thief (v. 6).

Jesus replied to this, however, "Leave her alone . . . it was meant that she should save this perfume for the day of My burial. You will always have the poor among you, but you will not always have Me" (vv. 7-8). This touching act of devotion on the part of Mary revealed that perhaps more than anyone else, as a result of her sitting at the feet of Jesus, she somehow comprehended that

He was going to die and intended this as a preparation and a demonstration of her devotion to Him.

While at the dinner, a crowd came out from Jerusalem not simply to see Jesus but also to see Lazarus as word of his restoration had been spread abroad (v. 9). The result of this was that the chief priests planned not simply to kill Jesus but to kill Lazarus because so many were believing in Jesus because of him (vv. 10-11).

### Jesus' Triumphal Entry into Jerusalem

*John 12:12-19; Matthew 21:1-9; Mark 11:1-10; Luke 19:29-38; cf. Zechariah 9:9.* The tidings of Lazarus' resurrection and the accumulation of Jesus' ministry caused the crowds to welcome Him with palm branches (John 12:12-13). John recorded that the crowds shouted, "Hosanna! Blessed is He who comes in the name of the Lord! Blessed is the King of Israel!" (v. 13) In addition to quoting and fulfilling Zechariah 9:9, the crowd also quoted from Psalm 118:25-26.

John recorded that the disciples at the time did not recognize the significance of what they had seen and heard, but after Jesus' glorification, they realized that this occasion was a fulfillment of prophecy. John also added that the resurrection of Lazarus and this event of entering Jerusalem triumphantly served to spread the Gospel so that many others believed in Jesus. This led the Pharisees to total exasperation, and they said, "See, this is getting us nowhere. Look how the whole world has gone after Him!" (v. 19)

### Jesus' Response to the Greeks Who Sought Him

*John 12:20-26.* Upon hearing of the Greeks wanting to see Him, Jesus said, "The hour has come for the Son of man to be glorified. I tell you the truth, unless a kernel of wheat falls to the ground and dies, it remains only a single seed. But if it dies, it produces many seeds. The man who loves his life will lose it, while the man who hates his life in this world will keep it for eternal life. Whoever serves Me must follow Me; and where I am My servant also will be. My Father will honor the one who serves Me" (vv. 23-26).

The issues facing Jesus were far greater than that of granting the Greeks an interview. Instead, Jesus was facing the imminent fulfillment that He was to die. He pointed out, however, that just as wheat when it dies produces much more than the single grain that is planted, so when Jesus died, it would produce many seeds (v. 24). This led to the larger principle that in order to gain your life you need to lose it, and those that are willing to lose it gain it (v. 25).

Jesus stated further, "Whoever serves Me must follow Me; and where I am, My servant also will be. My Father will honor the one who serves Me" (v. 26). In this pronouncement Jesus was anticipating His death and also the challenge of those who would follow Him. He promised that those who do serve Him will be honored by God the Father (v. 26).

### Jesus' Struggle with the Approaching Hour of His Death

*John 12:27-36.* As Jesus contemplated His coming crucifixion, He said, "Now My heart is troubled, and what shall I say? 'Father, save Me from this hour'? No, it was for this very reason I came to this hour. Father, glorify Your name!" (vv. 27-28) In response to Jesus' pronouncement, Scripture records, "Then a voice came from heaven, 'I have glorified it, and will glorify it again.' The crowd that was there and heard it said it had thundered; others said an angel had spoken to Him" (vv. 28-29).

In response to what the crowd had said, Jesus said, " 'This voice was for your benefit, not Mine. Now is the time for judgment on this world; now the prince of this world will be driven out. But I, when I am lifted up from the earth, will draw all men to Myself.' He said this to show the kind of death He was going to die" (vv. 30-33). This prediction is another allusion to His crucifixion, and being lifted up refers back to John 3:14; 8:28; 12:32, 34.

Though the allusion of being lifted up referred to His death, it seems that the crowd had some understanding that it was referring to the fact that Jesus would not be with them forever. They spoke up, "We have heard from the Law that the Christ will remain forever, so how can you say, 'The Son of man must be lifted up'? Who is this 'Son of man'?" (v. 34) Jesus did not answer them directly but warned them that the light was not going to be with them forever (vv. 35-36). They should put their trust in Him while it was still open to them. The incident closed with Jesus hiding Himself from them (v. 36).

*John 12:37-50.* John concluded with the sad fulfillment of Isaiah who prophesied their hardness of heart and blindness of eyes when it came to spiritual truth (vv. 37-40; Isa. 6:10; 53:1). In spite of the blindness of some, however, even some of the leaders of Israel were beginning to believe in Him (John 12:42-43). In conclusion, John recorded Jesus' statement that those who hear will be held responsible and judged by what they do with what they see and hear (vv. 44-50).

## *Jesus' Pronouncement at the Occasion of the Passover and His Washing the Disciples' Feet*

*John 13:1-20.* On the fateful night before His crucifixion, Jesus had gathered with His disciples to observe the Passover feast. Jesus Himself was looking beyond the immediate events of His death, resurrection, and later ascension into heaven to the present age between Pentecost and the Rapture when God's previously undisclosed plan to call a people from the church would be fulfilled. This discourse of John 13–17 is called the Upper Room Discourse, but only the first two chapters were actually delivered in the Upper Room. As the observance of the Passover supper was underway, Jesus, knowing that Judas Iscariot had agreed to betray Him and that He had come from God and was returning to God (vv. 2-3), He took a basin of water and a towel and began to wipe the disciples' feet. Though not prophecy in itself, it anticipated the ministry of the disciples after Jesus was gone.

There was an uneasy silence in the room as He went from one to another as they reclined, with their heads toward the table and their feet away from the table, on a couch that was only a short distance from the ground. It was customary when being invited to dinner to have a slave wash guests' feet after their contact with the dirty streets. None of the disciples wanted to volunteer for this because it would be admitting that they were not the greatest, and now they were being rebuked by the fact that Jesus took this lowly work.

When He came to Peter, Peter said, "You shall never wash my feet" (v. 8). Jesus replied to Peter, however, "Unless I wash you, you have no part with Me" (v. 8). Peter then replied, "not just my feet but my hands and my head as well!" (v. 9) The reply of Jesus distinguished a person having a bath where his whole body is washed and having only his feet washed. Jesus told Peter, "A person who has had a bath needs only to wash his feet; his whole body is clean. And you are clean, though not every one of you" (v. 10). Jesus, of course, was referring to Judas Iscariot (v. 11).

Upon completing the task, Jesus asked him, "Do you understand what I have done for you?" (v. 12) Jesus said, "Now that I, your Lord and Teacher, have washed your feet, you also should wash one another's feet. I have set you an example that you should do as I have done for you" (vv. 14-15).

Jesus then predicted, "I am not referring to all of you; I know those I have chosen. But this is to fulfill the Scripture: 'He who shares My bread has lifted up his heel against Me.' I am telling you now before it happens, so that when it does happen you will believe that I am He" (vv. 18-19). In this interchange with His disciples, Jesus predicted again that Judas Iscariot was going to betray Him to the chief priests.

### Jesus Predicts His Betrayal by Judas Iscariot, His Denial by Peter, and His Departure

*John 13:21-38; cf. Matthew 26:21-25, 30-35; Mark 14:18-21, 26-31; Luke 22:21-23, 31-34.* After referring to the importance of accepting Him, Jesus said plainly, "I tell you the truth, one of you is going to betray Me" (John 13:21). The disciples did not know what to do about this statement (v. 22). But John the beloved disciple, who apparently was next to Christ at the table, asked Jesus, "Lord, who is it?" (v. 25) Jesus answered, " 'It is the one to whom I will give this piece of bread when I have dipped it in the dish.' Then, dipping the piece of bread, He gave it to Judas Iscariot, son of Simon. As soon as Judas took the bread, Satan entered into him" (vv. 26-27).

Apparently, only John the Apostle knew of the identification of Judas Iscariot as the one who would betray Jesus. Judas himself, after he had taken the bread, went out (v. 30).

Jesus then announced to His disciples, "Now is the Son of man glorified and God is glorified in Him. If God is glorified in Him, God will glorify the Son in Himself, and will glorify Him at once" (vv. 31-32).

Jesus then announced prophetically that He was not going to be with them much longer. He said, "My children, I will be with you only a little longer. You will look for Me, and just as I told the Jews, so I tell you now: Where I am going, you cannot come" (v. 33).

In the light of His separation from His disciples, Jesus gave them a new commandment, "A new command I give you: Love one another. As I have loved you, so you must love one another. All men will know that you are My disciples, if you love one another" (vv. 34-35).

The disciples did not concern themselves with the command of loving one another. As a matter of fact they had been contending among themselves as to which would be the greatest (Luke 22:24). But they were very much interested in the fact that Jesus was leaving them. Simon Peter asked Jesus the question, "Lord, where are You going?" (v. 36) Jesus replied, "Where I am going, you cannot follow now, but you will follow later" (v. 36). Peter persisted, however, and asked, "Lord, why can't I follow You now? I will lay down my life for You" (v. 37). Jesus answered Peter, "Will you really lay down your life for Me? I tell you the truth, before the rooster crows, you will disown Me three times!" (v. 38) No doubt, Peter was sincere in his profession of loyalty to Jesus Christ, but he did not know how weak he was. The prophecy of Jesus that he would deny the Lord three times before the cock would crow was to be literally fulfilled the following morning.

### Jesus' Revelation of God's Provision
### for His Troubled Disciples

*John 14:1-31.* The disciples were deeply troubled. They had heard Jesus announce that one was going to betray Him. They had heard Him tell Peter that he was going to deny Him three times. Most of all, they were concerned about the fact that Jesus said He was going to leave them and they could not follow then (13:36). At this point in their last night together, Jesus prophetically outlined God's provisions for them as troubled disciples in a troubled world.

Jesus, first of all, exhorted them to not be troubled, but instead, He said, "Trust in God; trust also in Me" (14:1). This command can be literally translated, "Keep on trusting in God; keep on trusting in Me." The secret of the untroubled heart in a troubled world is complete trust in God. In exhorting them to do this, He was giving the whole answer. Recognizing, however, that all of us, including the disciples, are weak, the rest of the chapter outlined the support basis for this trust in God.

In the light of His departure, Jesus promised them that He would return, "In My Father's house are many rooms; if it were not so, I would have told you. I am going there to prepare a place for you. And if I go and prepare a place for you, I will come back and take you to be with Me that you also may be where I am" (vv. 2-3).

This was an entirely new revelation to be contrasted to Christ's earlier revelation concerning His second coming to judge the world. This was a coming with an entirely different context, and its purpose was to take them out of the world and take them to the Father's house which clearly refers to heaven where Jesus has gone before to prepare a place for them. This is the first instance in the New Testament to what Paul later referred to as the Rapture of the church (1 Cor. 15:51-58; 1 Thes. 4:13-18).

The disciples were both emotionally and theologically unprepared to receive this truth which John recorded many years later in this

# PREDICTED EVENTS RELATING TO THE CHURCH

1. Rise of liberalism and rejection of fundamental biblical doctrines permeate the professing church.
2. The rise of Communism and atheism as major opponents of Christianity.
3. The ecumenical movement promoting a world church organized in 1948.
4. Increased moral chaos resulting from departure from biblical doctrines.
5. Increasing evidence of spiritism, the occult, and Satan worship.
6. The Rapture of the church.
7. Lifting of the restraint of sin by the Holy Spirit.
8. Super church movement gains power and forms a world church.
9. World church works with the Antichrist to secure world domination.
10. Super church is destroyed by the ten kings supporting the Antichrist to pave the way for worship of the world ruler as God.
11. Those who have come to believe in Christ as Saviour since the Rapture suffer persecution because they refuse to worship the world ruler.
12. Second coming of Christ occurs, and remaining Christians in the world are rescued and enter the millennial kingdom.
13. After the Millennium the church is placed in the New Jerusalem in the new earth.

Gospel. They did comprehend, however, that He was going to leave them. This was a devastating truth to them because they had been with Christ for three-and-a-half years and had left their homes and their occupations in order to be His disciples. They simply did not understand what Jesus meant when He said He was going to leave them. Scripture recorded that Jesus had closed His remarks, "You know the way to the place where I am going" (John 14:4).

Thomas, as he contemplated this sentence, did not know where Jesus was going, and probably the other disciples had the same problem. Thomas said to Jesus, "Lord, we don't know where You are going, so how can we know the way?" (v. 5) This was a logical statement because if one does not know his destination, he does not know where he is going. This is a profound truth that affects all of our lives. Knowing our ultimate destination is a part of God's program of reassuring troubled disciples. On the other hand, Jesus was referring to heaven, and certainly Thomas and the other disciples should have known that this was their ultimate destination.

Jesus' answer to Thomas was both profound and simple, "I am the way and the truth and the life. No one comes to the Father except through Me" (v. 6). There are few statements in any language or any book that can rival this for profound truth. Jesus is the way or the road to heaven, a truth that is not accepted by the world but is the mainstay of Christians who put their trust in God.

Jesus also said, "I am the truth." All things are true because of God's laws and revelation, and Jesus is the source of this order in the universe. All truth is true only as it is related in some way to Jesus Christ as the truth.

Jesus also declared, "and the life" (v. 6). Again, the profound truth that only in Jesus eternal life and blessing in the life to come are possible. All the philosophies of the world and the schemes of men have never been able to substitute anything for God's plan of Jesus as the way to heaven as the ultimate test of truth and the ultimate bestower of eternal life.

In addition to having Jesus Christ as the way, the truth, and the life, the disciples also had a Heavenly Father. Jesus said, "If you really knew Me, you would know My Father as well. From now on, you do know Him and have seen Him" (v. 7). This time Philip spoke up, "Lord, show us the Father and that will be enough for us" (v. 8).

Jesus' reply to Philip was at the heart of the Christian faith. Jesus said, "Don't you know Me, Philip, even after I have been among you such a long time? Anyone who has seen Me has seen the Father. How can you say, 'Show us the Father'? Don't you believe that I am in the Father, and that the Father is in Me? The words I say to you are not just my own. Rather, it is the Father, living in Me, who is doing this work. Believe Me when I say that I am in the Father and the Father is in Me; or at least believe on the evidence of the miracles themselves" (vv. 9-11).

As God the Father has not been visible to man, the only way the

Father can be known is through His revelation in Jesus Christ. As God and Jesus have the same attributes as God the Father, and as any true son, He was the replica, in effect, of His Father, though existing from eternity past, even as the Father has existed.

Jesus brought this thought of the Father to its climax when He said, "I tell you the truth, anyone who has faith in Me will do what I have been doing. He will do even greater things than these, because I am going to the Father" (v. 12).

The startling statement that the disciples of Jesus could do greater works than Jesus Himself gave the disciples pause. The secret, of course, is the fact that Jesus said not that they would be greater than Jesus or do greater things in themselves than Jesus; but in a partnership of Jesus at the right hand of God the Father and their ministry on earth, they would be able to accomplish more in that relationship than Jesus Christ could if He had remained on earth as an individual. The disciples could achieve multiplication of their numbers, reach out to more in the world as many individuals than even Jesus on earth would have been able to reach. Even the experience of leading one soul to Christ is in a sense a greater miracle than the Creation of the entire world. The Creation of the world did not cost God anything as He could speak and it would be done. But the salvation of a soul involved the death of His Son on the cross. The prediction that more had been accomplished in the world is seen in that millions of people have come to put their trust in Jesus through the centuries through the work of many individual disciples.

In keeping with this promise to be partners with Him at the Father's right hand, Jesus urged them to pray, "And I will do whatever you ask in My name, so that the Son may bring glory to the Father. You may ask Me for anything in My name, and I will do it" (vv. 13-14). This, again, is a saying that confounds the wisdom of the world. The plan is that prayer in the name of Jesus by a disciple will ultimately be prayer in the will of God. Like a check requiring two signatures, any request signed by a believer, if it is signed also by Jesus Christ and it is in His name, will justify the hope of the prayer being answered.

Another important facet in God's provision for troubled disciples was the promise of the indwelling of the Holy Spirit. Jesus said, "And I will ask the Father, and He will give you another Counselor to be with you forever—the Spirit of Truth. The world cannot accept Him because it neither sees Him nor knows Him. But you know Him, for He lives with you and will be in you" (vv. 16-17).

This prophecy anticipated the dispensational change on the Day of Pentecost. In the Old Testament, only a few were indwelt permanently and always with a view to special service for God. Beginning at Pentecost, every believer will be indwelt by the Spirit and have the same resource in the time of trouble. Even though Christ was going to leave them, He said, "I will not leave you as orphans; I will come to you" (v. 18). The amazing truth in this chapter is that not only the Holy Spirit will indwell every believer but also Jesus Christ will indwell every believer, a truth that was never mentioned in the Old Testament and was not realized by any of the saints prior to the Day of Pentecost. Though the world will not be able to see Jesus, they will be able to realize that He is in heaven and, in effect, they will see Him (v. 19). Also, because Jesus Christ lives, they will also live (v. 19).

In addition to the great truth that Christ Himself was going to indwell believers, an additional dispensational truth, characteristic of the present age from Pentecost, was predicted in verse 20, "On that day you will realize that I am in My Father, and you are in Me, and I am in you." The expression, "I am in you," refers to Christ indwelling, but the fact that "you are in Me" presents a truth foreign to the Old Testament but realized by the Christians baptized into Christ. The gracious provision of God is not only that God is in us but that we are vitally related to Jesus Christ and share the same eternal life. It is not too much to say that verse 20 is one of the great revelations of the New Testament and characterizes the present age as a distinct dispensation.

Once again, Jesus referred to the need to obey His commands and to love Him. He promised, "He who loves Me will be loved by My Father, and I too will love him and show Myself to him" (v. 21). The disciples did not show too much interest in the fact of the love of Christ or being loved by the Father, but Judas, not Iscariot, asked the question, "But, Lord, why do You intend to show Yourself to us and not to the world?" (v. 22) Jesus replied to the point that a new relationship existed between Jesus and the disciples as well as the Father and the disciples. Jesus said, "If anyone loves Me, he will obey My teaching. My Father will love him, and We will come to him and make Our home with him" (v. 23). Here is an additional fact that not only Jesus and the Holy Spirit would indwell a believer but also God the Father will make their body His home.

Those who do not love Jesus and obey Him know nothing of this marvelous truth (v. 24).

Something of the tremendous future ministry of the Holy Spirit to the disciples was indicated in Jesus' pronouncement, "All this I have spoken while still with you. But the Counselor, the Holy Spirit, whom the Father will send in My name, will teach you all things and will remind you of everything I have said to you" (vv. 25-26). This was to be realized, particularly by the disciples and the Apostle John who was writing the Gospel of John many years after the events that are described, but it is also true that the Holy Spirit reminds all believers of the truth of God while we are listening to His teaching.

The final work of God on behalf of the troubled disciples was His marvelous peace, "Peace I leave with you; My peace I give you. I do not give to you as the world gives. Do not let your hearts be troubled and do not be afraid" (v. 27). This remarkable statement came from Jesus who knew in the next twenty-four hours He would die the awful death of crucifixion and His body would be in the tomb. What did Jesus mean by "My peace"? The peace which Christ was referring to goes beyond the prophecy of the death and resurrection of Christ and beyond ascension to the ultimate disposal and judgment of all things.

Jesus knew that in the end God would triumph and that His death on the cross would be rewarded by the heritage of millions of souls being saved through His death. He also knew that though the disciples were troubled, their troubles were temporary and their ultimate peace was to be realized. The peace that Christ gives is more than a psychological peace, more than an act of human will, and one of the marvelous things that comes when a disciple of Jesus who puts his faith in God and realizes the tremendous assets and provisions God has made for him as a Christian. Because of this, it is possible to be at peace even though a disciple may live in a troubled world.

Jesus again referred to His departure and said that He was predicting it in advance and that they would know it was of God for Him to go to the Father and to come back (vv. 28-29). He told them that after He departed, "the prince of this world is coming. He has no hold on Me, but the world must learn that I love the Father and that I do exactly what My Father has commanded Me" (vv. 30-31). His reference to the "prince of this world" is a reference to Satan, and

He was referring, of course, to the continued activity of Satan during the period that Jesus was going back to the Father. The ultimate triumph over Satan, however, was assured. At this point in their evening together, they left the Upper Room and proceeded toward the Garden of Gethsemane.

### Jesus as the Vine and the Disciples as the Branches

*John 15:1-8.* In opening His discussion of the disciples as those who would bear fruit for God, Jesus declared, "I am the true vine" (v. 1). This is the seventh "I am" of Christ as recorded in the Gospel of John. In John 6:35 Jesus declared, "I am the Bread of Life." In John 8:12 Jesus revealed, "I am the Light of the world." In John 10:7, 9 Jesus stated, "I am the gate." In John 10:11, 14 Jesus affirmed, "I am the Good Shepherd." In John 11:25 Jesus stated, "I am the resurrection and the life." In John 14:6 Jesus declared, "I am the way and the truth and the life."

In this final declaration, "I am the true Vine," Jesus was comparing Himself to Israel as a vine which was planted but did not bear fruit (cf. Isa. 5:1-7). Enlarging on the figure, He declared, "My Father is the gardener. He cuts off every branch in Me that bears no fruit, while every branch that does bear fruit He trims clean so that it will be even more fruitful" (John 15:1-2).

When Jesus stated that the branches were in the vine, He was using a figure of speech. In 14:20 He said, "You are in Me." Believers since the Day of Pentecost have been baptized and placed in Christ. This is a relationship that will never change and is part of God's plan of grace for those who put their trust in Christ. In John 15, however, where it speaks of being "in the vine," He is talking not about position but about fruitfulness. A branch appears superficially to be in the vine, but if there is no fruit, it is pruned. The gardener views it as only a superficial connection to the vine. He is not talking here about the security of a believer in Christ but rather about the state of fruitfulness that exists in a true believer but does not exist in one who is merely a professing Christian.

To the disciples Jesus said, "You are already clean because of the word I have spoken to you" (v. 3). In keeping with the illustration, the disciples cannot expect to bear fruit unless they remain in the vine which would enable them to bear fruit. Jesus again affirmed that "I am the Vine; you are the branches. If a man remains in Me and I in him, he will bear much fruit; apart from Me you can do nothing" (v. 5). As in the case of a grapevine, however, some

427

branches will not maintain a living connection with the vine and will be pruned. Accordingly, Jesus said, "If anyone does not remain in Me, he is like a branch that is thrown away and withers; such branches are picked up, thrown into the fire and burned" (v. 6).

Various interpretations have arisen concerning this statement as expressing the idea that a person, once saved, can be lost. But Jesus contradicted such interpretation. In the Gospel of John Jesus affirmed that eternal life cannot be lost (John 5:24). It is ultimately a question of what God does rather than what man does in contrast here to fruitfulness which depends on what man does in depending and drawing life from the vine. Jesus had frequently talked about the genuineness of salvation which could not be lost in the Gospel of John (1 Cor. 3:15; 9:27; 2 Cor. 5:10). The best explanation, however, is that it is referring to professing Christians who outwardly are joined to Christ but actually have no living connection and therefore cannot bear the fruit that can be expected of a fruitful branch. The branches do not become fruitful branches by bearing fruit; they become fruitful branches because of their abiding connection with the life of the vine.

If the disciples remain in vital relationship to Jesus Christ and are drawing on Him for fruitfulness, He promised, "If you remain in Me and My words remain in you, ask whatever you wish, and it will be given you. This is to My Father's glory, that you bear much fruit, showing yourself to be My disciples" (vv. 7-8). In the discourse on the vine, three degrees of fruitfulness are mentioned: bearing fruit (v. 2), being "more fruitful" (v. 2), and bearing "much fruit" (v. 8). One of the marks of a fruitful Christian is that he is in prayer fellowship with God and God can answer his prayers because they are to His glory.

### The Importance of Living in a Love Relationship

*John 15:9-14.* Earlier Jesus had declared that the disciples' love for one another was to be a distinguishing characteristic of their relationship (13:35). In keeping with this, He commanded them to love each other as Jesus had loved them (v. 34). In repeating this theme, Jesus first of all reminded them that He had been loved by the Father and, in keeping with this, had loved the disciples. The command was, "Now remain in My love. If you obey My commands, you will remain in My love, just as I have obeyed My Father's commands and remain in His love" (vv. 9-10). In talking about the love relationship, obviously, Jesus was calling their attention to the fact that if God loves them and they love God, it would be relatively easy to obey God's commands, and obeying His commands would be an evidence of their mutual love for each other. Obedience is at once the demonstration of love.

Now Jesus adds a further dimension, "I have told you this so that My joy may be in you and that your joy may be complete" (v. 11). The fruitful Christian life is not only one in which there is mutual love between God and the disciples, but this relationship also brings great joy, and without this relationship, joy would never be complete.

Christ then extended the command again as in John 13:34-35, "Love each other as I have loved you" (15:12). The supreme evidence of this love is Christ's own love for them to be demonstrated the next day as He laid down His life for them. Jesus said, "Greater love has no one than this, that he lay down his life for his friends" (v. 13). As they obey Christ and enter into this relationship, they qualify as His friends.

### The New Relationship of Being Friends of God

*John 15:15-17.* Though in the New Testament Paul and others delighted to call themselves servants, or slaves, of God, the relationship of Jesus to His disciples was much deeper than that. Instead of being a servant, they are actually His friends and associates, "I no longer call you servants, because a servant does not know his master's business. Instead, I have called you friends, for everything that I learned from My Father I have made known to you" (v. 15). This relationship did not come from the disciples choosing Jesus, but rather from Jesus choosing them and giving them the appointment to be fruit bearers and those that manifest the love of God, "You did not choose Me, but I chose you and appointed you to go and bear fruit — fruit that will last. Then the Father will give you whatever you ask in My name. This is My command: Love each other" (vv. 16-17).

### The World Will Hate True Disciples of Jesus

*John 15:18-25.* Just as the relationship of a disciple to God and to Jesus was one of love, so, by contrast, the world will hate them because they also hated Christ. Jesus said, "If the world hates you, keep in mind that it hated Me first. If you belonged to the world, it would love you as its own. As it is, you do not belong to the world, but I have chosen you out of the world. That is why the world hates you. Remember the words I spoke to you: 'No servant is greater than his master.' If they persecuted Me, they will persecute you also" (vv. 18-20). Jesus declared the world guilty because they rejected Christ and did not pay attention to His miracles (vv. 21-25).

### The Coming of the Holy Spirit as Counselor

*John 15:26-27.* As a final word of encouragement to His disciples, just as Jesus had done in 14:26, He assured His disciples that the Spirit of Truth would come and would testify to them concerning Jesus (15:26). Just as the Spirit testified to them, so they too must be a testimony for God because they had seen firsthand His miracles and heard His public ministry (v. 27). Taken as a whole, the Upper Room Discourse looks beyond the death and resurrection of Christ and His ascension into heaven and is a prediction concerning the moral and spiritual characteristics of the world while Jesus is with the Father.

### The Disciples to Experience Persecution

*John 16:1-4; cf. Matthew 24:9-10; Luke 21:16-19.* Having mentioned their coming persecution (John 15:18-20), Jesus now detailed some of their future experiences. The disciples would be put out of the synagogue, and those who killed them would think they were serving God (v. 2). The reason for this persecution is that they do not know the Father or Jesus (v. 3). As He will be absent from them, He tells them now so that they will realize that prophecy is being fulfilled when it occurs.

### The Work of the Holy Spirit After
### Jesus Returns to the Father

*John 16:7-15.* Though the disciples dreaded Jesus leaving them and could not understand it, Jesus stated that it was best for Him to go so that the Counselor, the Holy Spirit, could come. In respect to the world, the Holy Spirit would bring conviction concerning guilt in regard to sin, conviction of the righteousness of God in comparison to their unrighteousness, and of coming judgment on sin (v. 8). Jesus enlarged on the truth that will be communicated. Those who receive the revelation of the Holy Spirit will understand that their sin which keeps them from being saved is the sin of unbelief (v. 9). They will be convinced of righteousness because Jesus, who is the perfect example of righteousness, will be with the Father and not able to model righteousness (v. 10). In regard to God's coming judgment on sin, they need to know that in the death of Christ the prince of this world, Satan, stands condemned and his sentence will ultimately be fulfilled.

In contrast to the convicting work of the Spirit in the unsaved who hear the Gospel, the Spirit of God will also communicate to Christians. Jesus said, "I have much more to say to you, more than you can now bear. But when He, the Spirit of Truth, comes, He will guide you into all truth. He will not speak on His own; He will speak only what He hears, and He will tell you what is yet to come. He will bring glory to Me by taking from what is Mine and making it known to you" (vv. 12-14).

In general, the Holy Spirit will make known the meaning of Scripture to believers in Christ. For the disciples, there may have been an additional special communication of reminding them what Jesus said while He was with them and making them understand it. The process of revelation will bring glory to Christ (v. 14).

### Jesus' Prediction of His Death, Resurrection, and Second Coming

*John 16:16-33.* Jesus told the disciples, "In a little while you will see Me no more, and then after a little while you will see Me" (v. 16). The disciples did not understand Jesus (vv. 17-18). Jesus then enlarged on this prophecy, "I tell you the truth, you will weep and mourn while the world rejoices. You will grieve, but your grief will turn to joy. A woman giving birth to a child has pain because her time has come; but when her baby is born she forgets the anguish because of her joy that a child is born into the world. So with you: Now is your time of grief, but I will see you again and you will rejoice, and no one will take away your joy" (vv. 20-22).

In this passage Jesus was predicting His death and resurrection. In His death, they would grieve and be in pain; in His resurrection, they would have their grief turned to joy.

In the period after the resurrection of Christ, Jesus instructed them, "In that day you will no longer ask Me anything. I tell you the truth, My Father will give you whatever you ask in My name. Until now you have not asked for anything in My name. Ask and you will receive, and your joy will be complete" (vv. 23-24). While Jesus was with them, of course, they could ask Him for explanation of what He said and would have opportunity to have direct communication. After He left, however, Jesus assured them that the Father would reveal to them what they need to know and would give whatever they need. Though what Jesus said was only partially understood by the disciples, He assured them of the Father's love. He tells them plainly He is going back to the Father (vv. 25-28).

431

When the disciples said now they understood and put their trust in Christ, Jesus said, "You believe at last!" (v. 31) Jesus then went on to predict how they would scatter at the time of His crucifixion and leave Jesus alone. Jesus summarized His message to them, "I have told you these things, so that in Me you may have peace. In this world you will have trouble. But take heart! I have overcome the world" (v. 33).

### The Predictive Character of Jesus' High Priestly Prayer

*John 17:1-26.* John 17 is a marvelous revelation of how Jesus prays to the Father. Though, strictly speaking, it is not prophecy, the fact that all of His prayers will be answered indicates the prophetic future for the disciples in many particulars. In His prayer, Jesus rejoiced that God had given Him authority to give eternal life. Jesus asked that His ministry would glorify the Father and the Father, in turn, would glorify the Son (vv. 2-5). Jesus rejoiced that the disciples had come to faith in Him and they had regarded Him as coming from God and they believed that Jesus had been sent by the Father (vv. 6-8).

Jesus then prayed for the disciples. Because He no longer would be in the world when He went to the Father, He asked the Father to protect them and give them a unity that is similar to the unity of the Trinity (vv. 10-11). Jesus rejoiced in that He had kept all the disciples except Judas Iscariot (v. 12).

The objective of Jesus' prayer is that the disciples would have the full joy of fellowship with Him (v. 13). Though they were hated by the world, Jesus prayed that God would protect them from "the evil one" (vv. 14-15). As the disciples would have the task of witnessing to an evil world, Jesus prayed for their sanctification, "Sanctify them by the truth; Your word is truth. As you sent Me into the world, I have sent them into the world. For them I sanctify Myself, that they too may be truly sanctified" (vv. 17-19).

This prayer for sanctification is unusual as normally in the Bible sanctification relates to a Christian's position in Christ as embodied in the word "saint" and other aspects of truth. The ongoing, progressive sanctification of believers is mentioned only occasionally in Scripture and is related to this prayer of Christ that the disciples may be sanctified, that is, set apart as holy to God and used by God as a holy entity (vv. 17-19).

Jesus, however, prayed also for those who were not among the disciples at that time, having in view the larger outreach of the church to Gentiles as well as Jews. He prayed that all believers will be one in Christ (vv. 20-21). Their unity would be in the fact that the Father is in them and they are in the Father (v. 21). Jesus spoke again of the unity of believers, a theme running through the entire prayer. Jesus said, "I in them and You in Me. May they be brought to complete unity to let the world know that You sent Me and have loved them even as You have loved Me" (v. 23).

Having prayed for His disciples who would remain in the world, He asked that they will be in glory and see the glory of Christ, "Father, I want those You have given Me to be with Me where I am, and to see My glory, the glory You have given Me because You loved Me before the Creation of the world" (v. 24). The prayer concluded with Christ's anticipating that the love between the Father and the Son will characterize the love of believers (vv. 25-26).

The High Priestly Prayer of Christ emphasized the glory of God, the love relationship between the Father and the Son and the disciples, provision for the disciples' protection in the wicked world, the joy of being a disciple, their protection in the wicked world, their progressive sanctification through the truth of God, and the theme of unity in the Father, Son, and the believers in Christ which is one of the unusual features of the Church Age.

### Jesus' Arrest and Betrayal

*John 18:1-11; Matthew 26:36-56; Mark 14:32-50; Luke 22:39-53.* Jesus and His disciples had gone to a garden across the Brook Kidron, and there Judas found Him as he was leading a detachment of soldiers to arrest Jesus (John 18:1-3). As they arrested Him, however, Jesus urged them to let the disciples go (vv. 4-8). John added the comment, "This happened so that the words He had spoken would be fulfilled: 'I have not lost one of those You gave Me' " (v. 9). Peter, in his zeal to defend Christ, cut off the high priest's servant's ear. Jesus rebuked Peter, however, and healed and restored the ear (Luke 22:49-51).

### Jesus' Arrest and Peter's Denial as Fulfillment of Scripture

*John 18:12–19:16.* John's account of the trial and condemnation of Jesus leading up to His crucifixion is not in itself prophecy but fulfilled predictions of both the Old and New Testaments concerning the fact that Jesus would die.

### The Crucifixion of Jesus as Fulfillment of Prophecy

*John 19:16-37.* In giving the details of the crucifixion of Christ, John pointed out that there are several fulfillments of prophecy. One concerns the garment of Christ which was seamless which they cast lots as was predicted in Psalm 22:18, "They divided My garments among them and cast lots for My clothing" (John 19:24; Ps. 22:18).

When Jesus declared, "I am thirsty" (John 19:28), John also mentioned that Scripture had been fulfilled. He was referring to Psalm 69:21. Jesus, the One who could give the water of life (John 4:14; 7:38-39), here is suffering for the sins of the world. With His final statement, "It is finished" (19:30), Jesus indicated that He has completed the work of redemption and the price has been paid in full.

### The Death and Resurrection of Christ as Fulfillment of Scripture

*John 19:31-42; cf. Matthew 27:51-66; Mark 15:33-47; Luke 23:45-49.* The fact that they did not break Jesus' legs (John 19:32-33) fulfilled the Scriptures, "Not one of His bones will be broken" (v. 36; cf. the prediction in Ex. 12:46; Num. 9:12; Ps. 34:20). John also quoted Scripture, "They will look on the One they have pierced" (John 19:37; cf. Zech. 12:10).

The fact that Jesus was buried in the tomb of Joseph of Arimathea fulfilled the allusion in Isaiah 53:9, indicating that He would be buried with the rich.

### The Resurrection as Fulfillment of Prophecy

*John 20:1-18; cf. Matthew 28:1-15; Mark 16:1-14; Luke 24:1-32.* In His resurrection, Christ fulfilled the prophecies of the Old and New Testaments relative to His resurrection. Jesus revealed Himself first to Mary Magdalene (Mark 16:9-11; John 20:11-18); then to the women returning a second time to the tomb (Matt. 28:8-10); to Peter (Luke 24:34; 1 Cor. 15:5); the disciples on the road to Emmaus (Mark 16:12; Luke 24:30-32); to the disciples on the day of His resurrection in the evening, though Thomas was absent (Mark 16:14; Luke 24:36-43; John 20:19-25); a week later to all the disciples, including Thomas (John 20:26-31; 1 Cor. 15:5).

Though the events of His resurrection were a fulfillment of prophecy, Jesus Himself did not introduce many new prophecies in John 20. In His conversation with Mary Magdalene, Jesus told her He was ascending to God the Father, and it was not proper for her to hold Him to earth. His ascension took place forty days later (Acts 1:9-10). In John 20:23 He told the disciples, "If you forgive anyone his sins, they are forgiven; if you do not forgive them, they are not forgiven." The disciples had the power to acknowledge that sins were forgiven, but on the same basis as other Christians, that is, on

# APPEARANCES OF JESUS
# AFTER THE RESURRECTION

1. To Mary Magdalene when she returned to the tomb (John 20:11-17; cf. Mark 16:9-11).
2. To the other women as they were returning to the tomb a second time (Matt. 28:9-10).
3. To Peter in the afternoon of Resurrection Day (Luke 24:34; 1 Cor. 15:5).
4. To the disciples on the road to Emmaus (Mark 16:12-13; Luke 24:13-35).
5. To the ten disciples (Mark 16:14; Luke 24:36-43; John 20:19-23).
6. To the eleven disciples a week after His resurrection, Thomas being present (John 20:26-29).
7. To the seven disciples by the Sea of Galilee (John 21:1-23).
8. To 500 people as reported by Paul (1 Cor. 15:6).
9. To James, the Lord's brother (1 Cor. 15:7).
10. To the eleven disciples on a mountain in Galilee (Matt. 28:16-20; Mark 16:15-18).
11. At the time of His ascension from the Mount of Olives (Luke 24:44-53; Acts 1:3-9).
12. To Stephen at the time of his martyrdom (Acts 7:55-56).
13. To Paul on the road to Damascus (Acts 9:3-6; 22:6-11; 26:13-18).
14. To Paul in Arabia (Gal. 1:12, 17).
15. To Paul in the temple (Acts 22:17-21).
16. To Paul in the prison in Caesarea (Acts 23:11).
17. The final appearance of Christ was to the Apostle John at the beginning of the revelation given to him (Rev. 1:12-20).

the basis of the Word of God and its promises.

### Jesus' Final Appearances to the Disciples

*John 21.* An additional appearance of Christ occurred a week after His resurrection when He met several of the disciples by the Sea of Galilee (vv. 1-2). In His touching interview with Peter relative to Peter's love for Him, Jesus added the prophecy, "I tell you the truth, when you were younger you dressed yourself and went

435

where you wanted; but when you are old you will stretch out your hands, and someone else will dress you and lead you where you do not want to go" (v. 18). The prophecy indicated that Peter would be crucified (v. 19).

The Gospel of John closed with the statement, "Jesus did many other things as well. If every one of them were written down, I suppose that even the whole world would not have room for the books that would be written" (v. 25).

# 10

# PROPHECY IN
# THE BOOK OF ACTS

# HISTORY OF THE EARLY CHURCH

As indicated by the title of the book, the Acts of the Apostles is largely a report on the activities of the early church from the time of Pentecost to Paul's ministry in Rome. If Paul endured two Roman imprisonments, the Book of Acts carries us through the two years that Paul ministered in Rome in his first imprisonment.

Because the nature of the book deals with history rather than prophecy, there are relatively few prophecies included in the Book of Acts. Those that are included are essential to the historical narrative.

## The Coming of the Holy Spirit

*Acts 1:1-8.* In many respects the Book of Acts is a continuation of the Gospel of Luke, also written by Luke. In His postresurrection ministry, Jesus had instructed the disciples, "Do not leave Jerusalem, but wait for the gift My Father promised, which you have heard Me speak about. For John baptized with water, but in a few days you will be baptized with the Holy Spirit" (vv. 4-5). The record of the fulfillment of this prophecy is given in Acts 2.

While Jesus was still with them, the disciples asked Him, "Lord, are You at this time going to restore the kingdom to Israel?" (1:6) It is most illuminating that at this point, after three-and-a-half years of listening to Christ teach and going through the experiences of His death and resurrection and post-resurrection ministry, the disciples were still not clear concerning the kingdom promises of the Old Testament. Jesus answered their question, "It is not for you to know the times or dates the Father has set by His own authority" (v. 7). If they were incorrect in their expectation of literal fulfillment of the Old Testament promises of a kingdom on earth, this would have been a proper time to correct the disciples. The answer that Jesus gave, that it was not for them to know the time or the date, that is, the general time or the particular time, indicated the event was still ahead, but God had not seen fit to reveal to them how these prophecies were to be fulfilled.

From the perspective of almost 2,000 years, it is obvious that God is fulfilling in this present age His purpose, unannounced in the Old Testament, of calling out a people of both Jews and Gentiles to form the church of Christ. It is also abundantly clear that the church does not fulfill the promises of the kingdom on earth as given to the people of Israel. As the Book of Acts progresses, the disciples gradually realized that God was carrying out this program for Jew and

Gentile first, and after this period, which is really a time of Gentile blessing, that He would resume His plan and purpose to fulfill the kingdom promise to Israel in connection with the second coming of Christ.

More important than the time of the kingdom which God has not seen fit to reveal, Jesus revealed to them the coming of the Holy Spirit which would be the main factor in the present dispensation. He told them, "But you will receive power when the Holy Spirit comes on you; and you will be My witnesses in Jerusalem, and in all Judea and Samaria, and to the ends of the earth" (v. 8). In subsequent events in the Book of Acts, including Acts 2, the literal fulfillment of this promise was illustrated. All the Gospels agree with this that it was a duty of those left behind at the Ascension to evangelize the world (Matt. 28:18-20; Mark 16:15-18; Luke 24:47-48; John 20:21-22).

### Jesus' Ascension and Promise of Return

*Acts 1:9-11.* No sooner had He answered their question than He was literally taken up from before their eyes and bodily rose from earth to the heavens. A cloud enveloped Him and hid Him from their sight. Scripture recorded, "They were looking intently up into the sky as He was going, when suddenly two men dressed in white stood beside them. 'Men of Galilee,' they said, 'why do you stand here looking into the sky? This same Jesus, who has been taken from you into heaven, will come back in the same way you have seen Him go into heaven' " (vv. 10-11). The departure of Jesus was bodily, visibly, gradually, and with a cloud. These same factors enter into His second coming as portrayed in other Scriptures, including Revelation 19:11-18. Following these introductory prophecies in the Book of Acts, only occasional prophecies are mentioned in the course of the book.

### Peter's Pronouncement on the Occasion of
### Healing the Crippled Man in the Temple

*Acts 3:11-26.* As the people looked expectantly on Peter and John because of the healing of the crippled man, Peter delivered his sermonette, pointing out the background of Jesus and His being crucified (vv. 13-15). Peter announced that this crippled man had been healed by faith in Jesus (v. 16). Peter further informed them that though they acted in ignorance, what they did fulfilled the prophecies of the Old Testament indicating Christ would suffer.

On the basis of this, Peter exhorted them, "Repent, then, and turn to God, so that your sins may be wiped out, that times of refreshing may come from the Lord, and that He may send the Christ, who has been appointed for you—even Jesus. He must remain in heaven until the time comes for God to restore everything, as He promised long ago through His holy prophets. For Moses said, 'The Lord your God will raise up for you a Prophet like me from among your own people; you must listen to everything He tells you. Anyone who does not listen to Him will be completely cut off from among his people.' Indeed, all the prophets from Samuel on, as many as have spoken, have foretold these days. And you are heirs of the prophets and of the covenant God made with your fathers. He said to Abraham, 'Through your offspring all peoples on earth will be blessed.' When God raised up His servant, He sent Him first to you to bless you by turning each of you from your wicked ways" (vv. 19-26). Peter gave the certain prediction that Jesus is now in heaven and that the time of restoration promised Israel through the holy prophets is still future pending His return.

### The Prediction of the Severe Famine

*Acts 11:27-30.* In connection with Peter's indication of his ministry to the Gentiles in Acts 11 and the justification of his going to Cornelius with the Gospel, the prophecy was given by some prophets coming from Jerusalem to Antioch that there would be a famine throughout the Roman world (vv. 27-28). In response to this, the disciples took an offering and sent it to Judea, carried by Barnabas and Saul (vv. 29-30).

### Paul's Sermon on Mars' Hill

*Acts 17:22-34.* Paul, attempting to reach the hostile crowd in Corinth, preached his sermon, teaching that Jesus was indeed appointed the judge of all the earth. In connection with this, Paul declared, "In the past God overlooked such ignorance, but now He commands all people everywhere to repent. For He has set a day when He will judge the world with justice by the Man He has appointed. He has given proof of this to all men by raising Him from the dead" (vv. 30-31). Then, as now, the unbelieving world was not prepared to accept the concept of future judgment.

### Paul's Final Message to the Church at Ephesus

*Acts 20:18-31.* Paul delivered his final message to the Ephesian church to the leaders of the church at Ephesus who came to meet him at Miletus. He told them he was going to Jerusalem and that he had been warned prophetically that he would face hardship in prison

(v. 23). Paul announced also, "Now I know that none of you among whom I have gone about preaching the kingdom will ever see me again. Therefore, I declare to you today that I am innocent of the blood of all men. For I have not hesitated to proclaim to you the whole will of God" (vv. 25-27).

Paul also exhorted them, "Keep watch over yourselves and all the flock of which the Holy Spirit has made you overseers. Be shepherds of the church of God, which He bought with His own blood. I know that after I leave, savage wolves will come in among you and will not spare the flock. Even from your own number men will arise and distort the truth in order to draw away disciples after them. So be on your guard! Remember that for three years I never stopped warning each of you night and day with tears" (vv. 28-31). Scripture does not record the details of this disruption of the Ephesian church, but it seems to have gone on for several generations after Paul in spite of the problems he prophesied.

### Prophecy of Paul Going to Rome

*Acts 23:11.* In connection with Paul's being arrested and defending himself before the Sanhedrin, the meeting ended in turmoil when Paul stated that he was being persecuted because of his hope in the resurrection (Acts 23:6-10). The result was that the commander had to rescue Paul from them.

On the night following Acts recorded, "The Lord stood near Paul and said, 'Take courage! As you have testified about Me in Jerusalem, so you must also testify in Rome' " (v. 11). This was subsequently fulfilled in the Book of Acts.

### Safety from the Storm

*Acts 27:21-25.* In connection with Paul's sailing to Rome, the ship ran into a storm and for many days they were in danger of shipwreck. At this time of trouble, Paul had a special revelation given to him. Acts recorded, "After the men had gone a long time without food, Paul stood up before them and said: 'Men, you should have taken my advice not to sail from Crete; then you would have spared yourselves this damage and loss. But now I urge you to keep up your courage, because not one of you will be lost; only the ship will be destroyed. Last night an angel of God whose I am and whom I serve stood beside me and said, "Do not be afraid, Paul. You must stand trial before Caesar; and God has graciously given you the lives of all who sail with you." So keep up your courage, men, for I have faith in God that it will happen just as He told me' " (vv. 21-

25). As Acts recorded, the ship ran aground on the Isle of Malta, and all the people on board were safe. "In this way everyone reached land in safety" (v. 44). This prophecy of Paul was further reinforced in verse 34 when Paul told them they would survive and encouraged them to eat (vv. 33-36).

Though the Book of Acts is not primarily a prophetic book, it gives us historical background with which to set the tremendous revelations contained in the epistles and later books of the New Testament.

# 11

# PROPHECY IN
# THE PAULINE EPISTLES

## PROPHECY IN THE EPISTLE TO THE ROMANS

In the Epistle to the Romans, the Apostle Paul, guided by the Spirit, stated the basic theology of Scripture, including Old Testament revelation, but also the new revelation that came through the first coming of Christ. Many of the major doctrines of the Christian faith were to some extent revealed in the Old Testament, but fuller revelation came with the declaration of God's purpose to call out the church, composed of both Jews and Gentiles, to form a new entity which the Old Testament had not predicted.

The theology of the church provided a new, more comprehensive statement. Accordingly, in the Epistle to the Romans, the Apostle Paul presented the doctrine of sin and condemnation, the doctrine of justification by faith, the doctrine of sanctification, the relationship of God's present purpose in the church to His declared purposes for Israel, and the major principles of Christian life which is the practical application of the great doctrines of theology. As Paul was especially concerned with how the doctrine of the church related to the promises given to Israel, three chapters were devoted to this (Rom. 9–11).

It is probable that the Epistle to the Romans was preceded by the Letters to the Thessalonian church, the Epistle to the Galatians, and 1 Corinthians. Having stated particularly in the Thessalonian epistles and in 1 Corinthians the doctrine of the Rapture of the church, it was not considered necessary to restate this doctrine in the Epistle to the Romans.

As the epistle concerns itself primarily with the theology that existed at the time of Paul's writing the epistle, the book does not provide an extensive prophetic outline of the future. Only occasionally in Romans are future events predicted, but those that are mentioned are of essential character, including prophecies concerning Israel that will be fulfilled after the present age. Though the Epistle to the Romans emphasized the present situation at the time Paul lived, as is always the case, doctrine realized in the present has an implication and fulfillment in the future. Accordingly, when the epistle touches on prophecy, it deals with important future events.

### The Implications of a Doctrine of Sin
### to Future Divine Judgment

*Romans 2:5-16.* In the nature of sin and guilt, the doctrine has always a present application but faces also a future judgment. In dealing especially with Gentile sin and rebellion against God, Paul revealed that there will be certain divine judgment. He stated, "But because of your stubbornness and your unrepentant heart, you are storing up wrath against yourself for the day of God's wrath, when His righteous judgment will be revealed. God 'will give to each person according to what he has done.' To those who by persistence and doing good seek glory, honor and immortality, He will give eternal life. But for those who are self-seeking and reject the truth and follow evil, there will be wrath and anger" (vv. 5-8).

Earlier in this chapter Paul argued that all men have fallen short of God's moral standards and that therefore they should not pass judgment on others. He summarized this, "So when you, a mere man, pass judgment on them and yet do the same things, do you think you will escape God's judgment?" (v. 3) As Paul made clear later in this epistle, salvation is by faith and by grace as all have sinned.

There is, however, a different quality of life in those that are saved from those who are not saved. Those who persist in being unrepentant, as Paul stated, are facing certain judgment from God. In speaking of "the day of God's wrath," Paul is not referring to any specific day though, as Scripture unfolds the series of judgments that will characterize the judgment of all men, the final judgment will come at the end of the millennial kingdom (Rev. 20:11-15). Those who are saved have a different quality of life which demonstrates that they have come to God in repentance and faith. Accordingly, their manner of life will be rewarded and results in eternal life. The life of doing good and receiving eternal life is obviously not possible unless a person believes and accepts the truth of God's Gospel (Rom. 2:6-8).

Though Paul is dealing here primarily with Gentiles, he made clear that Jews are in the same situation, "There will be trouble and distress for every human being who does evil: first for the Jew, then for the Gentile; but glory, honor and peace for everyone who does good: first for the Jew, then for the Gentile. For God does not show favoritism" (vv. 9-11). The difference between Jew and Gentile is that the Jew has been given the revelation of the Law and the Gentiles have not, but this does not change the fundamental requirement of doing what is right in God's sight.

The distinction between those who sin who know the Law and those who do not is specifically faced, "All who sin apart from the

Law will also perish apart from the Law, and all who sin under the Law will be judged by the Law. For it is not those who hear the Law who are righteous in God's sight, but it is those who obey the Law who will be declared righteous" (vv. 12-13).

Paul used the word "law" in a number of different senses in his epistles. The point he is making is that those who are under the Mosaic Law who are Jews will be judged by it; but that the Gentiles also have a general moral law, and if they are living in the will of God, they will, to some extent, conform to the Mosaic Law in its moral teachings.

Paul stated, "(Indeed, when the Gentiles, who do not have the Law, do by nature things required by the Law, they are a law for themselves, even though they do not have the Law, since they show that the requirements of the Law are written on their hearts, their consciences also bearing witness, and their thoughts now accusing, now even defending them.) This will take place on the day when God will judge men's secrets through Jesus Christ, as my Gospel declares" (vv. 14-16).

Because all men have a conscience which to some extent distinguishes right from wrong, and because God deals with the hearts of men, even if they are not Jews under the Mosaic Law, they will be judged on the moral code which they recognize as witnessed by their conscience.

In dealing with the Day of Judgment, Paul had in mind that God will judge Christians at the time of the Rapture as brought out in his previous writing in 1 Corinthians 3:11-15; 9:24-27. The unsaved, however, will not be judged finally until after the millennial kingdom. In life, however, God also deals in judgment on those who rebel against Him, and they experience the wrath of God as it is expressed in history. The final judgment, however, determines the ultimate destiny of the soul. This will be especially evident at the Great Tribulation preceding the second coming of Christ.

### Reconciliation through Justification

*Romans 5:9-11; 6:8; 8:1.* Having demonstrated the need for salvation because of the universal condemnation described in Romans 1:18-20, and having expounded the doctrine of justification, revelation now turns to the wonderful reconciliation that justification provides, "Since we have now been justified by His blood, how much more shall we be saved from God's wrath through Him! For if, when we were God's enemies, we were reconciled to Him through the death of His Son, how much more, having been reconciled, shall we be saved through His life! Not only is this so, but we also rejoice in God through our Lord Jesus Christ, through whom we have now received reconcilation" (5:9-11).

Justification has declared the one who trusts in Christ to be righteous in his position before God because God sees him in the person and work of His Son. The argument is that if we were saved from God's wrath by justification in time, how much more, having been reconciled, Christians will enjoy salvation in this life and the life to come.

Paul later revealed further light on this subject of being seen in the life of Christ in Colossians 3:3-4, "For you died, and your life is now hidden with Christ in God. When Christ, who is your life, appears, then you also will appear with Him in glory." Justification as a particular act of God occurs at the moment of salvation. Thereafter, we enjoy justification because God sees us through His Son. This will become especially evident in the final judgments. Not only have we been justified already but we also have been reconciled to God by the death of His Son (Rom. 5:11).

Here, as in all of his discussions on salvation, Paul made clear that salvation is something that God does for those who trust in Christ, and justification and reconciliation are true for every believer from the moment of his salvation. The enjoyment of it in time and eternity demonstrates the wonderful fact of salvation in Christ.

A similar thought of how salvation is manifest in life is expressed in 6:8, "Now if we died with Christ, we believe that we will also live with Him." Just as death precedes resurrection, so those who are identified with Christ in His death are also identified with Him in His resurrection. This is a present benefit as well as a guarantee of future blessing. The one who is in Christ will not come into condemnation (8:1).

**Prophecy of a Believer as Son and Heir Inheriting Glory**
*Romans 8:12-39.* The true believer in Christ is described as having no condemnation (v. 1) and as one who is living under the control of the Holy Spirit. Even though this does not produce a perfect moral life, it nevertheless characterizes the believer who is living under the new nature rather than the old (v. 13). Present experience of salvation is the forerunner of that which is prophesied. If the believer is now a child of God (v. 17), then he is also the heir of God (v. 17). As such, we may share some sufferings in this present life, but we also

447

will share in the glory to come.

Contrasting our present suffering with future glory helps a Christian to realize what Paul states, "I consider that our present sufferings are not worth comparing with the glory that will be revealed in us" (v. 18). The sufferings of a Christian are paralleled by sufferings in the world as a whole for all creation is groaning and suffering like a woman giving birth (vv. 22-23). When a Christian experiences suffering, he all the more anticipates the full meaning of being adopted as a son of God. Though this takes place in our present life, when God recognizes a Christian as His son, it gives a basis for hope that ultimately the sufferings will cease and makes possible hoping patiently (v. 25). Even though a Christian may not know how to pray under some circumstances, the promise is given that the Holy Spirit will pray as his Intercessor (vv. 26-27).

Having been saved, a Christian enters into the divine process of ultimate glorification described by Paul, "For those God foreknew He also predestined to be conformed to the likeness of His Son, that He might be the firstborn among many brothers. And those He predestined, He also called; those He called, He also justified; those He justified, He also glorified" (vv. 29-30).

On the basis of God's sovereign work for a believer which will not be consummated until he is presented perfect in glory, Paul stated the great truth that a Christian can "know that in all things God works for the good of those who love Him, who have been called according to His purpose" (v. 28). The point is that a Christian was predestined before he was saved, he was called when he was saved, and justified. Now being justified and declared righteous by God, the next state will be one of glorification.

All of this, of course, is based on grace because a Christian has been chosen, and his salvation has been possible because God did not spare His own Son (v. 32). There is no danger of a Christian ever coming into condemnation and being declared lost. This is because they are seen in Christ who died and was resurrected and is supported by His present intercession in heaven, "Christ Jesus, who died — more than that, who was raised to life — is at the right hand of God and is also interceding for us" (v. 34).

The complete safety of the believer is presented in the classic conclusion of this chapter where Paul declared that nothing can separate a Christian from the love of Christ (v. 35). While it may be true that a Christian may face death and suffering as a martyr, it is also true that a Christian conquers through Christ who loved him.

Paul declared his own faith and the content of every Christian's faith, "For I am convinced that neither death nor life, neither angels nor demons, neither the present nor the future, nor any powers, neither height nor depth, nor anything else in all creation, will be able to separate us from the love of God that is in Christ Jesus our Lord" (vv. 38-39). This detailed summary covers the whole Gospel experience of man. Like all other aspects of our salvation, it is based on grace rather than reward. But having entered by faith into the grace which is in Christ Jesus, the believer has the certain hope that what is promised will be certainly fulfilled.

### God's Mercy Is Under His Sovereign Will

*Romans 9:10-33.* The doctrine of the sovereignty of God so firmly embedded in history and prophecy was discussed at length by Paul using Jacob and Esau as illustrations. Concerning this important point in God's manifesting His choice of Israel as a special nation, Paul declared, "Not only that, but Rebekah's children had one and the same father, our father Isaac. Yet, before the twins were born or had done anything good or bad—in order that God's purpose in election might stand: not by works but by Him who calls—she was told, 'The older will serve the younger.' Just as it is written: 'Jacob I loved, but Esau I hated' " (vv. 10-13).

The quotation referring to Jacob being loved and Esau being hated is derived from Malachi 1:2-3. This must be understood in the wider revelation of the entire Bible because John 3:16 declares that God loves the world which would include Esau. In other words, the choice is relative. Jacob He loved in advance, and Esau He did not. Now Paul brings up the question as to whether this is unjust, "What then shall we say? Is God unjust? Not at all! For He says to Moses, 'I will have mercy on whom I have mercy, and I will have compassion on whom I have compassion.' It does not, therefore, depend on man's desire or effort, but on God's mercy" (Rom. 9:14-16).

Using the illustration of Pharaoh, Paul pointed out that God's hardening of an unrepentant sinner is often based on additional offering of forgiveness. As in the case of Pharaoh, Paul wrote, " 'I raised you up for this very purpose, that I might display My power in you and that My name might be proclaimed in all the earth.' Therefore God has mercy on whom He wants to have mercy, and He hardens whom He wants to harden" (vv. 17-18). As Paul pointed out, the way God hardened Pharaoh's heart was by giving him repeated opportunities to yield to the will of God regarding Israel. The final chapter was written when Pharaoh pursued them in the Red Sea and was drowned. The hardening of Pharaoh's heart came not from the heart of God but from the heart of Pharaoh.

Paul used another illustration to demonstrate why God is sovereign. Using a potter making a clay pot, he asked the question, "Shall what is formed say to him who formed it, 'Why did you make me like this?' Does not the potter have the right to make out of the same lump of clay some pottery for noble purposes and some for common use?" (vv. 20-21)

The process of enduring with patience those who are destined to the wrath of God is justified by the fact that this makes the riches of the glory of His grace all the more evident, both for Jews and for Gentiles (vv. 23-24).

Recognizing the importance of this is a major doctrine of Scripture. Paul then quoted from Hosea 2:23, "I will call them 'My people' who are not My people; and I will call her 'My loved one' who is not My loved one" (Rom 9:25). This passage calls attention to a fine point in exegesis where interpretation and application are different. The passage quoted is to show that God in general is sovereign in His mercies, whether to Jew or Gentile. The quotation from Hosea 2:23, however, is in reference to Israel who, because of her sins, was declared not to be the people of God and then in grace is restored. The fact that he is referring to Israel, not Gentiles here as far as interpretation is concerned, is brought out in his further quotation of Hosea 1:10, "It will happen that in the very place where it was said to them, 'You are not My people,' they will be called 'sons of the living God' " (Rom. 9:26). Paul used this illustration of God's mercy with Israel, however, to support his concept of mercy also to the Gentiles and, while not interpreting the Book of Hosea, is making an application. At stake is the distinction made throughout Scripture that Israel are not Gentiles and Gentiles are not Israel, and this must be understood in this passage.

Further light is given from the Book of Isaiah (10:22-23), "Though the number of the Israelites be like the sand by the sea, only the remnant will be saved. For the Lord will carry out His sentence on earth with speed and finality" (Rom. 9:27-28). Even for Israel, the covenanted people, only those who come to the Lord will be received in mercy and grace, and probably the great bulk of the nation will be lost.

Paul further supported this in a quotation from Isaiah, "Unless the Lord Almighty had left us descendants, we would have become like Sodom, we would have been like Gomorrah" (v. 29).

As a conclusion to this complicated argument, Paul stated that the Gentiles, even though not the favored people of God, will have righteousness as they turn to God, but Israel, who would be normally considered as the ones who should pursue the law of righteousness, will not attain it because they do not put trust in Jesus Christ, "What then shall we say? That the Gentiles, who did not pursue righteousness, have obtained it, a righteousness that is by faith; but Israel, who pursued a law of righteousness, has not attained it. Why not? Because they pursued it not by faith but as if it were by works. They stumbled over the 'stumbling stone.' As it is written: 'See, I lay in Zion a stone that causes men to stumble and a rock that makes them fall, and the one who trusts in Him will never be put to shame' " (vv. 30-33).

Christ as the stone is presented in Scripture in various characterizations. He was the smitten rock (Ex. 17:6; 1 Cor. 10:4); He was portrayed as the foundation and chief cornerstone of the church (Eph. 2:20). Here, as is also true for the Jews at His first coming, He is a "stumbling block" (cf. 1 Cor. 1:23). He will be the stone which is the capstone of the corner when He comes in His second coming (Zech. 4:7). According to Daniel 2:34, He will be the smiting stone which destroys Gentile power. Also in verse 35, He will be the stone that expands and fills the earth when He takes over the earth as His kingdom. To unbelievers also He is a crushing stone (Matt. 21:44).

All of these illustrations combine to emphasize the sovereign character of God and, on the other hand, the responsibility of man to respond to God's message of grace and salvation. The same truth that saves one will condemn another. Taken as a whole, Romans 9 accounts for the extension of the Gospel to the Gentiles because the Jews did not respond in faith to Jesus Christ. This sets the stage for Romans 10, dealing with Israel's present opportunity, and Romans 11, Israel's future restoration.

### The Opportunity of Salvation in the Present Age

*Romans 10:8-21.* Though it is true that God has set aside Israel as a nation temporarily and moved in Gentiles for their blessing in the present age, it is also true that every individual, whether Jew or Gentile, can be saved by coming to Christ. Paul speaks of the word of faith which is the message of salvation, " 'The word is near you; it is in your mouth and in your heart,' that is, the word of faith we are proclaiming: That if you confess with your mouth, 'Jesus is Lord,' and believe in your heart that God raised Him from the dead, you will be saved. For it is with your heart that you believe and are justified, and it is with your mouth that you confess and are saved. As the Scripture says, 'Everyone who trusts in Him will never be put to shame' " (vv. 8-11).

Not only is the Gospel open to all, but both Jews and Gentiles can be saved in the same way, "For there is no difference between Jew and Gentile—the same Lord is Lord of all and richly blesses all who call on Him, for, 'Everyone who calls on the name of the Lord will be saved' " (vv. 12-13).

Here there is a repetition of the truth extended also in Romans 9:33 that individuals who trust in God, whether Jews or Gentiles, can be saved. Accordingly, though Israel as a nation was temporarily set aside, and progress in its prophetic program as outlined in the Old Testament has stopped, individual Jews can still be saved in exactly the same way that Gentiles can be saved.

### Israel's Glorious Future

*Romans 11:11-12.* As previously explained, Paul pointed out how Gentiles are receiving a blessing because Israel had rejected the Gospel. Paul restated this, "Again I ask: Did they stumble so as to fall beyond recovery? Not at all! Rather, because of their transgression, salvation has come to the Gentiles to make Israel envious. But if their transgression means riches for the world, and their loss means riches for the Gentiles, how much greater riches will their fullness bring!" (vv. 11-12)

The argument here is that if Israel being temporarily set aside has brought great riches to the Gentiles, how much more will the riches of God's grace be manifested when Israel will once again be restored. Just as Romans 9 dealt with Israel's failures in the past and Romans 10 their present opportunity to be saved, so Romans 11 paints a picture that Israel has a glorious future which will fulfill their expectation based on Old Testament prophecy.

### Israel's Return to Blessing

*Romans 11:22-24.* As Paul has brought out, Gentiles have been drafted into the place of blessing, the olive tree. The Jews, on the other hand, have been temporarily cut off as a nation. However, it will be easier for Israel to be grafted into their own olive tree than it was for the Gentiles to be grafted in, "After all, if you were cut out of an olive tree that is wild by nature, and contrary to nature were grafted into a cultivated olive tree, how much more readily will these, the natural branches, be grafted into their own olive tree!" (v. 24) Speaking to the Gentiles, he warned them that while Israel temporarily as a nation is not grafted in, it will be far easier for them to be grafted into the tree of blessing which they had in the Old Testament than it would be to graft in the Gentiles as is true in the present age.

The olive tree in Scripture represents the blessings that come through Abraham, to both Jews and to Gentiles. Because the Abrahamic Covenant had provision for Gentile blessing (Gen. 12:3), it was possible for the Gentiles to be grafted in, but most of the promises that are involved in the Abrahamic Covenant relate to the Jews, their future possession of the land, and their restoration spiritually. Accordingly, it is more natural for Israel to be grafted into the Abrahamic olive tree than it is for Gentiles.

### The Promise of Israel's Restoration

*Romans 11:25-27.* The outworking of God's present purpose of calling out both Jew and Gentile on an equal basis to form the body of Christ was not anticipated in the Old Testament. Its major features were mysteries, that is, truth that was not revealed in the Old Testament but which is revealed in the New Testament. In connection with this, Paul indicated he wanted Israel to understand this factor, "I do not want you to be ignorant of this mystery, brothers, so that you may not be conceited: Israel has experienced a hardening in part until the full number of the Gentiles has come in. And so all Israel will be saved, as it is written: 'The Deliverer will come from Zion; He will turn godlessness away from Jacob. And this is My covenant with them when I take away their sins' " (vv. 25-27).

In God's program the project of calling out His church of both Jews and Gentiles must be completed first (1 Cor. 12:12-13; Eph. 1:22-23; 4:11-13). What is being predicted here is that after the purpose of God for His church has been fulfilled, then God will deliver Israel (Rom. 11:25-26). The reference to Israel being saved is not in respect to freedom from the guilt of sin or the redemptive truth, but rather that Israel will be delivered from their enemies at the time of the Second Coming. As brought out in the quotation in verse 26 that a Deliverer will come, this assures, on the one hand, a completion of God's purpose for the Gentiles and, on the other hand, assures

Israel's restoration after this period is over. The answer to the question of whether God rejects His people (v. 1) is answered by the fact that God has not rejected them but will carry out His purposes as indicated in prophecy.

Prior to Israel's deliverance, however, during the present age they are experiencing "a hardening of heart," that is, many in Israel turn away from the Gospel. This will continue until God's purpose in His church is complete. Then there will be a revival in Israel and many will turn to the Lord.

The background of this is the New Testament doctrine of the Rapture of the church. When the church is taken out of the world in fulfillment of God's purpose for the church, Israel's present experience of hardening will also be removed and revival will come to Israel (v. 25). Their early conversion to the Gospel will help spread the Gospel throughout the world after the Rapture of the church as there are Israelites in every major nation who already know the languages and the people.

It is obvious from Scripture that not every individual Israelite will be saved from the guilt and power of sin. In Ezekiel 20:33-38, it is predicted that the rebels in Israel, those who were not saved prior to Christ's second coming, will be purged out, and only those converted will be allowed to enter the millennial kingdom. Accordingly, the deliverance in salvation which is referred to in verse 26, refers to a national deliverance, that is, a cessation of their persecution of the Gentiles. Those delivered are not necessarily saved in the sense of being saved from the guilt and power of sin. Though some expositors labor to try to prove that Israel has no future, the whole of Romans 11 teaches otherwise. It predicts that Israel does have a future once God's present purpose is fulfilled in the church.

The quotation in verses 26-27 is a combination of several verses in the Old Testament. What is being taught is that the Redeemer will come out of Zion, that He will turn ungodliness away from Jacob, and this will be a fulfillment of God's promise to extend mercy and salvation to Israel.

The Old Testament speaks of Christ's coming to Zion as well as coming from Zion (Pss. 14:7; 20:2; 53:6; 110:2; 128:5; 134:3; 135:21; Isa. 2:3; Joel 3:16; Amos 1:2). The point is that in the Second Coming, Christ comes both to Zion to rule over Israel and to rule the world, including the Gentiles. Zion here is used as a reference to Jerusalem as is common in Scripture.

The fulfillment predicted in Romans 11:25-27 is in keeping with the Abrahamic Covenant which promises that Israel will endure as a nation forever and that they ultimately will be restored spiritually and to their land politically. Though this truth is opposed by some scholars who do not accept a concept of a millennial kingdom after the Second Coming, the only way to understand these passages, dealing with truths such as the Scripture presents here, is to take literally the fact that Israel has a future as a nation and that that future is linked to the second coming of Christ.

In the verses which follow (vv. 28-32), a further statement is given of God's plan to give mercy to Israel and the certainty of that being fulfilled in the future. Chapter 11 of Romans closes with a remarkable statement of the wisdom of God in dealing with His purposes in the world, and especially with Israel.

### The Promise of Blessing to Those Committed to God

*Romans 12:1-2.* Promise was given to reveal God's will to those committed to God. It is important to note that the revelation of God's will is to individuals who have committed themselves to God before His will is revealed.

### The Future Judgment Seat of Christ

*Romans 14:9-12.* In Romans 14 the subject is how "gray" areas in the Christian life should be handled. A case in point is the question as to whether the Christian in the time of Paul could eat meat that had been previously offered to idols. The Christian community was divided on this, some saying meat is meat regardless what happened to it before they bought it, and, on the other hand, others claimed that by buying it they participated in the worship of idols it involved.

The exhortation which comes out of the situation is that we should not judge our Christian brethren, especially in areas where there is difference of opinion as to what is the right thing to do. As Paul pointed out, the important fact is that Christ died and was resurrected so that He might be Lord over both the dead and the living, "For this very reason, Christ died and returned to life so that he might be the Lord of both the dead and the living" (v. 9). In view of this, Paul declared that Christians should not judge each other, especially in the area of evaluating the ministry of a brother, "You, then, why do you judge your brother? Or why do you look down on your brother? For we will all stand before God's judgment seat" (v. 10).

Paul gives further exposition of the Judgment Seat of Christ in 1 Corinthians 3:11-15; 9:24-27; 2 Corinthians 5:10. The matter of judgment or evaluation of a brother's ministry is committed to Christ. Inasmuch as all Christians will stand before the Judgment Seat of Christ to be evaluated, believers should concentrate on their own problems instead of on the problems of others.

The absolute certainty of this judgment is stated in a quotation from Isaiah 45:23, " 'As surely as I live,' says the Lord, 'every knee will bow before Me; every tongue will confess to God' " (Rom. 14:11). Scriptures are clear in both the Old and New Testaments that every individual will stand before God as his Judge, not necessarily at the same time or for the same reason. The judgment at the Judgment Seat of Christ is for those who have been saved who will be evaluated then as to their contribution to the Lord's work.

Paul continued to summarize this, "So then, each of us will give an account of himself to God" (v. 12). The figure is that of a steward, or a trustee, who has responsibility for handling the business affairs of another and eventually reporting what he does with it. In life, Christians are endowed with spiritual and natural gifts that differ. No two Christians are exactly alike, and no two Christians have exactly the same opportunities, but each will be required to give an account for what he has done with them. Obviously, the more a person has, the greater is his responsibility.

The issue here is not success or amount of success, but rather the question of faithfulness in using properly what God has given to an individual Christian. Inasmuch as this is the main problem in a Christian's life, he should not turn aside to try to be a judge of his fellow Christians, except as it may be required in certain circumstances. Instead, he should be preoccupied with the fact that his own life is going to be judged, and he should give himself to things that will count in eternity.

### Gentiles to Praise the Lord

*Romans 15:8-13.* As Paul had previously explained, God's purpose in the present age is to call out Gentiles as well as Jews to form the body of Christ. Though the Old Testament did not anticipate the specific features of the body of Christ, it did make promises to the Gentiles and pictured them as singing praises to God. Paul stated, quoting from 2 Samuel 22:50; Psalm 18:49, "Therefore I will praise You among the Gentiles; I will sing hymns to Your name" (Rom. 15:9). He quoted additionally from Deuteronomy 32:43, "Rejoice,

O Gentiles, with His people" (Rom. 15:10). Paul again quoted from Psalm 117:1, "Praise the Lord, all you Gentiles, and sing praises to Him, all you peoples" (Rom. 15:11). His final quotation was from Isaiah 11:10, "The Root of Jesse will spring up, One who will arise to rule over the nations; the Gentiles will hope in Him" (Rom. 15:12). In each of these, it was anticipated that the Gentiles will praise the Lord, which to some extent is fulfilled in the present age, but will have its ultimate fulfillment in the millennial kingdom where Gentiles will be blessed as well as Jews.

Paul is arguing here for Jew and Gentile Christians to enter the full blessing of their fellowship one with the other and their enjoyment of God's mercy and grace. His final prayer was, "May the God of hope fill you with all joy and peace as you trust in Him, so that you may overflow with hope by the power of the Holy Spirit" (v. 13).

### The Prediction that Satan Will Be Crushed

*Romans 16:20.* In connection with the greetings to various Christians in Rome in which Paul exhorted them to serve the Lord with their full hearts, he prophesied, "The God of peace will soon crush Satan under your feet" (v. 20). Because the present age is of indeterminate length, and its length was unknown to Paul and others in the first century, it appeared to them that the final conquering of Satan will occur at the second coming of Christ and will be confirmed at the end of the Millennium. Throughout the history of the church, these prophecies have had the quality of being soon, or imminent, as the present age and its duration is indeterminate in length.

Taken as a whole, the Epistle to the Romans not only sets forth the great doctrines of sin, salvation, and sanctification, but also how this affects Israel in the present age and in the future where Israel's restoration is assured.

## PROPHECY IN 1 CORINTHIANS

Frequent reference to the prophetic future is found in 1 Corinthians, scattered more or less throughout the entire book. Most important are the prophecies of chapter 15, constituting a major contribution to prophetic truth.

### Introductory Prophecies in 1 Corinthians

*1 Corinthians 1:8-9.* Much of this epistle consists of rebuke and correction of the many problems which existed in the Corinthian church. It is, therefore, most significant that early in the first chapter he called attention to God's sovereign purpose that they will some-day be presented faultless in the presence of the Lord, "He will keep you strong to the end, so that you will be blameless on the Day of our Lord Jesus Christ. God, who has called you into fellowship with His Son Jesus Christ our Lord, is faithful" (vv. 8-9).

Though the epistle contains many exhortations and corrections of the problems in the Corinthian church, Paul had the long view, as stated in this passage, of how they will be presented perfect at the time of the Rapture of the church. The expression "Day of our Lord Jesus Christ" is apparently a reference to the Rapture. The same day is referred to as "the Day of the Lord" (1 Cor. 5:5; 2 Cor. 1:14), "the Day of Christ Jesus" (Phil. 1:6), and "the Day of Christ" (Phil. 1:10; 2:16). The context of these references indicate that they refer to the Rapture of the church.

As such, however, they are in contrast to references to the Day of the Lord as in 1 Thessalonians 5:1-11 which refers to the extend-ed period of time, beginning at the Rapture, extending through the time of Tribulation and Second Coming and even the millennial king-dom. It is a period in which God deals directly with the earth. The Rapture is the event which begins this extended period. At the Rapture of the church, the Corinthian church, for all its imperfec-tions, will be perfected, and every Christian in that church will be caught up to be with the Lord forever. In view of God's faithfulness in fulfilling His covenant promise to them, Paul had a basis for beginning his exhortations and corrections in the verses which follow.

### The Message of the Cross as Foolishness

*1 Corinthians 1:18-19.* One of the problems of the Corinthian church was that they greatly admired the intellectualism of Corinth with its philosophic teaching. By contrast, the Gospel was simple, Paul stated, "For the message of the Cross is foolishness to those who are perishing, but to us who are being saved it is the power of God" (v. 18). In support of this, he quoted Isaiah 29:14, "I will destroy the wisdom of the wise; the intelligence of the intelligent I will frustrate" (1 Cor. 1:19). In the passage which follows (vv. 20-31), Paul pointed out that the wisdom of man is foolishness with God, and the foolishness of the Gospel was declared to be the wisdom of God, "wisdom from God—that is, our righteousness, holiness and redemp-tion" (v. 30).

## The Wisdom of God

*1 Corinthians 2:6-12.* In keeping with his earlier discussion on God's wisdom as opposed to man's wisdom, Paul pointed out how the wisdom of God is a matter of divine revelation which far exceeds human wisdom. Paul stated, "We do, however, speak a message of wisdom among the mature, but not the wisdom of this age or of the rulers of this age, who are coming to nothing. No, we speak of God's secret wisdom, a wisdom that has been hidden and that God destined for our glory before time began. None of the rulers of this age understood it, for if they had, they would not have crucified the Lord of glory" (vv. 6-8).

The revealed wisdom of God far exceeds anything that man can devise by his own wisdom. This was further stated, "However, as it is written: 'No eye has seen, no ear has heard, no mind has conceived what God has prepared for those who love Him' — but God has revealed it to us by His Spirit" (vv. 9-10). The quotation Paul recorded is from Isaiah 64:4.

In the revelation which follows, the contrast between spiritual truth and natural truth is discussed and the world's evaluation of the wisdom of God as foolishness is because they do not spiritually understand the truth of God's revelation (1 Cor. 2:14). The spiritual truth which Paul stated here is the heart of the spiritual life and constitutes the truth which God reveals to those who are walking in fellowship with Him.

## The Judgment of a Believer's Works

*1 Corinthians 3:11-15.* In keeping with the previous discussion in 1 Corinthians concerning the wisdom of God which contrasts it to the wisdom of men, here Paul pointed out the difference in value that is made clear when what God values as worthwhile is contrasted to what the world values as worthwhile.

The Christian life is viewed here as a building which uses the foundation of Jesus Christ which is provided. This is in reference to salvation, without which it is impossible to build a Christian life. In the verses which follow, six materials are mentioned as being included in the building: "gold, silver, costly stones, wood, hay or straw" (v. 12). When the Rapture occurs, as referred to by "the Day" (v. 13), the quality of our life will be tested at the Judgment Seat of Christ.

The test will be that the building will be subjected to fire. Obviously, the wood, hay and stubble, representing different degrees of human worth, are all reduced to ashes. The gold, silver, and the costly stones survive because they are not combustible. They will constitute the basis for reward. The matter clearly refers to rewards, not salvation, because Paul stated, referring to the works being destroyed, "If it is burned up, he will suffer loss; he himself will be saved, but only as one escaping through the flames" (v. 15).

Paul didn't assign spiritual values to the gold, silver, and precious stone. In Scripture, gold is characteristically used for the glory of God and was therefore prominent in the tabernacle and in the temple. Whatever is done for the glory of God is represented by the gold. Silver is the metal of redemption (Num. 3:46-51). Whatever is done in evangelism or soul-winning is represented by silver. The costly stones were not identified as they represent so many ordinary tasks which, if fulfilled to the glory of God, will constitute a basis for reward. For other passages on the Judgment Seat of Christ, confer Romans 14:10-12; 1 Cor. 9:24-27; and 2 Cor. 5:10.

### The Lord, the Judge of His Servants

*1 Corinthians 4:1-5.* Because a Christian is a trustee of all that God has committed to him, whether natural or spiritual talents or opportunity, as a trustee, Christians should be faithful, "Now it is required that those who have been given a trust must prove faithful" (v. 2). Paul pointed out how the Lord will judge, but not until the appointed time (v. 5). A reassurance was given, "At that time each will receive his praise from God" (v. 5). Apparently, every Christian will have something that he has accomplished that is worthwhile from God's eternal point of view.

### God, the Ultimate Judge

*1 Corinthians 5:13.* In the fifth chapter Paul exhorted them to judge a case of immorality that existed in the church as well as other open sins. In this connection, they should not associate with sexually immoral people, those who are greedy, swindlers, or idolaters (v. 9). Though it is impossible to separate completely from the wicked world, we should not maintain fellowship with Christians who are obviously living as the world is living (v. 11). As a final statement in connection with this, even though we are not qualified to judge the outside world, he stated, "God will judge those outside. 'Expel the wicked man from among you' " (v. 13).

### The Saints as Judges

*1 Corinthians 6:1-3.* One of the problems in the Corinthian church was that some in the assembly were suing others in the assembly.

Paul sharply rebuked them, "If any of you has a dispute with another, dare he take it before the ungodly for judgment instead of before the saints? Do you not know that the saints will judge the world? And if you are to judge the world, are you not competent to judge trivial cases? Do you not know that we will judge angels? How much more the things of this life!" (vv. 1-3)

Scripture teaches we should not judge each other by evaluating others' actions. Here, however, is a case of dispute between Christians which Paul tells them should have been taken before the church to be settled. In the process he predicted that we will have part in judging the world (v. 2), and we will have part in judging angels (v. 3). If this is true, we are qualified to judge things that relate to this life.

### God to Judge the Wicked

*1 Corinthians 6:9-20.* Proceeding from judging disputes among Christians, Paul then pointed out how God will judge the wicked, including those who are sexually immoral, idolaters, adulterers, homosexuals, thieves, drunkards, slanderers, and swindlers (vv. 9-10). Those whose lives are characterized by these sins do not manifest that they are children of God. The Corinthians were reminded, however, that some of them once committed these sins, but that having come to Christ, Paul stated, "But you were washed, you were sanctified, you were justified in the name of the Lord Jesus Christ and by the Spirit of our God" (v. 11).

Though even Christians have freedom of choice in many matters, God is the ultimate Judge (v. 13). A Christian should not give himself to immorality in view of the fact that God who raised Jesus from the dead will also give us a resurrection body. Now, however, Christians are already members of the body of Christ. Under these circumstances, they should not unite with a prostitute (vv. 14-15). Paul's final argument was that the believer's body is the temple of God, "Do you not know that your body is a temple of the Holy Spirit, who is in you, whom you have received from God? You are not your own; you were bought at a price. Therefore honor God with your body" (vv. 19-20).

### Winning the Prize

*1 Corinthians 9:24-27.* In the preceding context, Paul discussed how he labored to win as many as possible (v. 19). Using the figure of a race, which was very familiar to those living in Corinth, the Christian life was compared to a race for a prize. Obviously, in running a race, one must compete, and this required strict training (v. 25). In the races at Corinth, it was customary to give a laurel wreath crown which in a few days would fade. By contrast, the Christian is endeavoring to gain a crown that will last forever (v. 25). In view of this, Paul found it necessary to limit himself to the rules of the race. He did not run aimlessly (v. 26). He does not fight simply by beating the air (v. 26). He makes his body submit and become his slave so that after he has exhorted others he himself would not be disqualified for the prize. The crown is not salvation, which is God's gift to those who trust in Christ; it is, rather, the future reward of one who is a Christian and seeks to honor Christ in his life. The reward will be received at the Judgment Seat of Christ (Rom. 14:10-12; 1 Cor. 3:11-15; 2 Cor. 5:10).

### The Resurrection of Christ Essential to Christian Faith

*1 Corinthians 15:12-19.* Having offered the proof of the resurrection of Christ in the preceding context (vv. 4-8), the resurrection of Christ is important because apart from this there would be a question as to whether Jesus was who He claimed to be, the Son of God who had the power to lay down His life and take it again (John 10:17-18). Paul, accordingly, stated, "And if Christ has not been raised, our preaching is useless and so is your faith" (1 Cor. 15:14). Again, he stated, "And if Christ has not been raised, your faith is futile; you are still in your sins" (v. 17). The fact of resurrection makes our hope extend into eternity, not to this life only (v. 19).

### The Order of the Resurrections

*1 Corinthians 15:20-28.* History records that Jesus died and that He rose again. As such, He is "the Firstfruits of those who have fallen asleep" (v. 20). Though others have been restored to life in both the Old and New Testaments, it may be assumed that they died again and returned to the grave. In Christ, a new order began with Christ receiving the body which will last for eternity. Because He has received a resurrection body, those who are raised after Him may also receive a similar body and will not die again. Dorcas, however, was merely restored to this life (Acts 9:36-42). It was proper for Christ to die and be resurrected first and then for others in their proper order to be resurrected (1 Cor. 15:22-23).

When human history has run its course and the millennial kingdom has been fulfilled, the final judgment on the wicked (Rev. 20:11-15) will take place, then Christ will be able to present the conquered world to God the Father, "Then the end will come, when

462

He hands over the kingdom to God the Father after He has destroyed all dominion, authority and power" (v. 24). In some sense, God's kingdom will continue forever as God necessarily directs His entire rule over creation.

### The Nature of the Resurrection Body

*1 Corinthians 15:35-50.* The question is raised concerning what kind of a body will be received in resurrection. Paul used the analogy of planting seed. Obviously, the body that will be resurrected is like the seed that is planted, but the seed itself perishes. Even in the natural world, men have bodies that are different than the bodies of animals or birds (v. 39). The inanimate bodies in space such as the sun, the moon, and the stars, likewise have different qualities (vv. 40-41).

The resurrection body, therefore, will have resemblance to the body that is sown or buried, but will be raised with different qualities, "So will it be with the resurrection of the dead. The body that is sown is perishable, it is raised imperishable; it is sown in dishonor, it is raised in glory; it is sown in weakness, it is raised in power; it is sown a natural body, it is raised a spiritual body" (vv. 42-44).

In our natural world, the natural body comes first, then later the body that is spiritual, or suited for heaven (vv. 45-46). Accordingly, in resurrection human beings will be given another human body and, especially in the case of the saved, will have a body that is rendered imperishable, holy, and suited for the service and worship of God. As Paul concluded, it is impossible for those in their natural bodies to go into eternity unchanged. That which is perishable must become imperishable (v. 50).

### The Mystery of the Resurrection of the Church

*1 Corinthians 15:51-58; cf. 1 Thessalonians 4:14-17.* Though the normal order for all men is to live, die, and then be subject to resurrection, there will be one grand exception at the end of the age. In history, Enoch and Elijah were caught up to heaven without dying (2 Kings 2:11; Heb. 11:5). At the Rapture of the church, however, a whole generation of those who are saved will be caught up to heaven without dying. This will constitute the grand exception to the normal rule of death and resurrection.

This translation without dying was revealed by Paul, "Listen, I tell you a mystery: We will not all sleep, but we will all be changed—in a flash, in the twinkling of an eye, at the last trumpet. For the trumpet will sound, the dead will be raised imperishable,

# MAJOR RESURRECTIONS

1. Resurrection of Jesus Christ (Matt. 28:1-7; Mark 16:1-7; Luke 24:1-8; John 20:1-10; Acts 2:24; 3:15; 4:32; 10:40; 17:3; Rom. 1:4; 4:25; 10:9; 1 Cor. 15:4; Eph. 1:20; 1 Thes. 4:14; 1 Peter 3:18).
2. The token resurrection of some saints at the time of the resurrection of Christ (Matt. 27:50-53).
3. The resurrection at the Rapture (1 Cor. 15:51-58; 1 Thes. 4:14-17).
4. The resurrection of the two witnesses (Rev. 11:3-13).
5. The resurrection of the Old Testament saints (Isa. 26:19-21; Ezek. 37:12-14; Dan. 12:1-3).
6. The resurrection of the Tribulation saints (Rev. 20:4-6).
7. The resurrection of the wicked dead (Rev. 20:11-15).

and we will be changed. For the perishable must clothe itself with the imperishable, and the mortal with immortality" (1 Cor. 15:51-53).

What can be known about the resurrection body? Much can be learned about our resurrection body by studying the resurrection body of Jesus Christ. From these Scriptures and this passage, it is obvious that those raised from the dead will share the Rapture with those who are living on earth at the time of the Rapture. Those who are raised and those who are translated will resemble what they were in earthly life. Jesus Christ was recognized, and though He had a new resurrection body, it still bore similarity to the body before the Crucifixion.

As is brought out in the doctrine of the Rapture (1 Thes. 4:14-17), not only will living Christians be caught up to heaven without dying, but those Christians who have died will be resurrected. Both will receive their new bodies which are suited for heaven. As Paul stated, they will be imperishable and never be subject to decay, and they will be immortal, not subject to death (1 Cor. 15:53). They will also be free from sin and be the objects of God's grace and blessing throughout eternity.

At the Rapture of the church, there will be a victory over death and the grave. Paul stated, "Death has been swallowed up in victory. Where, O death, is your victory? Where, O death, is your sting?" (vv. 54-55) In this quotation from the Old Testament, Paul was quoting Isaiah 25:8 which states that God will "swallow up death forever," and from Hosea 13:14 where God states, "I will ransom them from the power of the grave; I will redeem them from death. Where, O death, are your plagues? Where, O grave, is your destruction?" This doctrine is stated with greater clarity in the New Testament as Paul traced the victory through Jesus Christ, "But thanks be to God! He gives us the victory through our Lord Jesus Christ" (1 Cor. 15:57).

In light of the great doctrine of the resurrection and translation and the imminent hope of the Lord's return, believers are exhorted to make the most of their remaining time on earth. Paul stated, "Therefore, my dear brothers, stand firm. Let nothing move you. Always give yourselves fully to the work of the Lord, because you know that your labor in the Lord is not in vain" (v. 58). A believer should stand firm because he is standing on the rock Christ Jesus and on the sure promises of God. He should not allow the vicissitudes of life and the sorrows and burdens that come to move him away from confidence in God. While living out their life on earth, they are to engage in the work of the Lord, *always* as to time and *fully* as to extent, because they know that following this life at the Judgment Seat of Christ they will be rewarded and "your labor in the Lord is not in vain" (v. 58). This great passage dealing with the Rapture of the church coupled with Paul's earlier revelation of the Thessalonians (1 Thes. 4:14-17) constitute the principal passages on this great truth of the Lord's coming and the bright hope that it could be soon.

## PROPHECY IN 2 CORINTHIANS

Apart from the prophetic 2 Corinthians 5, the second epistle of Paul to the Corinthians has only two allusions, both to the day of the Rapture of the church. In 1:14, the reference to the Day of the Lord Jesus is a specific reference to the Rapture, concerning which Paul had earlier written the Thessalonians. In 4:14 he speaks of his and their resurrection, also a reference to the day of the Rapture (1 Thes. 4:13-18). Paul states that he will boast of the Corinthians at the Rapture (2 Cor. 1:14).

### The Promise of an Eternal House in Heaven

*2 Corinthians 5:1-9.* Continuing his revelation concerning the temporary nature of our present life and our present bodies, Paul unfolded the great truth that our present earthly bodies, which are so temporary, will be replaced by a body that will last forever (v. 1). Our present bodies have limitations and are subject to pain, illness, and death, and Christians long to have their permanent bodies (vv. 2-3), "Meanwhile we groan, longing to be clothed with our heavenly dwelling, because when we are clothed, we will not be found naked" (vv. 2-3). As Paul stated it, the "mortal may be swallowed up by life" (v. 4).

In facing the question as to whether Christians can be absolutely certain of their future resurrection, Paul pointed out that God has given us His Holy Spirit indwelling the believer, which is our seal and assurance of future resurrection (Eph. 4:30). As Paul stated it here, "Now it is God who has made us for this very purpose and has given us the Spirit as a deposit, guaranteeing what is to come" (2 Cor. 5:5).

As Christians, there are two different states. While in their present bodies, Christians are physically away from the Lord in that they are not in His presence in heaven, "Therefore we are always confident and know that as long as we are at home in the body we are away from the Lord. We live by faith, not by sight" (vv. 6-7).

The alternative of being with the Lord is attractive. However, as Paul had written earlier to the Philippians, "If I am to go on living in the body, this will mean fruitful labor for me. Yet what shall I choose? I do not know! I am torn between the two: I desire to depart and be with Christ, which is better by far; but it is more necessary for you that I remain in the body. Convinced of this, I know that I will remain, and I will continue with all of you for your progress and joy in the faith, so that through my being with you again your joy in Christ Jesus will overflow on account of me" (Phil. 1:22-26).

Paul stated, however, that while he was still in the body and in this life, "we make it our goal to please Him, whether we are at home in the body or away from it" (2 Cor. 5:9). Our present life presents opportunities for service and reward that will not be open to us in the intermediate state between death and resurrection or after resurrection in heaven.

### The Prophecy of the Judgment Seat of Christ

*2 Corinthians 5:10.* There are a number of reasons why a Christian should live his life with the Judgment Seat of Christ in view. Later in this chapter, Paul speaks of the compelling love of Christ, "For

466

Christ's love compels us, because we are convinced that One died for all, and therefore all died. And He died for all, that those who live should no longer live for themselves but for Him who died for them and was raised again" (vv. 14-15).

In verse 10 appeal is made on the basis of the Judgment Seat of Christ. Paul stated, "For we must all appear before the Judgment Seat of Christ, that each one may receive what is due him for the things done while in the body, whether good or bad" (v. 10). This is the central passage in the Bible on the Judgment Seat of Christ, and Paul alluded to it a number of times in his epistles (Rom. 14:10-12; 1 Cor. 3:11-15; 9:24-27). This was reinforced by the statement of Jesus, "Moreover, the Father judges no one, but has entrusted all judgment to the Son, that all may honor the Son as they honor the Father" (John 5:22-23).

The Judgment Seat of Christ must not be confused with other judgments, such as the judgment of the nations (Matt. 25:31-46), the judgment of Israel (Ezek. 20:33-38), the judgment of righteous Israel raised at the Second Coming (Dan. 12:1-2), or the judgment of the unsaved (Rev. 20:11-15). The Judgment Seat of Christ is peculiar in that it relates only to Christians and, apparently, is limited to those who have been saved between Pentecost and the Rapture.

According to Philippians 3:11, a Christian anticipates "the resurrection from the dead," literally "out from the dead," implying that only some are being raised. This is also confirmed by 1 Thessalonians 4:16 where those raised are referred to as "the dead in Christ." Instead of one general resurrection, Scriptures make plain that there will be a series of resurrections, beginning with the resurrection of Christ, including the resurrection of a small group of saints (Matt. 27:52-53), the resurrection at the Rapture, the resurrection of the two witnesses (Rev. 11:12), the resurrection of Old Testament saints (Dan. 12:1-2), the resurrection of the Tribulation martyrs (Rev. 20:4), and the resurrection of the wicked (Rev. 20:11-15).

From these Scriptures, it is clear that those present at the Judgment Seat of Christ are people who have been resurrected, or translated, at the Rapture of the church and are being judged not on the issue of salvation or justification but on the question of what they had done for God while still in the world. The expression "good or bad" (2 Cor. 5:10) refers to value, not morality, a truth

# MAJOR DIVINE JUDGMENTS

1. Judgment on Christ at the cross (John 1:29; Acts 20:28; Rom. 3:23-26; 5:9; 1 Cor. 15:3; 2 Cor. 5:15, 21; Gal. 1:4; Titus 2:14).
2. Contemporary judgment of believers' sins (1 Cor. 11:29-32; Heb. 12:5-6; 1 Peter 4:14-15; 1 John 1:9).
3. The Judgment Seat of Christ (Rom. 14:10-12; 1 Cor. 3:11-15; 9:24-27; 2 Cor. 5:10; Eph. 6:8).
4. The judgment of Israel (Ezek. 20:33-38; Matt. 24:42-51; 25:1-30).
5. The judgment of the nations (Matt. 25:31-46; Rev. 18:1-24; 19:17-19, 21; 20:7-9).
6. The judgment of Satan and fallen angels (Matt. 25:41; John 16:11; 2 Peter 2:4; Jude 6; Rev. 12:7-9; 20:1-3, 7-10).
7. The judgment of the Great White Throne (Rev. 20:11-15).

brought out in other passages dealing with the Judgment Seat of Christ. It is a solemn fact of Scripture that every Christian will give account of himself to God (Rom. 14:12). In view of that, there is not only the motivation of love to serve Christ but also the motivation of being found worthy to the extent that their works honored and glorified God.

## PROPHECY IN THE EPISTLE TO THE GALATIANS

Paul's Epistle to the Galatians deals largely with the question of legalism as it relates to salvation and as it relates to sanctification. Accordingly, prophetic revelation was not part of the revelation of this book.

However, because our life stretches on from time to eternity, it is impossible to have a correct view of life without a view of its culmination. Paul brought this to our attention in Galatians 6:7-10. In this passage he stated the law of the sower, that is, that what is sown determines what is reaped. Accordingly, one who lives in keeping with the sin nature will reap the judgment of God.

On the other hand, one who sows to please the Spirit will inherit eternal life (v. 8). Paul was not saying that good works are rewarded by eternal life, but rather that those who have good works demonstrate that they have eternal life and will reap its benefits. Accordingly, he exhorted the Galatians, "Let us not become weary in doing good, for at the proper time we will reap a harvest if we do not give up" (v. 9).

God allows what we sow to bring forth its harvest, whether good or evil. To some extent, God, however, intervenes in grace, and He does not always allow that which we have done wrong to have its inevitable judgment because He is dealing with us in grace based on our faith in Jesus Christ. It is obvious, however, that even under the grace of God, a Christian does not inherit a crop that he has not sown. The harvest may not be in this life; it may be in the life to come at the Judgment Seat of Christ. On this basis, he continued with his exhortation, "Therefore, as we have opportunity, let us do good to all people, especially those who belong to the family of believers" (v. 10).

## PROPHECY IN THE EPISTLE TO THE EPHESIANS

The Epistle to the Ephesians primarily concerns God's purpose for the church, a new line of truth not revealed in the Old Testament. Accordingly, prophecy is somewhat incidental to the revelation of the epistle, but, as is always the case, it has a natural climax to what is experienced in this life.

### The Prophecy that All Things
### Will Be Brought under Christ

*Ephesians 1:9-10.* Paul revealed that it is an important part of God's ultimate purpose of bringing all things under Christ. Paul referred to the riches of God's grace (vv. 7-8), and then stated, "And He made known to us the mystery of His will according to His good pleasure, which He purposed in Christ, to be put into effect when the times will have reached their fulfillment—to bring all things in heaven and on earth under one Head, even Christ" (vv. 9-10). Accordingly, Christ will be recognized as the Inheritor of the Davidic throne and King over Israel. He will also be recognized as Head over the church, and all things will be placed in subjection under Him. As the revelation which follows makes clear, Christians also will form part of this, having been predestined to share in this consummation of the mystery, God's revelation concerning the church.

### The Prophecy of Our Inheritance

*Ephesians 1:13-14.* Because the church is a part of this grand purpose of God, believers have, as Paul stated it, "heard the word of truth the Gospel of your salvation" (v. 13). As a part of our salvation also, we received the Holy Spirit as God's seal, or token, of ownership, "Having believed, you were marked in Him with a seal, the promised Holy Spirit, who is a deposit guaranteeing our inheritance until the redemption of those who are God's possession — to the praise of His glory" (vv. 13-14).

A part of the certainty of God's purpose being fulfilled in Christ, accordingly, is the presence of the Holy Spirit now and because of His presence as God's seal, our ultimate redemption. The redemption mentioned refers specifically to the resurrection of the body (Rom. 8:23), which includes all the dramatic transformation that will come in resurrection, or translation, for a Christian when he receives a new body, will be delivered completely from sin, and be equipped to serve the Lord throughout all eternity.

### Prophecy of the Glorious Inheritance of the Saints

*Ephesians 1:18-19.* In keeping with the revelation given in previous verses, Paul now speaks of his prayer for the Ephesians that they may now know something of the wonderful riches that will be theirs in their inheritance in Christ, "I pray also that the eyes of your heart may be enlightened in order that you may know the hope to which He has called you, the riches of His glorious inheritance in the saints, and His incomparably great power for us who believe" (vv. 18-19).

The salvation of a Christian has with it many tokens of the future, including the indwelling Holy Spirit which is a seal unto the day of redemption, a new nature desiring the things of God, and new experiences as God works in the lives of believers to sanctify and make them useful in His service. All of these, however, are tokens of that which is yet ahead which is far greater, which Paul referred to as "the riches of His glorious inheritance in the saints" (v. 18).

The point is that when a Christian's salvation is completed in heaven, he will be an illustration of the grace of God and the power of His resurrection. Accordingly, he will be glorious, that is, he will reflect the infinite perfections of God's handiwork. To some extent, this power of resurrection is experienced in this life, but its consummation will be complete in its transformation of a believer into the image of Christ.

### Prophecy of the Grace Revealed in the Church

*Ephesians 2:7.* In keeping with the wonderful fact that Jesus Christ will be seated in the heavenly realms, Christians will share His glory, and the purpose of this is that they manifest God's infinite grace, "in order that in the coming ages He might show the incomparable riches of His grace, expressed in His kindness to us in Christ Jesus" (v. 7). Angels do not know experientially anything about the grace of God though they observe how God works in the human race. Though all saints of all ages are a display of the grace of God, the church is especially selective. According to this Scripture, Christians will manifest the great riches of this grace. If anyone wants to know the grace of God, he should consider the state of a Christian in heaven made complete and perfect in the presence of God. All of this is grace, not human attainment.

### Prophecy of the Holy Spirit as a Seal of Our Redemption

*Ephesians 4:30.* In keeping with 1:13-14, Paul used the argument of a Christian being sealed unto the day of redemption, that is, his resurrection and perfection, as an argument why he should not grieve or sin in the presence of the Holy Spirit. As an important exhortation related to the spiritual life, Christians are exhorted not to grieve the Spirit, "And do not grieve the Holy Spirit of God, with whom you were sealed for the day of redemption" (v. 30).

The presence of the Holy Spirit is God's assurance that His purpose in grace for the church will be fulfilled completely. On that basis, Christians should be yielded to God and not allow sin in their lives that would grieve the presence of the indwelling Holy Spirit. Sin which grieves the Holy Spirit is sin which should be confessed and straightened out in keeping with the promise of 1 John 1:9, "If we confess our sins, He is faithful and just and will forgive our sins and purify us from all unrighteousness." The important reality of maintaining unbroken fellowship with God requires that sin be faced, confessed, and dealt with as soon as it is known by an individual Christian.

### Prophecy of God's Presentation of His Radiant Church

*Ephesians 5:25-27.* In dealing with the subject of husbands and wives (vv. 22-28), Paul drew the comparison of marriage in the relationship of Christ and the church. Husbands are to love their wives as Christ loved the church and gave Himself for her (v. 25). In addition to His sacrifice on the cross, there is a present undertaking of the church "to make her holy, cleansing her by the washing with water through the Word" (v. 26).

The present work of God in sanctification is outlined here as attempting to bring the church and its spiritual state up to the high level of our spiritual position in Christ. The cleansing "by the washing with water through the Word" refers to the cleansing power of the Word of God, not to the baptismal ceremony as some have taken it. This is the basic reason for expository preaching and the study of Scripture. The goal is not simply to comprehend the truth but to apply it in its sanctifying power to the individual life.

The ultimate goal prophetically is that Christ will "present her to Himself as a radiant church, without stain or wrinkle or any other blemish, but holy and blameless" (v. 27). By the grace of God, the church which is now on earth in its imperfections will be a church that is radiant in beauty and holiness. There will be no stain, that is, no defilement by sin; there will be no wrinkle, evidence of age and decay; and no blemishes—natural disfiguration. When the church is resurrected, or translated, individual believers will have bodies that are without sin and suited to serving the Holy God throughout eternity future. All of this work of sanctification comes from the fact that Christ died for the church, and subsequent sanctification grows out of this basic fact of Christ's giving Himself up for the church in His death on the cross.

Though a Christian's position is a sanctified position, now as a saint, his spiritual state will ultimately be brought up to the same perfect level of his position when he stands complete in God's presence after the Rapture of the church. These verses constitute an important revelation concerning God's present work for His church.

### Prophecy concerning Reward

*Ephesians 6:7-9.* Christians are exhorted to serve the Lord even as slaves serve their masters. If anything, a Christian should do better. As Paul expressed it, "Serve wholeheartedly, as if you were serving the Lord, not men" (v. 7). In their service for God, Christians are assured that the Lord will reward them for what has been done, and this is regardless of whether one is a slave or free, "because you know that the Lord will reward everyone for whatever good he does, whether he is slave or free" (v. 8). In view of the ultimate reward of the church in heaven, earthly masters are urged to treat their earthly slaves in a kind way (v. 9).

# PROPHECY IN THE EPISTLES TO THE PHILIPPIANS AND COLOSSIANS

Though the epistle of Paul to the Philippians is not considered a prophetic epistle because it deals primarily with other truths, nevertheless, its view of the Christian life extends from time into eternity, with references to the Rapture, the resurrection, the glorious bodies of the resurrected or translated saints, and the destruction of the wicked.

### Prophecy of the Day of Christ

*Philippians 1:6, 10; cf. 1 Corinthians 1:8; 5:5; 2 Corinthians 1:14; Philippians 2:11.* The day of Christ in Scripture needs to be distinguished from the more common expression "the Day of the Lord." The Day of the Lord normally has in view an extended period of time in which God deals in direct judgment in the world. This is developed, for instance, in 1 Thessalonians 5. The Day of Christ, which is referred to with various wordings, refers to the Rapture itself and the immediate results of the Rapture and therefore does not deal with judgment on the world.

In 1 Corinthians 1:7-8 Paul stated, "Therefore you do not lack any spiritual gift as you eagerly wait for our Lord Jesus Christ to be revealed. He will keep you strong to the end, so that you will be blameless on the Day of our Lord Jesus Christ."

In 1 Corinthians 5:5, there is reference in the context to the Rapture of the church though the expression that is used is the more common expression "the Day of the Lord." In Philippians 1:6, the expression "the Day of Christ Jesus" is used, and in Philippians 1:10 "the Day of Christ." In Philippians 2:16, the familiar expression "the Day of Christ" again is used in reference to the Rapture.

Though the varied wording does not in itself specify what day is in view, the context of these six references indicates a reference to the Rapture rather than to the Day of the Lord which will begin at the Rapture of the church and extend through the Tribulation and through the millennial kingdom, climaxing in the end of the Millennium. Paul has confidence that God who has begun a good work in the Philippian church will continue it until the day of the Rapture and that the Philippian church will be found "pure and blameless until the day of Christ" (1:10). As the Rapture of the church removes the church from the world, it will be immediately followed by the Judgment Seat of Christ in heaven when the works of believers will be evaluated and rewarded.

### Prophecy of the Life to Come

*Philippians 1:21-24.* Throughout Philippians Paul is viewing life as culminating in the life to come. Paul's objective was to live in such a manner that he would not be ashamed of the investment of his life once he was taken from this life to heaven. He also pointed out that the life to come is far better than life in the flesh here, "For to me, to live is Christ and to die is gain. If I am to go on living in the body, this will mean fruitful labor for me. Yet what shall I choose? I do not know! I am torn between the two: I desire to depart and be with Christ which is better by far; but it is more necessary for you that I remain in the body" (vv. 21-24).

In heaven Paul will be freed from the body of this flesh, will no longer have a sin nature, will be delivered from the limitations, weakness, and the mortality of this present life with its persecutions and difficulties, and will be free to serve the Lord without hindrance throughout eternity to come. In view of Paul's clear understanding of what heaven affords for a Christian, his belief that "to die is gain" (v. 21) is entirely understandable.

### Prophecy of the Exaltation of Jesus

*Philippians 2:9-11.* In exhorting the Philippian church to follow the humbling attitude of Christ when He became incarnate which ultimately led to the humiliation of the Cross, Paul also pointed out that Jesus Christ experienced His exaltation after suffering, a pattern which Christians will also follow. Paul stated this exaltation, "Therefore God exalted Him to the highest place and gave Him the name that is above every name, that at the name of Jesus every knee should bow, in heaven and on earth and under the earth, and every tongue confess that Jesus Christ is Lord, to the glory of God the Father" (vv. 9-11).

Jesus Christ will obviously have a higher place than any other person who had a human body. He will also experience universal worship with every knee bowing to Him. Those in heaven who bow the knee obviously refers to angels and saints who are in heaven; those on earth refer to men on earth still in their mortal bodies; and those "under the earth" (v. 10) apparently refers to Satan, the demon world, and even the souls in hell. Willingly or unwillingly, every tongue will confess the lordship of Jesus Christ, and this will bring glory to God the Father.

The certain triumph of Christ is here prophesied as it is in many other passages. The practical note is that while everyone will bow, for those who did not bow in life, it will be too late; and acknowledging Jesus as Lord will not lead to their salvation but to their eternal punishment. On the basis of Christ's experience and His prophetic hope, Christians are exhorted to follow His example.

### Prophecy of Paul's Boasting in the Day of Christ

*Philippians 2:16.* Another reference to the Rapture found here in the expression "the day of Christ" will be the occasion when the Philippian Christians will be judged. Paul stated that in that day his work among the Philippians will be honored, "as you hold out the Word of Life — in order that I may boast on the Day of Christ that I did not run or labor for nothing" (v. 16). Those faithful in preaching and teaching the Word do not necessarily see the fruit of their labors in visible form in this world, but at the Judgment Seat of Christ, after the Rapture, their deeds will be reflected in their true evaluation by Christ Himself.

### Prophecy of Attaining to the Resurrection from the Dead

*Philippians 3:10-11, 14.* In exhorting the Philippians and expressing his own desire "to know Christ and the power of His resurrection and the fellowship of sharing in His sufferings, becoming like Him in His death" (v. 10), Paul hoped that he would live until the Rapture of the church occurs and the resurrection of Christians will take place. At this time Paul and the other disciples did not know when the Rapture would occur, except that it was always regarded as an imminent event. Later in Paul's life, he was informed that he would be a martyr, and this is reflected in 2 Timothy. Whether or not Paul lived to that date, he pressed on "toward the goal to win the prize for which God has called me heavenward in Christ Jesus" (v. 14).

### Prophecy of the Destiny of the Wicked

*Philippians 3:18-19.* Though Paul stressed in his epistles the glorious destiny of Christians, he also painted the background of the destruction of the wicked. He stated, "For, as I have often told you before and now say it again even with tears, many live as enemies of the Cross of Christ. Their destiny is destruction, their god is their stomach, and their glory is in their shame. Their mind is on earthly things" (vv. 18-19). While warning against the way of the wicked, Paul was also painting a contrast of what should spur on the Christian in view of the fact that he is destined for glory. Those scheduled for destruction spend all their time on the present and live as enemies of the Cross. By contrast, Christians should further the work of God, should live for eternal values, and have in mind the glory that will be theirs in the Lord's presence.

### Prophecy of the Believer's Glorious Body in Heaven

*Philippians 3:20-21.* In contrast to the wicked whose destiny is destruction, though not annihilation, Paul referred to the fact that

Christians are citizens of heaven. Their expectation is in the future with the ultimate goal that they will have a glorious body in heaven, "But our citizenship is in heaven. And we eagerly await a Saviour from there, the Lord Jesus Christ, who, by the power that enables Him to bring everything under His control, will transform our lowly bodies so that they will be like His glorious body" (vv. 20-21). Though the Christian still is on earth, he is a citizen of heaven and is governed by the unseen power of God working in his life.

The same power that enables a Christian to bring his life under control will also ultimately transform the body he has in this life to a body "like His glorious body" (v. 21).

Paul is referring here to the fact that a believer's resurrection body will be patterned after the resurrection body of Christ. This body will be a body of flesh and bone, but a body without sin, decay, or death. In speaking of the believer's body as a glorious body, it does not mean that our bodies will emanate brilliant light as is sometimes true of God Himself, as in the transfiguration of Christ, and as revealed of God in heaven. The glory of which he is speaking here is in reference to the fact that the glory of God is the manifestation of God's infinite perfections. Though the believer may not have a body that glows with light in a similar way as the transfigured body of Christ (Matt. 17:1-2), his body will nevertheless reflect God's perfections.

A Christian's resurrection body will therefore be holy as God is holy, immortal as God is immortal, everlasting as God is everlasting, and will be a constant reminder of the extent of God's grace that took those who were justifiably destined for eternal punishment and transformed them into saints whose resurrection or translation introduced them to a life wholly committed to God.

Paul's Epistle to the Colossians concerns itself with problems in the Colossian church and not with prophecy, but there are a few allusions to the future as the goal for Christian life and testimony.

### Prophecy of the Inheritance of the Saints
*Colossians 1:12.* In itemizing the basic Christian standards for effective ministry, Paul spoke of giving proper thanks for our inheritance, "giving thanks to the Father, who has qualified you to share in the inheritance of the saints in the kingdom of light" (v. 12).

Though the details of a Christian's inheritance are not clear, it is one of the great truths of the Christian life that a Christian is promised future blessing and is a joint heir with Christ with a glorious inheritance awaiting him in heaven.

The Old Testament Scriptures abound in the laws of inheritance that existed in time in Israel. The New Testament carries this forward to the inheritance of Christians when they get to glory. In general, the inheritance refers to all the blessings Christians have been promised in Christ to which there is reference a number of times in the New Testament (Rom. 8:17; Gal. 3:29; Col. 3:24; Titus 3:7; Heb. 1:14; 6:17; 1 Peter 1:4). Blessings a Christian will receive in glory far exceed our capacity to understand it or visualize it now. They may be assured that God's grace is complete and that we will have a glorious future as God fulfills His promises to us.

### Prophecy of the Christian's Future Perfection

*Colossians 1:22-27*. In contrasting the tremendous change between being alienated from God because their behavior was characteristically evil, Christians have now been reconciled to God by Christ through His death and have the hope of being presented in moral and physical perfection in heaven. Paul expressed it, "But now He has reconciled you by Christ's physical body through death to present you holy in His sight, without blemish and free from accusation" (v. 22). Because not all the Colossian Christians were genuinely saved, he pointed out that our inheritance is only for those who continue in the faith, demonstrating that they are truly born again (v. 23).

Because it is believed the Colossian Christians were battling an error known as gnosticism which was supposed to give its adherents superior knowledge, the Apostle Paul here, as throughout the epistle, holds up the wonderful spiritual blessings that belong to a Christian in time and the glorious future, which is ours, which is beyond our knowledge or comprehension.

Paul also mentioned in connection with this the revelation of the mystery, the truth not revealed in the Old Testament, that in this dispensation Christ would indwell the believer, "To them God has chosen to make known among the Gentiles the glorious riches of this mystery, which is Christ in you, the hope of glory" (v. 27). This revelation far exceeds any of the so-called special knowledge of the Gnostics.

### The Promise of Appearing with Christ in Glory

*Colossians 3:4*. Having declared that the Christians are now raised with Christ spiritually and positionally in Christ are already with Him at the right hand of God, he exhorted them to set their minds on

477

things above (v. 2). Paul pictured, then, the ultimate goal, "When Christ, who is your life, appears, then you also will appear with Him in glory" (v. 4). The indwelling Christ who is the center of our lives now will be all the more a part of a Christian's life in heaven because He will be visibly present and will share something of the glory of heaven with Him.

**The Promise of Receiving an Inheritance from the Lord**

*Colossians 3:23-24.* After exhorting all classes of Christians—husbands, wives, children, fathers, and slaves—to living a life in keeping with their faith in Christ, the apostle adds the promise, "Whatever you do, work at it with all your heart, as working for the Lord, not for men, since you know that you will receive an inheritance from the Lord as a reward. It is the Lord Christ you are serving" (vv. 23-24).

Though all Christians will have an inheritance in Christ because it is based fundamentally on grace, it is nevertheless true that our inheritance is also a reward for faithful service to God in this present world. The point is that God is not settling all accounts now, and in heaven there will be reward for those who did not receive their reward in life.

## PROPHECY IN 1 THESSALONIANS

Probably the first of Paul's inspired epistles, 1 Thessalonians has a special place in that it was addressed to a young church. Paul founded this church on his second missionary journey when he spent three Sabbath Days preaching the Gospel. Though the Jews who rejected Paul's message stirred up trouble and forced Paul to leave, the young Christians in Thessalonica stood firm and formed the nucleus of the church there. To encourage them in their faith, Paul wrote his two epistles to them. Especially significant is the fact that the doctrine of the coming of the Lord and related events form one of the main doctrines of both 1 and 2 Thessalonians, with some reference to the coming of the Lord in every chapter. The instruction given by Paul in the field of prophecy was the basis for his enlarging on this teaching in his epistles. Especially significant is the detailed account of the Rapture in 4:13-18.

**The Hope of the Lord's Return**
**Encourages Faith and Endurance**

*1 Thessalonians 1:3.* In thanking God for His work of grace in the hearts of the Thessalonians, Paul refers to the importance of their hope in Christ, "We continually remember before our God and Father your work produced by faith, your labor prompted by love, and your endurance inspired by hope in our Lord Jesus Christ" (v. 3). The faith of the Thessalonians was well rounded and caused them to work faithfully for God. Their labor was also encouraged by their love for each other and their love for God. In their steadfastness, their endurance, according to Paul, was "inspired by hope in our Lord Jesus Christ" (v. 3). In 1 Thessalonians the hope of the Lord's return is seen as an integral part of our total faith and hope in God.

### Waiting for God's Son from Heaven

*1 Thessalonians 1:10.* The testimony of the Thessalonian church involved three time frames. Paul was assured that when he was there they had come to Christ in deep conviction of the Holy Spirit as this was manifested in their manner of life (vv. 4-5). They had a history of being faithful in persecution. Though they were in suffering, they remained true to God and became an example to the churches of the area (vv. 6-7). The truth they had received was not only sufficient for their own faith but became their message to those everywhere that heard of the Thessalonian church.

A summary of their present testimony was that "you turned to God from idols to serve the living and true God" (v. 9). In this way exercising faith and manifesting that faith in service, they were also looking forward to the coming of the Lord as a part of their Christian faith. They had a future time frame as Paul expressed it, "to wait for His Son from heaven, whom He raised from the dead—Jesus who rescues us from the coming wrath" (v. 10). Prophecy of the future was comprehended by the Thessalonian church in proper perspective with faith in what had already been accomplished in history in Christ.

### Living in Expectation of God's Coming Kingdom and Glory

*1 Thessalonians 2:12.* In his encouragement of the Thessalonians, Paul wrote that God had dealt with them as a father deals with his own children (v. 11), and he urged them to live in a worthy manner before God (v. 12). Their entire faith, life, and service, however, was in anticipation of God's future calling into His kingdom and glory. As he expressed it, "encouraging, comforting and urging you to live lives worthy of God, who calls you into His kingdom and glory" (v. 12). Throughout this epistle the coming of the Lord is linked as a natural outcome and encouragement to live for Christ in this present world. They were sure that while their present experience might involve persecution and trial, they were destined to be a part of God's kingdom with glory and blessing forever.

### The Wicked Destined for the Wrath of God

*1 Thessalonians 2:15-16.* Just as the Christian's life has as its goal God's blessing in eternity, so the wicked can anticipate experiencing God's wrath. Paul referred to Jews who were unbelievers, "who killed the Lord Jesus and the prophets and also drove us out. They displease God and are hostile to all men in their effort to keep us from speaking to the Gentiles so that they may be saved. In this way they always heap up their sins to the limit. The wrath of God has come upon them at last" (vv. 15-16). Written over all human experience is the fact that the present leads to the future and that the future is determined by what is done in the present. The wicked can only anticipate God's judgment in contrast to the righteous who will experience God's blessing.

### The Thessalonian Church to Be
### Paul's Glory and Joy in Heaven

*1 Thessalonians 2:19-20.* In speaking of his intense concern and love for the Thessalonian church, Paul indicated he had wanted to see them, but Satan had stopped him (vv. 17-18). In attempting to express his love and concern for them, Paul pointed out that not only was he involved with them at the present time, but he was looking forward to the time when they will be present in heaven, when they will be a source of joy and glory for him. He stated, "For what is our hope, our joy, or the crown in which we will glory in the presence of our Lord Jesus when He comes? Is it not you? Indeed, you are our glory and joy" (vv. 19-20).

Having stated that their present service and faithfulness to God would be rewarded in heaven, he now added this additional thought that because he had led them to Christ and encouraged them in their Christian life, he too would have the satisfaction of seeing them in the presence of the Lord, and that they would be the basis of Paul's glory and joy. In expressing this thought, the apostle was continuing in the line of revelation he had given earlier in the epistle that our present life is inexorably linked to that which is to come.

### Being Blameless and Holy When the Lord Comes

*1 Thessalonians 3:13.* In praying for them and urging them on in their Christian life, the apostle holds before the Thessalonian church the prospect of being recognized as those who are serving the

Lord, blameless and holy when the Lord comes. Paul stated, "May He strengthen your hearts so that you will be blameless and holy in the presence of our God and Father when our Lord Jesus comes with all His holy ones" (v. 13). This verse is commonly related to the Rapture of the church, that when Christ comes He will find His church on earth, serving Him effectively. The passage could, however, also be taken in regard to the arrival in heaven of those caught up at the Rapture. In heaven their holiness and faithfulness to God will be especially evident before God the Father and before saints and angels. Paul was not advocating here sinless perfection as something that could be attained in this life, but he does hold that it is possible for a Christian to live in such a way that he will manifest his desire to serve the Lord and be blameless in what he is doing.

## The Revelation of the Rapture of the Church

*1 Thessalonians 4:13-18.* Taking its place alongside 1 Corinthians 15:51-58, this passage in Thessalonians becomes one of the crucial revelations in regard to the Rapture of the church. Though the Old Testament and the Synoptic Gospels reveal much concerning the second coming of Christ, the specific revelation concerning Christ's coming to take His church out of the world, both living and dead, was not revealed until the night before His crucifixion in John 14:1-3. Because the apostles at that time did not understand the difference between the first and second comings of Christ, they could hardly be instructed in the difference between the Rapture of the church and Christ's second coming to judge and rule over the earth. A careful study of this passage in 1 Thessalonians will do much to set the matter in its proper biblical revelation.

Unlike passages that deal with the second coming of Christ and trace the tremendous world-shaking events which shall take place in the years preceding it, the Rapture of the church is always presented as the next event and, as such, one that is not dependent on immediate preceding events. The Rapture of the church, defined in 1 Thessalonians 4:17 as being "caught up together with them in the clouds to meet the Lord in the air," is a wonderful truth especially designed to encourage Christians.

Accordingly, Paul stated that he did not want the Thessalonians to be uninformed or ignorant concerning Christians who had died. Accordingly, they were not to grieve for them as the world does that has no hope. In this passage, as in all Scriptures, the sad lot of those who leave this world without faith in Christ is described in absolute terms of having "no hope" (v. 13). Only in Christ can one have hope of life to come in heaven.

The nature of their faith in Christ which prompts them to believe that they will be ready when Christ comes is stated in verse 14, "We believe that Jesus died and rose again and so we believe that God will bring with Jesus those who have fallen asleep in Him."

Though there may be debate as to what is absolutely fundamental in Christian doctrine, it is evident that faith in the fact that Christ died for the sins of the world and rose from the dead is essential to effective faith in Christ.

If one can accept the supernatural event of Christ's dying for sin and rising from the grave, he can also believe in the future Rapture of the church. This is defined as their faith "that God will bring with Jesus those who have fallen asleep in Him" (v. 14). Though the general truth of the resurrection of the dead is variously stated in Scripture in both the Old and New Testaments, a special revelation of the Rapture of a particular body of saints and the translation of those living at the time is nowhere linked to the doctrine of the Second Coming when Christ comes to establish His kingdom. At the Rapture believers are caught up to heaven. At the Second Coming believers remain on earth. Accordingly, the event that Paul was describing here is quite different than the second coming of Christ as it is normally defined.

In what sense will Jesus bring with Him those who have fallen asleep? This refers to Christians who have died and the expression of falling asleep is used to emphasize the fact that their death is temporary. When a Christian dies, his soul goes immediately to heaven (2 Cor. 5:6-8). On the occasion of the Rapture of the church, accordingly, Paul declared that Jesus would bring with Him the souls of those who have fallen asleep. The purpose is brought out for this in the verses which follow in that Jesus will cause their bodies to be raised from the dead and their souls will reenter their bodies.

The actual sequence of events was described by Paul, "According to the Lord's own word, we tell you that we who are still alive, who are left till the coming of the Lord, will certainly not precede those who have fallen asleep. For the Lord Himself will come down from heaven, with a loud command, with the voice of the archangel and with the trumpet call of God, and the dead in Christ will rise first.

After that, we who are still alive and are left will be caught up together with them in the clouds to meet the Lord in the air. And so we will be with the Lord forever" (1 Thes. 4:15-17).

This revelation was introduced as truth that is "According to the Lord's own word" (v. 15), that is, given to Paul by special revelation. Though Jesus introduced the doctrine of the Rapture in John 14:1-3, there was no exposition of it while He was still on earth. Accordingly, this revelation, given to Paul for the purpose of passing it on to the Thessalonian church, becomes an important additional revelation concerning the nature of the Rapture.

One of the questions which seems to have faced the Thessalonians is the question whether if the Lord came for the living, they would have to wait before they could see those who were resurrected from the dead. This thought was set at rest when Paul stated, "we who are still alive, who are left till the coming of the Lord, will certainly not precede those who have fallen asleep" (1 Thes. 4:15). In verse 16 the sequence of events is described. The Lord Jesus Himself will come down from heaven, that is, there will be a bodily return to the sphere of earth. Jesus will utter a loud command related to the resurrection of the dead and the translation of the living. This will be accompanied by the voice of the archangel. The archangel Michael, though not related to the order of events here, in view of the fact that he is the leader of the holy angels in their opposition to Satan, can understandably voice triumph and victory. This will be followed by the trumpet call of God. When this sounds, the event will take place. Christians who have died will rise first. Then, Christians still living, being translated into bodies suited for heaven, "will be caught up together with them in the clouds to meet the Lord in the air" (v. 17).

For all practical purposes, these events will take place at the same time. Those living on earth who are translated will not have to wait for the resurrection of Christians who have died because, as a matter of fact, they will be resurrected a moment before. In expressing the thought that those who "are left will be caught up together with them in the clouds" (v. 17), Paul was expressing the essential character of the Rapture which is a snatching up or a bodily lifting up of those on earth, whether living or resurrected, their meeting the Lord in the air, and then their triumphant return to heaven. This is described as being "with the Lord forever" (v. 17).

This is in keeping with the original revelation of the Rapture in

John 14:1-3 where Christ informed His disciples that He was coming for them to take them where He was, that is, in the Father's house in heaven. They will remain in heaven until the great events describing the period preceding the second coming of Christ will take place, and the church in heaven will participate in the grand procession described in Revelation 19 of Christ's return from heaven to earth to set up His earthly kingdom.

The mention of clouds (1 Thes. 4:17) is taken by some to be literal clouds as was true of His ascension (Acts 1:9). Some believe the great number of those raptured will resemble a cloud, similar to the reference of Hebrews 12:1. The glorious prospect is that once this takes place, there will be no more separations between Christ and His church.

The locale of their future is not permanent as they will be in heaven during the time preceding the Second Coming. They will be on earth during the millennial kingdom, and then will inhabit the new heaven and new earth in eternity. In each of these situations they will be with Christ in keeping with the symbolism of their marriage to Him as the heavenly Bridegroom. Though this passage is most informative concerning the nature of the Rapture, it is designed to be an encouragement to those who are living for Christ.

Most significant in this passage is the fact that there are no preceding events, that is, there are no world-shaking events described as leading up to this event. As a matter of fact, the church down through the centuries could expect momentarily the Rapture of the church, which hope continues today. By contrast, the second coming of Christ will be preceded by divine judgments on the world and followed by the establishing of Christ's earthly kingdom. No mention is made of that here, but the emphasis is placed on the wonderful fellowship Christians will enjoy with the Saviour. The wonderful hope of the Rapture of the church is a source of constant encouragement to those who put their trust in Him and who are looking for His coming.

### The Day of the Lord

*1 Thessalonians 5:1-11.* Coming immediately after the revelation concerning the Rapture of the church, it is natural to consider the question of when this will occur. Here the apostle appeals to a much larger doctrine of Scripture, the Day of the Lord, which is a time of special divine visitation mentioned often in the Old and New Testaments.

# THE DAY OF THE LORD

Pentecost

Church Age

Rapture

Period of Preparation — Ten Nations United

Seven-year Covenant Signed

70th Week

Period of Peace — 3½ Years of Peace

Covenant Broken

Period of Persecution — 3½ Years of Great Tribulation

Second Coming of Christ

Millennium

Great White Throne Judgment

New Heaven / New Earth / New Jerusalem

Day of the Lord — 2 Peter 3:10-11

Day of God — Eternity — 2 Peter 3:12

Paul stated, "Now, brothers, about times and dates we do not need to write to you, for you know very well that the Day of the Lord will come like a thief in the night" (vv. 1-2). As the Day of the Lord comes without warning, so also the Rapture. The placing of this doctrine next to the revelation of the Rapture is because of the similarity of both events not having signs prior to their beginning. Like a thief in the night, who comes without warning, the Rapture will occur and also the Day of the Lord will begin.

Mentioned frequently in the Old Testament, the Day of the Lord refers to any special period where God intervenes supernaturally, bringing judgment on the world. An outstanding illustration is the Book of Joel which has as its theme the Day of the Lord. The term is properly used of the crisis that occurred in the time of Joel brought on by the infestation of locusts which ruined their crops, bringing starvation and destruction.

Joel described it, "What a dreadful day! For the Day of the LORD is near; it will come like destruction from the Almighty" (Joel 1:15). The devastation in loss of crops was described graphically in verses 16-20. This, however, was not the only problem that they faced. They were also to experience the invading Assyrian armies which would conquer them, much as the locusts had conquered them. They were experiencing a day of judgment from God.

The day described in Joel was not a long period of time, but more than twenty-four hours. This impending Day of the Lord fulfilled in the Old Testament was an appeal by Joel to the people of Israel to return to the Lord. Joel wrote, " 'Even now,' declares the LORD, 'return to Me with all your heart, with fasting and weeping and mourning.' Rend your heart and not your garments. Return to the LORD your God, for He is gracious and compassionate, slow to anger and abounding in love, and He relents from sending calamity. Who knows? He may turn and have pity and leave behind a blessing—grain offerings and drink offerings for the LORD your God" (2:12-14).

The future period of God's intervention in the world will begin at the Rapture and will include the period of trouble preceding the second coming of Christ and the establishment of God's kingdom in the earth. The Day of the Lord also will include the millennial kingdom. The entire period before and after the second coming of Christ will constitute a special divine intervention and rule of righteousness on the earth in the way that is not being experienced in the present age. The teaching that the Day of the Lord does not begin until the Second Coming is refuted by the fact that it includes the Great Tribulation. Joel made it clear that the Day of the Lord included the Great Tribulation before the Second Coming (Joel 2:28–3:2). The time of restoration of Israel (Joel 3:16-21) following the Great Tribulation is related to the Second Coming and will be fulfilled in the Millennium.

The Day of the Lord will begin as a time period at the Rapture, but its major events will not begin immediately. The ten-nation kingdom must be formed in the final seven years before the Second Coming will begin. Because the Day of the Lord will begin as a time period at the time of the Rapture, the two events are linked as both beginning without warning and coming without a specific sign. Once the Day of the Lord begins, however, as it will after the Rapture, as time progresses there will be obvious signs that they are in the Day of the Lord and in the period leading up to the Second Coming just as there will be obvious evidences that the millennial kingdom has begun after the Second Coming. As the Rapture must precede the signs, it necessarily must occur when the Day of the Lord begins. (For further discussion see 2 Thes. 2.)

One of the important signs of the Day of the Lord is the fact that the people will be saying, "Peace and safety," when, as a matter of fact, "destruction will come on them suddenly, as labor pains on a pregnant woman, and they will not escape" (v. 3). The interpretation teaching that this is the period between the Rapture and the Second Coming fits very naturally into this period. According to Daniel 9:27, there will be a seven-year period leading up to the second coming of Christ. The first half of this period will be a time of peace when a covenant of peace will be made with Israel, as indicated in Daniel 9:27. During this period people will hail peace as having been achieved as mentioned in verse 3. Then suddenly the Great Tribulation will begin and they will not escape its judgment. The world-shaking judgments that precede the Second Coming are described graphically in Revelation 6–18.

Because Christians are forewarned that the Day of the Lord is coming and should not be surprised, they should live in the light of God's divine revelation, "But you, brothers, are not in darkness so that this day should surprise you like a thief. You are all sons of the light and sons of the day. We do not belong to the night or to the darkness" (vv. 4-5). The Day of the Lord is pictured here as a time of night for the world because it is a time of judgment in contrast to the Christian's day which is a day of light. The Christian's day will be climaxed by the Rapture; the day for the wicked will begin at that time, and the judgments related to the Day of the Lord will take place according to the time sequence of this period, with the great judgments occurring in the Great Tribulation, climaxing in the Second Coming. In addition to the references to the Day of the Lord in Joel, further description of the Day of the Lord is found in Isaiah 13:9-11; Zephaniah 1:14-18; 3:4-15.

Because Christians have been alerted, they should not be asleep but be "alert and self-controlled" (1 Thes. 5:6) in contrast to the world which drowns its sorrows in drinking (v. 7), a Christian should be, "self-controlled, putting on faith and love as a breastplate, and the hope of salvation as a helmet" (v. 8). The resource of a Christian in the period leading up to the Rapture will be one of faith in God, love for God and his fellow Christian, and the glorious hope of his future salvation which is described as a helmet.

The destinies of those who will be saved at the time of the Rapture and those who are not was brought out, "For God did not appoint us to suffer wrath but to receive salvation through our Lord Jesus Christ" (v. 9). For the Christian, his appointment is the Rapture; for the unsaved, his appointment is the Day of the Lord.

Paul realized that some Christians would have died before the Rapture and that others would be still living. Accordingly, he says of Christ, "He died for us so that, whether we are awake or asleep, we may live together with Him" (v. 10). By being awake, he was referring to Christians being still alive in the world, or asleep, to the fact that Christians have died and their bodies will be sleeping in the grave though their souls are in heaven. His conclusion here, as in the other prophetic truths revealed in this epistle, is a practical one, "Therefore encourage one another and build each other up, just as in fact you are doing" (v. 11).

### Being Blameless at the Coming of Our Lord Jesus Christ

*1 Thessalonians 5:23.* The extensive prophetic revelation as well as Paul's counsel and exhortation to live for God has its prophetic climax in his exhortation, "May your whole spirit, soul and body be kept blameless at the coming of our Lord Jesus Christ" (v. 23). In referring to Christians as having spirit, soul, and body, Paul was recognizing the essential elements of human personality. Christians have a body which will die, but will be resurrected. They also have a soul which refers to the psychological aspect of human life, and spirit, which seems to refer to their God-consciousness and religious experiences. Though it can be demonstrated in Scripture that all these terms are sometimes used synonymously for an individual, such as a spirit, soul, or body, and that the whole person is in view, nevertheless, these form the major constituent elements of human personality.

The reference to progressive sanctification obviously states that this is a work that only God can do. A believer in Christ can be part of the sanctification process by availing himself of the means to sanctification, such as the Word of God, prayer, fellowship with the Lord's people, and study of the Scriptures. In the end, however, God must do the sanctification or it will not be effective. Paul anticipated the ultimate when all Christians will stand in heaven complete, with a new body, without sin, blemish, or defilement.

## PROPHECY IN 2 THESSALONIANS

The young church at Thessalonica, since they had received Paul's first letter, had experienced false teaching on the part of some who came to visit the church. In addition to the persecutions they were facing from unbelievers, they now were dealing also with confusion and division in their midst. To remedy this situation, Paul wrote this epistle reminding them of what he had taught them when he was there and giving them further instruction on the major subject of the Day of the Lord and the man of lawlessness.

### The Coming Judgment of the Wicked
### and Reward of the Righteous

*2 Thessalonians 1:5-10.* Because the Thessalonian church was experiencing persecution from unbelievers, Paul assured them that, on the one hand, the righteous will be rewarded in the future and, on the other hand, the wicked will be punished. Paul wrote, "All this is evidence that God's judgment is right, and as a result you will be counted worthy of the kingdom of God, for which you are suffering. God is just: He will pay back trouble to those who trouble you and give relief to you who are troubled, and to us as well" (vv. 5-6). The truth that God will judge all men sometime in the future is taught in Scripture, but such a program is a comfort and a strength to those undergoing persecution because, on the one hand, they know that God will deal with their persecutors in judgment and, on the other hand, that they will be rewarded and blessed.

Our expectation appears in the further details which Paul gave when he stated that God will "give relief to you who are troubled, and to us as well. This will happen when the Lord Jesus is revealed from heaven in blazing fire with His powerful angels. He will punish those who do not know God and do not obey the Gospel of our Lord Jesus. They will be punished with everlasting destruction and shut off from the presence of the Lord and from the majesty of His power" (vv. 7-9).

Scripture reveals that there are several times when God deals in direct judgment on the world. Some of this will occur in what is referred to as the Great Tribulation, the forty-two-month period before the Second Coming. Some will occur at the second coming of Christ when people, living in the world who rebel against God and have not put their trust in Christ, will be judged unworthy of the millennial kingdom and be purged out. A further judgment is recorded in Revelation 20:11-15 where the wicked dead will be raised and judged. This is the final judgment.

The problem which some have with this passage is that the wicked unbelievers who are persecuting the Thessalonian church will not receive their final punishment until the judgment of the Great White Throne (vv. 11-15). Those who are punished at the time of Christ's second coming will be those living at that time who are unbelievers, but will not include those who persecuted the Thessalonian church who, of course, have died. The exact time is not indicated here because there are several periods of divine judgment.

The Thessalonians were assured that, in God's time and in God's way, those who persecute them will be punished, including their being shut out from the Lord. Because neither Paul nor the Thessalonian Christians knew when the Lord was coming, they could gather from this revelation the assurance that the wicked would be taken care of in God's program, whether sooner or later.

A further difficulty in explaining this passage is that this destruction is linked to the day of the Lord's glorification. According to 2 Thessalonians 1:10, the punishment of the wicked will be "on the day He comes to be glorified in His holy people and to be marveled at among all those who have believed. This includes you, because you believed our testimony to you" (v. 10).

The Lord will come at different times in the future program and will be glorified. He, first of all, was glorified when He went to heaven following His period on earth. He will be glorified and His majesty will be revealed also at the Second Coming when the world will be put under His power, judgment, and those who have trusted Him, referred to here as "His holy people," will be glorified. The glory of Christ again will be manifest at the end of the millennial kingdom at the Great White Throne judgment when He deals with the wicked dead and commits them to eternal punishment. Accordingly, the prophecy must be taken as not referring to a specific moment in the future program but to the fact that in the course of these various fulfillments of prophecy the wicked will be judged and Christ will be glorified.

### The Coming of the Day of the Lord
### in Relation to the Rapture

*2 Thessalonians 2:1-12.* In 1 Thessalonians 5, the apostle had pointed out to the Thessalonians that the Day of the Lord would begin at the time of the Rapture and that it would be a time period in which God deals in direct judgment in the world before the Second Coming and at the time of the Second Coming as well as in the millennial kingdom. In all this, God will deal directly with human sin in contrast to His withholding judgment in the present age.

The false teachers had come to Thessalonica, however, and told them they were already in the Day of the Lord, contradicting Paul's teaching, unsettling and alarming the Thessalonian church because they had understood Paul to say that they would not be in this period. Accordingly, Paul attempted to correct this difficulty by pointing out that the major events of the Day of the Lord had not occurred and that there was no evidence that the day had already begun.

The problem was stated in the opening verses of chapter 2, "Concerning the coming of our Lord Jesus Christ and our being gathered to Him, we ask you, brothers, not to become easily unsettled or alarmed by some prophecy, report or letter supposed to have come from us, saying that the Day of the Lord has already come. Don't let anyone deceive you in any way, for that day will not come until the rebellion occurs and the man of lawlessness is revealed, the man doomed to destruction. He opposes and exalts himself over everything that is called God or is worshiped, and even sets himself up in God's temple, proclaiming himself to be God" (vv. 1-4).

In approaching the interpretation of these verses, distinction must be made between the concept of the Day of the Lord *beginning* at a specific moment and the major events of the Day of the Lord *coming* which will occur some time after it has begun. The parallel is the ordinary twenty-four-hour period. The day actually *begins* at midnight, but no activity marks the day until one is raised from sleep to greet the morning. Then as the events of the day unfold, it is evident that a new day *has come.* The time period, accordingly, begins before the major events of the period *come.*

The same is true of the Day of the Lord. The time period *begins* at the Rapture of the church, but the major events do not *come* immediately. However, if the Day of the Lord has progressed very far, there will be unmistakable signs that they are in the Day of the Lord.

Paul, accordingly, warned them not to be deceived by any report that is received from him, a forged letter or report, because he did not send it. His view was expressed in his first letter to them which dated the Day of the Lord as following the Rapture.

The reasons why Paul was sure they were not in the Day of the Lord was that there were no signs of it. One of the major signs will be the emergence of a human leader, "the man of lawlessness" referred to as the "little horn" of Daniel 7:8, who, according to Daniel's prophecies, will bring together ten countries in a political confederacy that will be located in the Middle East. For a careful Bible student, he would be recognized at once when the event takes place seven years before the Second Coming because Daniel described him as first conquering three countries and then, apparently, all the remaining seven (vv. 8, 23-25). His prominence will be progressive. As there was no sign of his existence, it was proof that the Day of the Lord had not begun.

As Daniel stated, in addition to conquering the ten countries, he eventually "will devour the whole earth, trampling it down and crushing it" (v. 23). Before he conquers the world, after he has gained control of these ten countries, he will make a covenant with Israel, apparently settling peacefully the problems that exist between Israel and her neighbors (9:27). Though the details of this covenant are not revealed, it is clear from verse 27 that it is planned to last for seven years, that it was observed for the first three-and-a-half years and then broken, making Israel the object of his persecution the second half of the seven years which culminates in the second coming of Christ.

There will be unmistakable evidence then that they are in the Day of the Lord which comes by stages, first, when the ruler conquers three, then ten, then makes a seven-year covenant with Israel, observes it for three-and-a-half years, and then breaks it and desecrates the temple and persecutes the people of Israel. None of these events had occurred. Many Scriptures in the Old and New Testaments give further details on this process of fulfilled prophecy.

Paul's argument, accordingly, is that the Thessalonians had no proof at all that they were in the Day of the Lord and, as a matter of fact, this was contrary to what he had taught them when he was with them.

The key to the whole program of the Day of the Lord at its beginning is this "man of lawlessness" who may be identified with the "little horn" of Daniel 7:8 and the "ruler who will come" of 9:26 who prior to the second coming of Christ will desecrate the temple and become himself the object of terrible judgments from God as defined in Revelation 6–18. The "man of lawlessness" may also be identified as the ruler mentioned in Daniel 11:36-39 and as the beast out of the sea (Rev. 13:1-10). The "man of lawlessness" will become a world conquerer for forty-two months (vv. 5-7), and he will be the persecutor of Israel in that last forty-two-month period with countless martyrs (7:9-17).

In addition to the appearance of this man in fulfilling prophecies related to him which had not yet occurred, Paul pointed also to the fact that the one who is helping to restrain sin in the world, most probably a reference to the Holy Spirit, has not been "taken out of the way" (2 Thes. 2:7). This will occur at the Rapture when the church indwelt by the Spirit will be removed. It is evident from Scripture that God uses various means to restrain sin in the world, one of them being the presence of the Holy Spirit. Though the Holy Spirit is omnipresent and cannot be removed from the earth in the sense of restricting His access to the world, His restraining ministry apparently will be limited during the end time, and God will allow the wickedness of the wicked to have full display. This will begin after the Rapture. As the "man of lawlessness" will be revealed at least seven years before the Second Coming, the Rapture which removes the Holy Spirit must occur before the seven years begin. Hence, the fact that the Rapture had not taken place was another evidence that the teachers who had told them they were already in the Day of the Lord were teaching false doctrine.

At the time of the Second Coming the lawless one will be destroyed (v. 8; Rev. 19:20). Though his miraculous signs will deceive those who do not want to believe in Jesus as Saviour, the prophecy states that they will perish because they do not love the truth (2 Thes. 2:10). It is possible that some who are here worshiping the beast were unbelievers at the time of the Rapture of the church, and because of their settled unbelief against Jesus Christ, they were allowed to believe the lie rather than the truth and, of course, receive the judgment that this merits (vv. 10-12).

It is quite illuminating that the Thessalonian church early in the Church Age experienced what today is called posttribulationism, the idea that the Rapture occurs after the Day of the Lord has begun. Posttribulationism usually makes the Rapture a phase of the second coming of Christ to set up His kingdom. It is clear that Paul denied this teaching and affirmed that the Day of the Lord, which includes the activities of the future world ruler, must follow rather than precede the Rapture of the church. Though it is a popular view that the Rapture will be a part of the Second Coming, those who hold this view, generally speaking, are not able to assign specific fulfillment of prophecy in the period which precedes the Second Coming in spite of the fact that there are so many detailed prophecies at the Second Coming that require fulfillment. Paul obviously wanted the Thessalonians to have the challenge of believing that Christ would come at any time for them and the assurance that this event had not already occurred.

### Protection from the Evil One

*2 Thessalonians 3:1-5.* In view of the problems of being easily deceived by false teachers as well as other problems in the Christian life, Paul requested prayer that he and his companions "may be delivered from wicked and evil men, for not everyone has faith" (v. 2). As Paul anticipated God's faithfulness meeting his needs in answer to prayer, he also had confidence that the Thessalonian church would be strengthened and protected from the evil one (v. 3). His prayer for the Thessalonians was that they would continue in God's love and continue to serve the Lord (vv. 4-5).

# PROPHECY IN 1 AND 2 TIMOTHY, TITUS, AND PHILEMON

The pastoral letters to Timothy do not contain much prophecy as the problems with Timothy related to other areas of biblical truth.

When prophecy is mentioned, however, it is in harmony with other portions of Scripture.

### The Coming Appearing of the Lord Jesus Christ

*1 Timothy 6:14.* In connection with Paul's charge to Timothy to obey God and to have his testimony "without spot or blame" (v. 14), Paul viewed the Lord Jesus Christ as the final Judge of this situation who will judge Timothy at the time of His appearing. Though Christ will not appear to the entire world until the time of His second coming, He obviously will appear to those who are raptured in the period before these end-time events. At that time Timothy's exemplary life will be evaluated. The Christian life has its completion at the time of Christ's coming.

### The Apostasy to Come

*2 Timothy 3:1-9.* In Paul's final epistle addressed to Timothy, a detailed revelation was given concerning the extent of the departure, or apostasy, from Christ in the latter times. Paul stated, "There will be terrible times in the last days. People will be lovers of themselves, lovers of money, boastful, proud, abusive, disobedient to their parents, ungrateful, unholy, without love, unforgiving, slanderous, without self-control, brutal, not lovers of the good, treacherous, rash, conceited, lovers of pleasure rather than lovers of God—having a form of godliness but denying its power. Have nothing to do with them" (vv. 1-5).

In this detailed analysis of the wickedness of the human heart, Paul was referring, of course, to those who were unsaved, who may have a form of religion but turn away from it to manifest their true character. Apostasy, of course, was already present in the time that Paul lived, but with the progress of the present age, in spite of the dissemination of the truth and the availability of Scripture, the world undoubtedly will continue to follow the sinful description which the Apostle Paul gave here.

Paul gave further description of the character of the apostates, "They are the kind who worm their way into homes and gain control over weak-willed women, who are loaded down with sins and are swayed by all kinds of evil desires, always learning but never able to acknowledge the truth. Just as Jannes and Jambres opposed Moses, so also these men oppose the truth—men of depraved minds, who, as far as the faith is concerned, are rejected. But they will not get very far because, as in the case of those men, their folly will be clear to everyone" (vv. 6-9).

The apostasy that existed in Timothy's day and has continued to be manifest in human history is in contrast to the testimony of Christians. Paul characterized his life as being one of "faith, patience, love, endurance, persecutions, sufferings" (vv. 10-11). By contrast to the way of the wicked, Timothy also had been taught the Holy Scriptures from infancy (v. 15). Paul closed with the great affirmation, "All Scripture is God-breathed and is useful for teaching, rebuking, correcting and training in righteousness, so that the man of God may be thoroughly equipped for every good work" (vv. 16-17).

### Christ Jesus, the Future Judge

*2 Timothy 4:1.* In support of his solemn charge to Timothy to live for God, Paul called attention to the fact that Timothy would be judged by Jesus Christ at the time of His appearing. Though Paul speaks of the judgment of living and dead as if they occur at the same time, Scriptures make clear that the dead will not be judged until the end of the millennial kingdom (Rev. 20:11-15).

### The Promise of Being Brought Safely
### to Christ's Heavenly Kingdom

*2 Timothy 4:18.* Following his exhortation to Timothy and his evaluation of some who did not share Paul's devotion to God, Paul stated his assurance, "The Lord will rescue me from every evil attack and will bring me safely to His heavenly kingdom. To Him be glory forever and ever. Amen" (v. 18). As is clear from history, Paul shortly after writing this to Timothy was beheaded, but this does not contradict his anticipated promise that God would rescue him. The point is that through his execution Paul was immediately brought safely to the presence of the Lord where he would be free from all the limitations and problems of this life. What from the human point of view is a tragedy is often God's gracious provision for His own in view of His plans for them in eternity to come.

*Titus 2:13.* The epistle of Paul to Titus was largely concerned with pastoral counsel and advice as Titus was one of Paul's fellow workers. In appealing to Titus, Paul stated that the Gospel of salvation "teaches us to say 'No' to ungodliness and worldly passions, and to live self-controlled, upright and godly lives in this present age" (v. 12). As we live our lives in this world, we have a wonderful hope. As Paul expressed it, "while we wait for the blessed hope—the glorious appearing of our great God and Saviour, Jesus Christ" (v. 13). This hope, obviously, related to the Rapture of the church rather than the second coming of Christ to set up His kingdom, but the question has been raised as to why it is described as a "glorious appearing." At His second coming Jesus will appear in a glorious event described in Revelation 19:11-16, an event which all the world will see (1:7). On the other hand, the Rapture of the church is never described as visible to the world. The question therefore remains: How can the Rapture be described as a glorious event, as an event which reveals the glory of God? The answer is quite simple.

While the world will not see the glory of Christ at the time of the Rapture as they will at the time of the Second Coming, at the Rapture Christians will behold Him in His glory, and to them it will be a glorious appearing. As stated in 1 John 3:2, "What we will be has not yet been made known. But we know that when He appears, we shall be like Him, for we shall see Him as He is."

Christians will necessarily need to be changed into bodies that are sinless in order to behold the Lord in His holy glory. The fact that we will see Him as He is, that is, His glorious person, is evidence in John that the Christians will have been transformed which will make it possible for them to see Him in His glory. The expectation of seeing Christ as He is in glory is another reason to turn away from the glory of this world and live Christian lives before God while we are waiting for His coming.

Paul's Epistle to Philemon concerned the return of Onesimus who had escaped from Philemon even though he was a slave, but now had become a Christian and had ministered to Paul. The epistle does not have any allusion to the prophetic future.

# 12

# PROPHECY IN
# THE GENERAL EPISTLES

# PROPHECY IN THE EPISTLE TO THE HEBREWS

The purpose of the Epistle to the Hebrews was to confirm the Christian Jews in their faith and to support the teaching that the Christian faith superseded Judaism and fulfilled it. In general, the epistle serves to prove that the Christian faith was better, that Christ's priesthood was better than that of Aaron's, and that the New Covenant of grace was better than the Mosaic Covenant. The epistle was an encouragement to Christian Jews to remain true to the Christian faith.

Because of its major theme, Hebrews is not devoted to prophecy, but, as is always true of any declaration of the Christian faith, the prophetic future of a Christian serves to confirm the importance of living for Christ now.

### The Throne of God Is Forever

*Hebrews 1:1-9.* In comparing Christ to angels, the superiority of Christ is demonstrated by a number of facts. Christ is the Son having been begotten of the Father (v. 5) and angels are instructed to worship Him (v. 6). In contrast to angels who are made ministers, the Son has a throne forever and superior to all others, "But about the Son He says, 'Your throne, O God, will last forever and ever, and righteousness will be the scepter of Your kingdom. You have loved righteousness and hated wickedness; therefore God, Your God, has set You above Your companions by anointing You with the oil of joy' " (vv. 8-9). Christ is superior to angels inasmuch as His throne is for eternity because He is the Son of God.

### Christ, the Creator Who Exists Forever

*Hebrews 1:10-12.* Not only the throne of Christ continues forever, but also He continues forever as the Creator. Though creation will be destroyed, Jesus Christ remains the same forever, "O Lord, You laid the foundations of the earth, and the heavens are the work of Your hands. They will perish, but You remain; they will all wear out like a garment. You will roll them up like a robe; like a garment they will be changed. But You remain the same, and Your years will never end" (vv. 10-12).

### The Promise of Entering into God's Rest

*Hebrews 3:7-11; 4:1-11.* Israel had failed to enter into the rest of faith and the blessing of trusting God for redemption. Because of this, God declared that they would not enter into His rest (3:11; cf. vv. 7-10).

Readers of the epistle are warned of the danger of falling short of perfect faith and rest in Christ, "Therefore, since the promise of entering His rest still stands, let us be careful that none of you be found to have fallen short of it. For we also have had the Gospel preached to us, just as they did; but the message they heard was of no value to them, because those who heard did not combine it with faith" (4:1-2). As God rested from His work on the seventh day (v. 4), there is a place for believers also to rest in faith in God for their salvation, but the offer is limited in time, and the danger is not entering by faith into God's rest.

This is defined, "There remains, then, a Sabbath-rest for the people of God; for anyone who enters God's rest also rests from his own work, just as God did from His. Let us, therefore, make every effort to enter that rest, so that no one will fall by following their example of disobedience" (vv. 9-11). In the fuller revelation given in the New Testament, believers may now understand their rest in God in contrast to many in Israel in the Old Testament who did not enter into their rest.

### The Promise of the Better Covenant in Christ

*Hebrews 8:6-13.* The Mosaic Covenant had its limitations, both in its promises which did not offer salvation, and in its duration because it served only for a time. By contrast, a Christian trusting in Christ has a better New Covenant, of which Christ is the Mediator, "But the ministry Jesus has received is as superior to theirs as the covenant of which He is Mediator is superior to the old one, and it is founded on better promises" (v. 6). The New Covenant for Christians is better than the Mosaic Covenant (7:19; Rom. 8:3-4), better than the Mosaic Covenant because its promises are unconditional (Heb. 8:10, 12); because it brings personal revelation of divine truth to every believer (v. 11); it secures forgiveness of sins (v. 12; 10:17;) because it depends on a redemption wrought by Christ on the cross (1 Cor. 11:25; Heb. 9:11-12, 18-23); it also secures for Israel certain forgiveness and restoration in the future (10:9; cf. Jer. 31:31-40).

In support of the superiority of the New Covenant for Christians, evidence was given that even the Old Testament anticipated the passing of the Mosaic Covenant and the introduction of a New Covenant with Israel and the house of Judah (Heb. 8:8). Israel's New Covenant was not like the Mosaic Covenant which was temporary and conditional. Instead, as Jeremiah stated, " 'This is the covenant I will make with the house of Israel after that time,' declares the Lord. 'I will put My laws in their minds and write them on their hearts. I will be their God, and they will be My people' " (v. 10).

Israel was also promised universal revelation of God's grace to them, "No longer will a man teach his neighbor, or a man his brother, saying, 'Know the Lord,' because they will all know Me, from the least of them to the greatest. For I will forgive their wickedness and will remember their sins no more" (vv. 11-12). This was revealed to be fulfilled in the Millennium. The fact that these promises were made to Israel, forming a New Covenant replacing the Mosaic Covenant, is further evidence that those who put their confidence in the Mosaic Covenant are trusting something which is already antiquated, "By calling this covenant 'new,' He has made the first one obsolete; and what is obsolete and aging will soon disappear" (v. 13).

Interpreters of this covenant of Israel have had difficulty because of the question as to where the church, the believers of the present age, comes in. Some have held that the church is the true Israel and therefore inherits the promise along with Israel; others hold that the covenant is with Israel but that the church derives blessing from the covenant of Israel. None of these solutions seem to solve the problem of how the church can have a New Covenant that is different in its qualifications than the New Covenant with Israel.

Today it is still necessary to carry the Gospel to one's neighbor for all do not know the Gospel. This is evidence that the New Covenant with Israel is not now being fulfilled. The question is: Why does this epistle quote this prophecy from Jeremiah 31:31-40 in full here?

It is most important in understanding this Scripture to realize that the Epistle to the Hebrews does not claim that the church is inheriting the covenant with Israel; it claims only one aspect of the covenant, namely, that the covenant with Israel is a New Covenant, and as such even the Old Testament predicted that the Mosaic Covenant would be superseded. No other application is made in this context. This should have persuaded professing Christians among the Jews that they should not return to Moses.

Though scholars will continue to differ on their explanations, the simple solution to the whole problem is the fact that when Christ died on the cross, He provided grace, that is, unmerited favor with God for those who put their trust in Him, including forgiveness, eternal life, and promise of eternity in the presence of God. In a world that is run by law, including moral law, this new aspect is introduced and made possible by the fact that Christ died for the sins of the world on the cross. This doctrine of God's grace, of course, had its application in the Old Testament by faith.

Even under the Law, Israelites were forgiven when they confessed their sins. Salvation was possible in the Old Testament, not on the basis of keeping the Law but on the basis of faith in a God who is gracious. This anticipated, of course, the fact that Christ would die on the cross for the sins of the whole world.

Accordingly, the best solution to the problem is to recognize that Christ introduced by His death on the cross this covenant of grace which has many applications. One of its principal applications was to Israel in the Old Testament. It should be clear from Scripture that Israel's restoration in the future and deliverance at the second coming of Christ will not be due to any merit on their part but stems from the fact that God is a gracious God. The New Covenant, mentioned in Jeremiah 31, is a gracious covenant, based on God's grace, not on human merit.

The grace of God extended to Israel does not exhaust the grace of God. In the present age, Jews and Gentiles alike come to Christ in faith and are saved, forgiven, and given eternal life on the basis of the grace that is extended to them through the death of Christ.

The covenant of grace, accordingly, is extended principally to Israel in the Old Testament, to the church in the present age, and will be manifested in the gracious restoration of Israel in the future. The one act of dying on the cross makes it possible for Christ to extend grace to those who do not deserve it. This concept of grace, stemming from the death of Christ, can be extended to all acts of God's forgiveness and mercy, from Adam to the last human being in the world. Accordingly, while God's rule in different ages may be different, as under the Mosaic Law it was a rule of righteousness and in the present age a rule of grace, it is not necessary to confuse God's promises to Israel with God's promises to the church in that both these sets of promises stem from the death of Christ without complication to the others.

The salvation of any individual, from Adam to the present time and in the future, is based on grace, and forgiveness of those once saved as they fall short of the holiness of God is likewise made possible by the grace of God. This, however, should be a convincing evidence to Jewish Christians who were pondering whether their new relationship to Christ was better than their relationship to Moses. In every particular the New Testament application of grace exceeds that which was true in the Old Testament under Moses.

### The Certainty of Divine Judgment

*Hebrews 9:27-28.* A Christian living in this present age of grace is nevertheless reminded that it is part of God's righteous government that every individual will be judged. Normally, this is after his death, "Just as man is destined to die once, and after that to face judgment, so Christ was sacrificed once to take away the sins of many people; and He will appear a second time, not to bear sin, but to bring salvation to those who are waiting for Him" (vv. 27-28). The coming judgment for all men makes most clear the necessity of entering by faith into the grace of God which is provided through the death of Christ. Though judgment is certain, those who have entered into grace at the present age will find that their judgment is a gracious judgment when they are judged and will consist for the believer in an evaluation of his life and service as a basis for reward as brought out in the doctrine of the Judgment Seat of Christ (2 Cor. 5:10).

### The Promise of Eternal Sanctification

*Hebrews 10:14-18.* In keeping with the earlier discussion of the New Covenant, the superiority of the sacrifice of Christ, to the sacrifices in the Old Testament, is emphasized. As stated, "Because by one sacrifice He has made perfect forever those who are being made holy" (v. 14). As fulfilled by Israel in their millennial restoration, the New Covenant provides, "I will put My laws in their hearts, and I will write them on their minds." Then he adds: "Their sins and lawless acts I will remember no more" (vv. 16-17). Because the one offering of Christ is sufficient for time and eternity, the conclusion is, "And where these have been forgiven, there is no longer any sacrifice for sin" (v. 18). Accordingly, a Christian in the present age is not required to bring the offerings that the Jew had to bring in the Old Testament under the Mosaic Covenant. The Mosaic sacrifices were a temporary covering, looking forward typically to the sacrifice of Christ. Now that the sacrifice of Christ has taken place, they no longer are necessary.

### The Promise that Christ Will Come

*Hebrews 10:37.* As the Christian looks forward to relief from the present persecutions and difficulties, the promise is given, "For in just a very little while, 'He who is coming will come and will not delay' " (v. 37). The reference, no doubt, is to the Rapture of the church when every Christian, whether living or dead, will be caught up to be with the Lord. Necessarily, this will end the conflicts and problems of this life and constitute a part of the certain hope of a Christian as he looks to God to solve his problems.

### The Promise of Future Judgment on the Earth

*Hebrews 12:26.* In reviewing God's judgments in the past, a reminder is given that there is a future judgment coming, "At that time His voice shook the earth, but now He has promised, 'Once more I will shake not only the earth but also the heavens' " (v. 26). Prophetic Scripture enlarges on this in both the Old and New Testaments and describes the terrible judgments, including earthquakes, that will shake the earth prior to the second coming of Christ. This will be part of God's program of judgment on the wicked and will also end in the blessing and rescue of those who are saved. A reminder of the fragile character of our present world is also a reminder that eternal things that belong to the Christian faith are not subject to change or destruction.

### The Immutability of Jesus Christ

*Hebrews 13:8.* In considering the past, present, and future relating to the Christian faith, this reminder states, "Jesus Christ is the same yesterday and today and forever" (v. 8). Though there is progress in doctrine and progress in experience, and history records many changes, Jesus Christ in His deity is the same yesterday, today, and forever. Though in the Incarnation He partook of a human body, soul, and spirit, which continues throughout eternity after His resurrection, in His deity Jesus Christ is the same, having the same attributes, the same glory, and the same power. Christians, accordingly, in their faith in Christ are putting their confidence in things that cannot be changed because they are related to the person of Christ. Taken as a whole, prophecies of the Book of Hebrews serve to support and clarify the Christian faith as being God's answer to the need of man in time and eternity.

## PROPHECY IN THE EPISTLES OF JAMES AND 1 AND 2 PETER

The Epistle of James is largely devoted to practical Christian living and emphasis on moral and ethical teachings. Two mentions of the coming of Christ as related to the Christian life are included.

### The Promise of the Crown of Life

*James 1:12.* Those who will trust in the Lord in a time of trial are especially blessed, "Blessed is the man who perseveres under trial, because when he has stood the test, he will receive the crown of life that God has promised to those who love Him" (v. 12). Believers will be rewarded in heaven for their faithfulness to the Lord. Often these rewards are characterized as crowns (1 Cor. 9:25; Phil. 4:1; 1 Thes. 2:19; 2 Tim. 4:8; 1 Peter 5:4; Rev. 2:10; 3:11; 4:4, 10). The persecutions may bring humiliation and suffering on earth. The fact that we have eternal life will be a crown which will set us apart as belonging to the Lord.

### Waiting Patiently for the Lord's Coming

*James 5:7-8.* A comparison is made between believers waiting for the coming of the Lord and the farmer waiting for his crop to mature. Just as the harvest is certain ahead, so the coming of Christ will climax our earthly work, "Be patient, then, brothers, until the Lord's coming. See how the farmer waits for the land to yield its valuable crop and how patient he is for the autumn and spring rains. You too, be patient and stand firm, because the Lord's coming is near" (vv. 7-8). As James made clear, while we are waiting for the Lord's coming, we should be faithful in enduring suffering and be abundant in our service for the Lord. Especially, we should be engaged in prayer, recognizing that God hears and answers prayer (vv. 13-18).

### Prophecy of the Certainty of Our Inheritance

*1 Peter 1:4-5.* In keeping with the living hope given Christians through the resurrection of Christ (v. 3), they have a future inheritance that is being kept for them, "and into an inheritance that can never perish, spoil or fade—kept in heaven for you" (v. 4). Meanwhile, while Christians are waiting for their inheritance, God protects them, "who through faith are shielded by God's power until the coming of the salvation that is ready to be revealed in the last time" (v. 5). This inheritance is certain because of God's promise in grace. Peter goes on to say that persecutions and trials in Christ demonstrate the genuineness of our faith.

### Prophecy of Persecution which Will Refine Faith

*1 Peter 1:7.* On the one hand, our inheritance is certain because of God's promise; on the other hand, it is certain because our faith is demonstrated through persecution, "These have come so that your faith—of greater worth than gold, which perishes even though refined by fire—may be proved genuine and may result in praise, glory and honor when Jesus Christ is revealed" (v. 7). Though persecutions for the time being prove difficult in any Christian's life, he may be encouraged by the fact that his faithfulness under these circumstances prove the genuineness of his faith and therefore his right to receive the reward that will be his in heaven. His persecutions also will be cause for praising Jesus Christ.

### Prophecy that the Word of God Will Remain Forever

*1 Peter 1:25.* In contrast to that which is temporary as illustrated in grass and flowers in the field, the statement was made, "the Word of the Lord stands forever!" (v. 25) The Christian may observe that our present world is decaying and will not endure forever. By contrast, the things that belong to our Christian faith will never cease to be true and will be supported by the Word of God which stands forever.

### The Promise of the End Being Near Fulfillment

*1 Peter 4:7.* In the brief statement, "The end of all things is near" (v. 7), the fact that life will not go on forever should be an encouragement to Christians who are going through deep trouble. A Christian's pilgrimage on earth is temporary and soon may be cut short by the Rapture of the church. This should serve as a stimulus to faithful service and enduring where persecutions and trials may be the lot of an individual Christian.

### The Promised Welcome into God's Kingdom

*2 Peter 1:11.* In making sure that our faith in Christ is real, a Christian is reminded, "You will receive a rich welcome into the eternal kingdom of our Lord and Saviour Jesus Christ" (v. 11). Though the world may not always welcome Christians and their testimony, and there may be opposition and even a martyr's death as in the case of Peter, it is still true that we can anticipate, either through death or through Rapture, that we will be received and publicly acknowledged as a part of God's kingdom.

### Prophecy that Apostate Teachers Will Come

*2 Peter 2:1-22.* As Peter neared the end of his life, as his second epistle was written shortly before his death, he was overwhelmed by the evidence of corruption in doctrine and departure from the faith on the part of those who were apostates, that is, people who outwardly claim to be Christians but actually have no Christian faith. Accordingly, those who read his epistle are warned that these teachers will not only reject the truth themselves but will bring in teachings that are radical and destructive.

These false teachers were described, "But there were also false prophets among the people, just as there will be false teachers among you. They will secretly introduce destructive heresies, even denying the sovereign Lord who bought them—bringing swift destruction on themselves. Many will follow their shameful ways and will bring the way of truth into disrepute. In their greed these teachers will exploit you with stories they have made up. Their condemnation has long been hanging over them, and their destruction has not been sleeping" (vv. 1-3).

In dealing with heresies, Peter was not describing minor deviations from the faith but that which was essential to salvation and hope. The false teachers will be guilty of "even denying the sovereign Lord who bought them" (v. 1).

Of significance in this passage is the word for "redemption," translated "bought," and is used even of these false teachers. Scholars debate whether the death of Christ was limited in its efficacy to the elect or whether it includes all men. This is one of the central passages that demonstrate when Christ died, He died to make the whole world savable, dying even for those who do not turn to Christ and reject His proffered salvation. The condemnation of the wicked is all the greater because Christ died for them, and they rejected what He provided for them in grace.

The condemnation of the false teachers was seen in the light of God's judgment on the angels for whom there was no grace or mercy, "For if God did not spare angels when they sinned, but sent them to hell, putting them into gloomy dungeons to be held for judgment; if He did not spare the ancient world when He brought the Flood on its ungodly people, but protected Noah, a preacher of righteousness, and seven others; if he condemned the cities of Sodom and Gomorrah by burning them to ashes, and made them an example of what is going to happen to the ungodly; and if He rescued Lot, a righteous man, who was distressed by the filthy lives of lawless men (for that righteous man, living among them day after day, was tormented in his righteous soul by the lawless deeds he saw and heard)—if this is so, then the Lord knows how to rescue godly men from trials and to hold the unrighteous for the day of judgment, while continuing their punishment" (vv. 4-9).

Accordingly, if Christians are tormented by the terrible sins of the unsaved world, as Lot was in his day, they can rest assured, with Lot, that God's judgment in His proper time will take care of the wicked.

The utter lack of moral character of the wicked was described further in that they "slander celestial beings" (v. 10), in their "slanderous accusations against such beings in the presence of the Lord" (v. 11), and their blasphemy in essential doctrine which they do not understand (v. 12), though they are "blots and blemishes, reveling in their pleasures while they feast with you" (v. 13). Though it is true that their "eyes" are "full of adultery" and "they seduce the unstable" (v. 14), they will be judged in God's time and brought into proper punishment for their deeds.

Comparison is made between these false teachers and Balaam, a prophet of God (Num. 22) who was hired to curse Israel though he was kept from it (2 Peter 2:15-16). These false teachers "are springs without water and mists driven by a storm. Blackest darkness is reserved for them" (v. 17). Their winning oratory and their promise of freedom are not supported, and those who follow them will become "worse off at the end than they were at the beginning" (v. 20). This scathing denial of apostate teachers reflects God's approach to this important aspect of modern life where many reject the Word of God and substitute the religions of man instead. Peter assured that though in this life we may suffer persecution and trial in the end the righteous will triumph and the wicked will perish.

### Prophecy of Unbelief Regarding the Second Coming

*2 Peter 3:3-7.* In view of the prophetic outlook of this epistle, written so shortly before Peter's martyrdom, there is anticipation that there will be worldwide scoffing at the Second Coming. Peter declared, "First of all, you must understand that in the last days scoffers will come, scoffing and following their own evil desires. They will say, 'Where is this "coming" He promised? Ever since our fathers died, everything goes on as it has since the beginning of Creation' " (vv. 3-4).

The argument of scoffers is that due to the uniformity of nature, that is, always acting according to natural law, there is no room for a miraculous event, like a person returning who had once died. They argued that though God created the world (a concession on the part of unbelievers), since then He has dealt with the world entirely on the basis of natural laws. As they put it, "everything goes on as it has since the beginning of Creation" (v. 4).

These scoffers, however, have overlooked a great deal. If they are right, there is nothing to the accounts in the Bible of the many miracles that God performed, such as the miracle of the Flood and many miracles in connection with the freedom of Israel from Egypt, and, of course, most important, the supernatural event of Jesus Christ becoming incarnate.

Peter accused the scoffers of having a short memory and forgetting purposely, "But they deliberately forget that long ago by God's Word the heavens existed and the earth was formed out of water and with water" (v. 5). Though they passed by the question of the origin of all things by saying God created it, they failed to realize that this recognizes that God has supernatural power over natural laws and can change them or all of them as He wills.

Peter also accused them of forgetting the historical fact of the Flood. In verse 5 he mentioned that the "earth was formed out of water and by water," referring to the account of Genesis 1. However, in history there was added the account of Noah's flood when these same waters that were prominent in Creation now covered the earth and destroyed it, "By water also the world of that time was deluged and destroyed" (v. 6). The same Word of God, which predicted the Flood and fulfilled it, also predicted that there will be no further flood and that the next destruction of the world will be by fire, "By the same word the present heavens and earth are reserved for fire, being kept for the day of judgment and destruction of ungodly men" (v. 7).

### Prophecy of God's Judgment
### Though God Waits to Offer Salvation

*2 Peter 3:8-9.* The fact is, however, that the second coming of Christ did not occur immediately, as perhaps many of the early Christians anticipated. Here Peter introduced God's viewpoint of time as compared to man's, "But do not forget this one thing, dear friends: With the Lord a day is like a thousand years, and a thousand years are a like a day" (v. 8). This is a verse that is commonly misunderstood as meaning that a thousand years does not mean a thousand years. The contrast is not between literal and nonliteral meaning, but between the view of God and the view of man. For God who existed from all eternity past, a twenty-four-hour day could be like a thousand years of human history. If one attempted to write all the events of a single day—all that men did, all that animals did, all that occurred in the vegetable world, and other aspects of creation—it would be impossible to give a chronology of the work of one day. The facts of events in one day would be greater than a thousand years of human history as viewed by man. God looks at the world microscopically. He knows all about the tangled events that form a single twenty-four-hour day.

On the other hand, a thousand years of human history is also a brief time for God, who existed from all eternity past, and can be compared to man's experience of one twenty-four-hour day, When dealing with an infinite God who has always existed, one cannot argue therefore from time factors. The passage of 2,000 years since the first coming of Christ should not be any ground for viewing the Second Coming with uncertainty. As Peter expressed it, "The Lord is not slow in keeping His promise, as some understand slowness. He is patient with you, not wanting anyone to perish, but everyone to come to repentance" (v. 9).

Instead of being inattentive and slow in responding to the promise of the Second Coming, God has a loving purpose in wanting to extend the message of salvation and of gracious forgiveness to more individuals before the time of judgment comes. In other words, God is waiting for some to hear who have not heard. He is waiting for others to respond who have heard. He does not desire to punish anyone with eternal punishment; He wants all men to come to repentance.

Here we have the contrast between God's sovereign will and His desires. In the nature of a moral universe where men are given choices in creating the situation, God knew that not all would choose the right path. In His heart of love, which has provided grace for all men through Jesus Christ, God wants all to be saved and wants to give them all the time that is possible to hear and respond to the message. The fact is that, regardless of when the Lord came, there would be many who did not believe. The situation will be similar to that of the days of Noah, using an illustration in Scripture (Matt. 24:37-39). Though the ark took more than 100 years to build and Noah was faithful in telling people why it was being built, there seems to be no response to Noah's message except that on the part of his own family; his three sons and their wives shared this faith. At the time of the second coming of Christ, some will not be ready while others will be awaiting His coming.

### The Coming Destruction of the Earth

*2 Peter 3:10-14.* In earlier references to the Day of the Lord, as in 1 Thessalonians 5, the period was described as beginning with the

Rapture and continuing through the Tribulation period and ending at the end of the Millennium. Here the whole picture is again revealed with emphasis on the final end of it, "But the Day of the Lord will come like a thief. The heavens will disappear with a roar; the elements will be destroyed by fire, and the earth and everything in it will be laid bare" (v. 10). This will occur not at the beginning but at the end of the Day of the Lord which will be the end of the millennial kingdom (Rev. 20:11; 21:1). The description of the earth's being destroyed by fire is catastrophic and supports the conclusion that the new earth, created according to verse 1, will replace entirely our present earth. As scientists know, the earth is composed of atomic structure which is held together by the power of God. Just as God created it out of nothing, so He can dismiss it into nothing in preparation for the eternal state.

The practical application of all this, of course, is that Christians need to look at our present world as a temporary home. Peter asked the question, "Since everything will be destroyed in this way, what kind of people ought you to be? You ought to live holy and godly lives as you look forward to the Day of God and speed its coming" (2 Peter 3:11-12). In verse 12 a new expression is found which is not common in Scripture, "the Day of God." The question is naturally raised whether this is the Day of the Lord or whether it has a special meaning.

Though the conclusion may be debated, one point of view is that the Day of the Lord, which begins at the Rapture and ends at the Millennium, will be followed by the Day of God which is the day of eternity. Just as the Day of the Lord will end and then the Day of God will begin, so the future will bring about the various events which lie between.

Further light is cast on the subject of whether the earth will be restored or destroyed at the time of the creation of the new heavens and earth. As Peter declared, "That day will bring about the destruction of the heavens by fire, and the elements will melt in the heat" (v. 12). This description of the atomic destruction of the earth leads to the conclusion that the new earth will be entirely different with none of the geographic landmarks that relate to our present earth. There will be no more ocean, no more Red Sea, no more Jordan River, no sun or moon. The new earth will be entirely different as described in Revelation 21–22.

Though Christians are warned concerning the temporary nature of our present world, they also are assured that they can look forward to an eternal home, "But in keeping with His promise we are looking forward to a new heaven and a new earth, the home of righteousness" (2 Peter 3:13). This, of course, is the revelation of the new heaven and new earth, described in detail in Revelation 21–22. This is the ultimate goal of the Christian faith and the ultimate home of the redeemed of all ages.

In contemplating the majestic program of God, both in judgment and in restoration, Peter found that there was a practical application, "So then, dear friends, since you are looking forward to this, make every effort to be found spotless, blameless and at peace with Him" (2 Peter 3:14). This, of course, refers to the coming of the Lord for His church, which will be the Rapture, and our being with the Lord forever through the events which follow.

In the conclusion of 2 Peter, he pointed out the need for patience, faith, and anticipation, and the need to be on guard lest they fall from the faith.

# PROPHECY IN 1, 2, AND 3 JOHN
# AND THE EPISTLE OF JUDE

Prophecies in the Epistles of John significantly are related to the Christian walking in fellowship with the Father.

### The Temporary Desires of the World
### as Opposed to the Eternal Will of God

*1 John 2:17.* In the preceding context, John revealed that Christians should not love the world because all that is in the world is sinful, including the three major lines of temptation—the flesh or "the cravings of sinful man," the lust or desires of his eyes, and pride or boasting—and does not come from the Father but from the world (vv. 15-16). From the Christian's viewpoint of faith, the prediction is made, "The world and its desires pass away, but the man who does the will of God lives forever" (v. 17). Though John was primarily concerned with the effect of sin in the life of a Christian now and the need for walking in fellowship with God, this prophecy pointed out the eternal character of the will of God and the importance of a Christian emphasizing the things which are eternal in contrast to the temporary character of the things of the world.

### Being Confident before the Lord at His Appearing

*1 John 2:28.* As a climax to the preceding exhortation in which John warned his readers of apostasy and the importance of listening to the indwelling Holy Spirit as He distinguishes what is true and what is false, the reader is encouraged to continue serving the Lord so that he will not be ashamed before Christ at His coming, "And now, dear children, continue in Him, so that when He appears you may be confident and unashamed before Him at His coming" (v. 28). Though no Christian is able to lead a perfect life, the general tenor of his life serving the Lord or not serving the Lord will be evident at the time of divine judgment.

### The Promise to Be Like Christ

*1 John 3:2-3.* The previous exhortation to be serving Him when He comes is supported by the revelation of the love of the Father (v. 1). John pointed out the importance of being "called children of God" (v. 2) now, even if we do not know what we will be. John stated, "Dear friends, now we are children of God, and what we will be has not yet been made known. But we know that when He appears, we shall be like Him, for we shall see Him as He is" (v. 2).

The fact that a believer will be able to see Christ at His appearing indicates that a transformation of believers in the world will take place. Several times in Scripture it is made clear that man in his natural state cannot endure being in the presence of the holy God. Paul, for instance, was stricken blind when he saw the glorified Christ (Acts 9:8), and the Apostle John fell at the feet of Christ as though he were dead (Rev. 1:17). Accordingly, this Scripture makes clear that when we see Him, we are going to be like Him, that is, that we will be without sin and will be able to stand comfortably in the presence of the holy God because Christ, when He appears, will appear to us and we will see His glory (Titus 2:13).

A further incentive is given to Christians to live for Christ now so that their lives will be without criticism when they stand in His presence. The application of this is found in the next verse, "Everyone who has this hope in Him purifies himself, just as He is pure" (1 John 3:3). This passage refers to the present work of sanctification as "purifies" is in the present tense. The whole doctrine of sanctification reveals that Christians should progressively become more and more like Christ in their lives on the earth, and they have the prospect of being perfectly like Him when they see Him.

The elements of sanctification are revealed in Scripture. The indwelling presence of the Holy Spirit is the Christian's guide and teacher. As Christians yield to Christ, they will experience the sanctifying power of the Word of God. The experience of prayer and fellowship with God also is a sanctifying experience. Mingling with other Christians who are serving God also constitutes a work of sanctification. Accordingly, the hope of Christ's appearing is an imminent event, which could occur at any time, should spur a Christian to serve the Lord and continue in the process of sanctification in anticipation of the ultimate sanctification in Christ's presence.

The prophecies included in 1 John connect our present life with the hope of Christ's return in keeping with the major theme of the epistle. No prophecy is mentioned in the epistles of 2 John and 3 John.

### The Prophecy by Enoch of the Second Coming

*Jude 14-15.* Jude quoted from Enoch who, like Elijah, went to heaven without experiencing death (Heb. 11:5). This prophecy concerning the second coming of Christ emphasized the fact that He will be accompanied by thousands of angels, and on that occasion will judge the wickedness of ungodly people in keeping with Jude's previous statements concerning the extent of apostasy and God's judgment on them, "Enoch, the seventh from Adam, prophesied about these men: 'See, the Lord is coming with thousands upon thousands of His holy ones to judge everyone, and to convict all the ungodly of all the ungodly acts they have done in the ungodly way, and of all the harsh words ungodly sinners have spoken against Him' " (vv. 14-15).

This quotation from Enoch is not found elsewhere in the Bible. Because of the similarity of this to a statement in what is known as the "book of Enoch," one of the apocryphal books which was not included in the Bible, the question has been raised whether the quotation is from Enoch himself or from this writing which in itself was not inspired. Regardless of its source, this quotation in this book was here recorded as true under the inspiration of the Holy Spirit. Accordingly, whether this was a special revelation given to Enoch, which is similar to what was recorded in the book of Enoch, or whether he quoted from the apocryphal book of Enoch does not affect the truth or the accuracy of this prophecy.

A similar truth is emphasized in Revelation 19:11-21 when Christ returns. As included here in Jude's epistle, there is a reminder that God will deal with those who teach false doctrine and who are apostate concerning the faith. Their hypocrisy, wickedness, and unbelief is described graphically in the preceding verses. Accordingly, the reader is warned against apostates and against following their teaching and at the same time is alerted to the fact that the apostates are subject to God's searching judgments.

### The Keeping Power of God

*Jude 24-25.* At the conclusion of this book dealing primarily with the subject of apostasy, Jude gave reassurance to the Christian that he can experience the keeping power of God so that he will not fall into doctrinal error and will not follow the lead of the apostate teachers. Jude wrote, "To him who is able to keep you from falling and to present you before His glorious presence without fault and with great joy—to the only God our Saviour be glory, majesty, power and authority, through Jesus Christ our Lord, before all ages, now and forevermore! Amen" (vv. 24-25).

At the present time when apostates are teaching false doctrine, a Christian can be kept by the power of God from following their wrong teachings and their bad example. At the same time, a Christian is assured that the day will come when he will be presented to God as a trophy of His grace and that he will be without fault and with great joy. Jude enlarged on the nature of God which believers will see at that time, including His glory, majesty, power, and authority. This is an important reminder that while evil may seem to flourish, God in His time will judge it and manifest His holy and righteous perfections.

# 13

# GENERAL INTRODUCTION AND PROPHECY CONCERNING THE CHURCH IN REVELATION

## GENERAL INTRODUCTION TO PROPHECY
## IN THE BOOK OF REVELATION

The Book of Revelation, coming as a climax to preceding books of Scripture, brings to a conclusion the main themes of prophecy from both the Old and New Testaments. Because of their tremendous scope and detailed revelation, these prophecies will be considered under three divisions: (1) Prophecy in Revelation Concerning the Church (1–3); (2) John's Vision of Heaven and the End Time (4–18); and (3) Prophecy Concerning the Second Coming, the Millennium, and Eternal State (19–22).

The Book of Revelation is unique as the only New Testament book which is apocalyptic and similar in style to Old Testament books such as Ezekiel, Daniel, Joel, and Zechariah. The word "apocalyptic" is a transliteration of the Greek word *apokalypsis,* meaning "to uncover or disclose." The apocalyptic books in the Old Testament as well as the Book of Revelation in the New Testament differ, however, widely from apocalyptic writings which are outside the Bible which usually do not have a specific author and often are fanciful and impossible to organize theologically. An apocalyptic book is one which claims to be a divine revelation, usually revealing the future and presenting revelation in nonliteral terms which require interpretation.

Biblical books which are truly apocalyptic, however, not only contain this element but also plain prophecy in ordinary words, frequently explaining the vision or a symbol after the revelation is given symbolically. For this reason the interpretation of biblical books that are apocalyptic is not necessarily uncertain. An apocalyptic book requires interpretation based on the revelation given in the passage itself as well as in other books of prophetic character in Scripture.

Though some symbolic references in apocalyptic books are not certain of interpretation, most of them yield a literal meaning describing a future event or situation. Accordingly, in apocalyptic biblical books the main thought is one of revelation, whether given symbolically or in ordinary terms.

Because the Book of Revelation presents a specific eschatological future, including the concept of a literal extended period of terrible trouble, a literal second coming of Christ, a thousand-year kingdom following the Second Coming, and a new heaven and new earth as the ultimate residence of the saints, those who differ with these theological concepts tend to offer some form of interpretation of the Book of Revelation which will not lead to these theological conclusions. At least four divergent methods of interpretation have been employed.

1. Allegorical interpretation is an attempt to interpret the Book of Revelation in a nonliteral sense in which the interpreter finds some meaning other than the plain meaning of the term itself. Often this is claimed to be a spiritual interpretation as opposed to literalism, but this is a false antithesis. A literal interpretation may be the spiritual interpretation.

Though the Book of Revelation was regarded in the second century as genuine revelation, because of the rise of a school of theology in Alexandria, Egypt in the third century which attempted to make all the Bible one grand allegory, this same interpretation was applied to the Book of Revelation. This was acceptable to them because it would not confront them with theological points of view concerning the future which were unacceptable to them. Contemporary theologians, regardless of their theological point of view, recognize that the allegorical interpretation of the Bible as a whole is not justified and regard the school of Alexandria as basically heretical.

Saint Augustine of Hippo in the fourth and fifth centuries attempted to limit the viewpoint of allegory to eschatology instead of the entire Scripture, and this viewpoint was followed by many. The net result of the allegorical interpretation, however, is to deny that the Book of Revelation has anything specific to say about future events.

2. The preterist's approach to the Book of Revelation is similar to the allegorical method but is more limited in its application of nonliteral interpretation. Under this approach the Book of Revelation is regarded as a symbolic presentation of the conflicts of the early church, making it a symbolic history of the early church rather than a prophetic revelation in the future. This point of view claims that there are two basic approaches to the Book of Revelation, namely, the predictive or the descriptive, and they choose a descriptive view which eliminates the prophetic element. The scholars who oppose literal interpretation of the Book of Revelation tend to combine the preterist's view with some form of allegorical or nonliteral interpretation which will allow them to explain their point of view without contradiction of the Book of Revelation.

3. The historical approach to the Book of Revelation is one of the most popular which has been followed through the centuries of the Christian church.

Adopting a somewhat symbolic interpretation of the Book of Revelation similar to the preterist approach, interpreters claimed that the Book of Revelation is a symbolic history of the church which, in general, traces its struggles which issue in the ultimate triumph for the church. It, accordingly, has some predictive character. This is popular among the postmillenarians, whether conservative or liberal, and was held by theologians who were considered orthodox in other areas of theology.

One of the main problems of the historical view, however, is that each interpreter attempted to have the book climax with his generation, which led to a great variety of interpretations. Accordingly, it is impossible to find any two historical interpreters who provide the same interpretation of the Book of Revelation, and it leaves no pattern of significant truth with any consensus in support of it. Views that tend to avoid the theological climax of the Book of Revelation as a series of literal events tend to combine in one way or another a nonliteral approach which leaves interpretation in a state of confusion.

4. Because none of the preceding approaches has achieved any recognized consensus, many conservative scholars have turned to the futuristic approach, viewing the book as prophecy of the future, especially beginning in Revelation 4. Under this interpretation Revelation 4–18 deals with events that are yet future; Revelation 19 deals with a literal Second Coming; Revelation 20 deals with a future thousand-year reign of Christ on earth; and Revelation 21–22 is considered a description of the eternal state.

Following this interpretation, however, would require interpreters to be premillennial, holding the view that Christ will come back in His second coming first and that the thousand-year reign of Christ follows, in contrast to the postmillenarian who puts Christ's second coming at the end of the millennial reign. Countless variations, of course, occur in various interpretations of the book, but, generally speaking, the only view that provides any consensus is that of the futuristic view.

Under the futuristic view due recognition is given to the symbolic and the need for interpreting the symbols. Often this is done, however, in the very context of the revelation or can be determined by reference to other prophetic books in the Bible. Though some symbolic revelations are still not completely understood, a surprising number of passages yield to a factual conclusion regarding future events. Objections to the futuristic view usually are theological in nature as some resist the theological position taken by premillenarians. Often the accusation is made that the book would not bring sufficient comfort to those who read it throughout the history of the church if it was entirely futuristic. However, this point of view overlooks the fact that all prophecy to some extent is futuristic and constitutes a revelation of that which faith embraces.

Inasmuch as the futuristic view offers the only solid basis for consistent verifiable form of interpretation, this is the point of view adopted in this work.

Some of the symbols in the Book of Revelation are the widespread use of numbers which while taken literally also may have a symbolic meaning. These numbers include 3; 3 1/2; 4; 5; 6; 7; 10; 12; 24; 42; 666; 1,000; 1,260; 12,000; 144,000; 100 million; and 200 million. One of the most common numbers mentioned is the number 7 which has in it the concept of completion. The Book of Revelation includes 7 churches, 7 lampstands, 7 stars, 7 spirits of God, 7 seals on the scroll, 7 angels with 7 trumpets, 7 bowls containing the 7 last plagues, 7 thunders, 7,000 killed in the earthquake (Rev. 12), the dragon with 7 heads (13:1), 7 mountains (Rev. 17), and 7 kings. Many of the other numbers are frequently used throughout the Book of Revelation. Evidence points to the fact that these numbers are always used in a literal sense even though they may also have a symbolic sense; that is, if it declares that there are 7 stars, there are 7 stars, not 6 or 8, and so with other uses of the numbers.

One of the most significant references is to the forty-two months, or 1,260 days, which is the duration of the Great Tribulation (13:5). This refers to the last half of the seven-year period predicted in Daniel 9:27. Many interpreters find the entire seven years of verse 27 as the main subject of Revelation 6 through 18. The emphasis, however, seems to be on the last three-and-a-half years which is the predicted time of unprecedented trouble of which Christ Himself spoke (Matt. 24:21-22). Interpretation of the numbers will be given further attention as these appear in the Book of Revelation.

Symbols abound in the Book of Revelation. The following list of symbols published in the author's *The Revelation of Jesus Christ*

(Moody Press, 1966, pp. 29–30) will serve to demonstrate the symbolic character of many of the passages dealing with the future in the Book of Revelation.

The seven stars (1:16) represent seven angels (1:20).

The seven lampstands (1:13) represent seven churches (1:20).

The hidden manna (2:17) speaks of Christ in glory (cf. Ex. 16:33-34; Heb. 9:4).

The morning star (2:28) refers to Christ returning before the dawn, suggesting the Rapture of the church before the establishment of the kingdom (cf. Rev. 22:16; 2 Peter 1:19).

The key of David (3:7) represents the power to open and close doors (Isa. 22:22).

The seven lamps of fire represent the sevenfold Spirit of God (4:5).

The living creatures (4:7) portray the attributes of God.

The seven eyes represent the sevenfold Spirit of God (5:6).

The odors of the golden vials symbolize the prayers of the saints (5:8).

The four horses and their riders (6:1 ff.) represent successive events in the developing Tribulation.

The fallen star (9:1) is the angel of the abyss, probably Satan (9:11).

Many references are made to Jerusalem: the great city (11:8), Sodom and Egypt (11:8), which stand in contrast to the New Jerusalem, the heavenly city.

The stars of heaven (12:4) refer to fallen angels (12:9).

The woman and the child (12:1-2) seem to represent Israel and Christ (12:5-6).

Satan is variously described as the great dragon, the old serpent, and the devil (12:9; 20:2).

The time, times, and half a time (12:14) are the same as 1,260 days (12:6).

The beast out of the sea (13:1-10) is the future world ruler and his empire.

The beast out of the earth (13:11-17) is the false prophet (19:20).

The harlot (17:1) variously described as the great city (17:18), as Babylon the great (17:5), as the one who sits on seven hills (17:9), is usually interpreted as apostate Christendom.

The waters (17:1) on which the woman sits represent the peoples of the world (17:15).

The ten horns (17:12) are ten kings associated with the beast (13:1; 17:3, 7-8, 11-13, 16-17).

The Lamb is Lord of lords and King of kings (17:14).

Fine linen is symbolic of the righteous deeds of the saints (19:8).

The Rider of the white horse (19:11-16, 19) is clearly identified as Christ, the King of kings.

The lake of fire is described as the second death (20:14).

Jesus Christ is the Root and Offspring of David (22:16).

Though the Book of Revelation is often viewed as hopelessly contradictory and devoid of any factual information, with modern interpreters lacking the key to understanding its writings, actually, if the book is taken as having real meaning, surprisingly, a number of the symbolic passages yield specific prophecy of events in the future. This will be demonstrated in the interpretation of the book itself.

Few books of the Bible will do more to clarify the theology and thinking of a student of Scripture than a proper understanding of the Book of Revelation. It is unfortunate that even scholars have tended to make it a book that is impossible to understand by our present generation. For a commentary on the Book of Revelation, see the author's *The Revelation of Jesus Christ,* Moody Press, 1966.

## PROPHECY IN THE BOOK OF REVELATION CONCERNING THE CHURCH

### Prophecy of the Dramatic Revelation of Jesus Christ at His Second Coming

*Revelation 1:7-8.* The reader is challenged, "Look, He is coming with clouds, and every eye will see Him, even those who pierced Him; and all the peoples of the earth will mourn because of Him. So shall it be! Amen" (v. 7). Because this final book of the New Testament has as its central theme the revelation of Jesus Christ, that is, what the world will behold at the time of the Second Coming, this verse is especially significant, and, accordingly, the reader is urged to behold it.

When Christ was received by a cloud at the time of His ascension (Acts 1:9), and as three of the Gospels mention His coming in clouds (Matt. 24:30; 26:64; Mark 13:26; 14:62; Luke 21:27), so here Christ is coming with clouds which will reflect His glory. Unlike the occasion of His ascension, however, the clouds will not hinder people seeing Him, and it declares that "every eye will see Him" (Rev. 1:7).

The question is raised how, in a global situation with the world's population all over the globe, at any one moment every eye will be able to see Christ's coming to earth. The answer seems to be found in 19:11-16. The coming of Christ, unlike the Rapture, will not be an instantaneous event but will be a gigantic procession of holy angels and saints from heaven to earth. There is no reason why this should not take twenty-four hours with its termination on the Mount of Olives. In that period the earth will revolve, and regardless of what direction Christ comes from, people will be able to see His coming from their position on the earth.

The appearance of Christ at the Second Coming is contrasted to the Rapture of the church when nothing is said about the world seeing Him, and it is possible that the world will see nothing at the time of the Rapture. Only Christians will see His glory at the Rapture (Titus 2:13).

The fact that even those who pierced Him in His crucifixion will see Him at His second coming introduces a problem inasmuch as they were unsaved and at that time will be in hell and will not be in a position to see this event. This problem is solved, however, by the prediction in Zechariah 12:10, stating, "I will pour out on the house of David and the inhabitants of Jerusalem a spirit of grace and supplication. They will look on Me, the One they have pierced, and they will mourn for Him as one mourns for an only child, and grieve bitterly for Him as one grieves for a firstborn son." Those living at the time of the Second Coming in Israel will therefore be representatives of those in the first century who participated in the death of Christ. Though Gentiles performed the act of crucifixion, it was demanded by Jews who, according to the Scripture, "pierced" Christ. Jews living at the time of the Second Coming will accept responsibility.

The grief of Israel, however, will be shared by other peoples of the world because the death of Christ was required by the sins of the world. As the prediction states, "All the peoples of the earth will mourn because of Him" (Rev. 1:7). This is confirmed by Matthew 24:30 which states, "At that time the sign of the Son of man will appear in the sky, and all the nations of the earth will mourn. They will see the Son of man coming on the clouds of the sky, with power and great glory." The mourning of Israel will, no doubt, be caused by their identity with the people in Israel in the first century, but the mourning of all peoples of the earth will probably be because they are not saved and not ready for the coming of the Lord. The unbelief of the world and their rejection of Christ is referred to frequently in the Book of Revelation (6:15-17; 9:20-21; 16:9-11, 21). The verse closes with "Amen," meaning "so be it."

In concluding the salutation, John quotes Christ, " 'I am the Alpha and the Omega,' says the Lord God, 'who is, and who was, and who is to come, the Almighty' " (1:8). In using the term "Alpha and Omega," He is using the first and last letters of the Greek alphabet in keeping with the idea of Christ being from eternity past to eternity future. The expression "who is, and who was, and who is to come" is the same expression as the statement made of the Father in verse 4 and is climaxed by the term "the Almighty," an expression which is used ten times in the Book of Revelation. Because the last book of the Bible is primarily concerned with the revelation of Jesus Christ and His glory at the time of the Second Coming, it is fitting that these eight verses of introduction should introduce Christ as the eternal glorious God. The contrast, of course, is to His first coming when He was a Babe in Bethlehem, and His presence was revealed only to a few. In many respects the Book of Revelation is in contrast to the four Gospels which describe Christ in His first coming.

### The Patmos Vision

*Revelation 1:9-20.* In the first chapter of the Book of Revelation, John, on the Isle of Patmos where he was in exile, had a tremendous revelation of Jesus in His glory. Christ is described as "the First and the Last. I am the Living One; I was dead, and behold I am alive forever and ever!" (vv. 17-18) This was an experience for John which is now past, and though the first chapter of Revelation introduces the future coming of Christ, in general, the first chapter deals with things which were.

Beginning with the message to Ephesus and the other six churches, the narrative goes on to things which are, that is, which are present in the Church Age. Accordingly, though there is prophecy, it has to do with the present rather than the future (vv. 9-20).

Beginning in chapter 4, however, the entire narrative deals with events that are yet future, and only the interpretation which considers them as future can give any serious interpretation to the details of the prophecy that is recorded.

## Prophecy concerning the Church at Ephesus

*Revelation 2:1-7.* Beginning in chapter 2 prophetic messages are revealed to be communicated to the seven churches of Asia. These churches were specially selected for the purpose of this revelation as there were other churches of Asia not mentioned. They were in some sort of geographical relationship but were selected to represent the spiritual condition of various local churches. Accordingly, the messages were, first of all, to each of the churches as churches. Each message, however, is also addressed to individuals, and individual promises are given to those who hear. It is also true that throughout the history of the church and every generation similar churches would emerge which could profit by heeding the exhortation given to these seven churches. Some hold that these churches also, in general, represent the history of the church—the idea that the church in Ephesus represents the apostolic church, the others the progress of the church through the centuries, and the church at Laodicea as the final church at the time of Christ's coming. There is, however, no scriptural verification of this type of interpretation.

In addressing the church at Ephesus which earlier had been commended highly for its faithfulness to God, the corrective message was delivered, "Yet I hold this against you: You have forsaken your first love. Remember the height from which you have fallen! Repent and do the things you did at first. If you do not repent, I will come to you and remove your lampstand from its place. But you have this in your favor: You hate the practices of the Nicolaitans, which I also hate. He who has an ear, let him hear what the Spirit says to the churches. To him who overcomes, I will give the right to eat from the tree of life, which is in the paradise of God" (vv. 4-7).

The message to the church at Ephesus was addressed to "the angel of the church in Ephesus" (v. 1). Though the word for angel (Gr., *aggelos*) is properly translated "angel," it seems to be used here in the general sense of a messenger as it is doubtful whether God would commit the message to each of the churches to an angel. The word is sometimes used in Greek literature, as in Scripture, to refer to human messengers (Matt. 11:10; Mark 1:2; Luke 7:24, 27; 9:52). The church at Ephesus, a very prominent city on the western part of the Roman province of Asia, had enjoyed the ministry of Paul for three years (Acts 20:31). Timothy also had apparently served this church as pastor. Later, before his exile to the Isle of Patmos, the Apostle John had served as one of the pastors of this church. The church, therefore, was well established in doctrine and in faith, and in this message their basic orthodoxy and Christian faith was not questioned. Christ, however, had pointed out that the ardor of the first generation of Christians no longer was there because they had left their first love. As is historically true and often painfully experienced by individual Christians, devotion to Christ often declines long before doctrinal disagreement begins. The Ephesians were guilty of a defect of the heart rather than of the mind.

Some thirty years before the Apostle Paul had written the letter to the Ephesians and apparently had rich fellowship with them and included them in his constant prayers (Eph. 1:15-16). Paul was no longer on the scene, however, and the second and third generation of Christians which had followed somehow did not have the same zeal as their forebears. Genuine love is a test of Christian fellowship in relation to God, fellow Christians, and is characterized by not loving the world (cf. 1 Tim. 6:10; 1 John 2:15).

Christ urged them to repent, change their mind concerning their relationship to God, and go back to the attitudes and works which characterized them earlier. Failure to do this would cause Him to remove their lampstand. In Revelation 1:20 the lampstands are taken as representative of the churches and their distribution of God's truth. The warning to the Ephesian churches was delivered that they would no longer be a lampstand for God even though he commended them for hating the practices of the Nicolaitans (v. 6). It is believed that the Nicolaitans were Christians who professed faith but lived licentious lives. What is called "the practices of the Nicolaitans" in verse 6 is called "teaching of the Nicolaitans" in verse 15, a further progression and departure from God.

As is characteristic of the admonition to the churches, appeal is directed to the individual, and the promise is given, "To him who overcomes, I will give the right to eat from the tree of life, which is in the paradise of God" (v. 7). Though every Christian saved by grace will have the right to eat of the tree of life, it is possible to profess Christian faith while only achieving Christian profession without reality, and such will be judged in eternity as well as in time.

### The Prophecy to Smyrna

*Revelation 2:8-11.* The church at Smyrna was some thirty-five miles north of Ephesus, and, unlike Ephesus which is now a deserted city, Smyrna continues to be an important port and cosmopolitan wealthy city of 200,000 population. The city of Smyrna, however, was not a friendly place for the small Christian church that was located there. Those who professed Christ were opposed by ungodly Gentiles as well as Jews, referred to as "synagogue of Satan" (v. 9), and opposed by Satan as well. Christ urges them, however, "Do not be afraid of what you are about to suffer. I tell you, the devil will put some of you in prison to test you, and you will suffer persecution for ten days. Be faithful, even to the point of death, and I will give you the crown of life" (v. 10). The fact of their present and future suffering is clearly pointed out in this Scripture. The allusion to the "ten days" has aroused various interpretations. Probably the best point of view is that it is representative of a short but intensive period of suffering. They were urged to be faithful to God, even to the point of death, and they would be given "the crown of life" (v. 10). In contrast to their present persecution and afflictions, in heaven they will enjoy eternal life as a crown and token of God's blessing.

The problem of suffering in Christian experience is treated in Scripture from various points of view. In some cases it is a discipline (1 Cor. 11:30-32; cf. Heb. 12:3-13). Sometimes it is used as a preventative, keeping a Christian from sin (2 Cor. 12:7). Suffering obviously teaches a child of God things he could not learn any other way, and even Christ is said to have "learned obedience from what He suffered" (Heb. 5:8). Suffering often will bear the fruit of patience (Rom. 5:3-5). By its nature, suffering also clarifies the Christian's testimony and demonstrates the reality of his faith and commitment (Acts 9:16).

In this passage the church at Smyrna was encouraged first not to be afraid of suffering which was a reminder that they really did not need to be afraid as long as they were in God's hands. Also, though they apparently did not suffer martyrdom, they should be faithful to death as may be required. The suffering of the church at Smyrna was to continue in subsequent history as illustrated in the case of Polycarp who was bishop of the church at Smyrna and who died a martyr's death.

Their suffering, however, would lead to God's recognizing them as having eternal life, and they would have the crown of life (Rev. 2:10). In Scripture other crowns are mentioned, such as the crown for faithful shepherding (1 Peter 5:4) and the crown of gold which was an evidence of redemption (Rev. 4:4). The Thessalonians were to be Paul's crown of rejoicing (1 Thes. 2:19), and the corruptible crown, or the crown that would not decay, would be awarded for those showing self-control in the race of life (1 Cor. 9:25). In the Christian experience, suffering comes before the crown. It is used in Scripture as God's recognition of faithful commitment to the Lord.

An invitation is extended also to individuals, "He who has an ear, let him hear what the Spirit says to the churches. He who overcomes will not be hurt at all by the second death" (Rev. 2:11). Those who have eternal life do not have to fear eternal death which will be experienced by the unsaved (20:6, 15).

### The Prophecy concerning Pergamum

*Revelation 2:12-17.* The church at Pergamum may be described as a church in compromise with the world. Though they had remained true to their faith in God and one of their number, Antipas, had been martyred, they were nevertheless guilty of what is referred to as "the teaching of Balaam" (v. 14), practicing the sins of the world, and "the teaching of the Nicolaitans" (v. 15), referring to their living licentiously though claiming to be Christians. The word of Christ to them was sharp and to the point, "Repent therefore! Otherwise, I will soon come to you and will fight against them with the sword of My mouth" (v. 16).

The church at Pergamum was engulfed by a city that was largely pagan and devoted to idol worship. Pagan cults such as Athena, Asclepius, Dionysus, and Zeus had an important place in their local religious observances. The town also boasted a library of 200,000 volumes and was noted for its paper, and paper itself was called "pergamena." Today, only a small village named Bergama is found on the site of the ancient city. Though the church was in an unfavorable cultural situation, they, nevertheless, were required to bear true testimony for God and were coming short.

Christ declared that He would fight them with the sword of His mouth (v. 16). The sword referred to was a long sword like a spear, but it had the connotation of being a reference to the Word of God which has a doubled-edged character much like the sword. This sword is mentioned seven times in the Bible (Luke 2:35; Rev. 1:16; 2:12, 16; 6:8; 19:15, 21). As this sword is used referring to the sword out of the mouth of Christ (1:16), it supports the concept that the real reference here is to the Word of God in its penetrating and disciplinary character. The Word of God is a double-edged sword and, on the one hand, offers promises of grace and salvation to those who put their trust in Christ, and, on the other hand, promises condemnation to the unbeliever.

The city of Pergamum was so wicked that it was referred to by Christ as "where Satan has his throne" (2:13), fulfilled by the persecution of unbelievers in Pergamum and the custom to worship Esculapius, the serpent god. Under the evil influences of this city, it is understandable that those living there would be influenced by the teaching of Baal and the Nicolaitans, but Christ, nevertheless, judged it as evil and a basis for punishment of those in this church.

What was true of Pergamum and their failures has been too evident in the history of the church. When the world and its system of values take over, it leaves a Christian without the clear hope of serving Christ now and the hope of Christ's return for him.

As in the other messages, a personal invitation is given to those who will listen, "He who has an ear, let him hear what the Spirit says to the churches. To him who overcomes, I will give some of the hidden manna. I will also give him a white stone with a new name written on it, known only to him who receives it" (v. 17).

Spiritual decisions always begin with individuals, and those in the church at Pergamum were addressed. They were promised that if they would overcome by faith, they would be given hidden manna and a new name on a white stone. The hidden manna seems to refer to a believer being nourished by Jesus as the bread from heaven, much as the Israelites benefited by eating the hidden manna in the wilderness. The sustaining grace of God is experienced by those who give their hearts to the Lord.

The white stone is not identified by any particular jewel. Though it is not clear what the white stone represents, it has the new name of a Christian written on it and is a token of the individual believer being accepted by Christ.

### The Prophecy concerning Thyatira

*Revelation 2:18-29.* The charge against this church is that it tolerated apostasy. The town of Thyatira where the church was located is forty miles southeast of Pergamum, and the city was famous for the manufacture of purple dye. It is of interest that Christ selected this small church in an obscure location to represent one of the seven churches, but it clearly represented the tendency illustrated many times in the history of the church of a church departing from the faith and embracing apostasy.

ttle is mentioned about Thyatira outside the Book of Revelation. conversion of Lydia may have been the source of the evangeliza- ι of this city as Scripture records no other evangelistic effort ching the city. The conversion of Lydia mentions that she was m Thyatira and a seller of purple, "One of those listening was a ɔman named Lydia, a dealer in purple cloth from the city of Thyati- ., who was a worshiper of God. The Lord opened her heart to ɜspond to Paul's message" (Acts 16:14).

Though the church in Thyatira had many commendable features ,v. 19), Christ denounced her compromises, "Nevertheless, I have this against you: You tolerate that woman Jezebel, who calls herself a prophetess. By her teaching she misleads My servants into sexual immorality and the eating of food sacrificed to idols. I have given her time to repent of her immorality, but she is unwilling. So I will cast her on a bed of suffering, and I will make those who commit adultery with her suffer intensely, unless they repent of her ways. I will strike her children dead. Then all the churches will know that I am He who searches hearts and minds, and I will repay each of you according to your deeds" (vv. 20-23).

A principal criticism of the church at Thyatira was that they toler- ated a woman by the name of Jezebel. This was probably not her real name, but it would remind them of the role of Jezebel in history as the wife of Ahab. She attempted to combine the worship of Israel and that of Baal, but actually desired to destroy the true worship of God. Her wickedness is recorded in the Old Testament, including having Naboth killed as in 1 Kings 21:1-16. She did what she could to kill other prophets of the Lord and wanted to kill Elijah (1 Kings 19:2), but was kept from it. In her death her body was eaten by the dogs, fulfilling the prophecy of her death (21:23; cf. 2 Kings 9:33-35).

Appeal was made to the individual who will turn to God when Christ says, "Now I say to the rest of you in Thyatira, to you who do not hold to her teaching and have not learned Satan's so-called deep secrets (I will not impose any other burden on you): Only hold on to what you have until I come. To him who overcomes and does My will to the end, I will give authority over the nations — 'He will rule them with an iron scepter; he will dash them to pieces like pot- tery' — just as I have received authority from My Father. I will also give him the morning star. He who has an ear, let him hear what the Spirit says to the churches" (vv. 24-29).

Though it is apparent that revival of the church as a whole was unlikely, individuals in it could turn to the Lord and live for Him. God will judge those who do not but will reward those who turn to Him in faith. An unusual promise was given to the overcomer, "I will also give him the morning star" (v. 28). The one who overcomes will be given authority in God's millennial kingdom when Christ will have authority to rule (cf. Ps. 2).

The authority which Christ receives from the Father can be delegated to others who will reign with Him. Those who are true to Christ will also share His millennial reign. The reference to His rule in Revelation 2:27 is one of the first reminders of the second coming of Christ to be given in the letters to the churches. The concept of "rule" has in it the thought of shepherding the Lord's people which includes the sheep of Matthew 25:31-46 and the godly remnant of Israel in Ezekiel 20:33-38. The morning star is not explained but may refer to a star that appears just before the dawn, the darkest hour of the night. Christ will be that glorious One who will return at the close of the darkness of the Great Tribulation. As in other churches, the appeal is to hear and respond.

### The Prophecy to the Church at Sardis

*Revelation 3:3-5.* At the time this letter was addressed to Sardis, the city was a prominent one and obtained its wealth from textile manufacturing, jewelry trade, and the dye industry. Generally speaking, the city was pagan with many individual mystery cults. The temple of Artemis was one of the major points of interest. Archeologists have located the remains of a Christian church building adjacent to this temple, indicating, at least in part, the witness of the church at Sardis to its generation. The city has long since lost its prominence, and today only a small village, Sart, can be found in the ancient ruins.

The church described as spiritually dead (v. 1) has no commendation, and the message to the church is one of unrelieved judgment and warning to repent. Christ said, "Remember, therefore, what you have received and heard; obey it, and repent. But if you do not wake up, I will come like a thief, and you will not know at what time I will come to you" (v. 3).

Though the church as a whole could be characterized as a church without spiritual life, some individuals in the church were still attempting to serve the Lord. Christ said to them, "Yet you have a few people in Sardis who have not soiled their clothes. They will walk with Me, dressed in white, for they are worthy. He who overcomes will, like them, be dressed in white. I will never blot out his name from the book of life, but will acknowledge his name before My Father and His angels" (vv. 4-5).

When a church or a generation is labeled as apostate, as was the church at Sardis, some will be discovered in the midst of the group who are still serving the Lord. To them Christ extends assurance of their salvation and the promise that He will not blot out their name in the Book of Life. The Book of Life, later mentioned in 20:12, 15, is the record of those who have eternal life and who will spend eternity in the presence of the Saviour.

Scholars have debated what was meant by Christ's promising not to blot out their names out of the Book of Life. Two major views have emerged. One is that the Book of Life contains the names of everyone who was given physical life in the world and their names are blotted out when they have passed the point of no return as far as salvation is concerned, usually at death. The promise, then, would be one of assurance of their eternal salvation.

Another view which seems more probable is that the Book of Life contains those who have been born again and their names are entered at the time of their new birth. Though there is no record of anyone ever having his name blotted out of the book, the assurance given individuals in Sardis is one of assurance and certainty.

In contrast to the message to the few that were saved, the church as a whole was warned that God's judgment would fall on them at a time they did not expect. The city of Sardis had a peculiar geographic situation, and it was located on high ground surrounded by cliffs difficult to scale. Sardis tended to relax in confidence that the enemy could not reach them. However, twice in history they have experienced a sudden invasion by armies that did scale the cliffs. Their capture came suddenly and almost without warning. In a similar way, God is warning Sardis that God's judgment may come on them, and, of course, cliffs do not hinder God's judging a wicked city.

Whether the church as a whole heeded the message is not known, but as in the messages to the other churches, individuals were exhorted to hear, "He who has an ear, let him hear what the Spirit says to the churches" (3:6). In every situation no matter how far individuals may be from God, if the light of divine truth has penetrated at all, they sometimes bear faithful testimony in spite of their adverse circumstances. So it was to be at Sardis.

### The Prophecy to Philadelphia

*Revelation 3:9-12.* The city of Philadelphia is unusual in that its name means "brotherly love," an expression of affection found six other times in the New Testament (Rom. 12:10; 1 Thes. 4:9; Heb. 13:1; 1 Peter 1:22; 2 Peter 1:7). This is the only time it is used of a city. Philadelphia was located in an area that was rich in agricultural crops, especially grapes, and the population enjoyed a certain amount of prosperity.

The message to the church at Philadelphia is unusual in that it is almost entirely praise in contrast to the message of Sardis which is almost entirely condemnation. In the introduction to His message to Philadelphia, Christ had declared that there was an open door before the church at Philadelphia. Christ Himself had the key of David which opens God's treasury (v. 7). The church of Philadelphia was commended because, while its strength was small, it had been true to the name of Jesus (v. 8).

In the prophecy relating to the church at Philadelphia, Christ made the following statement, "I will make those who are of the synagogue of Satan, who claim to be Jews though they are not, but are liars—I will make them come and fall down at your feet and acknowledge that I have loved you" (v. 9). Though there was apparently opposition to the church on the part of certain Jews who were unbelievers, the promise is that they will have to acknowledge their faults either in time or eternity and recognize the love of God for the church of Philadelphia.

The church was also commended for enduring patiently (v. 10). Because of this Christ made a promise, "I will also keep you from the hour of trial that is going to come upon the whole world to test those who live on the earth" (v. 10). Most of the Book of Revelation concerns the Great Tribulation and the terrible judgments that will be poured out on the earth at that time. Accordingly, it is very significant that the church in Philadelphia was given the promise that they will be kept from this hour of trial. The language is explicit that they will not simply be kept from the persecution of that time and the great catastrophes that will occur, but they are going to be kept from the whole hour, indicating that God will protect them and they will not enter this period.

This must be seen in the light of the issue as to whether the church will go through the Tribulation or not. What is here promised to the Philadelphian church is, in effect, the promise that they will not enter the period of Tribulation which will come on the unbelieving world. Though the passage contains nothing that would intimate that the Philadelphian church would have to go through the trial, the careful selection of words indicates that they will not enter the period.

The preposition "from" in relation to the hour of trial (Gr., *ek*) must be understood as being kept from the entire period and not just deliverance at the end of the time of trouble. The passage states that they would be kept from the hour, not simply the events of the hour. The use of the preposition here coupled with "the hour" should make it clear that the deliverance is from the period, not deliverance through the period. If it were intended to teach that they would be kept through the time of trouble, it would be proper to use another preposition (Gr., *dia*), meaning "through."

The Book of Revelation sharply contrasts the 144,000 representatives of the twelve tribes of Israel (Rev. 7; 14) which will go through the period unscathed to the saints in general, both Jews and Gentiles, who will suffer martyrdom (7:9-17). Actually, the church is never mentioned by name throughout the entire period of the Tribulation (4:1–19:10). Though it may continue to be a subject of debate as to whether this clearly indicates a pretribulation Rapture, the passage certainly offers no comfort to those who predict that the church will go through the Tribulation. In keeping with the teaching of a pretribulational Rapture, the event of His coming is viewed as imminent in contrast to the Second Coming, described in Revelation 19, which has many preceding events, including the whole Tribulation (4:1–19:10). The Rapture of the church is always presented as an imminent event that could occur at any time. Accordingly, the promise for the Philadelphian church assured them that when the Lord came, they would be raptured and be taken out of the world before the time of trouble to follow. Because of the special promise to them, however, they were assured they would not go through this period of trouble.

As history unfolds, the Rapture has not taken place, and the Philadelphian church went to glory by means of death, but will be subject to resurrection at the time of the Rapture at the time of Christ's coming. The church at Philadelphia is the recipient of many promises, including the crown (3:11) and being made a pillar in the temple of God (v. 12). This, of course, has to be taken as a figure of speech because an individual human being could not be made into a pillar in the temple. What it refers to is that they will be standing in glory in contrast to others who have fallen.

Because Philadelphia was in an area subject to great earthquakes and had been destroyed several times by earthquakes, the concept of standing firm indicated the permanence of their salvation and reward. In addition, the promise was given that the name of God and the name of the city of God, the New Jerusalem, which is described, "which is coming down out of heaven from My God" (cf. 21:1-2), would be written on each individual in addition to "My new name" (3:12) which will indicate that he belongs to Christ.

As in the case of other messages to the churches, appeal is finally made to the individual, "He who has an ear, let him hear what the Spirit says to the churches" (v. 13). Even in Philadelphia there may have been some who were short of saving faith in Christ but going only through the outer form of religion. Accordingly, the message ultimately comes to the individual and concerns his own salvation. The message to the church at Philadelphia should be considered by each individual in relation to his faith in Christ and his hope for the future.

### The Prophecy to Laodicea

*Revelation 3:15-18.* The church at Laodicea described a church from a spiritual standpoint which was bankrupt and without a redeeming feature. Though they did not openly oppose the truth, they did not support the truth either, and were what Christ describes as "neither cold nor hot" (v. 15).

Christ stated, "So, because you are lukewarm—neither hot nor cold—I am about to spit you out of My mouth" (v. 16). The Laodicean church was guilty of having religion without sincere faith or zeal to serve the Lord. Part of their problem was that they were in a wealthy and self-sufficient city that had good income from the wool industry. Their lukewarm situation arose from their failure to comprehend their spiritual needs. They were being lulled to sleep by the financial sufficiency of their culture. This was brought out in what Christ had to say to them, "You say, 'I am rich; I have acquired wealth and do not need a thing.' But you do not realize that you are wretched, pitiful, poor, blind and naked" (v. 17). They were quite satisfied with being moral, religious, and outwardly conformed to the description of a Christian life. There is no indication that they were guilty of gross sins. Their problem was that they had not recognized their spiritual bankruptcy and their need to turn to Christ.

The adjectives used are graphic. The word "wretched" was used by Paul in referring to himself (Rom. 7:24) in his struggle with sin. The word "pitiful" was used by Paul in 1 Corinthians 15:19 for one who does not believe in the doctrine of the resurrection. The word used for "poor" was one meaning complete poverty which would reduce a person to begging. The situation was far from their minds. They were declared to be "blind," that is, unable to recognize spiritual truth and understand it. They were declared to be "naked" because they did not recognize their need to have spiritual garments.

Accordingly, Christ counseled them, "I counsel you to buy from Me gold refined in the fire, so you can become rich; and white clothes to wear, so you can cover your shameful nakedness; and salve to put on your eyes, so you can see" (Rev. 3:18). The Laodiceans characterized the world as it approaches life, seeing the outer garments of gold and silver as evidence of wealth but which is unable to see the spiritual needs of the individual who may have everything that wealth can buy. The garments which Christ provides for them will include real gold, used in Scripture to describe the glory of God. White raiment speaking of righteousness would cover their nakedness and is symbolical in reference to the righteousness of God which comes on those who put their trust in Christ. Their eye salve was to make them see.

In Laodicea there was at that time a treatment for eye soreness which was common in the Middle East. They knew what eye salve could do for one physically with sore eyes, and here this was to be transferred to their spiritual needs. In contrast to what wealth could buy, it is most significant that what is being provided here by God is something that cannot be earned or purchased by human wealth but has to be supplied by God Himself to those who put their trust in Him. As indicated in Isaiah 55:1, those who come to God have an invitation to receive what is necessary without money and without price.

Unfortunately, many churches in the twentieth century, in whole or in part, resemble the church at Laodicea that is self-sufficient in the things of this life but is in poverty concerning the things of God. Though no clear exhortation for repentance was demanded in connection with the need of the Laodicean church, they are warned that they will be cast out unless they turn to riches that are recognized by God—which would be a repentance, a change of mind concerning their spiritual condition.

### The Prophecy Given to Overcomers

*Revelation 3:19-21*. At the conclusion of the seven messages to the churches, a general invitation was given to those who will listen and come to Christ. First of all, Christ stated the general principle, "Those whom I love I rebuke and discipline. So be earnest, and repent" (v. 19). As is illustrated in all the messages to the churches, Christ stated that His purpose was not to judge but to bring them to repentance. An interesting fact is that He addresses them as "those whom I love" (Gr., *agapao*). The important fact is His rebuke and discipline stems from His love for them. The word "discipline" has in it the thought of child training taken from childhood to adulthood. The exhortation to self-judgment and repentance is another reminder that Christians who do not judge themselves will be judged, as stated by Paul in 1 Corinthians 11:31-32, "But if we judged ourselves, we would not come under judgment. When we are judged by the Lord, we are being disciplined so that we will not be condemned with the world." Because the believer has established an eternal relationship with God as one who is saved, it is revealed that God will not allow him to continue in sin indefinitely, but sooner or later, either in time or eternity, will deal with him.

Having urged them to have fellowship with Him, Christ now describes Himself as One who is waiting for them to come, "Here I am! I stand at the door and knock. If anyone hears My voice and opens the door, I will come in and eat with him, and he with Me" (Rev. 3:20). This passage has sometimes been construed to refer to salvation, but in the context it seems to refer to those who already are believers. The issue is not related to salvation by eating with Christ but to fellowship, nourishment, and spiritual growth. God does not force Himself on anyone but waits for believers to come in simple faith to receive from God that which only God can supply.

The concept of knocking and entering is found in Scripture, of which Luke 12:35-40 is an illustration. However, in this and many other instances, the thought is that Christ is on the outside and the others who are on the inside waiting for Him to come should open the door when He comes. Christ used this in a parable, "Be dressed ready for service and keep your lamps burning, like men waiting for their master to return from a wedding banquet, so that when he comes and knocks they can immediately open the door for him" (Luke 12:35-36).

The invitation Christ extends here for those who wish to come and eat with Him is a most gracious invitation and illustrates that fellowship with God is always available to those who are willing to put their trust in Christ and come to God. In that fellowship they will not only enjoy the presence of the Saviour but also the nourishment and the strengthening that comes from partaking from spiritual truth. They can be strengthened by dining on the things of God, the things of salvation, our wonderful hope, God's sustaining grace, and all the other blessings that are ours in Christ.

As Christ expresses it, "To him who overcomes, I will give the right to sit with Me on My throne, just as I overcame and sat down with My Father on His throne" (Rev. 3:21). Those who walk with Christ in fellowship in this life will also enjoy the right of fellowship and sharing in the throne of Christ in eternity to come. This invitation is extended to any in the churches who are faithful and who honor and serve the Lord. It is another illustration of the gracious provision God has made for those who trust Him.

The message to the churches closes with the same invitation repeated in the message of each church, "He who has an ear, let him hear what the Spirit says to the churches" (v. 22). God has spoken in words that should not be misunderstood, but so much depends on individuals hearing and responding to what they hear. The tragedy is that in so many cases no one is listening.

Taken as a whole, the messages to the seven churches represent the major spiritual problems of the church down through the ages. Ephesus represented the danger of forsaking the love that characterized believers when they first trusted Christ (2:4). Smyrna illustrated the danger of fear though otherwise they were faithful to God (v. 10). The church at Pergamum is a reminder of the constant danger of doctrinal compromise (vv. 14-15). The church at Thyatira illustrated moral compromise (v. 20). The church at Sardis illustrated the danger of spiritual deadness (3:1-2). The church at Philadelphia, though faithful, was warned against not holding fast to the things that they believed (v. 11). Laodicea illustrated the danger of lukewarmness (vv. 15-16), of outer religion without inner zeal and reality.

Though the Book of Revelation deals primarily with prophecy

concerning the future, it was written to help the churches of the present age understand the purposes of God and the great events that will characterize the end of the age.

# 14

# PROPHECY CONCERNING JOHN'S VISION OF HEAVEN AND THE END TIME

## JOHN'S VISION OF HEAVEN
### Prophecy of the Church in Heaven

*Revelation 4:1-11.* This chapter, following the revelation of the message to the seven churches, is introduced by the important phrase "after this." Most of the struggles of scholars attempting to interpret the Book of Revelation stem from a failure to understand that the Book of Revelation is a book of prophecy and that prophecy has a chronological order. This becomes the key to unlocking the Book of Revelation. As pointed out before (cf. 1:9-20), John was instructed, "Write, therefore, what you have seen, what is now and what will take place later" (v. 19). Simplistic as this statement is, it provides an inspired outline of the Book of Revelation, referring first to what was, that is, the experience of John seeing Jesus in His glory in chapter 1; "what is now," the messages to the seven churches which refer to the present age as the seven churches represent churches in this present age; and then "what will take place later," referring to that which is future. Confusion in the interpretation of Revelation stems almost entirely from the failure to observe this divine outline. The opening of chapter 4 with the phrase "after this," referring to the churches, should make clear that from chapter 4 on, the Book of Revelation is dealing with future events.

Apart from these indications in the text of the chronological outline, a number of important arguments support this concept so essential to understanding this book. One of the important and convincing arguments that the Book of Revelation chapter 4 and following relates to the future is that the events described, either in symbolic or other ways, find no literal fulfillment in the history of the church. The historical school of interpretation which regards the Book of Revelation as being fulfilled in history has been unable to provide any consensus on its interpretation and offers only confusion.

If the events described have any literal fulfillment, they, accordingly, must be fulfilled at some future time. This is in harmony with the concept that the book is prophecy rather than history or simply descriptive of the moral conflict that exists in the world. This also explains why, apart from the futuristic view which views Revelation as prophecy beginning in chapter 4, there has been no coherent, or majority interpretation, and each of the major views — allegorical, the preterist, and the historical view — when applied to this book yield entirely different answers according to the person doing the study. Only the futurist view provides any reasonable coherence between what the book states and what the fulfillment of its prophecy would indicate. Though there are some instances where interpretation is not entirely clear, other events stand out as being specific future events and provide enough guidance so that the Book of Revelation becomes a majestic unfolding of the future with the revelation of Christ at the Second Coming as its main theme.

One of the important conclusions in prophecy is the concept that the church composed of the saved of the present age will be in heaven while the great events of the Tribulation and of the end time take place. This is exactly what is described in Revelation 4–5. The church in heaven is in contrast to the great time of trouble which will take place on the earth prior to the second coming of Christ. Accordingly, though the specific prophecies of 4–5 are not the main burden of these two chapters, what is being described is a vision of heaven when the saints and angels and the sovereign God on His throne form an intelligent background for other events that shall take place both in heaven and on earth.

John stated at the opening of Revelation 4, "After this I looked, and there before me was a door standing open in heaven. And the voice I had first heard speaking to me like a trumpet said, 'Come up here, and I will show you what must take place after this' " (v. 1).

Actually, John was on the Isle of Patmos where he had been exiled, and the revelation was given to him at this location. In this instance, however, he stated, "At once I was in the Spirit, and there before me was a throne in heaven with someone sitting on it" (v. 2). It may be debated whether John was physically caught up to heaven or whether simply in his vision he is caught up to heaven. In either case, he saw the scene as he would if he had been present. The voice which provided the invitation, according to John, was the same voice he had heard in 1:10 where he was instructed to write the message to the seven churches (v. 11).

Because John's experience is similar to what will happen at the Rapture when the church is caught up to heaven, some have equated the two events, but, actually, John was not raptured, and his natural body was probably still on the Isle of Patmos. Accordingly, it is better to regard this as a special situation. It may be going beyond the intent of this passage to hint that the Rapture is going to take place in the period following the Church Age, but from the context in which the event is placed in the Book of Revelation, it is reasonable to conclude that the Rapture has taken place and that what John is seeing is a setting for events in heaven which will take place in heaven and earth in the period after the Rapture.

The word "church," prominent in chapters 2–3, does not reoccur until 22:16 though the bride mentioned in 19:7, no doubt, is a reference to the church. The total absence of any reference to the church or any synonym of the church in chapters 4–18 is highly significant because ordinarily the church would be in the center of the activities. Rather, Jews and Gentiles are spoken of separately as individuals who are saved or unsaved.

John's first experience upon arrival in heaven was to behold "a throne in heaven with someone sitting on it" (4:2). He described the personage on the throne in these words, "And the One who sat there had the appearance of jasper and carnelian. A rainbow, resembling an emerald, encircled the throne" (v. 3). The personage on the throne is said to resemble in His glory the jasper and the carnelian stones. The jasper, described in 21:11, is a clear stone in contrast to the jasper stone known on earth as an opaque stone. Accordingly, some have concluded that it may be a diamond in appearance. The carnelian stone is red in color like a ruby.

Though the colors of the stone, enhanced by the rainbow, resembling an emerald which is green in color, provide the glorious appearance, but the significance of these stones may be derived from their use in Israel. On the breastplate of the priest there were twelve stones, each representing a tribe of Israel. The high priest represented all twelve tribes before God when he performed his priestly functions. The jasper and the carnelian stones were the first and last of the twelve stones (cf. Ex. 28:17-21). Further, the jasper represented the tribe of Reuben, the first tribe, and the carnelian stone represented Benjamin, the youngest tribe. Mention of these two stones, accordingly, was intended to include all the twelve tribes of Israel.

Further, the names of Reuben and Benjamin have significance because Reuben has the meaning of "behold the son," and Benjamin means "son of my right hand." Christ, of course, fulfills both of these functions, and He is the first-begotten Son. Like Benjamin, He is "the Son of My right hand," also speaking of Christ in His relationship to God the Father. Taking all these things into consideration, it would seem best to interpret this passage as a description of

God the Father sitting on a throne. This is also supported by the fact that Christ is pictured in a different way in this passage as separate from the One on the throne, though actually He occupies the throne with the Father also. The main purpose of this vision, however, was to show the glory of God.

As John surveyed the scene in heaven, he also saw twenty-four other thrones and recorded, "Surrounding the throne were twenty-four other thrones, and seated on them were twenty-four elders. They were dressed in white and had crowns of gold on their heads" (Rev. 4:4). They are obviously a representative group. In Israel, for instance, the many priests were divided into twenty-four groups, and one priest would represent each of the twenty-four.

The question has been raised, however, as to whether these twenty-four elders represent all the saints, both Old and New Testament, or only the church of the present age, or perhaps are angelic figures. These and other interpretations have been advanced by scholars.

They were described as having white robes, speaking of righteousness in the presence of God, and wearing crowns of gold which were not the crown of a ruler (Gr., *diadem*), but rather the crown of a victor (Gr., *stephanos*), crowns awarded victors in the race. The implication is that these have already been rewarded as symbolized in the throne.

In reconstructing the events of the end time, if the church is raptured before the end-time events and is judged at the Judgment Seat of Christ, it would provide a plausible explanation that these twenty-four elders are representatives of the church. Additional revelation on this subject will be discussed in chapter 5.

John was then made aware of ominous sounds indicating divine judgment, "From the throne came flashes of lightning, rumblings and peals of thunder" (4:5). The setting in heaven foreshadows the judgments to come on the earth. A similar experience of thunders, lightnings, and trumpets was experienced in the giving of the Mosaic Law in Exodus 19:16. The scene in heaven which he saw was, of course, the forerunner of the terrible judgments to be inflicted on the earth in the period which followed.

John also recorded, "Before the throne, seven lamps were blazing. These are the seven spirits of God" (Rev. 4:5). Mention of these seven spirits is found earlier in 1:4; 3:1. Though no explanation was given, it is probably best to consider this a representation of the

Holy Spirit in a sevenfold way rather than consider them relating to seven angels which would be an alternate explanation.

The Holy Spirit, not ordinarily visible, on certain occasions has assumed physical form as here, and in the case of the Holy Spirit descending as a dove on Christ at His baptism (Matt. 3:16; Mark 1:10; Luke 3:22; John 1:32). On the Day of Pentecost the Holy Spirit was seen as "tongues of fire that separated and came to rest on each of them" (Acts 2:3). In this scene from heaven not only God the Father was revealed on the throne and Christ in the next chapter as the Lion of the tribe of Judah (Rev. 5:5) but the Holy Spirit as well, all three Persons of the Trinity being present. The term of "seven" in relation to the lamps and the spirits of God is in keeping with the concept that the number seven indicates perfection, and is in keeping also with the seven qualities or attributes of the Holy Spirit revealed in Isaiah 11:2-3.

John recorded, "Also before the throne there was what looked like a sea of glass, clear as crystal" (Rev. 4:6). Though the expression is not interpreted here, there seems to be a relationship to the laver or a bronze basin filled with water in the tabernacle in the Old Testament and the "sea" in the temple (1 Kings 7:23-25), both of them being washstands designed to provide the priest with water for cleansing. Together they represent the sanctifying power of the Word of God symbolized by the water. The sea of glass may represent the Word of God in its sanctifying power.

John also recorded, "In the center, around the throne, were four living creatures, and they were covered with eyes, in front and in back. The first living creature was like a lion, the second was like an ox, the third had a face like a man, the fourth was like a flying eagle. Each of the four living creatures had six wings and was covered with eyes all around, even under his wings" (Rev. 4:6-8). There is considerable diversity among interpreters concerning what the four living creatures represent. Probably the best interpretation is that they are physical embodiments of the attributes of God, as the seven lamps represent the Holy Spirit (v. 5). They are compared to a lion, ox, man, and flying eagle. Some relate this to the four Gospels, Matthew representing the lion or the king; Mark, the ox or servant; Luke, Man in His humanity; and the Gospel of John, the flying eagle representing the deity of Christ. Still others compare them to angels and find support in the fact they had six wings. Their ministry was to worship God, and John recorded, "Day and night they never stopped saying: 'Holy, holy, holy is the Lord God Almighty, who was, and is, and is to come' " (v. 8).

Their worship of God also is a call to the twenty-four elders to worship, "Whenever the living creatures give glory, honor and thanks to Him who sits on the throne and who lives forever and ever, the twenty-four elders fall down before Him who sits on the throne, and worship Him who lives forever and ever" (vv. 9-10). The twenty-four elders also give their praise to the Lord, "They lay their crowns before the throne and say: 'You are worthy, our Lord and God, to receive glory and honor and power, for You created all things, and by Your will they were created and have their being' " (vv. 10-11).

Though the entire content of chapter 4 is what John saw in heaven, it also is a revelation of the glory and honor given to God in the future and therefore has a prophetic base. Most important, it emphasizes what events will occur in heaven while end-time events take place on earth.

### Prophecy that Christ Will Be Worthy
### to Take the Seven-Sealed Scroll

*Revelation 5:1-10.* Attention now is focused on the fact that Jesus Christ is in heaven. This is in contrast to His later second coming when He will be in the earth for 1,000 years. John saw a scroll, parchment rolled up on a roller, written on both sides and sealed with seven seals in such a way that as the scroll unrolled, each seal must be successively broken.

John recorded this, "Then I saw in the right hand of Him who sat on the throne a scroll with writing on both sides and sealed with seven seals" (v. 1).

A mighty angel raised the question, "Who is worthy to break the seals and open the scroll?" (v. 2) A strong angel is mentioned in 10:1; 18:21. The loud voice would indicate that what is being said is of great importance and should demand the attention of everyone. John added, "But no one in heaven or on earth or under the earth could open the scroll or even look inside it. I wept and wept because no one was found who was worthy to open the scroll or look inside" (5:3-4).

One of the others comforted John who was weeping and told him, "Do not weep! See, the Lion of the tribe of Judah, the Root of David, has triumphed. He is able to open the scroll and its seven seals" (v. 5). The reference to Christ as the Lion is based on

Genesis 49:9-10. The tribe of Judah, the lion tribe, was the one from which Christ would come. The concept of Christ as the Root of David (Rev. 5:5), or a Descendant of David, was also prophesied in Isaiah 11:10. The characterization of Christ as a Lion calls attention to Christ as the sovereign Judge of the world, especially at His second coming, and is in contrast to His portrayal of a Lamb, speaking of meekness. This is the only reference to Christ as a Lion in the Book of Revelation in contrast to many references to Him as the Lamb.

John recorded what happened next, "Then I saw a Lamb, looking as if it had been slain, standing in the center of the throne, encircled by the four living creatures and the elders. He had seven horns and seven eyes, which are the seven spirits of God sent out into all the earth. He came and took the scroll from the right hand of Him who sat on the throne" (Rev. 5:6-7). The purpose of addressing Christ as the Lamb is to identify Christ as the Lamb who was sacrificed at His first coming, but also the same person as the glorified Christ of the Book of Revelation. Christ is both Lamb and Lion. Because the attributes of God are displayed by Christ, the four living creatures are also prominent in the picture.

The reference to horns seems to indicate authority (Dan. 7:24; Rev. 13:1). The seven eyes are identified as the seven spirits of God, most probably another reference to the Holy Spirit as in 5:6 (cf. Zech. 3:9; 4:10). The Lamb took the scroll, "He came and took the scroll from the right hand of Him who sat on the throne" (Rev. 5:7).

The same twenty-four elders who fell down before the One on the throne now fall down and worship the Lamb, indicating His deity and lordship, "And when He had taken it, the four living creatures and the twenty-four elders fell down before the Lamb. Each one had a harp and they were holding golden bowls full of incense, which are the prayers of the saints" (v. 8).

In recognizing the deity of the Lamb, the twenty-four elders sang a new song, "You are worthy to take the scroll and to open its seals, because You were slain, and with Your blood You purchased men for God from every tribe and language and people and nation. You have made them to be a kingdom and priests to serve our God, and they will reign on the earth" (vv. 9-10).

The translation of verses 9-10 in the NIV is somewhat different than that which was used for the KJV. In the KJV the song states, "for Thou wast slain, and hast redeemed us to God by Thy blood out of every kindred, and tongue, and people, and nation. And hast made us unto our God kings and priests: and we shall reign on the earth" (vv. 9-10). The difference is that in the KJV the song indicates that the four and twenty elders are those that are redeemed which would harmonize with the concept that they are representing the church. In the NIV a different manuscript changes this from first person to the third person. Instead of purchasing the twenty-four elders, it states, "You purchased men for God from every tribe and language and people and nation. You have made them to be a kingdom and priests to serve our God, and they will reign on the earth" (vv. 9-10).

The rendering of the *King James Version* makes necessary that the twenty-four elders are men and is conducive to supporting the concept that they are representatives of the church. In the revised translation of the NIV, it is made general and the statement is simply that Christ purchased men from all peoples and made them to be His subjects. The NIV translation would make it possible for the twenty-four elders to be something other than men, that is, angels, though it does not affirm this.

Scholars continue to differ on this subject. Manuscript evidence in support of the *King James Version* in verses 9-10 gives considerable support to the concept that the KJV is actually the best manuscript. The KJV would give the twenty-four elders a distinctive place in heaven, in contrast to angels, instead of being angels themselves. There is no solid reason why the twenty-four elders could not be redeemed men rather than angels regardless of which translation is accepted. The interpretation that they are angels is possible with the revised translation but is not supported by any direct statement. With either translation the twenty-four elders could be men.

### Prophecy of Angelic Worship of the Lamb

*Revelation 5:11-12.* In a general survey of what is going on in heaven, he next looked and heard a multitude of angels beyond number also worshiping the Lamb, "Then I looked and heard the voice of many angels, numbering thousands upon thousands, and ten thousand times ten thousand. They encircled the throne and the living creatures and the elders. In a loud voice they sang: 'Worthy is the Lamb, who was slain, to receive power and wealth and wisdom and strength and honor and glory and praise!' " (vv. 11-12)

The details of the angels worshiping the Lamb are significant.

First of all, there is the astounding number which places them beyond human estimation. They are declared here to sing which is unusual for angels. The singing of that large a group must have been most impressive and forms an important background to the final worship of the Lamb by the whole universe. The fact that this follows the worship of the twenty-four elders may be in contrast to human worship.

### The Worship of All Creation

*Revelation 5:13-14.* John recorded that he heard a mighty chorus not only of angels but of every creature in heaven and earth, "Then I heard every creature in heaven and on earth and under the earth and on the sea, and all that is in them, singing: 'To Him who sits on the throne and to the Lamb be praise and honor and glory and power, forever and ever!' The four living creatures said, 'Amen,' and the elders fell down and worshiped" (vv. 13-14). The glory of this heavenly scene is in sharp contrast to the dark scene on earth as a time of trouble begins. Christians who have previously endured temptation and trial and often persecution and martyrdom now are free from the ills of earth and leave to others the task of continued faithfulness to God which might lead to martyrdom of many. The significance of the fourth and fifth chapters of the Book of Revelation is to remind the reader of the dark scenes that are yet ahead for the Great Tribulation and the fact that in heaven there is victory, glory, and majesty, and that in God's good time His authority will be expressed in the earth in the millennial kingdom.

# PROPHECY IN REVELATION
# CONCERNING THE END TIME

As revealed in a study throughout Scripture, the events of the end time follow the Rapture of the church and culminate in the second coming of Christ. Immediately after the Rapture of the church, there will be a time period which may be called a period of preparation. In this period there will emerge a ten-nation group forming a political unit in the Middle East. A leader will emerge who will gain control first of three and then of all ten (cf. Dan. 7:8, 24-25). From this position of power he will be able to enter into a covenant with Israel, bringing to rest the relationship of Israel to her neighbors (9:27), and beginning the final seven-year countdown culminating in the Second Coming.

The first half of the seven years will be a time of peace as the

# MAJOR EVENTS OF UNFULFILLED PROPHECY

1. Rapture of the church (1 Cor. 15:51-58; 1 Thes. 4:13-18).
2. Revival of the Roman Empire; ten-nation confederacy formed (Dan. 7:7, 24; Rev. 13:1; 17:3, 12-13).
3. Rise of the Antichrist: the Middle East dictator (Dan. 7:8; Rev. 13:1-8).
4. The seven-year peace treaty with Israel: consummated seven years before the second coming of Christ (Dan. 9:27; Rev. 19:11-16).
5. Establishment of a world church (Rev. 17:1-15).
6. Russia springs a surprise attack on Israel four years before the second coming of Christ (Ezek. 38–39).
7. Peace treaty with Israel broken after three-and-a-half years: beginning of world government, world economic system, world atheistic religion, final three-and-a-half years before second coming of Christ (Dan. 7:23; Rev. 13:5-8, 15-17; 17:16-17).
8. Many Christians and Jews martyred who refused to worship world dictator (Rev. 7:9-17; 13:15).
9. Catastrophic divine judgments represented by seals, trumpets, and bowls poured out on the earth (Rev. 6–18).
10. World war breaks out focusing on the Middle East: Battle of Armageddon (Dan. 11:40-45; Rev. 9:13-21; 16:12-16).
11. Babylon destroyed (Rev. 18).
12. Second coming of Christ (Matt. 24:27-31; Rev. 19:11-21).
13. Judgment of wicked Jews and Gentiles (Ezek. 20:33-38; Matt. 25:31-46; Jude 14-15; Rev. 19:15-21; 20:1-4).
14. Satan bound for 1,000 years (Rev. 20:1-3).
15. Resurrection of Tribulation saints and Old Testament saints (Dan. 12:2; Rev. 20:4).
16. Millennial kingdom begins (Rev. 20:5-6).
17. Final rebellion at the end of the Millennium (Rev. 20:7-10).
18. Resurrection and final judgment of the wicked: Great White Throne judgment (Rev. 20:11-15).
19. Eternity begins: new heaven, new earth, New Jerusalem (Rev. 21:1-2).

covenant is observed. At the midpoint of the seven years, the covenant will be broken and the political leader will assume by proclamation the position of ruler over the entire world. This will begin the period of persecution, the final three-and-a-half years. For the next three-and-a-half years the world dictator, who previously led the ten nations, will head up a world empire, referred to in Daniel 7:25 as extending for a time, times, and half a time, that is, for a year, two years, and half a year. The end of his reign at the Second Coming will be preceded by a great world war (Dan. 11:40-45; Rev. 16:14-16).

The three time periods between the Rapture and the second coming of Christ therefore include an introductory period of unknown length, a period of peace of three-and-a-half years, and a period of great persecution for three-and-a-half years. The climax will be the second coming of Christ. Revelation 6–18 deals with the last seven years or, more specifically, the last three-and-a-half years preceding the Second Coming.

### The First Seal: World Conquest

*Revelation 6:1-2.* The scroll with seven seals introduced now becomes the key to understanding the events which were prophesied for this period. As the events are fulfilled, a seven-sealed scroll provides the major outline for events leading up to the Second Coming. Though many have attempted alternate views, probably the best approach is the view that the seven seals are the major events, or time periods, that out of the seventh seal will come a series of events described as seven trumpets, and out of the seventh trumpet will come a series of seven bowls of wrath: judgments on the world just preceding the Second Coming. The effect is a crescendo of judgments coming with increased severity and in increasing tempo as the Second Coming approaches. Though the Book of Revelation is not written necessarily in chronological order, as will be seen, this outline forms the chronological background and order of revelation of the Book of Revelation to which the Scriptures in this section may be related.

As John watched, he recorded that the Lamb opened the first seal, "I watched as the Lamb opened the first of the seven seals. Then I heard one of the four living creatures say in a voice like thunder, 'Come!' I looked, and there before me was a white horse! Its rider held a bow, and he was given a crown, and he rode out as a conqueror bent on conquest" (vv. 1-2). The symbolism of a white horse in the first century represented a conquering military leader. Later in Revelation Christ returns with the holy angels on white

JOHN'S VISION OF HEAVEN AND THE END TIME

# ORDER OF SEALS, TRUMPETS, AND BOWLS
## Revelation 6:1–16:21

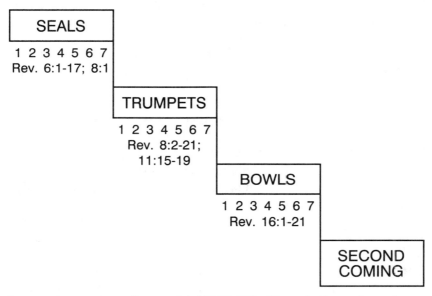

horses to conquer the world (19:11-21). Though there have been different interpretations concerning the white horse and its rider, the context would indicate that there is no real parallel between this rider and Christ as the rider of the white horse, and it is preferable to assume that this rider is the counterfeit Christ, or the Antichrist, the ruler who had previously gained control of the ten kingdoms in the Middle East.

In a description of the rider on the white horse, it states that he has a bow and a crown but does not mention an arrow. Though Scripture provides no interpretation of this, its probable meaning is that he becomes a conqueror without war. This seems to fit in all the other passages that relate to this world ruler. He apparently has risen to such power politically that no one is able to stand against him. In the later revelation of this same personage in Revelation 13, the question is asked, "Who is like the beast? Who can make war against him?" (Rev. 13:4) The answer, of course, is that no one is able to fight him.

The interpretation of the first seal raises the question as to where this occurs in end-time events. Probably the most popular view is that this introduces the final seven-year period. However, in the verses which immediately follow, it speaks of terrible disasters overtaking the world which apparently occur in the second half of the last seven years. Also, the world government begins at the middle of the seven years. Accordingly, it is probable that the Book of Revelation, though recognizing the events of the entire seven years, concentrates on the three-and-a-half years before the Second Coming as containing the most significant and recognizable signs of the Lord's return.

### The Second Seal: War

*Revelation 6:3-4.* John was then invited to consider the breaking of the second seal which reveals another horse and rider. John wrote, "When the Lamb opened the second seal, I heard the second living creature say, 'Come!' Then another horse came out, a fiery red one. Its rider was given power to take peace from the earth and to make men slay each other. To him was given a large sword" (vv. 3-4). As a white horse is symbolic of conquering, so a red horse would be symbolic of war. This is the specific interpretation given to the horse and its rider.

In the reference to war, it is not necessary to presume that this has in mind a particular war but rather that there are a series of wars in the end time, the most important of which will be at the end of the seven-year period just prior to the second coming of Christ (16:13-16). The last three-and-a-half years is a time when there is no peace.

### The Third Seal: Famine

*Revelation 6:5-6.* John was next invited to behold the opening of the third seal, and he wrote, "When the Lamb opened the third seal, I heard the third living creature say, 'Come!' I looked, and there before me was a black horse! Its rider was holding a pair of scales in his hand. Then I heard what sounded like a voice among the four living creatures, saying, 'A quart of wheat for a day's wages, and three quarts of barley for a day's wages, and do not damage the oil and the wine!' " (vv. 5-6)

The aftermath of war, which apparently continues to some extent throughout this entire period, brings famine, especially in the areas where war has devastated their crops. A day's wages was approximately sixteen cents, or a denarius. A quart of wheat would be sufficient only for one meal. If they bought barley, they could get three quarts, enough for three meals, but would have nothing left to buy oil, wine, or other necessities. The picture is one of famine.

The somber and death-dealing character of a famine is symbolized by the fact that the horse is black.

### The Fourth Seal: Death

*Revelation 6:7-8.* John was next invited to observe the opening of the fourth seal. "When the Lamb opened the fourth seal, I heard the voice of the fourth living creature say, 'Come!' I looked, and there before me was a pale horse! Its rider was named Death, and Hades was following close behind him. They were given power over a fourth of the earth to kill by sword, famine and plague, and by the wild beasts of the earth" (vv. 7-8). The revelation of the pale horse is quite dramatic as it is actually an unearthly color, somewhat like a pale green, the same word being used in Mark 6:39 and Revelation 8:7; 9:4. The rider is equally horrifying and is named "Death," and Hades follows close after. Because Hades is the abode of those who die, when a person dies in this situation, he goes to Hades. The most astounding part of the prophecy, however, is that these are given power over a fourth part of the earth, and instruments of death will include sword and famine, mentioned earlier in the preceding seals, but also plague and the wild beasts of the earth.

Earlier the question was raised as to what time frame chapter 6 and following falls in consideration that the last period preceding the Second Coming is divided into seven years, with the first half a time of peace and the second half a time of persecution. Though it is quite a popular interpretation to find the second half of the seven years in Revelation with the Great Tribulation not beginning until chapter 11, the fact that one-fourth of the earth is killed at this point would seem to indicate that the Tribulation is already underway.

If the earth's population at the time this occurs is 6 billion, one-fourth would mean the loss of life for 1.5 billion of the world's population. This would be more than if all of the people in North America, Central America, and South America were killed. It still would not equal what is described here. It, accordingly, is difficult to imagine this not being the Great Tribulation. If that is the case, inasmuch as the second and third seals, war and famine, are part of the process, it would seem to come back to them as well. Likewise, the first seal, because it is a conqueror of the entire world, seems to fit best the last three-and-a-half years which begin with the ruler taking political charge of the entire world.

The Bible has much to say concerning this final Great Tribulation. In Daniel 9:27 the last half of the final seven years leading up to the

Second Coming is the period in which the world ruler takes over and persecutes Israel and all who are not willing to obey him. The ruler at that time is the person mentioned in Daniel 9:26 as "the ruler who will come." In the words, "How awful that day will be! None will be like it. It will be a time of trouble for Jacob, but he will be saved out of it" (Jer. 30:7).

Christ added His word of explanation on this in describing the Great Tribulation in these words, "For then there will be great distress, unequaled from the beginning of the world until now—and never to be equaled again. If those days had not been cut short, no one would survive, but for the sake of the elect those days will be shortened" (Matt. 24:21-22).

The distinguishing characteristic of the Great Tribulation is that it is an unprecedented time of trouble, either before or after. Under this definition, the fourth seal qualifies because never in the history of the world has there been destruction of human life described here. If this is determined, the earlier seals could easily be seen as a part of the period. In general, this passage of Scripture makes clear that the world is headed for unprecedented trouble but that this will not occur until after the Rapture of the church. There are many indications, however, that the earth is vulnerable as our modern day has multiplied forms of destruction of human life. If the supernatural judgments of God be added to this, it is easy to see how the time of trouble will be described as unprecedented.

### The Fifth Seal: Martyrs

*Revelation 6:9-11.* John was invited to observe the opening of the fifth seal, and he recorded what he saw, "When he opened the fifth seal, I saw under the altar the souls of those who had been slain because of the Word of God and the testimony they had maintained. They called out in a loud voice, 'How long, Sovereign Lord, holy and true, until You judge the inhabitants of the earth and avenge our blood?' Then each of them was given a white robe and they were told to wait a little longer, until the number of their fellow servants and brothers who were to be killed as they had been was completed" (vv. 9-11).

The martyred dead were asking how long it would be before they would be avenged, that is, When will the Great Tribulation end and the Second Coming occur? They were given white robes and informed that there would be additional time during which some of their fellow servants and brothers would be killed.

One of the questions often raised in prophecy is the question of what the status of a saved person will be between the time he dies on earth and the time he is resurrected. Scriptures are clear that his soul will go immediately to heaven, but the question is: What will be the status of his body? This passage is one of a number that points to the conclusion that believers in Christ will have a temporary body prior to their resurrection body. It would be difficult to hang a robe on them if they did not have some physical body to hold it. Also attributed to them is the fact that they stand, which again would be impossible without a body (7:9; cf. Luke 16:22-24). A full description of the martyred dead is given in Revelation 7.

### The Sixth Seal: Catastrophic Judgment

*Revelation 6:12-17*. After observing these stirring scenes, John next recorded observing the opening of the sixth seal, "I watched as He opened the sixth seal. There was a great earthquake. The sun turned black like sackcloth made of goat hair, the whole moon turned blood red, and the stars in the sky fell to the earth, as late figs drop from a fig tree when shaken by a strong wind. The sky receded like a scroll, rolling up, and every mountain and island was removed from its place. Then the kings of the earth, the princes, the generals, the rich, the mighty, and every slave and every free man hid in caves and among the rocks of the mountains. They called to the mountains and rocks, 'Fall on us and hide us from the face of Him who sits on the throne and from the wrath of the Lamb! For the great day of Their wrath has come, and who can stand?' " (vv. 12-17)

It would be difficult to paint a scene more dramatic, more awful than that which is described in these verses. All the elements of catastrophic judgment are present: a great earthquake, the sun turning black, the moon becoming as blood, the stars of heaven falling like ripe figs, the heavens demonstrating major movements departing as a scroll, and on earth every mountain and island moving. The picture of God's judgment on the world at this time is so dramatic that some recoil from it and attempt to interpret it in a less than literal sense. They would hold that this simply refers to political and social instability that will characterize the end time. However, the objections to a symbolic interpretation for which there is no norm or guiding principle are such that it is far better to interpret it in its literal sense.

Though this scene is not the final judgment as recorded in Revelation 16 under the seventh bowl of wrath, it indicates that the entire last three-and-a-half years up to the second coming of Christ will be a period of unprecedented trial and trouble for the world as God deals in direct judgment on the world and all its sin. This passage also has support from Christ's own description of the Great Tribulation in Matthew 24 where He spoke of great earthquakes (v. 7). The heavens departing as a scroll is mentioned in Isaiah 34:4. The Book of Joel, dealing with the Great Tribulation at some length, speaks of earthquakes and the sun becoming black (Joel 2:2, 10, 30-31). The unbelieving world as far as salvation is concerned is stricken with terror but does not sense that there is any opportunity now to repent and to be saved. Instead, they recognize it as what they feared—a time of divine wrath and judgment. In referring to the period as a day, there is no intimation that this will be limited to twenty-four hours, but rather in the length of the time period required for the fulfillment of these prophecies.

In the light of the description of this terrible time of judgment, the prospect of the church being raptured before the time of wrath becomes all the more plausible and understandable. For the church to be forced to endure such a dramatic judgment can hardly be described as a blessed hope.

The question raised at the close of chapter 6, "who can stand?" (Rev. 6:17) made clear that only those who respond to the grace of God will be able to have a victorious climax. Whether this is fulfilled by the Rapture of the church—God's gracious intervention in taking the church from earth to heaven—or whether it refers to those saved after the Rapture who stand true, even to martyrdom, in this period of Great Tribulation, only those who are saved conquer and are victorious.

### Parenthetic Revelation I:
### The Martyred Dead in Heaven; The 144,000 of Israel

*Revelation 7:1-8.* Though the Book of Revelation in its fulfillment of prophecy methodically moves through the seven seals, the seven trumpets, and the seven bowls of the wrath of God in chronological sequence, some chapters of the Book of Revelation are parenthetic, that is, they view a subject without advancing the order of events in the Tribulation. Revelation 7 is one of these chapters. In chapter 6 there was chronological fulfillment as the first six seals were opened. Now the questions is raised as to whether anyone will be saved in the Great Tribulation.

This question is particularly relevant due to the fact that Scripture pictures the Holy Spirit as being removed at the time of the Rapture. According to 2 Thessalonians 2:7, the Holy Spirit will be removed in order to allow sin to manifest itself, "For the secret power of lawlessness is already at work; but the One who now holds it back will continue to do so till He is taken out of the way." Though many interpretations have been given of this passage, the most probable is that it is referring to the Holy Spirit who in some sense will be removed from the scene to permit the wickedness of the world to be displayed after the Rapture of the church.

The question naturally is raised then: How can anyone be saved apart from the Holy Spirit? The answer is that the removal of the Holy Spirit has to be qualified. The Spirit of God will be removed in the same sense that He came on the Day of Pentecost to indwell the church and to baptize the church into one body. These works of the Holy Spirit will cease, and the situation will return to what it was before Pentecost. Before Pentecost people were saved, and the Holy Spirit was working in the world because He is always omnipresent. So it will be in this period of the end time.

In Revelation chapter 7 two groups of the saved are mentioned: First, those who are protected and made able to go through the Great Tribulation; and, second, the great multitude of martyrs who are seen standing in heaven.

John recorded, "After this I saw four angels standing at the four corners of the earth, holding back the four winds of the earth to prevent any wind from blowing on the land or on the sea or on any tree. Then I saw another angel coming up from the east, having the seal of the living God. He called out in a loud voice to the four angels who had been given power to harm the land and the sea: 'Do not harm the land or the sea or the trees until we put a seal on the foreheads of the servants of our God' " (vv. 1-3).

John then wrote, "Then I heard the number of those who were sealed: 144,000 from all the tribes of Israel" (v. 4). Then follows the itemization of 12 tribes and 12,000 from each tribe of Israel that are sealed and protected. Certain questions arise in the examination of this group. As in all listings of the 12 tribes, 1 tribe has to be eliminated as the descendants of Joseph became 2 tribes. Accordingly, in the many listings in the Old and New Testaments never more than 12 tribes are listed. Often the tribe omitted is that of Levi. Here, however, it is the tribe of Dan. There is no explanation as to why Dan is omitted except perhaps that it was one of the smaller tribes.

Scholars also have stumbled on the question as to whether this refers to Israel. A common interpretation based on the concept that Israel is no longer subject to fulfilled prophecy is that this is actually a poetic presentation of the church. The fact is, however, that many Scriptures point to the future of Israel, as has been seen in previous study and is confirmed in the Book of Revelation. Jews and Gentiles are contrasted, and in this period of the Great Tribulation the church it is not even mentioned. Accordingly, an interpretation that takes these as literal individuals from Israel is preferable.

It is also clear, however, that not all Israelites are involved in this group of 144,000, and, no doubt, many Jews will perish in the Great Tribulation. Zechariah 13:8 says specifically, " 'In the whole land,' declares the LORD, 'two-thirds will be struck down and perish; yet one-third will be left in it.' " Accordingly, the sealing of the 144,000 does not refer to the entire nation of Israel but to specific individuals who are included. No explanation is given here concerning their peculiar situation, but in Revelation 14, at the end of the Great Tribulation, the 144,000 are seen again. They are pictured as redeemed, as pure, as purchased by God and blameless (Rev. 14:1-5).

It is sometimes asserted that these are evangelists who preach the Gospel in the time of the end. There is nothing in Scripture that indicates that they preach though their character and their preservation is in itself a sermon that God is able to keep those He desires to keep even in the time of the Great Tribulation. This passage makes clear that some Jews will be saved in the end time and that some will be preserved through to the end at the time of the Second Coming.

## The Multitude of Martyrs

*Revelation 7:9-17.* In this chapter also is presented another group which John described, "After this I looked and there before me was a great multitude that no one could count, from every nation, tribe, people and language, standing before the throne and in front of the Lamb. They were wearing white robes and were holding palm branches in their hands. And they cried out in a loud voice: 'Salvation belongs to our God, who sits on the throne, and to the Lamb' " (vv. 9-10). This group is notably different than the 144,000 because they are a great multitude which is unnumbered, individuals in the group relate to every nation, tribe, people, and language, and it is clear that they are no longer in earth but in heaven.

John went on to describe the scene, "All the angels were standing around the throne and around the elders and the four living creatures. They fell down on their faces before the throne and worshiped God, saying: 'Amen! Praise and glory and wisdom and thanks and honor and power and strength be to our God forever and ever. Amen!' " (vv. 11-12) The occasion of these standing before the throne moves the angels to worship. John then recorded the answer to the question as to who these are, "Then one of the elders asked me, 'These in white robes—who are they, and where did they come from?' I answered, 'Sir, you know.' And he said, 'These are they who have come out of the Great Tribulation; they have washed their robes and made them white in the blood of the Lamb' " (vv. 13-14).

In the verses which follow they are described as those who have served the Lord. They are promised that they will never suffer hunger, thirst, or heat again and that God will wipe away every tear (vv. 16-17). It is obvious that they are martyrs who died in the Great Tribulation. Because they would not worship the world ruler, they were killed, but they will be subject to resurrection on the return of Christ in order to enter the millennial kingdom as stated in Revelation 20:4.

Though there have been many confusing interpretations of this chapter which attempt to interpret the chapter nonliterally, the literal interpretation makes so much sense in view of the prophecies of the period that it is far better than any competing theory. What would be more natural than to select Jews as a token group testifying to God's keeping power? What would be more natural than to select an equal number from each tribe? After all, Israel, as prophesied in the Old Testament, plays an important part in the end time as even Christ predicted (Matt. 24:15-20). In the Great Tribulation the presentation of many martyrs in heaven from every nation is also a natural consequence of the Great Tribulation. If the literal interpretation makes sense, why seek any other?

A number of specific conclusions can also be reached. The question has sometimes been raised as to whether Israel is lost forever as a nation and the tribal distinction erased. From a human standpoint, it may be difficult to determine a Jew's tribal relationship today; but from the divine standpoint, God knows the Israelites and to which tribe they belong. The ten tribes are not lost, but are part of the twelve tribes that belong to the nation of Israel.

The record of the many martyrs beyond count who stand in heaven in this period also is a refutation of the concept that it will be comparatively easy for saints to go through this period and be preserved to the end. Accordingly, though the teaching that the church will go through this time of Tribulation and be triumphant at its end is advanced, the evidence points to the contrary. The very severity of the Great Tribulation and the number of martyrs here indicates that most of those who come to Christ in the end time will be faced with a choice, and a large percentage of them will be executed for failure to worship the world ruler. If the church were to go through this time of awful trouble, it is doubtful how more than a small fraction would be able to survive. In the Great Tribulation there is no protection from martyrdom except for these 144,000 mentioned specifically here. The reassuring word of God's provision for these martyred dead enriches the concept of how in heaven earth's sorrows will be erased, and all the saved will be the object of God's grace.

### The Seventh Seal:
### The Sounding of the First Four Trumpets

*Revelation 8:1-13.* With the opening of chapter 8, the chronological list of prophetic events is continued. John wrote, "When He opened the seventh seal, there was silence in heaven for about a half an hour" (v. 1). Though thirty minutes is not a long time, absolute silence for such a period was ominous and an indication of tremendous events to come. It could be compared to the report of the foreman of a jury who called for thirty minutes of silence before indicating his verdict.

John recorded, "And I saw the seven angels who stand before God, and to them were given seven trumpets. Another angel, who had a golden censer, came and stood at the altar. He was given much incense to offer, with the prayers of all the saints, on the golden altar before the throne. The smoke of the incense, together with the prayers of the saints, went up before God from the angel's hand. Then the angel took the censer, filled it with fire from the altar, and hurled it on the earth; and there came peals of thunder, rumblings, flashes of lightning and an earthquake. Then the seven angels who had the seven trumpets prepared to sound them" (vv. 2-6).

The trumpets which sounded and are described in this chapter describe the sequence chronologically of the various judgments that are poured out on the world. As presented in Revelation, the seventh seal includes all seven trumpets just as the seventh trumpet includes all the seven bowls of the wrath of God. The effect is a grand crescendo which indicates that each judgment will come with increased severity and rapidity in the time just before the Second Coming.

John recorded, "The first angel sounded his trumpet, and there came hail and fire mixed with blood, and it was hurled down upon the earth. A third of the earth was burned up, a third of the trees were burned up, and all the green grass was burned up" (v. 7).

These judgments on the earth can best be taken in their literal sense. It is not clear how the hail and fire could be mixed with blood, but in a supernatural event this was possible. The result was that a third of the earth, of the trees, and of the green grass were burned up. Characteristically, the trumpets deal with one-third of the earth in contrast to the bowls of wrath in Revelation 16 which extend to the entire earth. In general, the time of the Tribulation is a period of many judgmental changes in the world, including change in climate, temperature, and rainfall. The effect of having a third of the earth and a third of the trees and a third of the grass burned up will be catastrophic because it will destroy at least a third of the earth's crops.

The tendency of expositors of trying to symbolize prophecies and explain them as nonliteral tends to obscure the truth rather than to explain what is revealed. Though some parts of the Book of Revelation obviously are symbolic, the literal effect of this trumpet is very clear and should be understood in that sense. As in the case of the first four seals broken, so the first four trumpets form a unit, and one follows the other in somewhat complementary fashion.

The second trumpet was described by John, "The second angel sounded his trumpet, and something like a huge mountain, all ablaze, was thrown into the sea. A third of the sea turned into blood, a third of the living creatures in the sea died, and a third of the ships were destroyed" (vv. 8-9). Though some expositors try to explain this in less than literal fashion, however, the Great Tribulation is so awful that a literal interpretation is a reasonable explanation.

The explanation of a huge mountain being cast into the sea may be a reference to a large object falling from heaven. It was indicated earlier in the sixth seal that stars fell to earth, and, apparently, it is not an impossibility, especially in a supernatural situation like this, for a large material object to fall into the sea. Such, of course, would be devastating as it would cause mountainous tidal waves.

Also to be explained is the statement that "A third of the sea turned into blood" (v. 8), and the question is raised as to whether this could be literal blood. The same problem exists, of course, in the plagues on Egypt when the waters of the Nile were turned to blood. Some take this as the language of appearance—that it looked like blood, but whether there was a chemical change that we do not understand or whether it was supernaturally made to be blood, the devastating effect on the sea is indicated in that a third of the living creatures in the sea died and also a third of the ships were destroyed. These are catastrophic judgments and should not be explained away. In view of the fact that they are supernatural, we should not limit God in what He is desiring to do.

John then described the results of the sounding of the third trumpet, "The third angel sounded his trumpet, and a great star, blazing like a torch, fell from the sky on a third of the rivers and on the springs of water—the name of the star is Wormwood. A third of the waters turned bitter, and many people died from the waters that had become bitter" (vv. 10-11).

There have been many attempts to find some symbolic meaning to this third trumpet, but there has been no uniformity. The best explanation again is to take it in its literal sense. The star falling from heaven was undoubtedly a large object naturally blazing as it entered the atmosphere and apparently having chemicals that made the water bitter. It is called "Wormwood," possibly a reference to the experience of the Children of Israel at Marah (Ex. 15:23-25) where the waters were bitter and a tree had to be cast into the waters to sweeten it. Here the effect seems to be chemical and physical, and the result is that many people died from the waters that had become bitter. These judgments coincided with what Christ predicted that the events of the Great Tribulation would exceed any judgment of the past or the future (Matt. 24:21).

John recorded the events related to the fourth trumpet when it is sounded, and it brought to a close the first four trumpets, each affecting a third of the earth, "The fourth angel sounded his trumpet, and a third of the sun was struck, a third of the moon, and a third of the stars, so that a third of them turned dark. A third of the day was without light, and also a third of the night. As I watched, I heard an eagle that was flying in midair call out in a loud voice: 'Woe! Woe! Woe to the inhabitants of the earth, because of the trumpet blasts about to be sounded by the other three angels!' " (vv. 12-13)

This trumpet relates to heaven in contrast to the three preceding judgments which fell on the land, sea, rivers, and fountains of water. Though judgment will fall on heaven, the dramatic effect on the earth will be tremendous. To attempt a symbolic interpretation and consider this disruption of human government or society is not justified. It is far better to take this passage in its literal sense which is in keeping with all the prophecies preceding this period which describe it as a time of unprecedented trouble.

This is supported by the next three trumpets which are described as being even worse than the first four. In these judgments that relate to various parts of God's creation, it is significant that though God created them and they were good, now they are coming under divine judgment because of sin in the world. As the blessing of God is often interpreted as relating to the physical world in which we live, so the destruction and judgment on the world indicate God's purging of the world in preparation for the millennial kingdom. Though these judgments will be fearful, they will be only the beginning as the trumpets and later the bowls of the wrath of God speak of even greater disasters.

### The Fifth Trumpet and First Woe

*Revelation 9:1-11.* As the fifth and sixth trumpets sound, a further judgment, more terrible than anything they had experienced, came on the earth.

John wrote, "The fifth angel sounded his trumpet, and I saw a star that had fallen from the sky to the earth. The star was given the key to the shaft of the Abyss. When he opened the Abyss, smoke rose from it like smoke from a gigantic furnace. The sun and sky were darkened by the smoke from the Abyss. And out of the smoke locusts came down on the earth and were given power like that of scorpions of the earth. They were told not to harm the grass of the earth or any plant or tree, but only those people who did not have the seal of God on their foreheads. They were not given power to kill them, but only to torture them for five months. And the agony they suffered was like that of a sting of a scorpion when it strikes a man. During those days men will seek death, but will not find it; they will long to die, but death will elude them" (vv. 1-6).

As the trumpets sound, each trumpet presents a disaster worse than the disaster that preceded. The great star that fell in 8:10 was a literal portion of a star that fell to the earth as described. This star here, however, was different in that it was given the key to the Abyss, a place that is best described as a place of detention for the wicked angels or demon world. Satan would spend 1,000 years here during the millennial kingdom (20:3). The star apparently is an angel who has the power to open the shaft of the Abyss and, in effect, let loose the terrible judgment represented by the fifth trumpet.

As John watched, he saw smoke pouring from the Abyss, darkening the sky. Then out of the smoke he saw locusts come out who were like scorpions on earth. If the angel that descended (described in 9:1) was a prominent angel, the scorpions seem best explained as fallen angels or the demon world. Though they took on the appearance of locusts and were given the power of scorpions, they actually were neither. They were instructed, however, not to harm the grass or any plant or tree such as had been judged in 8:7, but only those people who do not have the seal of God on their foreheads. This would deliver from harm the 144,000 of 7:4. The question as to whether those who are saved who were not protected by the seal of God would be under this judgment is not answered, but it would seem to be contrary to God's purpose to allow this judgment which comes from God to strike a man who had actually been born again.

Though most of the trumpet judgments took place in a relatively short period of time, this trumpet is defined as introducing torture for five months. The pain was compared to that of a scorpion. In tropical climates where scorpions are large, they have the power to kill small children and to inflict terrible pain. Because of this, John stated that men will want to commit suicide but will be kept from it.

Further information is given on the nature of the locusts, "The locusts looked like horses prepared for battle. On their heads they wore something like crowns of gold, and their faces resembled human faces. Their hair was like women's hair, and their teeth were like lions' teeth. They had breastplates like breastplates of iron, and the sound of their wings was like the thundering of many horses and chariots rushing into battle. They had tails and stings like scorpions, and in their tails they had power to torment people for five months.

They had as king over them the angel of the Abyss, whose name in Hebrew is Abaddon, and in Greek, Apollyon" (vv. 7-11).

Interpreters have been tempted to find some obscure or non-literal meaning of this event, but the best approach is to take it quite literally, that is, the five months are months, not an extended period of time, but probably longer than that of some of the other trumpets. Though the pain of men who are stung by the scorpion was real and compared to the pain of being stung by a scorpion in ordinary life, it is obvious that this is a picture of supernatural judgment. Demons and angels can take on appearances other than human, and the description of the locusts who stung like scorpions does not fit any category of man or beast.

The one in charge of them is called in Hebrew, Abaddon, and in Greek, Apollyon, both meaning "destroyer." The fifth trumpet, though presenting problems of interpretation that are not fully resolved, nevertheless makes clear that their effect by far exceeds the destruction and catastrophe of the preceding trumpets. As such, this trumpet is a fitting introduction to the sixth and seventh trumpets which by far exceed anything that precedes them. The fifth trumpet having fulfilled the role of the first woe, the stage is now set for the two remaining woes to come.

### The Sixth Trumpet and Second Woe

*Revelation 9:13-21.* As John observed the scene, he recorded what he saw and heard, "The sixth angel sounded his trumpet, and I heard a voice coming from the horns of the golden altar that is before God. It said to the sixth angel who had the trumpet, 'Release the four angels who are bound at the great river Euphrates.' And the four angels who had been kept ready for this very hour and day and month and year were released to kill a third of mankind" (vv. 13-15).

John who was witnessing this event from the viewpoint of heaven refers to the golden altar with four horns. This altar is the altar of incense, and its introduction refers to the prayers of saints (cf. 8:3-4). The golden altar was the altar of incense within the temple or the tabernacle in contrast to the brass altar which was outside and was used for bloody sacrifices. The golden altar was used for burning incense and worshiping God.

The voice coming from the horns of the altar, probably the voice of an angel, addressed the sixth angel, " 'Release the four angels who are bound at the great river Euphrates.' And the four angels who had been kept ready for this very hour and day and month and year were released to kill a third of mankind. The number of the mounted troops was two hundred million. I heard their number" (9:14-16). The four angels mentioned here must refer to demons or fallen angels as holy angels are never bound. They are said to have been kept ready for the very hour, day, month, and year which means that they were kept for that very day and time when this was going to take place.

The release of the four demons made possible a chain of events that would kill a third of mankind. If the fourth seal (6:8) was able to kill a fourth of the world's population, this judgment would kill a third of the remainder which would leave the world's population at fifty percent or less, depending on how many died in other judgments that are mentioned. The fact that this Great Tribulation is defined as a time of unprecedented trouble certainly is supported by the facts that are given here.

An additional fact is given that the number of the mounted troups was 200 million. John stated, "I heard their number" (9:16). Amassing an army of 200 million is usually considered an impossibility. If an army this size were to be put in the field, its origin in Asia and such countries as China and India would certainly make possible this number of people. It has been long believed that in China, for instance, that the total number of their militia, including the home guard and everyone else in the military machine, numbers 200 million. The large number has raised question whether such an army could be assembled and supplied. It would be an overwhelming source of military power. It is interesting that John said he heard the number because, obviously, he could not count that many in any vision that would be given to him. As in other cases of numbers in the Book of Revelation, the numbers should be taken literally even though the literal number sometimes has a spiritual meaning as well.

That the army would come from the East is indicated by the fact that the four angels were in the Euphrates River, the eastern border of the Holy Land. This is confirmed by later reference in 16:12 how the River Euphrates is dried up, permitting the passage of the armies from the East. Today Russia has built a series of dams along the Euphrates River and makes possible drying up the river.

The army from the East is also mentioned in Daniel 11:44 as having part in the great final war before the Second Coming.

Having introduced the main significance of the great army, John gave further details concerning their character, "The horses and riders I saw in my vision looked like this: Their breastplates were fiery red, dark blue, and yellow as sulfur. The heads of the horses resembled the heads of lions, and out of their mouths came fire, smoke and sulfur. A third of mankind was killed by the three plagues of fire, smoke and sulfur that came out of their mouths. The power of the horses was in their mouths and in their tails; for their tails were like snakes, having heads with which they inflict injury" (Rev. 9:17-19).

The description of the horses does not resemble what is true of a horse, and some have suggested that they represent a form of modern warfare such as tanks which would be the source of fire power, smoke and sulfur. There is no explanation of the horses apart from what is given here. Some believe that the army is an army of demons—a supernatural force rather than a purely natural army. The devastating effect of such a large force, whether human or demonic, is in harmony with the result.

John went on to say, "The rest of mankind that were not killed with these plagues still did not repent of the work of their hands; they did not stop worshiping demons, and idols of gold, silver, bronze, stone and wood—idols that cannot see or hear or walk. Nor did they repent of their murders, their magic arts, their sexual immorality or their thefts" (vv. 20-21). Though they had observed God's terrible judgment which resulted in a third of the human race being put to death, they still would not repent of their evil deeds. The Book of Revelation, on the one hand, displays the mighty judgments of God but also the utter depravity of the human heart untouched by the grace of God. Though the wicked had the worship of idols as their religion, it did not redeem them or change them, and they continued in their life of sin.

### Parenthetic Revelation II:
### Angelic Announcement and the Two Witnesses

*Revelation 10:1-11.* Having carried the chain of events of the Great Tribulation through the sixth trumpet, John, before the seventh trumpet, introduced a parenthetical section which does not advance the series of events in the Great Tribulation.

John wrote, "Then I saw another mighty angel coming down from heaven. He was robed in a cloud, with a rainbow above his head; his face was like the sun, and his legs were like fiery pillars. He was holding a little scroll, which lay open in his hand. He planted his right foot on the sea and his left foot on the land, and he gave a loud shout like the roar of a lion. When he shouted, the voices of the seven thunders spoke. And when the seven thunders spoke, I was about to write; but I heard a voice from heaven saying, 'Seal up what the seven thunders have said and do not write it down' " (vv. 1-4).

The mighty angel is described in a way that almost is similar to the glory of God, and for this and other reasons, a number of interpreters believe that this is none other than the Lord Jesus Christ Himself appearing as an angel. Throughout the Old Testament Christ did appear as the Angel of Jehovah.

A number of reasons, however, militate against the concept that this is Christ Himself and leads to the conclusion that this is an angel who had been given great power by God.

The angel is introduced as "another" angel (Gr., *allon*) which identified the angel as of the same kind as the previous angels (v. 1). Though not the sixth angel mentioned in 9:13, and not the angel that sounds the seventh trumpet (11:15), the angel seems to come short of the attributes of God. As "the mighty angel," he is similar to the angel mentioned in 5:2.

The angel here also is said to come down from heaven, and there is no Scripture that indicates that Christ would return to the earth during the Great Tribulation prior to His second coming. Other angels are granted great power such as Michael who heads all the holy angels. The description of the angel, however, that he is "robed in a cloud, with a rainbow above his head" is very graphic. His feet are compared to "fiery pillars," and his face is compared to the brilliance of the sun. He is pictured as planting his feet on the ocean, his right foot on the sea and his left foot on the land, which is the opposite order, for usually the earth is mentioned before the sea (5:13; 7:1-3; 12:12; 14:7). Obviously, standing on the sea requires the supernatural stance that standing on the land might not require.

The most important fact about him is that he has a scroll in his hand (Gr., *biblaridon*). Accordingly, it should not be confused with the scroll mentioned in 5:1 in heaven (Gr., *biblion*). No information is given concerning what the scroll contains, but it probably represents the Word of God. In addition to all the other elements that make this angel an unusual person, John declares, "He gave a loud shout like the roar of a lion" (10:3). When this happens, John recorded that seven thunders spoke up (v. 4). Apparently, the thunders uttered something that John could understand and he was about to write it down when he was forbidden to do so (v. 4).

This mighty angel now makes the important announcement that there will be no more delay (v. 6). In the history of the saints in all ages God has been called on to fulfill His Word. The prospect of a great time of trouble preceding the second coming of Christ is found frequently in both the Old and New Testaments. Now its further fulfillment is predicted to follow immediately.

Because six trumpets have already sounded, John was informed that when the seventh trumpet sounds, it will introduce the mystery of God, apparently a reference to details about the second coming of Christ not previously revealed. The prophecy to be fulfilled will be the full revelation of the glory of God which will fulfill what the prophets had predicted.

Having brought to conclusion the first part of the announcement that there would be no delay, John was now informed concerning the second important event of this chapter. He wrote, "Then the voice that I had heard from heaven spoke to me once more: 'Go, take the scroll that lies open in the hand of the angel who is standing on the sea and on the land.' So I went to the angel and asked him to give me the little scroll. He said to me, 'Take it and eat it. It will turn your stomach sour, but in your mouth it will be as sweet as honey.' I took the little scroll from the angel's hand and ate it. It tasted as sweet as honey in my mouth, but when I had eaten it, my stomach turned sour. Then I was told, 'You must prophesy again about many peoples, nations, languages and kings' " (vv. 8-11).

This command to John to eat the book has a parallel in Ezekiel (Ezek. 2:9–3:4) and also in Jeremiah (Jer. 15:16-18). No comment is made in the Scripture concerning this act of eating the scroll, but it would seem most probable that this represents the Word of God. Heeding the scroll means to partake of its promises and contents as well as its predictions of judgment and live in keeping with its pronouncements.

The experience which John has that the Word is sweet, indicates the many wonderful promises of the Word of God, its marvelous grace, and its revelation of the love of God. The psalmist spoke in a similar way of the sweetness of the truth of the Lord (Ps. 19:9-10).

But the Word of God also has its bitter side. There are chapters that deal with divine judgment, and believers sometimes experience great difficulty, suffering, and even martyrdom. John himself was experiencing suffering as he was in exile here on the isle away from Christian friends and place of ministry and without normal comforts of life. The revelation which was being given to John also was bitter, and it indicated God's dealing in wrath with the wicked world.

The symbolism of inviting John to eat the scroll, however, extends to others who need the truth of the Word of God. Just as John partook of it, so those who face reception of the Word of God should accept it as from the Lord. Though the bitterness may appear at times in life and in this world, the ultimate glory of God will be the portion of all those who put their trust in Christ. John was also reassured that his stay on the Isle of Patmos was not permanent, and that he was destined to speak to many people (v. 11).

### Ministry of the Two Witnesses

*Revelation 11:1-13.* Continuing the parenthetical section, beginning with 10:1, John then recorded the strange case of the two witnesses that were raised by God for this period.

Before introducing the witnesses, however, he was given a reed and instructed to measure the temple. He wrote, "I was given a reed like a measuring rod and was told, 'Go and measure the temple of God and the altar, and count the worshipers there. But exclude the outer court; do not measure it, because it has been given to the Gentiles. They will trample on the holy city for 42 months'" (11:1-2).

No explanation is given of this command, but its symbolism probably is to the point that they are measured and found short. In the Great Tribulation the temple has already been desecrated, sacrifices stopped, and the worship of the world ruler installed instead (Dan. 9:27; 12:11-12; Matt. 24:15; 2 Thes. 2:4; Rev. 13:14-15). Measuring the temple will indicate the apostasy of the nation of Israel and their need for revival and restoration.

The Holy City, Jerusalem, according to the Scripture, will be trampled underfoot of Gentiles for the final forty-two months preceding the Second Coming. This has actually been true ever since 600 B.C. because from then to the time of the Great Tribulation, Israel never was in full possession of their holy places except by Gentile tolerance and permission. This is still true today as Israel could not retain its independence without the help of the United States. The forty-two months, however, refer to the Great Tribulation as a time when the holy place in the temple will be desecrated especially, and the Great Tribulation will run its course, climaxing in the second coming of Christ (13:5). Though there have been brief periods in the history of Israel when Israel temporarily retained control of the holy place, it will never be permanently theirs until the second coming of Christ.

John was then introduced to those who were called "two witnesses" who will be prophets in the end time. Their prophecy will cover 1,260 days, or forty-two months, the same length of time that the world ruler will possess the temple and turn it into a religous center for the worship of himself.

John described their unusual witness, " 'And I will give power to My two witnesses, and they will prophesy for 1,260 days, clothed in sackcloth.' These are the two olive trees and the two lampstands that stand before the Lord of the earth. If anyone tries to harm them, fire comes from their mouths and devours their enemies. This is how anyone who wants to harm them must die. These men have power to shut up the sky so that it will not rain during the time they are prophesying; and they have power to turn the waters into blood and to strike the earth with every kind of plague as often as they want" (11:3-6).

The reference to the two witnesses as being symbolized by the two olive trees and the two lampstands probably has reference to Zechariah 4 where the lampstand and two trees are discussed. The meaning of this to Zerubbabel, who was one of the important leaders in Israel in Zechariah's time, was that their witness was empowered by the oil from the olive tree, symbolic of being empowered by the Holy Spirit (Zech. 4:1-14).

Because the last seven years leading up to the second coming of Christ will be divided into two periods of 1,260 days each, it may be debated which of these two periods is in view here. The situation as described, however, clearly corresponds to the Great Tribulation when the holy place in the temple will be desecrated and the Jews will be under persecution. In that situation in the Great Tribulation where thousands have died as martyrs, the emergence of these two witnesses who cannot be killed introduces a world problem for those who are operating the world government.

The two witnesses, obviously, have unusual power comparable to the power of Elijah and some of the other prophets, and they can inflict plagues much as Moses did in Egypt. Because of the unusual character of these two witnesses, a great deal of speculation has arisen as to who they are. The Scriptures do not indicate any identification. Because Elijah and Enoch went to heaven without dying, some claim that these two witnesses are Enoch and Elijah returned to earth. However, the rule that it is appointed once to die was not only not observed in the case of Elijah and Enoch, but will be true of the entire church when the church is raptured from the earth. Others attempt to relate it to Elijah and Moses because the power and ministry of the two witnesses is similar.

In view of the fact that the Bible does not indicate who they are, it is probably safe to recognize them as two witnesses who will appear in the end time who are not related to any previous historical character.

The time comes, however, when God is going to permit the witnesses to be overcome. John wrote, "Now when they have finished their testimony, the beast that comes up from the Abyss will attack them, and overpower and kill them. Their bodies will lie in the street of the great city, which is figuratively called Sodom and Egypt, where also their Lord was crucified. For three-and-a-half days men from every people, tribe, language and nation will gaze on their bodies and refuse them burial. The inhabitants of the earth will gloat over them and will celebrate by sending each other gifts, because these two prophets had tormented those who live on the earth" (vv. 7-10).

The question has been raised concerning the fact that the entire world is able to gaze on their bodies though they actually are lying in the street of Jerusalem. In the modern world with television capability, this becomes something that could be easily fulfilled. Accordingly, all the greater impact would be achieved if their resurrection were also being telecast at the time it took place.

John continued, "But after the three-and-a-half days a breath of life from God entered them, and they stood on their feet, and terror struck those who saw them. Then they heard a loud voice from heaven saying to them, 'Come up here.' And they went up to heaven in a cloud, while their enemies looked on. At that very hour there was a severe earthquake and a tenth of the city collapsed. Seven thousand people were killed in the earthquake, and the survivors were terrified and gave glory to the God of heaven" (vv. 11-13).

The resurrection of the two witnesses becomes an important testimony to the world at a time when the world was given to the worship of the world ruler, and Satan seemed to be reigning supreme. Even though God was permitting the terrible events of the Great Tribulation to take place, including the catastrophes that will overtake most of the human race, it is also evident that God is still in control and can provide a ministry of testimony to the world even under these circumstances.

### The Seventh Trumpet and the Reaction in Heaven, the Third Woe

*Revelation 11:15-19.* The entire passage of Revelation from chapter 10 through chapter 14 is parenthetic and does not advance the narrative except for the injection at this point of the sounding of the seventh trumpet, the details of which will be unfolded in chapter 15. At the time of the seventh trumpet, the announcement from heaven is made, "The kingdom of the world has become the kingdom of our Lord and of His Christ, and He will reign forever and ever" (11:15).

The reaction in heaven is described and forms an ominous preparation for the tremendous catastrophes which will be a part of the bowls of the wrath of God contained in the seventh trumpet.

John recorded, "And the twenty-four elders, who were seated on their thrones before God, fell on their faces and worshiped God, saying: 'We give thanks to You, Lord God Almighty, the One who is and who was, because You have taken Your great power and have begun to reign. The nations were angry; and Your wrath has come. The time has come for judging the dead, and for rewarding Your servants the prophets and Your saints and those who reverence Your name, both small and great—and for destroying those who destroy the earth' " (vv. 16-18). Chronologically, the seventh trumpet is close to the time of the second coming of Christ as the contents of seventh trumpet, the bowls of wrath of Revelation 15–16, lead immediately to the time of the second coming of Christ.

Ominous sounds are heard in heaven pointing to the awfulness of the catastrophes that are yet ahead. John wrote, "Then God's temple in heaven was opened, and within His temple was seen the ark of His covenant. And there came flashes of lightning, rumblings, peals of thunder, an earthquake and a great hailstorm" (v. 19).

### Parenthetic Revelation III: Seven Important Personages

*Revelation 12:1-17.* The parenthetic section which began with 10:1 is interrupted by the sounding of the seventh trumpet now focused on important persons who will be prominent in the end times.

## The Woman with Child

John next recorded prophecy concerning a woman with a child, "A great and wondrous sign appeared in heaven: a woman clothed with the sun, with the moon under her feet and a crown of twelve stars on her head. She was pregnant and cried out in pain as she was about to give birth" (12:1-2).

One of the important problems in the interpretation of prophecy through the centuries of the church has been the tendency to take passages that relate to Israel and interpret them as dealing with the church in the present age. This problem appears in this chapter as some have said the woman represents the church. In order to make this prophecy relate to the church, it requires nonliteral interpretation without any real fulfillment of the predictive elements. A far better explanation is that this relates to Israel as this is supported by the details of the prophecy.

Seven important personages are presented in Revelation 12–14: (1) The woman representing Israel (12:1-5), (2) The dragon, or Satan (12:7-17; 13:1-2, 4, 11), (3) The Man-child, Christ (12:4-16), (4) Michael, representing the angels (vv. 7-9), (5) The remnant of Israel represented by the 144,000 (7:4-8; 14:1-5), (6) The beast out of the sea, the world dictator of the end time (13:1-8), (7) The beast out of the earth (vv. 11-17), a religious leader who is a false prophet and supports the world dictator. If the predictions of this portion of Revelation are to be properly interpreted, it is necessary to give close attention to the details concerning each person. The woman is not the church or Jesus Christ, but is Israel seen as the matrix from which Jesus Christ came.

In Scripture a woman is frequently used to represent different entities. For instance, Jezebel represents a false religion (2:20). The harlot of Revelation 17 is the apostate church of the end time. The bride, the Lamb's wife (19:7), represents the church joined to Christ in glory. Israel is also represented as the wife of Jehovah who was unfaithful. In this description true Israel, or that portion of Israel standing true to God, is in view.

The statement that she is "clothed with the sun, with the moon under her feet" (12:1) is an allusion to Joseph's dream in which he saw the saw the sun, moon, and eleven stars bowing down to him (Gen. 37:9). The sun and the moon in this context refer to Jacob and Rachel, the forebearers of Israel. The woman is also said to

576

have "a crown of twelve stars on her head" (v. 1). In Joseph's dream also the stars, or the sons of Israel, are intended with the twelfth star, including Joseph himself who was not in the dream as such.

Israel is obviously important in the history of the world and the outworking of the purposes of God, and so many blessings have been derived through the sons of Jacob, such as the Bible, the prophets, the apostles, and Christ Himself.

The fact that the woman is pregnant and in pain refers to the experience of Israel down through the centuries, waiting the coming of her Messiah. Her sufferings refer to the nation as a whole, not to Mary the mother of Jesus.

John recorded, "Then another sign appeared in heaven: an enormous red dragon with seven heads and ten horns and seven crowns on his head" (v. 3). This sign is called a "wonder" in the KJV, but the word for wonder is not used here. Rather, it is a "sign." The enormous red dragon with seven heads and ten horns and seven crowns on his heads refers to the Roman Empire (cf. Dan. 7:7; Rev. 13:1), particularly in the end time, but also to the power of the Roman Empire at the time of Christ's birth. Revelation 13 reveals more concerning this red dragon, with the ten horns representing ten countries constituting the nucleus of the beast's empire, the seven heads and seven crowns referring to the principal rulers of the empire either in history or in prophecy. John predicted that the tail of the beast will throw a third part of the stars to the earth, probably referring to the time of his power in the end time when he eventually will conquer the world at the beginning of the Great Tribulation.

The dragon is pictured as awaiting the birth of the man child to devour it as soon as it is born (12:4). This, of course, refers to the birth of Christ and the attempts of Herod to destroy the Infant Jesus. It was necessary for Joseph and Mary and Jesus to go to Egypt for the early years of Jesus' life in order to escape Herod's desire to destroy Him (Matt. 2:16-18). John then recorded, "She gave birth to a Son, a male child, who will rule all the nations with an iron scepter. And her child was snatched up to God and to His throne. The woman fled into the desert to a place prepared for her by God, where she might be taken care of for 1,260 days" (Rev. 12:5-6).

Expositors have argued concerning the identity of the child, some preferring it to represent the church rather than Christ Himself. The text, however, indicates that the child born is a male child. If it were the church, it would probably be in the feminine. He is also described as the one "who will rule all nations with an iron scepter" (v. 5). This is prophesied in Revelation 19:5 as referring to Christ and fulfilled in the millennial kingdom as predicted in Psalm 2:9, "You will rule them with an iron scepter; You will dash them to pieces like pottery." Christ is also prophesied as the Ruler over Israel, but here is pictured in a more gentle fashion (Luke 1:32-33).

The statement that the child will be "snatched up to God and to His throne" (12:5) has also been debated, some referring it to the deliverance from Egypt after Herod was dead. It is probable, however, that it refers to the ascension of Christ. The expression "snatched up" is too strong an expression to refer to the journey of Christ from Egypt to Nazareth. The same word is used of the Rapture of the church (1 Thes. 4:17), of Paul being caught up to heaven in his vision (2 Cor. 12:2, 4), and the catching up of Philip by the Spirit of God (Acts 8:39). If the church is represented by the twenty-four elders, it would seem to mix metaphors to refer to the church as a male child, especially as the church is referred to as the wife (Rev. 19:7-8).

The statement, "The woman fled into the desert to a place prepared for her by God, where she might be taken care of for 1,260 days" (12:6), is reference to Israel being preserved through the Great Tribulation. This is also predicted in Old Testament prophecy in Jeremiah 30:7, "How awful that day will be! None will be like it. It will be a time of trouble for Jacob, but he will be saved out of it." The 1,260 days is the exact length of the Great Tribulation which will culminate in the second coming of Christ. Though many in Israel will perish (Zech. 13:8), Israel as a nation will be preserved and be rescued by Christ when He comes (Ezek. 20:33-38; Rom. 11:26-27).

The beginning of the Great Tribulation, which is Israel's special time of trouble, is also marked by war in heaven. John wrote, "And there was war in heaven. Michael and his angels fought against the dragon, and the dragon and his angels fought back. But he was not strong enough, and they lost their place in heaven. The great dragon was hurled down—that ancient serpent called the devil, or Satan, who leads the whole world astray. He was hurled to the earth, and his angels with him" (Rev. 12:7-9). Earlier the Roman Empire is pictured as the dragon (v. 4), but here the dragon is identified as Satan himself who especially is in control of the world government at the period before the Second Coming. Until this event takes place, Satan is allowed in heaven and accuses the brethren as he did in the case of Job. The casting of Satan to the earth also marks the beginning of the most awful period in human history, the Great Tribulation.

John recorded the voice from heaven commemorating this event, "Now have come the salvation and the power and the kingdom of our God, and the authority of His Christ. For the accuser of our brothers, who accuses them before our God day and night, has been hurled down. They overcame him by the blood of the Lamb and by the word of their testimony; they did not love their lives so much as to shrink from death. Therefore rejoice, you heavens and you who dwell in them! But woe to the earth and the sea, because the devil has gone down to you! He is filled with fury, because he knows that his time is short" (vv. 10-12).

The long activity of Satan in heaven now comes to its close and with it the intensified activities of Satan on earth. Those who overcame Satan did so by "the blood of the Lamb" (v. 11), by their faithful testimony, and their willingness to be martyrs if necessary (v. 11). On earth there would continue to be many martyrs through the Great Tribulation. Satan knows prophecy and believes his time is short (v. 12).

Further attention is given to the activities of Satan during the Great Tribulation. John recorded, "When the dragon saw that he had been hurled to the earth, he pursued the woman who had given birth to the male child. The woman was given the two wings of a great eagle, so that she might fly to the place prepared for her in the desert, where she would be taken care of for a time, times and half a time, out of the serpent's reach" (vv. 13-14).

The time period here is the same as the 1,260 days mentioned earlier as the term "time" refers to one year, "times," two years, plus a half time or a total of three-and-a-half years (cf. Dan. 7:25; 12:7). As previously explained, though many in Israel will perish as warned by Christ (Matt. 24:15-22), some believe that there will be a specific place in the desert where Israel can flee; others take it as representative of the safety of those who survive. The description of Satan as the devil has in it the thought of slandering or defaming (Gr., *diabolos*) and is used some fourteen times in the Book of Job as well as elsewhere in Scripture (1 Chron. 21:1; Ps. 109:6; Zech. 3:1-2). Satan is the opponent of Christ, and just as Christ defends the believers, Satan accuses them.

John further recorded, "Then from his mouth the serpent spewed water like a river, to overtake the woman and sweep her away with the torrent. But the earth helped the woman by opening its mouth and swallowing the river that the dragon had spewed out of his mouth. Then the dragon was enraged at the woman and went off to make war against the rest of her offspring—those who obey God's commandments and hold to the testimony of Jesus" (vv. 15-17). Though the power of Satan is tremendous, so is the strength given believers in that hour who are said to conquer through the blood of the Lamb and their testimony (v. 11).

The flood which issues from Satan is probably a symbolic picture of all that Satan is doing to destroy Israel. This would include false teaching which in the end time would come in like a flood. Circumstances of the Great Tribulation also would test their faith sorely in the fulfillment of the promise of the Messiah's coming. Satan not only attempts to persecute Israel but all others who obey God's commandments. This is, of course, illustrated in Revelation 7:9-17 and the many other Scriptures that speak of the horrors of the Great Tribulation.

This chapter from the standpoint of time has to be considered as occurring before Revelation 6 if this is the time of the beginning of the Great Tribulation. Parenthetic sections which deal with specific subjects are not chronological in their presentation but give a broad view of the activities of the period.

**Parenthetic Revelation III: The Coming World Dictator**
*Revelation 13:1-10.* In this chapter prophecy focuses on the coming world government and the beast and the false prophet who lead it. This gathers in many prophecies throughout Scripture that speak of this crucial end time of three-and-a-half years, culminating in the second coming of Christ.

Having introduced the main characters of the end time, including Israel, the dragon, Christ, and Satan, the revelation given to John goes on to describe the important personages that dominate the Great Tribulation, including the beast, the coming world ruler, and the false prophet, the religious assistant of the beast who will support him throughout the period.

The chapter opens with a revelation of the world ruler as the dragon standing on the shore of the sea contemplating the scene. In the KJV, using a different text, it states that John stood on the shore of the sea. Which of the two readings is correct does not affect the outcome of this chapter. John wrote, "And I saw a beast coming out of the sea. He had ten horns and seven heads, with ten crowns on his horns, and on each head a blasphemous name. The beast I saw resembled a leopard, but had feet like those of a bear and a mouth like that of a lion. The dragon gave the beast his power and his throne and great authority" (vv. 1-2).

The identity of the beast is that it represents the revived Roman Empire and its ruler in the end time. Revelation here corresponds to the description given in Daniel 7:7-8; Revelation 12:3; 17:3, 7. This passage makes plain that the beast, the future world ruler, will come out of the Mediterranean situation with the sea representing the mass of humanity.

The empire is seen here in the form it will take after three of the ten nations that form its beginning are overthrown and come under the power of the beast (cf. Dan. 7:8). The ten horns represent ten governments as the horn is the symbol of political power, as illustrated in Daniel 7-8. The crowns are diadems or the emblem of governmental authority. Their blasphemous names indicate that they are opposed to God. Interpreters interpret the seven heads in various ways, sometimes phases of government which precede, but more likely referring to the principal authorities that headed these future governments.

John recorded, "The beast I saw resembled a leopard, but had feet like those of a bear and a mouth like that of a lion" (Rev. 13:2). In Daniel's description of the four great world empires preceding the kingdom from heaven in Daniel 7, the four great empires are described as beasts. The Babylonian power was represented as the lion (v. 4), the Medo-Persian Empire as the bear (v. 5), the leopard was Alexander the Great in his conquest (v. 6), and the beast of Revelation 13:1-7, who is not named, represented the future Roman Empire.

The first three of these empires, of course, are fulfilled prophecy, now history, and the first two of them were observed by Daniel himself. Though some attempt other explanations, the only empire since that of Alexander that is worthy of consideration is the Roman Empire, by far the greatest of all empires of the ancient world and one with the longest history as a world power and one with the greatest influence on subsequent civilization.

The point in having these three animals represented in the beast of the sea is that the final world ruler gathers into his power all the power of the preceding rulers and their territory, and as the Scriptures go on to teach, eventually becomes ruler over the entire globe, something that had never been accomplished before.

John also pointed out, "The dragon gave the beast his power and his throne and great authority" (v. 2). Behind the political government of the end time and its world rule is the power of Satan himself. The human world ruler is representative of Satan, much as Christ is the representative of God the Father. The final political power therefore is evil and opposed to everything that stands for the things of God.

John also gave a description of the beast and his worship and introduces some revelation that has caused a great deal of discussion. He wrote, "One of the heads of the beast seemed to have had a fatal wound, but the fatal wound had been healed. The whole world was astonished and followed the beast. Men worshiped the dragon because he had given authority to the beast, and they also worshiped the beast and asked, 'Who is like the beast? Who can make war against him?' " (vv. 3-4)

It is questionable whether Satan is able to raise one from the dead. It would be hard to explain how God would raise such a wicked person from the dead. There has been much discussion about the fatal wound that is described as being healed. Through the history of the church this description has suggested to various expositors the revival from the dead of some great personage of the past to assume this role, including such people as Judas Iscariot, Nero, and in more modern times, Mussolini, Hitler, and Stalin. The fact that there are so many possible candidates seems to militate against this explanation. It also has the problem that if Satan cannot raise one from the dead, it would require God to raise this person from the dead to fulfill his role.

Other explanations are better. One of the common ones is that what is described here is not the beast himself but the empire which he represents. The Roman Empire seemingly has been dead for centuries though it had a long history. The fact that it is resurrected at this time would seem to indicate that while the empire had a fatal wound that should have caused its demise, what we are seeing is a revival of the Roman Empire similar to the revival of a dead person.

Another possible explanation is that the ruler suffers an assassination attempt and is wounded with a wound that would normally cause death. It is within the power of Satan to heal, and it is possible that he would heal this ruler and restore him to life. In any event and regardless of what the interpretation is, the supernatural origin and special powers of this world ruler are revealed. As the world watched him, as the Scripture indicates, they were attracted to him as their world ruler and astonished at his powers.

Because a supernatural element was involved in his rule and supplemented by the supernatural power of Satan, they naturally ask the question of whether anyone was equal to the beast and who could make war with him. It is out of this background that the world worshiped the man and also worshiped Satan who is the power behind the world ruler. The final form of apostasy and departure from God is to worship a man instead of worshiping God and to worship Satan who sought to be like God (Isa. 14:14).

In the background of this description of the beast and the declaration that no one was able to stand against him, there may have been a fulfillment of Ezekiel 38–39 with a great war as Russia and her allies attacked Israel from the North only to be destroyed. With Russia probably the leading world power in the world, or at least in the Middle East, her destruction, as described in Ezekiel 38 and 39, would remove the only great military power in the world at that time. There is no indication that countries in the western hemisphere, such as the United States, would come into play at this time, and it is probable that they had less political power than they did previously.

The result of all this is that the beast out of the sea is able to become world leader and rule for the final three-and-a-half years, or forty-two months, leading up to the second coming of Christ. John recorded this, "The beast was given a mouth to utter proud words and blasphemies and to exercise his authority for forty-two months" (Rev. 13:5).

Like the rulers of the great empires of the past, and in particular those who headed up the Roman Empire who are described as having blasphemous names (v. 1), so the final ruler, a Gentile power, will engage in blasphemy against God. John wrote, "He opened his mouth to blaspheme God, and to slander His name and His dwelling place and those who live in heaven" (v. 6).

The extent of his power is stated next, "He was given power to make war against the saints and to conquer them. And he was given authority over every tribe, people, language and nation" (v. 7). The Scriptures leave no doubt that this is an actual political government that extends over the entire globe. This, of course, was in keeping with what Daniel predicted when he stated that the final world ruler "will devour the whole earth, trampling it down and crushing it" (Dan. 7:23). During most of the final three-and-a-half years, the world ruler has power to cause the saints to be martyred, as previously revealed in Revelation 7:9-17. His authority extended to the entire globe and to every people on the globe. Enforcing his position as leader, he is worshiped as God, "All inhabitants of the earth will worship the beast — all whose names have not been written in the Book of Life belonging to the Lamb that was slain from the Creation of the world" (13:8).

While the prophecy states that all on earth will worship the beast, there is the grand exception of those whose names are written in the Book of Life. There is some question whether the translation which indicates that the Lamb was slain from the Creation of the world is the proper interpretation. Though this translation follows the Greek order of words, the preferable interpretation is that "from the Creation of the world" refers to the Book of Life rather than to the Lamb.

Some problems have arisen in the interpretation of this passage. The Book of Life mentioned in Revelation 3:5 promises that those who are overcomers will not be blotted out of the book. They view the Book of Life as enrolling the saved when they are saved. Others believe that the book is not the book of the saved but the book of all living whose names are in the book until they pass the point of no return in death. A further reference in Revelation 22:19 probably is a reference to the Tree of Life rather than the Book of Life.

According to the best texts, the abundant evidence in Scripture that a soul once saved is saved eternally casts light on the interpretation of this passage. The resultant meaning is that those who are not saved will worship the beast, and those who are saved will not.

As frequently observed in the letters to the seven churches, invitations are given to the individual, "He who has an ear, let him hear. If anyone is to go into captivity, into captivity he will go. If anyone is to be killed with the sword, with the sword he will be killed. This calls for patient endurance and faithfulness on the part of the saints" (13:9-10).

This emphasizes the sovereignty of God which takes into consideration the response of individuals to the Gospel message. An invitation to those who hear is frequently found in the Scripture (Matt. 11:15; 13:9, 43; Mark 4:9, 23; 8:18; Luke 8:8; 14:34). The invitation here is not addressed to the churches as in Revelation 2–3 since the church has already been raptured, but to individuals. The saints can rest in the fact that God honors sincere faith in coming to Him. Though this may not prevent them from being martyred, it assures them, nevertheless, eternal blessing in the presence of God. On the other hand, those who are wicked and who deserve punishment will receive it in time or in eternity. The saints recognizing that God is not settling all accounts in this world, should have patience and endurance, trusting God who is handling their personal life.

Taken as a whole, this passage clearly predicts a future world government which will arise from the ruler in the Middle East who first conquers ten countries, then later is able to proclaim himself dictator of the whole world for the last three-and-a-half years preceding the second coming of Christ. The character of this period and the things that will occur in it support the concept that those in the church, who have put their trust in Christ and have been promised that they will not experience the wrath of God, will be raptured before this period begins, in fact, more than seven years before the second coming of Christ.

### Parenthetic Revelation III: The Beast out of the Land

*Revelation 13:11-18.* A second personage is introduced and John wrote, "Then I saw another beast, coming out of the earth. He had two horns like a lamb, but he spoke like a dragon. He exercised all the authority of the first beast on his behalf, and made the earth and its inhabitants worship the first beast, whose fatal wound had been healed" (vv. 11-12). Considerable attention has been given this passage by interpreters who try to determine who this person is. The fact that he comes out of the earth refers to the fact that he comes out of the world, not simply the land of Palestine. The fact that he had two horns would indicate he had some authority as a political character, and he also was pictured as a lamb which would point to the fact that he has religious character which is supported by the fact that he is called a prophet in Revelation 19:20. Though many attempts have been made to read into this passage more than it says, it does not indicate his racial background or his geographical background, and it is probable he was a Gentile revealed here to be a supporting character who has some of the supernatural power of the world ruler, but he uses this power to cause people to worship the world ruler.

In the process of supporting the rule of the world dictator, the beast out of the sea performs miraculous works, "And he performed great and miraculous signs, even causing fire to come down from heaven to earth in full view of men. Because of the signs he was given power to do on behalf of the first beast, he deceived the inhabitants of the earth. He ordered them to set up an image in honor of the beast who was wounded by the sword and yet lived" (vv. 13-14). It is often overlooked that Satan has miraculous powers though limited and less extensive than that of God.

As a false prophet, the beast out of the earth (v. 13) was able to provide some basis for belief in the beast out of the sea through the miracles he performed. As a part of his work in getting people to honor the first beast, he sets up an image of the beast which, though it is not stated, may well have been an idol depicting the beast himself. The image is referred to several times in this chapter and also six more times (Rev. 14:9, 11; 15:2; 16:2; 19:20; 20:4). Because the fire had come down from heaven, he, no doubt, compared himself to some of Elijah's miracles (2 Kings 1:10-12) or to the Day of Pentecost (Acts 2:3). Also, in Revelation 11:5 in connection with the two witnesses, they had the power to kill when the fire came out of their mouth.

Once the image had been made, he gave it the capacity to have breath, "He was given power to give breath to the image of the first beast, so that it could speak and cause all who refused to worship the image to be killed" (13:15). Though some have interpreted this as giving the image life, it is rather that he was able to contrive, either supernaturally or naturally, the impression that the beast was breathing. In any case, he caused people to worship this beast, and if they did not, they would be put to death.

One of the most commented-on aspects of his work was the introduction of a mark indicating the worshipers of the beast. John recorded, "He also forced everyone, small and great, rich and poor, free and slave, to receive a mark on his right hand or on his forehead, so that no one could buy or sell unless he had the mark, which is the name of the beast or the number of his name. This calls for wisdom. If anyone has insight, let him calculate the number of the beast, for it is man's number. His number is 666" (vv. 16-18).

The step requiring people to have a mark, either on their forehead or on their right hand, to identify them as worshipers of the beast, is not hard to understand as various types of identification are used for beasts today, such as cattle, fish, birds, and others. The enforcement applied to all, and the six classes of people referred to here cover the entire human race. Because this mark was absolutely essential to either buy or sell, it put tremendous pressure on Christians who would resist this as they would be helpless to conduct ordinary business and to care for their loved ones.

The number of the beast, as mentioned in verse 18, has called for extensive study. The Bible itself does not interpret the "666." Because in some languages the alphabet that is used has numerical value, some felt that this pointed to the beast as a character out of the past whose name in its numerical value would reveal the number "666." Accordingly, schemes abounded where many different names were suggested.

Probably the most widely recognized numerical system is found in Latin where the capital V represents 5, X represents 10, C represents 100, with corresponding values in other numbers. The task of the expositor was to find a name which, with the letters added up in their numerical equivalency, would add up to 666. Many characters of history were so identified, often using an alphabet that yielded the right numbers. All attempts to date to use this method have failed.

Though there may be more light cast on it at the time this prophecy is fulfilled, the passage itself declares that this number is "man's number." In the Book of Revelation the number "7" is one of the most significant numbers indicating perfection. Accordingly, there are seven seals, seven trumpets, seven bowls of the wrath of God, seven thunders, etc. This beast claims to be God, and if that were the case, he should be 777. This passage, in effect, says, No, you are only 666. You are short of deity even though you were originally created in the image and likeness of God. Most of the speculation on the meaning of this number is without profit or theological significance.

The important revelation of this chapter is that world history leading up to the second coming of Christ will be dominated by these two characters, especially in the last three-and-a-half years before the Second Coming. The world ruler will actually for a time exercise political authority over the entire world and the supporting character, the beast out of the earth, will give his support supernaturally and cause people to worship the world ruler. The worship of this world ruler and the recognition of Satan also as deity brings apostasy to its most dramatic revelation. The evil in Satan's and men's hearts is allowed its full manifestation but will be subject to the judgment of God at the time of the Second Coming.

### Parenthetic Revelation III:
### Vision of the 144,000 on Mount Zion

The parenthetical chapters, 12 through 14, have focused on important characters of the period. In chapter 12 Israel, Christ, Satan, and Michael are linked to the final great drama. In chapter 13 the future world ruler, the beast out of the sea, and his associate, the beast out of the earth, and the details of their world government are described. Chapter 14 may be summarized as a prediction of Christ in His ultimate triumph, the judgment of the wicked, and the pronouncements and visions supporting this are recorded.

*Revelation 14:1-5.* Expositors have had problems uniting on a specific interpretation, one of the problems being whether Mount Zion is a reference to earth or to heaven. A careful study of this chapter, however, does not support the concept that Zion here is heaven. The 144,000, introduced in chapter 7, were sealed to be kept safely through the Tribulation without losing their lives and are still in their natural bodies. They will go into the Millennium without dying. Accordingly, they would not be seen in heaven. Preferable is the interpretation that in prophetic vision John sees the triumph of the Lamb following His second coming and the 144,000 on Mount Zion as tokens of His keeping power and their induction to the millennial reign.

Scholars have had difficulty determining whether the 144,000 of chapter 14 is the same as that of chapter 7. Though various explanations have been given, it is preferable to regard them as the same group, as it would be most unlikely to have two different groups of 144,000 each, especially when the original 144,000 is based on 12 tribes of 12,000 each in order to arrive at this number. Scriptures record that they have the name of Christ and the name of the Father written on their foreheads, indicating possession and safety. It is rather obvious that while the 144,000 refers to Israel racially, they would not be preserved through the Great Tribulation unless they were also Christian.

There is nothing in Scripture that indicates that they are evangelists, as is often taught, or that they are prophets, but their role is one of illustrating the keeping power of God in this most awful period of the Tribulation.

John heard a sound from heaven which is compared to the roar of rushing waters or like a peal of thunder. It is, of course, a demonstration of divine power. The sound, however, has a musical quality as if played on the harp. Coupled with instrumental music, those before the throne sing a new song. This new song is not sung by the 144,000 on earth as they are in a different location, and it states simply that no one but the 144,000 could learn it. The heavenly choir is probably the martyred dead of the Tribulation mentioned in 7:9-17. The song mentioned, however, is not the same as that of the twenty-four elders in 5:9-10. In Revelation 5 the elders sing the song; in chapter 14 the song is sung to the four living creatures and the elders.

The 144,000 are also described, "These are those who did not defile themselves with women, for they kept themselves pure" (v. 4). They are described as "redeemed" (v. 3) and as those "offered as firstfruits to God and the Lamb" (v. 4). The implication from all these descriptive terms is that the 144,000 have been kept clear from doctrinal or moral impurity and that they are characterized as those who follow the Lamb wherever He goes (v. 4). Under ordinary circumstances, the married state is not regarded as less pure than the single state, but in the terrible period of the Great Tribulation, a normal married life would be impossible, and in order to serve the Lord without distraction, they remain unmarried.

The description of the 144,000 brings to the fore the importance of having a life of purity in the testimony of a Christian to the world. Christians are to be "holy and blameless," (Eph. 1:4); "holy and blameless" (Eph. 5:27), "without fault" (Jude 24). The 144,000 constituted an amazing testimony of the holiness of God in the midst of a generation that was utterly wicked and worshiping Satan.

### The Eternal Gospel Proclaimed

*Revelation 14:6-7.* John then recorded, "Then I saw another angel flying in midair, and he had the eternal Gospel to proclaim to those who live on the earth—to every nation, tribe, language and people" (v. 6). Because the word "Gospel" is used here, it has been presumed that he is talking about the way of salvation. As the context which follows indicates, however, what he is announcing is that God is going to judge the wicked. This is Gospel or Good News to those who have trusted in Christ, especially those living in the Great Tribulation, because it will signal the end of the Tribulation and the end of their deliverance from their enemies.

John continues, "He said in a loud voice, 'Fear God and give Him glory, because the hour of His judgment has come. Worship Him who made the heavens, the earth, the sea and the springs of water' " (v. 7). Just as the future holds a time of reward and blessing for the 144,000, so it holds judgment on the wicked who depart from God and blaspheme His name.

### Fall of Babylon Predicted

*Revelation 14:8.* The second angel makes another pronouncement, "A second angel followed and said, 'Fallen! Fallen is Babylon the Great, which made all the nations drink the maddening wine of her adulteries' " (v. 8). The announcement of Babylon's fall does not indicate that the end of the Great Tribulation has come but is rather an announcement of the future destruction of Babylon described in Revelation 18. The various pronouncements of this chapter are not necessarily a record that the event has taken place but that the event is impending.

### Judgment on the Worshipers of the Beast

*Revelation 14:9-12.* The worshipers of the beast have been previously described as being subject to judgment. Here we have a further pronouncement, "A third angel followed them and said in a loud voice: 'If anyone worships the beast and his image and receives his mark on the forehead or on the hand, he, too, will drink of the wine of God's fury, which has been poured full strength into the cup of his wrath. He will be tormented with burning sulfur in the presence of the holy angels and of the Lamb. And the smoke of their torment rises forever and ever. There is no rest day or night for those who worship the beast and his image, or for anyone who receives the mark of his name. This calls for patient endurance on the part of the saints who obey God's commandments and remain faithful to Jesus" (vv. 9-12).

Though the concept of eternal punishment is difficult for many to receive, it is clearly taught in the Word of God. Later revelation in the Book of Revelation indicates that those who die at the time of the second coming of Christ go to hades and will not be raised and cast into the lake of fire until after the thousand-year reign of Christ (20:11-15). Those who suffer from the hands of Satan and wicked men in the Great Tribulation have their comfort in the fact that their sufferings are temporary. The judgments on those who wickedly persecute them will be forever.

### The Dead of the Great Tribulation Blessed

*Revelation 14:13.* John heard another pronouncement, "Then I heard a voice from heaven say, 'Write: Blessed are the dead who die in the Lord from now on.' 'Yes,' says the Spirit, 'they will rest from their labor, for their deeds will follow them' " (v. 13). This is a passage of Scripture that applies only to those who die in the Great Tribulation and is not intended to be a universal recognition of death being a blessing.

The point is that in the Great Tribulation the saints will endure much suffering and persecution. When they suffer a martyr's death, they are immediately released and go to heaven. What this Scripture is revealing is that for those who trust in Christ, death will be better than life in the Great Tribulation because those who die immediately pass into the blessing of God. The fact that this pronouncement comes from heaven gives it special character. It is the fifth instance of a voice from heaven in Revelation (10:4, 8; 11:12; 14:2). Later in Revelation 18:4 and 21:3, there is again a direct communication from heaven, implying it is more important and urgent than other pronouncements.

### Judgment at the Second Coming

*Revelation 14:14-20.* The parenthetical section of Revelation 12–14 closes with an overall vision of Armageddon and God's judgment on the world. John recorded, "I looked, and there before me was a white cloud, and seated on the cloud was one 'like a son of man' with a crown of gold on his head and a sharp sickle in his hand. Then another angel came out of the temple and called in a loud voice to him who was sitting on the cloud, 'Take your sickle and reap, because the time to reap has come, for the harvest of the earth is ripe.' So he who was seated on the cloud swung his sickle over the earth, and the earth was harvested" (vv. 14-16).

The time of Armageddon (16:13-16) is a time of harvest when wickedness, which had reached its ultimate in the Great Tribulation, is judged, and the wicked, including Satan, the world ruler, and the false prophet, are likewise judged before God (19:20).

John further recorded, "Another angel came out of the temple in heaven, and he too had a sharp sickle. Still another angel, who had charge of the fire, came from the altar and called in a loud voice to him who had the sharp sickle, 'Take your sharp sickle and gather the clusters of grapes from the earth's vine, because its grapes are ripe.' The angel swung his sickle on the earth, gathered its grapes and threw them into the great winepress of God's wrath. They were trampled in the winepress outside the city, and the blood flowed out of the press, rising as high as the horses' bridles for a distance of 1,600 stadia" (14:17-20).

This passage is obviously talking about divine judgment, and the symbolism of the harvesting of grapes is taken as an illustration. The evil in the world has come to the ripe point where God can judge it at the time of Armageddon. Accordingly, the harvest is pictured as if they were gathering grapes and throwing them into the winepress which represents God's wrath. When the grapes are pressed, the blood is said to flow as high as the horses' bridles.

This judgment is pictured as one conducted by the angels. The angel of verse 17 is the fifth angel which is used as God's instrument in this chapter. A sixth angel also exhorts him to harvest the crop. The angels are acting, of course, under God's orders. The grapes are pictured as ready for harvest and bursting with juice. The use of a vine as figurative in the Bible is used of both Israel and the church, of Israel (Ps. 80:8, 14-15; Isa. 5:2-7; Jer. 2:21; Ezek. 17:5-8; Hosea 10:1) and of the church in John 15:1-6.

Though the vine was intended to bear righteous fruit, it brought wickedness, and this calls for the judgment of God. The judgment which is described here is later fulfilled after Christ's second coming as recorded in Revelation 19:15. The treading of grapes in the ordinary grape harvest resulting in the juice being produced in large quantities is used here of the terrible destruction brought on the armies that opposed Christ at His coming (vv. 17-21).

The grapes are said to rise as high as the horses' bridles and for a distance of 1,600 stadia, or 160 miles. It would be, of course, impossible to produce enough grape juice in one spot or let enough blood in one spot for a flood that would reach as high as a horse's bridle. It must be borne in mind that this is entirely an illustration and not literally fulfilled, but it no doubt speaks of the extent of the bloodletting in the final battle of Revelation 19 where, no doubt, actual blood is spattered as high as the horse's bridle. The fact that this extends 160 miles (1,600 stadia) indicates the scope of the battle of Armageddon which covers the whole Holy Land with the judgment of God on the armies that are there gathered covering the whole area where the armies are located.

Revelation 14 gathers in one perspective the major elements of the end-time judgments, including the 144,000 as a token of God's delivering power, the prediction of the fall of Babylon which is a major factor of the period of the second coming of Christ, the doom of the armies that oppose Christ at His second coming, the judgment on the world ruler, the beast and his assistant, the false prophet, the blessedness of those who die in the period of the Great Tribulation because of their immediate release to heaven, and, finally, the accuracy and justice of God's judgment on religious apostasy, and blasphemy against God which describes the end-time period.

Though the chapter deals with the period after the present age of grace, many truths are applied to our present age, including the necessity of salvation in Christ and the imperative character of walking before God in holiness and purity. In this age of grace where this judgment does not impend, there is still opportunity to receive the grace of God and to be saved and to be included in that glad number who will be raptured before these tragic end-time events will overtake the earth.

## The Great Tribulation Continued:
## The Bowl Judgments

Revelation 15 and 16 bring to a conclusion the chronological events of the Book of Revelation preceding the Second Coming. As previously brought out, the structure of Revelation depends first on the seven seals which are broken (6:1-17; 8:1), the seventh seal includes the seven trumpets (8:1-9:21; 11:15-19). The seven bowls of the wrath of God now being introduced are all included in the seventh trumpet. The order of events involves rapid increase in severity and in frequency of the judgments of God with the emphasis being on the seventh seal, the seven trumpets, and the seven bowls of the wrath of God. Parenthetic sections which intervene frequently in the Book of Revelation have to do with prophetic revelation concerning individuals and situations, but they do not advance the narrative chronologically (7:1-17; 10:1-11:14; 12-14; 17-19:10). Revelation 19:11 will occur immediately after chapter 16 following the seventh bowl of the wrath of God.

### The Seven Bowl Judgments Announced

*Revelation 15:1-8.* The revelation concerning the seven bowls is introduced by John, "I saw in heaven another great and marvelous sign: seven angels with the seven last plagues—last, because with them God's wrath is completed" (v. 1). This is another sign in sequence to two previous signs recorded in Revelation 12, the sign of the woman clothed with the sun (v. 1) and the sign appearing in heaven, referring to "an enormous red dragon with seven heads and ten horns and seven crowns on his heads" (v. 3). The three signs together concentrate attention on the woman—or Israel, on the world empire—the ultimate work of Satan, and the seven angels of the seven last plagues which bring out God's judgment on the wicked. The sign here presented in Revelation 15 is described as "great and marvelous," an expression which is found only here (v. 1), and concerning the deeds of God (v. 3).

The seven angels who are introduced here apparently are a different group than any mentioned previously, and the plagues concern a judgment of God which is different than anything which precedes it. Being seven in number, it gives the impression of completion, or fulfillment, of God's judgment on the wicked which is embraced in the phrase, "last, because with them God's wrath is completed" (v. 1). Tremendous as have been the judgments in the breaking of the seals and the sounding of the trumpets, these last judgments are obviously more extensive and more final than anything preceding. They are the expression of God's wrath (Gr., *thymos*), indicating not so much His judicial wrath as His anger. God's reaction to sin is, first of all, anger, and, second, wrath in the form of judgment.

John recorded further revelation, "And I saw what looked like a sea of glass mixed with fire and, standing beside the sea, those who had been victorious over the beast and his image and over the number of his name" (v. 2). The sea of glass here as well as in 4:6 is apparently the same entity and may signify the Word of God. The sea is not an ordinary sea because the heavenly hosts are pictured as standing on it, and it is designed to manifest the glory of God. With fire speaking of divine judgment, those standing on it reveal that some will not experience the wrath of God, whereas others will. Those standing on the sea of glass are described as "victorious over the beast and his image" (15:2).

The victorious group also is to be given harps, or lyres. The only musical instruments described in heaven are the harps, or lyres, and only certain personages in heaven have the harps. The martyred dead of the Tribulation are among those who play the harp.

John recorded that those who are victorious in standing on the sea of glass "sang the song of Moses the servant of God and the song of the Lamb" (v. 3). The statement implies that there is one song of Moses and another song of the Lamb. The song of Moses is often linked with the song sung by Moses in Exodus 15 when the Children of Israel were triumphant over Pharaoh and his hosts. Another suggestion, however, is that it refers to the song in Deuteronomy 32, also produced by Moses in presenting a comprehensive revelation of God's faithfulness to Israel and the certainty of Israel's enemies being defeated. The song of the Lamb is then recorded, "Great and marvelous are Your deeds, Lord God Almighty. Just and true are Your ways, King of the ages. Who will not fear You, O Lord, and bring glory to Your name? For You alone are holy. All nations will come and worship before You, for Your righteous acts have been revealed" (Rev. 15:3-4).

The question concerning who will fear the Lord and bring glory to Him is a question often addressed in Scripture. Jeremiah, for instance, asked the question, "Who should not revere You, O King of the nations?" (Jer. 10:7) The song of the nations worshiping the Lord recorded here by John is a frequent theme of the Old Testament which will be fulfilled, of course, in the millennial kingdom as well as in the eternal state (cf. Pss. 2:8-9; 24:1-10; 66:1-4; 72:8-12; 86:9; Isa. 2:2-4; 9:6-7; 66:18-23; Dan. 7:14; Zeph. 2:11; Zech. 14:9). Because God is righteous and holy, He will bring His judgments on men as indicated in the closing words of the song, "for Your righteous acts have been revealed" (Rev. 15:4).

From the vantage point of heaven, John recorded that he saw further, "After this I looked and in heaven the temple, that is, the tabernacle of the testimony, was opened. Out of the temple came the seven angels with the seven plagues. They were dressed in clean, shining linen and wore golden sashes around their chests. Then one of the four living creatures gave to the seven angels seven golden bowls filled with the wrath of God, who lives forever and ever. And the temple was filled with smoke from the glory of God and from His power, and no one could enter the temple until the seven plagues of the seven angels were completed" (vv. 5-8).

The temple (Gr., *naos*) indicates that the angels came out of the inner holy place. Though access by the priest was limited, angels, because they have no sin, are able to enter the holy place. What John has seen is, of course, symbolic of what is about to happen.

The angels were each given a bowl of the wrath of God which will be poured out in Revelation 16. Because this is a very dramatic consummation of God's judgment on a wicked world, the Scripture indicates that the smoke will fill the temple, in a way similar to when the cloud filled the tabernacle (Ex. 40:34-35). The whole scene is one that is ominous and indicating impending judgment on a wicked world.

### Seven Bowls of God's Judgment
### Ordered Poured Out on a Wicked World

*Revelation 16:1.* As John contemplated the scene before him, he heard "a loud voice from the temple saying to the seven angels, 'Go, pour out the seven bowls of God's wrath on the earth' " (v. 1). The voice from the temple could very well be the voice of God though the text does not indicate this. The "loud" voice (Gr., *megales)* is a characteristic word through this chapter as brought out in the KJV. In verse 1 a "great" voice, in verse 9 "intense" heat, in verse 12 the "great" Euphrates, in verse 14 the "great" day of God Almighty, in verse 18 a "severe" or great earthquake, in verse 19 the "great" city, also in verse 19 Babylon the "Great," in verse 21 "huge" or great hailstones, also in verse 21 a "terrible" or great plague. Everything about this chapter speaks of the climax as the greatest and most awful period of human history.

Because the seven bowls of the wrath of God are similar to the judgments of the trumpets and those of the seals, expositors have been tempted to equate them. Careful attention to the details, however, will point out the differences. It is true in the series of the trumpets and the bowls that the first ones deal with the earth, the next with the sea, the next with rivers and springs of water, the next with the sun, the next with darkness, the next with the Euphrates River, and the seventh a comprehensive judgment including all that is in the trumpets and all that is in the bowls and wrath of God which are summarized in the seventh bowl as a great earthquake and a great hailstorm.

Though the judgments are similar, notable differences are mentioned. The trumpet judgments extend to only one-third of the earth while the bowl judgments generally extend to the entire earth. There is really no problem of repetition of judgments as what the Scripture is revealing is that these judgments as the time progresses become increasingly worse and occurring in rapid chronological order. The seven bowls apparently occur one after the other in rapid sequence and immediately introduce the situation of the second coming of Christ. In Revelation 16 a series of judgments beyond anything ever mentioned before is revealed.

## The First Bowl

*Revelation 16:2.* In obedience to the voice from the temple, the first angel pours out his bowl. As John recorded, "The first angel went and poured out his bowl on the land, and ugly and painful sores broke out on the people who had the mark of the beast and worshiped his image" (v. 2). By contrast, in the first trumpet a third of the earth is burned up (8:7). In the first bowl of the wrath of God painful sores and afflictions are experienced by all those who worship the beast, the experience being similar to that experienced by the Egyptians (Ex. 9:9-11). The only ones who escape this judgment are those who have refused to worship the beast.

## The Second Bowl

*Revelation 16:3.* Following next, the second bowl is poured out, "The second angel poured out his bowl on the sea, and it turned into blood like that of a dead man, and every living thing in the sea died" (v. 3). In the second trumpet a third of the sea turned into blood (8:8). This judgment again seems to be similar to the judgment of the plagues in Egypt (Ex. 7:20-25) which was poured out on the River Nile, making it impossible to drink, and killing the fish in the river. In reference to the sea, it is possible that it may be limited to the Mediterranean, but the same word would be used if the entire world were involved.

## The Third Bowl

*Revelation 16:4-7.* John then recorded the pouring out of the third bowl, "The third angel poured out his bowl on the rivers and springs of water, and they became blood. Then I heard the angel in charge of the waters say: 'You are just in these judgments, You who are and who were, the Holy One, because You have so judged; for they have shed the blood of Your saints and prophets, and You have given them blood to drink as they deserve' " (vv. 4-6). In response to this, a voice is again heard from the altar, "Yes, Lord God Almighty, true and just are Your judgments" (v. 7).

Expositors tend to try to explain the judgment of the sea turning to blood as something not actually blood. If one accepts the omnipotence of God, of course, nothing is impossible, and the sea could become literal blood, or it may be the language of appearance; but in either case it is a terrible judgment, rendering the water unfit both for fish in the sea and for drinking on the part of man.

Attention is called in the third bowl to the martyrdom of saints and rejection of the prophets (vv. 4-5). The judgment was declared to be just (v. 5).

### The Fourth Bowl

*Revelation 16:8-9.* John then recorded the fourth bowl, "The fourth angel poured out his bowl on the sun, and the sun was given power to scorch people with fire. They were seared by the intense heat and they cursed the name of God, who had control over these plagues, but they refused to repent and glorify Him" (vv. 8-9). Similarities in contrast can be seen again between the fourth trumpet and the fourth bowl. The fourth bowl relates only to the sun and increases the sun's intensity. By contrast, the fourth trumpet darkened a third of the sun, moon, and stars (8:12). Though the sphere of the judgment was the same, the effect was different.

### The Fifth Bowl

*Revelation 16:10-11.* The fifth bowl was announced, "The fifth angel poured out his bowl on the throne of the beast, and his kingdom was plunged into darkness. Men gnawed their tongues in agony and cursed the God of heaven because of their pains and their sores, but they refused to repent of what they had done" (vv. 10-11). This judgment apparently increased the severity of the affliction of the first bowl and describes those associated with the beast and others as well as being in unusual agony. The familiar theme of failure to repent is repeated here (cf. 2:21; 9:20-21). When wicked men are confronted with the power of God, they do not easily come to the place of repentance, but instead enlarge their rebellion against God.

### The Sixth Bowl

*Revelation 16:12.* The sixth bowl introduces a number of interesting facts, "The sixth angel poured out his bowl on the great river Euphrates, and its water was dried up to prepare the way for the kings from the East" (v. 12).

When the sixth bowl was poured out, chronologically, the time of the Second Coming is very near. One of the major features of the period just before the Second Coming is a world war in which various parts of the world rebel against the world ruler who has taken power as the dictator some time before. In the light of this military conclusion to the Great Tribulation, the sixth bowl makes its own contribution in preparing the way for the kings of the East to cross the Euphrates.

Few portions of Revelation have called for more varied interpretations than this verse. A survey of a hundred commentaries on Revelation reveals fifty different theories, practically all trying to interpret what is meant by the "kings from the East" (v. 12) and also to determine whether the river Euphrates is literal or not. The numerous symbolic interpretations are its own confession that this is not the proper interpretation.

Accordingly, a literal interpretation of this is exactly what the text calls for, namely, that the Euphrates River will be dried up, and this will prepare for military invasion by the kings of the East, probably including rulers of China and other countries.

The implication from the text is that this is accomplished by supernatural means such as an earthquake though the method is not revealed. In the twentieth century, however, Russia has built a series of dams across the Euphrates River to capture water for irrigation purposes. The fact is that at certain times in the season when all the water is stored, the Euphrates River is dry. If it were flowing at ordinary rate, it would be a difficult river to cross because of the rough terrain on both sides of the river. With the riverbed dry, there would be no restriction of movement of a great army from the East.

Though this passage does not connect directly with the sixth trumpet, apparently the river is dried up in order for the great army of 200 million to cross it as indicated in the sixth trumpet (9:14-16). The two events are chronologically close together even though they belong to different series.

Though no further information is given about the sixth bowl, John then recorded a small parenthetic section, giving the overview of Armageddon.

### Parenthetic Revelation IV:
### Demonic Gathering of World Armies

*Revelation 16:13-14.* John wrote that he saw what revealed a coming world war, "Then I saw three evil spirits that looked like frogs; they came out of the mouth of the dragon, out of the mouth of the beast and out of the mouth of the false prophet. They are spirits of demons performing miraculous signs, and they go out to the kings of the whole world, to gather them for the battle on the great day of God Almighty" (vv. 13-14).

This revelation is a combination of literal and symbolic. Obviously, the evil spirits which looked like frogs were actually fallen angels who, apparently, respond to the direction of the dragon which is Satan and the world ruler and his associate, the false prophet. The evil spirits are sent throughout the world to entice the kings of the world to join in the great world war which will be underway in the Holy Land.

Obviously, as long as the world government was intact, there would be no war. The fact that there is war indicates rebellion against the rule of the world dictator toward the end of the Great Tribulation.

The gathering of the armies is in preparation for the Second Coming. Apparently Christ Himself proclaims the warning to be prepared, "Behold, I come like a thief! Blessed is he who stays awake and keeps his clothes with him, so that he may not go naked and be shamefully exposed" (v. 15). Though many events precede the Second Coming and Satan himself is aware that it is impending, many will be unprepared—"naked" and "shamefully exposed"—as far as God's righteousness is concerned.

The armies from all the world are gathered geographically to the Holy Land apparently to fight it out for power. The locale of the war is described as Armageddon. The term "Armageddon" geographically refers to the area eastward from Mount Megiddo in northern Israel and includes the large plain of Esdraelon. *Megiddo* is in the Hebrew a corresponding title to the Greek, Armageddon. This area has been the scene of great battles in the past, including that of Barak and the Canaanites (Jud. 4) and the victory of Gideon over the Midianites (Jud. 7). Saul and Josiah also were killed in this area. The valley is rather large, being fourteen miles wide and twenty miles long. Large as this area is, it obviously cannot contain the armies of millions of men, and it seems to be the marshaling point.

Actually, the armies are scattered up and down the Holy Land for a length of some 200 miles. Both World War I and World War II were identified by some as Armageddon, but subsequent history proved that they were wrong.

The enticement of the demons is apparently effective because the armies of the world assemble to fight it out in the Holy Land. The fact that the demons, including the efforts of the dragon, the world ruler, and the false prophet, openly invite a world war, seems to be a contradiction because in Revelation 13 the world government is put together by Satan in order to fulfill his imitation of the millennial world government. Satan and the world ruler and the false prophet are a trilogy compared to the Father, Son, and Holy Spirit who are in charge of the kingdom. Here, however, the same people are inviting countries of the world to fight it out which seems to be a contradiction.

The answer to this puzzle is found in Revelation 19 as the second coming of Christ is revealed. What Satan is doing is gathering all the military power of the world in a vain effort to contend with the army from heaven. It, of course, is futile because Christ speaks the word and the armies and their horses on both sides of the conflict are instantly killed in the awful judgment that occurs at the Second Coming.

As in other general prophecies dealing with many, there is also individual application as in 16:15, "Behold, I come like a thief! Blessed is he who stays awake and keeps his clothes with him, so that he may not go naked and be shamefully exposed." The symbolism of this verse is not explained in the text, but the individual is told to keep his clothes on in preparation for this event. Garments when used symbolically often refer to righteousness in life, and it may be that those who are saved at that time should continue to serve the Lord in a righteous fashion. Though many have been killed by the beast, many others have escaped up to this time as witnessed in the sheep in Matthew 25:31-46 and the remnant of Israel spoken of frequently in the Old Testament as in Ezekiel 20:33-38. Commentators generally agree that the seventh bowl is in preparation for the major events that follow such as the second coming of Christ.

### The Great Tribulation Continued: The Seventh Bowl of Divine Wrath and the Great Earthquake

*Revelation 16:17-18.* With the announcement of the seventh bowl, the final judgments on the earth preceding the Second Coming are revealed, "The seventh angel poured out his bowl into the air, and out of the temple came a loud voice from the throne, saying, 'It is done!' Then there came flashes of lightning, rumblings, peals of thunder and a severe earthquake. No earthquake like it has ever occurred since man has been on earth, so tremendous was the quake" (vv. 17-18).

Earthquakes have plagued the world throughout history. With increased population and building of cities, earthquakes now affect populous areas with increased casualties and destruction of property. This final earthquake that occurs before the second coming of

Christ eclipses all that has gone before.

### Destruction of the Great City

*Revelation 16:19.* John goes on to describe the destruction of the great city, "The great city split into three parts, and the cities of the nations collapsed. God remembered Babylon the Great and gave her the cup filled with the wine of the fury of His wrath" (v. 19).

The Scriptures declare that the great city split into three parts and that throughout the world the cities of the Gentiles would be shaken to pieces and collapse. The text does not indicate what great city is in view though Jerusalem was mentioned as a great city in 11:8. The Bible indicates that there will be tremendous changes in the land surrounding Jerusalem (cf. Zech. 14:4).

The problem that occurs with identifying Jerusalem as a city destroyed is that in Zechariah 14 at the time of the Second Coming, Jerusalem is still a city intact in spite of the earthquake which had destroyed the other cities of the world. If Jerusalem had been destroyed by an earthquake, the house-to-house fighting and other aspects of the final war, as recorded in Zechariah 14, could not have taken place.

Some expositors relate this to the city of Babylon on the Euphrates, and there are many indications in Scripture that this will be rebuilt and possibly made the capital city of the world empire. This seems to be confirmed by chapter 18. If Babylon is the city in view, the fact that it is divided into three parts is what happens according to Revelation 18, and the prophecy could be literally fulfilled in this way. This would be the climax of a long history of judgment on Babylon.

### Destruction of Islands, Mountains, and the Plague of Hail

*Revelation 16:20-21.* The destruction of the world was further described by John, "Every island fled away and the mountains could not be found. From the sky huge hailstones of about a hundred pounds each fell upon men. And they cursed God on account of the plague of hail, because the plague was so terrible" (vv. 20-21). The topographical nature of the world will be dramatically changed probably as the aftermath of the earthquake with islands and mountains disappearing with resultant loss of life and property. Huge waves in the ocean created by these changes will bring total destruction that is beyond description.

In addition to the earthquake, however, there will be a tremendous supernatural hailstorm with huge hailstones, weighing approximately 100 pounds each. Whatever is left from the earthquake in terms of building monuments of men will be beaten to pulp by these huge blocks of ice. As in previous judgments of God, however, it does not bring repentance or confession of sin, but, instead, men recognizing that the judgments came from God, curse God because of it (v. 21).

The world is now set for the second coming of Christ, but before this occurs, a parenthetic section dealing with Babylon is introduced.

### Parenthetic Revelation V:
### The Destruction of Ecclesiastical Babylon

*Revelation 17:1-18.* The Book of Revelation was written in the order in which the truth was revealed to John, but the events described are not necessarily in chronological order. This is especially true of Revelation 17 which probably occurred during the first half of the last seven years. Much confusion is manifested in interpretations of chapters 17–18, and there is some obscurity in the revelation itself. Probably the best solution is to regard chapter 17 as the destruction of ecclesiastical Babylon, or Babylon as a religion, and chapter 18, the destruction of Babylon as a city and as an empire.

John was invited by one of the angels who had the bowls of divine judgment to witness the punishment of ecclesiastical Babylon. By using the term ecclesiastical, it is not meant that Babylon is the true church in any sense of the term, but it is Babylon from a religious standpoint. An extensive study of the religions of Babylon demonstrate that many of them were carried over in part into Roman Catholicism and formed the background for some of the ceremonies. The Babylonian influence, however, is always contrary to the truth, and her final hour is described in this chapter.

John recorded his introduction to the judgment of the woman: "One of the seven angels who had the seven bowls came and said to me, 'Come, I will show you the punishment of the great prostitute, who sits on many waters. With her the kings of the earth committed adultery and the inhabitants of the earth were intoxicated with the wine of her adulteries.' Then the angel carried me away in the Spirit into a desert. There I saw a woman sitting on a scarlet beast that was covered with blasphemous names and had seven heads and ten horns. The woman was dressed in purple and scarlet, and was glittering with gold, precious stones and pearls. She held a golden cup in her hand, filled with abominable things and the filth of her adulteries. This title was written on her forehead:

MYSTERY
BABYLON THE GREAT
THE MOTHER OF PROSTITUTES
AND OF THE ABOMINATIONS OF THE EARTH.

I saw that the woman was drunk with the blood of the saints, the blood of those who bore testimony to Jesus" (vv. 1-6).

The great prostitute described in these verses is a portrayal of apostate Christendom in the end time. When the Rapture occurred, all true believers were caught up to be with the Lord, but left behind were many thousands of those who made some profession of faith in Christ and claimed to be Christians who were not born again. These constituted the apostate church which will dominate the scene politically and religiously up to the midpoint of that last seven years before the Second Coming.

The apostasy, called adultery and fornication here, of course refers to spiritual unfaithfulness, not to physical adultery. The church devoid of any redeeming influence is now completely united with the world, and, as the passage indicates, is working hand in glove with the political powers.

John saw a woman on a scarlet-colored beast with seven heads and ten horns. The beast is obviously the political empire described in 13:1-10. The fact that she is seated on the beast indicates that she is working with the beasts to attain common ends, that is, the subjugation of the entire world to their authority, and that the political power is supporting the apostate church. The woman wears the trappings of ceremonial religion in which purple and scarlet are prominent and which is often enhanced with precious stones. From the title written on her forehead, she is linked with the mystery of Babylon the Great. In referring to this identification as a mystery, because its ultimate truth is learned only by divine revelation, the influence of Babylon for evil is supported in Scripture from as early as Genesis 11 and continues through the revelation of the destruction of the city in Revelation 18.

Babylon is the title that covers all false religions that claim to be Christian in their content. Babylonian influence clearly crept into the church, and much of its ritual is similar to the Babylonian religious rites.

When Babylon was introduced in Genesis 11, her true character was revealed as rebelling against God and attempting to build a tower in recognition of her worship of heathen deities. Because this was contrary to the will of God, He confounded the language the people were using at that time so that they could not understand each other; hence, the term "Babel," meaning confusion, applies to the subsequent history of Babylon (cf. Gen. 11:9).

It should be borne in mind that the term "Babylon" applies to Babylonian religion; it also applies to the city of Babylon; and it applies to the empire of Babylon.

Babylon had a long history and rose to considerable prominence in the time of Hammurabi (1726–1686 B.C.). She reached her height of glory under Nebuchadnezzar who lived in what is known as the Neo-Babylonian period, beginning 600 years before Christ. It was in this period that Daniel wrote the Book of Daniel. Archeologists have uncovered much of the detail of this city, having been able to decipher the thousands of cuneiform tablets which were found in Babylon.

In this section, however, the revelation concentrates on the influence of Babylon religiously. Because the religion of Babylon was in the form of a secret religious rite in which they worshiped certain idols, it requires divine revelation to understand completely what they held. The wife of Nimrod, who was the founder of Babylon, headed up the mystery religion which characterized Babylon. She was given the name Semiramis, and according to the adherents' belief, she had a son conceived miraculously whose name was Tammuz. He was portrayed as a savior who fulfills the promise of deliverance given to Eve. This was, of course, a satanic description which permeates pagan religions.

The concept of woman and child was incorporated in various religious rites which were conducted by a priestly order which worshiped the woman and the child and is the background for the tendency in Roman Catholicism to glorify Mary the Mother of Jesus.

Throughout Scripture references are found concerning Babylonian worship such as Ezekiel's protest of weeping for Tammuz (Ezek. 8:14). Jeremiah objects to the heathen practice of offering cakes to Semiramis as the queen of heaven (Jer. 7:18). Offering of incense was also made to her as the queen of heaven (44:17-19, 25). An offshoot of this was the worship of Baal which was one of the pagan religions of Canaan, and Baal is often identified as the same person as Tammuz.

The mystery religions of Babylon permeated the ancient world, and with the decline of Babylon as a city and as empire, Babylonian religion found its way to Pergamum, the city in which one of the seven churches of Asia was located. Those who served as chief priests of this Babylonian cult were often related to Dagon the fish god and the "Keeper of the Bridge," that is, the bridge between man and Satan; and in recognition of this, the priests wore crowns in the form of a head of a fish.

As Christianity came in contact with the Babylonian religion, it created turmoil and confusion for the church. Through the centuries there has been a tendency for the church to be anchored in the world instead of in God, and modern liberalism has gone even farther in departing from the Scriptures. The prophecy concerning Babylon here as well as other allusions to religion in the Book of Revelation demonstrate that apostasy will have its final form in the Great Tribulation in the worship of the world ruler and Satan.

In the period of the first half of the seven years leading up to the second coming of Christ, Babylon combined with Romanism becomes a world religion — Christian in name, but not in content. Those who do come to Christ will be subject to her persecution, and the woman is described as "drunk with the blood of the saints" (Rev. 17:6). The apostate church has been unsparing in its persecution of those who have a true faith in Christ. Those who come to Christ in the end time will have the double problem of avoiding martyrdom at the hands of the political rulers and at the hands of the apostate church.

John was overwhelmed by this revelation and only partially understood it, and it was explained to him. He wrote, "When I saw her, I was greatly astonished. Then the angel said to me: 'Why are you astonished? I will explain to you the mystery of the woman and of the beast she rides, which has the seven heads and ten horns. The beast, which you saw, once was, now is not, and will come up out of the Abyss and go to his destruction. The inhabitants of the earth whose names have not been written in the Book of Life from the Creation of the world will be astonished when they see the beast, because he once was, now is not, and yet will come' " (vv. 6-8).

One of the outstanding, convincing arguments for worshiping the beast is the fact that he comes back from apparent death to life, as recorded in 13:3. The reference to the Abyss identifies the home of Satan and the demon world. The whole false religion found in Babylon is satanic in its origin and therefore is closely related to the demon world.

The purpose of the alliance between the woman and the beast is that both are seeking world domination. When this is finally achieved, as the end of this chapter indicates, the political power will no longer need the religious power to support it.

As previously discussed, the references to the beast as one who "once was, now is not, and yet will come" (17:8) has been taken as proof that the world leader is one who was resurrected from an earlier time on earth, including such possibilites as Judas Iscariot and Nero and other world rulers. The preferable interpretation, however, is either to regard the resurrection of the beast as the resurrection of the Roman Empire or to consider the possibility of a deadly wound suffered in the assassination attempt from which he is miraculously healed by Satan. In either case, the world ruler comes on the scene as a miraculous person.

Because of the seemingly miraculous qualities that enter into the world ruler, the unsaved, not in the Book of Life, will be astonished and will put their trust in this beast as God.

The angel goes on to refer to the seven heads as referring to seven kings, "This calls for a mind with wisdom. The seven heads are seven hills on which the woman sits. They are also seven kings. Five have fallen, one is, the other has not yet come; but when he does come, he must remain for a little while. The beast who once was, and now is not, is an eighth king. He belongs to the seven and is going to his destruction" (vv. 9-11).

This passage has caused great confusion among expositors who have had difficulty understanding what it means when it says that the seven heads are seven hills and that the woman sits on them. The statement, "This calls for a mind with wisdom," (v. 9) is clearly indicated by the history of interpretation of this passage.

One of the common explanations is to refer to the seven hills as the city of Rome which was known as "the city of seven hills." The ancient city of Rome was located on the left bank of the Tiber, and seven hills were named: Palatine, Aventine, Caelian, Equiline, Viminal, Quirimal, and Capitoline. As Rome grew in power and in size, it took in another hill, Janiculum, which was also numbered among the seven hills, and the hill Capitoline was omitted. Still later another hill, Pincian, north of ancient Rome, was added, requiring subtraction of one of the other hills.

The confusion of the seven heads of the beasts with the seven hills of Rome, however, arises from inattention to what the passage states. John was informed, "They are also seven kings" (v. 10). If the hills represent kings, then they do not refer to the seven hills of Rome, and the whole conclusion that Rome is the capital of ecclesiastical Babylon is brought into question. Further, a statement is made, "Five have fallen, one is, the other has not yet come; but when he does come, he must remain for a little while" (v. 10). This could not refer to hills. How can the five that are fallen and the one that is and the one not yet come be identified?

Some have identified the five as some of the more prominent rulers of ancient Rome, but it is difficult to select five who deserve this prominence. Accordingly, scholars have suggested that instead of the five referring to individual kings, they refer to the great nations of the past who were empires. This would include Egypt, Assyria, Babylon, Medo-Persia, Greece, and ancient Rome. As John viewed it, ancient Rome would be the sixth king, but later in history Rome would be revived and would be considered a seventh king. This is what John refers to when he stated, "the other has not yet come" (v. 10). This view at least is a possibility.

As the years progress leading up to the second coming of Christ, however, the ten-nation kingdom (Rev. 13), which was Rome revived, becomes a world empire which with its ruler is the eighth king. This is stated, "The beast who once was, and now is not, is an eighth king" (17:11).

This identification is a plausible explanation though not all expositors would agree. Important, however, to conclusions about this prophecy is that it eliminates the concept that Rome geographically is involved as the headquarters of political Babylon. It leaves open the question as to where ecclesiastical Babylon will have its seat of power. Perhaps more important, it opens the way for the possibility that political Babylon (revived Rome) will have its center of power in the rebuilt city of Babylon during the last three-and-a-half years leading up to the second coming of Christ. This would have its climax in Revelation 18 where the city is destroyed.

If the explanation of the seven heads of the beast is accepted, the question remains as to what the ten horns are.

The angel declared, "The ten horns you saw are ten kings who have not yet received a kingdom, but who for one hour will receive authority as kings along with the beast. They have one purpose and will give their power and authority to the beast" (vv. 12-13).

Based on a study of Daniel 7 and Revelation 13, the ten horns represent ten kingdoms which were banded together to form the nucleus of the revived Roman Empire which had power during the first half of the last seven years. Many have attempted to find ten kings in history that corresponded to these ten horns, but the quest is futile because, as a matter of fact, the ten horns do not exist until the revived Roman Empire comes about and will not have fulfillment until the first half of the last seven years is fulfilled. Further, it is clear that they are simultaneous in their rule, not successive. They are always viewed as ten kings in a unit rather than successive monarchs. They act unitedly as illustrated later in this chapter (17:16-17). As stated in verse 13, their purpose and place is to honor the world ruler.

The angel continues in his prediction, "They will make war against the Lamb, but the Lamb will overcome them because He is Lord of lords and King of kings — and with Him will be His called, chosen and faithful followers" (v. 14). Both the woman and the beast, the ecclesiastical and the political, are utterly opposed to God and those who put their trust in the Lord at that time.

The woman is described as one "who sits on many waters" (v. 1). This is now interpreted by the angel, "Then the angel said to me, 'The waters you saw, where the prostitute sits, are peoples, multitudes, nations and languages' " (v. 15). This indicates that the false religion promoted by the woman as well as the political power promoted by the beast are worldwide.

The next development, however, is a tremendous additional revelation, "The beast and the ten horns you saw will hate the prostitute. They will bring her to ruin and leave her naked; they will eat her flesh and burn her with fire. For God has put it into their hearts to accomplish His purpose by agreeing to give the beast their power to rule, until God's words are fulfilled" (vv. 16-17).

The same ecclesiastical apostate church, typified by the woman that was supported and brought into being with the help of the political ruler, the scarlet beast, is now destroyed. The question is a natural one of how this fits into the sequence of events.

In the overall picture of the last seven years leading up to the second coming of Christ, this passage indicates that in the first half of the seven years, this woman, representing the world religion, will have power, but probably will be a continuation of the world church movement in the present world from which the true church was raptured earlier in the sequence of events. Now having come to the midpoint of the seven years when the head of the ten nations takes over as world ruler, the apostate church is no longer useful and, as a matter of fact, is in the way. Accordingly, the ten nations destroy the woman and terminate her power and position.

The purpose behind this is that the world ruler will claim to be God Himself, and for the final three-and-a-half years, the world religion will consist in the worship of the world ruler and the worship of Satan who is recognized as the power behind the world ruler. This was stated in Revelation 13:4, "Men worshiped the dragon because he had given authority to the beast, and they also worshiped the beast and asked, 'Who is like the beast? Who can make war against him?' " The whole religious system having its source in ancient Babylon is brought to its close because the final form of religion, the worship of the world ruler, is atheism and does not need this support.

The final verse of the chapter brings in another concept, "The woman you saw is the great city that rules over the kings of the earth" (17:18).

This statement must be taken as representative of the religious character of Babylon depicted by the prostitute but also as a great city, possibly referring to the Vatican, which in history had ruled over the earth. The power of the Roman church to some extent was the extension of the influence of ancient Babylon throughout history, particularly in the period before the Protestant Reformation. The city here must be taken in less than a literal sense because it refers to the church which by its nature was not a city any more than it was a prostitute. The chapter which follows will deal with Roman power as centered in the city of Babylon.

### The Destruction of Political Babylon

*Revelation 18:1-24.* This chapter continues a prophetic revelation concerning Babylon with the context and meaning of this chapter as entirely different than the preceding chapter. Revelation 17 was probably fulfilled before the Great Tribulation began. By contrast, the events of Revelation 18 are probably fulfilled as a judgment at the time of the second coming of Christ.

Expositors have struggled with Revelation 17 and Revelation 18 in an attempt to find some reasonable explanation of the prophecies. Probably the best approach for Revelation 17 is to regard it as having its fulfillment in the world church movement which will be judged and destroyed three-and-a-half years before the second coming of Christ.

Revelation 18, however, deals specifically with a city that is essentially a political entity. The question is: When will this prophecy be fulfilled?

The interpretation of this chapter depends on the question whether Babylon will be rebuilt as the capital of the world in the end time or whether Babylon will be fulfilled by the role of Rome in the period preceding the Second Coming. As pointed out in the exegesis of Revelation 17, the concept that the seven hills refer to the city of Rome is found to be unsupportable in the context, and the evidence that the city of Rome will be in some sense the Babylon represented here does not have sufficient basis of support in other Scriptures to justify the conclusion.

Accordingly, the approach taken here is to anticipate Babylon as a city that will be rebuilt as the capital of the final world empire and will be destroyed physically as well as politically at the time of the Second Coming.

This conclusion is based on studies in the Old Testament concerning the prophecies there of the destruction of Babylon. In the Old Testament a number of prophecies point to sudden and catastrophic destruction of Babylon (Isa. 13:5-6, 10, 19-22; 14:1-6, 22, 25-26; Jer. 51). These prophecies anticipating the sudden destruction of Babylon were not fulfilled in history. When the Medes and the Persians took over Babylon in 539 B.C., they did not destroy the city of Babylon. The city of Babylon continued to be a population center through the time of Christ when there was a large colony of Jews living in the city. Actually, there was no act of sudden destruction, but Babylon gradually diminished as a city in the centuries following the first coming of Christ until today it is largely in ruins. Accordingly, the fulfillment of the promise in the Old Testament has not occurred. It is on this basis that some anticipate a rebuilt Babylon as a part of the world empire system prior to the second coming of Christ.

Revelation 18 fits into this picture very well because it describes a sudden catastrophic destruction of the city and with it the destruction of its political and commercial power. Presented as it is in connection with the second coming of Christ in the Book of Revelation, the implication is that the Old Testament fall of Babylon did not fulfill all the prophecies.

The announcement given in Revelation 18 is by "another angel" than the one who revealed the destruction of Babylon in Revelation 17. John described this, "After this I saw another angel coming down from heaven. He had great authority, and the earth was illuminated by his splendor" (18:1). This angel came down after chapter 17 chronologically, and in the order of revelation comes second. Actually, the destruction of chapter 17 and the destruction of chapter 18 are two separate events separated by three-and-one-half years.

John recorded, "With a mighty voice he shouted: 'Fallen! Fallen is Babylon the Great! She has become a home for demons and a haunt for every evil spirit, a haunt for every unclean and detestable bird. For all the nations have drunk the maddening wine of her adulteries. The kings of the earth committed adultery with her, and the merchants of the earth grew rich from her excessive luxuries' " (vv. 2-3). The fall of Babylon as prophesied here will be followed by being unpopulated, a center of demon power, and the home for wild animals. This never occurred in the history of Babylon.

Scriptures are not clear whether this destruction of Babylon is immediately before the Second Coming or immediately afterward. According to 16:19, however, the great earthquake that precedes the Second Coming will destroy the cities of the Gentiles, and it could be that Babylon was destroyed at the same time.

John then heard an additional revelation concerning the fall of Babylon, "Then I heard another voice from heaven say: 'Come out of her, My people, so that you will not share in her sins, so that you will not receive any of her plagues; for her sins are piled up to heaven, and God has remembered her crimes. Give back to her as she has given; pay her back double for what she has done. Mix her a double portion from her own cup. Give her as much torture and grief as the glory and luxury she gave herself. In her heart she boasts, "I sit as a queen; I am not a widow, and I will never mourn." Therefore in one day her plagues will overtake her: death, mourning and famine. She will be consumed by fire, for mighty is the Lord God who judges her' " (18:4-8).

Those living in Babylon in the end time who are Christians are urged to flee Babylon, much as the inhabitants of Babylon who were saved were urged to flee Babylon in the Old Testament (cf. Jer. 50:4-9; 51:6). Likewise, Lot was urged to leave Sodom (Gen. 19:15-20). The warning lest the plagues overtake them would seem to indicate that this may be subsequent to the seventh bowl of the wrath of God (Rev. 16:17-21). The statement that "her sins are piled up to heaven" (18:5) is a reminder of the Tower of Babel (Gen. 11:5-9), a reminder how God judged the Tower of Babel when it began the long history of Babylon.

Another voice from heaven exhorted them to punish Babylon in keeping with her illicit sins and luxuries. Again, the judgment does not come in a long, drawn-out situation but by the immediate judgment which will come on a given day. The exhortation to pay Babylon back double for what she has done is an application of the law of retribution. When she boasts that she is not a widow, she has in mind all her illicit love affairs with the kings on earth. The result is that Babylon will be destroyed and burned with fire (v. 8).

John recorded that the kings of the earth who had shared her illicit luxuries lamented her passing, "Terrified at her torment, they will stand far off and cry: 'Woe! Woe, O great city, O Babylon, city of power! In one hour your doom has come!' " (v. 10) Again, this judgment on Babylon occurs in a single day in contrast to the hundreds of years in which it gradually was left in ruins.

The voice from heaven continues its revelation, "The merchants of the earth will weep and mourn over her because no one buys their cargoes any more — cargoes of gold, silver, precious stones and pearls; fine linen, purple, silk and scarlet cloth; every sort of citron wood, and articles of every kind made of ivory, costly wood, bronze, iron and marble; cargoes of cinnamon and spice, of incense, myrrh and frankincense, of wine and olive oil, of fine flour and wheat; cattle and sheep; horses and carriages; and bodies and souls of men. They will say, 'The fruit you longed for is gone from you. All your riches and splendor have vanished, never to be recovered.' The merchants who sold these things and gained their wealth from her will stand far off, terrified at her torment. They will weep and mourn and cry out: 'Woe! Woe, O great city, dressed in fine linen, purple and scarlet, and glittering with gold, precious stones and pearls! In one hour such great wealth has been brought to ruin!' " (vv. 11-17)

This remarkable account of the products that were used by ancient Babylon indicates the extensive wealth of the city and the many costly things that were normally imported. Again, as the city is destroyed, the merchants lament its passing, and the reminder is given that this destruction takes place "In one hour" (v. 17).

There is no correspondence of the scene here with what happened to Babylon in the Old Testament, and this gives further basis for belief that this is a future situation where Babylon is rebuilt and then brought to ruin in connection with the events related to the second coming of Christ. The sea captains and merchants who had conveyed these rich products to Babylon also add their lament, "Every sea captain, and all who travel by ship, the sailors, and all who earn their living from the sea, will stand far off. When they see the smoke of her burning, they will exclaim, 'Was there ever a city like this great city?' They will throw dust on their heads, and with weeping and mourning cry out: 'Woe! Woe, O great city, where all who had ships on the sea became rich through her wealth! In one hour she has been brought to ruin!' " (vv. 17-19) Some have suggested that the Euphrates at that time will be opened to sea traffic which would account for the reference to ships and sailors.

Joining in the cry over Babylon is heaven itself. As John stated it, "Rejoice over her, O heaven! Rejoice, saints and apostles and prophets! God has judged her for the way she treated you" (v. 20).

The final description of the destruction of Babylon comes after an angel throws a millstone into the sea, symbolic of the destruction of Babylon, "Then a mighty angel picked up a boulder the size of a large millstone and threw it into the sea, and said: 'With such violence the great city of Babylon will be thrown down, never to be found again. The music of harpists and musicians, flute players and trumpeters, will never be heard in you again. No workman of any trade will ever be found in you again. The sound of a millstone will never be heard in you again. The light of a lamp will never shine in you again. The voice of bridegroom and bride will never be heard in you again. Your merchants were the world's great men. By your magic spell all the nations were led astray. In her was found the blood of prophets and of the saints, and of all who have been killed on the earth' " (vv. 21-24).

The prophecy is specific that life and events will come to a total stop in the ancient city of Babylon due to a sudden destruction that comes in one day. As this has never been fulfilled, it lends credence to the concept that Babylon will be rebuilt in the end time and then suffer this destruction at the time of the Second Coming.

# 15

# PROPHECY OF THE SECOND COMING, THE MILLENNIUM, AND THE ETERNAL STATE

# PROPHECY CONCERNING THE SECOND COMING OF CHRIST

## Announcement of the Second Coming of Christ

*Revelation 19:1-6.* Previous revelation in the book has been largely dealing with God's judgment on a wicked world. Now the theme changes to some extent because it will reveal God's blessed plan for His own. This chapter introduces the second coming of Christ which is the major theme of this entire book. All that precedes chapter 19 is by way of introduction. The Second Coming itself is presented in Revelation 19:11-21, and the chapters which follow, 20–22, are the aftermath of the Second Coming. The revelation of chapter 19 follows the preceding chapter in order of revelation to John as well as chronologically.

Accordingly, John wrote, "After this I heard what sounded like the roar of a great multitude in heaven shouting: 'Hallelujah! Salvation and glory and power belong to our God, for true and just are His judgments. He has condemned the great prostitute who corrupted the earth by her adulteries. He has avenged on her the blood of His servants.' And again they shouted: 'Hallelujah! The smoke from her goes up forever and ever.' The twenty-four elders and the four living creatures fell down and worshiped God, who was seated on the throne. And they cried: 'Amen, Hallelujah!' " (19:1-4)

John recorded the shouting of "a great multitude" (v. 1), precisely the same wording as 7:9. Accordingly, the multitude in heaven that is participating in this may well be the martyred saints of the Great Tribulation. The "Hallelujah" (19:1) is the first of four Hallelujahs in the New Testament, all of which are found in this chapter (vv. 1, 3-4, 6).

The English word "hallelujah" is from the Hebrew word "hallelujah" which means "praise the Lord." The Greek word *allelouia* is a transliteration from the Hebrew and has the same meaning. It is a time for rejoicing and praising God for the great victory that is going to be symbolized and realized by the second coming of Christ.

The multitude ascribes three major attributes to God: salvation, referring to deliverance from evil; glory, speaking of God's moral glory described in the judgments on sin; and power, revealed in His judgments on the harlot and evil in the period preceding the Second Coming. Some texts add a fourth, honor, referring to the fact that God is worthy of highest honor.

The attributes have been illustrated and confirmed in God's judgment on the prostitute (Rev. 17). The smoke of her torment continues forever (19:3) which refers first to judgment in hades prior to the judgment of the Great White Throne and afterward punishment in the lake of fire (20:14). Further praise is ascribed to God by the twenty-four elders and the four living creatures (19:4). If the multitude mentioned in this chapter refers to the Tribulation saints and the twenty-four elders represent the church prior to the Rapture, the revelation is one that they unite their praise of God. Anticipated is the fact that Jesus Christ will reign (v. 6).

### The Wedding Supper Announced

*Revelation 19:7-10.* John was next introduced to the wedding of the Lamb, literally, the "marriage supper" (Gr., *gamos*). This announcement has to be seen in the background of the ceremonies concerning marriage customs in the ancient world. At the time Christ was on earth there were three major aspects to this: (1) A marriage contract was consummated by parents of the bride and the bridegroom, and the parents of the bridegroom would pay a dowry to the parents of the bride. This was the legal marriage and would require a divorce to break the union. (2) The second step, which usually occurred a year later or at another suitable time, featured the bridegroom accompanied by his male friends going to the house of the bride at midnight with a torch parade through the streets. The bride would know he was coming and be ready with her maidens and would join the procession and go back to the home of the bridegroom. This is illustrated in the Parable of the Virgins in Matthew 25:1-13. (3) The third phase of the wedding was the marriage supper which might go on for days as illustrated in the wedding at Cana in John 2:1-12.

In view of this custom, it is significant that what is here announced is the wedding feast, or supper, and the implication is that the first two steps of the wedding have taken place. This would fit naturally into the prophetic fulfillment of this illustration in that the legal phase of the wedding was consummated on earth when an individual believer puts his trust in Christ as Saviour. He has been bought by the blood of Christ and now belongs to Christ in the sense of a betrothal. Accordingly, unfaithfulness for the bride in this situation is considered adultery.

The second phase of the marriage of the Lamb is illustrated in the Rapture of the church when Christ comes to claim His bride and take her to the Father's house. The marriage supper of the

Lamb would then follow as the third and final step.

As the narration of the events leading up to the Second Coming have been completed and the Second Coming itself is in view, it is significant that the wedding feast is now announced as if it were not consummated in heaven but was about to be consummated in connection with the Second Coming. Though many expositors believe that the wedding supper is in heaven, there is this evidence here at least that the wedding feast could be connected with the second coming of Christ. It should be remembered that this will not be be a literal feast with millions of people attending, but it is a symbolic concept where the guests, or friends, of the bride and the bridegroom will join in on the celebration of the marriage of the bridegroom and the bride.

The bride is presented as being ready with fine linen bright and clean which is defined as representing the righteous acts of the saints. Ephesians 5:25-27 speaks of the preparation of the bride, "Husbands, love your wives, just as Christ loved the church and gave Himself up for her to make her holy, cleansing her by the washing with water through the Word, and to present her to Himself as a radiant church, without stain or wrinkle or any other blemish, but holy and blameless."

In preparation for the marriage, the Saviour died on the cross for His church and became the sacrifice for her sin. This led to the present work of sanctification as the church is being cleansed during her period on earth with the washing of water through the Word, meaning the sanctifying truth of the Word of God is applied and in this way prepares the bride for her future role. The third and final stage is at the Rapture when the bride is presented in her perfection. There is no stain or discoloration, no wrinkle, no blemish, but in every respect the bride is holy and blameless. This, of course, is the result of the sanctifying work at the time of the Rapture when the church is made like Christ.

The invitation to attend the wedding supper is given further revelation as John wrote, "Then the angel said to me, 'Write: "Blessed are those who are invited to the wedding supper of the Lamb!" ' " (Rev. 19:9) Though the wedding feast is not said to take place here, it would seem reasonable that it would be part of the festivities on earth when the Lord Jesus Christ comes with all His saints.

John was overwhelmed by this revelation, and he fell at the feet of the angel who rebukes him, stating that he is not to be worshiped

(v. 10). The exhortation is left, "Worship God! For the testimony of Jesus is the spirit of prophecy" (v. 10). Prophecy has its central purpose in revealing the beauty and righteousness of Christ. This will be a part of the divine revelation in connection with the Second Coming.

This passage distinguishes those who are invited to the wedding feast and those who are not and also distinguishes the bride and those who are not the bride.

The figure of a marriage was used in the Old Testament of Israel pictured as the wife of Yahweh who was unfaithful but whose restoration spiritually will take place in the future. The figure of marriage is also used of the church where Christ is the Bridegroom and the church is the bride. The wedding feast to which the saints are invited, accordingly, includes the church as the bride of Christ and all others. This would include the Old Testament saints who are going to be raised at the Second Coming as well as the martyred dead of the Tribulation who form the multitude. The fact that God deals differently with different people such as Israel, the church, and various nations is in keeping with His sovereignty. Actually, no two individuals are going through the world in exactly the same situation or have exactly the same opportunities. God deals with each individual as well as each group on the basis of the qualities that are revealed in them.

### The Second Coming of Christ Described

*Revelation 19:11-21.* The preparatory revelation concerning the wedding supper of the Lamb is followed by the vision that John had of the second coming of Christ. He recorded, "I saw heaven standing open and there before me was a white horse, whose Rider is called Faithful and True" (v. 11).

Christ is seen here as bodily leaving heaven and coming to earth. The white horse is symbolic of victory. It was customary for Roman generals after a conquest to parade on white horses with their captive prisoners in the procession that followed. The fact that Christ comes on a white horse indicates that it is a time for His victory and for judgment on the wicked world.

John further recorded, "With justice He judges and makes war. His eyes are like blazing fire, and on His head are many crowns. He has a name written on Him that no one knows but He Himself. He is dressed in a robe dipped in blood, and His name is the Word of God. The armies of heaven were following Him, riding on white horses and dressed in fine linen, white and clean. Out of His mouth comes a sharp sword with which to strike down the nations. 'He will rule them with an iron scepter.' He treads the winepress of the fury of the wrath of God Almighty. On His robe and on His thigh He has this name written: KING OF KINGS AND LORD OF LORDS" (vv. 11-16).

What John recorded concerning the Second Coming is in sharp contrast to His first coming when He was born in Bethlehem and placed in a manger. Here He comes as the conquering King and Lord of lords. His purpose in coming is to execute justice on the world, and to accomplish this He will make war (v. 11). His glory was described by John, referring to His eyes blazing fire, speaking of His omniscience and omnipotence. The fact that He wears many crowns, signifying rulership, shows that He is indeed the proper King over all nations.

The name written on Him is not revealed. His robe made of white linen is dipped in blood, signifying that He comes on the basis of His sacrifice for sin and His victory over death. He is also called the "Word of God" by which it is meant that He, like the written Word, expresses who God is and illustrates the attributes of God.

He is accompanied by the hosts of heaven riding also on white horses, representing them as victorious, and dressed in fine linen, white and clean, signifying purity. Christ is pictured as having a sword in His mouth, and the word for "sword" indicates a long and usually large sword known as a Thracian sword (Gr., *hromphaia*). He will, of course, speak the word and will be able to bring judgment on the wicked. Psalm 2:9 is also quoted, referring to His reigning with an iron scepter (Rev. 19:15). His rule will be that of an absolute monarch, but perfectly righteous and just. He will also be One who brings judgment on the wicked, and the symbolism of a winepress pressing out the juice of grapes is used as a picture of His judgment on the wicked, "On His robe and on His thigh He has this name written: KING OF KINGS AND LORD OF LORDS" (v. 16).

Brief as this description of the Second Coming is, it is clear that when Christ comes in power, He will bring His judgment on the world, and will establish the millennial kingdom.

Other Scriptures bear out some of the details concerning the Second Coming. In Zechariah 14:3-4 the prediction is made, "Then the LORD will go out and fight against those nations, as He fights in the day of battle. On that day His feet will stand on the Mount of Olives, east of Jerusalem, and the Mount of Olives will be split in two from east to west, forming a great valley, with half of the mountain moving north and half moving south." This event distinguishes the second coming of Christ from the Rapture at which time no such event will take place.

Jesus Himself described His second coming in Matthew 24:27-31, "For as lightning that comes from the east is visible even in the west, so will be the coming of the Son of man. Wherever there is a carcass, there the vultures will gather. Immediately after the distress of those days 'the sun will be darkened, and the moon will not give its light; the stars will fall from the sky, and the heavenly bodies will be shaken.' At that time the sign of the Son of man will appear in the sky, and all the nations of the earth will mourn. They will see the Son of man coming on the clouds of the sky, with power and great glory. And He will send His angels with a loud trumpet call, and they will gather His elect from the four winds, from one end of the heavens to the other." The second coming of Christ and His presence on the earth brings to a climax the whole matter of judging the world and bringing in Christ's righteous kingdom.

John recorded some of the things that will occur after the second coming of Christ, "And I saw an angel standing in the sun, who cried in a loud voice to all the birds flying in midair, 'Come, gather together for the great supper of God, so that you may eat the flesh of kings, generals, and mighty men, of horses and their riders, and the flesh of all people, free and slave, small and great.' Then I saw the beast and the kings of the earth and their armies gathered together to make war against the rider on the horse and his army" (Rev. 19:17-19).

The fact that the angel speaks with a loud voice signifies that something important is about to happen (cf. 6:10; 7:2, 10; 10:3; 14:15; 18:2). The invitation to the birds to partake of the dead bodies that had been killed in the judgment on the army is in contrast to the invitation given earlier in this chapter to those who are invited to the wedding supper of the Lamb. Similarity can also be found in the prophecies of Ezekiel 39:17-20 at the conclusion of the invasion of Israel from the North with the bodies of the dead being eaten by birds. Ezekiel, however, referred to an earlier battle that occurred in the first half of the last seven years rather than to this, but the similarities are obvious. Similarity does not prove identity, however. A scene that is actually parallel to this is found in Matthew 24:28, where, again, birds feed on the carcasses.

The terrible judgment that is inflicted on the armies which had united to fight the army from heaven makes clear that God is no respecter of persons, and unbelievers who are great in the sight of the world are no better than others who are obscure.

The next step is to bring judgment to bear on the beast, the world ruler, and the false prophet associated with him. John recorded, "But the beast was captured, and with him the false prophet who had performed the miraculous signs on his behalf. With these signs he had deluded those who had received the mark of the beast and worshiped his image. The two of them were thrown alive into the fiery lake of burning sulfur" (Rev. 19:20).

Careful distinction needs to be made between this lake of fire and hades. Those who are unsaved who die before the second coming of Christ go to hades, as illustrated by the rich man after his death (Luke 16:23). Up to this point nobody had been cast into the lake of fire. Both the beast and the false prophet, however, now are cast directly into the lake of fire, and they will be joined 1,000 years later by those who are now in hades or those who are unsaved at the time of the end of the millennial kingdom. This marks the end, of course, of Gentile power and the world kingdom which was under the ruler of the beast out of the sea, and the beast out of the land, the false prophet who was associated with the beast out of the sea (13:1-18). As supported by the fact that the beast and the false prophet are still there in the lake of fire at the end of the Millennium, it is clear that the lake of fire is not annihilation, and also it does not serve as a sanctifying force because those who are in it remain in their wicked natures with bodies that are suited for eternal punishment. By contrast, believers in Christ will have new bodies that are holy and suited for the worship and service of God throughout eternity. The judgment of Christ on this army is summarized, "The rest of them were killed with the sword that came out of the mouth of the Rider on the horse, and all the birds gorged themselves on their flesh" (19:21).

## THE MILLENNIAL REIGN OF CHRIST
### Views of the Millennium

A major division in the theology of the church has been concerning the question whether there will be a 1,000-year reign of Christ after His second coming. Both the postmillennial and the amillennial views hold that fulfillment of the Millennium is achieved before His second coming, with amillenarians more or less explaining away any literal fulfillment. Accordingly, this chapter should be carefully studied to see what its contribution is and whether it teaches a kingdom on earth of which Christ will be King of kings and Lord of lords following His second coming. It will be seen that the events of Revelation 19:11–20:15 are chronologically presented with the events logically following the Second Coming as effect follows cause. There is no suggestion in the text of any interruption of the natural consequences of the Second Coming. For a discussion of the millennial kingdom, see the author's *The Millennial Kingdom,* Zondervan Publishing House.

Chapter 20 along with Revelation 19 form two of the most important chapters in the Scripture on prophecy of future events. Revelation 20, in particular, deals with the question as to whether there is a Millennium on earth after the second coming of Christ.

There are a bewildering number of diverse interpretations. Among those who are premillennial who view the kingdom as following the second coming of Christ, there are three schools of thought: those who follow a historical fulfillment of the Book of Revelation, believing that some events of Revelation 6–18 are being fulfilled now. They hold that the Second Advent and the kingdom which follows is literal, but that much of the preliminary material, Revelation 6–18, has in some sense been fulfilled.

In the twentieth century another form of premillennialism has arisen which emphasizes the soteriological character of it, and this point of view attempts to find some ground of common faith with the postmillennial and amillennial viewpoints. This form of premillennialism tends to downplay the role of Israel and the political character of the millennial kingdom.

The majority view among premillenarians, however, is that the kingdom following the second coming of Christ is a fulfillment of God's theocratic program, and in keeping with the promise given to David that his kingdom and throne would continue forever over Israel. Those who interpret the prophecies literally view Christ as reigning supremely over the entire world as a political leader, beginning with the Second Coming. This viewpoint is often called the dispensational point of view, but a preferable designation would be that they hold to a literal kingdom on earth. That such a kingdom is soteriological is also evident, and that it has spiritual qualities also is self-evident, but this view takes into consideration the fact that Christ fulfills in a literal way what was prophesied in the Scripture concerning the kingdom on earth.

The amillennial interpretation, which is probably the majority view of the church today, tends to minimize the promise of a kingdom on earth. Amillenarians are not all agreed as to how to arrive at this conclusion. Their viewpoint is called amillennial because their view is nonmillennial, that is, there will be no literal kingdom on earth with Christ reigning on the throne. The amillenarians vary a great deal as to how they arrive at this conclusion.

Some feel, like Augustine, that the entire present age is the millennial kingdom and that God is reigning in the hearts of men who put their trust in Him. This, of course, does not provide any literal fulfillment of the millennial kingdom.

Some hold that the millennial kingdom is being fulfilled in heaven through Christ's spiritual reign over the earth. Often they do not consider the period a literal 1,000 years, and they minimize the literal meaning of the prophecies relating to it.

Some amillenarians now hold that the Millennium will be fulfilled in the new heaven and new earth in eternity. Therefore, it does not need to be fulfilled now. The problem with all of these points of view characteristic of amillennialism and postmillennialism is that they do not provide an intelligent explanation of many passages in the Old Testament and in the New Testament which teach a literal kingdom. This is true also of Revelation 20.

### The Binding of Satan

*Revelation 20:1-3.* John recorded what he saw concerning the binding of Satan, "And I saw an angel coming down out of heaven, having the key to the Abyss and holding in his hand a great chain. He seized the dragon, that ancient serpent, who is the devil, or Satan, and bound him for a thousand years. He threw him into the Abyss, and locked and sealed it over him, to keep him from deceiving the nations anymore until the thousand years were ended. After that, he must be set free for a short time" (vv. 1-3). John saw an angel who had the key to the Abyss, the natural home of Satan and the fallen angels. As he watched, he saw the dragon, or Satan, bound with a great chain, thrown into the Abyss, and the opening was sealed and locked with the statement that it will not be opened until 1,000 years later. While he could see that Satan was being bound and cast into the Abyss with the obvious point being that Satan will be unable to be active any longer, in addition to what he saw he heard the interpretation that this binding of Satan could last 1,000 years and the purpose was to prevent Satan from deceiving the nations.

Inasmuch as the revelation of the duration is a matter of direct divine revelation which John was told, the 1,000 years must be also taken as a literal figure because it was revealed by God as the duration of this event. If God were in any way to try to describe the literal binding of Satan and his being inactive for 1,000 years, He could not have done it in any more graphic or clear way than He has done in these three verses.

The events of verses 1-3 are clearly chronological in order and in total support of the premillennial interpretation. The passage makes clear that Satan is not simply restricted, as some would teach, but he is totally inactive in the Millennium. By contrast, the New Testament teaches that Satan is still very much alive and well in the present age. In Acts 5:3 Ananias and Sapphira were declared to be filled with Satan and motivated by him in lying about their sale of property. In 2 Corinthians 4:3-4 the statement is made that Satan was very active in blinding the eyes of those who hear the Gospel so that they will not see it and understand it. In 11:14 Satan was declared to be an angel of light, appearing in religious guise, deceiving the church through false teaching. According to Ephesians 2:2, the unsaved are working in the power of Satan. In 1 Thessalonians 2:18 Satan was revealed to have hindered Paul in his desire to come to the Thessalonians. In 2 Timothy 2:26 unsaved people were declared to be taken captive and can only be saved by the grace of God. The most decisive text is in 1 Peter 5:8, "Be self-controlled and alert. Your enemy the devil prowls around like a roaring lion looking for someone to devour."

These passages teach dramatically that Satan is not bound in the present age, and though he is somewhat restricted by God, as in the case of Job, Christians can depend on God's protecting power. Satan is, nevertheless, very active in the world and a leader in all its rebellion against God. The 1,000 years will follow the Second Coming.

### The Resurrection of the Tribulation Saints

*Revelation 20:4-6.* With Satan out of the way, the revelation now turns to what God will do for the saints in this period. John wrote,

"I saw thrones on which were seated those who had been given authority to judge. And I saw the souls of those who had been beheaded because of their testimony for Jesus and because of the Word of God. They had not worshiped the beast or his image and had not received his mark on their foreheads or their hands. They came to life and reigned with Christ a thousand years" (v. 4).

Those who had refused to worship the beast had been executed, and a great host of martyrs went to heaven during the time of the Great Tribulation. This had happened in the three-and-one-half years preceding the Second Coming. They are described as "a great multitude" (7:9). Here they are resurrected and honored because they had not received the mark of the beast, and the purpose of the resurrection is that they would reign with Christ 1,000 years. This is a very clear support for a millennial kingdom following the second coming of Christ. The chronology is quite evident.

These martyred dead were killed in the period just before the Second Coming. Now Christ causes the saints who had been martyred in the Tribulation, which was only a short period before the Second Coming, to be resurrected in order to reign with Christ for 1,000 years. There is no way to avoid the implication that the Millennium is subsequent to the second coming of Christ in this passage as it is subsequent to the death and resurrection of the martyrs. As such, the premillennial view is supported.

The attempts to avoid premillennialism have required extreme methods of explaining away this passage. Some amillenarians interpret the resurrection of the martyred dead as their new birth. This, of course, would be entirely out of sequence because they were born again in the Great Tribulation and they were martyred in that situation. Now they are resurrected, and it could not refer to them as being born again on this occasion.

Scriptures go on to describe further their situation, "(The rest of the dead did not come to life until the thousand years were ended). This is the first resurrection. Blessed and holy are those who have part in the first resurrection. The second death has no power over them, but they will be priests of God and of Christ and will reign with Him for a thousand years" (20:5-6). This resurrection is "first" in the sense of being first or before the resurrection of the wicked. Obviously, Christ was the first to be raised if the resurrections of Scripture are numbered.

*Revelation 20:7-15.* The lot of those who are resurrected from the dead is declared to be a blessed event for them, and it promises that they will not be subject to the second death, referring to the judgment of the Great White Throne in verses 11-15. Furthermore, they are declared to be priests of God and Christ. This, apparently, refers to the fact that they will have a special significance as martyrs and will have a special role in the millennial kingdom.

The interpretation of this passage of Revelation illustrates an important point. While prophecy is sometimes presented in symbolic form which has to be interpreted, when the symbolic act is interpreted, one is not free to spiritualize the interpretation. In verses 1-6, while it is presented as a vision which needs interpretation, the interpretation, when given, speaks of the solid fact that Satan needs to be bound for 1,000 years and that the Tribulation saints will be resurrected to reign with Christ in the millennial kingdom. There is no ground for spiritualization of these statements, and that is why many conclude that the premillennial explanation of the second coming of Christ as preceding the Millennium is justifiably supported by Scripture.

The question has been raised concerning those who are seated on the throne to judge (v. 4). Many Scriptures contribute to the fact that saints will share in the reign of Christ. Jesus told His disciples, "And I confer on you a kingdom, just as My Father conferred one on Me, so that you may eat and drink at My table in My kingdom and sit on thrones, judging the twelve tribes of Israel" (Luke 22:29-30).

Obviously, those who reign with Christ will not have equal status but will be subject to Christ and be acting on His behalf. The millennial kingdom as such, however, is not discussed, except that it is clear that it will begin with the second coming of Christ and will end with judgment on the world and a creation of a new heaven and new earth.

### Major Features of the Millennium

The millennial kingdom, which will run its course before the events which climax it, is described at length in many passages in the Scripture. Though the exact figure of 1,000 years is not mentioned except in Revelation 20, the fact of a kingdom which has long duration is clearly the intent of the prophetic passages (Isa. 2:2-4; 11:4-9; Ps. 72; etc.). According to the Old Testament, Jerusalem will be the capital of the millennial kingdom (Isa. 2:3). War will cease (v. 4). The millennial kingdom will be characterized by righteousness, peace, and tranquility, and there will be justice for all the oppressed (11:3-5). Even the ferocity of beasts will be tamed (vv. 6-9). Isaiah summarized the thought in verse 9, "They will neither harm nor destroy on all My holy mountain, for the earth will be full of the knowledge of the LORD as the waters cover the sea," as indicated in Isaiah 11:11-16; Jeremiah 23:3-4, 8; 30:3-9; 31:3-14.

Psalm 72 as well as many other psalms give the glowing prophetic picture of the future Millennium. The future is described as flourishing, the government as righteous, and abundant peace is promised as long as the moon endures. All kings bow down before Christ, and His rule extends from sea to sea. The earth will be filled with the glory of God. The desire of nations for peace, righteousness, knowledge of the Lord, economic justice, and deliverance from Satan will all have its prophetic fulfillment. The major factors of the Millennium, including Christ's absolute power, will include the perfect and righteous government and ideal circumstances on the earth. In many respects the rule of Christ as the last Adam replaces what God had intended for Adam who was placed in charge of the Garden of Eden.

Many passages in the Old Testament emphasize the fact that Israel will have a prominent place. According to Ezekiel 20:33-38, at the time of the Second Coming Israel will experience a purging judgment, and only the righteous, godly remnant will be allowed to enter the kingdom. Israel, pictured in the Old Testament as being an untrue wife, will now be rejoined to Christ in the symbol of marriage and experience the love of Christ (Hosea 1:10-11; 2:14-23).

Though Israel will enjoy the blessings of being regathered to her ancient land and under the special rule of Christ, the rest of the world will also experience the rule of Christ as King of kings. The nation of Israel, however, will also have the benefits of the rule of David resurrected from the dead as a regent of Christ (Jer. 30:9; Ezek. 34:23-24; 37:24-25).

### The Final Rebellion against Christ

*Revelation 20:7-9.* John described the climax of the millennial kingdom, "When the thousand years are over, Satan will be released from his prison and will go out to deceive the nations in the four corners of the earth—Gog and Magog—to gather them for battle. In number they are like the sand on the seashore. They marched across the breadth of the earth and surrounded the camp of God's people, the city He loves. But fire came down from heaven and devoured them" (vv. 7-9).

At the end of the Millennium Satan will be released and will go out and deceive the nations (vv. 7-8). The nations are referred to as "Gog and Magog" (v. 8). This has confused some who try to connect this with Ezekiel 38 and 39. The war of Ezekiel is an invasion of Israel from the North by Russia and a few other nations. By a series of judgments from God, the armies are completely wiped out and months are spent in burying the bodies.

The battle here is totally different. Those who form the attackers come from all nations of the world, not just a few. They gather about the city of Jerusalem in attempting to capture the capital city, but fire comes down from heaven and devours them. The war of Ezekiel 38–39 is far north of Jerusalem. The time situation is different.

The war of Ezekiel 38–39 occurs at a time when Israel is at peace and not expecting war. The battle here is at the end of the millennial kingdom and is Satan's final attempt to conquer the world. There is no need to bury the dead bodies because they have been consumed by fire in contrast to Ezekiel 38–39. Life does not go on after this battle as in Ezekiel for the world immediately moves into the new heaven and new earth situation.

People have asked the question why Satan will be loosed from his prison after the 1,000 years. This action is in keeping with God's purpose to demonstrate in history that man left to his own devices will, nevertheless, sin against God. Even though the Millennium provided a perfect environment for humanity with abundant revelation of God's power, the evil heart of man is manifest in the fact that people reject Christ and follow Satan when he is loosed. The loosing of Satan also is a demonstration of the wickedness of Satan and the fallen angels and how even 1,000 years in confinement does not change this.

### Satan Cast into the Lake of Fire

*Revelation 20:10.* The wickedness of Satan is the basis for justifying God's judgment on Satan who is here thrown into the lake of burning sulfur (v. 10). Important to note is the fact that the beast and the false prophet, who had been thrown into the lake of burning sulfur 1,000 years before, are still there, demonstrating that this is not annihilation but continued punishment. The beast and the false prophet as well as the devil are included in the statement, "They will be tormented day and night forever and ever" (v. 10).

### The Great White Throne Judgment

*Revelation 20:11-15.* John then recorded the change in the scene and introduced the revelation concerning the Great White Throne and the judgment of the wicked dead. He wrote, "Then I saw a Great White Throne and Him who was seated on it. Earth and sky fled from His presence, and there was no place for them" (v. 11). Though the word "throne" appears some thirty times in the Book of Revelation, this is a reference to a throne different than any previously mentioned, and, accordingly, it is called "a Great White Throne." Unlike the previous thrones on earth or heaven, it is pictured as being in space and occupied by Christ Himself.

This is supported by the statement in John 5:22-23, "Moreover, the Father judges no one, but has entrusted all judgment to the Son, that all may honor the Son just as they honor the Father. He who does not honor the Son does not honor the Father, who sent Him." Like the Judgment Seat of Christ which took place in heaven before the Millennium, this judgment does not have its scene on earth but in space.

The fact that earth and sky fled from the presence of the One on the throne is in keeping with Revelation 21:1 where a new heaven and a new earth is introduced. As John watched, he saw this great judgment taking place, "And I saw the dead, great and small, standing before the throne, and books were opened. Another book was opened, which is the Book of Life. The dead were judged according to what they had done as recorded in the books. The sea gave up the dead that were in it, and death and Hades gave up the dead that were in them, and each person was judged according to what he had done. Then death and Hades were thrown into the lake of fire. The lake of fire is the second death. If anyone's name was not found written in the Book of Life, he was thrown into the lake of fire" (Rev. 20:12-15).

As this text makes plain, this is the final judgment. As the righteous have already been judged, this judgment relates to the wicked. This is the final resurrection in contrast to the first resurrection which had to do with the righteous (Dan. 12:2; John 5:29; Acts 24:15; Rev. 20:5).

The fact that both small and great are specified is similar to descriptions previously used in Revelation (11:18; 13:16; 19:5, 18).

Those standing before the throne come from all walks of life, but now are being judged on the basis of their works. According to Hebrews 9:27, everyone has to face Christ in judgment. The judgment is based on what occurs in the books which record their works and whether their names are in the Book of Life.

The Book of Life is presented as including the names of all who are genuinely saved. The description of this resurrection indicates that it is a universal resurrection of all that are yet in the grave, that is, the unrighteous. Special mention is made of the sea as giving up the dead in it because bodies lost at sea disintegrate and are scattered as far as the particles of their human bodies are concerned. This is no problem for an omnipotent God, and their bodies are raised from the dead in the sea. Hades is also declared to give up "the dead that were in it" (v. 13), and those in hades were thrown into the lake of fire.

Distinction in Scripture should be observed between hades, which is the place of the dead between death and resurrection, and the lake of fire which is the final destiny of those who are unsaved. The resurrection of the wicked is distinguished from the resurrection of the righteous in that there is no reward or recognition of righteousness on their part.

Like the righteous, they are given bodies which cannot be destroyed. But while the righteous receive bodies that are holy and suited for the presence of God, the wicked dead receive bodies that are indestructible and suited for eternal punishment. They are still wicked and still in rebellion against God. The Scriptures are very clear that if anyone's name is not found in the Book of Life, he will be thrown in the lake of fire.

Many have attempted to find some escape for the wicked so that they would not be the objects of eternal punishment. From a human viewpoint this may be desired, but the Bible never suggests that the punishment of the wicked continues only for a time. If the beast and the false prophet after 1,000 years in the lake of fire are still intact, it is obvious that those who are now being thrown into the lake of fire will, likewise, continue in the place of torment. Christ Himself emphasized the destiny of the wicked (Matt. 13:42; 25:41, 46). In Revelation 14:11 those who received the mark of the beast were declared to be the objects of eternal punishment. Scriptural revelation limits the destiny of mankind to either heaven or the lake of fire.

# THE NEW HEAVEN, NEW EARTH, AND NEW JERUSALEM
## General Description

*Revelation 21:1-8.* Having revealed the destruction of the old earth and the old heaven, John wrote that he saw what will take its place — a new heaven, new earth, and a New Jerusalem, "Then I saw a new heaven and a new earth, for the first heaven and the first earth had passed away, and there was no longer any sea" (v. 1). Scriptural revelation gives very little information about the new heaven and the new earth, except by inferring that it is quite different than our present earth. The only major characteristic mentioned is that there will not be any longer any sea in contrast to the present situation where most of the earth is covered with water. It is apparent as the narration goes on that the new earth is round because there are directions of north, south, east, and west (v. 13), but there is no indication as to whether the new earth is larger or smaller than our present earth.

Instead of focusing on the new earth and a new heaven, Revelation deals with the subject of the Holy City, the New Jerusalem. John wrote, "I saw the Holy City, the New Jerusalem, coming down out of heaven from God, prepared as a bride beautifully dressed for her husband" (v. 2). The New Jerusalem is totally different than the old Jerusalem on the present earth and is created to be the center of population in the new earth.

Without explanation John stated that the New Jerusalem comes down out of heaven from God. Though the new earth and new heaven are created at this time, apparently the New Jerusalem was created earlier. As the New Jerusalem will not be on the millennial earth, some have postulated the possibility that the New Jerusalem will be a satellite city over the earth during the Millennium and as such would be the home of resurrected and translated saints. They would be able to go from the New Jerusalem to the millennial earth much as people today have their home in the country and go to the office in the city. This would solve the problem of where the millions of resurrected and translated people live during the period when on earth there will be a population still living their natural lives, and no picture of the millennial earth takes into consideration the millions of those who are not in their natural bodies but who are serving the Lord. Because this has such a slender basis, however, it is a doctrine that cannot be dogmatically held.

The New Jerusalem is mentioned earlier in Scripture in a few passages (Isa. 65:17; 66:22; 2 Peter 3:13; Rev. 3:12). Several of these predictions of the New Jerusalem were found in a context where millennial truth is being discussed, and this has confused expositors as to how to relate the New Jerusalem to the millennial period. The answer is that in revealing future events, often events that are separated by time are merged as if they were in existence together. This is especially true, for instance, of the first and second comings of Christ which in the Old Testament often are mentioned in the same verse (Isa. 61:1-2; cf. Luke 4:17-19). In a similar way in Daniel 12:2, the resurrection of the righteous and the wicked are mentioned in the same verse, but later revelation reveals that there will be 1,000 years between the resurrection of the righteous and the resurrection of the wicked. In Malachi 4:5 the second coming of Christ is followed in verse 6 by reference to His first coming. In the New Testament as well, similar events are put together that were separated by time as in 2 Peter 3:10-13 which refers to the beginning of the Day of the Lord but then recounts events such as the destruction of the heaven and the earth which will take place at the end of the Day of the Lord as well as the end of the Millennium.

The absence of any sea in the new earth also makes it clear that this is not the Millennium as some have tried to hold, for bodies of water occur frequently in millennial passages (Ps. 72:8; Isa. 11:9, 11; Ezek. 47:10, 15, 17-18, 20; 48:28; Zech. 9:10; 14:8). The tendency of some contemporary scholars to try to find fulfillment of the Millennium in the new heaven and the new earth ignores these important differences in description of the new earth as compared to the old earth. In the revelation to John of the new earth, new heaven, and New Jerusalem, it should be remembered that what John is seeing prophetically is what will happen in the future, not what was existing at the time he lived on earth. Accordingly, John was projected forward in the history of the world to the time following the end of the Millennium when this important change of scene will take place.

Some scholars also have been confused because the city is referred to as "prepared as a bride beautifully dressed for her husband" (Rev. 21:2). Some have tried to spiritualize the New Jerusalem as if it were a company of people. As Revelation continues, however, it is quite clear that it is a literal city that is intended, and the reference to it being beautiful like a beautiful bride is only a way to refer to its beauty and its newness. The setting of the New Jerusalem in the new earth is God's provision of a happy home for saints of all ages. Though not revealed in the Old Testament in any great length, Abram, who looked for God's fulfillment in regard to the millennial kingdom, also looked for a heavenly city (Heb. 11:10-16; cf. 12:22-24).

In the New Jerusalem God will make His residence; in fact, the New Jerusalem will be His temple. John wrote, "He will wipe every tear from their eyes. There will be no more death or mourning or crying or pain, for the old order of things has passed away" (Rev. 21:4). In making this statement, the revelation does not mean that we will start crying in heaven and then have our crying eased, but, rather, it will be foreign to the whole setting. It will be a time of rejoicing in the grace of God and the opportunity and privilege of worship and service for the Lord. The situation will be entirely a new order as John recorded, "He who was seated on the throne said, 'I am making everything new!' Then He said, 'Write this down, for these words are trustworthy and true' " (v. 5).

In a further summary of the character of heaven and of the New Jerusalem, John wrote, "He said to me: 'It is done. I am the Alpha and the Omega, the Beginning and the End. To him who is thirsty I will give to drink without cost from the spring of the water of life. He who overcomes will inherit all this, and I will be his God and He will be My son. But the cowardly, the unbelieving, the vile, the murderers, the sexually immoral, those who practice magic arts, the idolaters and all liars—their place will be in the fiery lake of burning sulfur. This is the second death' " (vv. 6-8).

In referring to Himself as "the Alpha and the Omega, the Beginning and the End" (v. 6), Christ is saying that He is the first and the last as the first and last letters of the Greek alphabet are mentioned, and this is further defined as the beginning and the end. Christ is the eternal One, and the truths He is talking about are truths that will last forever.

The wonder of salvation by grace and drinking of the spring of the water of life are part of the wonderful provision God has made for those who put their trust in Him. This refers to how abundant our new life in Christ is as indicated in the invitation of Isaiah 55:1 and that of Christ in John 4:10, 13-14. The promise that all things will be inherited by those who overcome by faith and that God will be his God and he will be God's son is the illustration of the abundant grace that Christians have in Christ and how marvelous our inheritance is (cf. Matt. 5:5; 19:29; 25:34; 1 Cor. 6:9-10; Heb. 1:14; 9:15; 1 Peter 1:4; 3:9; 1 John 5:5).

Overcoming by faith is also mentioned as a ground of reward in Christ's messages to the seven churches (Rev. 2–3) and is itemized as a hope and an expectation of Paul, "So then, no more boasting about men! All things are yours, whether Paul or Apollos or Cephas or the world or life or death or the present or the future—all are yours, and you are of Christ, and Christ is of God" (1 Cor. 3:21-23).

Those whose lives are characterized by disregard of God and disregard of His moral commandments will be excluded. This revelation does not mean that if at one time in their lives some people were engaged in these immoral acts that they cannot be saved, but, rather, it is if the quality of their life as a whole is characterized by these sins, their destiny will be the lake of fire. In Scripture as in common life sometimes people with a sordid background are saved, forgiven, justified, and bound for heaven. Those who do not respond to faith in Christ have to face the fact that their destiny is the second death, the fiery lake of burning sulfur.

### The New Jerusalem

*Revelation 21:9-27.* Having surveyed the general character of the new earth and the New Jerusalem, John was then introduced to the Holy City, Jerusalem, mentioned in verse 2. Scholars who otherwise agree on interpretation of prophecy have raised the question as to whether this section, beginning in verse 9, is a recapitulation, taking them back to the millennial kingdom, or whether it is in chronological order here and a description of the new heaven and new earth and New Jerusalem as that which will follow the Millennium.

Though worthy scholars can be named on both sides of this argument, in view of the fact that all has been chronological from chapter 19:11 up to this point, it would seem most logical for the narration to continue chronologically, having introduced the New Jerusalem now to describe it in detail. Having introduced the subject in 21:2-8 which most expositors recognize as the eternal state, it would follow that verse 9 also is referring to the eternal state and not a millennial situation. As the details of the city unfold, it is clear that it is not a millennial situation for there is no room for such a large city as the heavenly city, the New Jerusalem, to be placed on the Holy Land during the millennial kingdom. Scriptures instead describe the city in the Millennium in entirely different terms (Ezek. 40–48).

The revelation that is given in these closing verses of the Book of Revelation provide a vista for comprehending the beauty of the eternal situation in which Christians will find themselves when they are in the New Jerusalem and in the new earth.

One of the problems of interpretation is the question of how far nonliteral interpretation should figure in understanding this passage. As a general rule, the basis for interpretation is best understood as providing a literal view of what is revealed, but that the contents of what is seen may have spiritual meaning beyond the physical.

John wrote, "One of the seven angels who had the seven bowls full of the seven last plagues came and said to me, 'Come, I will show you the bride, the wife of the Lamb.' And he carried me away in the Spirit to a mountain great and high, and showed me the Holy City, Jerusalem, coming down out of heaven from God" (Rev. 21:9-10). The problem mentioned in verse 2 of how a city could also be a bride carries over to this description. Actually, the bride of Christ is composed of people, those who have accepted Christ in the present age and who form the church, the body of Christ. In showing John the Holy City, there is a relationship to the bride in that the beauty of the Holy City is similar to the beauty of the bride. Obviously, a literal meaning cannot be that it is both a city and a bride, and so one must complement the other.

John in his statement went on, "It shone with the glory of God, and its brilliance was like that of a very precious jewel, like a jasper, clear as crystal" (v. 11). Beginning with this verse, a number of precious jewels are mentioned as being characteristic of the New Jerusalem. Sometimes, however, it is difficult to ascertain exactly which jewel is in mind.

The city as a whole is like a precious jewel, like a jasper clear as crystal, according to John. In our present earth the jasper stone is not clear but opaque, indicating that while the jewel looks like a jasper, it actually could be some other jewel. The description which follows pictures Jerusalem as a gigantic jewel piece aglow with the glory of God and a beautiful setting for God's grace to be made evident in the lives of those who have trusted Him.

John described the city, "It had a great, high wall with twelve gates, and with twelve angels at the gates. On the gates were written the names of the twelve tribes of Israel. There were three gates on the east, three on the north, three on the south and three on the west" (vv. 12-13). The city as described by John is a very impressive one even by present standards. Though some have said that the city is not a literal city and merely symbolizes the church, the body of Christ, it seems best to consider it a literal city which, nevertheless, in its elements represents the church in some of its qualities. The wall of the city is described as great and high which illustrates the fact that not everyone is qualified to enter into the blessings of the city. The number "twelve" is very prominent in the description of the city as seen in the twelve gates, the twelve angels, the twelve tribes of Israel (v. 12), the twelve foundations (v. 14), the twelve Apostles (v. 14), the twelve pearls (v. 21), and the twelve kinds of fruit (22:2). The city is also said to be 12,000 stadia in length and the wall to be 144 cubits in width, 144 being twelve times twelve. The fact that the twelve gates have the names of the twelve tribes of Israel (21:12) makes clear that Israel will be part of the populace of this city.

In Ezekiel 48:31-34 the twelve gates of the millennial temple are mentioned: Reuben, Judah, and Levi, going west to east on the north side; going north to south on the east side, Joseph, Benjamin, and Dan; on the west side, moving from north to south, Naphtali, Asher, and Gad; and on the south side, proceeding from east to west, Simeon, Issachar, and Zebulun. Nothing is said here about the names of the twelve tribes on the particular gates. It may or may not be true that the same order is followed here as in the millennial temple.

John in his description of the city continued, "There were three gates on the east, three on the north, three on the south and three on the west. The wall of the city had twelve foundations, and on them were the names of the twelve Apostles of the Lamb" (Rev. 21:13-14). Though the names of the twelve Apostles were not given, it is clear that just as the names of Israel on the gates of the city prove that Israel is in the New Jerusalem, so the names of the apostles on the twelve foundations prove that the church will be in the New Jerusalem. In fact, as all the facts are put together, the New Jerusalem will be the home of all the saints of all ages and the holy angels as well as God Himself.

The immensity of this city is brought out by John's statement of the angel measuring the city, "The angel who talked with me had a measuring rod of gold to measure the city, its gates and its walls. The city was laid out like a square, as long as it is wide. He measured the city with a rod and found it to be 12,000 stadia in length, and as wide and as high as it is long." He measured its wall, and it was 144 cubits thick (or high) by man's measurement, which the angel was using. The city, therefore, is a large city, larger than any city known today, and especially unusual in that it is as high as it is long. The 12,000 stadia translated into modern terms amount to about 1,400 miles. The city as such would be far too large to place on the millennial earth, but in the new earth there will be plenty of room.

In this city, as brought out, both Jew and Gentile will be inhabiting the city along with the saints of all other ages. Significant is the fact, however, that a Jew is not automatically recognized as belonging to the church and the church is not automatically related to Israel. The distinctions between the racial Jew and the church composed of both Jews and Gentiles is maintained in this revelation.

In Hebrews 12:22-24 the inhabitants of the city are itemized, "But you have come to Mount Zion, to the heavenly Jerusalem, the city of the living God. You have come to thousands upon thousands of angels in joyful assembly, to the church of the firstborn, whose names are written in heaven. You have come to God, the Judge of all men, to the spirits of righteous men made perfect, to Jesus the Mediator of a New Covenant, and to the sprinkled blood that speaks a better word than the blood of Abel." In the New Jerusalem will be both angels and the church and all others who could be called righteous regardless of their dispensational background. In the city also will be God the Father, God the Son, and God the Holy Spirit.

John described in detail the beautiful stones relating to the wall, "The wall was made of jasper, and the city of pure gold, as pure as glass. The foundations of the city walls were decorated with every kind of precious stone. The first foundation was jasper, the second sapphire, the third chalcedony, the fourth emerald, the fifth sardonyx, the sixth carnelian, the seventh chrysolite, the eighth beryl, the ninth topaz, the tenth chrysoprase, the eleventh jacinth, and the twelfth amethyst" (Rev. 21:18-20).

These stones, having varied colors and glowing with the glory of God, present an amazingly beautiful spectacle for John as he gazed on the city. The jasper stone, mentioned first, is apparently like our present jasper stone but clear as crystal. Built on the jasper stone, which is the bottom layer of the foundation, was a brilliant sapphire in appearance like a diamond in color. The third foundation of chalcedony was an agate stone from Chalcedon, modern Turkey, and it is believed to have been sky blue with stripes of other colors. The fourth foundation, the emerald, introduces the familiar bright green color. The sardonyx is a red and white stone. The sixth foundation, carnelian, also identified as Sardius stone, was a stone usually found in a honey color. It is used with jasper in Revelation 4:3, describing the glory of God on the throne.

The seventh foundation is chrysolite which is thought to have been a gold color, and possibly different from the modern chrysolite stone which is pale green. The eighth foundation, the beryl, is a deep sea green. The ninth foundation, the topaz, is yellow green, and transparent. The tenth foundation, chrysoprase, introduces another green color. The eleventh foundation, jacinth, is violet in color. The twelfth foundation, the amethyst, is commonly a purple.

In seeing these many colors with the brilliant light of the glory of God in the New Jerusalem, John saw a scene of indescribable beauty worthy of the God who had created it. If Christians can be thrilled by the use of colors and the creations of men, how much greater will be the New Jerusalem which comes from the creative hand of God.

John also referred to the twelve gates, "The twelve gates were twelve pearls, each gate made of a single pearl" (21:21). Obviously, these transcend any pearl such as we know in this life and are large stones, but beautiful like a pearl. The streets to the city are declared to be of pure gold like transparent glass (v. 21). It is possible that all the materials of this city are translucent, and the glory of God will go through them and light up the city in a blaze of color.

John next itemized things he did not see, "I did not see a temple in the city, because the Lord God Almighty and the Lamb are its temple" (v. 22). There apparently will be no sun or moon needed to bring light to the earth because the glory of God will lighten the New Jerusalem (v. 23). There will be no night either because the glory of God will illuminate the city continuously (v. 25). John stated, "The nations will walk by its light, and the kings of the earth will bring their splendor into it" (v. 24).

The nations, referring to the Gentiles, will bring their glory and honor into the city to the glory of God (v. 26). Anything that is impure, however, or is shameful or deceitful is shut out of the city and not permitted to inhabit it, as John stated it, "but only those whose names are written in the Lamb's Book of Life" (v. 27) will be allowed in the city. Though the description of John is graphic and presents a beautiful display of the glory of God, it is obvious that the real city which believers will see in the eternal state will far exceed the possibility of describing it in words.

### The Final Revelation concerning the City and the Eternal State

*Revelation 22:1-21.* As John recorded the final chapter of the Book of Revelation featuring the major features of the life and circumstances of the saints in eternity, the judgment of the wicked is viewed as past and eternity stretches before the believer. It is a time of unqualified blessing. John recorded, "Then the angel showed me the river of the water of life, as clear as crystal, flowing from the throne of God and of the Lamb" (v. 1). In keeping with the holiness and perfection of the eternal state, the water of life issued from the throne of God and of the Lamb. Scriptures mention other streams in the Millennium, and this revelation should not be confused with the river that flows from the millennial sanctuary (Ezek. 47:1, 12) nor with the record of the living waters going forth from Jerusalem (Zech. 14:8). The water of life speaks of the purity, the power, and the holiness of the eternal life in the heavenly city. Significant is the fact that the water proceeds from the throne of God and of the Lamb. Though the throne of Christ is different than the throne of David and the millennial throne on which He sat throughout the millennial kingdom, this indicates that Christ is still with God the Father reigning over the eternal state.

In addition to picturing the water of life, John also recorded the tree of life in the city. The water of life which John pictured in Revelation 22:1 also is said to flow "down the middle of the great street of the city. On each side of the river stood the tree of life, bearing twelve crops of fruit, yielding its fruit every month. And the leaves of the tree are for the healing of the nations" (v. 2).

This verse has confused expositors because it is hard to visualize how the same tree could be on both sides of the river which flows down the great street of the city. Several solutions are possible. The stream may be very narrow flowing down the street, and the tree of life may be very large in the sense that it is over the entire street. Some offer the opinion that the tree of life is a collective term and that there is more than one tree, and hence the tree of life

640

would be on both sides of the street.

A number of problems confront the interpretation of this passage besides the attempt to reconstruct visually what is described. The tree of life here seems to be a reference to what is mentioned in the Garden of Eden (Gen. 3:22, 24) where it is stated that if Adam and Eve had eaten of the tree of life they would have lived forever in their fallen state. It was preferable that they go through death into a new order of a resurrection body and all that this entails.

Further, the statement is that the tree of life bears twelve crops of fruit which, apparently, are subject to being eaten. Most significant is the fact that "the leaves of the tree are for the healing of the nations" (Rev. 22:2). The question is fairly asked why healing would be necessary in a situation where there is no sickness, no death, no sorrow, and no crime. The word for healing (Gr., *therapeian*) is in the English the word "therapeutic." Accordingly, rather than healing, it could be understood as that which brings health. The leaves of the tree, then, would be described as bringing enjoyment of life in the New Jerusalem. Accordingly, as it may not be necessary to partake of the leaves of the tree in order to enjoy the eternal state forever, it apparently provides an avenue by which enjoyment can be enhanced. The healing is also said to extend to the nations (Gr., *ethne*), literally, the Gentiles or the peoples. Though frequently used to distinguish Gentiles from Israel, the word would include all races in a context such as this.

As if to answer the question of whether these verses imply imperfection in the eternal state, John stated, "No longer will there be any curse. The throne of God and of the Lamb will be in the city, and His servants will serve Him" (v. 3). All that spoke of sin and its penalties is wiped away in heaven, and there is nothing left that is a reminder of sin. All are blessed, not cursed. In support of this conclusion, it is revealed that God's throne and that of the Lamb will be in the city. The question is often raised: What will Christians do in heaven? The Scriptures are very simple in stating the fact, as this verse does, that "His servants will serve Him" (v. 3). In a situation where every child of God will be profoundly grateful for God's grace in bringing them to this place where they can enjoy the blessings of eternal life, the love of the saints for God will show itself in an eager desire to serve God. Whatever the humble task or the important task assigned to an individual, it will bring great satisfaction to be able to do something for God who has done so much for him.

The intimacy of the servants of God with God is indicated in that the saints will be able to see the face of God, and His name will be on their foreheads. John wrote, "They will see His face, and His name will be on their foreheads" (v. 4). The identification with God is mentioned several times previously in the Book of Revelation (2:17; 3:12; 7:3; 14:1). Seeing the face of God is something that could not have been accomplished prior to the saints' resurrection and glorification. The fact that they will be able to see the face of God demonstrates that they are perfectly holy by the grace of God.

Just as there will be wonderful experience of relationship and service to God, so they will enjoy the glory of God, "There will be no more night. They will not need the light of a lamp or the light of the sun, for the Lord God will give them light. And they will reign forever and ever" (22:5). Darkness will be banished in the eternal state. The New Jerusalem made of translucent materials will be an amazing, beautiful sight as the light streams through all the various colors, not leaving any shadows. The sun and the moon will be no more because they are no longer needed, but the glory of God will be the light of the city (21:23). Their blessed state is that they will reign with Christ forever.

As a climax to this revelation, John recorded, "The angel said to me, 'These words are trustworthy and true. The Lord, the God of the spirits of the prophets, sent His angel to show His servants the things that must soon take place' " (22:6).

An amazing record of God's faithfulness and sovereignty is demonstrated in history and climaxing in the eternal state. God has put down evil and judged Satan and men. No longer will men rebel against God, but God will be sovereign in time and eternity. No trace of sin will taint the kingdom of God, but the holiness that is God's own spiritual quality will be shared with the saints. Where there once was death, now there will be resurrection life; where there once was judgment and curse, there now is removal and redemption; where there once was darkness, now there is light; where there was once ugliness, now there is beauty. Joys replace sorrow; holiness, sin; and men, instead of serving themselves and Satan, will worship God, serve Christ, and be like Christ in spiritual quality.

Spiritually, there will be perfect restoration. In the conduct of government, there will be perfect administration. The servants shall be transformed into the likeness of God. They will clearly be identified with His name on their foreheads. No artificial means of light is necessary because God provides perfect illumination.

John was well aware, however, that the battle of the ages had not yet been consummated and John still lived in the wicked world where he was in exile on the Isle of Patmos. To him and to others caught still in the world's sinful state, the angel said, "Behold, I am coming soon! Blessed is he who keeps the words of the prophecy in this book" (v. 7). Though it is impossible to date the coming of Christ, the fact that the Rapture of the church is an imminent event which requires preparation in advance serves to alert believers that the events of the end time may be impending.

John was overwhelmed by the abundance of revelation given to him, and he recorded, "I, John, am the one who heard and saw these things. And when I had heard and seen them, I fell down to worship at the feet of the angel who had been showing them to me. But he said to me, 'Do not do it! I am a fellow servant with you and with your brothers the prophets and of all who keep the words of this book. Worship God!' " (vv. 8-9)

The angel also gave John a practical word as to how this truth should be used as John recorded, "Then he told me, 'Do not seal up the words of the prophecy of this book, because the time is near. Let him who does wrong continue to do wrong; let him who is vile continue to be vile; let him who does right continue to do right; and let him who is holy continue to be holy' " (vv. 10-11). In giving John these instructions, the angel is not indifferent to the need for moral change, but is stating that in view of the Lord's imminent return, it will not be possible to correct things in earth prior to His coming. The angel as well as John struggles with the evil in the world, but he is not to be worshiped.

John then recorded that the announcement of Christ's coming is repeated, "Behold, I am coming soon! My reward is with Me, and I will give to everyone according to what he has done. I am the Alpha and the Omega, the First and the Last, the Beginning and the End. Blessed are those who wash their robes, that they may have the right to the tree of life and may go through the gates into the city. Outside are the dogs, those who practice magic arts, the sexually immoral, the murderers, the idolaters and everyone who loves and practices falsehood. I, Jesus, have sent My angel to give you this testimony for the churches. I am the Root and the Offspring of David, and the bright Morning Star" (vv. 12-16). In this final pronouncement by Jesus Himself, John was again reminded that Christ is coming like the morning star just before dawn, and when He comes it will be an abrupt event. It will be a time of judgment on the wicked and a time of reward for the saints. Christ again points out that He is Alpha and Omega, the first and last letters of the Greek alphabet, and the First and Last in terms of time, and the Beginning and End in terms of creation (1:8, 11, 17; 2:8; 21:6).

John also recorded the final beatitude of seven in the Book of Revelation (1:3; 14:13; 16:15; 19:9; 20:6; 22:7, 14). The statement, "Blessed are those who wash their robes" (v. 14), differs from the text used in the KJV where the phrase is translated, "that do His commandments." Textual evidence seems to be in favor of the NIV translation, and it is preferable to base our hope of salvation on the fact that our robes have been washed and made clean rather than on our obedience to God. The important point is that believers are now justified to enter into the city because they have been rendered holy before God and therefore have a right to the tree of life.

In contrast to believers who will enjoy eternal life, unbelievers, who are described as "dogs," will not be allowed to enter the city. The reference to "dogs" is not to the animal but rather to those of sinful character who do not qualify for the presence of God. Their lives have been characterized by immorality and living falsehood, and their lives have been untouched by the grace of God.

Once again, Jesus points out that He is the Son of David and the bright Morning Star. Though He fulfills all that was promised David, the Morning Star speaks of the bright promise of the future.

The reference to "the churches" is of significance because this is the first reference to the word "church" (Gr., *ekklesia)* since the message to the seven churches. The reason for this is that the church is not involved in the Great Tribulation.

The final message of the Book of Revelation is an invitation to partake of the water of life freely, "The Spirit and the bride say, 'Come!' And let him who hears say, 'Come!' Whoever is thirsty, let him come; and whoever wishes, let him take the free gift of the water of life" (v. 17).

Prophecy was written, on one hand, to warn the sinner of God's judgment on him in the future with its appeal to come to God for the grace that He offers. By contrast also, prophecy describes for the saint the blessings that will be his in eternity because he serves

God in time. Readers of the Book of Revelation who do not have the gift of eternal life are urged, accordingly, to accept the gift as God's free offer to be born again by faith in Christ and to be qualified to participate in what God has planned for those who love Him.

A final word of warning was recorded by John, "I warn everyone who hears the words of the prophecy of this book: If anyone adds anything to them, God will add to him the plagues described in this book. And if anyone takes words away from this book of prophecy, God will take away from him his share in the tree of life and in the Holy City, which are described in this book" (vv. 18-19).

It obviously is a tremendous sin to tamper with the Word of God, to discard it as unworthy, or to live without taking heed to it. The Bible in a number of passages warns against tampering with the Word of God (Deut. 4:2; 12:32; Prov. 30:6; Rev. 1:3). Because the Book is inspired of God, one can neither add nor subtract from that which is revealed. In the light of current neglect of the Book of Revelation in the church today, it points to a serious fault in failing to take into consideration the picture that is painted of end times.

As a final word from Christ, John recorded, "He who testifies to these things says, 'Yes, I am coming soon' " (22:20). The concept of Christ's coming soon has to be interpreted as a warning that He could come at any time but that when He comes it will be sudden. The time for preparation for the coming of the Lord is the period preceding His coming. John added the prayer, "Amen. Come, Lord Jesus" (v. 20). John closed this tremendous revelation with the simple statement, "The grace of the Lord Jesus be with God's people. Amen" (v. 21).

The Book of Revelation, placed last in the Scriptures, introduced the broad theme of the Revelation of Jesus Christ in the opening verses. Subsequently, the major events that followed revealed the power, the righteousness, the sovereignty of Christ and also His marvelous grace for those who come to Him in faith. The Bible does not present in any other book quite as stark a picture of the awfulness of sin, the certainty of divine judgment, and, by contrast, the wonder of being a child of God who is promised eternal blessing in the presence of the Saviour. In a sense, all the prophetic revelation, from Genesis up to the Book of Revelation, finds its summation and its climax in the Book of Revelation. Those who read the Book of Revelation today and are captured by its graphic revelation should sense the fact that while these events have not yet been fulfilled, they could be very quickly, and the time for preparation for end-time events is now.

# TOPICAL INDEX

Baasha, kingdom of Israel, judgment
pronounced on for forsaking
God  63–64
Babylon
to carry off treasures from Jerusalem
to Babylon  108
to conquer the land  307
Daniel's first vision  229–31
to defeat and invade Egypt  147–48
destroyed  603–9
destroyed at the Second Coming
611–14
destruction of  112, 151–54
ecclesiastical, destroyed  603–9
fall of  227–28
fall predicted  590
four woes predicted  308
God's judgment on it  99
history as a false religion  603–6
to be judged  308
judged  323–24
judged after seventy years of Israel's
Captivity  134–35
leaders described as being in the
realm of the dead  100
political, destroyed  610–14
prediction of her victory over
Judah  307–8
prophecy against  102–3
rebuilt in the end time  614
represented in Nebuchadnezzar's
image  218
sword of God's judgment on
Israel  170
Babylonian Captivity, to begin after
Hezekiah's death  69
Balaam
doctrine of  37
prophecies of  37
Barak, prophecies of  45
Baruch, would escape disaster because
he was Jeremiah's
secretary  147–48
Bathsheba  348
Beast
exercised authority for forty-two
months  583
mark of  586–87
number of  587
out of the land  585–88
out of the sea  229–34, 580–84
universal ruler  583–84

worshiped as God  584
worshipers to be judged  590–91
wound of  582–83
Beatitudes  365–66
Belshazzar
death of, predicted and
fulfilled  227–28
feast of  223–28
feast of, writing on the wall interpreted by Daniel  227
Ben-Hadad, king of Aram, though re-
covering from illness, would die  68
Bethsaida, judgment pronounced
on  355
The blessed man, delights in the Law of
God  76
Blessing on Christians
see Christians
Book of Life  631
Bowl judgments
announced  593–603
introduced by seven angels  593–94
Bowls
first, of wrath  596–97
second, of wrath  597
third, of wrath  597–98
fourth, of wrath  598
fifth, of wrath  598
sixth, of wrath  598–99
seventh, of wrath  601–3
Cain  23
Canaanites, victory over them
promised  44
Capernaum, judgment pronounced
on  355
Christ
see Jesus Christ
Christians
appear with Christ in glory  477–78
authority to judge  532
to be blameless at Rapture  480–81,
488–89
entering into God's rest  500–501
to be glorified  448
to have a glorious body in
heaven  475–76
Paul's glory and joy  480
to be heirs of God  448
inheritance of  469–70, 476–77,
506–7, 635
judged at the judgment seat of
Christ  455–56

654

655

# 14

| | |
|---|---|
| 8:00 | |
| 8:30 | |
| 9:00 | |
| 9:30 | |
| 10:00 | |
| 10:30 | |
| 11:00 | |
| 11:30 | |
| 12:00 | |
| 12:30 | |
| 1:00 | |
| 1:30 | |
| 2:00 | |
| 2:30 | |
| 3:00 | |
| 3:30 | |
| 4:00 | |
| 4:30 | |
| 5:00 | |

January 2006

| S | M | T | W | T | F | S |
|---|---|---|---|---|---|---|
| 1 | 2 | 3 | 4 | 5 | 6 | 7 |
| 8 | 9 | **10** | 11 | 12 | 13 | 14 |
| 15 | **16** | 17 | 18 | 19 | 20 | 21 |
| 22 | 23 | 24 | 25 | 26 | 27 | 28 |
| **29** | **30** | 31 | | | | |

# 13

AT-A-GLANCE ®

December 2005

| S | M | T | W | T | F | S |
|---|---|---|---|---|---|---|
| | | | | 1 | 2 | 3 |
| 4 | 5 | 6 | **7** | 8 | 9 | 10 |
| 11 | **12** | 13 | 14 | 15 | 16 | 17 |
| 18 | 19 | 20 | **21** | 22 | 23 | 24 |
| **25** | **26** | 27 | 28 | 29 | 30 | 31 |

February 2006

| S | M | T | W | T | F | S |
|---|---|---|---|---|---|---|
| | | | 1 | 2 | 3 | 4 |
| **5** | 6 | 7 | **8** | 9 | 10 | 1 |
| **12** | 13 | **14** | 15 | 16 | 17 | 1 |
| 19 | **20** | 21 | **22** | 23 | **24** | 2 |
| 26 | 27 | 28 | | | | |

**Friday, January 13**

659

# SCRIPTURE INDEX

670

679

681

682